PSYCHOLOGY 93/94

Twenty-Third Edition

Editor

Karen G. Duffy
SUNY College, Geneseo

Karen G. Duffy holds a doctorate in psychology from Michigan State University and is currently a professor of psychology at SUNY at Geneseo. She sits on the executive board of the New York State Employees Assistance Program and is a certified community and family mediator. She is a member of the American Psychological Society and the Eastern Psychological Association.

Cover illustration by Mike Eagle

Annual Editions
A Library of Information from the Public Press

The Dushkin Publishing Group, Inc.
Sluice Dock, Guilford, Connecticut 06437

The Annual Editions Series

Annual Editions is a series of over 55 volumes designed to provide the reader with convenient, low-cost access to a wide range of current, carefully selected articles from some of the most important magazines, newspapers, and journals published today. Annual Editions are updated on an annual basis through a continuous monitoring of over 300 periodical sources. All Annual Editions have a number of features designed to make them particularly useful, including topic guides, annotated tables of contents, unit overviews, and indexes. For the teacher using Annual Editions in the classroom, an Instructor's Resource Guide with test questions is available for each volume.

VOLUMES AVAILABLE

Africa
Aging
American Government
American History, Pre-Civil War
American History, Post-Civil War
Anthropology
Biology
Business Ethics
Canadian Politics
China
Commonwealth of Independent States
Comparative Politics
Computers in Education
Computers in Business
Computers in Society
Criminal Justice
Drugs, Society, and Behavior
Dying, Death, and Bereavement
Early Childhood Education
Economics
Educating Exceptional Children
Education
Educational Psychology
Environment
Geography
Global Issues
Health
Human Development
Human Resources
Human Sexuality
India and South Asia

International Business
Japan and the Pacific Rim
Latin America
Life Management
Macroeconomics
Management
Marketing
Marriage and Family
Microeconomics
Middle East and the Islamic World
Money and Banking
Nutrition
Personal Growth and Behavior
Physical Anthropology
Psychology
Public Administration
Race and Ethnic Relations
Social Problems
Sociology
State and Local Government
Third World
Urban Society
Violence and Terrorism
Western Civilization, Pre-Reformation
Western Civilization, Post-Reformation
Western Europe
World History, Pre-Modern
World History, Modern
World Politics

Library of Congress Cataloging in Publication Data
Main entry under title: Annual Editions: Psychology. 1993/94.
    1. Psychology—Periodicals. I. Duffy, Karen G., *comp.* II. Title: Psychology.
ISBN 1–56134–211–4   150'.5   79–180263
BF 149.A58

Twenty-Third Edition

Manufactured by The Banta Company, Harrisonburg, Virginia 22801

Editors/ Advisory Board

EDITOR

Karen G. Duffy
SUNY College, Geneseo

ADVISORY BOARD

Michael Atkinson
University of Western Ontario

Joanna B. Boehnert
University of Guelph

Linda Bosmajian
Hood College

John Cross
St. Louis University

Linda K. Davis
Mt. Hood Community College

Thomas Eckle
Modesta Junior College

Roland S. Englehart
University of Windsor

Florine A. Greenberg
Northern Virginia Community
College

C. Harry Hui
University of Hong Kong

Nancy E. Kelley
Indiana University-
Purdue University

David B. Miller
University of Connecticut
Storrs

Carroll Mitchell
Cecil Community College

Terry F. Pettijohn
Ohio State University
Marion

Virginia F. Saunders
San Francisco State University

Harry Strub
The University of Winnipeg

Larry R. Vandervert
Spokane Falls Community College

David Wolfe
Ocean County College

Members of the Advisory Board
are instrumental in the final
selection of articles for each
edition of Annual Editions. Their
review of articles for content,
level, currentness, and
appropriateness provides critical
direction to the editor and staff.
We think you'll find their careful
consideration well reflected in
this volume.

STAFF

Ian A. Nielsen, Publisher
Brenda S. Filley, Production Manager
Roberta Monaco, Editor
Addie Raucci, Administrative Editor
Cheryl Greenleaf, Permissions Editor
Diane Barker, Editorial Assistant
Lisa Holmes-Doebrick, Administrative Coordinator
Charles Vitelli, Designer
Shawn Callahan, Graphics
Meredith Scheld, Graphics
Steve Shumaker, Graphics
Lara M. Johnson, Graphics
Libra A. Cusack, Typesetting Supervisor
Juliana Arbo, Typesetter

To the Reader

In publishing ANNUAL EDITIONS we recognize the enormous role played by the magazines, newspapers, and journals of the *public press* in providing current, first-rate educational information in a broad spectrum of interest areas. Within the articles, the best scientists, practitioners, researchers, and commentators draw issues into new perspective as accepted theories and viewpoints are called into account by new events, recent discoveries change old facts, and fresh debate breaks out over important controversies.

Many of the articles resulting from this enormous editorial effort are appropriate for students, researchers, and professionals seeking accurate, current material to help bridge the gap between principles and theories and the real world. These articles, however, become more useful for study when those of lasting value are carefully *collected, organized, indexed,* and *reproduced* in a *low-cost format,* which provides easy and permanent access when the material is needed. That is the role played by *Annual Editions.* Under the direction of each volume's *Editor,* who is an expert in the subject area, and with the guidance of an *Advisory Board,* we seek each year to provide in each *ANNUAL EDITION* a current, well-balanced, carefully selected collection of the best of the public press for your study and enjoyment. We think you'll find this volume useful, and we hope you'll take a moment to let us know what you think.

Ronnie's parents could not understand why he did not want to be picked up and cuddled as his older sister had when she was an infant. As an infant, Ronnie did not respond to his parents' smiles, words, or attempts to amuse him. By the age of two, Ronnie's parents knew that he was not like other children. He spoke no English, was very temperamental, and often rocked himself for hours. Ronnie is autistic. His parents feel that some of Ronnie's behavior may be their fault; they both work long hours as young professionals and leave both children with an older woman during the weekdays. Ronnie's pediatrician assures his parents that their reasoning, while logical, probably holds no merit because the causes of autism are little understood. What can we do about children like Ronnie? From where does autism come? Can autism be treated or reversed? Can autism be prevented?

Psychologists attempt to answer these and other questions in a specific way, with scientific methods. Researchers, using carefully planned methods, try to discover the answers to the complexities of human behavior, normal or not. Many of the scientific results of psychological research are published in professional journals and therefore are difficult for the layperson to understand.

Annual Editions: Psychology 93/94 is designed to meet the needs of laypeople and beginning level students curious about psychology. This annual edition provides a vast selection of readable and informative articles from popular magazines and newspapers. These articles are written by journalists and a few are written by psychologists whose writing styles are uncluttered and clear yet retain the excitement of the discovery of scientific knowledge.

The particular articles selected for this volume were chosen to be representative of current work in psychology. They were selected because they are accurate in their reporting and provide examples of the types of psychological research discussed in most introductory psychology classes. As in any science, some of the findings discussed in this collection are startling, while others will confirm what we already suspected. Some will invite speculation about social and personal implications; others will demand careful thought about potential misuse of the applications of research findings. You will be expected to make the investment of effort and critical judgment needed to answer such questions and concerns.

We hope you find this collection of articles readable and useful. We suggest that you look at the organization of this book, and compare it to the organization of your textbook and course syllabus or outline. By examining the topic guide provided after the table of contents, you can identify those articles most appropriate for any particular unit of study in your course. Your instructor may provide some help in this effort. As you read the articles, try to connect their contents with the principles you are learning from your text and classroom lectures. Some of the articles will help you better understand a specific area of research, while others are designed to help you connect and integrate information from various research efforts. Both of these strategies are important in learning about psychology or any other science; it is only through intensive investigation and subsequent integration of the findings of many scientists that we are able to discover and apply new knowledge.

Please take time to provide us with some feedback to guide the annual revision of this anthology by completing and returning the article rating form in the back of the book. With your help, this collection will be even better next year. Thank you.

Karen Grover Duffy

Karen Grover Duffy
Editor

Contents

Unit 1

The Science of Psychology

Three articles examine psychology as the science of behavior.

Unit 2

Biological Bases of Behavior

Six selections discuss the biological bases of behavior. Topics include brain functions and the brain's control over the body.

The concepts in bold italics are developed in the article. For further expansion please refer to the Topic Guide, the Index, and the Glossary.

Unit 3

Perceptual Processes

Four articles discuss the impact of the senses on human perceptual processes.

The concepts in bold italics are developed in the article. For further expansion please refer to the Topic Guide, the Index, and the Glossary.

Unit 4

Learning and Remembering

Four selections examine how operant conditioning, positive reinforcement, and memory interact during the learning process.

Unit 5

Cognitive Processes

Six articles examine how social skills, common sense, and intelligence affect human cognitive processes.

The concepts in bold italics are developed in the article. For further expansion please refer to the Topic Guide, the Index, and the Glossary.

Unit
6

Emotion and Motivation

Five articles discuss the influences of stress, mental states, and emotion on the mental and physical health of the individual.

The concepts in bold italics are developed in the article. For further expansion please refer to the Topic Guide, the Index, and the Glossary.

Unit 7

Development

Six articles consider the importance of experience, discipline, familial support, and physiological aging during the normal human development process.

Unit 8

Personality Processes

Five selections discuss a few of the processes by which personalities are developed. Topics include sex differences, state of mind, and cynicism.

The concepts in bold italics are developed in the article. For further expansion please refer to the Topic Guide, the Index, and the Glossary.

Unit 9

Social Processes

Four selections discuss how the individual's social
development is affected by genes, stereotypes,
prejudice, and self-help.

Unit 10

Psychological Disorders

Four articles examine several psychological disorders.
Topics include unexpected behavior, the impact of
depression on a person's well-being, and schizophrenia.

The concepts in bold italics are developed in the article. For further expansion please refer to the Topic Guide, the Index, and the Glossary.

Unit 11

Psychological Treatments

Three selections discuss a few psychological treatments, including psychoanalysis, psychotherapy to alleviate depression, and self-care.

The concepts in bold italics are developed in the article. For further expansion please refer to the Topic Guide, the Index, and the Glossary.

Topic Guide

This topic guide suggests how the selections in this book relate to topics of traditional concern to psychology students and professionals. It is useful for locating articles that relate to each other for reading and research. The guide is arranged alphabetically according to topic. Articles may, of course, treat topics that do not appear in the topic guide. In turn, entries in the topic guide do not necessarily constitute a comprehensive listing of all the contents of each selection.

TOPIC AREA	TREATED IN:	TOPIC AREA	TREATED IN:
Adolescence	31. Children in Gangs 36. Girls' Self-Esteem Is Lost on Way to Adolescence	**Depression**	44. Mood Disorders: A Sad State of Mind 45. Winning the War Against Clinical Depression 48. Depression: The Growing Role of Drug Therapies
Aging	23. Mental Gymnastics 32. Meeting the Challenges of an Aging Nation 33. Silent Saviors	**Disease/Illness**	8. Pleasurable Chemistry 26. Stress: The "Type A" Hypothesis 38. Tapping the Healing Power of Positive Thinking
Animals	3. Ratting on Psychologists 17. Dreams of a Rat	**Dreams/Sleep**	17. Dreams of a Rat 24. Where Emotions Come From 25. Happy or Sad, A Mood Can Prove Contagious 44. Mood Disorders: A Sad State of Mind
Artificial Intelligence	20. Brains at Work		
Bipolar Disorder	44. Mood Disorders: A Sad State of Mind	**Experimental Psychology**	1. Psychology: The Core Discipline 2. Liberal Education, Study in Depth, and the Arts and Science Major—Psychology
Brain	4. Mapping the Brain 5. Mind and Brain 8. Pleasurable Chemistry 13. Consciousness Raising 20. Brains at Work 21. Brain Yields New Clues on Its Organization for Language	**Femininity**	36. Girls' Self-Esteem Is Lost on Way to Adolescence 41. Blame It on Feminism
Child Abuse	30. Sad Legacy of Abuse: The Search for Remedies	**Genetics**	6. What a Child Is Given 7. Study Links Genes to Sexual Orientation 9. Sizing Up the Sexes
Children	6. What a Child Is Given 14. How Kids Learn 29. Putting Children First 30. Sad Legacy of Abuse: A Search for Remedies 31. Children in Gangs 39. Are You Raising an Optimist?	**Gestalt Psychology**	10. Legacy of Gestalt Psychology
		Groups/Group Dynamics	42. Groupthink: Taking Easy Way Out of a Tough Decision 49. Recovery Fever
Cognition	13. Consciousness Raising 18. New Perspective on Cognitive Development in Infancy 20. Brains at Work 22. Probability Blindness: Neither Rational nor Capricious 23. Mental Gymnastics	**History of Psychology**	1. Psychology: The Core Discipline
		Homosexuality	7. Study Links Genes to Sexual Orientation
Conditioning	15. Town B. F. Skinner Boxed	**Intelligence/IQ Tests**	19. New Views of Human Intelligence
Conflict	43. Resolving Conflicts: Step by Step		
Culture	32. Meeting the Challenges of an Aging Nation 40. Where Do We Stand?	**Language**	21. Brain Yields New Clues on Its Organization for Language
Death	34. Bright Lights, Big Mystery	**Learning**	14. How Kids Learn 15. Town B. F. Skinner Boxed

The Science of Psychology

Little did Wilhelm Wundt realize his monumental contribution to science when he opened the first psychological laboratory to examine consciousness in Germany in 1879. Today Wundt would barely recognize the science of psychology as he knew it.

Psychology today is defined as the science of mental activity and behavior. This definition reflects the two parent disciplines from which psychology emerged: philosophy and biology.

Compared to its parents, psychology is very much a new discipline. Some aspects of modern psychology are particularly biological, such as neuroscience, sensation and perception, and behavioral genetics. Other aspects are more philosophical, such as the study of personality.

Today psychologists work in a variety of settings. Many psychologists are academics, teaching and researching psychology on university campuses. Others work in applied settings such as hospitals, mental health clinics, industry, and schools. Industrial psychologists specialize in human performance in organizational settings, while clinical psychologists are concerned about the assessment, diagnosis, and treatment of individuals with a variety of mental health problems.

Psychology is one of the most popular academic majors on today's college campuses. The first two articles explore psychology as a major. In the first article, "Psychology: The Core Discipline," Raymond Fowler, a former president of the American Psychological Association, reviews the history of psychology and ponders the ever-widening gap between researchers and practitioners in psychology. Fowler also discusses why psychology is one of the most popular majors in this country. In the companion or second article, several psychologists discuss psychology as a liberal arts major in "Liberal Education, Study in Depth, and the Arts and Science Major—Psychology." This article reviews some of the history of psychology, conflicts among contemporary psychologists, and curricular options within psychology.

Psychological research, the basis for all advances in psychology, is considered in the last article in this first unit. In "Ratting on Psychologists," Lawrence LeShan criticizes American psychologists for using animal models to study human behavior. The animal examined most often, of course, is the white rat. LeShan is convinced that psychologists have lost track of human qualities in their laboratories as well as in their applied, but still artificial, settings.

Looking Ahead: Challenge Questions

Do you think that the emergence of applied areas in psychology (such as clinical psychology) has hurt or advanced scientific psychology?

Which area of psychology do you think is the most valuable and why? About which area of psychology is the public most aware? About which other areas of psychology do you think the public ought to be informed?

What trends shaped psychology as we know it today? How is psychology related to other disciplines on campus? What concepts do you think are core to psychology, that is, what should all psychology majors know? Should there be a common core of knowledge within a discipline such as psychology?

Why are animal models useful for the study of human behavior? What are the limitations of using animals to study human behavior? Why is the white rat the model of choice, especially for behaviorists? Do you think most research conducted in laboratories is useful or useless? Need laboratory settings always be artificial?

Unit 1

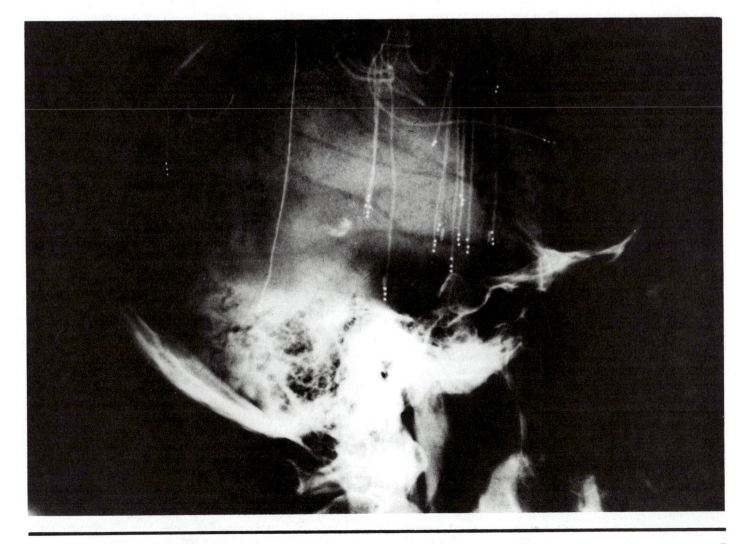

Psychology: The Core Discipline

Raymond D. Fowler
University of Tennessee

Giving a presidential address for the American Psychological Association (APA) is not a responsibility that I take lightly nor, I suppose, have any of my predecessors. Being 96th in the progression of APA presidents is more intimidating than reassuring, but it does include the benefit of being able to look to one's seniors for guidance and inspiration. As I considered what I wanted to say today, I found it very helpful to read what other presidents have said and to review the progress and the problems of our Association and our discipline through their eyes.

APA presidential addresses have been of two major types. Most presidents have used the occasion to summarize their own substantive contributions or to describe recent developments in a particular subarea of psychology. Other presidents, particularly during times of conflict and change within the Association, have examined the structure of our discipline and how psychologists relate to each other and to the larger society. Because we are certainly in one of those recurring seasons of discontent, those presidential addresses are the ones that I found most instructive and that I kept returning to as I prepared to give my own.

Three of the early presidents, who served during a period when the discipline was trying to define itself and its mission, gave presidential addresses that expressed their vision of how psychology might develop in future years.

Granville Stanley Hall, who had brought together the founding group of APA a few months earlier, was elected president at the first APA convention in Philadelphia in December 1892. Soon afterwards, President Hall (in Woodworth, 1943, p. 18) said that psychology "is showing itself . . . to be the long hoped for, long delayed science of man, to which all other sciences are bringing their ripest and best thoughts, [and] is introducing a period that will be known hereafter as the psychological era of scientific thought." Brave words indeed for the president of an association with only 31 members.

George Ladd, our second president, gave a presidential address that he called a "cheering reminder that this Association should enter upon its career with a sufficiently generous estimate of its privileges and its responsibility" (in Hilgard, 1978, p. 21). Always on the lookout for cheering reminders, I read it with interest. Ladd described the rapidly developing science of psychology and then went on to present a remarkable projection of the future professional role of psychology in education, medicine, mental health, law, and child rearing.

Our eighth president, John Dewey, was the first president to focus on the relationship of psychology to society. In his presidential address entitled "Psychology and Social Practice," he examined ethical issues in the application of psychology. Even so great a mind as Dewey's recognized that there are limitations in what one can hope to accomplish in a presidential address. He began: "In coming before you I had hoped to deal with the problem of the relation of psychology to the social sciences—and through them to social practice, to life itself. . . . That discussion is not ready today" (in Hilgard, 1978, p. 65).

So, even in the first decade of our existence as a discipline and as an association, our presidents had foreseen that psychology would be a science and a profession while contributing to the public good.

Our early presidents were enthusiastic and visionary about the prospects for the new discipline. Subsequent presidents, who have had ample opportunities to see the problems of our discipline and our Association, have also been notably optimistic about our prospects. I will return frequently to what these distinguished psychologists have said about psychology in an effort to recapture some of their hope and enthusiasm for our collective futures.

A theme that has been prominent in the speeches of our presidents is the potential impact that psychology as a discipline could have on society. Our fourth president, James McKeen Cattell (1937), once noted in a "backward" glance written some years after his presidency, "It is possible that the development of psychology as a science and its application to the control of human conduct—individual and collective—may in the course of the coming century be as significant for civilization as has been the industrial revolution" (p. 1). Speaking more recently, George Miller, our 77th president, once noted that if the stated goals of scientific psychology were to be realized, the social and personal implications would far outrun the implications of atomic energy or recombinant DNA.

It is in that spirit that I have used the term *core discipline* as a metaphor to express the significance of psychology as a field of knowledge and the important destiny it has to fulfill. We have a large responsibility, as temporary custodians of the discipline, to promote and integrate the science and practice of psychology for the benefit of society.

The term *discipline* is used in the academic world to refer to the knowledge and information base of a broad field of study and instruction. The discipline of psychology includes both its science and its applications. A *core discipline* is one that provides a basic core of knowledge that is used by other disciplines. That is, a core discipline contains concepts and content that are basic to the effective functioning of other disciplines.

For example, mathematics may be regarded as a core discipline for the physical sciences. Most physical scientists take courses in mathematics and use mathematics in conceptualizing and solving their problems. Mathematics provides a common language across the sciences.

The study of psychology was synthesized from many other disciplines, including: education, philosophy, psychology, and medicine.

The science of psychology, because it deals with the fundamental understanding of behavior, serves as a core discipline for other social sciences concerned with human behavior. Psychological terms, concepts, and methodology are common across the social sciences. Most of the professions that deal with problems of living draw heavily on both the knowledge base of scientific psychology and the technology of professional psychology.

Another reason that I characterize psychology as a core discipline is that it deals with problems and issues that are essential and fundamental. I believe that the failure to understand human behavior is at the core of most of the world's most serious problems. As George Miller (1969) said in his presidential address, "The most urgent problems of our world today are the problems we have made for ourselves. . . . They are human problems whose solutions will require us to change our behavior and our social institutions" (p. 1063).

When we look at society's problems, we often focus on peripheral or technological issues. Automobile accidents are seen as a result of poor highway design, and low industrial productivity is viewed as the result of inadequate or poorly designed machinery. As the technological problems are solved, the residual problems—the core problems—are usually found to be problems of human behavior. Automobile accidents occur mostly as a result of human error—irresponsible driving, intoxication, and the like, and a major factor in low industrial productivity is improper use of human resources—inadequate training, management, and incentives. Compared with the technological and mechanical matters, the human problems are much more difficult to overcome. They are the core problems, and it is these that psychology addresses.

If you doubt that the core problems of our world relate to human behavior, think for a minute about the problems that most endanger our species. Overpopulation, which dooms increasingly large portions of our world to poverty, misery, and starvation, is most certainly caused by human behavior. And overpopulation is only one of many such problems. Our decisions with respect to energy policy and land development are resulting in the gradual destruction of our tropical rainforests, our wetlands, and much of our arable land while simultaneously threatening our oceans, our freshwater supplies, our air, and the ozone layer that protects our planet. The decisions made by a few powerful government leaders could determine whether there will be any human beings to inhabit our world.

At a more personal level, we know now that 7 of the 10 major causes of death in the United States are primarily behavioral, not medical or physical, in nature. Our behavior contributes to heart disease, alcoholism, drug addiction, homicide, suicide, automobile accidents, many forms of cancer, and a host of other self-inflicted forms of torture and death. As Lewis Lipsett (1989) said, "behavior kills."

Certainly, few could deny that human behavior, the subject matter of our discipline, is at the core of many of the most fundamental concerns of the inhabitants of the planet.

As a core discipline, psychology contains both scientific knowledge about human behavior and methods of applying that knowledge. A good profession must be based on good science, and both the science and the profession are ultimately legitimated by serving the public.

Psychology as a Science

When the founders of the APA announced the formation of a new organization, they were also announcing the establishment of a new discipline. Psychology emerged from philosophy as a self-designated science. The methods of this new science were borrowed from the physical sciences, as John Stuart Mill had advised almost a century earlier. James McKeen Cattell was the first American to complete a dissertation in psychology under Wilhelm Wundt. In his youthful enthusiasm for his very young discipline, he wrote to his parents that "psychology is likely to be the science of the next thirty years—at all events, the science in which most progress will be made" (Sokal, 1981, quoted in Benjamin, 1986, p. 941).

The founders of our discipline saw psychology as integrating knowledge from many sources. They themselves were recruited from a number of disciplines. They included educators, philosophers, physiologists, and physicians. They believed that psychology would not only bring together like-minded scholars from different disciplines but would also bring the concepts of those many disciplines to bear on the understanding of human behavior and thought.

The path of scientific progress has not been easy. From the beginning, psychology has been torn between the urge to know more and more about less and less, or less and less about more and more. Psychology has been criticized both for being preoccupied with trivial problems that ignore the larger picture and for trying to encompass too much.

In a delightful conversation between four developmental psychologists on the future of their specialty, Urie Bronfenbrenner expressed himself on the dangers of too narrow a view by relating the following tale by the great Russian fabulist Krilov, in which a man spoke of his visit to the zoo and all the creatures that he saw there:

"The tiny flies and beetles, the ladybirds, jewel-like butterflies, and insects with heads no bigger than a pin. What marvels!"

"And did you see the elephant?" asked his friend.

"Oh, do they have one there? I guess I must have missed the elephant." (Bronfenbrenner, Kessel, Kessen, & White, 1986, p. 1219)

The other side of the criticism that psychological researchers take on too little is the assertion that psychology as a discipline tries to take on too much. This problem is usually posed as a question: Can psychology be a unified science?

The delights of being part of a discipline that is rich in diversity sometimes seem outweighed by the problems of finding unifying themes and principles. Those who observe that psychology is split along the lines of science and practice greatly oversimplify and underestimate the problem of unity in the discipline of psychology. Of course there is a discontinuity between a science and a profession, because each is different in role and function, but the more fundamental issue is whether psychology, per se, can be ordered to a characteristic set of phenomena.

To Sigmund Koch (1969) the answer was clear: *"Psychology,"* he said, *cannot be a coherent science* or indeed a coherent field of scholarship" (p. 65, emphasis in original). These are strong words, indeed, from the one scholar delegated by the APA and the National Science Foundation to assess the status of psychology as a science. For Koch, the problem was not in the methodology of our discipline but in the scope of our domain. The fundamental flaw that keeps psychology from being a coherent discipline can be found, Koch believed, in the subject matter. "Anything so awesome as the total domain comprised by the functioning of all organisms," he said, "can hardly be thought to be the subject matter of a coherent discipline" (p. 65).

To me, there is something both quixotic and appealing about a discipline that strives for so much despite the odds. None can doubt that we have taken on a worthy challenge. Nor can we reasonably claim that we have mastered the unwieldy beast. Must we then give up the goal of psychology as a unified science? Or are we, as a very young discipline, simply too impatient? Arthur Staats (1983), in his book *Psychology's Crisis of Disunity,* expressed hope for our future. He observed,

Today's psychologist, is bewildered by all but a small corner of the fragmented science. The optimistic message in the present work, nevertheless, is that what psychology has achieved in its 100 or so years of self-conscious striving does provide the raw materials for making the leap to the status of a unified science.

I share that sense of optimism. We must continue to search for the "grand unifying principles." The solution to the problems of diversity cannot be more fragmentation. As a science and as a discipline, psychology must continue to seek the common threads that connect and unite. As Kessen (in Bronfenbrenner et al., 1986) pointed out, "It's perfectly all right for people to till their own garden, but once in a while they are going to have to talk over the fence" (p. 1224).

Psychology as a Profession

The lack of integration within the science of psychology is echoed in the lack of integration between our science and our profession. Psychology began as a science, and its professional aspects developed much later. As Don Peterson (1976) observed, "Having emerged from philosophy as a natural science, neither of which have a tradition of direct service, developing as a profession required a lengthy process of redefinition, which is still underway" (p. 572).

We spent our first 50 years building a science base for the discipline, with little attention to applications, but it would be incorrect to suppose that our founders intended a science without a profession. It is clear from the addresses of our earliest presidents that they foresaw the development of a profession of psychology that could use the knowledge base of our science to benefit humanity.

This is nowhere more clear than in the address of our second president, George Trumbull Ladd of Yale University. Professor Ladd had the great misfortune of serving as president between G. Stanley Hall and William James, thus dooming himself to relative obscurity. His presidential address was not even abstracted in Ernest Hilgard's (1978) collection of APA presidential addresses, but when I located his original 1893 speech, I was astonished by his vision of how a profession might develop.

After reviewing the progress made by the new science, Ladd (1894) expressed his view that psychology would provide the behavioral foundation for the other social sciences. He then focused on the impact scientific psychology could have through its applications:

The obligation to be of practical benefit [is] heavily laid upon psychology. The more I study and teach this science, the deeper does the impression become that it is able and destined to contribute greatly to the welfare of mankind. . . .

The science of psychology may be expected to make large contributions toward the improvement of the art and practice of teaching, [and] the science of psychology may be expected to contribute much to the science and practice of medicine. . . . Even modern surgery has already been guided by the help which physiological psychology has rendered in the . . . localization of cerebral function. Looked at from a truly rational point of view, what can be more amazing than the fact that thousands of doctors are today treating patients suffering from "mental" disease, who themselves never made the slightest study of mental phenomena, sane or abnormal? With so many quacks, on the one side, medicating the mind with drugs, is it greatly to be wondered at that there are so many cranks on the other side? In the diagnosis and treatment of the insane [and] the incorrigible, scientific psychology is surely destined to exert a growing influence. (pp. 19–20)

Ladd predicted that psychologists would be called upon to give courtroom testimony to distinguish between "the insane and the sane criminal" and that "the advantages of prolonged psychological investigation for the improvement of jurisprudence" would be recognized. He expressed the hope that we could expect "to see our science contributing to [improvements] in the school, in the courtroom, the prison, and the asylum," and even in the home where, he believed, "parental influence . . . may . . . be helped and blessed in no small degree by the recent rapid advances of human psychology" (p. 21).

In 1937, 41 years after he gave his presidential address, James McKeen Cattell was asked to comment on psychology as a profession in the first issue of the *Journal of Consulting Psychology.* He said,

All of the professions need a science of psychology and a profession of psychology. The present function of a physician, a lawyer, a clergyman, a teacher or a man of business is to a considerable extent that of an amateur psychologist. In the inevitable specialization of modern society, there will become increasing need of those who can be paid for expert psychological advice . . . in the end, there will be not only a science but also a profession of psychology. (p. 3)

At the time Cattell spoke, almost halfway into our first century, there were only 3,000 members of APA, and almost all were employed in academic settings. During the years following World War II, the profession of psychology, which had represented a tiny minority of psychologists, began to develop. Thousands of postwar students were attracted to industrial, organizational, school, and clinical psychology. In 1979, the number of psychologists employed in academic settings still exceeded the number employed in all nonacademic settings. Ten years later, educational institutions are still the largest single employer of psychologists, but they are no longer equal to all others combined. This pattern is characteristic of all of the scientific disciplines. The nation has shifted from an agricultural and industrial economy to a service economy, and the predominant locus of scientific employment has shifted from the university to business, government, consulting, and the delivery of services. It would be remarkable if psychology had remained untouched by these national trends.

It is important to remember, however, that growth in psychology is not a zero-sum game. The increase in the number of applied professional psychologists did not

Professional psychology has emerged almost entirely in the last third of our first century.

cause a reduction in the number of academic researchers. To the contrary, academic psychology continued to increase at a faster rate than most of the other academic disciplines.

Some argue that the emergence of professional psychology hurt the development of our science. But it may be argued that the opposite is true. The increased resources available to academic psychology in the form of research grants and new positions resulted largely from the increased visibility of psychology as an applied discipline. During both world wars, but especially during World War II, psychologists, particularly our scientists, demonstrated that the knowledge base of psychology could be applied to the nation's benefit in time of national crisis. This had the dual effect of increasing our public acceptance and justifying our claims that additional research could result in still more benefits to the nation. The national enthusiasm for psychology attracted undergraduate and graduate students in unprecedented numbers. No similar growth occurred in the other social sciences, which do not have applied or professional aspects. Psychology departments grew in size and resources because they had both a science and a profession. And the profession gained credibility because of its scientific foundation.

The relation between science and practice in a discipline could be (and often is) viewed as hierarchical, with science on top and knowledge trickling down to the practitioner on the bottom. This view is generally accepted by scientists and practitioners alike, but it could as readily be seen in reverse, with science as the foundation upon which practice is built, and practice as the part of the discipline that fulfills the goal of service to the public.

Part of the conflict between scientific and professional psychology is based on a syllogism: Psychology is a science; therefore all psychologists must be scientists. Abraham Flexner pointed out long ago that the fundamental attitude of the professional practitioner should resemble that of the scientist in terms of systematic observation, hypothesis building, and cautious judgement. But the belief that all practitioners should be scientists, or vice versa, is a misconception. As Flexner (1925) said, "The assertion that the intellectual attitude of the investigator and the practitioner should be identical does not mean that . . . investigation and treatment coincide; it does not mean that practitioners should all be experimenters or that investigators must all be practitioners" (p. 12).

The changing face of American psychology has, I believe, been widely misunderstood. The fact that large numbers of psychologists are being trained primarily for applied positions rather than academic–research positions does not mean that psychology will be less able to develop as a scientific discipline. We are currently producing enough academic–research PhDs to fill all of the available positions, and we will soon be increasing that production to meet the needs of the next century. The proportion of our scientists who graduate from the major research institutions has not decreased, and the absolute number of scientist–practitioners who graduate from those same institutions has remained constant. The large growth of new doctorates outside the major research institutions is made up of professional psychologists, and they are coming, as one might expect, from professionally oriented programs, not from the major research departments.

Professional psychology has emerged almost entirely in the last third of our first century. This growth took place during a period in which most of the new opportunities for employment occurred outside academic settings, especially in the health-care sector. The changing face of American psychology involves the development of an additional face—a professional face—and not the demise of our already well-established academic–research face. Psychology has not *become* a profession; rather, psychology has *added* a profession to the academic science foundation that already existed.

There may still be a few people who actively discourage the application of psychology on the grounds that it compromises the purity of our science, but surely such is a minority view in our discipline. Most psychologists recognize the importance of applying psychology, and throughout our history there has been great optimism that the application of psychology can benefit humanity.

Similarly, there may be a few who believe that the profession of psychology has outgrown its scientific base and that professional psychologists no longer need a close connection with academic–research psychology. But they represent, I believe, an even smaller minority.

As we have seen so vividly, the intrinsic differences between science and practice often result in conflict. As William Bevan (1982), our 90th president said, "We differ in motivation and goals, in priorities, in intellectual styles, in human values, and in temperament, and we won't find peace by glossing over these differences" (p. 1310).

I think you will agree with me that whatever we have been doing lately, we certainly have not been "glossing over our differences." But I believe that increasing numbers of us are ready to shift from a preoccupation with our differences to an examination of how our diversity can contribute to psychology as a whole. Bevan (1982) commented that "the problems which ultimately will tax us most severely [are] the problems of balance and interrelatedness between our basic and applied concerns" (p. 1303). It seems to me that it is that interrelatedness that has been most seriously neglected to the detriment of our discipline and our Association. It is that balance that we most need to achieve.

How does a profession build on science? Harrison (1984) pointed out that it is almost always a reciprocal relationship. Rather than saying that science drives practice or that practice drives science, it would be more accurate to say that they are synergistic.

Thus, the solution to our problem as a discipline is at once very simple and very difficult. How can we achieve the synergy that is necessary if psychology is to contribute what it has the potential to contribute? How can we develop that reciprocal relationship between the science and the profession and, more important, between scientists and professionals?

In an address to Psi Chi at the 1988 APA convention, I said, "During the first six months of my presidency, our association has been far more fractionated and divided than it has ever been in my experience. . . . If I have a single, primary personal goal during this year, it is to do

all I can to maintain a unitary APA, and as matters have developed that has become an increasingly difficult goal" (Fowler, 1988, p. 3).

As I assume my new role as chief executive officer of APA, that observation is no less true and my primary goal is unchanged. I know that most psychologists would prefer a unitary APA that can represent all of psychology, although many doubt that it can be achieved. I firmly believe that it can and will be achieved. In his 1893 APA presidential address, George Ladd (1894) noted that the future success of American psychology depended "very largely upon the action, individually and in corporate fashion, of the members of this Association" (p. 11). I believe that is no less true today.

I am continually told that the American Psychological Association is in a state of crisis. I do not deny that, but I like to remind myself that a crisis is defined as a turning point, an unstable or crucial period the outcome of which will make a decisive difference for better or worse. The choice of whether the outcome of our crisis will be for better or worse is a choice that will be made by human beings, not by circumstances or by fate. It is our choice to make.

We have, throughout our history, faced many troubling periods that threatened our unity, and through cooperation and good will we have surmounted them. Although some people see APA as rigid and resistant to change, it has, in fact, been surprisingly flexible in accommodating itself to new conditions, especially when these new conditions threatened the unity of psychology. For most of our history, the demands for change have come from applied psychologists; more recently academic–research psychologists have found the organizational structure unsatisfactory.

In 1917, and again in 1937, applied psychologists became so dissatisfied with APA that they founded new national associations to represent them. In response, APA modified its structure, admitted members of the new associations as members of APA, and changed its bylaws in ways that were supportive of professional psychology. The changes were not made as rapidly as some would have liked, but they were made and they succeeded in

---

Academicians and practitioners have different activities and different priorities.

---

keeping APA united. Once again we have reached a time when some members feel frustrated and disenfranchised by our structure, and once again we need to find ways to meet the needs of those members.

Why is it important to preserve APA as a unitary association representing the science and profession of psychology? Surely the advantages of a common voice in advocacy and in public image are apparent to all. During the past decade the effectiveness of our science advocacy has become the envy of many other scientific organizations. We have become a significant and responsible factor in national policy decisions, and more recently our professional advocacy has developed as a significant force at the national and state levels.

But I believe there are more important reasons to keep APA together. I hope I will not sound grandiose when I say that I consider the American Psychological Association a vital national asset and that I believe we have a responsibility to preserve it for the public good.

The history of APA is the history of American psychology. APA helped to establish the science of psychology by providing scientific conventions, by publishing the major psychological journals, and by preserving and disseminating our knowledge base. Psychology has become one of the most successful scientific disciplines, and APA has long been the leader among the world's national psychological associations.

While promoting and preserving scientific psychology, APA has also helped to nourish and guide the development of the profession of psychology. In a few short years, professional psychology has moved from being a very minor player to being one of the major health care disciplines. Psychology has already surpassed the other mental health professions, with over 50 million hours of mental health care services provided by psychologists each year. By providing strong professional and ethical standards and vigorously enforcing them, APA has helped to make psychology a highly regarded profession as well.

Both our science and our profession have achieved a considerable measure of respect. Why do we not respect each other? Academicians and practitioners have different activities and different priorities—but why can we not value each other's differences? John Gardner could have been speaking of the discipline of psychology when he attributed the problems of modern society to "a loss of mutual trust."

The early presidents of APA were all scientists and academicians because there was, of course, no profession of psychology then. They had the foresight and vision to realize that psychological science had the potential to contribute greatly to the solution of human problems. They also had a conviction that one day a profession would grow from the foundation of our science. I believe it would have surprised them to see how successful psychology has been in establishing a science and a profession—and how unsuccessful we have sometimes been in learning to get along with each other.

There are psychologists who say that we must be either a professional association or an academic association. I believe that there is no reason that we should limit ourselves to being only one or the other. National surveys indicate that just over 40% of all psychologists in this country are employed in academic settings, a similar number are health care service providers, and 20% are employed in a wide variety of government, business, applied, and research settings. If APA is to continue to represent psychologists in all of these settings, we must somehow regain our sense of mutual trust.

There are some who foresee a grim future for psychology: exodus of our best scientists to other disciplines and the gradual withering away of our science; separation of our professional training programs from our scientific knowledge base and our profession from our science; and Balkanization of our strong national association into a number of smaller groups speaking for their special concerns but not for the entire discipline of psychology.

We can achieve such self-destruction if we choose, but I have too much respect for my colleagues to believe that will happen. Our predecessors found ways to reconcile their differences and to coexist. I cannot believe that we are less intelligent or less generous. The process must begin with individual acts of mutual respect and restraint in the uses of power. I know of many who are already working to achieve this. I believe we have already begun to turn the corner in this crisis and that we will find solutions to our mutual dilemma.

My vision for psychology is not defeat and disintegration. I believe we can enter our second century as a unitary association and a unified discipline. In its first century, psychology established itself as a major discipline with a strong science and a vigorous profession. Our prospects for the second century are limited only by our vision and our personal decisions.

The economic future of America and of the world depends on training, management, leadership, knowledge exchange, and the effective application of artificial intelligence. All these are the natural province of psychology. The major issues in health care, the fastest growing industry, are no longer disease and infection, but life-styles and prevention, which are psychological, not medical, issues. Physiological, social, clinical, and health psychologists will make important contributions to the nation's health through scientific research and professional application. Psychology will be a major player in what the National Institute of Mental Health has called the Decade of the Brain. Psychologists will use the developing technologies of brain mapping and genetic mapping to further explain human thought and behavior.

We can build, among ourselves and with colleagues in related disciplines, cooperative and synergistic relationships. Instead of fragmenting, we can bring ourselves together to make our knowledge base work for the benefit of humanity. In a new period of almost unlimited technological growth, the discipline of psychology can bring both the intellectual and the humanistic vision to finally justify the brave words of G. Stanley Hall and make our second century a golden age for all of psychology.

REFERENCES

Benjamin, L. T. (1986). Why don't they understand us? A history of psychology's public image. *American Psychologist, 41,* 941–946.

Bevan, W. (1982). A sermon of sorts in three plus parts. *American Psychologist, 37,* 1303–1322.

Bronfenbrenner, U., Kessel, F., Kessen, W., & White, S. (1986). Toward a critical social history of developmental psychology: A propaedeutic discussion. *American Psychologist, 41,* 1218–1230.

Cattell, J. McK. (1937). Retrospect: Psychology as a profession. *Journal of Consulting Psychology, 1,* 1–3.

1. SCIENCE OF PSYCHOLOGY

Flexner, A. (1925). *Medical education: A comparative study.* New York: Macmillan.

Fowler, R. D. (1988). Address. *Psy Chi Newsletter, 14*(4), 1, 3–5.

Harrison, A. J. (1984). Science, engineering, and technology [Editorial]. *Science, 223,* 543.

Hilgard, E. (1978). *American psychology in historical perspective.* Washington, DC: American Psychological Association.

Koch, S. (1959). *Psychology: A study of a science.* New York: McGraw-Hill.

Koch, S. (1969). Psychology cannot be a coherent science. *Psychology Today, 3,* 14, 64–68.

Ladd, G. T. (1894). President's address before the New York meeting of the American Psychological Association. *Psychological Review, 1,* 1–21.

Lipsitt, L. P. (1989, June). *Behavior is a life and death matter: Risk factors in development.* Invited lecture presented at the meeting of the American Psychological Society, Alexandria, VA.

Miller, G. A. (1969). Psychology as a means of promoting human welfare. *American Psychologist, 24,* 1063–1075.

Peterson, D. R. (1976). Is psychology a profession? *American Psychologist, 31,* 572–581.

Sokal, M. M. (1981). *An education in psychology: James McKeen Cattell's journal and letters from Germany and England, 1880–1888.* Cambridge, MA: MIT Press.

Staats, A. (1983). *Psychology's crisis of disunity: Philosophy and method for a unified science.* New York: Praeger.

Woodworth, R. S. (1943). The adolescence of American psychology. *Psychological Review, 50,* 10–32.

Liberal Education, Study in Depth, and the Arts and Sciences Major—Psychology

Thomas V. McGovern   *Arizona State University West*
Laurel Furumoto   *Wellesley College*
Diane F. Halpern   *California State University, San Bernardino*
Gregory A. Kimble   *Duke University*
Wilbert J. McKeachie   *University of Michigan*

Undergraduate psychology is considered one of the contemporary arts and sciences majors that achieve liberal-education and study-in-depth goals. Past reports on the psychology major are reviewed as a preamble to defining the field of study and the conflicts that contributed to that definition. Eight common goals for the major are identified that are adaptable to a variety of institutional settings and resources. A common framework for course requirements is suggested and 4 curricular models to achieve the common goals are described. Assessment of the major as a program and evaluation of students and their learning are also described.

We teach psychology in an array of institutional settings. Our students bring to their undergraduate classes different cultural heritages and a range of academic preparation. The American Psychological Association (APA) urged us to draw on our collective experiences as classroom teachers, as scholars, and as administrators in framing this report. We listened to the voices of many colleagues. We tried, as William James (1902/1958) said in describing the task of exploring another type of experience, to ex-

amine "the roots and the fruits" of teaching psychology. Psychologists have reflected periodically on the objectives of undergraduate education, on what courses best prepare students to attain these objectives, on research designed to understand how students learn, and on innovative pedagogy that enlivens the work of faculty and students in the classroom, laboratory, and field settings.

Past Reports

In 1951, six psychologists met at Cornell University to "audit" the undergraduate curriculum. In their report, *Improving Undergraduate Instruction in Psychology* (Buxton et al., 1952), they identified "intellectual development and a liberal education" as primary objectives for undergraduate work. A secondary objective was "a knowledge of psychology, its research findings, its major problems, its theoretical integration and its contributions" (pp. 2–3).

Ten years later, another study group met at the University of Michigan. They were concerned that teaching had lost its prestige and that research consumed most faculties' energy and creativity. Using survey data collected from 411 departments, they discussed the curriculum, professional and vocational training, the introductory course, methods courses in experimental psychology and statistics, and three model curricula. The authors of *Undergraduate Curricula in Psychology* (McKeachie & Milholland, 1961) characterized psychology as a liberal arts discipline that emphasizes breadth rather than narrow specialization.

In *Undergraduate Education in Psychology,* Kulik (1973) reported on data gathered from 463 baccalaureate programs, 99 two-year institutions, and 17 site-visit case studies. From analyses of these data he argued that no single curriculum could encompass the diversity of student needs and educational settings, and concluded that "pluralism may be a valuable concept in the design of programs in psychology" (p. 203). Moreover, the report questioned whether curricula such as those of liberal arts colleges best met the ideals of liberal education: "Is it

This article was completed as part of a national review of arts and sciences majors initiated by the Association of American Colleges as part of its continuing commitment to advance and strengthen undergraduate liberal learning. The American Psychological Association was 1 of 12 learned societies contributing to this review. Each participating learned society convened a task force to address a common set of questions about purposes and practices of liberal arts majors; individual task forces further explored issues in their particular fields. The authors of this article were named by the APA Committee on Undergraduate Education, of which Thomas V. McGovern was chair, and the APA Education and Training Board.

Generous funding for the project and dissemination of the reports was provided by the Fund for the Improvement of Postsecondary Education (FIPSE) and the Ford Foundation.

Correspondence concerning this article should be addressed to Thomas V. McGovern, Arizona State University West, Arts & Sciences, 4701 West Thunderbird Road, Phoenix, AZ 85069-7100.

conceivable that for some students, occupationally oriented programs may provide a better road?" (pp. 202–203)

A special issue of the journal *Teaching of Psychology* (Morris, 1982) was devoted to "Undergraduate Psychology Education in the Next Decade." The APA (1983b) conducted a telephone survey of psychology departments. Scheirer and Rogers's (1985) report, *The Undergraduate Psychology Curriculum 1984,* mapped the terrain of an increasingly complex field taught in many different academic environments.

The reports issued in the 1950s and 1960s affirmed undergraduate psychology as one of the disciplines in the liberal arts, emphasizing breadth, content, scientific methodology, and intellectual sophistication. Its aim was to teach students to ask questions about behavior and to understand the ingredients of good answers. In the 1970s, against a background of changes in the field and in the demography of higher education, Kulik (1973) advocated "curricular pluralism" in recognition of the developing conflicts in psychology that will be described in the next section. By the 1980s, however, faculty members still were attempting to resolve the tensions between scientific and applied concerns and between breadth and depth through distribution of curriculum requirements: introductory psychology, methods courses, and then a mix-and-match menu based on the expertise of faculty and the needs of particular student populations at the institution.

Defining the Field of Study

Our report, then, builds on a 40-year tradition of studying undergraduate education in psychology, a tradition shaped by conflicts that have emerged from new developments in the field. The most common definitions of psychology describe it as the science of the behavior of individual organisms. Even William James, who preferred to define psychology as the science of mental life, recognized that mental processes always exist for purposes of doing. Psychology encompasses the roles of groups and the functions of parts of individual organisms. The former often are the context in terms of which individual behavior is to be understood; the latter provide neurophysiological foundations for the concepts that apply to individual behavior. Physiological psychologists (whose work is sometimes indistinguishable from one or another of the biological sciences) and social psychologists (whose work is sometimes indistinguishable from sociologists, cultural anthropologists, or political scientists) are so different in what they do that communication is difficult and conflict probable.

The differing interests of the physiological and social psychologists reflect the branching of the field in the last 50 years. In the 1930s there were still "schools" of psychology—behaviorism, functionalism, Gestalt psychology, and the like—that attempted to embrace the entire subject matter of the field. By the 1940s, these schools had given way to smaller but still "grand" theories that sought to explain such phenomena as learning, perception, and social action. Even these smaller theories were displaced gradually by the current theorizing that tends to focus on specific types of learning, perception, motivation, psychotherapy, and the like. The potential for

misunderstanding and conflict growing out of extreme specialization is obvious.

Another source of stress is that there essentially are two sciences of psychology (Cronbach, 1957). One is traditional experimental psychology, modeled after physics. Its procedures involve the manipulation of causal variables. In principle, this science permits both the prediction and the control of behavior. The second science of psychology, psychometric psychology, derives from the development of mental tests and is modeled on astronomy. Its procedures involve assessments of behavior, usually with the aid of tests, for the purpose of predicting, but not controlling, behavior in some other situation. These two sciences have different outlooks. Experimental psychology concentrates on averages; psychometric psychology is concerned with individual differences and variation. They use different statistics: Experimental psychology uses techniques of hypothesis testing, whereas psychometric psychology uses correlational procedures. Again, the potential for conflict is clear.

Differences in temperament and values also invite conflict. Kimble's (1984) study of "Psychology's Two Cultures" identified six dimensions on which psychologists differ:

(a) most important scholarly values (scientific vs. humanistic), (b) lawfulness of behavior (determinism vs. indeterminism), (c) basic source of knowledge (observation vs. intuition), (d) appropriate setting for discovery (laboratory vs. field study/case history), (e) generality of laws (nomothetic vs. idiographic), (f) appropriate level of analysis (elementism vs. holism). Psychologists associated with institutions and programs devoted to the natural science aspects of the field occupy the positions identified with the first-mentioned terms in the six polarities. (p. 833)

These polarities are associated with the ways that psychologists earn a living. Many traditional research and academic psychologists endorse the scientific values. By contrast, health service providers endorse the humanistic values. Identification by teaching faculty with either of these two polarities has implications for the shaping of an undergraduate curriculum.

Comments from faculty members on an earlier draft of this article reflected the polarities identified by Kimble (1984). Some psychologists advocated teaching the science of psychology in depth, through a structured sequence of required content courses and associated laboratory experiences. Others proposed a track approach to undergraduate training. One track might emphasize general concepts, critical thinking, and a liberal arts approach. A second track suggested by a few psychologists might focus on students' preparation for postbaccalaureate settings or positions (e.g., as behavioral technicians in community mental health agencies or personnel officers in corporate settings). These preprofessional track options would enable students who intend to work after completing their undergraduate degree to have in-depth experience that helps them focus their major field courses, field work experiences, and electives on a career specialization.

Comments on an earlier draft of this article also pointed to different views on how best to integrate gender, ethnicity, culture, and class into the study of psychology (see Bronstein & Quina, 1988). Most psychologists would acknowledge that faculty members must challenge campus racism and sexism, but there is less agreement on how to do so. Gender, ethnicity, culture, and class are seen by some teachers as issues that challenge the contemporary curricula. Such a challenge also questions traditional research methodologies that are empirical, quantitative, and positivist, and may advocate alternative psychological methods that are contextual, interpretive, and more qualitative. Other psychologists believe that, although these topics and the new knowledge generated by research have legitimacy in the discipline, they should be subtopics best left to treatments determined by an instructor's sensitivities and commitments.

This article will not reconcile all of the conflicts that faculty discussions generate. We believe that differences can be explained to students to foster in them the capacity to make connections between seemingly disparate arguments and knowledge bases. This means that teachers will see psychology as an evolving subject matter best understood from an array of differing perspectives. The primary goal is not to demand that the student master fixed content, but rather to teach the student how to struggle with ambiguity, how to reflect on this experience, and how to ask more sophisticated questions about behavior and experience.

This article is organized in six sections: Orienting Assumptions, Undergraduate Psychology Students, Common Goals, Measurement and Evaluation of Major Field Outcomes, Structure of the Major, and Student Learning and Self-Evaluation.

Orienting Assumptions

Five assumptions guided our discussions. These assumptions are consistent with the evolving perspective on the curriculum described in earlier psychology reports and with our understanding of the psychology major in the context of contemporary American higher education. These assumptions were as follows:

1. Institutions vary in their missions and in the characteristics of their students. In every generation, from the mid-1800s (Rudolph, 1977) through World War II, the Korean war, and the Vietnam war (Gamson, 1984) to the present, universities and colleges have served new student populations. As student heterogeneity increased, uniform curricula and undergraduate programs became increasingly problematic. Balancing curricular coherence with responsiveness to new knowledge, new students, and new epistemologies is always a difficult task (Astin, 1985).

2. A liberal arts education in general, and the study of psychology in particular, is a preparation for lifelong learning, thinking, and action; it emphasizes specialized and general knowledge and skills. The skills required to be a successful student do not always match those required to be a good citizen or a happy and productive person. For example, there are differences between academic and nonacademic life in the type of intelligence that is most useful (abstract intelligence vs. social or practical intelligence or aesthetic sensitivity); the knowledge that is most prized (generalized knowledge vs. specific, informal, nonverbal, and implicit real-life knowledge); the definition and solution of problems (defining problems by type and yielding to simple elegant solutions vs. recognizing the problems and juggling numerous possible solutions); and the employment of resources (rewarding "pure thought" exercised in independent isolation vs. cooperating toward a common, negotiated goal). Definitions of liberal education may need some rethinking. (See Jeavons, 1989, and Resnick, 1987, for a discussion.)

3. The definition of curricular goals begins with a specific group of faculty and their departmental and institutional culture (Appley, 1970), and their specific understanding of the discipline in the context of changing knowledge and changing student profiles. We think there should be no universally prescribed course of study in undergraduate psychology, no hard and fast requirements such as those suggested for doctoral training in APA-accredited programs. Instead, we advocate curricular pluralism. Coherence across curricula should be based on the common goals suggested in a later section of this article.

4. Researchers have established that faculty do not teach in only one way and students do not learn in only one way.

5. Students should expect feedback from faculty. Evaluation and assessment should not be tied solely to the task of assigning grades. Assessment of students and programs is best accomplished through multiple methods. Students must also acquire the skill to evaluate their own progress and accomplishment of integrated learning.

Undergraduate Psychology Students

In 1987, more than 42,000 students received baccalaureate degrees in psychology, almost 2,000 more than in the previous year. This was the second consecutive year in which the number of degrees increased, reversing a downward trend from the more than 50,000 degrees awarded in 1976. As shown in Table 1, the decline in enrollments between 1976 and 1986 was entirely due to the declining number of degrees awarded to men in this period.

Howard et al. (1986) analyzed the changing demographics of psychology students, shifts in gender and ethnic composition of graduate and undergraduate student groups, advances in health-care provider specialties, and the declining interest in employment in traditional academic and research settings. They found that the dramatic increases in the numbers of women in undergraduate and graduate student bodies have not been matched by similar gains in the achievement of tenure and salary parity by women academics.

It is not known why there has been such a significant increase in the numbers of women in psychology programs, nor what consequences the gender shift in enrollments will have on the field. For example, has classroom pedagogy become more responsive to potential differences between men and women in ways of knowing and discourse (Belenky, Clinchy, Goldberger, & Tarule, 1986; Clinchy, 1989)? As Howard et al. (1986) concluded, demographic changes should have a "profound effect on the field both now and in the future" (p. 1326).

Common Goals

In spite of the diversity of settings in which the under-

Table 1
Bachelor's Degree Recipients in Psychology (1976–1987)

Year	Total	Women n	Women %	Men n	Men %
1976	50,363	27,376	54	22,987	46
1977	47,794	27,102	57	20,962	43
1978	45,057	26,540	59	18,517	41
1979	43,012	26,363	61	16,649	39
1980	42,513	26,923	63	15,590	37
1981	41,364	26,917	65	14,447	35
1982	41,539	27,783	67	13,756	33
1983	40,825	27,597	68	13,228	32
1984	40,375	27,426	68	12,949	32
1985	40,237	27,422	68	12,815	32
1986	40,937	28,246	69	12,691	31
1987	42,868	29,536	69	13,332	31

Note. Data are from *Academic Science/Engineering: Graduate Enrollment and Support Detailed Statistical Tables* (Surveys of Science Resource Series) by the National Science Foundation, 1988, Washington, DC: Author. Data are in the public domain.

graduate degree in psychology is completed, we believe that common goals can be identified. The eight goals offered here as guidelines may lend coherence to the psychology curriculum. We recognize that specific course requirements will be different in different institutions. The works of Halpern (1988) and McGovern and Hawks (1986, 1988) were particularly helpful in generating these guidelines.

Knowledge Base

There are significant facts, theories, and issues in psychology that a student needs to know. Faculty members' training and their interpretations of the field determine what they label as significant. Comparison of past reports, especially of Buxton et al. (1952) with Scheirer and Rogers (1985), indicates that the content of the field changes. Nevertheless, there are common continuing foci, such as biopsychology, learning, cognition, social psychology, developmental psychology, personality, abnormal psychology and adjustment, and principles of psychological tests and measurements. Partly on the basis of analysis of chapter titles and major themes in introductory psychology textbooks published between 1890 and 1987, Matarazzo (1987) concluded that "there is only one psychology, no specialties, but many applications" (p. 893).

The critical goal of teaching is to help students develop a conceptual framework that embraces relevant facts and concepts rather than isolated bits of knowledge, and to help them achieve a base for lifelong learning rather than a static, encyclopedic knowledge of the current state of the field. Because knowledge in the field and in parallel disciplines grows so rapidly, teachers need to recognize the principle that less is more in coverage of content knowledge in individual courses and in the curriculum as a whole.

Thinking Skills

Advanced work in the discipline requires skills in learning, critical thinking, and reasoning—skills that come in part from working with quantitative information in statistics or experimental methods courses and from critical reading of original texts in all courses. Psychology students also need to gain familiarity with qualitative methods and to develop a disciplined curiosity about human behavior and experience. Even at the introductory level, students should be able to inquire about behavioral antecedents and consequences and to view with amiable skepticism the explanations and conclusions in popular media reports on psychology and other social sciences. As they advance, psychology students should learn to think critically about themselves, including their differences and their similarities with others; to evaluate their attitudes about people who are different from themselves; and to know how gender, race, ethnicity, culture, and class affect all human perspectives and experiences.

Language Skills

Research in the pedagogy of composition and its cognitive psychology bases should encourage teaching that gives explicit attention to the development of students' thinking, reading, and writing skills (McGovern & Hogshead, 1990). Psychology students should be able to comprehend the discourse of the discipline used in textbooks and scientific journal articles, and should be able to present written arguments in the language of the discipline, using the elements of style and the presentation of scientific information described in the *Publication Manual of the American Psychological Association* (3rd ed.; APA, 1983a).

Information Gathering and Synthesis Skills

Psychology majors should be able to gather information from a library, from computerized information and bibliographic systems, and from other sources to present a persuasive argument.

Research Methods and Statistical Skills

The skills to use experimental methods, statistics, and qualitative methods are essential. These skills should be fostered in separate courses, developed in laboratory work, and reinforced by the use of critical discussion of research findings and methods in every course. Whatever the mode of instruction, students should become increasingly independent in posing questions about the study of behavior and experience and in selecting effective methods to answer those questions. Through repeated exposure to the methods of psychology, students majoring in psychology should develop growing sophistication about research strategies and their limitations, including such issues as the drawing of causal conclusions from experimental versus correlational results.

Interpersonal Skills

Interpersonal awareness, sensitivity, and expanded self-knowledge can be fostered by the study of psychology. The ability to monitor one's own behavior; to be sensitive to differences and similarities in the way people are treated because of gender, race, ethnicity, culture, and class; and to work effectively in groups are outcomes that should complement the cognitive achievements of the traditional course of study in psychology.

History of Psychology

It is important for psychology majors to have an understanding of the history of the discipline that goes beyond knowledge of major figures and their contributions and includes the sociocultural context in which psychology emerged. Through such knowledge, students may better appreciate the evolution of the methods of psychology, its theoretical conflicts, its sociopolitical uses, and its place in the broader intellectual traditions of the humanities, sciences, and social sciences (Furumoto, 1989).

Ethics and Values

The *Ethical Principles of Psychologists* (APA, 1990) were empirically derived from critical incidents submitted by scientists and practitioners. Since 1948, when the first APA committee met to fashion a code of ethics, the discipline's emphasis has always been on the educational value of espousing a set of ethical principles for psychologists. Undergraduate students should learn to use these principles to understand conflicts, to generate alternative responses, and to act on their judgments. Recognizing the dignity of the person, promoting human welfare, and maintaining academic and scientific integrity are examples of such principles. A particularly important social and ethical responsibility of faculty members is to promote their students' understanding of gender, race, ethnicity, culture, and class issues in psychological theory, research, and practice.

Measurement and Evaluation of Major Field Outcomes

Outcomes to be evaluated must be consistent with the mission and goals of a particular college or university. At the departmental level, the goals for the major should be viewed in this broader context. Thus, the important outcomes for psychology intersect with the broader goals found in an institution's mission statement or those suggested as a minimum required curriculum in the Association of American Colleges (AAC; 1985) report—literacy, working with quantitative information, science, historical consciousness, values, and multicultural experiences.

A hallmark of effective assessment in psychology is a multimethod approach (Halpern, 1988). Archival strategies such as transcript analyses; surveys of students, alumni, and employers (McGovern & Carr, 1989); portfolios of laboratory reports and class papers; performance on standardized tests such as the Graduate Record Examination; locally developed comprehensive examinations; and senior theses and research projects are all potential sources of evaluation information.

Any evaluation of the undergraduate psychology program should be initiated internally and validated by external consultants. Evaluation is an opportunity for periodic reflection and should be a stimulus for growth and renewal.

Despite the increasing emphasis on assessment as a tool of program and institutional evaluation, students gain most from assessment that takes place in individual courses. Effective use of multiple testing procedures in the classroom accomplishes multiple goals: Students gauge their understanding of new and increasingly complex material; faculty members gauge the clarity of their presentation of this material; and faculty members and students shape one another's expectations for learning.

Structure of the Major

Most psychology curricula have a beginning, a middle, and an end. The beginning includes an introductory course that exposes students to topics in the discipline. Methods courses in research and statistics and, in some departments, a course in principles of psychometrics and individual differences, follow the introductory experience. The methods courses enable students to read and evaluate the research presented in content courses as the knowledge base of the major. Many departments organize these requirements with a distribution model in which students sample several courses offered in cognitive psychology, developmental psychology, social and personality psychology, biopsychology, and so on. Finally, a course in history and systems of psychology, an advanced general psychology course, or a senior seminar on selected topics in psychology may serve as a capstone for content. The senior research project completed in a campus laboratory or the senior fieldwork, practicum, or internship completed in an applied setting may be offered either as a requirement or as an elective. The curricular models displayed in the Appendix are traditional and alternative structures for organizing a sequence of learning.

The *generalist model* displayed in Model 1 of the Appendix most closely approximates the traditional curricular structure. Consistent with our working premise that less is more—that students' capacity to develop thinking, learning, reasoning, language, and methodological skills is facilitated by an iterative exposure to less content—we recommend reducing the number of survey courses. This requires two courses in the traditional knowledge base of offerings, followed by two more specialized courses in the same area and with a laboratory.

The *thematic models* in Models 2 (developmental psychology), 3 (biological psychology), and 4 (health psychology) of the Appendix are possible examples of curricula that extend our notion of less is more even further. Instead of the traditional introductory course that covers 14 to 16 subfields of psychology in a single semester, students would be introduced to one area (e.g., life span developmental, Model 2) that treats all of the topics included in traditional introductory courses in the context of an integrative perspective. Subsequent methods courses could be generalist in nature (e.g., Models 2 and 3) or continue with the theme introduced in the first course by exposing students to more and more complex research and statistical methods on the thematic topic (e.g., Model 4).

Continuing with the developmental psychology thematic model as an example, the survey courses would broaden the students' knowledge by exposing them to two facets of human development in which they must necessarily integrate other subfields of psychology that influence the developmental literature. Specialized courses with laboratories would follow these two survey courses.

Critics of the thematic model (which could be designed equally well for social psychology, cognitive psychology, or other areas in the traditional knowledge base) might argue that it is not psychology because it is too narrow and specialized. We would agree that, although this is not a traditional approach, it can foster both breadth and specialization and encourage students to integrate their learning in a more coherent manner. In large, research-oriented institutions in which distinguished senior faculty often do not teach undergraduates, the thematic model has the potential for bringing such individuals back to the baccalaureate enterprise. Scholars, graduate students, and undergraduates enrolled in a thematic track may be more likely to work together in and out of the classroom. In sum, we see both the generalist and the thematic models as worthy of consideration because they reflect what is now happening and what we believe could be designed to facilitate students' integrated learning.

All four models include an integrated senior-year project to be completed in an applied field setting off campus (e.g., a mental health agency or a corporate personnel office), on campus (e.g., a university peer counseling services), or in a research setting (e.g., a neurosurgery laboratory or a survey research laboratory). Another example for this senior-year experience could be in a traditional classroom with one or more faculty teaching the history and systems, advanced general psychology, or special topics courses. Senior-year applied experiences enable students to test their accumulated knowledge, skills, and ethical sensitivities. Furthermore, applied experiences integrate for the students the goal of liberal learning espoused by most teachers—that is, to be reflective about all of one's experiences. In contrast, a senior-year classroom experience emphasizes the integration of what has been learned up to that point, but focuses more sharply on traditional intellectual outcomes for study in the major.

We recommend an additional component for all undergraduate majors in psychology. An interpersonal skills and group process laboratory to develop students' ability to work in groups is included in all of our proposed models. Whenever possible, we recommend that this laboratory (or the senior-year applied project) be combined with a community-service component. A volunteer experience should be an integral part of every student's undergraduate education. Such an experience would give psychology majors an opportunity to apply interpersonal problem-solving and decision-making skills, develop their leadership potential, and provide career-related insights. Supervised community service can instill a sense of responsibility that is critical for informed citizenship.

In sum, our assumptions, common goals for the major, and proposed curricular models converge to expose students to many ideas and perspectives and give them conceptual structures whereby they can think in psychological terms. We want to emphasize teaching for the transfer of learning. Our students should be able to recognize concepts and skills in a variety of contexts and apply them appropriately. They should be able to look at relationships, make connections, and struggle with ambiguity. To accomplish this, our curricular models stress students having the experience of practicing (talking, writing, doing) psychology and listening to psychologists and others talking about the discipline from personal and scholarly perspectives.

As every past report has stressed, the content of courses and structures of curricula are necessary but not sufficient conditions for effective education in a field. Good teaching is essential. Good teaching in psychology is characterized by the active involvement of students—that is, more talking by students and less by teachers. Good teaching, whether in a large auditorium, a smaller classroom, or a laboratory, uses technology directly or indirectly to enhance students' learning and enthusiasm. For example, computers can be used in many ways to enhance students' learning. They can be used as tools to develop statistical and research methods skills and to demonstrate and simulate psychological research. They can be used for student practice and as programmed learning devices. They can be used to teach problem-solving strategies and to further develop the complex thinking abilities learned through critical reading and writing tasks.

Good teaching requires that teachers continually renew their craft by exploring how their students learn most effectively. Katz (1988) summarized this process well:

How does our field look from the point of view of the learner? . . . we want to build a cognitive science upon which teaching is based, and we cannot leave it to the specialists alone, good as they may be. We the teachers, as *clinicians of cognitive science* [italics added] in our classrooms, need to articulate what we do. (p. 183)

Student Learning and Self-Evaluation

The learning process and the influence of college on students have been studied by psychologists for many years (e.g., Astin, 1977, 1985; Chickering & Associates, 1984; Feldman & Newcomb, 1976). We recommend that teachers use this literature to design individual courses in the same way that they can use the past literature to design their overall curricula.

A National Institute of Education (1984) report, *Involvement in Learning: Realizing the Potential of American Higher Education*, recommended three critical conditions of excellence in the learning process: student involvement, clear and high expectations, and regular and periodic assessment and feedback. In specifying learning goals and measurable outcomes, teachers could consider the eight goals that we proposed earlier in this article, use whatever local modifications seem necessary, and gather reactions from their students about how the current curriculum enables students to achieve these goals. Grading in individual courses provides discrete markers for students about their mastery of knowledge in one content area, but useful evaluation must also include periodic, cumulative evaluation points. Such points can be embedded in required courses or field experiences and be designed to help students evaluate their progress.

As students gradually become independent learners, the department's advising system should enable students and faculty members to work together to gauge progress, analyze roadblocks, and plan for the future beyond the baccalaureate program. Effective departmental advising systems include informational resources (e.g., brochures, handouts, videotapes) on career planning, postbaccalaureate employment, and graduate or professional school opportunities and requirements. Ware and Millard (1987) and Woods (1988) have developed excellent handbooks for these purposes. Departmental chairs and deans can help make advising much more effective by including this work in promotion and tenure decisions and in annual performance evaluations.

Summary

The world of the 1990s is different from the world described by Buxton et al. (1952), McKeachie and Milholland (1961), and Kulik (1973). In the year 2000 and beyond, the knowledge base of psychology may include few of the content areas described in this article. Hybrid departments are growing out of the combinations of knowledge generated by scientists and humanists in collaborative disciplines. Undergraduates now are studying social ecology, behavioral medicine, health psychology, neuroscience, and cognitive science.

Is there a canon in psychology? If there is, it is probably in evolving methodologies for the study of behavior, emotion, and cognition. These methods enabled psychologists and their students to study such problems as racism, educational testing, and computer-assisted learning when the knowledge and social norms in these areas were shifting rapidly.

As one contributor to contemporary undergraduate liberal learning, psychology should sustain its popularity and efficacy. Psychology has the potential to touch the whole lives of students—their intellectual development, their emotional growth, and their behavioral skills. The uniqueness of psychology is in the ability of its teachers to incorporate what Mann (1982) labeled the scientific, healing, and wisdom functions in their teaching of undergraduates. As the group of psychologists who met in Ann Arbor to review the undergraduate curriculum stated more than 30 years ago:

We want our students, in encountering the concrete material of human life, to be skillful in (a) recognizing aspects or properties of it that psychology has helped them to see more clearly, and (b) recognizing processes and relationships they would not have known about except as a consequence of their study of psychology . . . which, also, commonly involves some emotional involvement on their part. (McKeachie & Milholland, 1961, p. 88)

REFERENCES

American Psychological Association. (1983a). *Publication manual of the American Psychological Association* (3rd ed.). Washington DC: Author.

American Psychological Association. (1983b). *Results: Phase 1 survey of undergraduate department chairs.* Washington DC: Author.

American Psychological Association. (1990). Ethical principles of psychologists (Amended June 2, 1989). *American Psychologist, 45,* 390–395.

Appley, M. H. (1970). The place of psychology in the university. *American Psychologist, 25,* 387–390.

Association of American Colleges. (1985). *Integrity in the college curriculum: A report to the academic community.* Washington DC: Author.

Astin, A. W. (1977). *Four critical years.* San Francisco: Jossey-Bass.

Astin, A. W. (1985). *Achieving educational excellence.* San Francisco: Jossey-Bass.

Belenky, M. F., Clinchy, B. M., Goldberger, N. R., & Tarule, J. M. (1986). *Women's ways of knowing. The development of self, voice and mind.* New York: Basic Books.

Bronstein, P. A., & Quina, K. (Eds.). (1988). *Teaching a psychology of people: Resources for gender and sociocultural awareness.* Washington DC: American Psychological Association.

Buxton, C. E., Cofer, C. N., Gustad, J. W., MacLeod, R. B., McKeachie, W. J., & Wolfle, D. (1952). *Improving undergraduate instruction in psychology.* New York: Macmillan.

Chickering, A. W., & Associates. (1984). *The modern American college.* San Francisco: Jossey-Bass.

Clinchy, B. (1989). On critical thinking and connected knowing. *Liberal Education, 75*(3), 14–19.

Cronbach, L. J. (1957). The two disciplines of scientific psychology. *American Psychologist, 12,* 671–684.

Feldman, K. A., & Newcomb, T. M. (1976). *The impact of college on students.* San Francisco: Jossey-Bass.

Furumoto, L. (1989). The new history of psychology. In I. S. Cohen (Ed.), *The G. Stanley Hall Lecture Series* (pp. 5–34). Washington, DC: American Psychological Association.

Gamson, Z. (1984). *Liberating education.* San Francisco: Jossey-Bass.

Halpern, D. F. (1988). Assessing student outcomes for psychology majors. *Teaching of Psychology, 15,* 181–186.

Howard, A., Pion, G. M., Gottfredson, G. D., Flatteau, P. E., Oskamp, S., Pfafflin, S. M., Bray, D. W., & Burstein, A. G. (1986). The changing face of American psychology: A report from the Committee on Employment and Human Resources. *American Psychologist, 41,* 1311–1327.

James, W. (1958). *The varieties of religious experience.* New York: Mentor Books. (Original work published 1902)

Jeavons, T. H. (1989). Connecting the curriculum and the community. *Liberal Education, 75*(3), 20–25.

Katz, J. (1988). Does teaching help students learn? In B. A. Kimball (Ed.), *Teaching undergraduates. Essays from the Lilly Endowment workshop on liberal arts* (pp. 173–184). Buffalo, NY: Prometheus Books.

Kimble, G. A. (1984). Psychology's two cultures. *American Psychologist, 39,* 833–839.

Kulik, J. (1973). *Undergraduate education in psychology.* Washington, DC: American Psychological Association.

Mann, R. D. (1982). The curriculum and context of psychology. *Teaching of Psychology, 9,* 9–14.

Matarazzo, J. D. (1987). There is only one psychology, no specialties, but many applications. *American Psychologist, 42,* 893–903.

McGovern, T. V., & Carr, K. (1989). Carving out the niche. A review of alumni surveys on undergraduate psychology majors. *Teaching of Psychology, 16,* 52–57.

McGovern, T. V., & Hawks, B. K. (1986). The varieties of undergraduate experience. *Teaching of Psychology, 13,* 174–181.

1. SCIENCE OF PSYCHOLOGY

McGovern, T. V., & Hawks, B. K. (1988). The liberating science and art of undergraduate psychology. *American Psychologist, 43,* 108–114.

McGovern, T. V., & Hogshead, D. L. (1990). Learning about writing, thinking about teaching. *Teaching of Psychology, 17,* 5–10.

McKeachie, W. J., & Milholland, J. E. (1961). *Undergraduate curricula in psychology.* Fair Lawn, NJ: Scott, Foresman.

Morris, C. G. (Ed.). (1982). Undergraduate psychology education in the next decade [Special Issue]. *Teaching of Psychology, 9*(1).

National Institute of Education. (1984). *Involvement in learning: Realizing the potential of American higher education* (Report of the Study Group on the Condition of Excellence in American Higher Education). Washington DC: Author.

National Science Foundation. (1988). *Academic science/engineering: Graduate enrollment and support detailed statistical tables* (Survey of Science Resource Series). Washington, DC: Author.

Resnick, L. (1987). Learning in school and out. *Educational Researcher, 16,* 13–20.

Rudolph, F. (1977). *Curriculum: A history of the American undergraduate course of study since 1636.* San Francisco: Jossey-Bass.

Scheirer, C. J., & Rogers, A. M. (1985). *The undergraduate psychology curriculum 1984.* Washington DC: American Psychological Association.

Ware, M. E., & Millard, R. J. (Eds.). (1987). *Handbook on student development: Advising, career development, and field placement.* Hillsdale, NJ: Erlbaum.

Woods, P. J. (Ed.). (1988). *Is psychology for them? A guide to undergraduate advising.* Washington, DC: American Psychological Association.

APPENDIX

Model 1
Generalist Model: Undergraduate Psychology

Introductory Psychology (1)
Methods courses (3)
  Statistics; Research Methods; Psychometrics and Individual Differences
Survey courses in knowledge base (2)
  Examples: Social Psychology; Personality; Physiological Psychology
Specialized courses with laboratories to follow up survey courses (2)
  Examples (matched to above survey courses): Group Dynamics; Behavior Modification; Animal Learning
Integrated senior-year project or seminar (1)
  Examples: History and Systems; Advanced General; Special Topics; Senior Research; Honors Research; Field Work and Seminar
Interpersonal skills and group process laboratory for community service (1)
Electives

Model 2
Thematic Model: Developmental Psychology

Life Span Developmental Psychology (1)
Methods courses (3)
  Statistics; Research Methods; Psychometrics and Individual Differences
Survey courses in thematic knowledge base (2)
  Cognitive Development; Social/Personality Development
Specialized courses with laboratories to follow up survey courses (2)
  Examples: Child Psychology; Psychology of Adolescence; Adulthood; Psychology of Aging
Integrated senior-year project or seminar (1)
  Examples: History and Systems; Advanced General; Special Topics; Senior Research; Honors Research; Field Work and Seminar
Interpersonal skills and group process laboratory for community service (1)
Electives

Model 3
Thematic Model: Biological Psychology

Biological Psychology (1)
Methods courses (3)
  Statistics; Research Methods; Psychometrics and Individual Differences
Survey courses in thematic knowledge base (2)
  Brain and Behavior; Evolution of Behavior
Specialized courses with laboratories to follow up survey courses (2)
  Examples: Sensation and Perception; Learning and Cognition; Emotion and Motivation; Health Psychology; Personality and Pathology
Integrated senior-year project or seminar (1)
  Examples: History and Systems; Advanced General; Special Topics; Senior Research; Honors Research; Field Work and Seminar
Interpersonal skills and group process laboratory for community service (1)
Electives

Model 4
Thematic Model: Health Psychology

Health Psychology (1)
Methods courses (3)
  Statistics; Research Methods in Health and Clinical Psychology; Psychometric Methods and Individual Differences
Survey courses in thematic knowledge base (2)
  Psychology of Personality or Social Psychology; Biological Bases of Behavior or Learning and Adaptive Behavior
Specialized courses with laboratories to follow up survey courses (2)
  Examples: Abnormal Psychology; Child Clinical Psychology; Stress and Coping; Psychology of Prevention; Psychology of Women; Experimental Approaches to Personality; Hormones and Behavior; Motivation and Emotion
Integrated senior year project or seminar (1)
  Examples: History and Systems; Advanced General Psychology; Independent Research; Honors Research; Field Work and Seminar
Interpersonal skills and group process laboratory for community service (1)
Electives

Ratting on Psychologists

How the science of human behavior and inner thought became the science of rat learning.

Lawrence LeShan

A disastrous decision made early on in the history of psychology explains its modern-day shortcomings. Eager to achieve the same scientific grace enjoyed by 19th century physicists and chemists, psychologists headed into the laboratory—and most of them never left.

The pitfalls of studying human behavior—let alone consciousness—in the laboratory are easy to illustrate. Look at what we know about the white rat. When its sex life first came under professional scrutiny, it was found to be quite atypical for mammals: It followed no cyclical patterns, and was always initiated by the male. The female seemed generally unresponsive or resistant, and often gave the impression of being bored. This phenomenon was observed over and over again and recorded in a great many professional papers.

Along came the ethologists, who study animal patterns of behavior under natural conditions. They reported that in the wild, the sexual behavior of rats was very different. It followed cyclical patterns and was always initiated by the female. The way she initiated it was to come within three or four body lengths of the male.

Since it is impossible for the female to get more than three or four body lengths *away* from the male in a laboratory cage, this meant that from the male point of view, the female was constantly "coming on" to him, whereas she thought he was a sex maniac. Behavior in the laboratory, in other words, was clearly irrelevant to behavior outside of it.

The point I want to make is that most of the time, our laboratories are highly artificial situations that seriously distort the behavior—and therefore our interpretations—of humans or whatever other species we are studying. The question is whether we can learn *anything* worthwhile about human consciousness and human behavior there.

One widely reported set of experiments shows just how easy it is to go wrong in the laboratory. In the Milgram study, a student subject was shown a person in a different room, strapped into a chair with electrodes attached to him. (Unknown to the subject, this person was really another experimenter hooked up to fake electrodes.) The job of the person strapped into the chair, the subject was told, was to learn to respond correctly to cue words. Every time he goofed, the student was to give him an electric shock. The shocks were to increase in intensity along with the number of wrong answers.

It was not in fact a learning experiment, but rather a study to see how the student subjects would react to being told to give someone else painful shocks. At 75 volts, the pretend-subject would give mild grunts, at 315 volts, violent screams; at 330 volts there was silence. The maximum level was 450 volts.

A group of 39 psychiatrists was asked to predict how far students from Yale University would go. Their almost unanimous consensus was that only 4 percent would reach 300 volts, and that a tiny pathological fringe—fewer than one in 1,000—would go to 450 volts.

In fact, more than 60 percent of the Yale students went all

From *Hippocrates*, January/February 1991, pp. 71-75. From *The Dilemma of Psychology* by Lawrence LeShan. Copyright © 1991 by Lawrence LeShan, Ph.D. Published by E. P. Dutton, USA, Inc.

FIFTY MINUTES WITH A STRANGER

No laboratory experiment is more artificial than making an appointment with a total stranger, walking into an unfamiliar office, and being expected to talk about the intimate details of one's life within a 50-minute time frame. Therapists judge a patient on the basis of a short acquaintance in a highly structured situation. And they tend to be remarkably resistant to changing this initial impression.

Many years ago Richard Renneker, a highly trained psychoanalyst, installed one-way mirrors in several of his colleagues' offices, with their consent and that of their patients. In filming their behavior, he observed to his horror that the therapists usually made up their minds about a patient in the first session, and that almost nothing the patients did or said thereafter could change their minds.

When he brought his filmed demonstrations of this to his colleagues and asked for their help in remedying the situation, they solved the problem by abruptly taking away his research grant and dismissing him from the Chicago Psychoanalytic Institute.

We all know that when we meet someone new, it takes a long time to decipher the major thrusts of his personality. Therapists usually understand this with people they meet outside their offices. Inside, however, they can become so filled with pride of profession that they forget it completely.

I recall, for example, one patient who brought to the first session a dream of an atomic explosion in a subway. This convinced the therapist that the patient had a weak ego that could be easily disrupted. Although the patient had a strong and resilient ego that had stood up and continued to stand up under much stress, nothing that happened in the next four years of psychotherapy could convince the therapist that she was wrong and should reevaluate her opinion. Not only was the entire process of therapy a waste of time and money, but it did much damage to the patient's feelings about himself.

Thirty and 40 years ago, professional therapists tried to hold their impressions and check them against projective tests. They waited until they could compare their initial impressions with the Rorschach Test, the Thematic Apperception Test, or a social work evaluation. Today, however, psychotherapists have grown so arrogant that they judge another human being on the basis of what he or she does in the course of one or two hours, in as artificial a situation as is possible to find on this planet.

the way. In Italy, South Africa, and Australia, the percentage turned out to be somewhat higher. In Munich, the percentage was 85 percent.

Although there was a great deal of shock over how "sick" the subjects—and possibly the whole human race—were shown to be, this study ignored a major variable: The subjects had been completely removed from their normal environments and placed in one with different rules. The new rules were, "Forget everything you have been taught in the past. Forget your ethical standards and beliefs. There is only one law or morality here: Obey the experimenter." By agreeing to be subjects in the experiment, they agreed to obey these laws as long as they were in the laboratory.

In further studies, when the subjects were told they could choose the level of administered shock, they always chose the lowest level. The follow-up research points to a far different interpretation of the Milgram study: It shows that Milgram is actually a study of how a laboratory setting acts to constrain human behavior.

The psychologist David Bannister puts it this way: "In order to behave like scientists, we must construct situations in which our subjects can behave as little like human beings as possible, and we do this to allow ourselves to make statements about the nature of their humanity."

Further, it soon became clear that humans were poor subjects for behavioristic experiments. Instead of asking if, perhaps, behavioristic models did not apply to human beings, behaviorists decided to find better subjects.

When the American psychologist went hunting human behavior, he found one animal—the albino rat. He reasoned that since all behavior consists of reflexes, and since one reflex is very like another, studying the behavior of one species will yield information on the behavior of all species. Therefore, we might as well use animals we can give shocks to, that we don't have to pay, and whose lives we can completely control.

In the two major behaviorist psychology journals, *The Journal of Animal Behavior* and *The Journal of Comparative and Physiological Behavior*, the more articles that were published over time, the fewer species they covered. As we published more and more in this field, it was literally about less and less. The end of the story is well known. Edwin Chase Tolman dedicated his book *Purposive Behavior in Animals and Man* to the white rat.

Very few rats have learned to march in military formations, cheat on income taxes, or compose the Fifth Symphony.

How this happened is analogous to a group of scientists living in Venice and wanting to study cars. Since cars run so poorly on or under water and there are no roads available, the scientists decide to study canoes instead so that through them they can better understand cars.

Canoes are about as similar to cars as rats are to human beings. On the one side, both are mammals. On the other, both are human-made objects that transport people faster and more efficiently than they could go on their own. Rats and canoes are easier and cheaper to obtain for experimental purposes than people and cars.

The problem with this solution is that each species is very different and that one generalizes at one's peril. Chickens will starve if they're prevented from learning to peck while young. If, however, you keep swallows from flying, they still fly flawlessly at the first opportunity. Rats reared in darkness have no trouble seeing when brought into light, whereas apes raised this way are functionally blind, and only slowly regain their visual ability.

Very few rats have learned to march in military formations, cheat on income taxes, turn the design of female decoration over to males who prefer other males as sexual partners, or any other of the common behaviors of the human race. Nor have they learned to establish a Red Cross for disaster relief, to compose the Fifth Symphony, or to paint *Christina's World*.

The special things that make us human can't be studied in the laboratory. By adapting a scientific method that was not feasible for studying humans, we lost contact with them. Then, instead of changing our method, we changed our subjects of study. The human being was lost, and psychology became the study of the trivial.

Biological Bases of Behavior

As a child, Nancy vowed she did not want to turn out like either of her parents. Nancy's mother was very passive and acquiescent about her father's drinking. When Dad was drunk, Mom always called him in "sick" at work and acted as if there were nothing wrong at home. Nancy's childhood was a nightmare. Her father's behavior was unpredictable. If he drank a little he was happy, most of the time. If he drank a lot, which was usually the case, he became belligerent. But here was Nancy, in the alcohol rehabilitation unit of a large state hospital. Nancy's employer could no longer tolerate her on-the-job mistakes nor her unexplained absences from work and referred her there. As Nancy pondered her fate, she wondered whether her genes preordained her to follow in her father's inebriated footsteps or whether the stress of her childhood had brought her to this point in her life. After all, being the child of an alcoholic is not easy.

Just as Nancy is, psychologists are concerned with discovering the causes of human behavior. Once the cause is known, treatments for problematic behaviors can be developed. In fact, certain behaviors might even be prevented when the cause is known. But for Nancy, prevention was too late.

One of the paths to understanding humans is to understand the biological underpinnings of their behavior. Genes and chromosomes, the body's chemistry (as found in hormones, neurotransmitters, and enzymes), and the central nervous system are all implicated in human behavior. All represent the biological aspects of behavior and ought, therefore, to be worthy of study by psychologists.

Physiological psychologists and other similar psychologists are the ones who often examine the role of biology in behavior. The neuroscientist is especially interested in brain functioning; the psychopharmacologist is interested in the effect of various psychopharmacologic agents or psychoactive drugs on behavior.

These psychologists often utilize one of two techniques to understand the biology-behavior connection. Animal studies involving manipulation, stimulation, or destruction of certain parts of the brain offer one method of study. However, of late, animal rights activists have questioned the validity and ethical correctness of maiming animals to advance the human condition. Therefore, for scientists there is a second technique available that includes the examination of unfortunate individuals whose brains are defective at birth or damaged later by accidents or disease. We can also use animal models to understand

genetics; with animal models we can control reproduction and develop various strains of animals if necessary. Such tactics with humans would be considered extremely unethical. However, by studying an individual's behavior in comparison to natural and adoptive parents we can begin to understand the role of genetics in human behavior.

The articles in this unit are designed to familiarize you with the various knowledge psychologists have gleaned by using these two techniques as well as others to study physiological processes and mechanisms in human behavior. Each article should interest you and make you more curious about the role of biology in human endeavors.

In the first article, "Mapping the Brain," techniques for conducting brain research or studying the function of various parts of the brain are discussed. The article also provides some interesting and challenging puzzles to introduce you to how the brain functions in thought, emotions, and language. A comparison article, "Mind and Brain" indicates that the newest research points to a positive biological explanation of mental events.

In the third article, "What a Child Is Given," Deborah Franklin points out that behavior is a function of the genotype-environment interaction, an interaction that begins prenatally and includes interaction with the organism's internal biochemical environment. Interestingly enough, as geneticists come even closer to mapping the human genome, behavior geneticists provide stronger and stronger evidence that environmental events play a critical role in structuring how the individual's genotype will be expressed. In the next article, heredity is also highlighted. In "Study Links Genes to Sexual Orientation," new and interesting research which suggests that homosexuality is inherited rather than learned is divulged. The study from which this conclusion is drawn compared identical and fraternal twins, another research technique for examining the role of nature versus nurture.

Our emphasis next shifts to biochemistry. In "A Pleasurable Chemistry," Janet Hopson reviews research that delineates the role of endorphins, which seem to be the body's natural opiates, in athletic events, pain control, and even the immune system.

Finally, both of these determinants of behavior, biology and environment are discussed in "Sizing Up the Sexes," an article that addresses differences between men and women and to what these differences ought to be ascribed.

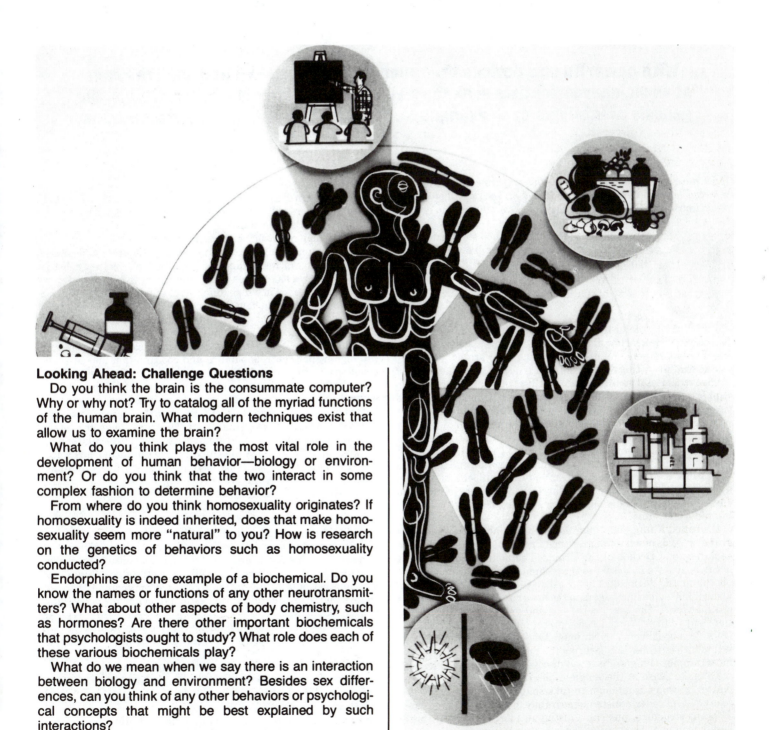

Looking Ahead: Challenge Questions

Do you think the brain is the consummate computer? Why or why not? Try to catalog all of the myriad functions of the human brain. What modern techniques exist that allow us to examine the brain?

What do you think plays the most vital role in the development of human behavior—biology or environment? Or do you think that the two interact in some complex fashion to determine behavior?

From where do you think homosexuality originates? If homosexuality is indeed inherited, does that make homosexuality seem more "natural" to you? How is research on the genetics of behaviors such as homosexuality conducted?

Endorphins are one example of a biochemical. Do you know the names or functions of any other neurotransmitters? What about other aspects of body chemistry, such as hormones? Are there other important biochemicals that psychologists ought to study? What role does each of these various biochemicals play?

What do we mean when we say there is an interaction between biology and environment? Besides sex differences, can you think of any other behaviors or psychological concepts that might be best explained by such interactions?

MAPPING THE BRAIN

With powerful new devices that peer through the skull and see the brain at work, neuroscientists seek the wellsprings of thoughts and emotions, the genesis of intelligence and language. They hope, in short, to read your mind.

If you have one of 1,000 test copies of this magazine, sometime while you read this article a specially embedded microchip will give you a mild electric shock. If you have an ordinary copy, there is no danger.

Deep inside your brain, a little knob-shaped organ no bigger than a chickpea is going like gangbusters right now (at least if you're the gullible type). The organ is called the amygdala, and when neuroscientists gave volunteers a version of this warning—that sometime during an experiment they might receive an electric shock—the nerve cells in the volunteers' amygdalae lit up like telephone lines during the World Series earthquake. How did the scientists know? They were reading their volunteers' minds—by mapping their brains.

It seems only fitting that, with 1492 in the air, one of the greatest uncharted territories in science is finally attracting its own cartographers. The terrain is the gelatinous three-pound world called the Brain, and the map makers' sextants are devices that stare right through the solid wall of the skull. The maps they are slowly piecing together will carry labels even more provocative than the 15th century's "Disappointment Islands." They will show, with the precision of the best atlas, the islands of emotion and the seas of semantics, the land of forethought and the peninsula of musical appreciation. They will show, in short, exactly where in the brain cognition, feelings, language and everything else that makes us human comes from.

It's called a functional map of the brain, and it is one of the grandest goals of what Congress and President George Bush have declared the "Decade of the Brain." The neuroscientists might actually achieve it, thanks to the technologies that open windows on the mind. With 100 billion cells—neurons—each sprouting about 1,000 sylphlike fingers to reach out and touch another, it's quite a view. "The brain is the last and greatest biological frontier," says James Watson, codiscoverer of the double helix that is DNA. In a book from the National Academy of Sciences released last month entitled "Discovering the Brain," Watson calls it "the most complex thing we have yet discovered in our universe."

To make sense of the jungle of neurons and swamps of gray matter, it won't be enough to take snapshots with, say, a CAT scanner. Computer-assisted tomography produces lovely pictures of brain structure, but can't distinguish between a live brain and a dead one. The challenge for brain cartography is to move

beyond structure—all the cranial continents have been identified—to create a detailed diagram of which parts do what. For that, the map makers rely on an alphabet soup of technologies, from PETs to SQUIDs (page 68), that pinpoint neural activity in all its electrical, magnetic and chemical glory.

Each technique adds a different piece to the neural puzzle. Some magnetic imaging, for instance, is so spatially precise it can distinguish structures as small as a millimeter, but is much too slow to reveal the sequence in which different clumps of neurons blink on during a thought. But together, the technologies are yielding a map as detailed as that expected to be drawn for human DNA—though much more interesting. For instance, neuroscientists thought that the cerebellum was the patron saint of the clumsy, the region that controls balance and coordination and so keeps people from stumbling. New studies suggest that the cerebellum may also house the memory of rote movements: touch-typing or violin fingering may originate in the same place as the command not to trip over your own two feet. "Perhaps the brain can package a task very efficiently, even take it out of the conscious world [of the cortex] and just run the program unconsciously," speculates neurologist John Mazziotta of the University of California, Los Angeles. The mapping expeditions have also perked up philosophy. Once again, eminent thinkers are dueling over whether the mind is anything more than the brain.

The lofty abilities of the brain reside in the cortex, the quarter-inch-thick cap of grooved tissue that runs from the eyebrows to the ears. The cortex consists of two hemispheres, a left and a right, each composed of four distinct lobes (diagram, page 67) and connected by a highway of fibers called the corpus callosum. Studies of patients with brain lesions, as well as electrical stimulation of conscious patients during brain surgery, have pinpointed scores of regions that seem to specialize in particular jobs. Some make sense of what the eyes see. Others distinguish irregular from regular verbs. But research on brain-damaged people always runs the risk that they aren't representative. The power of the new imaging techniques is that they peer inside the minds of the healthy. "They allow us to study how the living brain performs sophisticated mental functions," says neuroscientist Eric Kandel of Columbia University. "With them, we can address the most complicated questions in all science."

Some of the maps confirm what studies of brain-damaged patients had already shown. Last November, for instance, research-

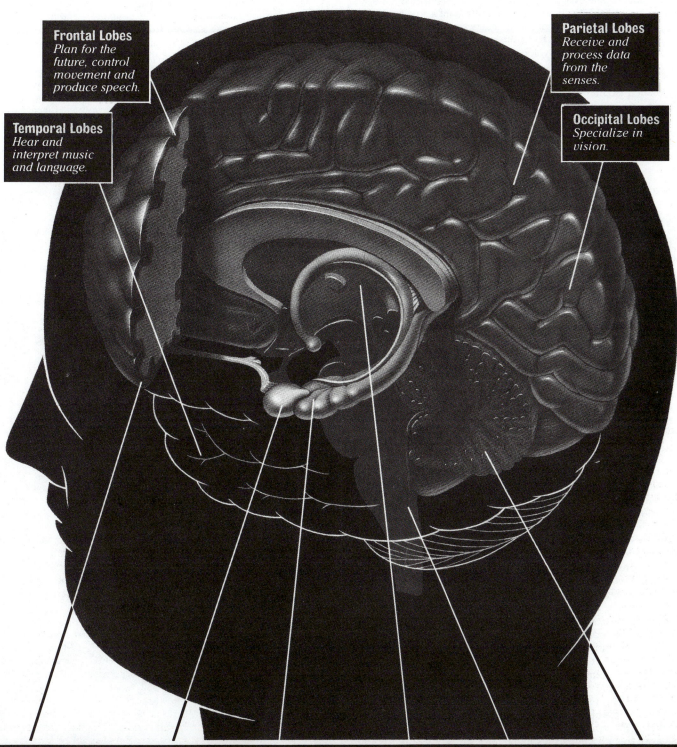

Frontal Lobes
Plan for the future, control movement and produce speech.

Parietal Lobes
Receive and process data from the senses.

Temporal Lobes
Hear and interpret music and language.

Occipital Lobes
Specialize in vision.

Cerebral Cortex
Covers the four lobes that make up the left and right hemispheres of the brain. It is just a few millimeters thick.

Amygdala
Generates emotions from perceptions and thoughts.

Hippocampus
Consolidates recently acquired information, somehow turning short-term memory into long term.

Thalamus
Takes sensory information and relays it to the cortex.

Brainstem
Controls automatic body functions like breathing. It is the junction between the brain and the spine.

Cerebellum
Governs muscle coordination and the learning of rote movements.

ers reported on a PET (positron emission tomography) study confirming that the hippocampus, a little sea-horse-shaped structure deep inside the brain, is necessary for forming and retrieving memories of facts and events (NEWSWEEK, Nov. 25, 1991). That's just what studies of amnesiacs had found. But while confirmation of old notions is nice, what the brain mappers really want is to stumble upon a Northwest Passage, connections that were totally unexpected, symphonies of neurons that had gone completely unheard. PET may do that. For a PET scan, volunteers are injected with radioactive glucose. Glucose, the body's fuel, mixes with the blood and wends its way to the brain. The more active a part of the brain is, the more glucose it uses. PET sensors arrayed around the head of a volunteer, who sits in a modified dentist's chair with his head behind black felt to keep out distractions, pinpoint the source of the radioactivity, and hence the heightened activity. They send the data to computers that produce two-dimensional drawings showing the neural hot spots.

brain thinks, lots of extraneous or inefficient neural circuits crackle. Intelligence, in this model, is a function not of effort but of efficiency. Intelligence "may involve learning what brain areas *not* to use," says Haier.

One key to intelligence may be "pruning." At birth, a baby's brain is a rat's nest of jumbled neurons. It uses up more and more glucose until the child is about 5, when it is roughly twice as active as an adult's. Then glucose use and the number of circuits plummet until the early teen years. This is called neural pruning, and Haier speculates it's the key to neural efficiency. More intelligent people may get that way by more pruning, which leaves remaining circuits much more efficient. Might pruning explain the link between genius and madness? "Overpruning may result in the high intelligence often associated with creativity, but hyperpruning may result in psychopathology," suggests Haier. No one has a clue as to why some brains prune their circuits like prize bonsai and others let them proliferate

PET is hardly the only technique to discover that the brain is organized in weird ways. Take music—as a team at New York University did. It has pioneered the use of the SQUID (superconducting quantum interference device), which senses tiny changes in magnetic fields. (When neurons fire, they create an electric current; electric fields induce magnetic fields, so magnetic changes indicate neural activity.) The device looks like a hair dryer from hell. When the NYU scientists aimed a SQUID at a brain listening to various notes, they found an eerie reflection of the black and white keys on a piano. NYU physicist Samuel Williamson and psychologist Lloyd Kaufman saw not only that the brain hears loud sounds in a totally different place from quieter sounds, but also that the areas that hear tones are laid out like a keyboard. "The distance between brain areas that hear low C and middle C is the same as the distance between areas that hear middle C and high C—just like on a piano," says Williamson.

In another unexpected find, brain systems that learn and remember faces turn out to reside in a completely different neighborhood from those that learn and recall man-made objects. The memory of a face activates a region in the right part of the brain that specializes in spatial configurations. The memory of a kitchen spatula, in contrast, activates areas that govern movement and touch. "What counts is how the brain acquires the knowledge," says neuroscientist Antonio Damasio of the University of Iowa College of Medicine. "The brain lays down knowledge in the very same systems that are engaged with the interactions"—in the case of a spatula, the memory resides in that part of the cortex that originally processed how the spatula felt and how the hands moved it.

Imagine four squares and form them into an "L." Now imagine two squares side by side. Fit the pieces into a smooth rectangle.

An area near the left side of the back of your head snapped to attention, especially if you're doing this without pencil and paper. It's one of the brain's centers for spatial reasoning—no surprise there. The astonishing thing is how hard it works. At the Brain Imaging Center at UC, Irvine, Richard Haier had volunteers play the computer game Tetris while in a PET scanner. In Tetris, players move and rotate squares, in various configurations such as an "I" or an "L," to create a solid block. This year, Haier found that people used lots of mental energy while learning Tetris, but after practicing for several weeks their brains burned much less energy—even though their scores had improved 700 percent. "Watching someone play Tetris at an advanced level, you might think, 'That person's brain must really be active'," says Haier. However, "[their] brains were actually not working as hard as when they played for the first time." Even more intriguing, the greater a volunteer's drop in the energy his brain used, the higher his IQ.

Intelligence, then, may be a matter of efficiency—neural efficiency. Smart brains may get away with less work because they use fewer neurons or circuits, or both. Conversely, when a less smart

WINDOWS ON THE MIND?

Each scanning device has strengths and weaknesses. PET accurately tracks brain function, but can't resolve structures less than .5 inch apart. MRI can't detect function, but can distinguish structures even .05 inch apart.

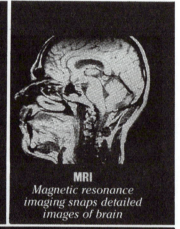

MRI
Magnetic resonance imaging snaps detailed images of brain

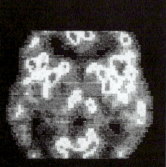

PET
Positron emission tomography tracks blood flow, a proxy for brain activity

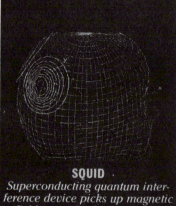

SQUID
Superconducting quantum interference device picks up magnetic fields, a mark of brain action

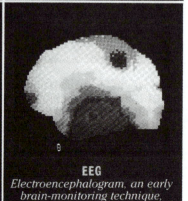

SPECT
Single-photon emission computerized tomography tracks blood flow, a sign of activity

EEG
Electroencephalogram, an early brain-monitoring technique, detects electrical activity

like out-of-control wisteria. Edward Scissorhands, call Dr. Frankenstein.

Decide whether any words in this sentence rhyme. Now name an animal with a very long neck.

Your vision center, at the back of your head right behind your eyes, has been buzzing with activity as you read. That's to be expected. But until recently, scientists thought that all language skills—reading, writing and rhyming—were contained within a single brain circuit. They were wrong. Naming and reading are governed from two different places. You can thank several clusters of neurons scattered across the cortex for coming up with "giraffe"; that's where naming comes from. But these clusters are not necessarily involved in reading. Similarly, regions that process spoken language, midway back on the left side of your head, told you that no words in the sentence rhymed. That spot had been basically dormant until then: contrary to psych texts, words do not have to be pronounced in the mind's ear in order for the brain to assign them a meaning. In the new model, the brain processes words by sight *or* sound. The result goes to the left frontal lobe, which imparts meaning to information received by either sense.

That finding undercuts psychologists' certainty that language is processed like a football play. Scholars had thought that to speak aloud a written word, the printed word had to pass from the visual cortex that saw it to the area that decoded it. From there, it was lateraled to the area in the frontal lobe that pronounces it. Touchdown! "The surprise is that when you see a word, and say it, it doesn't pass through the auditory part of the brain at all," says neuroscientist and PET pioneer Marcus Raichle of Washington University in St. Louis. "The old idea was that before you could say a word, the brain must change a visual code into a sound code. We don't see that at all." In fact, auditory areas of the brain are not active when one speaks, says Raichle: "You don't listen to what you say in the same way that you hear what others say."

Board. Tweal. Nlpfz.

Your visual cortex is still on the job, seeing words. But so are areas way outside the vision centers. To get at the great questions of language, Raichle and colleagues started small—with single words. As words flashed by on a computer screen, one per second, the PET volunteers' visual cortex lit up, as expected. But so did dime-size clusters of neurons way outside the vision centers, on the left side of the brain. Perhaps they hold the meanings of words. Call it Semantic Central. These same areas lit up when the volunteers saw nonwords that nevertheless obeyed rules of English— "tweal"—as if the brain were scrambling to assign a meaning to something that by all rights should have one. These semantic areas stayed dark when the volunteers saw consonant letter strings—*nlpfz*. Since babies aren't born knowing which letters form words and which don't, the brain has apparently learned what conforms to rules of English spelling and what does not. And it has carved out special zones that do nothing but analyze these rule-obeying strings of letters.

Supply a verb for each noun: pencil, oven, broom. And tell which animals in this list are dangerous: tapir, lion, lamb.

Two clusters in your cerebral cortex lit up. One, in the left frontal lobe, kicks in when the brain deals with meanings. But it gets bored easily. If you were asked to supply verbs for the same nouns, or analyze the same animals, over and over, the region wouldn't life a neuron: it seems to play a role only "in the acquisition of a new skill, in this case linguistic," says Raichle. Then it bows out. The brain can still provide "write" for "pencil," but seems to do so on automatic pilot. In addition, to focus on the word problems, the "anterior cingulate gyrus" turns on, as it does whenever "subjects are told to pay attention," says Raichle. It also shines with activity when researchers ask volunteers to read words for colors—red, orange, yellow—written in the "wrong" color ink, such as "red" written in blue. Some neural arbiter must choose which processing center, that for reading "red" or naming blue, to activate. As the brain tries to resolve the conflict, the front of something called the cingulate cortex, located an inch or so beneath the center line of the front of the scalp, positively glows.

COURTESY HAIER & BUCHSBAUM (TOP & MIDDLE), COURTESY BUCHSBAUM (BOTTOM)

PETTING THE BRAIN

LEARNING
The brain of a novice computer-game player (left) is very active; with practice, the brain uses less energy

MENTAL RETARDATION
The brain of a retarded patient (left) is much more active than that of a normal volunteer

DEPRESSION
The brain of a clinically depressed person shows less activity (right) than that of a healthy person

Scans make it clear that the brain is a society of specialists. Different grape-size regions process proper but not common nouns, for instance. Not only that, separate zones also harbor tiny fragments of a larger idea, says Antonio Damasio. It can be an idea as lofty as Truth or as mundane as silver candlesticks. The Ph.D.s haven't figured out Truth yet, but they think they have a pretty good idea how your mind's eye sees the candlestick. PET scans show that these fragments come together in time but not in space, thanks to an as-yet-undiscovered maestro that takes the disparate tones and melds them into perfect harmony.

2. BIOLOGICAL BASES OF BEHAVIOR

Fragments of knowledge are scattered around the brain, especially in the back of the cortex. Areas closer to the front contain what Damasio calls "combinatorial codes," which assemble information from the rear. Damasio has christened these "convergence zones"; their location varies from one person to the next. A convergence zone recalls where in the back office the different attributes of the candlestick are stored. When it's time to reconstruct the silver candlestick, the convergence zone activates all the relevant storage sites simultaneously. One bundle of nerves sends in a pulse that means "silver," another shoots out "cylinder shaped," another offers "burns." "Our sensory experiences happen in different places," says Damasio. "There must be an area where the facts converge."

PETs have seen clues to convergence zones in people who, because of brain lesions, cannot name famous faces. They register a flicker of recognition, but deny they know whose face it is. The knowledge exists, says Damasio, but is "unavailable to consciousness." The lesion has apparently disrupted the links between the memories for various parts of a face—the shapes of its features, the tone of its skin—tucked away in the right part of the cortex and the memory of the name in another back office. The fragments remain, but the convergence zone cannot bring them together.

Sing "Row, Row, Row Your Boat." Lift your finger when you come to a four-letter word.

If you're female, tiny spots on both sides of your brain light up. If you're male, only one side does. That's the kind of map Cecile Naylor of the Bowman Gray School of Medicine saw when she scanned brains of people who had been marked with a radioactive tracer that homes in on active areas. In one task, they listened to words and raised a finger when they heard one four letters long. Women's mental acrobatics were all over the brain; men's were compartmentalized. In women but not in men, some areas associated with vision lit up. "You wonder if females are using more of a visual strategy than males," says Naylor. Perhaps they see the spelled word in their mind's eye and then count letters.

New windows into the brain are ready to open. Robert Turner of the National Institutes of Health recalls "the awe-inspiring experience" of lying inside a colossal MRI (magnetic resonance imaging) magnet as images flashed on and off before his eyes. The machine recorded changes in his brain that came 50 milliseconds apart. "You can see different areas light up at different times," marvels Turner. NYU uses five SQUIDs to spy on the brain; the Japanese are hard at work on a 200-SQUID array. At Massachusetts General Hospital, researchers are putting the finishing touches on "ecoplanar MRI," which snaps a picture of the brain in just 45 milliseconds. The brain's cartographers are poised to glimpse thoughts, feelings and memories as they spring from one tiny clump of cells, ignite others and blossom into an idea or a passion, a creative leap or a unique insight. When they do, science may truly have read the mind.

SHARON BEGLEY *in St. Louis with* LYNDA WRIGHT *in Los Angeles,* VERNON CHURCH *in New York and* MARY HAGER *in Washington*

Mind and Brain

The biological foundations of consciousness, memory and other attributes of mind have begun to emerge; an overview of this most profound of all research efforts

Gerald D. Fischbach

Gerald D. Fischbach is Nathan Marsh Pusey Professor of Neurobiology and chairman of the department of neurobiology at Harvard Medical School and Massachusetts General Hospital. After graduating from Colgate University in 1960, he earned his medical degree at Cornell University Medical School in 1965 and received an honorary M.A. from Harvard University in 1978. Fischbach is also a member of the National Academy of Sciences, the National Institute of Medicine and the American Academy of Arts and Sciences. He is a past-president of the Society for Neuroscience and serves on several foundation boards and university advisory panels.

Ruth gave me a piece of her mind this morning. I am grateful, of course, but I don't know where to put it or, for that matter, what it is. I suppose that the imperatives belong in the limbic system and the geographic information in the hippocampus, but I am not sure. My problem also troubled René Descartes. Three centuries ago he described the mind as an extracorporeal entity that was expressed through the pineal gland. Descartes was wrong about the pineal, but the debate he stimulated regarding the relation between mind and brain rages on. How does the nonmaterial mind influence the brain, and vice versa?

In addressing this issue, Descartes was at a disadvantage. He did not realize the human brain was the most complex structure in the known universe, complex enough to coordinate the fingers of a concert pianist or to create a three-dimensional landscape from light that falls on a two-dimensional retina. He did not know that the machinery of the brain is constructed and maintained jointly by genes and by experience. And he certainly did not know that the current version is the result of millions of years of evolution. It is difficult to understand the brain because, unlike a computer, it was not built with specific purposes or principles of design in mind. Natural

[Ed. note: Refer to *Scientific American*, Sept. 1992 for additional data referenced in this article.]

selection, the engine of evolution, is responsible.

If Descartes had known these things, he might have wondered, along with modern neurobiologists, whether the brain is complex enough to account for the mystery of human imagination, of memory and mood. Philosophical inquiry must be supplemented by experiments that now are among the most urgent, challenging and exciting in all of science. Our survival and probably the survival of this planet depend on a more complete understanding of the human mind. If we agree to think of the mind as a collection of mental processes rather than as a substance or spirit, it becomes easier to get on with the necessary empirical studies. In this context the adjective is less provocative than the noun.

The authors of the articles in this special issue of *Scientific American* and their colleagues have been pressing the search for the neural basis of mental phenomena. They assume that mental events can be correlated with patterns of nerve impulses in the brain. To appreciate the meaning of this assumption fully, one must consider how nerve cells, or neurons, work; how they communicate with one another; how they are organized into local or distributed networks, and how the connections between neurons change with experience. It is also important to define clearly the mental phenomena that need to be explained. Remarkable advances have been made at each level of analysis. Intriguing correlations have in fact begun to emerge between mental attributes and the patterns of nerve impulses that flare and fade in time and space, somewhere inside the brain.

The most striking features of the human brain are the large, seemingly symmetric cerebral hemispheres that sit astride the central core, which extends down to the spinal cord. The corrugated hemispheres are covered by a cell-rich, laminated cortex two millimeters in thickness. The cerebral cortex can be subdivided by morphological and functional criteria into numerous sensory receiving areas, motor-control areas and less well-defined areas in which associative events take place. Many observers assume that here, in the interface between input and output, the grand syntheses of mental life must occur.

It may not be that simple. Mind is often equated with consciousness, a subjective sense of self-awareness. A vigilant inner core that does the sensing and moving is a powerful metaphor, but there is no a priori reason to assign a particular locus to consciousness or even to assume that such global awareness exists as a physiologically unified entity. Moreover, there is more to mind than consciousness or the cerebral cortex. Urges, moods, desires and subconscious forms of learning are mental phenomena in the broad view. We are not zombies. Affect depends on the function of neurons in the same manner as does conscious thought.

And so we return to the organ itself. The brain immediately confronts us with its great complexity. The human brain weighs only three to four pounds but contains about 100 billion neurons. Although that extraordinary number is of the same order of magnitude as the number of stars in the Milky Way, it cannot account for the complexity of the brain. The liver probably contains 100 million cells, but 1,000 livers do not add up to a rich inner life.

Part of the complexity lies in the diversity of nerve cells, which Santiago Ramón y Cajal, the father of modern brain science, described as "the mysterious butterflies of the soul, the beating of whose wings may some day—who knows?—clarify the secret of mental life." Cajal began his monumental studies of adult and embryonic neurons about 100 years ago, when he came across Camillo Golgi's method of staining neurons with silver salts. The great advantage of this technique, which led Cajal to his neuron doctrine, is that silver impregnates some cells in their entirety but leaves the majority untouched. Individuals thus emerged from the forest. Seeing them, Cajal realized immediately that the brain was made up of discrete units rather than a continuous net. He described neurons as polarized cells that receive signals on highly branched extensions of their bodies, called dendrites, and send the information along unbranched extensions, called axons. The Golgi stain revealed a great variety of cell-body shapes, dendritic arbors and axon lengths. Cajal discerned a basic distinction between cells having short axons that communicate with neighbors and cells having long axons that project to other regions.

Shape is not the only source of variation among neurons. Diversity is even greater if molecular differences are considered. Whereas all cells contain the same set of genes, individual cells express, or activate, only a small subset. In the brain, selective gene expression has been found within such seemingly homogeneous populations as the amacrine cells in the retina, the Purkinje cells in the cerebellum and the motor neurons in the spinal cord. Beyond the structural and molecular differences, even more refined distinctions among neurons can be made if their inputs and projections are taken into account. Is it possible that each neuron is unique? This is certainly not the case in all but the most trivial circumstances. Yet the fact that the brain is not made up of interchangeable parts cannot be ignored.

In the face of this astounding diversity, it is a relief to learn that simplifications can be made. Several years ago Vernon B. Mountcastle, working on the somatosensory cortex, and David H. Hubel and Torsten N. Wiesel, working on the visual cortex, produced an important insight. They observed that neurons of similar function are grouped together in columns or slabs that extend through the thickness of the cortex. A typical module in the visual cortex whose component cells respond to a line of a particular orientation measures approximately one tenth of a millimeter across. The module could include more than 100,000 cells, the great majority of which participate in local circuits devoted to a particular function.

Another simplification is that all neurons conduct information in much the same way. Information travels along axons in the form of brief electrical impulses called action potentials, the beating wings of Cajal's butterflies. Action potentials, which measure about 100 millivolts in amplitude and one millisecond in duration, result from the movement of positively charged sodium ions across the surface membrane from the extracellular fluid into the cell interior, or cytoplasm.

The sodium concentration in the extracellular space is about 10 times the intracellular concentration. The resting membrane maintains a voltage gradient of -70 millivolts; the cytoplasm is negatively charged with respect to the outside. But sodium does not enter rapidly because the resting membrane does not allow these ions easy access. Physical or chemical stimuli that decrease the voltage gradient, or depolarize the membrane, increase sodium permeability. Sodium influx further depolarizes the membrane, thus increasing sodium permeability even more.

At a critical potential called the threshold, the positive feedback produces a regenerative event that forces the membrane potential to reverse in sign. That is, the inside of the cell becomes positive with respect to the outside. After about one millisecond the sodium permeability declines, and the membrane potential returns to -70 millivolts, its resting value. The sodium permeability mechanism remains refractory for a few milliseconds after each explosion. This limits to 200 per second or less the rate at which action potentials can be generated.

Although axons look like insulated wires, they do not conduct impulses in the same way. They are not good cables: the resistance along the axis is too high and the membrane resistance too low. The positive charge that enters the axon during the action potential is dissipated in one or two millimeters. To travel distances that may reach many centimeters, the action potential must be frequently regenerated along the way. The need to boost repeatedly the current limits the maximum speed at which an impulse travels to about 100 meters per second. That is less than one millionth of the speed at which an electrical signal moves in a copper wire. Thus, action potentials are relatively low frequency, stereotypical signals that are conducted at a snail's pace. Fleeting thoughts must depend on the relative timing of impulses conducted over many axons in parallel and on the thousands of connections made by each one.

The brain is not a syncytium, at least not a simple one. Action potentials cannot jump from one cell to another. Most often, communication between neurons is mediated by chemical transmitters that are released at specialized contacts called synapses. When an action potential arrives at the axon terminal, transmitters are released from small vesicles in which they are packaged into a cleft 20 nanometers in width that separates presynaptic and postsynaptic membranes. Calcium ions enter the nerve terminal during the peak of the action potential. Their movement provides the cue for synchronized exocytosis, the coordinated release of the neurotransmitter molecules.

Once released, transmitters bind to postsynaptic receptors, triggering a change in membrane permeability. The effect is excitatory when the movement of charge brings the membrane closer to the threshold for action-potential generation. It is inhibitory when the membrane is stabilized near its resting value. Each synapse produces only a small effect. To set the intensity (action-potential frequency) of its output, each neuron must continually integrate up to 1,000 synaptic inputs, which do not add up in a simple linear manner. Each neuron is a sophisticated computer.

Many different kinds of transmitters have been identified in the brain, and this variety has enormous implications for brain function. Since the first neurotransmitter was identified in 1921, the list of candidates has grown at an increasing pace. Fifty is close to the mark. We have learned a great deal about how transmitters are synthesized, how they are released and how they activate receptors in the postsynaptic membrane.

This level of analysis is particularly relevant for psychiatric and neurological disorders that shed light on the workings of the mind. For example, drugs that alleviate anxiety, such as Valium, augment the action of gamma-aminobutyric acid (GABA), an important inhibitory transmitter. Antidepressants, such as Prozac, enhance the action of serotonin, an indoleamine with a wide variety of functions. Cocaine facilitates the action of dopamine, whereas certain antipsychotics antagonize this catecholamine. Nicotine activates acetylcholine receptors, which are distributed throughout the cerebral cortex. Further insight into the chemical bases of thinking and behavior depends on obtaining more precise data regarding the sites of action of these potent agents and on the discovery of more selective ligands, molecules that bind to receptors.

The power of the molecule-to-mind approach can be illustrated by recent advances in the pharmacologic treatment of schizophrenia, the most common and the most devastating of all thought disorders. The classic antipsychotic drugs include the phenothiazines (for example, Thorazine) and the butyrophenones (for example, Haldol). These agents ameliorate hallucinations, delusions, disorganized thinking and inappropriate af-

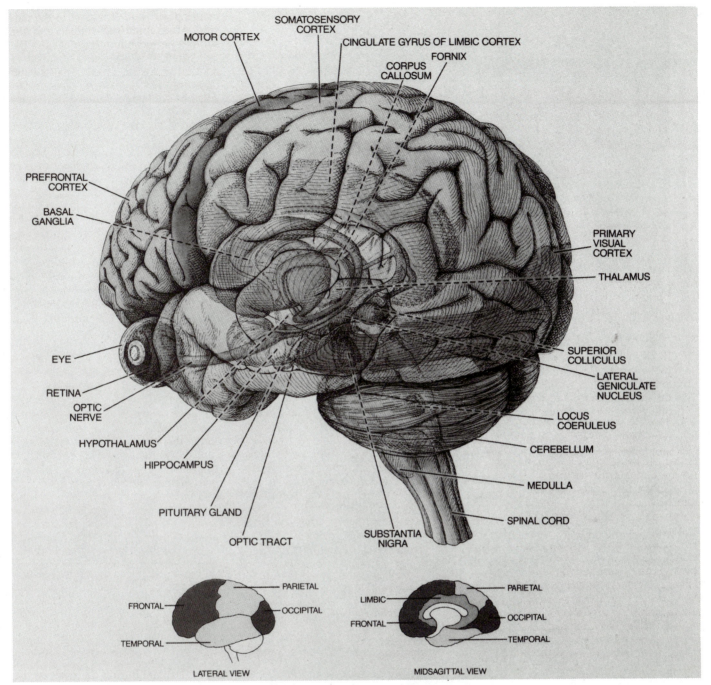

MOTOR CORTEX

SOMATOSENSORY CORTEX

CINGULATE GYRUS OF LIMBIC CORTEX

FORNIX

CORPUS CALLOSUM

PREFRONTAL CORTEX

BASAL GANGLIA

PRIMARY VISUAL CORTEX

THALAMUS

EYE

RETINA

OPTIC NERVE

HYPOTHALAMUS

HIPPOCAMPUS

PITUITARY GLAND

OPTIC TRACT

SUBSTANTIA NIGRA

SUPERIOR COLLICULUS

LATERAL GENICULATE NUCLEUS

LOCUS COERULEUS

CEREBELLUM

MEDULLA

SPINAL CORD

PARIETAL

FRONTAL

OCCIPITAL

TEMPORAL

LATERAL VIEW

PARIETAL

LIMBIC

FRONTAL

OCCIPITAL

TEMPORAL

MIDSAGITTAL VIEW

The Brain: Organ of the Mind

For good reason, the human brain is sometimes hailed as the most complex object in the universe. It comprises a trillion cells, 100 billion of them neurons linked in networks that give rise to intelligence, creativity, emotion, consciousness and memory. Large anatomic subdivisions in the brain offer a rough map of its capabilities. At a very gross level, the brain is bilaterally symmetric, its left and right hemispheres connected by the corpus callosum and other axonal bridges. Its base consists of structures such as the medulla, which regulates the autonomic functions (including respiration, circulation and digestion), and the cerebellum, which coordinates movement. Within lies the limbic system, a collection of structures involved in emotional behavior, long-term memory and other functions.

The highly convoluted surface of the cerebral hemispheres—the cortex (from the Latin word for bark)—is about two millimeters thick and has a total surface area of about 1.5 meters, approximately that of an office desk. The most evolutionarily ancient part of the cortex is part of the limbic system. The larger, younger neocortex is divided into frontal, temporal, parietal and occipital lobes that are separated by particularly deep sulci, or folds. Most thought and perception take place as nerve impulses, called action potentials, move across and through the cortex. Some brain regions with specialized functions have been studied in detail, such as the motor cortex, the somatosensory cortex and the visual pathway. From the collective activity of all the brain regions emerges the most fascinating neurological phenomenon of all: the mind.

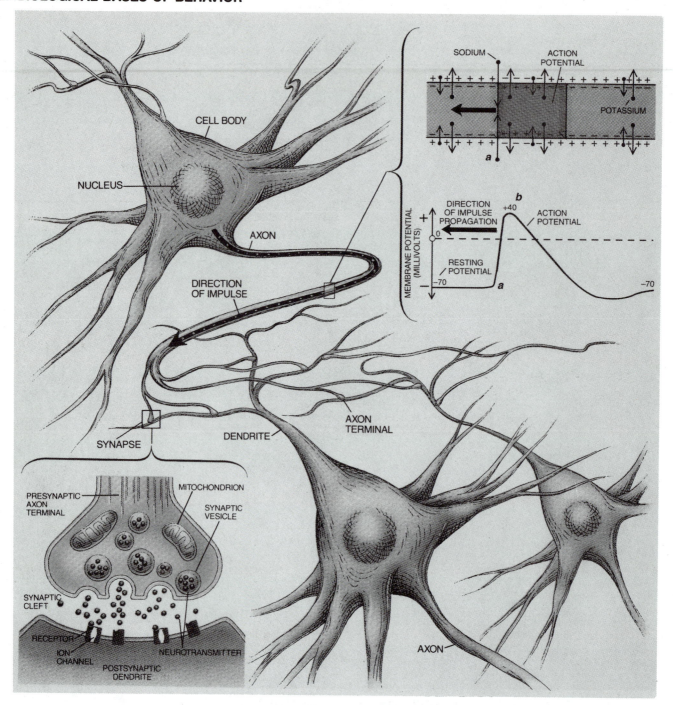

How Neurons Communicate

Aneuron that has been excited conveys information to other neurons by generating impulses known as action potentials. These signals propagate like waves down the length of the cell's single axon and are converted to chemical signals at synapses, the contact points between neurons.

When a neuron is at rest, its external membrane maintains an electrical potential difference of about −70 millivolts (the inner surface is negative relative to the outer surface). At rest, the membrane is more permeable to potassium ions than to sodium ions, as indicated by the lengths of the dark arrows in the inset at the top right. When the cell is stimulated, the permeability to sodium in-creases, leading to an inrush of positive charges (*a*). This inrush triggers an impulse—a momentary reversal (*b*) of the membrane potential. The impulse is initiated at the junction of the cell body and the axon and is conducted away from the cell body (*bold arrows*).

When the impulse reaches the axon terminals of the presynaptic neuron, it induces the release of neurotransmitter molecules (*inset at bottom left*). Transmitters diffuse across a narrow cleft and bind to receptors in the postsynaptic membrane. Such binding leads to the opening of ion channels and often, in turn, to the generation of action potentials in the postsynaptic neuron. For the sake of clarity, several elements are drawn larger than scale.

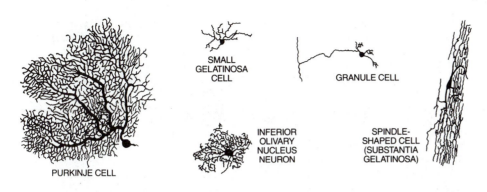

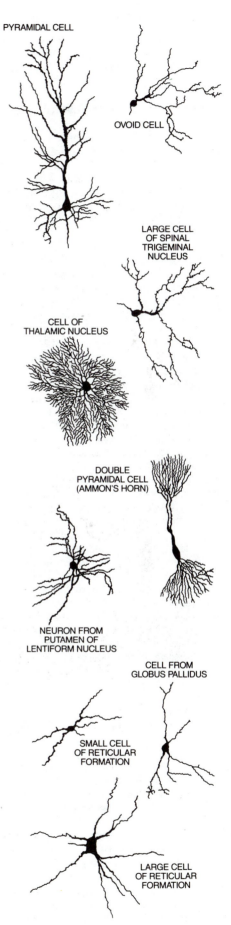

PYRAMIDAL CELL

OVOID CELL

SMALL GELATINOSA CELL

GRANULE CELL

INFERIOR OLIVARY NUCLEUS NEURON

SPINDLE-SHAPED CELL (SUBSTANTIA GELATINOSA)

PURKINJE CELL

LARGE CELL OF SPINAL TRIGEMINAL NUCLEUS

CELL OF THALAMIC NUCLEUS

DOUBLE PYRAMIDAL CELL (AMMON'S HORN)

NEURON FROM PUTAMEN OF LENTIFORM NUCLEUS

CELL FROM GLOBUS PALLIDUS

SMALL CELL OF RETICULAR FORMATION

LARGE CELL OF RETICULAR FORMATION

STRUCTURAL VARIETY OF NEURONS (*shown as tracings from Golgi stains*) contributes to the vast capacity of the brain to store, retrieve, use and express information, as well as to experience emotion and control movement.

fect—the "positive" symptoms of schizophrenia that are most evident during acute psychotic episodes. They are not as effective in treating autism and paucity of speech—"negative" symptoms that are prominent during interpsychotic intervals. Moreover, they all produce subtle, abnormal movements when administered to treat acute episodes of illness (hence the name "neuroleptics"). When administered for a long time, they often cause a devastating disorder called tardive dyskinesia. Involuntary and at times incessant writhing movements of the limbs and trunk characterize the disorder, which can persist long after the drug is discontinued.

Why would an agent that affects mental function also produce motor symptoms? The answer lies in the fact that conventional antipsychotics prevent the binding of dopamine to its receptors. To appreciate the importance of this insight, one must know that dopamine-containing nerve cell bodies, gathered deep in the midbrain in a region known as the ventral tegmentum, project their axons widely to the prefrontal cortex as well as to subcortical structures, including the basal ganglia, which are involved in many aspects of motor control. The prefrontal cortex is particularly relevant to schizophrenia because it contains circuits that are active during manipulation of symbolic information and in a type of short-term memory called working memory. Neurons in this region may form a central processing unit of sorts.

A new drug, clozapine, affects the negative as well as the positive symptoms of schizophrenia. Most important, clozapine does not lead to tardive dyskinesia. The discovery of additional members of the dopamine receptor family may provide the explanation for the unique efficacy and selectivity of this antipsychotic.

Transmitter receptors can be grouped into two large (and growing) superfamilies based on their amino acid sequence and on presumptions about the shape that the molecules assume as part of the cell membrane in which they are embedded. A more detailed receptor classification scheme has emerged. It incorporates molecular architecture as well as the more traditional criteria of ligand binding and function. Based on the added molecular information, one receptor superfamily consists of ion channels, proteins that can form aqueous pores through which ions cross the membrane. They underlie the changes in permeability discussed above. The other superfamily, which includes the dopamine receptors, does not form channels. Instead its members interact with a neighboring membrane protein that cleaves a high-energy phosphate bond from guanosine triphosphate. This process initiates a cascade of biochemical reactions. Such G protein–mediated effects are slow in onset, and they last longer than directly gated receptor responses. It is therefore unlikely that they mediate rapid, point-to-point synaptic transmission in the brain. Rather they modulate the way ion channels respond to stimuli. They set the gain of the system much as the pedals on a piano modulate the action of the keys.

The first dopamine receptor gene was isolated four years ago. The search was based on the presumption that the receptor would resemble other receptors that were known to couple to G proteins. This powerful "homology" screening strategy led in short order to the identification of four more dopamine receptors. One of the recent additions, imaginatively named D_4, has attracted considerable attention. The receptor binds dopamine and clozapine with extraordinarily high affinity. Of equal importance, the D_4 gene is apparently not expressed in the basal ganglia, a finding that may explain the absence of tardive dyskinesia. Precise localization of the D_4 receptor within the prefrontal cortex may reveal the origin of hallucinations or at least a component of the neural machinery that has gone awry in schizophrenia.

The slow rate at which psychoactive drugs work presents a puzzle. Drug receptor interactions are immediate, yet symptoms of schizophrenia, depression and other disorders do not resolve for several weeks. The first consequences of drug binding cannot be the sole explanation for their efficacy. This issue leads to a more general consideration of mechanisms by which the environment might change the brain.

Investigation of dopamine synapses has also provided information about the curse of drug addiction. Cocaine, which binds to and inhibits a protein that transports dopamine away from its site of action, is one of the most powerful reinforcing drugs known. Recent studies point to a neural pathway that may be a target of all addictive substances—amphetamines, nicotine, alcohol and opiates. Within this pathway, the nucleus accumbens, a small subdivision of the basal ganglia, appears to be particularly important. Further studies of neurons in this region will certainly sharpen understanding of drug-seeking behavior. They may reveal mechanisms of motivation in general.

The structural, functional and molecular variety that has been described so far would seem to provide a sufficiently complete basis for mental function. Yet another dimension must be considered: plasticity, the tendency of synapses and neuronal circuits to change as a result of activity. Plasticity weaves the tapestry on which the continuity of mental life depends. Action potentials not only encode information, their metabolic aftereffects alter the circuits over which they are transmitted.

Synaptic plasticity is the basis for the informative connectionist neural models that Geoffrey E. Hinton describes. More generally, plasticity multiplies the complexity provided by any fixed cast of molecular characters or cellular functions. Hence, it provides an even richer substrate for mental phenomena.

From the brief tour of synaptic biology presented above, you can imagine many ways that synaptic efficacy might be altered. For example, transmitter release can be enhanced by a small increase in the amount of calcium that enters a nerve terminal with each action potential. The probability of postsynaptic receptor activation can be changed, and on a longer time scale, variations in activity can alter the number of functional receptors. Increases or decreases in the number of receptors, which take time to occur, may account for the delayed effect of psychotherapeutic agents. Beyond changes in the function of synapses, activity may alter the number or location of synapses themselves. Axons sprout new endings when their neighbors become silent, and the terminal branches of dendritic arbors are constantly remodeled.

In their discussion of plasticity and learning, Eric R. Kandel and Robert D. Hawkins review evidence that short-term synaptic changes associated with simple forms of learning are accompanied by molecular modification of proteins. One such modification is phosphorylation, the addition or attachment of a phosphate group. Phosphorylation has a profound effect on the function of proteins. It is commonly stimulated by transmitters and drugs that act via G protein-coupled receptors. But proteins are degraded on a time scale that ranges from minutes to days. Maintenance of memories that may last a lifetime requires more stable alterations, such as those associated with persistent changes in gene expression. A recently discovered family of genes called immediate early genes (IEGs), which are activated rapidly by brief bursts of action potentials, may provide a crucial link. As expected of master switches that initiate long-term changes in the brain, IEGs encode transcription factors, proteins that regulate the expression of other genes.

Some evidence has been obtained that impulse activity increases the expression of genes that encode trophic factors, proteins that promote the survival of neurons. The adage "use it or lose it" may soon have a specific biochemical correlate. The actions of each transcription factor and their relevance remain to be determined, however.

Another focus of inquiry into the basis of memory is the phenomenon of long-term potentiation (LTP), a persistent increase in synaptic efficacy that follows brief periods of stimulation. Attention has focused on synapses in the hippocampus because clinical and experimental data have implicated this region of the cortex in forms of memory that require conscious deliberation. At certain synapses in the hippocampus, LTP may last for weeks. At the same junctions, LTP meets the "Hebbian" criterion for learning in that it requires coincident presynaptic and postsynaptic activity. LTP does not occur if the postsynaptic neuron is rendered inactive during the priming, presynaptic stimulation. Donald O. Hebb suggested this relation in his 1949 book *The Organization of Behavior* as a basis for the formation of new neural ensembles during learning. It has been repeated often enough to have achieved the force of law.

Synaptic transmission in the hippocampus is mediated by glutamate, the most common excitatory transmitter in the brain, and LTP of the Hebbian type is blocked by aminophosphonovaleric acid (APV), a selective antagonist of one type of glutamate receptor. APV also diminishes the ability of rats to learn tasks that require spatial cues. This is probably not a coincidence, but it remains to be shown that these observations are causally related. The gene that encodes the APV-sensitive glutamate receptor has been cloned in recent months. We can therefore expect tests in transgenic mice bearing mutated receptors to be conducted in the near future. The work will not be straightforward. The plasticity of the brain and the likelihood that natural selection has provided alternative routes to such an important end may complicate matters.

Although the forces leading to plastic changes in the mature brain are ubiquitous and unrelenting, it is important to emphasize the precision and overall stability of the wiring diagram. We could not sense the environment or move in a coordinated manner, let alone think, if it were otherwise. All studies of higher brain function must take into account the precise way in which neurons are connected to one another.

Pathways in the brain have been traced by means of a variety of molecules that are transported along axons. Such reporter molecules can be visualized once the tissue is properly prepared. Connections have also been traced by fine-tipped microelectrodes positioned close enough to a nerve cell body or an axon to detect the small currents generated as an action potential passes by. Each technique has revealed ordered, topographic maps in the cerebral cortex. The body surface is represented in the postcentral gyrus of the cerebral cortex even though the cortical neurons are three synapses away from sensory receptors in the skin. Likewise, a point-to-point map of the visual world is evident in the primary visual cortex at the occipital pole at the back of the brain. Order is evident at each of the early relays on route to the cortex, and topographic order has also been found in projections from the primary cortices to higher centers.

To appreciate just how precise the wiring diagram can be, we need only consider a fundamental discovery made about 30 years ago by Hubel and Wiesel. They determined that neurons in the primary visual cortex (V1) respond to line segments or edges of a particular orientation rather than to the small spots of light that activate the input neurons in the retina and lateral geniculate nucleus of the thalamus. The response implies that neurons in V1 are connected, via the lateral geniculate nucleus, to retinal ganglion cells that lie along a line of the preferred orientation.

We know the anatomy of the major sensory and motor systems in some detail. In contrast, the pattern of connections within the intervening association cortices and the large subcortical nuclei of the cerebral hemispheres is not clearly defined. Goldman-Rakic's experiments are designed to decipher the wiring diagram of the monkey's prefrontal cortex in order to provide a more complete anatomy of memory. Our lack of information about similar connections in the human brain is glaring. Unlike the molecular building blocks and the functions of individual neurons, it cannot be assumed that the intricacies of cortical connectivity will be conserved in different species. The intricacy of this network, after all, is what distinguishes *Homo sapiens* from all other forms of life. An effort akin to the genome project may be called for.

How does the specificity of synaptic connections come about during development? Carla J. Shatz reviews mechanisms by which axons are guided to their appropriate targets in the visual and other systems. The initial stages of axon outgrowth and pathway selection are thought to occur independently of activity. The genetically determined part of the program is evident in the remarkably complete wiring diagram that forms during embryonic life. But once the advancing tips of the axons arrive in the appropriate region, the choices of particular targets are influenced by nerve impulses originating within the brain or stimulated by events in the world itself. Synapse formation during a critical period of development may depend on a type of competition between axons in which those that are activated appropriately are favored.

Steroid hormones also influence the formation of synapses during early development at least in certain regions of the brain. Anatomic, physiological and behavioral data indicate that the brains of males and females are not identical.

The pattern of information flow in the brain during the performance of mental tasks cannot easily be determined by anatomic studies of the circuit diagram or by studies of plasticity. Neural correlates of higher mental functions are being sought directly in awake primates trained to perform tasks that require judgment, planning or memory, or all three capacities. This demanding approach requires sophisticated instrumentation, sophisticated experimental design and months of training until the monkey thinks the same thoughts as the investigator. All-night sessions spent listening to amplified action potentials generated by one or a few neurons followed by days of data analysis are the rule. Progress is slow, but important generalizations have emerged.

One of the most important principles is that sensory systems are arranged in a hierarchical manner. That is, neurons respond to increasingly abstract aspects of complex stimuli as the distance—measured in numbers of synapses from the source—grows. The fact that neurons in V1 respond to lines rather than spots makes the case. Another important principle, discussed by Semir Zeki, is that information does not travel along a single pathway. Rather, different features of a single percept are processed in parallel pathways. A tennis player who wanders to the net from time to time will be alarmed to learn that the movement, color and shape of a tennis ball are processed in different cortical visual centers. Separation of these information streams begins in the retina; they remain segregated in the lateral geniculate nucleus and the primary visual cortex en route to the higher visual centers.

An analogous situation has been found in the auditory system. Mark Konishi and his colleagues at the California Institute of Technology have shown that the localization of sound sources by the barn owl depends on interaural phase and amplitude differences. Phase differences indicate location along the azimuth, whereas amplitude differences signal elevation. Phase and amplitude signals are processed in different pathways through three synaptic relays in the brain. It seems likely that this type of parallel processing characterizes other sensory systems, association cortices and motor pathways as well.

Where is the information reassembled? When does the subject become aware of the approaching ball? The receptive fields of neurons in higher centers are larger than those found in earlier relay stations, so they monitor a larger fraction of the external world. Zeki describes a model that depends on feedback connections from cells with large receptive fields to the cells in the primary visual cortex that have high spatial resolution. Such feedback circuits might coordinate the activity of cells in the primary cortex that have high spatial resolution and cells that respond to more abstract features of the stimulus no matter where it is located. Francis Crick and Christof Koch address the role in visual awareness of a 40-cycle-per-second oscillation in firing rate that is observed throughout the cortex. The oscillations, discovered by Wolf J. Singer and his colleagues at the Max Planck Institute for Brain Research in Frankfurt, may synchronize the firing of neurons that respond to different components of a perceptual scene and hence may be a direct neural correlate of awareness.

Konishi has identified the first neurons in the owl's brain that respond to a combination of interaural phase and amplitude differences but not to either parameter presented alone. These neurons, located deep in the animal's brain in a region called the inferior colliculus, activate a motor program that results in the owl's turning toward the sound source.

In the monkey's visual system, "face cells" located in the inferior temporal sulcus represent perhaps the highest level of abstraction yet identified. These neurons respond to faces but not to other visual stimuli. Similar cells may be present in our own brains. Lesions in the corresponding area of the temporal lobe result in prosopagnosia, a remarkably selective deficit in which the ability to recognize faces is lost. In the zebra finch's auditory system (birds again), a high level of abstraction is evident in neurons found in each male's brain that respond to the complex song of his father but not to pure tones or to the songs of other males of the same species.

How many neurons must change their firing rate to signal a coherent percept or gestalt? The most extreme view holds that one cell may do the job. Is there one face cell per face? Such a supposition seems unlikely on first principles: we lose thousands of neurons every day, so overcommitment to one would be unwise. A more compelling argument comes from recent experiments that have shown face cells to be broadly tuned, responding to faces with similar features rather than to one face alone. The number of neurons that must be activated before recognition emerges is not known, but the data are consistent with a sparse coding rather than global or diffuse activation.

Face cells have their counterparts on the motor side. "Command" neurons have been identified in certain invertebrates that trigger all-or-none, fixed-action patterns, such as stereotypical escape behaviors. Apostolos P. Georgopoulos of Johns Hopkins University has found command neurons of a kind in the monkey's motor cortex (precentral gyrus) that encode the direction of forelimb movement. The firing of these neurons is not associated with the contraction of a particular muscle or with the force of the coordinated movement. Like face cells in the temporal lobe, individual motor cortex neurons are broadly tuned.

The vector obtained by summing the firing frequencies of many neurons is better correlated with the direction of movement than is the activity of any individual cell. The vector becomes evident several milliseconds *before* the appropriate muscles contract and the arm actually moves. It must be a sign of motor planning. The vector is usually derived from less than 100 neurons, so sparse coding may be the rule in the motor cortex as it is in the temporal sulcus.

An important next step at this level of analysis is to produce mental phenomena by focal electrical stimulation. A beginning has been made by William Newsome and his colleagues at Stanford University. They trained monkeys to decide on the direction of movement of dots displayed in random positions on a screen. When the number of dots that showed net movement was set near the threshold for a consistent judgment about the population as a whole, focal stimulation of the V5 region in the cortex influenced the monkey's perceptual judgments.

Strokes and other unfortunate "experiments of nature" have also provided important insights regarding neural correlates of mental phenomena. Antonio R. and Hanna Damasio continue a long tradition of research in their studies of language disorders among neurological patients. This work requires careful examination with a battery of tests designed to elicit the most subtle deficits. Here is an example of the pressing need to define the mental phenomena that need to be explained. The Damasios propose the view that language can be considered a three-part system: word formation, concept representation and mediation between the two. If, as they suggest, language has evolved as a tool to compress concepts and communicate them in an efficient manner, a clear view of its functional anatomy brings us to the crux of the mind matter.

The very real experience of phantom limbs cautions against quick acceptance of sparse coding or even of localization as a universal mechanism. Amputated limbs, experiments of nature of another sort, may be experienced as an integral part of the body or "self." A deep and burning pain is a distressing component of the syndrome. It is impossible to find a local area in which such sensations are experienced. Attempts have been made to abolish phantom pain by cutting peripheral nerves, by destroying ascending pathways and by removing sensory regions of the brain. All attempts have failed to eliminate the perception of pain. It may be that the emotional response we call pain requires activation of neurons in widely dispersed regions of the brain.

The future of cognitive neuroscience depends on our ability to study the living human brain. Positron emission tomography (PET) and functional magnetic resonance imaging (MRI) hold great promise in this regard. These noninvasive imaging techniques depend on tight coupling between neuronal activity, energy consumption and regional blood flow. These relations were pointed out by Sir Charles Scott Sherrington in 1890 and later placed on a quantitative basis by Seymour S. Kety and Louis Sokoloff of the National Institute of Mental Health. The brain is never completely at rest. Furthermore, the increases in regional blood flow that MRI and PET detect are not large (they are on the order of 20 to 50 percent). So PET and MRI measurements depend on sophisticated subtraction algorithms that allow one to distinguish the pattern of blood flow during the mental task from the resting, or control, pattern. Assignment of the changes in blood flow to specific structures depends on accurately superimposing the computed images on precise anatomic maps.

At present, neither technique provides the spatial resolution to visualize single cortical columns. Moreover, the slow temporal resolution of both imaging techniques demands that mental tasks be repeated over and over again during the recording session. Technical advances, especially related to rapid MRI scanning, are sure to follow. Even with the current limitations, the advantages of working with humans, who can think on command, are overwhelming.

In sum, we can expect advances at an increasing rate on all levels of investigation relevant to the mind. We will soon know exactly how many transmitters and transmitter receptors there are in the brain and where each one is concentrated. We will also have a more complete picture of neurotransmitter actions, including multiple interactions of jointly released modulators. And we will learn much more about molecules that affect neuronal differentiation and degeneration. Molecules of the mind are not unique. Many of the neurotransmitters are common amino acids found throughout the body. Likewise, no new principles or molecules specific to the brain have emerged in studies of hormone regulation or of trophic factors that influence the survival and differentiation of neurons. The great challenge, then, is to determine how these molecules modulate the functional wiring diagram of the brain and how this functional nerve net gives rise to mental phenomena.

Ultimately, it will be essential to specify what exactly it means to say that mental events are correlated with electrical signals. Certainly, there is a need for theory at this level of analysis, and as emphasized by Crick and Koch, this effort has become one of the most exciting aspects of cognitive neuroscience.

Is the mind an emergent property of the brain's electrical and metabolic activity? An emergent property is one that cannot be accounted for solely by considering the component parts one at a time. For example, the heart beats because its pacemaker depends on the influx and efflux of certain ions. But the automaticity cannot be understood without considering the magnitude and kinetics of all the fluxes together. Once that is accomplished, what is left to explain in physiological terms? In an analogous manner, biological explanations of mental events may become evident once the component neural functions are more clearly defined. We will then have a more appropriate vocabulary for describing the emergent mind.

WHAT A CHILD IS GIVEN

We have long accepted that chromosomes form our physical selves. Now, scientists say they also provide a blueprint for personality.

Deborah Franklin

Deborah Franklin, who lives in San Francisco, is a staff writer at Hippocrates magazine.

On the August morning in 1971 when Marietta Spencer first met the birth family of her adopted son, Paul, she was prepared to be nervous. In the four years that she had worked as a social worker for the Children's Home Society of Minnesota, in St. Paul, Spencer had arranged and guided many such meetings. She had seen firsthand the fears and confusion stirred up when strangers, joined at the heart by adoption, examine the potent ties among them. But what Spencer wasn't prepared for, as she and Paul and the rest of the family spent a day swapping stories with a score of her son's birth relatives in their home in northern Germany, was how familiar all these strangers would seem.

It was more than physical appearance, she decided, though Paul's tall, slight build, blue eyes and narrow smile were echoed throughout the birth family, who had not seen the boy since they had arranged for his adoption 17 years earlier. It had more to do with the way one of the birth mother's brothers tossed a pillow up atop a bookcase to punctuate a joke, and with the jokes themselves—no slapstick here, only very dry, occasional one-liners. The conversational tone was familiar, too—mostly quiet and spare of excess emotion.

Like Paul, a gifted pianist, they reserved their passion for music; three of the birth mother's brothers had played for years in the local orchestra. In this German family of the woman who had died soon after giving birth to Paul, Spencer saw striking reflections of her son's personality.

"I felt such a tremendous sense of relief, as I realized, of course, this is Paul, here are the roots of who he is," she recalls.

For Paul, the encounter sparked a friendship that he pursued, returning again to visit the family on his own. For Spencer, it hammered home a lesson that scientific studies of the last 20 years have validated: A newborn child is not a formless bit of clay waiting to be shaped by parents or anybody else.

Rather, the core of many behaviors and most personality traits—the determinants of whether we're shy or extroverted, even the kinds of jokes we find funny and the kinds of people we like—seem largely embedded in the coils of chromosomes that our parents pass to us at conception. The question today is no longer whether genetics influence personality, but rather how much, and in what ways?

The answers, emerging in the last few years primarily from long-term studies of twins and adopted children, bring increasing clarity to the nature/nurture debate: While environmental forces *can* help shape temperament, it is apparently equally true that genes can dictate an individual's response to those environmental forces.

The cumulative evidence also suggests that it's not full-blown personality traits that are inherited, but rather predilections. And, in an interesting turnabout, that information has already begun to change the process of adoption itself. At many adoption agencies, a child is no longer passed from one family to another like a closely held secret. Instead, birth parents fill out lengthy questionnaires that probe not only their medical histories, but also their interests, talents and goals; that information is presented to the adoptive parents as a part of the child's birthright.

Spencer is unsentimental about the value of this information.

"A genetic history—psychological as well as medical—is something like a child's washing instructions," she ways. "When you buy a sweater, you want to know all about its fabric content. How much more important is it to know everything you can about the care and feeding of the child you are about to nuture?"

Not long ago, such views were scandalous. James Watson, Francis Crick and Maurice Wilkins were awarded a 1962 Nobel Prize for puzzling out the structure of the human genetic code, and the medical discoveries that their work has spawned—genetic clues to Tay-Sachs disease, sickle-cell anemia and hemophilia, for example—have been universally heralded. But the notion that psychological traits and behavioral disorders may also be genetically rooted has had more difficulty escaping the pall of Nazi experiments in eugenics during World War II.

Irving Gottesman, a psychologist at the University of Virginia, has studied genetic influences in intelligence, criminality and mental illness for 30 years and has some chilling memories. "At one point, I was invited to speak at the University of Texas," he says. "When I arrived, there were flyers all over campus with the title of my talk and a large swastika, implying that my work was somehow fascist." Gottesman, who is Jewish and lost several members of his family in the Holocaust, was both unnerved and outraged.

"That was the moment I first realized that it's important to say not only what I believe but what I don't believe," he says, "and to explain not only what the results of my studies mean, but also what they don't mean."

Many political activists of the 1960's and 70's, wary that genetic theories might ultimately be used to justify social inequality, attacked anyone who suggested that it wasn't within the DNA of each person to be a mathematical genius, a concert pianist or a gifted statesman. "Potential" was the buzzword; any mention of limits was deemed reactionary. It was all right to talk to your veterinarian about a sweet-tempered pup, but heaven forbid you should suggest that your child had an inherent nature. Still, even then, in a few psychology departments scattered around the world, researchers were stubbornly chipping away at the idea that every aspect of personality is learned.

It is within the family that the alchemy of nurture and nature works its strongest magic, and it is by studying families—of twins and adopted children—that behavioral geneticists have best succeeded in untangling those forces. Thomas J. Bouchard at the University of Minnesota heads one of the most dramatic of such studies.

Since 1979, Bouchard has specialized in the examination of adult identical and fraternal twins who were separated soon after their birth and reared in separate families, separate worlds. To date, he has found about 100 twin pairs—60 of them identical—and has brought each to his laboratory for a week of tests.

These days, when newspapers carry stories every other week of scientists closing in on the gene that causes one or another illness, such as cystic fibrosis or Huntington's disease, it is tempting to think of all genetic research in terms of test tubes and bits of chopped-up DNA. But those aren't a behavioral geneticist's tools. Bouchard does take many physical measurements—of heart rhythms, brainwave patterns and motor skills, for example—but most of his tests are done with pencil and paper.

He finds that identical twins reared in completely different families and communities answer the 15,000 questions he asks in remarkably similar ways. In fact, in questions that reveal traits as diverse as leadership ability, traditionalism or irritability, for example, they respond just as identical twins would who grew up in the same family. When measuring traditionalism—a composite trait that includes showing respect for authority, endorsing strict child-rearing practices and valuing the esteem of the community—the similarities between twins reared in different families were striking.

What elevates these findings above the level of what Mark Twain, borrowing from Disraeli, disparaged as "lies, damned lies, and statistics," is that these are very well-controlled statistics. By focusing on identical twins reared apart, Bouchard has found individuals who have all of their genes—and perhaps only their genes—in common. The clincher is that he and his colleagues run the same battery of tests on three other types of twins: identical pairs raised in the same families, fraternal twins reared together and fraternal twins reared apart.

Remember that identical twins arise from the fertilization of a single egg that splits in half shortly after conception, while fraternal twins are the product of *two* fertilized eggs. Identical twins have in common all their genes; fraternal twins, on average, half. By comparing the degree of similarity among twins in each of

Adoptions lend insight—what do we get from nature and what from nurture?

these four categories, Bouchard is able to look trait by trait and see how much each is influenced by genetics. In measuring I.Q., for example, Bouchard found that identical twins reared apart were more similar than fraternal twins reared together.

Internationally, there are two other major, ongoing studies of identical twins reared apart—one in Sweden, the other in Finland—encompassing more than 7,000 pairs of twins all told. Together with earlier, smaller studies, this research has allowed behavioral geneticists to begin to speak confidently about the influence of genes on a number of human characteristics.

Though the debate over the value of intelligence quotient tests continues, for example, there is ample evidence that whatever it is they measure is in large part inherited. Studies of some 100,000 children and adults internationally suggest that genes are 50 percent to 70 percent responsible for an individual's I.Q. "That's not to say that you can't reduce anybody's I.Q. to zero if you hit them over the head hard enough," says John C. Loehlin, a behavioral geneticist at the University of Texas at Austin. Physical or psychological abuse, malnutrition or even a lack of intellectual stimulation can act as environmental bludgeons to native intelligence. However, Loehlin adds, "The idea that, if raised in the same environment, we would all have the same I.Q. has pretty much been laid to rest."

The findings are trickiest to understand where what we call personality is concerned. Research of the last decade shows that genetics are as influential as environment on characteristics as varied as extraversion, motivation for achievement, leadership, conscientiousness and conservatism. But whether some traits are more genetically controlled than others is much harder to tease apart. Like Bouchard and others, Robert Plomin, a developmental psychologist at Pennsylvania State University, is trying to do just that in a study of nearly 700 pairs of Swedish twins.

"The interesting question today," says Plomin, "is, 'Are there any traits that *aren't* significantly affected by genetics?' " He thinks he has found one: agreeableness, or as he calls it, "niceness"—whether a person is more trusting, sympathetic and cooperative, or cynical, callous and antagonistic. "We found that where a person tends to fall on that scale is much more influenced by environment—mostly early environment—that by genes," Plomin says, "and as a parent, I find that very reassuring."

The same studies continue to shed light on behavioral disorders such as alcoholism—a particularly complicated area of inquiry, since research shows that "situational" alcoholism caused by environmental factors such as war and unemployment skews the findings.

Men appear to be much more susceptible to the disorder than women; an alcoholic father is a strong indicator of a possible problem in a son. Conventional wisdom holds that about 25 percent of the male relatives of alcoholics are problem drinkers themselves, as compared with less than 5 percent of the general population. Perhaps the best evidence for a genetic link comes from a 1987 adoption study in Sweden, which found that the adopted sons of alcoholic birth fathers were four times more likely to grow up to be alcoholic than were members of a control group. A smaller study of adopted daughters of alcoholic birth mothers found they were three times more likely to have the disorder.

Recent adoption and twin studies also suggest that there's a genetic link to most—but not all—forms of schizophrenia. The likelihood that a child or sibling of someone with schizophrenia will develop the disorder is about 12 percent—12 times higher than the risk for everyone else—and if one identical twin has schizophrenia, the other has a 50 percent chance of developing the illness. Researchers suspect that a constellation of genes, working in combination with environmental forces, triggers the disease.

Both adoptive and twin studies confirm that clinical depression, particularly the bipolar manic-depressive variety, has a strong genetic component. According to one of the largest studies, in Denmark in 1977, if one identical twin suffers from bipolar manic depression, the other has a 79 percent likelihood of having the same disorder. Among fraternal twins, that correlation is only 19 percent.

The genetic study of criminality has replaced the study of I.Q. as the most controversial area of behavioral genetics. It is also one of the most speculative. In the mid-1960's, a theory was put forward, based on several studies of felons, that men with an extra Y choromosome were more aggressive than the average male. But further research disproved the finding. More recent adoption and twin studies, says Gottesman, indicate that if there *is* a genetic component to criminal behavior, it is slight.

MARIETTA SPENCER'S SECOND-FLOOR OFFICE AT THE CHILdren's Home Society overlooks a shaded avenue on the residential fringe of St. Paul. On her way upstairs after lunch one afternoon last spring, she walked through the examining room, where a nurse gently prodded and poked a line-up of infants, waiting for adoption, who had been brought to the society by their foster mothers for routine check-ups. Spencer paused to play with a strikingly serious 3-month-old girl. After getting a smile from the child, she moved on.

"Even at this age, children have such obviously different temperaments," Spencer said. "Every child comes into the world with a genetic history. You can't expect them to let go of that, like so much baggage, just because they've been adopted into a new family."

These views were confirmed in the mid-1970's, Spencer said, when "people who had been adopted as children were coming back to us for more information. Some wanted to meet their birth parents, but many just wanted to know more about them, as a way of knowing more about themselves." Even if sympathetic, most adoption workers at the time had little information to offer. Disorders like depression, schizophrenia and alcoholism carried a much stronger social stigma then, and were commonly thought to be either failures of character or environmentally induced. Rather, the emphasis was on integrating the child into the new family as quickly as possible, and for some families that even meant denying the child was adopted.

To help the adopted learn more about their backgrounds, Spencer assembled a team of social workers whose main job was and continues to be detective

---

Twins, raised apart and together, form the basis for the new findings.

---

work; they've answered 1,600 requests for information since 1977. They locate birth parents wherever possible, discreetly contact them and—if and when the individuals are willing—fill in the history of the adopted child.

"Anything that might be even partially inherited, and provide useful information for the adopted person, we'll ask about," Spencer says. She steps into her office and pulls open a file drawer filled with folders detailing the lives of her clients.

One particularly thick file belongs to Robert Morse. He and his family weren't much interested in questions of personality when they sought Spencer's help eight years ago; they were afraid for the boy's life. Though apparently healthy when adopted soon after birth, Morse, now 21, nearly died at age 5 from a bout with Crohn's disease, an intestinal disorder that kept him from absorbing nutrients from food. He recovered, but went on to develop arthritis at 12. The pain was so intense that at times he couldn't walk.

"I was starting to feel like a time bomb," Morse remembers, "wondering what was going to happen to me next." While hospitalized, he had plenty to wonder about. Without any medical history to work from, doctors were forced to perform painful test after painful test to come up with a definitive diagnosis of juvenile chronic arthritis, which has sometimes been associated with Crohn's disease.

"They asked if we had any illness like this in the family," Morse recalls. "All we knew from my records was that my birth mother was of Swedish extraction and allergic to hollyhocks."

Spencer, whose agency had arranged the adoption, had more information, which eventually led her to Sally Boyum, a 39-year-old whose avocation is acting. In 1967, on the day of her fiancé's funeral—he had drowned in a boating accident—Boyum had discovered she was pregnant. Grief-stricken, she arranged for an adoption. Though she didn't think to mention it at the time of the adoption—"Both Jim and I had always been so healthy"—there was a history of Crohn's disease and intestinal illness in her family. Several of her close relatives, Boyum would later learn, had bone abnormalities and the same type of arthritis as Morse.

"At first I didn't want to meet with Sally, and she didn't push it," Morse says. "I had the medical information, and that was enough." But after a few weeks of gentle encouragement from his parents, he changed his mind.

"Apparently Jim—my birth father—was a terrible tease, and so am I," Morse says. "Both my folks have a good sense of humor, but teasing—calling up on the phone and pretending to be someone else, for example—that's a kind of joking that I do, but they don't" The list goes on. "At school, or in the fraternity, I've always been a coalition-builder—it's one of the things I do best," says Morse, "and that's a role that Sally plays too." Then there's acting—a love of playing to the crowd that for Sally Boyum is also a passion.

One piece of information, Morse says, has changed his life: Many members of both sides of the family struggled with alcoholism. "Like a lot of kids in college, I used to go out and drink a lot on the weekends," he says. "Now I know that's a danger for me, and I've stopped."

MARY ANNE MAISER, WHO SUPERVISES SOCIAL WORKERS at the Children's Home Society, works in an office dotted with photographs of her three daughters, the oldest of whom, Laura, is adopted. "At the time my husband and I adopted Laura, social workers were taught—and taught clients—that each baby is a tabula rasa," Maiser says. "But by the time Laura was a year old, I knew something was wrong." She was an extremely difficult child, even alienated.

Over the years, the family sought help from a therapist. It wasn't until age 17 that Laura was diagnosed with bipolar disorder, or manic-depressive illness. Around that time, after two years of trying, Maiser was able to get more information about Laura's birth family; she had been adopted through a different agency in another state. The agency revealed that within months of Laura's adoption, her biological father had been hospitalized. "You can guess the diagnosis," Maiser says. "Bipolar disorder and schizophrenia."

If she had been given the information earlier, would it have made a difference? Maiser's voice gets tight and her mouth forms a resolute line. "Laura had so much pain and went undiagnosed for so long," she says. "She didn't just need family therapy, she needed lithium."

Despite such testimonials, some people still argue that wrapping an adopted child in genetic history does more damage than good. Laura had only about a 15 percent chance of inheriting her biological father's illness. If the disorder had never appeared, might not the label itself have twisted her life?

Marietta Spencer dismisses such objections: "Everyone I have ever worked with has said it is always better to know the history than not to know. Because, believe me, it's the parents who *don't* know who imagine the worst if they have a child who seems to be troubled."

For his part, Plomin thinks it's at least as important to tell adoptive parents that the birth father was an alcoholic as to alert them to their child's tiny risk of inheriting a rare disease. "Even if you have a genetic vulnerability," he points out, "you don't become an alcoholic unless you drink a lot over a long period. If you have the genetic history ahead of time, and you see the symptoms developing, you may be more likely to get help early."

If adoption agencies are going to do everything they can to maximize the chances of harmony in a family, should they perhaps go one step further and take temperamental factors into account when "matching" a child to new parents?

Spencer, while stressing that genetic history isn't the *only* factor to consider in an adoption, thinks it shouldn't be ignored. "Adoption, like marriage, is a process of family building, and empathy is very important," she says.

While Spencer might have a point, Plomin says, accurately predicting whether family members will be sympathetic or antagonistic to each other—in essence, predicting the chemistry of relationships—is much more difficult than she imagines. And even if adoption workers could give long, detailed personality tests to both sets of parents, they would still be a long way from predicting the baby's temperament.

Moreover, Plomin cautions, the current infatuation with genetic influences has obscured the very real importance of environment in human development. "More and more, I find myself standing up before funding committees and the public to say, 'Hey, wait a minute everybody, hold on. It's not *all* genetic.'"

In fact, Plomin's most recent research suggests that the influences of genes and the environment may be intractably intertwined. He asked participants in the Swedish twin study, who were an average of 59 years old, to fill out questionnaires about their parents, siblings and childhood experiences. The questions were phrased so as to get at the respondents' perceptions of their families—how cohesive, or emotionally demonstrative the families were, for example, or how much stress parents had placed on achievement, organization, discipline or culture.

The results were striking: identical twins reared in different families described their early childhood environments as remarkably similar—almost as similar as if they had been raised in the same family. Fraternal twins, on the other hand, even when raised in the same family, described that family very differently.

"You can interpret the finding in one of two ways," Plomin says. "Maybe, because of their identical genes, identical twins perceive their environment in a quite similar way—sort of like looking at the world through the same shade of gray- or rose-colored glasses. But it

In matters of human development, 'It's not all genetic,' as one researcher stresses. 'The trait develops via the environment,' says another.

is also possible—and we think quite likely—that their parents and others respond to them similarly because of genetically influenced quirks of personality that they share."

Bouchard is finding much the same thing in his study; . . . He cites the example of one pair of identical twins from Britain, now middle-aged, who were separated soon after birth. One was adopted by a working-class family with little time or money for books. The other grew up exposed to a rich library as the daughter of a university professor. "From early childhood, both women loved to read," Bouchard says. "One had only to walk out into the living room and pull books off the shelf. The other went every week to the library and came home with a huge stack. Though one had to work a little harder at it than the other, they both ended up creating functionally similar environments."

However, "if one of those women had been raised in a family with *no* access to libraries, she would have been dramatically different from her sister," he explains. "The trait develops via the environment."

If the behavioral geneticists are right, then those who fear the tyranny of biological determinism can rest a little easier. Genes aren't the sole ingredient of the personality soup, they are merely the well-seasoned stock. That message should be liberating for all parents—and children.

Study links genes to sexual orientation

Tina Adler
Monitor staff

Which sex men are sexually attracted to is probably between 50 percent to 70 percent genetic, researchers have found in one of the largest twins studies of the origins of homosexuality, published in the December 1991 *Archives of General Psychiatry.*

"The reason why male sexual orientation runs in families appears to be genetic and not environmental," said the study's lead author, psychologist J. Michael Bailey. This study confirms the results of other, smaller twins studies, some researchers familiar with the field said, and would contribute to their understanding of the biological roots of sexual orientation. But some researchers question whether findings from twins studies can be applied to the general population.

"You have to take the [study's] exact figures with a grain of salt," but all in all, the 50 percent finding is very significant, said Simon LeVay, a neurobiologist at the Salk Institute for Biological Studies. "It's another point of pretty strong evidence" that there is a genetic component to sexual orientation, he said.

LeVay had a study published in *Science* last fall describing differences in homosexual and heterosexual men's brains. He found that a section of the hypothalamus that helps regulate sexual behavior was smaller in gay men than in straight men. (See the November 1991 *APA Monitor*.)

"This confirmed and strengthened other studies," said Len Heston at the Washington Institute for Mental Research and Training, which is part of the University of Washington. He is a psychiatrist who has done twins research on homosexuality.

The researchers, including co-author and psychiatrist Richard Pillard of Boston University School of Medicine, studied about 110 fraternal and identical male twins and 46 adoptive men and their brothers. All the subjects were 19 to 65 years old, with a mean age of 33. At least one in each pair was homosexual or bisexual, and answered the researchers' advertisement for gay or bisexual men who had a male twin or an adoptive or "genetically unrelated" brother with whom they started living at least by age 2.

With the subjects' permission, the researchers sent a questionnaire to the subjects' brothers, of whom 127 responded. The researchers gathered information about brothers who didn't respond from the brother in the study.

The researchers determined sexual orientation by asking the subjects questions, including: "Are you attracted to men?" and "Are you attracted to women?" If a subject did not want his brother contacted, or if the brother didn't respond, the researchers asked the subject about his brother's sexual orientation.

Bailey and his colleagues have recently completed a similar study of women. They are not yet able to publicize the findings because of the restrictions of the journal they want to publish in. They hope to present the data at the American Psychological Association convention in August in Washington, D.C., however.

In this current study, they found that the more genetically similar the brothers were, the more likely both were to be homosexual. Fifty-two percent of the 56 sets of identical twins were both gay. Twenty-two percent of the 54 fraternal twin sets were both gay. And only 11 percent of adopted brothers were both gay. This suggests a genetic component to sexual orientation because identical twins share the same genes, whereas fraternal twins are no more similarly genetic than non-twin siblings, Bailey said.

However, none of these figures describes the magnitude of the influence of genes on sexual orientation. That figure is called a "heritability estimate"—Bailey and Pillard's 50 percent to 70 percent figure—and is the proportion of behavioral variability that is caused by genetic differences, Bailey said.

Bailey said his heritability estimate could be as low as 30 percent, although he doubts it. Heritability estimates are rough estimates, in part because they use the base rate of homosexuality in the population, which people disagree on. They used two common estimates: 10 percent and 4 percent, Bailey said. Also, any sampling bias in the study affects the heritability estimate, the authors wrote.

But Leon Kamin, a psychologist at Northeastern University, said twins studies do not show that any trait is heritable. Twin studies "tell you absolutely nothing" about the influence of genes versus the environment, he said. "There is nothing new here." Identical twins share many more experiences than do other siblings and are more apt to be similar in all regards, he asserted.

Moreover, Kamin said, the researchers did not include in their heritability estimate their finding that only 9 percent of the subjects' non-twin siblings were homosexual. This is lower than what Bailey and Pillard found for adopted brothers and fraternal twins. If homosexuality had a large genetic component, then siblings should be more apt to be alike than adopted brothers, and as similar as fraternal siblings, who are no more genetically similar than non-twin siblings, Kamin said.

Other studies have found the rate of homosexuality among non-twin siblings of a homosexual male to be about 22 percent, said Bailey. He and Pillard acknowledge in the paper that their 9 percent figure is unusual and should be replicated to better understand what it means.

How a gene or set of genes could help determine a person's sexual orientation is still unclear. The genes could do their work by affecting the area of the hypothalamus that LeVay found differs in gay and straight men. Or the genes could cause a biological characteristic in people that makes others treat them a certain way. Bailey and LeVay said they believe it is the former.

Since genes only account for about half of the variability, other factors play a big role in determining sexual orientation, Bailey and others agreed. Although psychologists once thought the parents' relationship with the child determined sexual orienta-

tion, scientists now play down the role of parenting. Bailey suspects the strongest non-genetic influence on sexual orientation is biological—the hormones that fetuses are exposed to. Simply having certain genes does not necessarily make a person gay— for one, the gene must be activated, said Heston, and whether the gene is activated or not is just chance.

Because Bailey and Pillard's study found homosexuality to be strongly influenced by a person's biology, "a lot of people think this [study] says something about whether people can choose to be straight," Bailey said. But the study "really can't" do that. Just because sexual orientation "is biological doesn't mean it is immutable," he said. However, he added, research does show that one's sexual orientation is very difficult to change.

In phone or during in-person interviews, the researchers asked the participants about their behavior and interests as children to get a sense of whether they tended to act like typical boys or not. They found that homosexuals "who behaved like typical boys during childhood do not appear to have been influenced particularly by external events during and after childhood compared with homosexuals who behaved atypically from an early age," they wrote. This suggests that the causes of effeminate and masculine homosexuality are similar, Bailey said.

And identical twins who were both homosexual also tended to be similar in how typical or atypical they were as children. "This suggests that among homosexuals, individual differences in [the] development [of homosexuality] are largely determined by genetic and/or shared environmental factors," they wrote. More research needs to be done of homosexual siblings to see which it is, however, they wrote.

This study is more thorough and is considerably larger than previous studies with similar findings, other researchers said, but they and the authors acknowledged it wasn't without its faults.

A problem with twins studies is that unique characteristics of being a twin may make the find-

ings unapplicable to a general population, LeVay said. For example, twins may both be gay because they were exposed in the womb to the same hormones that influence sexual orientation, as opposed to sharing certain genes.

Also, advertising in gay publications does not necessarily guarantee a representative sample. "The sampling method in this study falls short of the ideal genetic epidemiological study, which would involve systematic sampling from a well-specified population," the authors acknowledged.

It's also difficult to score people as being gay or straight, Heston said. For example, he studied a set of identical twins who were raised apart. One grew up in a city and was definitely homosexual. His twin grew up on a farm and got married and had children. But from age 16 to 22 the married twin had had a sexual affair with an older man, Heston said. The married brother may have continued a homosexual relationship if he had grown up in an environment where homosexuality was more common or accepted, Heston said.

A surprisingly small 11 percent of Bailey and Pillard's subjects were bisexual, which Bailey said suggests that "bisexuality is not the most common orientation," as some researchers have said. But LeVay said that the 11 percent figure is probably off. People will say they are either straight or gay if asked to identify their sexual orientation, but more detailed questionnaires turn up more bisexuality, LeVay said.

Few studies have been done on sexual orientation from a behavior-genetics perspective, the authors wrote. However, those that have been done have found a similar genetic influence on sexual orientation, Bailey said.

Heston studied at the University of Minnesota two other sets of twins raised apart, in which at least one of the twins was homosexual. It wasn't a large enough study to reveal any telling results, but it did yield some interesting stories.

One set of twins discovered each other after one walked into a gay bar and was mistaken for his brother, whom he had never known existed.

A Pleasurable Chemistry

Endorphins, the body's natural narcotics, aren't something we have to run after. They're everywhere.

Janet L. Hopson

Janet L. Hopson, who lives in Oakland, California, gets endorphin highs by contributing to Psychology Today.

Welcome aboard the biochemical bandwagon of the 1980s. The magical, morphine-like brain chemicals called endorphins are getting a lot of play. First we heard they were responsible for runner's high and several other cheap thrills. Now we're hearing that they play a role in almost every human experience from birth to death, including much that is pleasurable, painful and lusty along the way.

Consider the following: crying, laughing, thrills from music, acupuncture, placebos, stress, depression, chili peppers, compulsive gambling, aerobics, trauma, masochism, massage, labor and delivery, appetite, immunity, near-death experiences, playing with pets. Each, it is claimed, is somehow involved with endorphins. Serious endorphin researchers pooh-pooh many or most of these claims but, skeptics notwithstanding, the field has clearly sprinted a long way past runner's high.

Endorphin research had its start in the early 1970s with the unexpected discovery of opiate receptors in the brain. If we have these receptors, researchers reasoned, then it is likely that the body produces some sort of opiate- or morphine-like chemicals. And that's exactly what was found, a set of relatively small biochemicals dubbed "opioid peptides" or "endorphins" (short for "endogenous morphines") that plug into the receptors. In other words, these palliative peptides are sloshing around in our brains, spines and bloodstreams, apparently acting just like morphine. In fact, morphine's long list of narcotic effects was used as a treasure map for where scientists might hunt out natural opiates in the body. Morphine slows the pulse and depresses breathing, so they searched in the heart and lungs. Morphine deadens pain, so they looked in the central and peripheral nervous systems. It disturbs digestion and elimination, so they explored the gut. It savages the sex drive, so they probed the reproductive and endocrine systems. It triggers euphoria, so they scrutinized mood.

Nearly everywhere researchers looked, endorphins or their receptors were present. But what were they doing: transmitting nerve impulses, alleviating pain, triggering hormone release, doing several of these things simultaneously or disintegrating at high speed and doing nothing at all? In the past decade, a trickle of scientific papers has become a tidal wave, but still no one seems entirely certain of what, collectively, the endorphins are doing to us or for us at any given time.

Researchers do have modern-day sextants for their search, including drugs such as naloxone and naltrexone. These drugs, known as opiate blockers, pop into the endorphin receptors and block the peptides' normal activity, giving researchers some idea of what their natural roles might be. Whatever endorphins are doing, however, it must be fairly subtle. As one researcher points out, people injected with opiate blockers may feel a little more pain or a little less "high," but no one gasps for breath, suffers a seizure or collapses in a coma.

Subtle or not, endorphins are there, and researchers are beginning to get answers to questions about how they touch our daily lives—pain, exercise, appetite, reproduction and emotions.

•ANSWERS ON ANALGESIA: A man falls off a ladder, takes one look at his right hand—now cantilevered at a sickening angle—and knows he has a broken bone. Surprisingly, he feels little pain or anxiety until hours later, when he's home from the emergency room. This physiological grace period, which closely resembles a sojourn on morphine, is a common survival mechanism in the animal world, and researchers are confident that brain opiates are responsible for such cases of natural pain relief. The question is how do they work and, more to the point, how can we make them work for us?

The answers aren't in, but researchers have located a pain control system in the periaquaductal gray (PAG), a tiny region in the center of the brain, and interestingly, it produces opioid peptides. While no one fully understands how this center operates, physicians can now jolt it with electric current to lessen chronic pain.

One day in 1976, as Navy veteran Dennis Hough was working at a hospital's psychiatric unit, a disturbed patient snapped Hough's back and ruptured three of his vertebral discs. Five years later, after two failed back operations, Hough was bedridden with constant shooting pains in his legs, back and shoulders

From *Psychology Today*, July/August 1988, pp. 29-30, 32-33. Copyright © 1988 by Sussex Publishers, Inc.

and was depressed to the point of suicide. Doctors were just then pioneering a technique of implanting platinum electrodes in the PAG, and Hough soon underwent the skull drilling and emplacement. He remembers it as "the most barbaric thing I've ever experienced, including my tour of duty in Vietnam," but the results were worth the ordeal; For the past seven years, Hough has been able to stimulate his brain's own endorphins four times a day by producing a radio signal from a transmitter on his belt. The procedure is delicate—too much current and his eyes flutter, too little and the pain returns in less than six hours. But it works dependably, and Hough not only holds down an office job now but is engaged to be married.

Researchers would obviously like to find an easier way to stimulate the brain's own painkillers, and while they have yet to find it, workers in many labs are actively developing new drugs and treatments. Some physicians have tried direct spinal injections of endorphins to alleviate postoperative pain. And even the most cynical now seem to agree that acupuncture works its magic by somehow triggering the release of endorphins. There may, however, be an even easier path to pain relief: the power of the mind.

Several years ago, neurobiologist Jon Levine, at the University of California, San Francisco, discovered that the placebo effect (relief) based on no known action other than the patient's belief in a treatment) can itself be blocked by naloxone and must therefore be based on endorphins. Just last year Levine was able to quantify the effects: One shot of placebo can equal the relief of 6 to 8 milligrams of morphine, a low but fairly typical dose.

Another line of research suggests that endorphins may be involved in self-inflicted injury—a surprisingly common veterinary and medical complaint and one that, in many cases, can also be prevented with naloxone. Paul Millard Hardy, a behavioral neurologist at Boston's New England Medical Center, believes that animals may boost endorphin levels through self-inflicted pain and then "get caught in a self-reinforcing positive feedback loop." He thinks something similar may occur in compulsive daredevils and in some cases of deliberate self-injury. One young woman he studied had injected pesticide into her own veins by spraying Raid into an intravenous needle. This appalling act, she told Hardy, "made her feel better, calmer and almost high."

Hardy also thinks endorphin release might explain why some autistic children constantly injure themselves by banging their heads. Because exercise is believed to be an alternate route to endorphin release, Hardy and physician Kiyo Kitahara set up a twice-a-day exercise program for a group of autistic children. He qualifies the evidence as "very anecdotal at this point" but calls the results "phenomenal."

•RUNNER'S HIGH, RUNNER'S CALM: For most people, "endorphins" are synonymous with "runner's high," a feeling of well-being that comes after an aerobic workout. Many people claim to have experienced this "high," and remarkable incidents are legion. Take, for example, San Francisco runner Don Paul, who placed 10th in the 1979 San Francisco Marathon and wound up with his ankle in a cast the next day. Paul had run the 26 miles only vaguely aware of what turned out to be a serious stress fracture. Observers on the sidelines had to tell him he was "listing badly to one side for the last six miles." He now runs 90 miles per week in preparation for the U.S. men's Olympic marathon trial and says that when he trains at the level, he feels "constantly great. Wonderful."

Is runner's high a real phenomenon based on endorphins? And can those brain opiates result in "exercise addiction"? Or, as many skeptics hold, are the effects on mood largely psychological? Most studies with humans have found rising levels of endorphins in the blood during exercise.

However, says exercise physiologist Peter Farrell of Pennsylvania State University, "when we look at animal studies, we don't see a concurrent increase in the brain." Most circulating peptides fail to cross into the brain, he explains, so explaining moods like runner's high based on endorphin levels in the blood is questionable. Adds placebo expert Jon Levine, "Looking for mood changes based on the circulating blood is like putting a voltmeter to the outside of a computer and saying 'Now I know how it works.'" Nevertheless, Farrell exercises religiously: "I'm not going to waste my lifetime sitting around getting sclerotic just because something's not proven yet."

Murray Allen, a physician and kinesiologist at Canada's Simon Fraser University, is far more convinced about the endorphin connection. He recently conducted his own study correlating positive moods and exercise—moods that could be blocked by infusing the runner with naloxone. Allen thinks these moods are "Mother Nature's way of rewarding us for staying fit" but insists that aerobic exercisers don't get "high." Opioid peptides "slow down and inhibit excess activity in the brain," he says. "Many researchers have been chasing after psychedelic, excitable responses." The actual effect, he says, is "runner's calm" and extremes leading to exhaustion usually negate it.

In a very similar experiment last year, a research team at Georgia State University found the mood-endorphin link more elusive. Team member and psychologist Wade Silverman of Atlanta explains that only those people who experience "runner's high" on the track also noticed it in the lab. Older people and those who ran fewer, not more, miles per week were also more likely to show a "high" on the test. "People who run a lot—50 miles per week or more—are often drudges, masochists, running junkies," says Silverman. "They don't really enjoy it. It hurts." For optimum benefits. Silverman recommends running no more than three miles per day four times a week.

Silverman and Lewis Maharam, a sports medicine internist at Manhattan's New York Infirmary/Beekman Downtown Hospital, both agree that powerful psychological factors—including heightened sense of self-esteem and self-discipline—contribute to the "high" in those who exercise moderately. Maharam would still like to isolate and quantify the role of endorphins, however, so he could help patients "harness the high." He would like to give people "proper exercise prescriptions," he says, "to stimulate the greatest enjoyment and benefit from exercise. If we could encourage the 'high' early on, maybe we could get people to want to keep exercising from the start."

The questions surrounding exercise, mood and circulating endorphins remain. But even if opioids released into the bloodstream from, say, the adrenal glands don't enter the brain and give a "high" or a "calm," several studies show that endorphins in the blood do bolster the immune system's activity. One way or the other, regular moderate exercise seems destined to make us happy.

•APPETITE CLOCKS AND BLOCKS: Few things in life are more basic to survival and yet more pleasurable than eating good food—and where survival and pleasure intersect, can the endorphins be far behind? To keep from starving, an animal needs to know when, what and how much to eat, and researchers immediately suspected that opioid peptides might help control appetite and satiety. People, after all, have long claimed that specific foods such as chili peppers or sweets give them a "high." And those unmistakably "high" on morphine or heroin experience constipation, cravings and other gastrointestinal glitches.

Indeed, investigators quickly located opiate receptors in the alimentary tract and found a region of the rat's hypothalamus that—when injected with tiny amounts of beta endorphin—will trigger noshing of particular nutrients. Even a satiated rat will dig heartily into fats, proteins or sweets when injected with the peptide. Neurobiologist Sarah Leibowitz and her colleagues at Rockefeller University produced this result and also found that opiate blockers would prevent the snack attack—strong evidence that endorphins help regulate appetite. The opiates "probably enhance the hedonic, pleasurable, rewarding properties" of fats, proteins and sweets—foods that can help satiate an animal far longer than carbohydrates so it can survive extended periods without eating.

Intriguingly, rats crave carbohydrates at the beginning of their 12-hour activity cycles, but they like fats, proteins or sweets before retiring—a hint that endorphins control not just the nature but the timing of appetites. Leibowitz suspects that endorphins also help control cravings in response to stress and starvation, and that disturbed endorphin systems may, in part, underlie obesity and eating disorders. Obese people given opiate blockers, for example, tend to eat less; bulimics often gorge on fat-rich foods; both bulimics and anorexics often have abnormal levels of endorphins; and in anorexics, food deprivation enhances the release of opiates in the brain. This brain opiate reward, some speculate, may reinforce the anorexic's self-starvation much as self-injury seems to be rewarding to an autistic child.

Researchers such as Leibowitz are hoping to learn enough about the chemistry of appetite to fashion a binge-blocking drug as well as more effective behavioral approaches to over- or undereating. In the meantime, people who try boosting their own endorphins through exercise, mirth or music may notice a vexing increase in their taste for fattening treats.

•PUBERTY, PREGNANCY AND PEPTIDES: Evolution has equipped animals with two great appetites—the hunger for food to prevent short-term disintegration and the hunger for sex and reproduction to prevent longer-term genetic oblivion. While some endorphin researchers were studying opioids and food hunger, others began searching for a sex role—and they found it.

Once again, drug addiction pointed the way: Users of morphine and heroin often complain of impotence and frigidity that fade when they kick their habits. Could natural opioids have some biochemical dampening effect on reproduction? Yes, says Theodore Cicero of Washington University Medical School. Endorphins, he says, "play an integral role—probably the dominant role—in regulating reproductive hormone cycles."

This formerly small corner of endorphin research has "exploded into a huge area of neurobiology," Cicero says, and researchers now think the opioid peptides help fine-tune many—perhaps all—of the nervous and hormonal pathways that together keep the body operating normally.

Cicero and his colleagues have tracked the byzantine biochemical loops through which endorphins, the brain, the body's master gland (the pituitary), the master's master (the hypothalamus) and the gonads exchange signals to ensure that an adult animal can reproduce when times are good but not when the environment is hostile. Cicero's work helped show that beta endorphin rules the hypothalamus and thus, indirectly, the pituitary and gonads.

The Washington University group also sees "a perfect parallel" between the brain's ability to produce endorphins and the onset of puberty: As the opioid system matures, so does the body sexually. A juvenile rat with endorphins blocked by naloxone undergoes puberty earlier; a young rat given opiates matures far later than normal and its offspring can have disturbed hormonal systems. Cicero calls the results "frightening" and adds, "there couldn't possibly be a worse time for a person to take drugs than during late childhood or adolescence."

Endorphins play a critical role in a later reproductive phase, as well: pregnancy and labor. Women in their third trimester sometimes notice that the pain and pressure of, say, a blood pressure cuff, is far less pronounced than before or after pregnancy. Alan Gintzler and his colleagues at the State University of New York Health Science Center in Brooklyn found that opioid peptides produced inside the spinal cord probably muffle pain and perhaps elevate mood to help a woman deal with the increasing physical stress of pregnancy. Endorphin activity builds throughout pregnancy and reaches a peak just before and during labor. Some have speculated that the tenfold drop from peak endorphin levels within 24 hours of delivery may greatly contribute to postpartum depression.

•CHILLS, THRILLS, LAUGHTER AND TEARS: Just as the effects of morphine go beyond the physical, claims for the opioid peptides extend to purely esthetic and emotional, with speculation falling on everything from the pleasure of playing with pets and the transcendence of near-death experiences to shivers over sonatas and the feeling of well-being that comes with a rousing laugh or a good cry.

Avram Goldstein of Stanford University, a pioneer in peptide research, recently collected a group of volunteers who get a spine-tingling thrill from their favorite music and gave them either a placebo or an opiate blocker during a listening session. Their shivers declined with the blocker—tantalizing evidence that endorphins mediate rapture, even though the mechanics are anyone's guess.

Former *Saturday Review* editor Norman Cousins may have spawned a different supposition about endorphins and emotion when he literally laughed himself out of the sometimes fatal disease ankylosing spondylitis. He found that 10 minutes of belly laughing before bed gave him two hours of painfree sleep. Before long, someone credited endorphins with the effect, and by now the claim is commonplace. For example, Matt Weinstein, a humor consultant from Berkeley, California, frequently mentions a possible link between endorphins, laughter and health in his lectures on humor in the workplace. His company's motto: If you take yourself too seriously, there's an excellent chance you may end up seriously ill.

Weinstein agrees with laughter researcher William Fry, a psychiatrist at Stanford's medical school, that evidence is currently circumstantial. Fry tried to confirm the laughter-endorphin link experimentally, but the most accurate way to assess it would be to tap the cerebrospinal fluid. That, Fry says, "is not only a difficult procedure but it's not conducive to laughter" and could result in a fountain of spinal fluid gushing out with the first good guffaw. Confirmation clearly awaits a less ghoulish methodology. But in the meantime, Fry is convinced that mirth and playfulness can diminish fear, anger and depression. At the very least, he says, laughter is a good aerobic exercise that ventilates the lungs and leaves the muscles relaxed. Fry advises patients to take their own humor inventory, then amass a library of books, tapes and gags that dependably trigger hilarity.

Another William Frey, this one at the University of Minnesota, studies the role of tears in emotion, stress and health. "The physiology of the brain when we experience a change in emotional state from sad to angry to happy or vice versa is an absolutely unexplored frontier," Frey says. And emotional tears are a fascinating guidepost because "they are unique to human beings and are our natural excretory response to strong emotion." Since all other bodily fluids are involved in removing something, he reasons, logic dictates that tears wash something away, too. Frey correctly predicted that tears would contain the three biochemicals that build up during stress: leucine-enkephalin, an endorphin, and the hormones prolactin and ACTH. These biochemicals are found in both emotional tears and tears from chopping onions, a different sort of stress.

Frey is uncertain whether tears simply carry off excess endorphins that collect in the stressed brain or whether those peptides have some activity in the tear ducts, eyes, nose or throat. Regardless, he cites evidence that people with ulcers and colitis tend to cry less than the average, and he concludes that a person who feels like crying "should go ahead and do it! I can't think of any other physical excretory process that humans alone can do, so why suppress it and its possibly healthful effects?"

All in all, the accumulated evidence suggests that if you want to use your endorphins, you should live the unfettered natural life. Laugh! Cry! Thrill to music! Reach puberty. Get pregnant. Get aerobic. Get hungry, Eat! Lest this sound like a song from *Fiddler on the Roof*, however, remember that stress or injury may be even quicker ways to pump out home-brew opioids. The bottom line is this: Endorphins are so fundamental to normal physiological functioning that we don't have to seek them out at all. We probably surf life's pleasures and pains on a wave of endorphins already.

Test yourself by imagining the following: the sound of chalk squeaking across a blackboard; a pink rose sparkling with dew; embracing your favorite movie star; chocolate-mocha mousse cake; smashing your thumb with a hammer. If any of these thoughts sent the tiniest tingle down your spine, then you have have just proved the point.

Sizing Up The Sexes

Scientists are discovering that gender differences have as much to do with the biology of the brain as with the way we are raised

CHRISTINE GORMAN

What are little boys made of?
What are little boys made of?
Frogs and snails
And puppy dogs' tails,
That's what little boys are made of.

What are little girls made of?
What are little girls made of?
Sugar and spice
And all that's nice,
That's what little girls are made of.
　　—Anonymous

Many scientists rely on elaborately complex and costly equipment to probe the mysteries confronting humankind. Not Melissa Hines. The UCLA behavioral scientist is hoping to solve one of life's oldest riddles with a toybox full of police cars, Lincoln Logs and Barbie dolls. For the past two years, Hines and her colleagues have tried to determine the origins of gender differences by capturing on videotape the squeals of delight, furrows of concentration and myriad decisions that children from 2 1/2 to 8 make while playing. Although both sexes play with all the toys available in Hines' laboratory, her work confirms what most parents (and more than a few aunts, uncles and nursery-school teachers) already know. As a group, the boys favor sports cars, fire trucks and Lincoln Logs, while the girls are drawn more often to dolls and kitchen toys.

But one batch of girls defies expectations and consistently prefers the boy toys. These youngsters have a rare genetic ab-normality that caused them to produce elevated levels of testosterone, among other hormones, during their embryonic development. On average, they play with the same toys as the boys in the same ways and just as often. Could it be that the high levels of testosterone present in their bodies before birth have left a permanent imprint on their brains, affecting their later behavior? Or did their parents, knowing of their disorder, somehow subtly influence their choices? If the first explanation is true and biology determines the choice, Hines wonders, "Why would you evolve to want to play with a truck?"

Not so long ago, any career-minded researcher would have hesitated to ask such questions. During the feminist revolution of the 1970s, talk of inborn differences in the behavior of men and women was distinctly unfashionable, even taboo. Men dominated fields like architecture and engineering, it was argued, because of social, not hormonal, pressures. Women did the vast majority

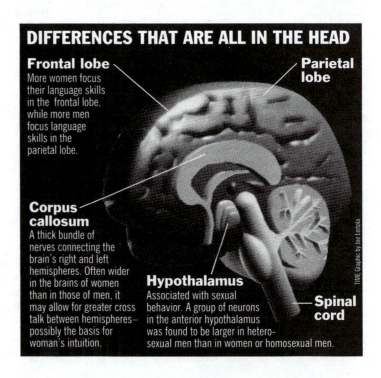

DIFFERENCES THAT ARE ALL IN THE HEAD

Frontal lobe
More women focus their language skills in the frontal lobe, while more men focus language skills in the parietal lobe.

Parietal lobe

Corpus callosum
A thick bundle of nerves connecting the brain's right and left hemispheres. Often wider in the brains of women than in those of men, it may allow for greater cross talk between hemispheres—possibly the basis for woman's intuition.

Hypothalamus
Associated with sexual behavior. A group of neurons in the anterior hypothalamus was found to be larger in heterosexual men than in women or homosexual men.

Spinal cord

TIME Graphic by Joe Lertola

of society's child rearing because few other options were available to them. Once sexism was abolished, so the argument ran, the world would become a perfectly equitable, androgynous place, aside from a few anatomical details.

But biology has a funny way of confounding expectations. Rather than disappear, the evidence for innate sexual differences only began to mount. In medicine, researchers documented that heart disease strikes men at a younger age than it does women and that women have a more moderate physiological response to stress. Researchers found subtle neurological differences between the sexes both in the brain's structure and in its functioning. In addition, another generation of parents discovered that, despite their best efforts to give baseballs to their daughters and sewing kits to their sons, girls still flocked to dollhouses while boys clambered into tree forts. Perhaps nature is more important than nurture after all.

Even professional skeptics have been converted. "When I was younger, I believed that 100% of sex differences were due to the environment," says Jerre Levy, professor of psychology at the University of Chicago. Her own toddler toppled that utopian notion. "My daughter was 15 months old, and I had just dressed her in her teeny little nightie. Some guests arrived, and she came into the room, knowing full well that she looked adorable. She came in with this saucy little walk, cocking her head, blinking her eyes, especially at the men. You never saw such flirtation in your life." After 20 years spent studying the brain, Levy is convinced: "I'm sure there are biologically based differences in our behavior."

Now that it is O.K. to admit the possibility, the search for sexual differences has expanded into nearly every branch of the life sciences. Anthropologists have debunked Margaret Mead's work on the extreme variability of gender roles in New Guinea. Psychologists are untangling the complex interplay between hormones and aggression. But the most provocative, if as yet inconclusive, discoveries of all stem from the pioneering exploration of a tiny 3-lb. universe: the human brain. In fact, some researchers predict that the confirmation of innate differences in behavior could lead to an unprecedented understanding of the mind.

Some of the findings seem merely curious. For example, more men than women are lefthanded, reflecting the dominance of the brain's right hemisphere. By contrast, more women listen equally with both ears while men favor the right one.

Other revelations are bound to provoke more controversy. Psychology tests, for instance, consistently support the notion that men and women perceive the world in subtly different ways. Males excel

EMOTIONS

FEMALE INTUITION: THERE MAY BE SOMETHING TO IT

Do women really possess an ability to read other people's hidden motives and meanings? To some degree, they do. When shown pictures of actors portraying various feelings, women outscore men in identifying the correct emotion. They also surpass men in determining the emotional content of taped conversation in which the words have been garbled. This ability may result from society's emphasis on raising girls to be sensitive. But some researchers speculate that it has arisen to give women greater skill in interpreting the cues of toddlers before they are able to speak.

MALE INSENSITIVITY: IT'S A CULTURAL RELIC

If men seem less adept at deciphering emotions, it is a "trained incompetence," says Harvard psychologist Ronald Levant. Young boys are told to ignore pain and not to cry. Some anthropologists argue that this psychic wound is inflicted to separate boys from their mothers and prepare them for warfare. Many men, says Levant, can recognize their emotions only as a physical buzz or tightness in the throat—a situation that can be reversed, he insists, with training.

at rotating three-dimensional objects in their head. Females prove better at reading emotions of people in photographs. A growing number of scientists believe the discrepancies reflect functional differences in the brains of men and women. If true, then some misunderstandings between the sexes may have more to do with crossed wiring than cross-purposes.

Most of the gender differences that have been uncovered so far are, statistically speaking, quite small. "Even the largest differences in cognitive function are not as large as the difference in male and female height," Hines notes. "You still see a lot of overlap." Otherwise, women could never read maps and men would always be lefthanded. That kind of flexibility within the sexes reveals just how complex a puzzle gender actually is, requiring pieces from biology, sociology and culture.

Ironically, researchers are not entirely sure how or even why humans produce two sexes in the first place. (Why not just one—or even three—as in some species?)

What is clear is that the two sexes originate with two distinct chromosomes. Women bear a double dose of the large X chromosome, while men usually possess a single X and a short, stumpy Y chromosome. In 1990 British scientists reported they had identified a single gene on the Y chromosome that determines maleness. Like some kind of biomolecular Paul Revere, this master gene rouses a host of its compatriots to the complex task of turning a fetus into a boy. Without such a signal, all human embryos would develop into girls. "I have all the genes for being male except this one, and my husband has all the genes for being female," marvels evolutionary psychologist Leda Cosmides, of the University of California at Santa Barbara. "The only difference is which genes got turned on."

Yet even this snippet of DNA is not enough to ensure a masculine result. An elevated level of the hormone testosterone is also required during the pregnancy. Where does it come from? The fetus' own undescended testes. In those rare cases in which the tiny body does not respond to the hormone, a genetically male fetus develops sex organs that look like a clitoris and vagina rather than a penis. Such people look and act female. The majority marry and adopt children.

The influence of the sex hormones extends into the nervous system. Both males and females produce androgens, such as testosterone, and estrogens—although in different amounts. (Men and women who make no testosterone generally lack a libido.) Researchers suspect that an excess of testosterone before birth enables the right hemisphere to dominate the brain, resulting in lefthandedness. Since testosterone levels are higher in boys than in girls, that would explain why more boys are southpaws.

Subtle sex-linked preferences have been detected as early as 52 hours after birth. In studies of 72 newborns, University of Chicago psychologist Martha McClintock and her students found that a toe-fanning reflex was stronger in the left foot for 60% of the males, while all the females favored their right. However, apart from such reflexes in the hands, legs and feet, the team could find no other differences in the babies' responses.

One obvious place to look for gender differences is in the hypothalamus, a lusty little organ perched over the brain stem that, when sufficiently provoked, consumes a person with rage, thirst, hunger or desire. In animals, a region at the front of the organ controls sexual function and is somewhat larger in males than in females. But its size need not remain constant. Studies of tropical fish by Stanford University neurobiologist Russell Fernald reveal that certain cells in this tiny region of the brain swell markedly in an individual male whenever he comes to dominate a school. Unfortunately for the piscine pasha, the cells will also shrink if he loses control of his harem to another male.

Many researchers suspect that, in humans too, sexual preferences are controlled by the hypothalamus. Based on a study of 41 autopsied brains, Simon Le-Vay of the Salk Institute for Biological Studies announced last summer that he had found a region in the hypothalamus that was on average twice as large in heterosexual men as in either women or homosexual men. LeVay's findings support the idea that varying hormone levels before birth may immutably stamp the developing brain in one erotic direction or another.

These prenatal fluctuations may also steer boys toward more rambunctious behavior than girls. June Reinisch, director of the Kinsey Institute for Research in Sex, Gender and Reproduction at Indiana University, in a pioneering study of eight pairs of brothers and 17 pairs of sisters ages 6 to 18 uncovered a complex interplay between hormones and aggression. As a group, the young males gave more belligerent answers than did the females on a multiple-choice test in which they had to imagine their response to stressful situations. But siblings who had been exposed in utero to synthetic antimiscarriage hormones that mimic testosterone were the most combative of all. The affected boys proved significantly more aggressive than their unaffected brothers, and the drug-exposed girls were much more contentious than their unexposed

PERCEPTION

HE CAN READ A MAP BLINDFOLDED, BUT CAN HE FIND HIS SOCKS?

It's a classic scene of marital discord on the road. Husband: "Do I turn right?" Wife, madly rotating the map: "I'm not sure where we are." Whether men read maps better is unclear, but they do excel at thinking in three dimensions. This may be due to ancient evolutionary pressures related to hunting, which requires orienting oneself while pursuing prey.

IF LOST IN A FOREST, WOMEN WILL NOTICE THE TREES

Such prehistoric pursuits may have conferred a comparable advantage on women. In experiments in mock offices, women proved 70% better than men at remembering the location of items found on a desktop—perhaps reflecting evolutionary pressure on generations of women who foraged for their food. Foragers must recall complex patterns formed of apparently unconnected items.

sisters. Reinisch could not determine, however, whether this childhood aggression would translate into greater ambition or competitiveness in the adult world.

While most of the gender differences

uncovered so far seem to fall under the purview of the hypothalamus, researchers have begun noting discrepancies in other parts of the brain as well. For the past nine years, neuroscientists have debated whether the corpus callosum, a thick bundle of nerves that allows the right half of the brain to communicate with the left, is larger in women than in men. If it is, and if size corresponds to function, then the greater crosstalk between the hemispheres might explain enigmatic phenomena like female intuition, which is supposed to accord women greater ability to read emotional clues.

These conjectures about the corpus callosum have been hard to prove because the structure's girth varies dramatically with both age and health. Studies of autopsied material are of little use because brain tissue undergoes such dramatic changes in the hours after death. Neuroanatomist Laura Allen and neuroendocrinologist Roger Gorski of UCLA decided to try to circumvent some of these problems by obtaining brain scans from live, apparently healthy people. In their investigation of 146 subjects, published in April, they confirmed that parts of the corpus callosum were up to 23% wider in women than in men. They also measured thicker connections between the two hemispheres in other parts of women's brains.

Encouraged by the discovery of such structural differences, many researchers have begun looking for dichotomies of

TEST YOURSELF: A SAMPLER OF GENDER-SENSITIVE QUESTIONS

❶ Which two figures on the right are identical to the figure in the square?

Percent scoring both answers correctly:
Females: **41%**   Males: **64%**

❷ **Study the objects in group A for one minute and cover it up. Then look at group B and put an X through the figures not in the original array. Score one point for each item correctly crossed out and subtract one point for each item incorrectly crossed out.**

Female average : **15**
Male average : **12**

❸ **Name as many synonyms for the following words as you can in three minutes:**

clear dark strong wild

Female average: **4.1** synonyms per word
Male average: **2.2** synonyms per word

Answers: question 1: 1 and 3; question 2: perfect score, 20

LANGUAGE

IN CHOOSING HER WORDS, A WOMAN REALLY USES HER HEAD

For both sexes, the principal language centers of the brain are usually concentrated in the left hemisphere. But preliminary neurological studies show that women make use of both sides of their brain during even the simplest verbal tasks, like spelling. As a result, a woman's appreciation of everyday speech appears to be enhanced by input from various cerebral regions, including those that control vision and feelings. This greater access to the brain's imagery and depth may help explain why girls often begin speaking earlier than boys, enunciate more clearly as tots and develop a larger vocabulary.

IF JOHNNY CAN'T READ, IS IT BECAUSE HE IS A BOY?

Visit a typical remedial-reading class, and you'll find that the boys outnumber the girls 3 to 1. Stuttering affects four times as many boys as girls. Many researchers have used these and other lopsided ratios to support the argument that males, on average, are less verbally fluent than females. However, the discrepancy could also reflect less effort by teachers or parents to find reading-impaired girls. Whatever the case, boys often catch up with their female peers in high school. In the past few years, boys have even begun outscoring girls on the verbal portion of the Scholastic Aptitude Test.

Is Sex Really Necessary?

Birds do it. Bees do it. But dandelions don't. The prodigious spread of these winsome weeds underscores a little-appreciated biological fact. Contrary to human experience, sex is not essential to reproduction. "Quite the opposite," exclaims anthropologist John Tooby of the University of California at Santa Barbara. "From an engineer's standpoint, sexual reproduction is insane. It's like trying to build an automobile by randomly taking parts out of two older models and piecing them together to make a brand-new car." In the time that process takes, asexual organisms can often churn out multiple generations of clones, gaining a distinct edge in the evolutionary numbers game. And therein lies the puzzle: If sex is such an inefficient way to reproduce, why is it so widespread?

Sex almost certainly originated nearly 3.5 billion years ago as a mechanism for repairing the DNA of bacteria. Because ancient earth was such a violent place, the genes of these unicellular organisms would have been frequently damaged by intense heat and ultraviolet radiation. "Conjugation"—the intricate process in which one bacterium infuses genetic material into another—provided an ingenious, if cumbersome, solution to this problem, although bacteria continued to rely on asexual reproduction to increase their numbers.

Animal sex, however, is a more recent invention. Biologist Lynn Margulis of the University of Massachusetts at Amherst believes the evolutionary roots of egg and sperm cells can be traced back to a group of organisms known as protists that first appeared some 1.5 billion years ago. (Modern examples include protozoa, giant kelp and malaria parasites.) During periods of starvation, Margulis conjectures, one protist was driven to devour another. Sometimes this cannibalistic meal was incompletely digested, and the nuclei of prey and predator fused. By joining forces, the fused cells were better able to survive adversity, and because they survived, their penchant for union was passed on to their distant descendants.

From this vantage point, human sexuality seems little more than a wondrous accident, born of a kind of original sin among protozoa. Most population biologists, however, believe sex was maintained over evolutionary time because it somehow enhanced survival. The mixing and matching of parental genes, they argue, provide organisms with a novel mechanism for generating genetically different offspring, thereby increasing the odds that their progeny could exploit new niches in a changing environment and, by virtue of their diversity, have a better chance of surviving the assaults of bacteria and other tiny germs that rapidly evolve tricks for eluding their hosts' defenses.

However sex came about, it is clearly responsible for many of the most remarkable features of the world around us, from the curvaceousness of human females to the shimmering tails of peacocks to a lion's majestic mane. For the appearance of sex necessitated the evolution of a kaleidoscope of secondary characteristics that enabled males and females of each species to recognize one another and connect.

The influence of sex extends far beyond the realm of physical traits. For instance, the inescapable fact that women have eggs and men sperm has spurred the development of separate and often conflicting reproductive strategies. University of Michigan psychologist David Buss has found that men and women react very differently to questions about infidelity. Men tend to be far more upset by a lover's sexual infidelity than do women: just imagining their partner in bed with another man sends their heart rate soaring by almost five beats a minute. Says Buss: "That's the equivalent of drinking three cups of coffee at one time." Why is this so? Because, Buss explains, human egg fertilization occurs internally, and thus a man can never be certain that a child borne by his mate is really his. On the other hand, because women invest more time and energy in bearing and caring for children, they react more strongly to a threat of emotional infidelity. What women fear most is the loss of their mates' long-term commitment and support.

The celebrated war between the sexes, in other words, is not a figment of the imagination but derives from the evolutionary history of sex—from that magic moment long, long ago when our unicellular ancestors entwined in immortal embrace.
—*By J. Madeleine Nash/Chicago*

function as well. At the Bowman Gray Medical School in Winston-Salem, N.C., Cecile Naylor has determined that men and women enlist widely varying parts of their brain when asked to spell words. By monitoring increases in blood flow, the neuropsychologist found that women use both sides of their head when spelling while men use primarily their left side. Because the area activated on the right side is used in understanding emotions, the women apparently tap a wider range of experience for their task. Intriguingly, the effect occurred only with spelling and not during a memory test.

Researchers speculate that the greater communication between the two sides of the brain could impair a woman's performance of certain highly specialized visual-spatial tasks. For example, the ability to tell directions on a map without physically having to rotate it appears stronger in those individuals whose brains restrict the process to the right hemisphere. Any crosstalk between the two sides apparently distracts the brain from its job. Sure enough, several studies have shown that this mental-rotation skill is indeed more tightly focused in men's brains than in women's.

But how did it get to be that way? So far, none of the gender scientists have figured out whether nature or nurture is more important. "Nothing is ever equal, even in the beginning," observes Janice Juraska, a biopsychologist at the University of Illinois at Urbana-Champaign. She points out, for instance, that mother rats lick their male offspring more frequently than they do their daughters. However, Juraska has demonstrated that it is possible to reverse some inequities by manipulating environmental factors. Female rats have fewer nerve connections than males into the hippocampus, a brain region associated with spatial relations and memory. But when Juraska "enriched" the cages of the females with stimulating toys, the females developed more of these neuronal connections. "Hormones do affect things—it's crazy to deny that," says the researcher. "But there's no telling which way sex differences might go if we completely changed the environment." For humans, educational enrichment could perhaps enhance a woman's ability to work in three dimensions and a man's ability to interpret emotions. Says Juraska: "There's nothing about human brains that is so stuck that a different way of doing things couldn't change it enormously."

Nowhere is this complex interaction between nature and nurture more apparent than in the unique human abilities of speaking, reading and writing. No one is born knowing French, for example; it must be learned, changing the brain forever. Even so, language skills are linked to specific cerebral centers. In a remarkable series of experiments, neurosurgeon George Ojemann of the University of

Washington has produced scores of detailed maps of people's individual language centers.

First, Ojemann tested his patients' verbal intelligence using a written exam. Then, during neurosurgery—which was performed under a local anesthetic—he asked them to name aloud a series of objects found in a steady stream of black-and-white photos. Periodically, he touched different parts of the brain with an electrode that temporarily blocked the activity of that region. (This does not hurt because the brain has no sense of pain.) By noting when his patients made mistakes, the surgeon was able to determine which sites were essential to naming.

Several complex sexual differences emerged. Men with lower verbal IQs were more likely to have their language skills located toward the back of the brain. In a number of women, regardless of IQ, the naming ability was restricted to the frontal lobe. This disparity could help explain why strokes that affect the rear of the brain seem to be more devastating to men than to women.

Intriguingly, the sexual differences are far less significant in people with higher verbal IQs. Their language skills developed in a more intermediate part of the brain. And yet, no two patterns were ever identical. "That to me is the most important finding," Ojemann says. "Instead of these sites being laid down more or less the same in everyone, they're laid down in subtly different places." Language is scattered randomly across these cerebral centers, he hypothesizes, because the skills evolved so recently.

What no one knows for sure is just how hardwired the brain is. How far and at what stage can the brain's extraordinary flexibility be pushed? Several studies suggest that the junior high years are key. Girls show the same aptitudes for math as boys until about the seventh grade, when more and more girls develop math phobia. Coincidentally, that is the age at which boys start to shine and catch up to girls in reading.

By one account, the gap between men and women for at least some mental skills has actually started to shrink. By looking at 25 years' worth of data from academic tests, Janet Hyde, professor of psychology and women's studies at the University of Wisconsin at Madison, discovered that overall gender differences for verbal and mathematical skills dramatically decreased after 1974. One possible explanation, Hyde notes, is that "Americans have

HOW OTHER SPECIES DO IT

Humans think there's nothing more natural than males and females in mutual pursuit of the urge to be fruitful and multiply. But nature follows more than one script. Not every species has two sexes, for example. And even when it does, neither their behavior nor their origin necessarily conforms to human notions of propriety. Some of the more bizarre cases in point:

TURTLES

Among most reptiles, males are literally made in the shade. The gender of a turtle hatchling, for instance, is determined not by sex chromosomes but by the temperature at which it was incubated. Eggs that develop in nests located in sunny areas, where it is warm and toasty, give rise to females. Eggs nestled in shady places, where it may be 5°C (10°F) cooler, will yield a crop of males.

WHIPTAIL LIZARDS

For some varieties of these lizards there's no such thing as a battle of the sexes. All of them are female. In a process known as parthenogenesis, they produce eggs that hatch without ever being fertilized. Yet, because they evolved from lizards that come in two sexes, pairs of these single-minded creatures will take turns imitating males and mount each other. The act apparently stimulates greater egg production.

JACANA BIRDS

Females usually rule the roost on every shore, marsh and rice field where these long-legged "lily trotters" abound. They are generally larger than the males, which are saddled with the duties of building the nest, incubating the eggs and raising the chicks. In fact in some varieties, female Casanovas regularly jilt their domestic-minded mates and search for more sexually available males.

CICHLIDS

These fish come in three sexes: brightly hued macho males, paler females, and male wimps that look and act like females. There are only a few sexually active males in a school. But the minute a piscine Lothario dies, an ambitious wimp rises to the occasion. His brain unleashes sex hormones that bring color to his scales and make him feisty, but he can revert to pallid impotence if challenged by a more macho fish.

changed their socialization and educational patterns over the past few decades. They are treating males and females with greater similarity."

Even so, women still have not caught up with men on the mental-rotation test. Fascinated by the persistence of that gap, psychologists Irwin Silverman and Marion Eals of York University in Ontario wondered if there were any spatial tasks at which women outperformed men. Looking at it from the point of view of human evolution, Silverman and Eals reasoned that while men may have developed strong spatial skills in response to evolutionary pressures to be successful hunters, women would have needed other types of visual skills to excel as gatherers and foragers of food.

The psychologists therefore designed a test focused on the ability to discern and later recall the location of objects in a complex, random pattern. In series of tests, student volunteers were given a minute to study a drawing that contained such unrelated objects as an elephant, a guitar and a cat. Then Silverman and Eals presented their subjects with a second drawing containing additional objects and told them to cross out those items that had been added and circle any that had moved. Sure enough, the women consistently surpassed the men in giving correct answers.

What made the psychologists really sit up and take notice, however, was the fact that the women scored much better on the mental-rotation test while they were menstruating. Specifically, they improved their scores by 50% to 100% whenever their estrogen levels were at their lowest. It is not clear why this should be. However, Silverman and Eals are trying to find out if women exhibit a similar hormonal effect for any other visual tasks.

Oddly enough, men may possess a similar hormonal response, according to new research reported in November by Doreen Kimura, a psychologist at the University of Western Ontario. In her study of 138 adults, Kimura found that males perform better on mental-rotation tests in the spring, when their testosterone levels are low, rather than in the fall, when they are higher. Men are also subject to a daily cycle, with testosterone levels lowest around 8 p.m. and peaking around 4 a.m. Thus, says June Reinisch of the Kinsey Institute: "When people say women can't be trusted because they cycle every month, my response is that men cycle every day, so they should only be allowed to negotiate peace treaties in the evening."

Far from strengthening stereotypes about who women and men truly are or how they should behave, research into innate sexual differences only underscores humanity's awesome adaptability. "Gender is really a complex business," says Reinisch. "There's no question that hormones have an effect. But what does that have to do with the fact that I like to wear pink ribbons and you like to wear baseball gloves? Probably something, but we don't know what."

Even the concept of what an innate difference represents is changing. The physical and chemical differences between the brains of the two sexes may be malleable and subject to change by experience: certainly an event or act of learning can directly affect the brain's biochemistry and physiology. And so, in the final analysis, it may be impossible to say where nature ends and nurture begins because the two are so intimately linked.

—**Reported by**
J. Madeleine Nash/Los Angeles

Perceptual Processes

Susan and her roommate have been friends since freshmen year. Because they share so much in common, they decided in their sophomore year to become roommates. They both want to travel abroad one day, both date men from the same fraternity, are education majors, and want to work with young children after graduation from college. Today they are at the local art museum. As they walk around the galleries, Susan is astonished at her roommate's taste in art. Whatever her roommate likes, Susan hates. The paintings and sculptures that Susan admires are the very ones her roommate turns up her nose at. "How can our tastes in art be so different?" Susan wonders.

What Susan and her roommate are experiencing is a difference in perception, or the interpretation of the sensory stimulation provided by the artwork. Perception and its sister area of psychology, sensation, are the focus of this unit.

For many years in psychology, it was popular to consider sensation and perception as two distinct processes. Sensation was defined in passive terms as the simple event of some stimulus energy (i.e., a sound wave) impinging on the body or on a specific sense organ, which then reflexively transmitted appropriate information to the central nervous system. Both passivity and simple reflexes were stressed. Perception, on the other hand, was defined as an integrative and interpretive process that the higher centers of the brain supposedly accomplished based on the sensory information and available memories for similar events.

The Gestalt psychologists, early German researchers, were convinced that perception was a higher order function compared to sensation. They believed that the whole stimulus was more than the sum of its individual sensory parts. Gestalt psychologists believed this statement was made true by the process of perception. For example, some of you listen to a song and hear individually the words, the loudness, and the harmony as well as the main melody. However, you do not really hear each of these units; what you hear is a whole song. If the song is pleasant to you, you may declare that you like the song. If the song is raucous to you, you may believe that you do not like it. However, even the songs you first hear and do not like may become liked after repeated exposure to those songs. Hence perception, according to these early Gestalt psychologists, was a more advanced and complicated process than sensation.

This dichotomy of sensation and perception is no longer widely accepted. The revolution came in the mid-1960s when psychologist James Gibson published a then-radical treatise (*The Senses Considered as Perceptual Systems*, Boston: Houghton Mifflin, 1966) in which he reasoned that perceptual processes included all sensory events that were seen as directed by a searching central nervous system. Also, this view provided that certain perceptual patterns, such as recognition of a piece of artwork, may be species-specific. That is, all humans, independent of learning history, should share some perceptual repertoires.

The articles in this unit were selected to help you understand perceptual processes better. In "The Legacy of Gestalt Psychology," Irvin Rock and Stephen Palmer reveal some of the principles of this early school of psychology that emphasized the study of perceptual processes. Armed with this historical information, you should better understand the articles that follow.

In the next article, "Are We Led by the Nose?" Terence Monmaney discusses olfaction or the sense of smell. Not only is smell important, it is much more acute in humans than you might think.

We next turn to articles that are on the fringe of the traditional study of sensation and perception. In "Research Probes What the Mind Senses Unaware," Daniel Goleman discusses the process of subliminal perception. Under the influence of subliminal perception, we supposedly hear or see stimuli below threshold or normal detectable levels. The article examines whether there is any veracity to this concept by examining the fascinating notion of the unconscious. Freud believed that simple subliminal messages can have an influence on us without our awareness. In this article, cognitive psychologists disagree and offer an alternative explanation.

The article "Consciousness Raising" explores the conscious experience and its relation to the unconscious perception.

Looking Ahead: Challenge Questions

What are some of the main principles of Gestalt psychology? Which ones seem to have survived intact in psychology as we know it today?

Can you rank order the senses, that is, place them in a hierarchy of importance? Do you think that olfaction is an important sense in humans?

Do you believe in the unconscious? Is there evidence that subliminal messages influence us? Whom do you think is right, the Freudian psychologist or the cognitive psychologist, in the debate over the efficacy of subliminal messages? Given what you have already learned in psychology, as a fledgling psychologist, should you base your response to the previous question on intuition or science?

The Legacy of Gestalt Psychology

Since its inception early in this century, Gestalt theory has made significant contributions to the study of perception, learning and social psychology. These contributions remain influential today

Irvin Rock and Stephen Palmer

IRVIN ROCK and STEPHEN PALMER, both at the University of California, Berkeley, collaborate on studies of visual perception. Despite their different backgrounds, they share an interest in many phenomena uncovered by Gestalt psychologists. Rock received his training at the New School for Social Research under students of the founding fathers of Gestalt, including Solomon Asch, Hans Wallach, Mary Henle and Martin Scheerer. He completed his Ph.D. there in 1952. Palmer was trained at the University of California, San Diego, in the more modern tradition of information processing, under the guidance of Donald Norman and David Rumelhart. His doctoral dissertation, completed in 1975, attempted to investigate Gestalt ideas in terms of information processing. Rock and Palmer are currently pursuing several research projects that extend and revise Gestalt theories of perceptual grouping and frame of reference.

Like many important movements in science, Gestalt psychology was born of a revolt against the intellectual establishment of its time. Today several concepts that Gestalt theorists proposed early in this century have been incorporated into modern understanding of perception, learning and thought—indeed into our very language and culture. Many people have heard the phrase "the whole Gestalt" or have seen pictures that demonstrate Gestalt principles, such as the one that looks now like a vase, now like two profiles face to face. But few outside of academic psychology know what the movement was about or what has happened to the ideas on which it was based.

Gestalt psychology started in Germany, but after the rise of Nazism its founders—Max Wertheimer, Wolfgang Köhler and Kurt Koffka—moved to the U.S., where some of their students remain active. The Gestaltists contributed more to the study of perception than to other areas of psychology—*Gestalt* is German for "pattern" or "shape," although "configuration" comes closer to its intended meaning—but they also made important advances in education, learning, thinking and social psychology. Some of their ideas have not survived, but others continue to influence the work of modern psychologists.

Gestalt psychology was launched in 1912 when Wertheimer, then at the Institute of Psychology in Frankfurt am Main, published a paper on a visual illusion called apparent motion. Apparent motion is the perception of movement that results from viewing a rapid sequence of stationary images, as in the movies. This phenomenon indicated to Wertheimer that the perception of the whole (movement) was radically different from the perception of its components (static images).

The idea that the whole is different from the sum of its parts—the central tenet of Gestalt psychology—challenged the then prevailing theory of Structuralism. In particular, the Gestaltists rejected elementarism, a basic Structuralist assumption that complex perceptions could be understood by identifying the elementary parts of experience. Structuralists believed a trained observer could break down the fundamental elements of perception into primitive sensations, such as the points that make a square or the particular pitches in a melody. They maintained that a square was just the experience of a particular set of points stimulating the retina; a melody was just the experience of a sequence of distinct tones that became associated with one another in the listener's mind. Their view has been described as "mental chemistry" because it assumes that perceptions can be analyzed component by component, much as molecules can be broken down into atoms.

The Gestaltists attacked this theory. What people perceived, they held, is not merely a sum or sequence of sensations but the whole configuration of which they are part. The location or size of a square's image can be altered so that entirely different retinal sensations are produced, yet the perception is still that of a square. How else could people experience the same melody when it is transposed in key? All the corresponding pitches are now different, yet only a few musicians with perfect pitch would notice any change.

Gestalt theorists maintained that the parts of a square—or the tones of a melody—interact with one another and in so doing produce a perceived whole that is distinct from the sum of its parts. Shape and melody are examples of what they called emergent properties: overall qualities of an experience that are not inherent in its components. Emergent properties are not unique to mental phenomena, however. The properties of table salt, for instance, are very different from those of its constituents, sodium (a corrosive metal) and chlorine (a poisonous gas). Even the characteristics of a society are distinct from those of the individuals who compose it.

Emergent quality illustrates one meaning of the Gestalt concept of organization. The Gestaltists also believed

 From *Scientific American*, December 1990, pp. 84-90.

organization was necessary to explain why human beings see the world as composed of distinct objects. They pointed out that because the retinal image is nothing but an array of varying intensities and frequencies of light, the rays coming from different parts of the same object have no more affinity for one another than those coming from two different objects. It follows that the ability to perceive objects—such as stones, trees and houses—must be an organization achieved by the nervous system. The realization that the perception of separate objects was not achieved solely by the "picture" focused on the retina was one of the Gestaltists' most important contributions.

To explain how perceptions of individual objects are formed, Wertheimer proposed that the visual system organizes parts into wholes based on laws of grouping. Elements tend to be grouped perceptually if they are close together, similar to one another, form a closed contour or move in the same direction [*see illustration on page 62*]. Most often these laws lead to an accurate representation of the objects in a scene, but they can also lead to inaccurate ones, as in the case of camouflage.

Another important aspect of organization, called figure-ground perception, was discovered in 1921 by Danish psychologist Edgar Rubin. Rubin pointed out that even if all the parts of a connected region are grouped together properly, it can be interpreted either as an object (figure) or as the surface behind it (ground) [*see lower illustration on next page*]. He formulated a set of laws that describe the conditions under which a region would tend to be seen as figure rather than as ground.

The Gestaltists further discovered that certain structures determine a frame of reference with respect to which other objects are perceived. Many people have reported experiencing an instance of this phenomenon, called induced motion, when a neighboring train slowly pulls out of the station, producing the impression that one's own train has begun to move in the opposite direction, although it is actually stationary. Another example of this phenomenon occurs when an observer is inside a tilted room. The walls of the room define the vertical and horizontal axes of the frame, causing a chandelier to look strangely askew and the observer's own body to feel tilted, despite the fact that both are perfectly aligned with gravity. In each case, the visual system takes a large, surrounding structure to define the perceptual standard—stillness or uprightness—

and construes other objects, including one's self, in terms of these standards.

A final aspect of the Gestalt concept of organization deals with what they called the principle of *Prägnanz,* which states that when stimuli are ambiguous, the perception will be as "good" (meaning simple, regular and symmetric) as the "prevailing conditions" allow. The prevailing conditions refer to the information being registered by the retina. Obviously, the visual system does not convert any pattern into the simplest shape. An irregular triangle, for example, is not seen as a circle, because perception must account for the nature of the retinal image. But in cases where the image is ambiguous, such as a partly hidden figure [*see lower illustration on page 61*], the viewer tends to perceive the simplest shape consistent with the information available.

Gestalt theorists sought to understand these and other perceptual phenomena in physiologic terms. They posited a very direct connection between experience and physiology in their doctrine of isomorphism, which states that a subjective experience and its underlying neural event have similar structures. Wertheimer's analysis of apparent movement illustrates this idea. When two lights in nearby locations are turned on and off at the proper alternation rate, the observer sees a single light moving back and forth [see "The Illusion of Movement," by Paul A. Kolers; SCIENTIFIC AMERICAN, October, 1964]. Wertheimer argued that this perception was caused by electric energy in the brain flowing between the two locations stimulated by the lights—in other words, the physiological event had the same structure as the perception it gave rise to.

The flowing of electric energy in the brain did not refer to the transmission of electric signals along individual neurons, as dictated by the standard view of neurophysiology. Such a neuronal system did not seem capable of explaining the kind of interaction and organization Gestalt theorists had in mind, so they suggested that direct current flowed through brain tissue. They held that stimuli created electric fields in the brain that interacted with one another and converged toward a state of minimum energy. Köhler, who was well versed in the physics of the day, argued that the brain was only one example of many physical systems—which he called physical *Gestalten*—that evolve toward a state of equilibrium. Soap bubbles, for instance, start

out in various shapes, but they always change over time into perfect spheres because that is the minimum energy state for a soap film.

Consistent with their doctrine of isomorphism, the Gestaltists believed that the convergence of electric brain fields toward a minimum energy state provided the mechanism for *Prägnanz:* perceptions were simplified when the underlying brain event reached a state of equilibrium.

Although Köhler's theory of electric brain fields is no longer taken seriously, many other ideas that emerged from Gestalt psychology continue to influence today's perception theorists. In some cases, Gestalt views have been extended and in others revised, but one cannot read a contemporary perception textbook without finding a wealth of ideas that originated with the Gestalt movement.

Wertheimer's laws of grouping have withstood the test of time. In fact, not one of them has been refuted, and no new ones have been added to his original list, until our own recent proposals. One of us (Palmer) suggested a law of enclosure, or common region, referring to an observer's tendency to group elements that are located within the same perceived region [*see illustration on page 62*]. The second law, connectedness, which we postulated jointly, may be the most fundamental principle of grouping yet uncovered. Connectedness refers to the powerful tendency of the visual system to perceive any uniform, connected region—such as a spot, line or more extended area—as a single unit. Connectedness is a particularly good candidate for a law of grouping because it is perhaps the most diagnostic property of objects in the environment. We suspect Wertheimer missed this important principle because he failed to realize that an explanation was required for why each element in his configurations was itself perceived as a single entity.

Although the validity of the laws of grouping has not been seriously challenged, the stage at which they operate in the visual system is being reassessed. The Gestalt position implicitly assumes that grouping must occur early in visual processing. So when Wertheimer discussed principles such as proximity, he presumably referred to retinal proximity: how close the stimuli were to one another on the retina. It is possible, however, that these grouping principles operate later in visual processing, after depth and lighting conditions have been perceived.

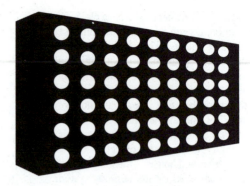

LATTICE OF GLOWING BEADS is organized vertically into columns (*left panel*). When it is tilted backward (*right pan-el*), observers still perceive columns even though the retinal images of the beads are now closer together horizontally.

To disentangle these two hypotheses, one of us (Rock) performed an experiment with Leonard Brosgole some years ago. Luminous beads were strung on parallel strings and suspended in the dark so that they appeared as a lattice of glowing dots. Because the beads were closer to one another vertically than horizontally, observers saw them as organized into columns [*see illustration above*]. We then tilted the display backward so that the retinal images of the beads were closer together horizontally, although the beads themselves of course remained closer vertically. When observers viewed this display, they continued to see the beads in columns, indicating that grouping was based on perceived proximity in three-dimensional space rather than on actual proximity on the retina. Grouping by proximity must therefore occur after depth perception. We have reached similar conclusions for the principles of common region and connectedness, as well as for similarity grouping by lightness.

New experimental methods have further advanced the understanding of grouping and have also suggested links to the underlying physiology. Jacob Beck of the University of Oregon pioneered the study of texture segregation, a form of grouping elements by similarity when they are perceived as a pattern rather than as individual forms. In one experiment he presented observers with a field of three different types of elements side by side: L's (or reversed L's), T's and tilted T's [*see top illustration on page 63*]. The observers were to say at which boundary there was a more natural break in the pattern.

Beck found that the boundary between the upright and tilted T's was much more evident than the one between the L's and the T's. This reveals—somewhat surprisingly from the Gestalt point of view—that the orientation of the elements is a more powerful factor than their overall shape. These and related findings have forged theoretical connections between the separation of textures and the activity of cells in the visual cortex that respond strongly to differences in the orientation of component lines and edges [see "Brain Mechanisms of Vision," by David H. Hubel and Torsten N. Wiesel; SCIENTIFIC AMERICAN, September, 1979].

Other techniques have provided ways of testing the Gestalt idea that wholes are perceptually dominant. David Navon, now at the University of Haifa in Israel, performed a study to determine whether wholes are perceived before parts, or vice versa. Using large letters composed of small letters, he measured the time observers needed to identify the large (global) or small (local) letters [*see middle illustration on page 63*]. In some cases, the large and small letters were the same (consistent); in others, they were different (conflicting).

If whole figures are perceptually primary, as the Gestaltists held, global letters should be identified faster than local ones; if parts are primary, as others believe, the reverse should be true. Another prediction of the Gestalt viewpoint is that if the whole is perceived first, conflicting local letters should not affect the naming of the global ones, but conflicting letters at the global level should slow naming of the local ones. Again, part-to-whole theorists predict the opposite. Navon's results supported the Gestalt predictions on both counts. Later investigators have found

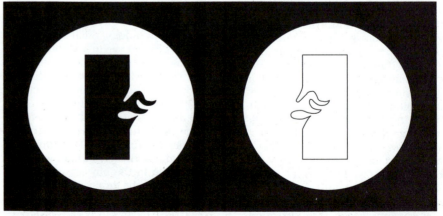

FIGURE-GROUND ORGANIZATION is fundamental to perception. Either side of the pattern on the left can be perceived as figure or as ground. Although the two shapes on the right share the same contour, they seem very different.

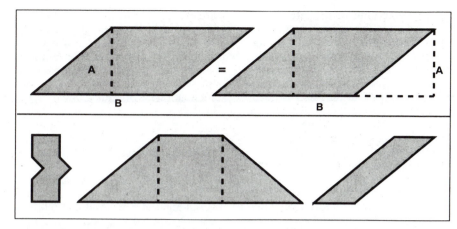

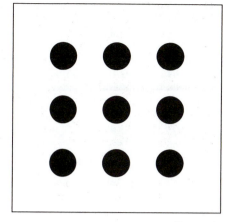

UNDERSTANDING that a parallelogram's area is equivalent to that of a rectangle's (*top panel*) makes finding the areas of other shapes (*bottom panel*) easier. Learning by understanding allows insights to be transferred to analogous situations.

CONNECT the dots by drawing four straight lines without lifting pencil from paper. (Solution on page 63, at bottom.)

these results to be less pervasive than Gestalt theory would suggest by showing that responses depend on factors like the absolute and relative size of the letters.

Another concept of Gestalt theory that is very much alive is the principle of *Prägnanz*—the idea that the visual system converges on the most regular and symmetric perception consistent with sensory information. The vague Gestalt notion of "goodness" has now been clarified. Emanuel Leeuwenberg and Hans Buffart, then at the University of Nijmegen, advanced a theory that specifies the amount of information in various perceptions—"good" ones contain little information, and "bad" ones contain a lot—and have predicted how people will perceive partly hidden figures, among other phenomena. Wendell R. Garner of Yale University has shown that good patterns can be matched more quickly, re-

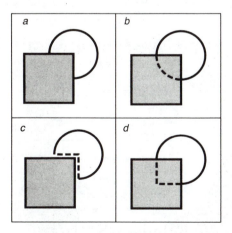

OBSCURED FIGURE illustrates the idea of *Prägnanz*. Given an ambiguous pattern (*a*), observers perceive simple shapes (*b*) instead of complex ones (*c*, *d*).

membered better and described more succinctly than bad ones.

In contrast to their theories of perception, Gestaltists' ideas about electric fields in the brain have been resoundingly rejected by modern physiologists. Concepts similar to Köhler's notions about physical *Gestalten,* however, have resurfaced under the guise of neural networks. According to neural-network theorists, mental processes result from the dynamic behavior of many interconnected computing units, which can be thought of as neurons. Each unit's behavior can be characterized by its state of activation—much like a neuron's firing rate—and units affect one another by excitatory or inhibitory connections—much like synapses. The entire system is initially activated by an external stimulus that affects some subset of the units. Activation then propagates through the network until it reaches an equilibrium state of minimum energy [see "Collective Computation in Neuronlike Circuits," by David W. Tank and John J. Hopfield; SCIENTIFIC AMERICAN, December, 1987]. In short, these networks can be thought of as examples of physical *Gestalten.* Although this work is still in its infancy, neural-network models of perception promise to open a whole new chapter of Gestalt theory.

Beyond revolutionizing the study of perception, Gestalt theorists enriched the fields of learning, memory and thinking—with important implications for education—and social psychology. Early Gestalt ideas about thinking clashed with those of the emerging Behaviorist movement. A forerunner of that school, Edward L. Thorndike, concluded from his studies that animals solved problems by trial

and error rather than by thought or understanding. In one now famous experiment, he placed a cat in a cage from which it could escape by pulling a hanging string that opened the door latch. In the process of thrashing about, the cat would inadvertently tug the string and be released. After many such trials, it would pull the string the moment it was returned to the cage. Thorndike concluded that the cat did not use intelligence but gradually developed an association.

Gestalt theorists vehemently denounced this kind of experiment and the conclusions drawn from it. They objected that the situation actually prevented any display of intelligence in problem solving because the cat could hardly be expected to understand the hidden mechanism that related tugging on the string to opening the door. In contrast, Köhler performed experiments with chimpanzees while he was isolated on the island of Tenerife during World War I in which both the requirements for a solution and the means to achieve it were perceptually evident. Köhler observed chimps discovering how to retrieve bananas from outside their cage with a stick.

These findings conflicted with Behaviorist dogma in at least two important ways. First, the chimps arrived at the solution suddenly, in a flash of "insight," rather than gradually. This was possible, Köhler argued, because the nature of the problem was perceptually apparent, unlike the string-latch mechanism. Second, the errors made by the chimps were not random, as predicted by Behaviorist theory, but displayed intelligence and comprehension.

Although no one has explained how insight occurs, the Gestaltists did illuminate certain aspects of how understanding could be achieved. One way humans can do it, unlike animals, is by having something explained to them. Mere listening is not enough, of course, for the listener must achieve the same cognitive structure as the explainer in order to become aware of the essential connections among the relevant facts. Listeners do not have to go through the same creative process as did the original problem solver to arrive at the solution, but their final state of comprehension must be similar.

The educational implications of achieving insight through explanation cannot be overestimated. Not only is it satisfying to grasp the solution to a problem, but it is far less likely to be forgotten than rote memorization, and it can be readily transferred to related new problems. Wertheimer showed, for instance, that once children realize why the area of a parallelogram equals its base times its altitude [*see upper left illustration on preceeding page*], they can find the areas of other geometric figures without having to memorize the formulas. Many modern educators critical of rote learning advocate teaching students to think creatively to achieve insight. Few realize that these "revolutionary" ideas about education originated with Gestalt psychologists.

Gestalt theorists also struggled to describe the creative process through which a person achieves original insight in everyday life. They proposed that problems have certain demands that are readily grasped, which lead people to attempt nonrandom solutions [see "Problem-Solving," by Martin Scheerer; SCIENTIFIC AMERICAN, April, 1963]. Becoming fixated on one hypothesis or one function of an object—often without realizing it [*see upper right illustration on preceeding page*]—is the chief obstacle to insight. When people let go of implicit assumptions, their understanding of a problem is sometimes dramatically reorganized, enabling them suddenly to "see" the solution, complete with the accompanying "aha!" experience.

Modern researchers on human problem solving have not yet explained insight, but they have abandoned the Behaviorist idea of blind trial and error in favor of one more consistent with Gestalt ideas about the value of comprehension. One promising focus of recent research has been the use of analogies in problem solving: those who understand one topic can apply this knowledge elsewhere through analogy.

The Gestaltists made further inroads against the Behaviorist approach in the realm of social psychology. Beginning in the late 1930s, three investigators—Kurt Lewin, Fritz Heider and Solomon E. Asch—rejected the idea that social behavior could be explained solely as a response conditioned by societal rewards, such as approval or praise. Rather, they argued, people make sense of the behavior of others by attributing to them feelings, perception, goals, beliefs and intentions—a view known as attribution theory. As obvious as this idea sounds, it was a radical departure from the prevailing Behaviorist approach, which minimized or denied subjective states of mind. Attribution theory has since displaced Behaviorism as the dominant view in social psychology.

Few of Lewin's ideas have survived in contemporary psychology, but the work of Heider and Asch has had lasting influence. Heider applied Gestalt ideas about object perception to the perception of others. One cornerstone of his theory was the idea of attribution: that people try to account for one another's behavior in terms of deeper causal explanations, such as motives and intentions, using context and behavioral consistencies. Heider also developed the concept of balance: the idea that individuals prefer harmonious cognitive relations. For instance, if Jane likes person X and thinks X likes person Y, then the system of beliefs will be balanced if Jane also likes Y—and imbalanced if she does not. This idea echoes the principle of *Prägnanz:* the tendency to achieve the best or most basic organization.

Heider's seminal work on balance theory is related to the late Leon Festinger's theory of cognitive dissonance. Because Festinger believed people seek to reduce inconsistencies in their beliefs, feelings and behavior, he studied how people's choices affect their subsequent beliefs and attitudes. He reasoned that when a rejected alternative (say, a sporty but temperamental car) is in many ways more desirable than the chosen one (a staid but reliable car), the fact that it was not chosen will produce an inner state of disharmony—or dissonance, as Festinger called it—which produces pressure toward eliminating it. One way to reduce dissonance is to reevaluate the relative attractiveness of the alternatives, such as devaluing the unchosen one (sporty cars are too dangerous anyway), thereby enhancing the chosen one.

Asch, who worked with Wertheimer at the New School for Social Research, directly extended Gestalt theory to social psychology. He contended that attitudes are rooted in beliefs, that beliefs are rooted in information and that beliefs tend to be rational rather than molded by "suggestion," as early social psychologists thought. His emphasis on human rationality conflicted with the seeming irrationality of phenomena such as racial prejudice. Asch argued, however, that even prejudice can be understood as being reasonable and rooted in information, albeit misinformation. For example, if children depend on parents and other respected adults and have little reason to mistrust them, accepting adult opinions about an ethnic or racial group is a reasonable thing to do. Moreover, children get little if any information from other sources to contradict what they have been told by their parents.

Asch also challenged the Behaviorist assumption that beliefs and attitudes result from suggestions based on the prestige of the source. For instance, American college students were known to change their opinion of a statement depending on who they believed had made it. When told Thomas Jefferson had said "a little rebellion, now and then, is a good thing, and as necessary in the political world as storms in the physical," they often strongly agreed. If

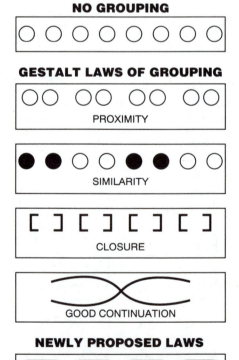

NO GROUPING

GESTALT LAWS OF GROUPING

PROXIMITY

SIMILARITY

CLOSURE

GOOD CONTINUATION

NEWLY PROPOSED LAWS

COMMON REGION

CONNECTEDNESS

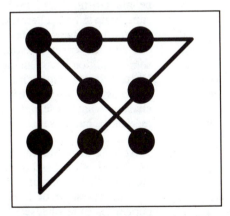

TEXTURE SEGREGATION is based on the dissimilarity of elements. The boundary between upright and tilted **T**'s is clearer than between upright **T**'s and **L**'s.

GLOBAL PRECEDENCE allows larger letters to be recognized more rapidly than smaller ones, whether or not the latter are consistent. Identifying small letters, in contrast, takes longer when they conflict with the global letter.

DOTS can be connected by extending the lines beyond them. People assume incorrectly that they may not do this.

the same statement was attributed to Lenin, their agreement with the statement diminished considerably.

These results superficially support the idea that the acceptability of the source strongly influences a person's opinions. But Asch believed there was a rational basis for such decisions. He proposed that people understood the statement differently depending on who was thought to have said it. Indeed, Asch found that students who attributed the statement to Lenin interpreted "rebellion" to mean the complete overthrow of the socioeconomic system. Those who attributed it to Jefferson usually had a less violent interpretation, such as moderate social or political reform [see "Opinions and Social Pressure," by Solomon E. Asch; SCIENTIFIC AMERICAN, November, 1955].

This aspect of Asch's work represents an extension of the Gestalt concept of part-whole contextual effects that was developed to explain perceptual phenomena. The part in this case was the statement, which had different meanings when embedded within the whole (all that one knows about the author, be he Jefferson or Lenin). The idea of the whole resulting from the organization of parts is illustrated by Asch's experiment on how people form impressions of personalities from lists of traits. Asch found that when people arrive at a unified impression of a person, certain traits are pivotal: substituting one for the other in a list of otherwise identical traits would entirely change the overall impression. Even the same trait will be perceived differently as a function of another trait. Thus, the meaning of being "determined" in a warm person is not quite the same as being "determined" in a cold person.

In some ways, the Gestalt movement, despite its acknowledged impact on several areas of psychology, has always been regarded rather skeptically by the scientific establishment. This opinion was certainly true in the 1920s and 1930s when the dominant theories were Structuralism and Behaviorism, schools that the Gestaltists attacked vehemently—and successfully. Yet such skepticism persists today for several reasons. First, Gestalt psychology sought to investigate subjective experience, as in perception, which Behaviorists rejected as an improper subject for scientific inquiry. Second, although Gestaltists did perform many well-controlled experiments, their best-known phenomena were often presented as straightforward demonstrations, such as the figures illustrating the laws of grouping. Third, their theories were usually expressed qualitatively and fell short of current standards of precision. Moreover, their views about brain function have been largely discredited by modern neurophysiologists. And last, but certainly not least, the theoretical approach they advocated seems to deny one of the most basic tenets of the scientific method—that wholes can be understood by reducing them to a set of parts.

These formidable obstacles to the acceptance of Gestalt ideas should be weighed against their considerable accomplishments. The list of major perceptual phenomena they elucidated—grouping, figure-ground organization, frames of reference, figural goodness and apparent motion, just to name the ones mentioned in this article—is impressive. Although it is logically possible that these discoveries could have been made independently of their methods and theoretical beliefs, it seems unlikely. The Gestalt attack against Structuralism was devastatingly effective.

In addition, the Gestaltists were victorious over the Behaviorists in their clash regarding the nature of learning, thinking and social psychology. Although behavioral methods are adhered to by modern psychologists, Behaviorist theory has been abandoned in favor of a cognitive approach more in line with Gestalt thinking. The theoretical problems they raised about perceptual organization, insight, learning and human rationality remain among the deepest and most complex in psychology.

Even though Gestalt ideas about electric brain fields were erroneous, the more general proposal that the brain is a dynamic system converging toward equilibrium in an energy function—physical *Gestalten* in Köhler's terminology—may turn out to be correct. The remarkable surge of interest in neural-network models attests to the fact that Gestalt theories are very much alive today and that their place in psychological history is assured.

FURTHER READING

A SOURCE BOOK OF GESTALT PSYCHOLOGY. Prepared by Willis Davis Ellis. Humanities Press, 1938.

GESTALT PSYCHOLOGY. Wolfgang Köhler. Liveright, 1970.

THE MENTALITY OF APES. Wolfgang Köhler. Liveright, 1976.

PERCEPTUAL ORGANIZATION. Edited by Michael Kubovy and James R. Pomerantz. Lawrence Erlbaum Associates, 1981.

PARALLEL DISTRIBUTED PROCESSING: EXPLORATIONS IN THE MICROSTRUCTURE OF COGNITION, Vol. 1: FOUNDATIONS. David E. Rumelhart, James L. McClelland and the PDP Research Group. The MIT Press, 1986.

SOCIAL PSYCHOLOGY. Solomon E. Asch. Oxford University Press, 1987.

ARE WE LED BY THE NOSE?

T E R E N C E   M O N M A N E Y

Terence Monmaney writes about health for Newsweek.

> What a rat smells in the womb is what it seeks in a mate. What mammals smelled 100 million years ago may have led to the human forebrain.

On a rainy October night in Chicago 11 years ago, 33-year-old mathematician David Griffin* stepped off a curb and into the path of a Dodge van. He was on his usual after-dinner walk, although he was perhaps feeling an unusual need for it—the buffet supper of turkey and potatoes and fixings had not fully agreed with him.

Griffin considered himself something of an epicure, with an ability to taste and smell that was the functional equivalent of perfect pitch. Impressed once, for instance, by the exotic flavor of some broiled fish he had eaten in a restaurant in Pisa, he divined the secret recipe and re-created the dish, down to the basting of lime juice, rosemary, and mustard.

The van was moving about five miles an hour when it hit him. He cracked his skull on the pavement. His recovery

---

*This is not his real name, but all the details of his case are true.

was good, and during the eight days he spent in the hospital he did not have any remarkable symptoms. True, he noticed that the hospital food was terribly bland and yet very salty, but that was clearly just a sign of his good taste. It appeared he would suffer no deep or lasting injury. The day after returning home he poured his father a snifter of pear brandy—sweet, ethereal, redolent of fruit ripening in a sun-washed orchard—and discovered he could smell absolutely nothing. "I was devastated," he says.

The doctors said that if he still couldn't smell anything after six months to a year, he probably never would. The blow, they explained, apparently tore nerves connecting his brain and nose. Griffin's taste buds worked fine, so at least he sensed the salty, bitter, sour, and sweet ingredients in food. Seven years

went by. His condition unchanged, Griffin sued the van's driver and won a modest settlement.

These days—well, he has resigned himself to an odorless existence, rationalizing that it certainly could be worse. Yet he has learned it is a hazardous as well as a hollow way of life. Shortly after the accident his apartment building caught fire; he awoke to the shouts of neighbors, not to the smell of smoke that might have alerted him sooner. He cannot detect leaking gas. He has been poisoned by spoiled food. But Griffin says he suffers a more profound loss: deprived now of the rush of memory that an odor can let loose, he feels cut off from moments in his own past. "Think about rotting leaves or a campfire or a roast or a Christmas tree—I enjoyed those smells so much. I miss not being able to experience

them again and be reminded of other times. A dimension of my life is missing. I feel empty, in a sort of limbo."

Approximately one out of every 15 victims of head trauma wakes up in a permanently odorless world. Accidents are the leading cause of anosmia (loss of smell) in people Griffin's age. Influenza, brain tumors, allergies, and the uncertain effects of old age are other reasons some 2 million people in the United States can't smell anything. No surveys have charted what these people miss most, but it's safe to say their lives lack spice.

At least three quarters of the flavors in food and drink are not tastes but aromas. The volatile essences of black pepper or blue cheese are breathed into passageways originating at the back of the mouth and delivered to olfactory nerve endings high in the nasal cavities.

Sex without smells is not quite the same either, according to Robert Henkin, former director of the Center for Sensory Disorders, Georgetown University. He says about one in four people with little or no smelling ability loses some

Between your eyes, just below the forebrain, some 20 million
olfactory nerves hang from the roof of each nasal cavity; their wispy cilia
bathed in mucus, swaying in the currents like sea grass.

sex drive. This is hardly the loss suffered by a male golden hamster with such a disability—remove that part of his brain devoted to olfaction and he'll give up mating entirely. But it suggests how our lives are enriched by olfactory signals, however unconsciously we tune them in.

The mysterious way smells refresh memories fascinates novelists as well as neuroscientists. Proust said the aroma of lime-flower tea and madeleines launched his monumental *Remembrances of Things Past*. Kipling, in his poem "Lichtenberg," wrote that the pungence of rain-soaked acacia meant home. That smell should be the most nostalgic sense seems logical. Compared with sights, sounds, and touch, odors are messages that last; the smell of burned gunpowder lingers long after the firecracker has sparkled and popped.

Unlike some other animals, we don't much rely on our noses to get around anymore, although some curious new experiments suggest we could if we were so inclined. Researchers at the Monell Chemical Senses Center in Philadelphia have shown that humans can smell the difference between two mice that are identical except for a small set of genes on one chromosome. People can in fact distinguish the urine of these two mice. If we close our eyes and lower our noses, we might not only find the urine-marked trails mice leave but tell one mouse's route from another's.

But we don't often track odors— we just keep track of them. The close tie between odors and

memory is more than happy coincidence; without it, odors would be meaningless. You can't identify an odor you've never experienced any more than you can recognize a face you've never seen.

The most primitive and evocative of the senses, smell is also the most intimate. Odors give you away. Everyone knows you can't hide alcohol on the breath. The urine of children with the genetic disease phenylketonuria is mousy. Intimate, too, is the very act of smelling. You have to inhale the stimulus, bring it inside, before you know what to make of it. "Touch seems to reside in the object touched..." Helen Keller wrote, "and odor seems to reside not in the object smelt, but in the organ."

The smelling organ turns out to be a lot more complicated than scientists imagined it would be: Chemicals flowing into some hollow tubes and reacting with a bunch of nerves—what could be simpler? But there are two strange things about olfactory nerves. For one, they constantly replace themselves, the only nerves we have capable of rebirth. One by one they die after a month or so, and new nerves sprout from cells in the nasal lining, growing thin filaments that seek the brain like seedlings pushing toward sunlight.

The reason olfactory nerves probably need to renew themselves is the other strange thing. Protected merely by a film of mucus, they are the only nerve endings out in the open. In the nose, in other words, the brain directly confronts and tries to sort out the world.

Michael Shipley, a neurobiologist at the University

of Cincinnati College of Medicine, is one of the new breed of olfaction researchers trying to get to the brain through the nose. "I've got a hunch if we can come close to understanding how the brain keeps track of odors," he says, "we'll be a long way toward understanding how it processes other kinds of information."

Between your eyes, just below the forebrain, some 20 million olfactory nerves hang from the roof of each nasal cavity, their wispy cilia bathed in mucus, swaying in the currents like sea grass. Just here, where olfactory nerves greet odorants dissolved in mucus, researchers have for decades drawn a blank. What nobody understands is what everybody wants to know: Why do things smell the way they do?

Solving the problem would be easier if all odors could be broken down into a few elements, as visible light can be separated into its spectral colors. The retina can faithfully reproduce a scene, in color, by means of a few sensory cell types, such as those dedicated to picking up red, green, or blue. But there is no odor spectrum. Olfactory nerves must recognize each odorant individually.

Many scientists imagine that olfactory receptors work like other receptors—like, say, the specialized protein on a muscle cell that receives the hormone insulin in the way a lock admits a key, and passes along insulin's message to break down more glucose. One problem with this idea, though, is that it doesn't account for the smell of a new car. While it's conceivable that olfactory nerves have evolved receptors for

natural odorants, surely humans haven't had time to evolve receptors devoted specifically to smelling the vinyl odors in a new car's interior. Around 10,500 chemical compounds are invented or discovered each week, and many are smelly.

Another idea, publicized by physician-essayist Lewis Thomas a decade ago, suggests that the immune and smelling systems, both dedicated to recognizing new, foreign substances, perform that task in much the same way. Recently, researchers at the Johns Hopkins Medical School offered some support for the theory. They discovered a protein in the nasal linings of cows that binds specifically to six different types of smelly chemicals, including pyrazines, which give scent to bell peppers. This pyrazine-binding protein, they say, looks and behaves somewhat like a disease-fighting antibody protein. From this bit of evidence it would appear that our smelling and immune systems literally come to grips with the outside by tailoring a protein to fit new materials encountered.

This theory of made-to-odor receptors represents a promising new approach, but it probably won't tell the whole story even if it holds up. Neurobiologist Robert Gesteland of the University of Cincinnati College of Medicine says, "Since these nerve cells are sitting out there in the fluid, accessible to the world—anything that gets into the fluid in your nose is certainly going to get to those

Boys and girls both start smelling right away. We're generally outfitted to smell days before birth, so it is possible to get a whiff of the world in the womb. Perhaps from spicy amniotic fluid we begin to acquire a taste for garlic.

cells—probably a few different receptor mechanisms have evolved. And no experiment so far favors one mechanism over another."

Seeing, touching, hearing—the neurons controlling these senses are relatively "hard wired," a fact of life the brain seems to have taken advantage of. It keeps track of stimuli by sending them down dedicated circuits. A dot of light on the retina, for instance, sets off an impulse through the optic nerve that activates brain cells corresponding to just that point on the retina.

Gordon Shepherd, a Yale University neuroscientist, believes olfaction works in a manner something like that of the other senses, despite its obvious differences. In his view, an odorant first stimulates particular receptors, which then transmit a signal to neurons dedicated to that odor in the olfactory bulbs, two matchstick-size brain structures above the nasal cavities. Those cells relay the news to brain centers involved, ultimately, in behavior appropriate to that odor. When researchers in Shepherd's lab analyzed the olfactory bulbs of newborn rats, they found that certain odors—especially those associated with the mother rat's nipples—were processed by a particular patch of cells on the bulbs, the makings of a kind of olfactory circuit. One stimulus, one circuit, one response—presented with the odor, the newborn suckles.

Walter Freeman, a neurophysiologist at the University of California, Berkeley, doesn't believe in olfactory circuits. He measures brain waves emanating from the

olfactory bulb of a rabbit while it sniffs an odor. When a rabbit is presented with an odor for the first time, according to Freeman's studies, its olfactory bulbs give off brain waves in fairly disordered fashion. After several exposures to an odor, a pattern emerges, and thereafter that odor prompts that pattern of neuronal activity—the sign of recognition.

The essence of Freeman's view is that olfactory neurons—and perhaps all neurons devoted to the senses—are not hard wired to perform single tasks but are creative; given a stimulus, they improvise a song of brain waves to go with it, and later sing the theme whenever cued. When Freeman speaks of neurons in action, he refers not to circuits but to ensembles.

Freeman's and Shepherd's views of olfactory-signal processing may simply be different versions of the same reality. It is too early to tell. But it's important to know, because the stakes are high: an understanding of the means by which the brain turns stimulus into sensation. Many olfaction researchers believe that even those who study vision and hearing (the so-called higher senses) and touch will have to turn to olfaction for inspiration. Ultimately, sensory biologists are in pursuit of the answer to the same question: How does a particular clump of neurons in the brain generate the awareness of an F-sharp, say, or a 1983 chardonnay?

Richard Doty is in a glistening steel room showing off his olfactometer. Fluorescent lights shine through chrome grids in the ceiling, and the walls and floors are

paneled with stainless steel. The room, in a University of Pennsylvania hospital, is as odorproof as can be.

The olfactometer is a closet-size machine connected by steel piping to a thing on a table that looks like a glass octopus with 11 tentacles. You put your nostril over the tip of a tentacle and the machine serves up a precisely measured wisp of, say, phenylethyl alcohol, an essence of rose. Then you indicate whether or not you detect it. In this way Doty measures smelling thresholds.

From the looks of this room you might get the idea that olfaction research is so advanced that the only task remaining is to add more decimal places to existing data. Yet smelling isn't such a precise experience. Your sensitivity to phenylethyl alcohols depends on your health, your allergies, whether you're tired or rested, whether you smelled it an hour ago, the humidity, the elevation above sea level, your age, and your sex.

So, the exquisite high-tech instruments so impressive to funding agencies won't necessarily solve the mysteries of human smelling. Consider Doty's low-tech success. He recently settled two much-debated questions—does smelling ability decline with age, and are men or women better smellers?—using a $20 scratch-and-sniff test.

It comes in a letter-size envelope and consists of 40 scratch-and-sniff patches: bubble gum, paint thinner, menthol, cherry, leather,

skunk, pizza. Next to each patch are the words, "This odor smells most like," followed by four choices. One is correct. At his lawyer's request, David Griffin, the mathematician struck by a van, took the test twice, and the scores helped convince the judge of Griffin's anosmia. He scored 9 and 8 out of 40. A score of 35 or better is considered normal. By now the researchers have administered the University of Pennsylvania Smell Identification Test to more than 5,000 people—males and females, white and black Americans, Korean-Americans, native Japanese (they had trouble recognizing cherry), some 50 five-year-olds, and many over 90.

Doty and his coworkers discovered that smelling power does fade late in life and that the sense is sharpest around middle age: The average score for 20- to 50-year-olds was 37. The average for 75-year-olds was 30. What's more, a quarter of the people between 65 and 80, and half of those over 80, appear anosmic. As the researchers concluded, "it is not surprising that many elderly persons complain that food lacks flavor and that the elderly account for a disproportionate number of accidental gas poisoning cases each year."

In a study published last May, these investigators showed that patients with Alzheimer's disease are unusually likely to have smelling deficits. Of 25 men and women diagnosed with Alzheimer's, all but 2 scored lower on the test than age-matched control subjects without the degenerative disease. "It's interesting that in a disease like Alzheimer's, where memory loss is a major dysfunction, there is also a problem with olfaction," Doty says. Researchers at Stanford and other universities have also demonstrated that memory and smelling often fade together in Alzheimer's patients. Olfaction may even sometimes disappear before other problems become evident, Doty says. Scratching and sniffing could turn out to be an effective and inexpensive screening tool for the disease.

Digging deeper into the test results, Doty found that at every age, women scored better on the smelling test than men, in all ethnic groups tested so far. At peak performance, by those subjects around middle age, the differences were slight—a point or less, on average. At the extremes it was more dramatic. Five-year-old boys scored an average of 27, while girls of the same age scored 34. At the other end, 65-year-old men averaged 33, compared with the 36 scored by 65-year-old women.

Doty can't explain the sex differences, but he may have ruled out one popular theory. Researchers who previously said women are superior smellers often gave credit to ovarian hormones like estrogen. After all, pregnant women, who are besieged by hormones, are considered especially acute smellers. But, Doty asks, if ovarian hormones are the key, why are five-year-old girls, years shy of puberty, better smellers than five-year-old boys?

Whatever their differences, boys and girls both start smelling right away. We're born with a set of olfactory nerves and bulbs already in working order. We're generally outfitted to smell days before birth, so it is possible we get a whiff of the world in the womb. Researchers have even suggested, and not entirely in jest, that from spicy

ILLUSTRATION BY MICHAEL REINGOLD

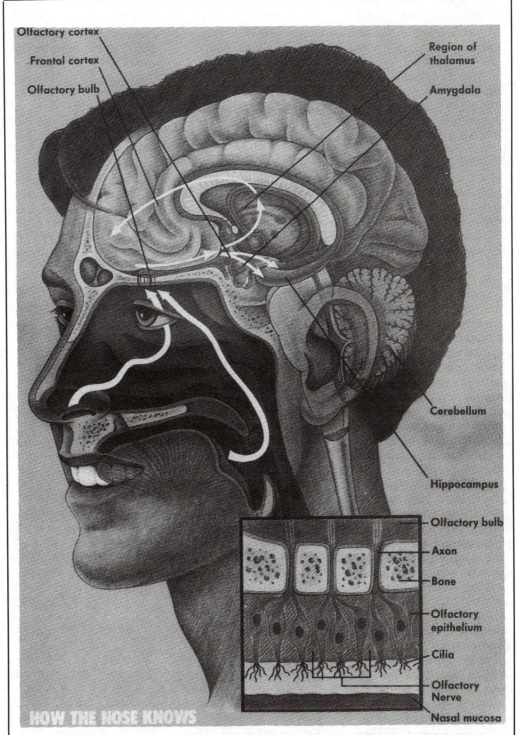

HOW THE NOSE KNOWS

Olfactory cortex
Frontal cortex
Olfactory bulb
Region of thalamus
Amygdala
Cerebellum
Hippocampus
Olfactory bulb
Axon
Bone
Olfactory epithelium
Cilia
Olfactory Nerve
Nasal mucosa

Aromas enter the nasal cavities through the nose and the back of the mouth, swirl around, and flow up to the top, where they encounter the mucus-bathed cilia of millions of tiny olfactory nerve cells. The aromatic molecules react with specific nerve receptors and send signals to the olfactory bulbs. That is where the signal begins to be interpreted; you become aware that you've smelled something, but you still can't identify what it is. The message is then relayed to the olfactory cortex, which puts a label on the odor ("The sea!"). From there it travels down two pathways: to the thalamus and cerebral cortex, where, for example, smell and sight are compared ("I smell the sea, but I'm in the Midwest. Why?"), and to the amygdala and hippocampus, structures that handle emotion and memory. It is there that an experience associated with a smell can be recalled ("The seaside cottage of childhood summers...").

amniotic fluid we might begin to acquire a taste for garlic, or cigarettes.

Rats, anyway, learn a thing or two about their mothers in utero, according to experiments done at Johns Hopkins by psychologists Elliot Blass and Patricia Pedersen, who now works in Shepherd's lab at Yale. A rat pup, born deaf and blind, smells the way to its mother's nipples, homing in on the already familiar odor of amniotic fluid on her underside. They found that if they injected a pregnant rat with citral, a lemon scent, a few days before she gave birth, the pups would prefer citral-rinsed nipples to their own mother's.

Blass and psychologist Thomas Fillion, of Yale, completed further experiments showing how odors shape behavior. Again the experiments were done on rats, and again the researchers can't say what the findings mean for the rest of us. But you have to wonder. They say odors that rats experience while suckling can be a sexual turn-on later in life.

Each experiment began with a litter of pups that were suckled by mothers whose nipples and genitals were painted with citral. After weaning, the male pups were isolated from both citral odors and females until they reached sexual maturity, at about 100 days. Then the rats were introduced to a female in heat—either a normal female or one with citral-scented genitals.

Blass and Fillion found that males exposed to citral while suckling were more eager to mate with citral-scented females and finished mating more quickly—an average of five minutes, or 30 percent, faster than when mating with normal females. "These findings," the researchers concluded, "suggest that, at least for this mammal, the degree to which

a feminine feature is sexually arousing to adult males can be established in the context of suckling."

That's exciting to the male rat, apparently, is not any particular odor—fragrance of lemon furniture polish will do—but the sensation associated with it. "There's a learning process going on," Fillion says. "My intuition is that suckling is such a powerful experience, and the arousal provided by it is so powerful, it's an ideal time and place for any mammal to learn an important sensory cue." Far from coldly objectifying rat sex, Blass and Fillion have revealed its poignance, showing it is in part a rat's pursuit of infantile satisfactions.

No equivalent studies have been done on humans, but research does show that babies experience and recognize maternal odors while suckling. The first such study was done a decade ago at the University of California, San Francisco, by Michael Russell, then a graduate student. A two-day-old infant, he showed, would not respond to a cotton pad worn for three hours in its mother's bra. Yet most six-week-olds tested did begin suckling if they smelled a cotton pad worn by their mothers, although they didn't respond to a pad worn in the bra of an unfamiliar lactating woman. Writing in *Nature,* Russell also noted that most infants were obviously attracted to their mother's scent and often repulsed by a stranger's. Russell concluded: "The existence of olfactory maternal attraction suggests that humans have a pheromonal system and that it operates at a very early age."

A pheromone is a substance that is produced by an organism and that elicits a

specific and unlearned response in another member of the same species. At least that's how researchers defined it in 1959, after collecting several examples of chemicals that insects use to communicate—ant trail markers, queen-bee anointments, and so forth. By the mid-1970s there was an increased interest in human pheromones, and Russell's study was considered by many as support for the substances' existence.

But critics say Russell never ruled out the possibility that the infants were merely recognizing ordinary odors, even traces of their own saliva. What Russell called "olfactory maternal attraction," they said, was simply the infant's recognition, after learning, of their mothers' body odor.

The strongest case for a human pheromone involves menstrual synchrony. Psychologist Martha McClintock wasn't the first to notice that when women live together in close quarters for months at a time, their menstrual cycles begin to coincide. But her 1970 study of women in a college dormitory documented synchrony so thoroughly that the phenomenon is now widely known as the McClintock effect. And she made the crucial observation that many of the dormitory residents adopted the rhythms of a certain few women—perhaps, she said, because they broadcast a chemical signal, a pheromone, that the other women heeded.

Skeptics have said women achieve menstrual synchrony because they eat, study, wash, vacation, talk, and stay up all night together; shared stresses and joys regulate their cycles, not chemical messages. Still, late last year, researchers at the Monell Chemical Senses Center and the University of Penn-

sylvania offered the firmest evidence yet that pheromones mediate the McClintock effect. George Preti and Winnifred Cutler exposed 10 women with normal cycles to underarm sweat from other women. The subjects were daubed under the nose every few days with the female sweat. After three months, the subjects' cycles began to coincide with sweat-donors' cycles—evidence, the researchers say, that a pheromone in sweat mediates menstrual synchrony (other women, controls, were daubed with alcohol and showed no significant change). "Pheromone effects are real in human beings," Preti grandly told the *Washington Post,* "and the anecdotal evidence suggests they even occur here in the United States, where we're all deodorized and perfumized."

Maybe so. But Doty doesn't believe that humans, like moths, have automatic or built-in responses to certain odors or pheromones; instead, he says, we interpret odors much as we do visual or auditory signals: "If I'm walking down the street and see a woman with beautiful blond hair and I get sort of excited—you don't say blond hair is a *visual* one. Our idea of what is attractive depends on styles we grow up with, what we see on TV, what society values. In some cultures blond hair is unattractive. The same thing occurs in the sense of smell. Smelling is just a way of extracting information from chemicals in the environment. The *meaning* that information may have is affected by locale and learning and memory, by the context of the experience."

That is partly what makes the smell of smoke pleasant at a barbeque, not so welcome in a movie theater. Even a rat can learn that an odor's message depends on

Researchers at the Monell Chemical Senses Center have shown
that humans can smell the difference between two mice that are identical
except for a small set of genes on one chromosome.

the context. Trained to anticipate a rewarding sip of water after smelling the banana odor of amyl acetate, a rat will quickly learn to avoid amyl acetate if the "reward" is changed to an electric shock. A silkworm moth is less flexible. It is difficult to imagine training the moth not to respond to bombykol, a mating pheromone secreted by females that males can detect from miles away.

Psychologist William Cain's experiments at the Pierce Foundation at Yale spell out how important the context is. Cain asked a dozen undergraduates to identify by smell alone 80 familiar things, such as baby powder, burned toast, shoe polish, and popcorn. The samples were kept in opaque jars and the students, eyes closed, sniffed them through cloth. They could identify fewer than half. "They knew the smell was familiar," says Cain. "They just couldn't always name it."

It happens all the time. You've smelled it before, you like it—but what is the spice in that dish, what is it about that perfume? Cain, Shipley, and others believe

odors often leave us dumb because brain centers concerned with language are not richly connected to the olfactory cortex.

For most of us, as Cain's study suggests, smelling is somehow remote from the higher cognitive functions. You cannot really conjure up an odor in the way you can imagine a face or voice. Nor can you manipulate that image as you can rotate an imaginary cube, for example, or put words in someone's mouth. And while odors evoke memories, the opposite is not generally true.

That's because there are different brain structures for detecting and remembering odors, according to Gary Lynch, a neurobiologist at the University of California, Irvine. After the olfactory bulbs receive and sort a signal, they relay it to several places—to the olfactory cortex (to make you aware you smell something), and from there to centers involved in memory (most importantly the hippocampus, which connects to higher visual centers). Although information flows from olfactory bulbs to hippocampus to visual cortex, prompting a memory, visual information can't make it back to odor-sensing areas of the olfactory cortex.

Kipling saw this memory lane as a one-way street in "Lichtenberg." After reaching town and its smell of wattle, or acacia, a cascade of memories—"the picnics and brass-bands"—is let loose, courtesy of hippocampal connection:

"It all came over me in one
    act
Quick as a shot through the
    brain—
With the smell of the wattle
    round Lichtenberg,
Riding in, in the rain."

Lynch believes that the kind of memory we use to store facts began to emerge in some primitive mammal 100 million years ago, as a means of keeping track of odors. It was only a matter of time before a more advanced smeller made a breakthrough, rousing the image corresponding to an odor— "mother," say—without actually smelling her. In this evolutionary view, the collections of neurons originally designed to process olfactory information gave rise to higher forms of memory and cognition; the human forebrain, seat of art making and history writing and joke telling, is basically a souped-up smelling machine.

You can take this as an insult to your intelligence or a

celebration of your nose. But the more neuroscientists learn about smelling, the more it looks right for this sophisticated new role. Olfactory nerves in flux, receptors arising to each smelly occasion, bulbs creating patterns of neuronal activity for each odorant, memory linking the sensation of odor with whatever happens to be around—you'd expect this sort of creativity of the sense that introduced learning and memory into the world.

Brainy snobs, our noses up in the air, we don't follow odor trails anymore. We work in skyscrapers where the windows don't open, drive around in climate-controlled cars, hide behind "five-day deodorant protection," gobble up processed cheese. We are starting to act like birds, too high up and fast-moving to heed earthly chemical signals.

Even as our lives become more rarefied, the orphan sense, as Lynch calls it, is turning into one of the premier problems in biology. "Olfaction has always been in the back shed of neuroscience," Walter Freeman says. "The reason is largely emotional, I think. It has always been thought of as primitive. It's not glamorous. Olfaction is—it's *smells*."

Research Probes What the Mind Senses Unaware

New findings fuel debate about the power of messages directed to the unconscious.

Daniel Goleman

The power of subliminal messages is taken as an article of faith by many people. Critics of advertising often take for granted the power of "hidden persuaders." Many parents stand convinced that messages buried in rock music are poisoning their children's minds. And for vendors of audio tapes, the power of the imperceptible exhortation to strengthen memory or take off pounds is more than an article of faith—it is a profit center.

But scientists studying the mind's ability to register information outside awareness are locked in debate about the power of messages directed to the unconscious mind. Some, most of whom are cognitive psychologists, say there is no credible scientific evidence that hidden messages can persuade or cure. But psychoanalytic researchers claim their data show that certain kinds of subliminal messages can have great persuasive and therapeutic impact. Both sides agree that popular understanding of subliminal persuasion is largely naive, crediting it with powers that it simply does not have.

"There's a huge gap between the scientific data on subliminal perception and the extravagant claims made for it," said Timothy Moore, a psychologist at York University in Toronto. "For example, I regard subliminal tapes as a form of health fraud."

Even psychologists who say some subliminal messages can have therapeutic effects are skeptical about commercial tapes. "On the whole, the tapes do not work," said Dr. Howard Shevrin, a psychologist at the University of Michigan. "A uniform, off-the-rack message is not likely to have an effect, and can even have negative effects. However, the right message under the right circumstances might be therapeutic, but you have to tailor it to the individual."

On Sunday Dr. Moore was the chairman of a panel on subliminal messages at the annual meeting of the American Psychological Association in Boston. The panel of cognitive psychologists declared that the lore about subliminal perception is largely nonsense.

The matter is of more than academic interest. The scientific debate has spilled over into the courtroom in the trial of a rock band, Judas Priest.

The parents of two men who killed themselves after listening to an album by the band contend that the suicides were caused by a subliminal message, "Do it!" on a song portraying a hopeless view of life. Testifying last week as an expert witness for the defense, Dr. Moore said the assumption that embedded messages can compel such a strong reaction is wrong. Dr. Shevrin, a witness for the parents, disagrees. "As I read the evidence, including my own work, the subliminal message could have been a contributory cause to the suicides," he said.

Solid Tests Are Recent

Only recently have there been well-conducted scientific tests of subliminal messages. The results do not support the commercial claims made for subliminal tapes.

In a study reported at the psychological association's meeting, two subliminal tapes were given to volunteers, who used them for six to 20 sessions over several weeks. One tape was to improve self-esteem, the other to boost memory. Listeners heard only a sound like that of ocean waves; the messages about memory or self-esteem were beneath the threshold of conscious awareness, the manufacturer said.

But in the experiment half the volunteers received tapes with the labels reversed: what was labeled the self-esteem tape, for example, was actually the memory tape. Changes in self-esteem or memory were measured by 12 different psychological tests.

We asked, do you believe your memory or self-esteem has improved since you've used this tape?" said Anthony Greenwald, a psychologist at the University of Washington, who did the studies. "About 50 percent said they had improved on memory or self-esteem, but the effect was a result of the labels, not the tapes. Those with the tapes labeled for memory said they had better memory, those with tapes labeled self-esteem said they felt better about themselves. But there was virtually no change on the objective measures of self-esteem or memory."

'Today's Snake Oil'

Anthony Pratkanis, a psychologist at the University of California at Santa-Cruz, said: "Subliminal tapes are today's snake oil. There's no evidence that there is subliminal perception of their message. There's no evidence of any perception at all, let alone evidence that they work."

Subliminal tape companies typically

support their claims through testimonials by satisfied customers, rather than by citing specific studies of their tapes' effectiveness.

Despite the conclusion that the effects of subliminal tapes are simply due to suggestion, Dr. Greenwald and other researchers concede that there is scientific evidence for the mind's ability to perceive without conscious awareness. But they deny that subliminal perceptions can lead to the kinds of effects like better bowling made in commercial claims.

Studies of subliminal message don't back claims for them.

There is much debate among scientists, however, over the power of messages received outside a person's awareness to affect how people act, as well as over the conditions under which such effects occur. The debate tends to split along disciplinary lines, with cognitive scientists, who study how the mind takes in and stores information, disputing the power of subliminal messages and researchers with a psychoanalytic bent upholding it. The cognitive scientists tend to be scornful of the psychoanalytic research as poorly conducted. But the analysts discount the cognitive research as trivial.

Tests With Flashing Words

In a typical cognitive science approach to studying perception that goes on outside conscious awareness, volunteers watch a screen on which words are displayed for a 30th to a 50th of a second so all they see is a flash of light. The volunteer is asked to decide whether the string of letters makes a word or is nonsense.

Just after the word is flashed, a gridlike pattern flashes to help insure that the word does not register in awareness. Then, a half second later, a string of letters is displayed so that it can be plainly seen. The volunteer is asked to decide whether this string of letters makes a word or is nonsense. If the meaning of the initial word is somehow related to that of the word that follows (for example, "day" and "night"), then people can more quickly and accurately identify the second as a word rather than a nonsense string of letters.

This effect, known as priming, is widely accepted among cognitive psychologists as strong evidence that the mind registers information outside awareness. Even so, they do not see its implications as going far.

"There's nothing very powerful that's performed by the unconscious in these experiments," said Dr. Greenwald. "It suggests a primitive, crude brain, not the potent unconscious that psychoanalysis calls for."

For their part, psychoanalytic researchers have been carrying out more pointed studies. In one, for instance, volunteers are exposed to a four-milli-second flash of the message "Mommy and I are One." Some researchers have found that seeing the message, improves volunteers' performance on a dart game, as well as on a variety of measures of emotional well-being.

The rationale is psychoanalytic. "The phrase evokes the positive state of an infant feeling united with her mother," said Joel Weinberger, a psychologist at Adelphi University. "In theory, it makes people feel secure and safe. In adulthood, it's an emotionally reparative experience; it makes you feel good about yourself."

In an article to be published in the Clinical Psychology Review, Dr. Weinberger, with Richard Hardaway, used a statistical technique to combine results from 72 different studies, using a total of 2,562 subjects, all exposed to the phrase "Mommy and I are one." "There definitely is an effect," Dr. Weinberger said.

Dr. Weinberger cites the studies as scientific evidence that there is "something like a psychodynamic unconscious," as analysts take for granted.

The cognitive scientists remain unpersuaded. "I don't find the evidence that 'Mommy and I are one' is a magic phrase very compelling," said Dr. Greenwald, adding that the methods used in the studies do not insure that the message was, in fact, outside the awareness of those volunteers tested.

Psychoanalytic researchers, on the other hand, criticize cognitive scientists for failing to use words that are emotionally meaningful to the people being tested. Were they to do so, the psychoanalysts say, they would find stronger effects.

For instance, Dr. Shevrin uses individually selected words and phrases in subliminal tests of patients being treated for problems like extreme shyness. In the experiments, the phrases were flashed to the patients for one thousandth of a second. Using a computerized analysis of brain waves, Dr. Shevrin found that the patients had brain responses showing more reaction to the emotionally meaningful phrases than to neutral ones.

"The evidence says to me," said Dr. Shevrin, "that there is a Freudian unconscious, and it is a potent force in mental life."

Consciousness Raising

Theories abound regarding the vexing nature of conscious experience

A 17th-century interpretation of the mind with separate parts for the senses, imagination, and intellect.

BRUCE BOWER

Like a chameleon that splashes a new array of colors across its skin each time it scurries from one place to another, consciousness — the awareness of oneself and the surrounding world, as well as the sense of free will — takes on a unique look and texture from one person to the next. Indeed, the chameleon's iridescent repertoire seems narrow compared to such conscious adventures as savoring a good meal, harboring envy toward a successful colleague, making plans for the arrival of a baby, and pondering the meaning of life.

For much of the 20th century, scientists have shunned the slippery, subjective trappings of consciousness that intrigued their predecessors in the 1800s. Instead, psychologists concentrated on the external rewards and punishments that shape behaviors (an approach known as behaviorism), while neuroscientists and biologists searched for a few glimmers of insight into how the brain works.

In another academic corner, philosophers continued their long-standing practice of devising logical arguments — "thought experiments" and "possible world" scenarios — to explain the relationship of mind to brain.

Over the last 30 years, these separate disciplines, as well as several others, have gradually banded — some might say straggled — together under the umbrella of "cognitive science" to study the mind and how it emanates from the brain's tangle of neurons and gray matter.

Several developments helped spur this cognitive convergence: Neuroscientists gained a better understanding of brain-cell function and the duties of various brain structures; powerful new digital computers gave rise to a search for "artificial intelligence" and theories of the brain as a highly complex computer; and psychologists and linguists delved into unconscious directives guiding language, memory, perception, and other remarkable mental feats.

Philosophers ambled out of scholarly seclusion to apply cognitive research findings to their thoughts about thought itself.

Only recently, however, has the study of consciousness gained widespread respectability in cognitive science, which has long concentrated on the unconscious mental world.

"For the first time in many years, cognitive scientists of all kinds are interested in consciousness and its relation to the unconscious," says psychologist John Kihlstrom of the University of Arizona in Tucson. "We now have some scientific tools to study this issue."

This trend provides hope that cognitive scientists may someday develop more sophisticated theories of the mind based on data drawn from diverse disciplines. If so, investigations of memory, perception, and other mental activities would undoubtedly undergo radical changes.

For now, of course, scientists of the mind disagree plenty about the nature of consciousness. To make matters stickier, investigators routinely accuse one another of misunderstanding and misinterpreting their respective theories and data. But they share a general affinity for the philosophical concept of materialism, which holds that the brain and its billions of neural minions somehow give rise to the mind.

In contrast, 17th-century French philosopher Rene Descartes expounded the long dominant opposing belief that the mind, or "soul," exists separately from the physical brain and interacts with sensory information shuttled by the brain to a central location — the pineal gland — from which conscious experience arises. Scientists have yet to unravel the function of the pineal gland, but it no longer passes for the seat of consciousness.

Nonetheless, cognitive scientists, who sensibly reject Descartes' argument for an ethereal mind, often erroneously cling to his notion that the brain harbors a kind of central theater where its diverse contents "all come together" in an unconscious dress rehearsal for conscious experience, argues philosopher Daniel C. Dennett of Tufts University in Medford, Mass. The "stream of consciousness" that seems to connect us to ourselves and the world around us, long espoused by philosophers and psychologists, evaporates in the harsh light of cognitive science findings, he asserts.

Dennett offers instead a "multiple drafts" model of consciousness, which he presents in his book *Consciousness Explained* (1991, Little, Brown and Co.). Dennett and psychologist Marcel Kinsbourne of Boston University elaborate on this model and defend it against critics in the June BEHAVIORAL AND BRAIN SCIENCES.

Dennett essentially holds that the brain unconsciously processes numerous streams of information simultaneously. The streams sometimes coalesce, sometimes conflict, but undergo continual revision, or "editing," as time passes and the brain gathers new information. Thus each stream represents a temporary draft that may or may not contribute to a conscious experience.

If, indeed, the brain creates multiple, ever-changing interpretations of experience, researchers cannot pin down the first appearance of a conscious thought to a precise moment, and the distinction between what happens before and after the onset of consciousness remains cloudy, Dennett contends. For this reason, he rejects popular theories that the brain rushes to "fill in" missing information before consciousness occurs, as exemplified by the fact that one perceives a coherent visual field despite a natural blind spot in the retina of both eyes (SN: 4/27/91, p.262). Likewise, he disputes the notion that the brain creates bogus memories after consciousness commences — say, wrongly recalling that a passing jogger wore glasses because she instantly brought to mind a friend who wears glasses.

Dennett compares human consciousness to an evolved "virtual machine," a sort of computer software program that shapes the activities of its hardware—the brain. The logical structure of the virtual machine relies on flexible rules that can incorporate one or more drafts into consciousness, fostering the deluded intuition that a single stream of consciousness pours forth, he asserts.

Feelings and experiences unique to each person arise from the bundles of innate and learned dispositions deposited in networks of neurons throughout the brain, he proposes. For instance, a person's perception of the red color of a Santa Claus suit goes beyond simply seeing red; it emerges from the acuteness of his or her color vision, comparisons of the red suit with stored representations of other red items, and doubtless other red-related drafts in the brain.

Over the years, the brain's virtual machine composes the shifting representations of an individual's "self," which are based largely on social experiences, Dennett argues. The self exists as a crucial fiction for getting around in the world, not a real thing; if all goes well, the created self endows its owner with the capacity for free will and moral responsibility, he holds.

Several scientific findings undermine the idea of a unified, time-specific consciousness, Dennett points out. Consider the "color phi," or apparent motion phenomenon. Volunteers watch a screen on which two dots separated by a small space briefly flash in rapid succession, creating the impression of a single dot that moves from one point to the other. If experimenters present two dots of different colors — say, red followed by green — the single red dot appears to move and transform itself into a green dot before the second flash occurs.

When a lot happens in a short time, as in color phi, the brain makes simplifying assumptions, Dennett argues. The brain processes that calculate the color of the second dot and falsely determine that motion took place occur at about the same time and influence a third process, which concludes that the first dot moved over and changed color on the way. In what seems like a stream of consciousness to the observer, drafts in the brain rapidly construct an interpretation of what happened that does not coincide with the actual sequence of observed events.

Perceptual "filling in," or an instantaneous memory revision by the brain, cannot explain color phi, because the various drafts that make up the phenomenon do not reach awareness at precisely the same moment, Dennett contends.

He and Kinsbourne also use the multiple drafts model to reinterpret provocative studies directed by physiologist Benjamin Libet of the University of California, San Francisco. In one set of studies, Libet's team observed a delay of up to one-half second before volunteers reported feeling a tingle in their right hand, whether experimenters induced the tingle by electrically stimulating the appropriate spot in the brain or delivering a mild electrical pulse to the right hand. This result provoked considerable surprise, since direct stimulation of the brain should enter awareness more quickly than a tingle that travels from the hand to the brain.

No good explanation exists for these results, Libet says. Perhaps people perceived the sensations as occurring equally fast because both stimuli produce a distinct electrical reaction about one-fiftieth of a second after being delivered, he speculates.

Libet's explanation proves inadequate, Dennett argues, because consciousness does not occur at an absolute time in a central brain location. Several brain processes, or drafts, must interpret jolts to brain tissue and skin. Hasty cerebral editing of these drafts produces a subjective sense that a tingle on the hand occurred as quickly as a tingle express-delivered by the brain.

Dennett also remains skeptical of Libet's claims to have shown that the decision to flex a finger begins unconsciously about one-third of a second before aware-ness of the decision, although volunteers can consciously veto the act of flexing before it actually occurs (SN: 4/26/86, p. 266). According to Libet, this finding suggests that free will, if it exists, selects among and controls unconscious urges rather than initiating those urges.

Again, Libet charted self-reports that reflected volunteers' inaccurate intuitions that they had decided to flex a finger at a specific time, Dennett contends. Depending on how researchers test and question a study participant, they will tap into different cerebral drafts and the volunteer's experience and self-reports of what happened when will vary, he asserts.

Libet considers Dennett's multiple drafts model a "philosophical construction" that has yet to yield testable scientific theories. But some investigators point to related evidence that supports the model.

For example, studies of brain-damaged and healthy people find that diverse types of sensory information do not converge on a single brain structure, notes neurologist Antonio R. Damasio of the University of Iowa College of Medicine in Iowa City. Many brain systems generate the sense of self as well as the false intuition that experience or consciousness happens at one site, Damasio maintains. However, brain activity in each system may undergo integration to produce multiple coherent versions of experience, he asserts.

A perceptual illusion discovered in 1976 taps into different drafts of the same conscious experience, contends psychologist Andy Young of Durham University in England. When volunteers watch a videotape of a person mouthing the sound "ga," which is synchronized with the sound "ba" on the soundtrack, most report hearing the sound "da." An explanation for the "fusion" of the visual and auditory sounds into a kind of compromise sound remains unclear, Young says. "Da" corresponds to one draft of the experience, but another draft — "ba" — emerges if participants close their eyes during the screening, relying only on hearing, he asserts.

Consciousness of this type evolved as a side effect in brains capable of seamlessly processing numerous plans and memories independently of immediate environmental concerns, argues psychologist Bruce Bridgeman of the University of California, Santa Cruz. The many plans correspond to multiple drafts, and awareness arises only when it serves a function, such as perceiving particular objects in the world, Bridgeman holds. He rejects the notion of consciousness as a monitor of mental life.

Perhaps Dennett's most controversial

assertion involves the claim that human consciousness stems from a virtual machine existing in the brain's voluminous system of interconnected neurons. This argument, a staple of many artificial intelligence advocates and sometimes referred to as "strong AI," holds that a properly programmed computer would possess a conscious self.

Thinking and consciousness — as well as conscience — indeed apply to computers as well as humans, argues neurobiologist Andrei S. Monin of the Russian Academy of Sciences in Moscow. Thinking systems, whether human or machine, employ step-by-step processes or programs — what mathematicians call algorithms — to receive and remember information, Monin contends in the Aug. 1 PROCEEDINGS OF THE NATIONAL ACADEMY OF SCIENCES. Some set of algorithms in the human brain compares one's knowledge, intentions, decisions, and actions with new information to produce consciousness, or "co-knowledge," he theorizes.

The first consciousness algorithm separates the individual from the surrounding environment and creates self-awareness, according to Monin. A program for self-identification and other aspects of consciousness can conceivably be worked out for modern computers, he asserts.

An algorithm must also exist for generating conscience, or the sense that some acts are good and others evil, Monin adds. This algorithm undoubtedly responds to various social and family influences — and it may play little or no role in the consciousness of some criminals and despots — but artificial intelligence researchers should begin to experiment with "conscience programs" built into computers, Monin contends.

"It's not that you can't imagine a conscious robot," Dennett tells those who doubt such assertions, citing the friendly R2D2 and C3PO from "Star Wars" and the ominous Hal in "2001: A Space Odyssey." "It's that you can't imagine how a robot could be conscious."

Some critics charge that Dennett himself fails to grasp a fundamental problem: Achieving conscious understanding and insight requires something other than computations and algorithms. In his book *The Emperor's New Mind: Concerning Computers, Minds, and the Laws of Physics* (1989, Oxford University Press), Roger Penrose argues that quantum physics' subatomic forces, which operate in indeterminate and unprogrammable ways, interact within the brain to produce the rich variety of conscious experience. Modern physics currently cannot explain the quantum leaps the brain makes on the road to feeling an emotion or discerning sophisticated mathematical relations,

says Penrose, a mathematical physicist at the University of Oxford in England.

John Eccles, a neurophysiologist at the Max Planck Institute for Brain Research in Frankfurt, Germany, and a Nobel laureate in medicine, agrees with Penrose's dismissal of strong AI. But unlike most researchers, he attempts to update Descartes' theory of a nonmaterial mind.

Consciousness began to evolve more than 200 million years ago in the earliest mammals, Eccles maintains in the Aug. 15 PROCEEDINGS OF THE NATIONAL ACADEMY OF SCIENCES. It proved advantageous as a way to experience the surrounding world and guide behavior beyond simple reflexes, he proposes. Mammalian brains evolved increasingly complex and numerous bundles of pyramidal cells, or "dendrons," capable of interacting through quantum physics with a non-physical mental world composed of "psychons," each corresponding roughly to an idea or feeling, Eccles proposes.

This theory only accounts for "simple consciousness," Eccles adds. The unique experience of human self-consciousness lies beyond scientific understanding, at least for now, he concludes.

Eccles maintains a minority viewpoint, but even some investigators who consider the mind a product of the brain still reject Dennett's multiple drafts model. His approach "explains away" consciousness by assuming it can never really be pinned down to a particular time or place, these critics assert.

Psychologists Stephen M. Kosslyn of Harvard University and Olivier Koenig of the University of Geneva in Switzerland offer an alternative theory in their book *Wet Mind: The New Cognitive Neuroscience* (1992, The Free Press). Consciousness serves as a kind of check that signals whether different brain states are in proper balance and mesh properly, they contend.

Neural discharges of electricity in different areas of the brain that process the same stimulus apparently emit a shared electromagnetic rhythm that helps to stitch together a unified representation of the stimulus, Kosslyn and Koenig note. In this way, for example, neural discharges underlying representations of "ball," "red," "large," and "moving to the right," link up at the appropriate time. Consciousness has the same relation to these interconnected discharges as a chord does to individual notes played on a guitar: It exists as an interaction of brain events that produce consonance or dissonance.

If neural balance reigns, only the contents of consciousness — an object in view, the meaning of a statement, and so on — reach awareness, according to Koss-

lyn and Koenig. When dissonance arises, people become aware of and reflect on their conscious state.

The two psychologists agree with Libet that conscious experiences lag slightly behind the brain events that evoke them. Thus, brain processes that work rapidly — the calculation of an object's orientation, for example — evade awareness, while slower processes, which coordinate perception, memory, and movement, enter consciousness more easily, they argue.

Other investigators accept Dennett's insistence on multiple drafts in the brain but still maintain that some type of "chief editor" ties them together for conscious presentation.

The brain takes one or more drafts and constructs a stream of consciousness that goes through constant flux and change, holds psychologist Max Velmans of the University of London in England. Although usually thought of as necessary for choice, learning, memory, planning, reflection, and creativity, consciousness performs none of those functions, Velmans proposes in the December 1991 BEHAVIORAL AND BRAIN SCIENCES. Unconscious brain activity guides these abilities and produces the potential for focused attention and awareness of the results of automatic brain processes, he argues.

"Consciousness neither interacts with the brain nor can it be reduced to a state or function of the brain," Velmans contends. Yet consciousness serves a purpose, he adds—it allows an individual to experience enough of the world to endow his or her survival with a sense of purpose. In a nutshell, consciousness gives us the will to get on with our lives, even though unconscious processes orchestrate our thoughts and feelings.

Some investigators take Velmans' argument a step further by treating consciousness as a useless by-product of the brain. In fact, the term "consciousness" captures nothing over and above an individual's experiences, argues philosopher Stephen Priest of the University of Edinburgh in Scotland.

"The onus is on the advocate of consciousness to prove that it exists," he writes in *Theories of Mind* (1992, Houghton Mifflin).

Abundant evidence points to the operation of various mental domains that regulate bona fide conscious states, responds Arizona psychologist John Kihlstrom. Neodissociation theory, developed in the 1970s by Stanford University psychologist Ernest R. Hilgard, offers a useful framework for understanding the relation of conscious to unconscious mental activity, Kihlstrom contended at the recent annual meeting of the American Psychological Association in Washington, D.C.

Hilgard characterized the mind as a set of separate units or subsystems that monitor, organize, and control different aspects of mental functioning. Ideally, the various units communicate both with each other and with an "executive ego," which translates information into conscious awareness and intentions, much like the central cerebral theater derided by Dennett. If lines of communication between the executive ego and various subsystems break, divisions in consciousness occur, according to Hilgard's theory.

One such division appears among brain-damaged patients with "blindsight," Kihlstrom maintains. In these cases, people report no ability to see objects in front of them but nearly always offer correct guesses about the location, form, and orientation of these objects. Brain damage apparently disrupts one of two visual subsystems, he asserts; appropriate responses to visual stimuli remain, but the subjective sense of seeing things in the world fades.

A communication breakdown between an intact subsystem and the executive ego explains the alterations of consciousness provoked by hypnosis, Kihlstrom contends. For instance, a hypnotized volunteer reports no pain upon submerging her hand in a bucket of ice because the appropriate subsystem processes the painful stimulus without sending a memo to the executive ego. The subsystem still generates its own effects, such as increasing the volunteer's heart rate as her hand gets colder, despite the absence of subjective pain.

Neodissociation theory also explains why the rapid or incomplete presentation of a stimulus, such as a word, often creates an unconscious, or "implicit," memory in the absence of any conscious recollection of that stimulus, Kihlstrom proposes. A briefly flashed word enters a verbal subsystem before it can hook up with the executive ego, he argues; thus, indirect cues, such as an ambiguous fragment of the same word with several letters missing, quickly evoke the previously viewed word by tapping into the unconscious subsystem where it resides. Research on implicit memory has mushroomed in the past several years (SN: 11/17/90, p.312).

Multiple personality disorder, a condition usually stoked by severe abuse during childhood, appears to involve two or more different executive egos that take turns controlling conscious thoughts and actions, Kihlstrom suggests. Ordinarily, people display awareness of their various social roles—son, spouse, parent, scientist, and so on. One's ability to juggle these many roles dissolves in multiple personality disorder, he says.

Another group of psychologists, in the spirit of Dennett's multiple drafts model, eschews the concept of a central personality or executive ego. Instead, they argue that the average person creates multiple "selves" that go beyond the social roles Kihlstrom cites. As social companions and situations change, the individual creates—consciously and unconsciously—a fundamentally different personality, rather than a variation on a basic, underlying personality, maintain psychologists such as Hazel R. Markus of the University of Michigan in Ann Arbor.

Unlike multiple personality disorder, these many selves are not obvious to one another and do not have separate memories, according to these researchers.

Although the argument for multiple selves remains a minority viewpoint among psychologists, it strikes another blow at the central theater of consciousness Dennett hopes to demolish.

Computer scientist Drew McDermott of Yale University summarizes the multiple drafts model in this way: "I am a character in a story my brain is making up. Consciousness is a property I have by virtue of my brain's attributing it to me. My story doesn't have to cohere completely to be useful."

If brains make up your sense of self as a useful fiction, canons of morality and spirituality may need an overhaul, McDermott contends.

"If people are valuable, it is not because they are imperishable souls connected to bodies only for a brief sojourn," he asserts. "For now, we just have to take it as a postulate that creatures that invent conscious selves are to be cherished and protected more than other information-processing systems."

Learning and Remembering

Do you remember your first week of classes at college? There were so many new buildings' and people's names to remember. And you had to recall accurately where all your classes were as well as your professors' names. Just remembering your class schedule was problematic enough. For those of you who lived in dormitories, the difficulties multiplied. You had to remember where your dorm was, recall the names of individuals living on your floor, and learn how to locomote from your dormitory to other places on campus, such as the dining halls and library. Then came examination time. Did you ever think you would survive college exams? The material in terms of difficulty level and amount was perhaps more than you thought you could handle. What a stressful time you experienced when you first came to campus! Much of what created the stress was the strain on your learning and memory systems, two complicated processes unto themselves. Indeed, most of you survived just fine and with your memories, learning strategies, and mental health intact.

The processes you depended on in the above example are the processes of learning and memory, two processes that are some of the oldest processes studied by psychologists. Today, with their sophisticated experimental techniques, psychologists have detected several types of memory processes, and they have also discovered what makes learning more complete so that subsequent memory is more accurate. We also discovered that humans are not the only organisms capable of these processes; all types of animals can learn, even if the organism is as simple as an earthworm or an amoeba.

Psychologists know, too, that rote learning and practice are not the only forms of learning. For instance, at this point in time in your introductory psychology class, you might be studying operant and classical conditioning, two very simple but nonetheless important forms of learning by both humans and simple organisms. Both types of conditioning can occur without our awareness or active participation. The articles in this unit examine the processes of learning and remembering (or its reciprocal, forgetting).

What kind of instructional environment is most beneficial for learning? The "back-to-basics" approach to instruction emphasizes repetition, drill, and sustained attention in a highly structured classroom setting. Another approach, "open education," emphasizes self-pacing and exploration in an unstructured setting. In the first article in this unit, Barbara Kantrowitz and Pat Wingert review evidence suggesting that children learn best when the learning environment is based on the concept of "developmentally appropriate practice." This approach, firmly grounded in the knowledge gained from scientific studies of child development, stresses matching educational programs to the child's developmental level. Implementing "developmentally appropriate practice" in American schools, however, will require extensive retraining of teachers and actively involving more parents in the education of children.

In the next article, "The Town B. F. Skinner Boxed," the story is told of a Mexican town that is experimenting with Skinnerian principles of operant conditioning. In this small town, Skinner's ideas are put into practice; thus, the whole community has become a social laboratory of sorts. If you're curious about what a Skinnerian town is like, read this article.

While the first two articles pertain to learning in its various forms, the remaining two relate to memory, the process of retention after learning has occurred. In "Gone But Not Forgotten," Bruce Bower, the author, examines both implicit and explicit memory but focuses on implicit memory. Implicit memory involves the unintentional retrieval of previously learned material in situations that do not ask for that information. Research on memory, implicit memory included, has revealed that there appears to be several distinct memory systems in the brain. Surprisingly, research has also shown that implicit memory is very influential in everyday life, perhaps more influential than explicit memory. This may mean that Freud was right; there are memories stored in our psyches that influence us without our complete awareness. In the final article, "Dreams of a Rat," June Kinoshita discusses the purpose of dreams. Contrary to the Freudian idea that dreams are unconscious wish fulfillments, recent research suggests that dreams are the way the brain sifts through new information and consolidates it with the old information so it is better remembered.

Looking Ahead: Challenge Questions

What was your schooling in early childhood like? Do you think that the processes and environment experi-

enced could have been improved? How so? What are the differences between back-to-basics education and open education? How will schools, teachers, and parents have to change if open education is adopted?

What are the basic tenets of Skinnerian psychology? How can Skinnerian principles be practiced or put into effect in everyday life? Would you want to live in a community such as the one in Mexico? Why?

How is brain functioning related to the ability to remember? What part of the brain seems to be responsible for

memories? What would life be like if this area of the brain were destroyed? Can you think of techniques we could use to get along in daily life if we were not able to store memories?

Do you believe that dreams are wish fulfillments of the unconscious? Is there any research evidence supporting this contention? What other function might dreams serve? Can you recall any of your dreams? Do any of your dreams support the wish fulfillment or the memory consolidation theory of dreaming?

How Kids Learn

BARBARA KANTROWITZ & PAT WINGERT

Ages 5 through 8 are wonder years. That's when children begin learning to study, to reason, to cooperate. We can put them in desks and drill them all day. Or we can keep them moving, touching, exploring. The experts favor a hands-on approach, but changing the way schools teach isn't easy. The stakes are high and parents can help.

With Howard Manly in Atlanta and bureau reports

It's time for number games in Janet Gill's kindergarten class at the Greenbrook School in South Brunswick, N.J. With hardly any prodding from their teacher, 23 five- and six-year-olds pull out geometric puzzles, playing cards and counting equipment from the shelves lining the room. At one round table, a group of youngsters fits together brightly colored wooden shapes. One little girl forms a hexagon out of triangles. The others, obviously impressed, gather round to count up how many parts are needed to make the whole.

After about half an hour, the children get ready for story time. They pack up their counting equipment and settle in a circle around Gill. She holds up a giant book about a zany character called Mrs. Wishy-washy who insists on giving farm animals a bath. The children recite the whimsical lines along with Gill, obviously enjoying one of their favorite tales. (The hallway is lined with drawings depicting the children's own interpretation of the book; they've taken a few literary liberties, like substituting unicorns and dinosaurs for cows and pigs.) After the first reading, Gill asks for volunteers to act out the various parts in the book. Lots of hands shoot up. Gill picks out four children and

they play their parts enthusiastically. There isn't a bored face in the room.

This isn't reading, writing and arithmetic the way most people remember it. Like a growing number of public- and private-school educators, the principals and teachers in South Brunswick believe that children between the ages of 5 and 8 have to be taught differently from older children. They recognize that young children learn best through active, hands-on teaching methods like games and dramatic play. They know that children in this age group develop at varying rates and schools have to allow for these differences. They also believe that youngsters' social growth is as essential as their academic achievement. Says Joan Warren, a teacher consultant in South Brunswick: "Our programs are designed to fit the child instead of making the child fit the school."

Educators call this kind of teaching "developmentally appropriate practice"—a curriculum based on what scientists know about how young children learn. These ideas have been slowly emerging through research conducted over the last century, particularly in the past 30 years. Some of the tenets have appeared

The Lives and Times of Children

Each youngster proceeds at his own pace, but the learning curve of a child is fairly predictable. Their drive to learn is awesome, and careful adults can nourish it. The biggest mistake is pushing a child too hard, too soon.

● Infants and Toddlers

They're born to learn. The first important lesson is trust, and they learn that from their relationships with their parents or other caring adults. Later, babies will begin to explore the world around them and experiment with independence. As they mature, infants slowly develop gross motor (sitting, crawling, walking) and fine motor (picking up tiny objects) skills. Generally, they remain egocentric and are unable to share or wait their turn. New skills are perfected through repetition, such as the babbling that leads to speaking.

■ 18 months to 3 years

Usually toilet training becomes the prime learning activity. Children tend to concentrate on language development and large-muscle control through activities like climbing on jungle gyms. Attention spans lengthen enough to listen to uncomplicated stories and carry on conversations. Vocabulary expands to about 200 words. They enjoy playing with one other child, or a small group, for short periods, and learn that others have feelings too. They continue to look to parents for encouragement and protection, while beginning to accept limits on their behavior.

▲ 3-year-olds

Generally, they're interested in doing things for themselves and trying to keep up with older children. Their ability to quietly listen to stories and music remains limited. They begin telling stories and jokes. Physical growth slows, but large-muscle development continues as children run, jump and ride tricycles. They begin to deal with cause and effect; it's time to plant seeds and watch them grow.

● 4-year-olds

They develop better small motor skills, such as cutting with scissors, painting, working with puzzles and building things.

They can master colors, sizes and shapes. They should be read to and should be encouraged to watch others write; let them scribble on paper but try to keep them away from walls.

■ 5-year-olds

They begin to understand counting as a one-to-one correlation. Improved memories make it easier for them to recognize meaningful words, and with sharper fine motor skills, some children will be able to write their own names.

▲ Both 4s and 5s

Both groups learn best by interacting with people and concrete objects and by trying to solve real problems. They can learn from stories and books, but only in ways that relate to their own experience. Socially, these children are increasingly interested in activities outside their immediate family. They can play in groups for longer periods, learning lessons in cooperation and negotiation. Physically, large-muscle development continues, and skills such as balancing emerge.

● 6-year-olds

Interest in their peers continues to increase, and they become acutely aware of comparisons between themselves and others. It's a taste of adolescence: does the group accept them? Speech is usually well developed, and children are able to joke and tease. They have a strong sense of true and false and are eager for clear rules and definitions. However, they have a difficult time differentiating between minor and major infractions. Generally, children this age are more mature mentally than physically and unable to sit still for long periods. They learn better by firsthand experiences. Learning by doing also encourages children's "disposition" to use the knowledge and skills they're acquiring.

■ 7- to 8-year-olds

During this period, children begin developing the ability to think about and solve problems in their heads, but some will continue to rely on fingers and toes to help them find the right answer. Not until they're 11 are most kids capable of thinking purely symbolically; they still use real objects to give the symbols—such as numbers—meaning. At this stage they listen better and engage in give and take. Generally, physical growth continues to slow, while athletic abilities improve—children are able to hit a softball, skip rope or balance on a beam. Sitting for long periods is still more tiring than running and jumping.

under other names—progressivism in the 1920s, open education in the 1970s. But they've never been the norm. Now, educators say that may be about to change. "The entire early-childhood profession has amassed itself in unison behind these principles," says Yale education professor Sharon Lynn Kagan. In the last few years, many of the major education organizations in the country—including the National Association for the Education of Young Children and the National Association of State Boards of Education—have endorsed remarkably similar plans for revamping kindergarten through third grade.

Bolstered by opinions from the experts, individual states are beginning to take action. Both California and New York have appointed task forces to recommend changes for the earliest grades. And scores of individual school districts like South Brunswick, figuring that young minds are a terrible thing to waste, are pushing ahead on their own.

The evidence gathered from research in child development is so compelling that even groups like the Council for Basic Education, for years a major supporter of the traditional format, have revised their thinking. "The idea of putting small children in front of workbooks and asking them to sit at their desks all day is a nightmare vision," says Patte Barth, associate editor of Basic Education, the council's newsletter.

At this point, there's no way of knowing how soon change will come or how widespread it will be. However, there's a growing recognition of the importance of the early grades. For the past few years, most of the public's attention has focused on older children, especially teenagers. "That's a Band-Aid kind of approach," says Anne Dillman, a member of the New Jersey State Board of Education. "When the product doesn't come out right, you try and fix it at the end. But we really have to start at the beginning." Demographics have contributed to the sense of urgency. The baby boomlet has replaced the baby-bust generation of the 1970s. More kids in elementary school means more parents asking if there's a better way to teach. And researchers say there is a better way. "We've made remarkable breakthroughs in understanding the development of children, the development of learning and the climate that enhances that," says Ernest Boyer of The Carnegie Foundation for the Advancement of Teaching. But, he adds, too often, "what we know in theory and what we're doing in the classroom are very different."

The early grades pose special challenges because that's when children's attitudes toward school and learning are shaped, says Tufts University psychologist David Elkind. As youngsters move from home or preschool into the larger, more competitive world of elementary school, they begin to make judgments about their own abilities. If they feel inadequate, they may give up. Intellectually, they're also in transition, moving from the intensely physical exploration habits of infancy and toddlerhood to more abstract reasoning. Children are born wanting to learn. A baby can spend hours studying his hands; a toddler is fascinated by watching sand pour through a sieve. What looks like play to an adult is actually the work of childhood, developing an understanding of the world. Studies show that the most effective way to teach young kids is to capitalize on their natural inclination to learn through play.

But in the 1980s, many schools have tried to do just the opposite, pressure instead of challenge. The "back to basics" movement meant that teaching methods intended for high school students were imposed on first graders. The lesson of the day was more: more homework, more tests, more discipline. Children should be behind their desks, not roaming around the room. Teachers should be at the head of the classrooms, drilling knowledge into their charges. Much of this was a reaction against the trend toward open education in the '70s. Based on the British system, it allowed children to develop at their own pace within a highly structured classroom. But too many teachers and principals who tried open education thought that it meant simply tearing down classroom walls and letting children do whatever they wanted. The results were often disastrous. "Because it was done wrong, there was a backlash against it," says Sue Bredekamp of the National Association for the Education of Young Children.

At the same time, parents, too, were demanding more from their elementary schools. By the mid-1980s, the majority of 3- and 4-year-olds were attending some form of pre-school. And their parents expected these classroom veterans to be reading by the second semester of kindergarten. But the truth is that many 5-year-olds aren't ready for reading—or most of the other academic tasks that come easily to older children—no matter how many years of school they've completed. "We're confusing the numbers of years children have been in school with brain development," says Martha Denckla, a professor of neurology and pediatrics at Johns Hopkins University. "Just because a child goes to day care at age 3 doesn't mean the human brain mutates into an older brain. A 5-year-old's brain is still a 5-year-old's brain."

As part of the return to basics, parents and districts demanded hard evidence that their children were learning. And some communities took extreme measures. In 1985 Georgia became the first state to require 6-year-olds to pass a standardized test before entering first grade. More than two dozen other states proposed similar legislation. In the beginning Georgia's move was hailed as a "pioneering" effort to get kids off to a good start. Instead, concedes state school superintendent Werner Rogers, "We got off on the wrong foot." Five-year-olds who used to spend their days fingerpainting or singing were hunched over ditto sheets, preparing for the big exam. "We would have to spend a month just teaching kids how to take the test," says Beth Hunnings, a kindergarten teacher in suburban Atlanta. This year Georgia altered the tests in favor of a more flexible evaluation; other states have changed their minds as well.

The intense, early pressure has taken an early toll. Kindergartners are struggling with homework. First graders are taking spelling tests before they even understand how to read. Second graders feel like failures. "During this critical period," says David Elkind in his book "Miseducation," "the child's bud-

In Japan, First Grade Isn't a Boot Camp

Japanese students have the highest math and science test scores in the world. More than 90 percent graduate from high school. Illiteracy is virtually nonexistent in Japan. Most Americans attribute this success to a rigid system that sets youngsters on a lock-step march from cradle to college. In fact, the early years of Japanese schooling are anything but a boot camp; the atmosphere is warm and nurturing. From kindergarten through third grade, the goal is not only academic but also social—teaching kids to be part of a group so they can be good citizens as well as good students. "Getting along with others is not just a means for keeping the peace in the classroom but something which is a valued end in itself," says American researcher Merry White, author of "The Japanese Educational Challenge."

Lessons in living and working together grow naturally out of the Japanese culture. Starting in kindergarten, youngsters learn to work in teams, with brighter students often helping slower ones. All children are told they can succeed if they persist and work hard. Japanese teachers are expected to be extremely patient with young children. They go over lessons step by step and repeat instructions as often as necessary. "The key is not to scold [children] for small mistakes," says Yukio Ueda, principal of Mita Elementary School in Tokyo. Instead, he says, teachers concentrate on praising and encouraging their young charges.

As a result, the classrooms are relaxed and cheerful, even when they're filled with rows of desks. On one recent afternoon a class of second graders at Ueda's school was working on an art project. Their assignment was to build a roof with poles made of rolled-up newspapers. The children worked in small groups, occasionally asking their teacher for help. The room was filled with the sound of eager youngsters chatting about how to get the job done. In another second-grade class, the subject was math. Maniko Inoue, the teacher, suggested a number game to practice multiplication. After a few minutes of playing it, one boy stood up and proposed changing the rules just a bit to make it more fun. Inoue listened carefully and then asked if the other students agreed. They cheered, "Yes, yes," and the game continued according to the new rules.

Academics are far from neglected in the early grades. The Education Ministry sets curriculum standards and goals for each school year. For example, third graders by the end of the year are supposed to be able to read and write 508 characters (out of some 2,000 considered essential to basic literacy). Teachers have time for play and lessons: Japanese children attend school for 240 days, compared with about 180 in the United States.

Mothers' role: Not all the teaching goes on in the classroom. Parents, especially mothers, play a key role in education. Although most kindergartens do not teach writing or numbers in any systematic way, more than 80 percent of Japanese children learn to read or write to some extent before they enter school. "It is as if mothers had their own built-in curriculum," says Shigefumi Nagano, a director of the National Institute for Educational Research. "The first game they teach is to count numbers up to 10."

For all their success in the early grades, the Japanese are worried they're not doing well enough. After a recent national curriculum review, officials were alarmed by what Education Minister Takeo Nishioka described as excessive "bullying and misconduct" among children—the result, according to some Japanese, of too much emphasis on material values. So three years from now, first and second graders will no longer be studying social studies and science. Instead, children will spend more time learning how to be good citizens. That's "back to basics"—Japanese style.

BARBARA KANTROWITZ *with* HIDEKO TAKAYAMA *in Tokyo*

---

ding sense of competence is frequently under attack, not only from inappropriate instructional practices . . . but also from the hundred and one feelings of hurt, frustration and rejection that mark a child's entrance into the world of schooling, competition and peer-group involvement." Adults under similar stress can rationalize setbacks or put them in perspective based on previous experiences; young children have none of these defenses. Schools that demand too much too soon are setting kids off on the road to failure.

It doesn't have to be this way. Most experts on child development and early-childhood education believe that young children learn much more readily if the teaching methods meet their special needs:

Differences in thinking: The most important ingredient of the nontraditional approach is hands-on learning. Research begun by Swiss psychologist Jean Piaget indicates that somewhere between the ages of 6 and 9, children begin to think abstractly instead of concretely. Younger children learn much more by touching and seeing and smelling and tasting than by just listening. In other words, 6-year-olds can easily understand addition and subtraction if they have actual objects to count instead of a series of numbers written on a blackboard. Lectures don't help. Kids learn to reason and communicate by engaging in conversation. Yet most teachers still talk at, not with, their pupils.

Physical activity: When they get to be 10 or 11, children can sit still for sustained periods. But until they are physically ready for long periods of inactivity, they need to be active in the classroom. "A young child has to make a conscious effort to sit still," says Denckla. "A large chunk of children can't do it for very long. It's a very energy-consuming activity for them." Small children actually get more tired if they have to sit still and listen to a teacher talk than if they're allowed to move around in the classroom. The frontal lobe, the part of the brain that applies the brakes to children's natural energy and curiosity, is still immature in 6- to 9-year-olds, Denckla says. As the lobe develops, so

4. LEARNING AND REMEMBERING

does what Denckla describes as "boredom tolerance." Simply put, learning by doing is much less boring to young children.

Language development: In this age group, experts say language development should not be broken down into isolated skills—reading, writing and speaking. Children first learn to reason and to express themselves by talking. They can dictate stories to a teacher before they actually read or write. Later, their first attempts at composition do not need to be letter perfect; the important thing is that they learn to communicate ideas. But in many classrooms, grammar and spelling have become more important than content. While mastering the technical aspects of writing is essential as a child gets older, educators warn against emphasizing form over content in the early grades. Books should also be interesting to kids—not just words strung together solely for the purpose of pedag-

ogy. Psychologist Katherine Nelson of the City University of New York says that her extensive laboratory and observational work indicates that kids can learn language—speaking, writing or reading—only if it is presented in a way that makes sense to them. But many teachers still use texts that are so boring they'd put anybody to sleep.

Socialization: A youngster's social development has a profound effect on his academic progress. Kids who have trouble getting along with their classmates can end up behind academically as well and have a higher incidence of dropping out. In the early grades especially, experts say youngsters should be encouraged to work in groups rather than individually so that teachers can spot children who may be having problems making friends. "When children work on a project," says University of Illinois education professor Lillian Katz, "they learn to work together, to disagree, to speculate,

The early years of a child's education are indeed wonder years. They begin learning to socialize, to study, and to reason. More and more education experts are favoring a hands-on approach to introducing young children to the mysteries of their surroundings.

to take turns and de-escalate tensions. These skills can't be learned through lecture. We all know people who have wonderful technical skills but don't have any social skills. Relationships should be the first 'R'."

Feelings of competence and self-esteem: At this age, children are also learning to judge themselves in relation to others. For most children, school marks the first time that their goals are not set by an internal clock but by the outside world. Just as the 1-year-old struggles to walk, 6-year-olds are struggling to meet adult expectations. Young kids don't know how to distinguish between effort and ability, says Tynette Hills, coordinator of early-childhood education for the state of New Jersey. If they try hard to do something and fail, they may conclude that they will never be able to accomplish a particular task. The effects of obvious methods of comparison, such as posting grades, can be serious. Says Hills: "A child who has had his confidence really damaged needs a rescue operation."

Rates of growth: Between the ages of 5 and 9, there's a wide range of development for children of normal intelligence. "What's appropriate for one child may not be appropriate for another," says Dr. Perry Dyke, a member of the California State Board of Education. "We've got to have the teachers and the staff reach children at whatever level they may be at . . . That takes very sophisticated teaching." A child's pace is almost impossible to predict beforehand. Some kids learn to read on their own by kindergarten; others are still struggling to decode words two or three years later. But by the beginning of the fourth grade, children with very different histories often read on the same level. Sometimes, there's a sudden "spurt" of learning, much like a growth spurt, and a child who has been behind all year will catch up in just a few weeks. Ernest Boyer and others think that multigrade classrooms, where two or three grades are mixed, are a good solution to this problem—and a way to avoid the "tracking" that can hurt a child's self-esteem. In an ungraded classroom, for example, an older child who is having problems in a particular area can practice by tutoring younger kids.

Putting these principles into practice has never been easy. Forty years ago Milwaukee abolished report cards and started sending home ungraded evaluations for kindergarten through third grade. "If anything was developmentally appropriate, those ungraded classes were," says Millie Hoffman, a curriculum specialist with the Milwaukee schools. When the back-to-basics movement geared up nationally in the early 1980s, the city bowed to pressure. Parents started demanding letter grades on report cards. A traditional, direct-teaching approach was introduced into the school system after some students began getting low scores on standardized tests. The school board ordered basal readers with controlled vocabularies and contrived stories. Milwaukee kindergarten teachers were so up-

A Primer for Parents

When visiting a school, trust your eyes. What you see is what your child is going to get.

● Teachers should talk to small groups of children or individual youngsters; they shouldn't just lecture.

■ Children should be working on projects, active experiments and play; they shouldn't be at their desks all day filling in workbooks.

▲ Children should be dictating and writing their own stories or reading real books.

● The classroom layout should have reading and art areas and space for children to work in groups.

■ Children should create freehand artwork, not just color or paste together adult drawings.

▲ Most importantly, watch the children's faces. Are they intellectually engaged, eager and happy? If they look bored or scared, they probably are.

set by these changes that they convinced the board that their students didn't need most of the standardized tests and the workbooks that go along with the readers.

Some schools have been able to keep the progressive format. Olive School in Arlington Heights, Ill., has had a nontraditional curriculum for 22 years. "We've been able to do it because parents are involved, the teachers really care and the children do well," says principal Mary Stitt. "We feel confident that we know what's best for kids." Teachers say they spend a lot of time educating parents about the teaching methods. "Parents always think school should be the way it was for them," says first-grade teacher Cathy Sauer. "As if everything else can change and progress but education is supposed to stay the same. I find that parents want their children to like school, to get along with other children and to be good thinkers. When they see that happening, they become convinced."

Parental involvement is especially important when schools switch from a traditional to a new format. Four years ago, Anne Norford, principal of the Brownsville Elementary School in Albemarle County, Va., began to convert her school. Parents volunteer regularly and that helps. But the transition has not been completely smooth. Several teachers refused to switch over to the more active format. Most of them have since left the school, Norford says. There's no question that some teachers have trouble implementing the developmentally appropriate approach. "Our teachers are not all trained for it," says Yale's Kagan. "It takes a lot of savvy and skill." A successful child-centered classroom seems to function effortlessly as youngsters move from activity to activity. But there's a lot of planning behind it—and that's the responsibility of the individual teacher. "One of the biggest problems," says Norford, "is trying to come up with a program

83

that every teacher can do—not just the cadre of single people who are willing to work 90 hours a week." Teachers also have to participate actively in classroom activities and give up the automatic mantle of authority that comes from standing at the blackboard.

Teachers do better when they're involved in the planning and decision making. When the South Brunswick, N.J., schools decided in the early 1980s to change to a new format, the district spent several years studying a variety of curricula. Teachers participated in that research. A laboratory school was set up in the summer so that teachers could test materials. "We had the support of the teachers because teachers were part of the process," says teacher consultant Joan Warren.

One residue of the back-to-basics movement is the demand for accountability. Children who are taught in nontraditional classrooms can score slightly lower on commonly used standardized tests. That's because most current tests are geared to the old ways. Children are usually quizzed on specific skills, such as vocabulary or addition, not on the concepts behind those skills. "The standardized tests usually call for one-word answers," says Carolyn Topping, principal of Mesa Elementary School in Boulder, Colo. "There may be three words in a row, two of which are misspelled and the child is asked to circle the correctly spelled word. But the tests never ask, 'Does the child know how to write a paragraph?'"

Even if the tests were revised to reflect different kinds of knowledge, there are serious questions about the reliability of tests on young children. The results can vary widely, depending on many factors—a child's mood, his ability to manipulate a pencil (a difficult skill for many kids), his reaction to the person administering the test. "I'm appalled at all the testing we're doing of small children," says Vanderbilt University professor Chester Finn, a former assistant secretary of education under the Reagan administration. He favors regular informal reviews and teacher evaluations to make sure a student understands an idea before moving on to the next level of difficulty.

Tests are the simplest method of judging the effectiveness of a classroom—if not always the most accurate. But there are other ways to tell if children are learning. If youngsters are excited by what they are doing, they're probably laughing and talking to one another and to their teacher. That communication is part of the learning process. "People think that school has to be either free play or all worksheets," says Illinois professor Katz. "The truth is that neither is enough. There has to be a balance between spontaneous play and teacher-directed work." And, she adds, "you have to have the other component. Your class has to have intellectual life."

Katz, author of "Engaging Children's Minds," describes two different elementary-school classes she visited recently. In one, children spent the entire morning making identical pictures of traffic lights. There was no attempt to relate the pictures to anything else the class was doing. In the other class, youngsters were investigating a school bus. They wrote to the district and asked if they could have a bus parked in their lot for a few days. They studied it, figured out what all the parts were for and talked about traffic rules. Then, in the classroom, they built their own bus out of cardboard. They had fun, but they also practiced writing, problem solving, even a little arithmetic. Says Katz: "When the class had their parents' night, the teacher was ready with reports on how each child was doing. But all the parents wanted to see was the bus because their children had been coming home and talking about it for weeks." That's the kind of education kids deserve. Anything less should get an "F."

The Town
B. F. Skinner Boxed

In the dusty reaches of the Mexican desert, a handful of utopians are trying to prove that what worked for the psychologist's pigeons can work for humans, too.

Steve Fishman

Steve Fishman is a contributing editor.

LATELY IVAN, who is two years old, has been emitting some undesirable verbal behavior.

Where Ivan lives, the Code of Children's Behavior is quite explicit about what is desirable: Orderliness and cleanliness, for example; singing, laughing, dancing. And speaking positively.

"Great!" "I like it." "I'm happy"—these are the kinds of statements Ivan should be making. But Ivan has been negative. Linda, the leader of the committee on children's behavior, reports that he has been saying things like "The sky is not blue," or "You can't run," or "No, that is not yours, that is everyone's"—which could be considered desirable "sharing behavior," if it weren't for all the other negatives.

It's Thursday night and the committee is holding its weekly meeting in the children's house, where the community's four youngest children live. In these get-togethers, the adults discuss everything about the kids, from how they ought to behave to what medical care they should receive to how long their hair should be. The eleven adults listening to Linda's recitation of Ivan's negatives—two biological parents and nine "behavioral" parents—sit in the dining room clumped around the long, low children's table.

Linda explains that for the past week, the grownups who care for the youngest children have been wearing counters around their necks—little silvery devices like those that ticket takers use to click off the number of people entering a theater. Every time Ivan, who has brown bangs, brown eyes, and a voice that penetrates like a foghorn, has emitted a negative verbal behavior, *click*. "I don't like the beans." *Click.* "It's too cold outside." *Click.*

Linda holds up a piece of peach-colored graph paper with penciled peaks: Ivan has averaged 18 negative verbal behaviors per day. She poses the crucial question: "Should we intervene now to correct Ivan's behavior?"

WELCOME TO LOS HORCONES, a tiny enclave in the barely hospitable stretches of Mexico's Sonora Desert, 175 miles south of the U.S. border. Here 26 adults and children are attempting to live according to the teachings of the late Harvard behaviorist Burrhus Frederic (B.F.) Skinner—one of the most widely recognized and most often maligned of psychologists.

In the cultural lab they call home, this outpost community of Mexicans has been at it for 17 years, experimenting with Skinner's ideas, working away on themselves and their children. So that no visitor will miss the point, there is this welcome sign at the edge of their land, written in both Spanish and English: "We apply the science of behavior to the design of a new society."

The idea, first Skinner's and now theirs, is as ambitious as it sounds: By the methodical application of the science of behaviorism, the little band at Los Horcones believes it can transform selfish human beings into cooperative, sharing ones.

Until his death this past August, B.F. Skinner argued that his psychology was both potent and practical. His fundamental discoveries, made 55 years ago, rest on this idea: If any particular behavior is reinforced, it will continue. If not, it will cease.

For pigeons, Skinner found, reinforcement came in the form of dry, hard food pellets. What a hungry pigeon wouldn't do for the promise of a pellet! Climb stairs, peck a key 10,000 times, even guide a missile—which Skinner demonstrated to U.S. Army officials in World War II.

Give Skinner some lab time—he was one of psychology's first great experimenters—and he'd figure out which reinforcers, administered how often and for how long, would not only make people share but make them *like* to share. "We can *make* men adequate for group living," boasted the protagonist in Skinner's classic 1948 utopian novel, *Walden Two*.

Over the past two decades, Skinner's behaviorism and his

ideas about what motivates people have largely been supplanted in the world of academic psychology. The trend now is toward cognitive psychology, which concentrates on the unconscious causes of human behavior, processes that cognitive psychologists say cannot or should not be subject to systems of reward and punishment.

But in this desert proving ground, behaviorism is as alive as the tarantulas that take up guard on the drainpipes, as hardy as the boa constrictors that swallow live rabbits whole. In the children's house and the other whitewashed bungalows of the community of Los Horcones, behaviorism still has a shot.

"It's true," says Juan Robinson, the community's coordinator of adult behavior. "A person can be made to enjoy what he did not at first enjoy."

Take Ivan.

IVAN'S BIOLOGICAL PARENTS, Luciano Coronado Paredes, 26, and Maria Guadalupe Cosio de Coronado, 26, better known as Lucho and Lupita, sit in the tiny children's chairs with the other adults. They met elsewhere, but heard about Los Horcones and were married here. They vowed to put the community first. "If you ever decide to leave, just go, don't even tell me," said Lupita. Both Ivan and his brother Sebastian, aged four, were born at Los Horcones, and live together in the children's house.

Lucho and Lupita are tired after a long day's work, and remain quiet even when the subject is their younger son. Lucho, in fact, peruses a book on rabbits while Linda's discussion goes on. "Did you know," he asks a neighbor, "that rabbits eat their food twice?" No one is really worried about Ivan. It is just behavior, after all. Ivan used to cry when he wanted something, instead of asking for it. That took but a few weeks to correct.

An approach is suggested for Ivan's negative emissions—straightforward Skinnerian science. When Ivan says something positive, he'll be reinforced with attention—hugs and kisses, pats on the head, and M&Ms. His negative comments will be ignored (but still counted with the clickers). Punishment isn't shunned out of principle; it is just, as Skinner saw it, that the consequences can turn out to be troublesome.

Linda (the children all call her La Linda) asks if everyone agrees. In the community's open family, all decisions must be made unanimously. One by one, the adults, all of whom are considered parents, nod. "Adults are difficult to change," says a parent. "Pigeons and children are easy."

B. F. SKINNER experimented on pigeons and also on rats. In his crucial experiments of the 1930s, he demonstrated that by offering a simple food pellet as a "reinforcer"—a term first used by the famed Russian physiologist Ivan Pavlov—he could condition laboratory rats to press a bar when a light came on, to hold it down for as long as 30 seconds, and to keep pressing harder.

To Skinner, humans were bigger and more complex but not fundamentally different from lab animals. For the right reinforcers, he claimed, they would do almost anything.

Critics denounced Skinner's science, when it came to humans, as simplistic, manipulative, and reductionist—as well as downright unflattering. They argued that people, unlike pigeons, have rich inner lives and complex, hidden motivations. What, for goodness' sake, of a person's free will? cried the critics.

Skinner harrumphed. Free will, he said, was illusory. He preferred to talk about the predictability of people.

The late psychologist wasn't, however, a cold, impersonal manipulator. Rather, he seems to have been as cheery and optimistic as a handyman who says, Hey, I can fix that. After his wife complained that the first years of child-rearing were hell, he devised the "baby tender," a glass-enclosed, temperature-controlled crib that eliminated the need to change the baby's clothes so often. His own daughter tried it out and became the notorious baby in the "Skinner box." After noticing how dull his other daughter's grammar school was, Skinner built a "teaching machine," decades ahead of today's interactive learning systems.

In the same problem-solving spirit, the late behaviorist sat down in 1947 and in seven weeks wrote the book outlining his plan to ease society's woes through behaviorism. In Skinner's utopia, 1,000 citizens work four hours a day for no money, share their children, develop their artistic talents. As literature, *Walden Two* is a bore, freighted with long arguments between the proselytizing Frazier and his skeptical foil, a character named Castle. But the ideas have had a long life.

The book became a staple of college psychology classes as behaviorism flourished in the 1950s and 1960s. Two million copies are in print today. To a disposed mind, it can read like a do-it-yourself kit.

IN THE LATE 1960s, Juan Robinson, a handsome young middle-class Mexican (descended from a Scottish grandfather), was a university psychology student in Mexico City. Robinson read *Walden Two* and quickly became a convert.

In 1972, on the dusty edge of the Mexican town of Hermosillo, he and his wife, Mireya Bustamente Norberto, then 21, decided to give behaviorism a practical try. They founded a school for retarded children, many of them so unmanageable that their parents were prepared to ship them to an institution. Subjected to behavioral techniques, the 20 students fell into line.

Consider the case of Luis, an autistic teen who threw as many as three tantrums a day. Did Luis sit quietly? Very nice, the behaviorists said, and handed him a coin. Shake hands? Very good. Another coin. Do anything but throw a fit? One more coin. Merchant Luis began bartering half hours of appropriate behavior—he even did chores!—for coins redeemable for meals, and his tantrums virtually ceased. "We can modify antisocial behavior," Juan concluded, "in three months."

At the end of the school day, Juan and Mireya hosted gatherings. Linda (La Linda), just 19, a volunteer at the school, attended; so did her husband, Ramon Armendariz, 21. Juan, old man of the group at 24, would break out his copy of *Walden Two* and read aloud. Juan's voice is high and breathy, like the sound produced by blowing air into a Coke bottle. Night after night, his audience listened to that eerie hoot go on about how, with the aid of Skinner's science, a new society could be formed.

Among the small following, the idea started to take. They would start a community called Los Horcones—or "the pillars"—of a new society, nothing less. It would be a living experiment, a "cultural lab." They would be the researchers, they and their children the pigeons. Together they'd take Skinner's behaviorism another step down the road.

They drafted a Code of Adult Behavior—41 pages in a green

The little band at Los Horcones believes it can transform human nature.

"Adults are difficult to change," says a resident. "Pigeons and children are easy."

plastic binder, written in a style about as lively as a traffic ticket's—and in it they spelled out the details of the communitarian lifestyle. All adults would be parents to all children. Residents would be discouraged from saying "mine" and encouraged to say "ours"—as in "This is our daughter," even if one was not a blood relation. If an adult was working and a child asked a question, the adult would drop everything and explain what was going on. In addition, the older children would serve as teachers for the younger ones. Casual sex would not be considered a good example for "our" children.

In general, residents were to keep the community in mind at all times. They had to stop getting satisfaction from receiving more—whether pie or praise—and start getting excited about giving more. "Have approving thoughts about others" was a key dictum. The worst adjective that could be applied to someone at Los Horcones was "individualistic."

In all, six young urban friends gave up the career track in society—"the outside"—and moved to the countryside to build houses and to farm. They knew nothing about these endeavors, and Ramon recalls that for a few moments in 1973, the idea of building a new society with these ragtag city kids seemed like a very silly idea. It was dawn and the brand new behaviorists found themselves circling a fawn and white Guernsey cow, trying to figure out how to milk it.

IN 1980, THE CITIZENS of Los Horcones departed that first desolate site for the current patch of desert: an even more remote 250 acres of brush, cactus, and mesquite, 40 miles from Hermosillo. The new land might as well have been a stretch of concrete. They dug a small reservoir and carved out irrigation ditches to compensate for the parching lack of rain, and they hauled in trees. With a mania for systems, they not only planted but numbered every one of them. "Orderliness," Mireya says with a chortle, "is reinforcing."

Today Los Horcones is an oasis. "Everywhere you look, there we have done something," says Lucho. Vegetables grow in flawless stripes on seven acres. Orchards produce grapefruits as big as melons and lemons the size of baseballs. There are pigs, rabbits, chickens, 13 cows, electric milking machines, and a cheese factory. The community is, in fact, 75 percent food self-sufficient, buying only such staples as rice and flour. They have a Caterpillar tractor, trucks, and a school bus converted into a touring vehicle—sleeps nine—for occasional group forays to the outside world.

There's a basketball court and a plaza where they hold pig roasts and dances for guests from Hermosillo. They've dug a swimming hole, called Walden Pond, and built wood and metal shops. There's a dormitory for the dozen or so mentally impaired children they care for, which earns them cash to buy supplies. Luis is still there, helping to milk the cows for coins. The huge main house has a living room, communal dining room, and an office featuring a couple of computers. A lab contains cages of cooing pigeons used in behavioral experiments.

This has taken considerable work, far more than the four hours a day Skinner projected in his book. "I did like to play sports, but for me, it's not so important now," says Lucho, who, as all the adults do, works six and a half days a week. What's

important to him now? "Building a building, fixing a toilet," he says simply.

The only space an adult can call his or her own at Los Horcones is one of the 25 assigned white stucco residences, each no more than a bedroom. Meager quarters for a private life, but the idea, after all, was to build a place where people shared not only space but belongings and emotions. The bedrooms are starkly utilitarian, with perhaps a table, an overhead fan—and no closets.

That's because the clothes at Los Horcones belong to everybody and are stored in one building: rows of jeans, neatly pressed and arranged by size, rows of shirts on hangers. First come, first served; too bad what goes best with your eyes. "I have four or five shirts I like," says Ramon. "I don't care who uses them. How could you build a community on sharing and be worried about who uses shirts?"

At first, it's fair to say, newcomers couldn't believe they had to do this clothes-swap thing. Even those dedicated to the design of a new society found it strange to see someone else in the clothes they were wearing yesterday.

And yet, in the long run, sharing clothes has turned out to be one of the easier things to adjust to. Some of the less tangible behaviors have been tougher to master. The main hurdle for the individual and for the new society is this: How can someone who's been reared to believe that if you don't look out for yourself, no one else will, suddenly believe that other people's happiness is your happiness, too?

"It's like being born again," says Juan.

But how to be reborn?

FORTUNATELY, A DAY AT LOS HORCONES is chock-full of strategies. Every activity can, it seems, be a form of reinforcement. Not only do the residents pick beans side by side, and take turns cooking together, they hold meetings to air any thoughts about how everyone behaved during the picking and cooking.

If you don't show up where you are supposed to, or if your tone of voice is too authoritarian, someone will take note of it. Alcohol, and even coffee, are allowed only in moderation because they aren't good for you. The place is like a big self-improvement camp, with lots of monitors. Lucho wrote in his notebook how many times his coworker was late for his shift at the cheese factory. That way, he said, there would be no argument when they were both sitting down with the behavior coordinator, trying to improve the situation.

If the extended family's kindhearted badgering can't haul a newcomer into line, there are, of course, other weapons for promoting utopia in the desert. That's where Skinner's science comes in. "That's right," says Juan, "we have the technology to change behavior."

In theory, no behavior is beyond the technology's reach. One woman—who prefers to remain anonymous, so we'll call her Susan—was interested in improving her relationship with her husband, so she designed a self-management program. She translated relationship-with-husband into graphable entities—positive verbal contacts, or PVCs, and negative verbal contacts, NVCs. She collected the data on a notepad she hid in her pocket, and after nine days she checked her chart: on average, 3.5 PVCs and 1.8 NVCs per day. Secretly, she also tallied her husband's

Here, the clothes belong to everyone. How could you build a community based on sharing and be worried about who wears what shirt?

communications. His score: 2.5 PVCs and 1.5 NVCs.

For Susan, or anyone, to learn a new behavior, it's essential to figure out what reinforces that behavior. Busi, 15 years old, taught Sebastian, just four, how to read in an astonishingly quick 15 hours. As he sounded out words, syllable by syllable, she patted his head and pushed a few of his reinforcers, Fruit Loops, into his mouth. But pats and sweets don't work for everybody. There is also the "participative reinforcer." To reward someone for cooking a nice meal, you not only applaud—though they like applause here—you offer to help afterwards with the dishes.

The most reliable reinforcer, though, is what the behaviorists at Los Horcones call a "natural" one, in which the person practicing a new behavior is reinforced by the consequences of that behavior. When Linda, for instance, discovered that she didn't run to other people's babies when they cried, she made herself run. The babies smiled in her arms, which, she explained, reinforced her response, naturally.

Susan, too, chose a natural reinforcer: her husband's response. She set a goal for herself: She would emit seven PVCs a day, and drop her NVCs to zero. Her husband had no idea about this particular behavior management program—it's hard to always know who's managing whose behavior at Los Horcones—but Susan noted that his PVCs increased to almost eight a day and his NVCs fell to zero. Both their PVCs up, Susan felt a lot better about their relationship.

PVCs? NVCs? They make lovely points on a graph, but are they love? It's not a distinction that behaviorists are troubled by. They're interested in observable behavior, not hidden recesses of the psyche. "How can you see what is inside except by the outside product?" explains Linda. "Anyone can imagine that if you, as a wife, have more pleasing interactions with your husband, you feel like he loves you more."

Despite the behaviorist lingo and the laboratory overtones, there is a bit of common sense to all this. A baby's smile can make someone feel good. And many people know that lending a hand, the essence of "participative reinforcement," or making tender comments, as Susan did to increase her PVCs, brings returns in good will. The difference is that at Los Horcones, these insights are applied in a deliberated system.

What's more, in a community that's also a behaviorism laboratory, reinforcers are the object of methodical study. Every morning, Linda experiments with the little ones. One current topic: Can children learn to consider future consequences? Linda doles out the investigative tool: M&M's. "you can eat it now," she tells the two- through seven-year-olds, "but if you wait until I say 'eat,' you get another." On a wall are the graphs she has charted; the lines reveal that the children will wait up to four minutes.

Los Horcones may, in fact, be one of the most self-studied communities in history. The results of the group's self-scrutiny, 20 papers, have been published in academic journals over the past 15 years—each signed communally, of course: "Los Horcones." The articles have examined the steps the community has taken to make its system of government by consensus more democratic, or revealed some of the reinforcers they've discovered to be most effective in motivating people to clean their rooms (candy and praise for a 14-year-old) or help harvest the crops (participation rather than sweets).

Still, when it comes to human overhaul, there are sticky areas. Even the technology, apparently, cannot always correct a history of individualistic living. Jealousy, for instance. That most individualistic of emotions, which says this is mine and not yours, seems to be stubborn as hell.

At Los Horcones possessiveness is discouraged. You aren't supposed to waltz into the dining room where the kids slide from one adult's lap to another's and check that your child or your husband has enough of Lupita's special rabbit-garlic stew on his or her plate. Spouses rarely sit together, often don't acknowledge each other, and a visitor doesn't at first know who the pairs are. One couple who became too much of a couple, walking hand in hand and generally behaving like honeymooners, was booted out. The community may be sexually monogamous, but it is emotionally polygamous. "You're married to everyone," Lupita explains.

"Yes, I had jealousy," says Ramon. "I went to Juan, the behavior manager. Here, your problem is everybody's. We had long meetings about it. It helped, though I think behaviors that you have when you are an adult you can't entirely get rid of."

CLEARLY, THE BRIGHTEST HOPES for the redesigned society are the people without an individualistic past, those who have benefited from the technology starting at the earliest stages of their lives: the children. If anyone is to carry out the caring and cooperative ideal, it ought to be those who have grown up here. "I never wanted kids before this," says Ramon, who is the father of four. "I didn't think I had anything to offer them, not until Los Horcones."

The children receive an enormous amount of attention from lots of adults. They're bright and outgoing, and from all appearances, feel capable and loved and useful. Skinner himself, who met the youngsters on several visits they paid to the United States, approved. "They've done wonderful things with their children," he said.

The first wave of the community's children are teenagers now. They have spent weekends with friends from the outside, and have had their friends visit them at Los Horcones. They know their upbringing has been different, but they dismiss the issue with a big shrug.

Ask them, for instance: If you had a problem, would you go to your mother?

"Sometimes when I have a problem I go to La Linda because she is the coordinator of child behavior," says Esteban, 12, son of Juan and Mireya.

Or you could ask: Who won the game of Monopoly?

"I think we all did," one child says. " We were all rich."

Or, Wouldn't you like a little pocket money?

Another shrug, confused, like when you try to explain something to a cat. "I have the money I need," says a teenager named Javier. "Whenever I go to town, they give me some money to buy a soda or something."

Or, Wouldn't you like to live somewhere else?

"I can't stand to stay away more than a couple of days," says Busi, her hands filled with fruit from the orchard.

Still, when it comes to human overhaul, there are sticky areas. Jealousy, for instance.

The community may be sexually monogamous, but it is emotionally polygamous.

None of the kids can; but none have had to. That may all change. The teenagers may soon be sent to Tucson, Arizona, to a branch of the community to be opened there, so they can enroll at the University of Arizona—not for a diploma, just to attend classes and learn. The prospect of this exodus makes some nervous, and not just the kids.

Who knows how many of the five teenagers will return? Or will these behaviorally brought up young people make their lives elsewhere?

"I accept both possibilities," says Juan.

WALDEN TWO was a community of a thousand people; Los Horcones hovers at 25 to 30, and can seem at times on the verge of depopulating. They would like to boost the population to 100 or 200; that would be much more reinforcing. Then at midday, children could greet workers with fresh lemonade and maybe a band would be playing.

"Then, even the people we lost would return," says Ramon. As it is now, members, even those who share the ideals, fall away, beyond the reach of the technology. Over the past 17 years, 60 people have come and gone—from South America, the United States, even as far away as Europe. Perhaps some were simply lonely, or seeking food and shelter, or curious because they'd heard about the community or seen an ad. (Yes, Los Horcones advertised in the local newspaper.) They stayed a few months or a couple of years, and drifted away. Leaving is the worst anticommunitarian behavior, and yet, it would seem, the toughest to change.

Last spring, just as the counter revealed that four in five of tiny, horn-voiced Ivan's commentaries were positive, Lupita and Lucho packed up their sons and left for Lupita's family home in Hermosillo. Lucho said he had wearied of trying, against his nature, to put the community first, whether by working more or organizing better. Lupita was torn, but followed her husband.

Lucho had succeeded through behavioral self-management in giving more approval to the kids, but he had never found a program that would make him think less often of his family and himself. "I just didn't want to change for what the community was offering me," he says. "It was simply that."

It was an awful failure of the technology—that was the shared analysis of the members who remained, though the discussions weren't so analytical. There were tears. The departure was like a divorce, an angry divorce.

With the exception of one founder who stayed 12 years before leaving, Lupita and Lucho had been there longer than any of the dozens who had passed through. But years spent at the community were evidently no guarantee of continued commitment.

Outside Los Horcones, Lucho said, things seemed easier. "Here it's not the same as starting a new society and defining everything. Here, the rules of the game are easy. I feel energized to do something. I think this energy I got at Los Horcones, and I am thankful for that." He got other things, too, like knowledge of how to make cheese, which is the business he and Lupita have chosen to go into for themselves—competing, of all things, for Los Horcones's customers.

Maybe Lucho would have liked some other reinforcers: additional time for himself, more trips outside the community, perhaps a few more economic incentives?

"If there had been those, I would have felt much better," Lucho said after he left.

And now, into this 17-year-old utopia, new "experimental" reinforcers soon may be creeping: credits for work, and paid vacations. That's what Los Horcones is considering. "People won't try to live communitarianly if they are not earning something more individualistic," says Juan pragmatically.

Individual rewards for living together? It sounds against the grain. Could behaviorism have pecked up against its limits?

"With investigation, you rise above the limits," says Juan, faithful as Skinner's *Walden Two* hero, Frazier. "We must investigate in more detail the variables that control these problems."

As the late great experimenter himself might have said: Back to the lab.

Not only do the residents pick beans together, and share kitchen duties, they meet to discuss how everyone behaved during the picking and cooking.

Gone But Not Forgotten

Scientists uncover pervasive, unconscious influences on memory

BRUCE BOWER

Donald M. Thomson, an Australian psychologist and lawyer, undoubtedly will never forget the day 15 years ago when he walked into a Sydney police station on routine court-related business and was arrested for assault and rape in a weird turn of events worthy of an Alfred Hitchcock movie.

The evening before his arrest, Thomson appeared on a local television program, where he discussed psychological research on eyewitness testimony and how people might best remember the faces of criminals observed during a robbery. As he spoke, a Sydney woman watching the show was attacked, raped and left unconscious in her apartment. When she awoke several hours later, she called the police and named Thomson as her assailant.

The following day, after Thomson's arrest, the woman confidently selected him as the perpetrator from a lineup of possible rapists at the police station.

Thomson, of course, professed his innocence. "The police didn't believe me at first," he recalls, "but I had appeared on a live television show when the crime occurred, so I had a good alibi."

Officials quickly dropped the charges when they realized the woman had unwittingly substituted Thomson's televised face for that of her attacker. "She had apparently watched my television appearance very closely, but it's not clear if she ever actually saw her assailant's face," says Thomson, now at Monash University in Clayton, Australia.

The real rapist was never apprehended.

Memory researchers from Los Angeles to London still talk about Thomson's bizarre brush with the law (with inevitable embellishments and distortions, according to Thomson), and many cite it as a dramatic demonstration of how no-doubt-about-it recollections can march to the misleading beat of an unconscious drummer. Over the last decade, in fact, laboratory investigations of "implicit memory" — the unintentional retrieval of previously studied information on tests that do not ask for that information — have surged faster than Thomson's blood pressure on the day he was wrongly accused.

"Most researchers now agree that implicit memory is more influential than explicit, conscious memory," says psychologist Robert G. Crowder of Yale University.

But opinions differ concerning the implications of implicit memory findings for an overall understanding of how memory works. One school of thought, endorsed mainly by those who study brain-damaged and amnesic patients, holds that several memory systems in the brain handle different types of implicit and explicit knowledge. Another camp, populated primarily by researchers who study healthy volunteers, regards memory as a single entity. These investigators theorize that successful performance on any memory test reflects a match between the mental processes or operations used in the initial learning of an item and those used in remembering it.

For much of the past century such a dispute was unthinkable, as psychologists focused almost exclusively on explicit, conscious memories of previous experiences. Study participants typically were asked either to recall what they had already seen — say, a list of five common nouns — or to pick out previously studied items from among two or more choices on "recollection tests."

But current memory investigations often delve into what psychologists call the "cognitive unconscious" — mental processes that operate outside of awareness but nevertheless influence conscious thoughts and actions. Considerable inspiration for this approach comes from the work of psychologist William James, who in 1890 contrasted the automatic nature of numerous habitual behaviors — driving a car, to use a modern example — with the consciously controlled use of reason.

Sigmund Freud's notion that our conscious mental lives reflect unconscious conflicts and emotions pitted against psychological defense mechanisms rarely accommodates controlled laboratory experiments, and thus gets little attention from explorers of the cognitive unconscious.

A series of ground-breaking studies with amnesic patients, conducted in England during the 1970s, paved the way for implicit memory research. One investigation found that brain-damaged men with no conscious memory of words they had just read showed a marked preference for the same words on implicit tests. For instance, the amnesics had no idea they had read a list of five-letter words including "table," but when told to complete the word stem "tab-" with whatever came to mind, they responded with "table" as often as healthy study participants did. Amnesics also mentioned previously studied but consciously forgotten words after viewing fragmented versions of the words, in which segments of each letter were omitted and the word's identity was ambiguous.

Other researchers went on to probe the unconscious memories of amnesics with different implicit tasks. For instance, amnesics shown a list of common idioms, including the item SOUR-GRAPES, were asked to write down the first word that came to mind upon seeing a cue such as SOUR-?. In most cases, they wrote down previously studied idiomatic completions. In a test of explicit memory, however, the amnesics were at a loss to remember previously studied words when instructed to use SOUR-? and other half-completed items as cues.

As research proceeded through the 1980s, the subtle staying power of implicit memory and the relative fragility of explicit memory grew more evident. Among the findings:

• Some brain-damaged patients who have no conscious memory for faces nonetheless show preferences for previously viewed faces on implicit tests.

• Although children and the elderly display poor recognition memory compared with young adults, the effects of prior study on word-stem completion and other implicit memory tasks remain stable from the wonder years through the golden years.

• While drugs such as alcohol dampen conscious recall and recognition, implicit memory remains largely impervious to these substances.

Implicit memory resists even the numbing effects of surgical anesthesia, according to a report in the September PSYCHOLOGICAL SCIENCE. Researchers led by John F. Kihlstrom of the University of Arizona in Tucson played tape recordings of pairs of related words (such as "house-chair") to 25 anesthetized hospital patients during surgery. Two weeks later, the patients could not recall having heard the words. When told the first word from each pair, they still had no recollection of the matching word. But when asked to report the first word that came to mind upon hearing half of each word pair, most participants responded with the other half heard under anesthesia.

Some scientists say such results indicate that implicit and explicit tests tap into distinct memory systems housed in different brain regions. In his influential book *Memory and Brain* (1987, New York, Oxford University Press), psychologist Larry R. Squire of the Veterans Administration Medical Center in San Diego draws a line between "declarative" and "procedural" memory systems. In Squire's view, declarative memory—thought to reside mainly in the brain's outer layer — holds the consciously remembered, factual and personal knowledge plumbed by explicit tests. He suggests the procedural system — with a home base in deeper brain structures — underlies the fluid, automatic performance of skilled behaviors, forms of learning such as classical conditioning, and unconscious preferences displayed on many implicit memory tasks.

In classical conditioning, an automatic response comes under the control of a formerly neutral stimulus. Pavlov's dogs provide the classic example: After several instances of hearing a bell just before receiving food, they salivated at the mere sound of the bell.

However, emerging evidence suggests that a large category of implicit memory operates independently of Squire's declarative and procedural systems, asserts psychologist Daniel L. Schacter of the University of Arizona.

In the Jan. 19 SCIENCE, he and Endel Tulving of the University of Toronto propose that a "perceptual representation system" directs a common type of im-

plicit memory known as priming. As in the British studies of amnesics, tests of priming involve the presentation of reduced perceptual information about previously observed words, pictures of objects or other items. Study participants then attempt to name or categorize incomplete items with whatever comes to mind. Priming occurs when responses predominantly refer to items already seen.

Whereas memories for motor skills, personal events or factual information lodge in specific brain regions, the perceptual representation system distributes different perceptual versions of particular words and objects throughout the brain, Schacter contends. Moreover, each

---

"Misleading unconscious inferences create serious questions about the accuracy of much eyewitness testimony, even when the witnesses are confident and sincere."

---

of the multiple perceptual forms assumed by an item apparently responds to its own memory cues.

For example, in an unpublished study directed by Tulving, volunteers saw a list of words, such as AARDVARK and UMBRELLA. They later filled in three-letter fragments (say, -A-D — R- and U — R — L-), and then five-letter fragments that included the three letters already seen (-ARD-AR- and U-BR—LA). Tulving found that individuals completing a three-letter fragment with a previously studied word did not show priming for the five-letter fragment of the same word, and vice versa.

Schacters says studies of brain-damaged patients by his group and others

suggest that the perceptual representation system contains a subsystem that promotes priming by granting mental access to a word's visual form, not its meaning. Some patients with brain injuries can read aloud but have little or no understanding of written words, he notes. They correctly pronounce printed words that cannot be sounded out, such as "cough" or "blood," although they haven't the faintest idea what the words signify.

Schacter theorizes that another subsystem handles structural knowledge about objects and shapes that can exist in three-dimensional form. In studies he and his colleagues describe in an upcoming JOURNAL OF EXPERIMENTAL PSYCHOLOGY: LEARNING, MEMORY AND COGNITION, college students were shown line drawings of physically possible and impossible three-dimensional objects on a computer screen for 5 seconds. Participants then viewed for 0.1 second each previously seen object—as well as a new series of possible and impossible 3-D objects — and were asked to decide whether each drawing was structurally feasible. The 0.1-second flashes allowed no time for conscious mental manipulations of the drawings.

Volunteers accurately categorized only the possible objects presented previously. This, says Schacter, suggests that priming through the perceptual representation system depends on perceiving objects as "structured wholes."

Other pursuers of the cognitive unconscious perceive memory itself as a structured whole, lacking separate brain systems but obeying a few general principles.

According to these researchers, one such maxim holds that performance on any type of memory test improves when initial learning and later testing involve the same mental operations or forms of information. Most explicit tests engage the learning and memory of word meanings and semantic concepts, whereas implicit tests usually begin and end with perceptual information, observes Henry L. Roediger of Rice University in Houston. Thus, test design — rather than separate memory systems in the brain — guarantees striking differences between an individual's performance on most implicit and explicit tasks, he argues.

Roediger buttresses his point by noting that two implicit tests focusing on different types of information also produce contrasting results. In a 1987 study published in MEMORY & COGNITION, he and a colleague had subjects study a list of words and pictures of common objects before taking one of two implicit memory tests. One was a word-stem completion test with stems corresponding to previously studied words, the names of already studied pictures and new items. The other test required identification of incomplete pictures corresponding to previously studied pictures, already studied words and new objects.

Prior study of pictures produced substantial unintentional memory only for corresponding picture fragments, not for picture fragments based on words in the original list. Likewise, previously seen words were generated mainly by corresponding word stems rather than by stems based on pictures. In other words, memory improved when the study and test conditions tweaked a common mental operation, such as verbal or perceptual processing, Roediger maintains.

Differences between conscious recall and recognition provide further ammunition for Roediger's argument, which he outlines in the September AMERICAN PSYCHOLOGIST. For instance, while healthy volunteers recall commonly used words more often than rarely used words, they identify rarely used words more accurately than common words on multiple-choice recognition tests. Roediger concludes that when individuals attempt to recall words in the absence of memory cues, automatic mental operations engaged by reading familiar words apparently kick into gear; when several choices consciously prod memory, the more deliberate mental manipulations used with unusual words take precedence.

Conscious judgments may also reflect often-deceptive unconscious inferences, contends Larry L. Jacoby of McMaster University in Hamilton, Ontario.

Jacoby regards data from implicit and explicit memory experiments as potentially misleading. Conscious recollection partially pumps up performance on some implicit tasks, including word-stem completions, Jacoby maintains. Unconscious memories sometimes influence responses on explicit tests or spark the spontaneous conscious recall of prior events, he adds.

Yet researchers can exploit a natural opposition between unconscious and conscious memories, Jacoby says.

In a series of studies, Jacoby and his colleagues found that unconscious exposure to a word quickened the conscious perception of the same word on an ensuing memory test and created an illusion of familiarity with the word. Conscious exposure to the word produced no such effect.

For example, college students in one experiment prepared for a recognition test by studying a word list. Then, just before the test, they viewed new words

flashed for a fraction of a second on a computer screen — just long enough for unconscious perception. New words also showed up on the recognition test, and students often mislabeled them as previously studied words, Jacoby and Kevin Whitehouse of McMaster report in the March 1989 JOURNAL OF EXPERIMENTAL PSYCHOLOGY: GENERAL.

"The flashed word produced more fluent perceptual processing of the new test word, which was interpreted as familiarity," Jacoby says.

When flashed words were shown long enough for conscious perception, students correctly labeled them as "new" on the subsequent recognition test.

In a related study described in the same issue, Jacoby and several associates made up nonfamous names and presented them on a computer screen, asking students to read the names aloud. They told all the students in advance that the names (such as Sebastian Weisdorf and Valerie Marsh) were not well known. Some volunteers devoted their full attention to the task; others were asked to read the names while listening for runs of three odd-numbered digits in a continuous string of numbers announced through a loudspeaker.

All students then rated whether or not names on a test list were famous. The new list included previously read names, new nonfamous names, and famous names (such as Satchel Paige and Minnie Pearl).

Volunteers who had been distracted by the loudspeaker during the initial name-reading task showed poor conscious recollection of the names they had read, but they often judged those names as famous when rating the test list. Students who had given full attention to reading the first list remembered most of the names later on and judged them as nonfamous.

"False fame" judgments also occurred when students gave full attention to the initial list of nonfamous names and then responded to the test list while listening for odd-numbered digits.

In both instances, divided attention blocked conscious recognition of nonfamous names, while an unconscious familiarity with each moniker bred mistaken fame judgments, Jacoby says.

Even something as basic as the perception of sound can become skewed by unconscious influences, he adds. In one study, Jacoby's research team presented previously heard and new sentences against an unchanging background of noise and asked students to judge the loudness of the noise. Students judged loudness as substantially lower upon hearing the old sentences. Jacoby asserts that previous exposure made these sentences easier to perceive through the din of the test situation, and that participants

misattributed this to a lower noise level.

This phenomenon often occurs outside the lab, he adds, citing the experience of learning a foreign language as a case in point. At first, native speakers seem to speak so rapidly that one cannot make out separate words. As facility with the language increases, the speech rate of native speakers seems to slow and distinct words pop out of the verbal stream. Thus, Jacoby says, a typical language student automatically perceives the accumulation of fluency as a slowing of native speakers' speech rates.

Jacoby draws a lesson from the pranks played by unconscious influences: "Mundane, rather than traumatic, experiences exert the most unconscious effects on perception and behavior," he suggests.

And those mundane influences can have traumatic consequences, as in cases of unconscious plagiarism. Consider the respected psychiatrist who resigned last year as head of a major psychiatric hospital amid accusations that one of his published papers contained paragraphs with wording identical to that in another researcher's previously published report on the same subject. The psychiatrist said he had seen the other paper, but he maintained that any resemblance between the two works was unintentional.

Jacoby says his studies of the cognitive unconscious suggest that, unbeknownst to some plagiarizers, previously read material may automatically bubble to the surface during an attempt to write about a similar topic.

Subtle, unconscious influences also play tricks on eyewitness accounts of crimes, as starkly illustrated by the false rape accusation levied at Donald Thomson, says psychologist Robert A. Bjork of the University of California, Los Angeles.

"Misleading unconscious inferences create serious questions about the accuracy of much eyewitness testimony, even when the witnesses are confident and sincere," remarks Bjork, who frequently testifies in court on the fallibility of eyewitness memories.

No single theory neatly pulls together all the data on unconscious or implicit memory, Bjork adds. But in his view, the new generation of studies shoots down the intuitive and widespread belief that memory works like a tape recorder, storing pristine bits of information for playback later on.

"People misunderstand their own memories to a great degree," he argues. "They think memories etch themselves into the brain, when memory actually involves unconscious interpretations of previous experiences."

RODENTS ARE HINTING THAT FREUD GOT IT WRONG. DREAMS AREN'T FOR INFANTILE WISH FULFILLMENT. THEY'RE FOR LEARNING THE LESSONS OF SURVIVAL.

dreams
of a rat

J U N E   K I N O S H I T A

June Kinoshita, a former editor at Sci- entific American, *just finished a Knight science journalism fellowship at MIT that gave her free run of the university. Now she's working on a travel guide to Tokyo and a book on neuroscience. In the January 1991* Discover *she wrote about a gene that makes mice male.*

Jonathan Winson is fascinated by dreams. To be specific, he is fascinated by the machinations of the brain that produce a dream's evanescent images. But Winson hasn't spent his professional years in an analyst's armchair, listening to patients free-associate about their nocturnal fantasies. His domain has been a laboratory stacked to the ceiling with electronic equipment and laced with a whiff of animal odors.

Winson, at 69, is now leaving the hands-on part of his lab research to others. But just a couple of years ago he could still often be seen in his lab at Rockefeller University in New York fighting a quiet battle of wills with one of his subjects: a rat intent on crawling inside the sleeve of Winson's tweed jacket while he gently restrained it. At those moments, Winson, with his mild gray eyes and grizzled raft of hair, seemed like a kindly uncle minding a restless child.

The rat was wearing what looked like a tiny pillbox hat. A thin ribbon of wire trailed from the hat to an overhead pulley, then ran across the ceiling and down to an electronic box a few feet away. The wire was picking up signals from a minute electrode implanted under the hat, in the rat's brain. Every time a particular nerve cell, or neuron, fired, the electrode relayed the signal to the wire, which sent it to the electronic box, which recorded the event with a sharp click.

Using electrodes like this one to eavesdrop on the ephemeral conversations of neurons, Winson was testing an idea that had obsessed him for years— the idea that dreaming reflects a biological process by which the brain sifts through new information and incorporates it into its existing memory. The notion smacks of the obvious; we've all had dreams triggered by daytime events that inspire remembrances of things past. Yet what seems obvious can be notoriously hard to prove scientifically. After all, no one really knows why we sleep. As for why we dream, that's always been the province of psychoanalysts and psychologists, not of physiologists.

By recording the activity of these rats' neurons, however, Winson has provided the first neurological evidence that information from an animal's waking hours is indeed reprocessed by the dreaming brain. Moreover, his findings may shed some light on *why* we dream periodically during sleep. Winson suspects that the brain uses these periods to carry out one of life's more important tasks: to integrate new experiences with old ones and come up with a strategy for survival. "The contents of dreams in early life," he says, "reflect the building of a plan for behavior—a core plan that profoundly influences reaction to experiences in later life."

Winson is not the first to suppose there might be a fundamental link between dreaming and memory. Freud himself intuited the connection and even tried to derive a dream theory from neurobiological mechanisms. But given the paucity of knowledge about the brain at the time, the attempt fizzled, and Freud turned increasingly to psychological motives to explain dreams.

In Freud's psychoanalytic view, dreams consist of infantile wishes and emotions that pop up in sleep. The ego, like a censor, normally represses these unacceptable feelings completely. But when the ego gets sleepy and relaxes its guard, the unconscious desires sneak through to manifest themselves in dreams. These feelings, however, are so upsetting that they would disrupt sleep if they appeared undisguised. So the censorial, if drowsy, ego cloaks them in cryptic symbols. That's why Freud believed you could analyze the oddball contents of a person's dreams to glimpse the workings of his unconscious mind and understand his psyche.

Yet despite its great influence, Freud's theory has had its foundations steadily gnawed away by modern neuroscience. By the 1930s neurophysiologists were using the electroencephalogram to study electrical activity in the human cerebral cortex, the brain's furrowed rind, which is the seat of perception and thought. Their recordings would show that most of a person's night is spent in slow-wave

WINSON IS NOT THE FIRST TO SUPPOSE THERE MIGHT BE A LINK BETWEEN DREAMING AND MEMORY. FREUD HIMSELF INTUITED THE CONNECTION.

sleep, marked by large, slow brain waves. The recordings of a waking person, in contrast, jitter in small, rapid waves.

In the early 1950s Eugene Aserinsky, a graduate student at the University of Chicago, pasted electrodes to his 10-year-old son's face to record eye movements while the boy slept. Aserinsky discovered that at certain times of the night his son's eyes skittered back and forth in unison. During such episodes of rapid eye movements, or REMs, breathing quickened and the heart beat faster. The muscles went limp and the body lay still, save for faint twitches of the extremities.

REM episodes had another oddity. Brain waves recorded at these times were small and fast, like those of a waking brain, not large and slow as was typical during sleep. Aserinsky and his adviser, Nathaniel Kleitman, suspected that the skittish eye movements coincided with dreams. Sleep labs around the world substantiated the hunch: when people were woken during REM sleep, 95 percent of the time they confirmed that they had been dreaming. Soon after this discovery another Kleitman protégé, William Dement, confirmed that REM sleep came in cycles, typically four or five times a night. Altogether, adult humans spent almost two hours a night dreaming.

even more astounding revelations were to follow. Experiments with cats soon showed that neurons in the cerebral cortex hammered away during REM sleep, as though the animals were wide awake. The brain was clearly intensely active, yet it wasn't getting any sensory input. Nor was it driving the body to move in response to its commands, as it would in waking animals. Why? The answer lay in the brain stem, the stalklike lower brain connecting the spinal cord to the cerebral cortex. There Michel Jouvet, a French researcher, found regions that functioned like some internal clock, periodically triggering REM sleep and its accompanying burst of brain activity; Jouvet also discovered a cluster of brain stem neurons that inter-

cepted commands from the cortex to the spinal cord. When Jouvet destroyed those neurons, the slumbering cats got up, pounced on invisible mice, and arched their backs; they were acting out their dreams.

So Freud had it wrong. It wasn't repressed desires but a neuronal clock in the brain stem that sent the brain into a dream state four or five times a night. Based on such findings, psychiatrist Allan Hobson of Harvard proposed in 1977 a radical new theory of dreams. It was the brain stem's random excitement of the cortex, he said, that accounted for the hallucinatory bizarreness of dreams. Our dreams were the vivid by-products of a purely physiological process.

Hobson, now 59, is an animated man with riveting blue eyes and snow white hair that spills over his shirt collar. His office at the Massachusetts Mental Health Center in Boston is cluttered with photos, mementos, and images of brains, among them several ink drawings of brain cells resembling leafless shrubs. Hobson's fingers caress a delicate ink drawing of nerve-cell bodies overlaid by the dark branches of their outstretched axons. "Some of these may have been by Cajal himself," he says, referring to the great Spanish neuroscientist Santiago Ramón y Cajal, a contemporary of Freud's.

Dreams are bizarre, Hobson argues, not because the Freudian ego disguises hidden wishes, but because neurons in the brain stem bombard the visual cortex with random signals as the eyes dart about during REM sleep. These signals, called PGO spikes, apparently convey information about the direction of the moving eyes, says Hobson, but the brain tries to interpret them as real visual data.

"So according to our theory," explains Hobson, "the visual system gets a barrage of signals, and it says, What's this? And it goes into its memory stores, looks for a match, and says, Well, that's sort of like this high rise I was in. What was going on there? Well, so and so was there. And there's a story generated to go with that notion. Then a new set of signals arises,

incompatible with the previous data set, and the story changes: Oh, now it's my grandmother's house."

It's this barrage of brain stem signals, says Hobson, that directs the images and abrupt scene shifts in dreams. Dreams are our awareness of this organic brain activity, which probably serves a variety of purposes. Among other things, Hobson speculates, "REM sleep may allow us to rev our cerebral motor and actively test all our circuits in a reliably patterned way."

Yet brain stem signals, as even Hobson agrees, are not the whole story. "The REM state is generated by the brain stem and transmitted to the cortex, but the cortex feeds back," says Barbara Jones, a brain stem expert at McGill University in Montreal. "If you remove the cortex, the PGO spikes become very much simplified. You can't say information flows in just one direction. There's a circuit."

This evidence suggests that a higher cortical process may help orchestrate whatever goes on in the brain once REM sleep begins. But what could that be? That's precisely the question that Winson has seized on. He believes that sleep—and in particular, REM sleep—triggers the reprocessing and consolidating of daytime information into memory.

Winson thinks the key to unlocking the mystery of REM sleep and dreams lies in a part of the brain called the hippocampus (from the Greek word for sea horse, which it resembles). We have a pair of these six-inch-long structures, one buried on each side of the brain where the cortex buckles inward at the temples, and they are crucial to memory. This discovery was made inadvertently in the early 1950s when a neurosurgeon tried to subdue a patient's intractable epilepsy by slicing out the brain tissue—including the hippocampus—where his seizures ignited. The operation left the patient unable to form new memories. After a moment's absence, he could no longer recognize people he had conversed with for hours.

Around that same time researchers discovered that during certain activities the hippocampus produced a distinctive

REM SLEEP APPEARS LATE IN EVOLUTION. ONLY MAMMALS HAVE IT, AND WITH ONE DOCUMENTED EXCEPTION, EVERY TERRESTRIAL MAMMAL HAS IT.

rhythm, which became known as theta rhythm. The activity, recorded by an electrode and displayed on a paper tracing, showed up as alternating peaks and valleys of voltage, six peaks per second. Rabbits, cats, and rats, it was found, all generated theta rhythm when exploring a strange place. Rabbits also produced it when startled by a predator, and cats when they were stalking prey. The common denominator of these behaviors seemed to be that all were important to the animals' survival.

Then, in 1969, theta rhythm was found during another behavior that these mammals shared: REM sleep.

Back in 1969, Winson hadn't yet embarked on his career in neuroscience. Soon after he'd received his Ph.D. in mathematics from Columbia, his father had become ill, and Winson had taken over the family manufacturing business. But he had long been intrigued by the way the brain processes memory, and this discovery linking theta rhythm to REM sleep sparked an epiphany. "The hippocampus is central to memory," he recalls thinking. "And here's this theta rhythm occurring in the hippocampus during activities that are important for the animals' survival. And now here it is again in REM sleep. I said to myself, Something's got to be going on."

In a mid-life career switch, Winson became a guest investigator in a neuroscience lab at Rockefeller. His studies of rats in the early 1970s demonstrated that theta waves were produced in two regions of the hippocampus. Other researchers found theta waves generated in the entorhinal cortex, a staging area for information entering and leaving the hippocampus.

Winson wondered what would happen if he knocked out the neurons, located in an adjoining part of the brain, that pace the oscillations, thereby silencing the theta rhythm without harming the hippocampus itself. When he did this, he found that rats that had learned to use spatial cues to find a spot in a maze could no longer do so. Without theta rhythm, their spatial memory was obliterated.

Theta rhythm was evidently essential for hippocampal function, which in turn was essential for memory. But how was theta rhythm involved in integrating and utilizing memories? To answer that question, one needs to address a fundamental riddle: How is memory formed? How is a friend's face, an episode of *L.A. Law*, or a calculus formula captured inside our heads?

Most neuroscientists think memories are encoded over a sprawling network of neurons in the brain. According to the going theory, a novel experience creates a pattern of firing in the network. Later, a reminder of that experience, or an attempt to recall it, triggers the same firing pattern. The pattern represents the memory. How is it stored? Neurobiologists believe a physical change at the synapses—the junctions where one neuron communicates with another—is responsible. As neurons fire in a pattern, their synaptic connections become strengthened to conduct the signals more readily, thereby etching the pattern more firmly into the network.

Compelling evidence for such strengthening was first found in 1972. Researchers discovered that if they buzzed a nerve pathway in the hippocampus with a rapid tattoo of electric pulses, neurons in the pathway fired more readily upon subsequent stimulation. The synaptic connections did indeed appear to have been strengthened. This change, called long-term potentiation, or LTP, has become the working model for how memories are stored.

Of course, the LTP observed in 1972 was caused by a prolonged and artificial pattern of electric pulses, quite unlike anything known to occur in the brain. But in 1986 some researchers suggested there might be a natural stimulus for LTP, at least in lower mammals like rats. That natural stimulus, they said, could be theta rhythm. In experiments on the rat hippocampus, electric pulses produced LTP most effectively when they were applied at the theta rate.

What kind of information is etched into memory by theta-rhythm-induced LTP? "In rats," Winson observes, "theta rhythm is perfectly synchronized with whisker movement, sniffing, and the firing of neurons in the olfactory bulb as the animal explores its environment." Could theta waves be the agency through which such sensory information is stored in long-term memory? When Winson's group applied short electric pulses to the hippocampus at the peak of theta rhythm—simulating the way cells normally fire in the hippocampus in response to sensory stimuli—they found that they did indeed induce LTP.

Now the pieces of the puzzle were starting to fit together. As a rat explores its surroundings, theta waves wash over its hippocampus. At the same time, sensory signals from its whiskers and nose burst out in synchrony. These signals coincide with the pulsing of theta waves in the hippocampus and activate LTP, leaving a memory trace. Later, in REM sleep, theta waves turn on again and reactivate those neuronal circuits, allowing the memory trace to be reaccessed and integrated with old memories.

It was a nifty hypothesis. But the evidence was still circumstantial. To help clinch his case, Winson needed to prove that new information actually gets reprocessed during REM sleep. The problem was how to do the experiment. It may take thousands, perhaps even millions, of neurons to represent the memory of a single event, yet an experimenter can monitor only a very few using implanted electrodes. How could Winson be sure that the activity of a neuron corresponded to a specific piece of information?

about four years ago Winson and his then graduate student Constantine Pavlides came up with a solution. Rats have rather unusual neurons in the hippocampus known as place neurons, which encode a rat's brain map of its physical space. When a rat runs around an open maze in a lab, for example, it orients itself by various landmarks in the room—a wall clock, a window—and each place neuron becomes responsive to a

"I'M SAYING THE INFORMATION CHOSEN FOR REPROCESSING IS NOT RANDOM. IN OTHER WORDS, THE CONTENTS OF DREAMS ARE NOT RANDOM."

unique locale. Winson and Pavlides realized they could monitor the processing of spatial information in a rat by recording from just one place neuron. If the waking animal traversed a location that made the place neuron fire, the same neuron should later fire energetically during REM sleep—assuming, of course, that their theory was correct.

As a first step they carried out an exploratory test to map the location on the maze that would excite the neuron they were recording. They placed one of their pillbox-wearing rats at the center of a maze that had eight arms radiating out like the spokes of a wheel. The maze looked like a giant stationary fan upended at the top of a pole, giving the rat a panoramic view of its surroundings. The rat immediately began to explore. It pattered up and down one arm—whiskers twitching, sniffing, observing its environment—then returned to the maze's center and pattered down another arm. Just as it crossed one spot, a barrage of clicks sounding like a toy machine gun broke out from the recording equipment. Moments later, as the rat continued onward, the sound died away. But when the rat doubled back and recrossed the spot, the machine gun noise chattered out again. The electrode had tuned into a place neuron for that spot on the maze.

Pavlides next blocked access to the spot and let the rat wander elsewhere in the maze. The monitor picked up only sporadic signals from the neuron, which was just ticking as the rat went about its business.

Now came the crucial part of the experiment. After a while the rat curled up to snooze. A second probe broadcast theta waves as the animal entered REM sleep. The place neuron stirred and broke out in a burst of signals—over and over again.

Many months and several rats later Winson and Pavlides combed through the data. Winson's eyes twinkle with pleasure as he recalls the outcome. A consistent pattern had emerged. "Each time a rat hit its trigger spot in the maze, the place neuron fired rapidly. Then the

rat moved on to the rest of the maze, and the neuron quieted down. But during REM sleep the place neuron hammered away again, at the rapid rate that's effective for inducing LTP. It was a very compelling result."

The place-neuron experiment provided the first direct evidence that the brain is reprocessing daytime information during sleep. But why does the brain go to the trouble? Why doesn't it just process everything at once while it's awake?

Evolution suggests a reason. REM sleep appears late in evolutionary history. Only mammals have it, and, with one documented exception, every terrestrial mammal has it. The curious exception is the echidna, or spiny anteater. This small Australian animal, which looks like an overfed hedgehog with a beak, is a monotreme, the most primitive kind of mammal—so primitive that it lays eggs, like a reptile. In addition to lacking REM sleep, the echidna is exceptional in one other respect. Its prefrontal cortex is huge, larger relative to the rest of the brain than that of any other mammal, humans included.

The brain of the echidna, Winson explains, has to perform two functions at once. It has to react to any new environmental challenge based on its previous experience, and it has to update that strategy with whatever is new in that experience. So nature provided it with an oversize prefrontal cortex, the part of the brain where, it's believed, survival strategies are devised and stored.

But the echidna's large prefrontal cortex amounted to an evolutionary impasse. Mammalian evolution could not proceed further, because there wasn't enough room in the skull to accommodate more brain tissue. To get past that, higher mammals had to come up with a method of using brain space more efficiently—namely, REM sleep. REM sleep, Winson proposes, lets the brain reprocess information taken in during the day so it can get more done in a limited space. If our brain didn't use this "offline" scheme, our prefrontal cortex would have to be so big we'd need a

wheelbarrow to trundle it around. "Indeed, if nature hadn't hit upon REM sleep," Winson likes to say, "we would never have evolved."

So what does this brain activity imply about dreams, the nocturnal images that flit through our sleeping minds? Freud believed that dreams were driven by unconscious desires. But according to Hobson, dream images are instigated by random signals shooting up from the brain stem to the visual cortex and other parts of the forebrain. The classic flight dream, he speculates, is more likely evoked by an uprolling of the eyeballs during REM sleep than erotic impulses, as Freud would have it. If dreams reflect psychological concerns, that's because the cortex then tries to make sense of this random neuronal activity and its *interpretation* may reveal something about a person's psychological state. It's like interpreting a physiological Rorschach inkblot. We try to read meaning into the inchoate inky smudge, but its shape (like the brain activity of dreams) is random.

Dreams, Hobson concludes, dealing his coup de grace to Freudian theory, are not a covert manifestation of hidden feelings. "No disguise, no censorship," he exclaims. "Trying to interpret the bizarre, incongruous elements in dreams is like attributing symbolic content to the utterings of a person with Alzheimer's disease! You're trying to account psychodynamically for a process that is organic."

"Dreams are not disguised," Winson concurs. On that point both researchers agree. But on the question of their meaning, Winson parts company with Hobson. Winson's experiments in the hippocampus have convinced him that the contents of our dreams *are* significant. "I'm saying the information chosen for reprocessing is not random," he asserts. "In other words, the contents of dreams are not random."

Some dream studies certainly seem to support this idea. In the late 1970s one experiment had student volunteers outfitted with goggles that made the world appear red. With each successive night, .

the students' dreams became systematically more red. Even dreams of events that took place long before they ever wore goggles sometimes took on a red tint, indicating an integration of newer and older information.

Winson also believes that the contents of our dreams can be symbolic. He suspects that dream symbols arise from the associative quality of our memories. This is the quality that enables us to link the form of a rose not only to its perfume, hue, velvet texture, and spiky thorns—information that smites our senses in one moment of time—but also to Valentine's Day and the sayings of Gertrude Stein, information we accrue in scattered episodes. No one yet knows for sure how our brains make such associations. But presumably, since memories are linked in our minds, they must also be physically linked in the neuronal networks in our brains.

Our dreams, Winson thinks, tend to be stated in visual images and scenarios— that is, in symbolic form—because the memory mechanism involved is so ancient, inherited from lower mammals before language evolved. As a result, abstract concepts can only be expressed in images, not represented by words. What's more, he points out, a symbol permits several concepts to be compressed into one image.

So, for example, you might dream that you are late for an exam and running down a long hall, opening one door after another, trying to find the examination room. This is the kind of dream we tend to have when we're worried about meeting a deadline for a report or a delivery date for a shipment. According to Winson's theory, the sleeping brain searches around in its memory networks and lands on an image that expresses several ideas—frustration, fear of failure, desire to succeed, anxiety—in a concise and undisguised manner. But there may be a bizarre component in that dream as well. Perhaps you're wearing a funny outfit as you race down the hall, a child's outfit reminiscent of some other time when you experienced similar feelings. So the precise meaning of any dream, even a classic anxiety dream, can only be gleaned from the context of your life and memory associations.

Winson's view, in other words, doesn't offer a new interpretation of dreams so much as it provides a biological and evolutionary rationale for the phenomenon of dreaming. In a similar spirit, he thinks REM sleep may offer a way to account biologically for the formation of the unconscious. Psychoanalytic studies, for example, indicate that the unconscious mind is shaped in early childhood. Winson notes that our neural circuits are quite plastic in early life, when we must rapidly build our cognitive framework— a core of knowledge that we'll use to integrate subsequent experiences and interpret them for future reference. This

process is most intensive in young children. Two-year-olds spend three hours a night in REM sleep, a third more time than adults do. In children, Winson suspects that much of this time is spent building up coping strategies to get them through life.

"All of this is quite speculative, of course," he says, and deftly changes the subject. "My main interest is to clarify how memory is processed in REM sleep."

Winson's eyes regain their twinkle as he describes the plan of his latest experiment. In his 1978 experiment to gauge the importance of theta rhythm, Winson wiped out the rhythm completely. As a result, rats were deprived of theta both as they explored the maze and during REM sleep. But in 1990, he relates, Robert Vertes, of Florida Atlantic University at Boca Raton, pinpointed a part of the brain stem that drives theta rhythm *exclusively* during REM sleep. And that has enabled Winson and Vertes to design a maze experiment to see what happens to the memory of rats when only those neurons are knocked out.

If Winson is on target, these rats will still experience theta waves when awake and thus have no difficulty exploring a maze. But without theta in REM sleep, the processing of these daytime memories will be impossible. A series of mnemonic tests comparing these animals with control animals will then start to tease out just how this process works. Whatever the outcome, science will come one step closer to knowing whether we are, after all, such stuff as dreams are made on.

Cognitive Processes

Cognitive psychology has grown faster than most other specialties in psychology in the past 20 years in response to new computer technology, as well as the growth of psycholinguistics. Computer technology has prompted an interest in artificial intelligence, the mimicking of human intelligence by machines. Similarly the study of psycholinguistics has prompted the examination of the influence of language on thought and vice versa.

While interest in these two developments has nearly eclipsed interest in more traditional areas of cognition, such as intelligence and creativity, we cannot ignore in this anthology these traditional areas. With regard to intelligence, one persistent problem has been the difficulty of defining just what intelligence is. David Wechsler, author of several of the most popular intelligence tests in current clinical use, defines intelligence as the global capacity of the individual to act purposefully, to think rationally, and to deal effectively with the environment. Other psychologists have proposed more complex definitions. The problem arises when we try to develop tests that validly and reliably measure such concepts. Edward Boring once suggested that we define intelligence as whatever it is that an intelligence test measures!

Psychologists know less about creativity than we do about intelligence. Both constructs, intelligence and creativity, are fairly abstract and difficult to measure. Beyond that, everyone values creativity but few claim to be creative. Psychologists are looking for ways to enhance creativity in the average human being and are on the brink of understanding the process better as well as being able to measure and stimulate it better, too.

In this unit of the book, we will focus on cognitive processes. Some, such as intelligence and creativity, would traditionally be included here; others, such as metacognition, thinking about thinking, could not have appeared even seven years ago because they are so new.

In the first article, "A New Perspective on Cognitive Development in Infancy," we look at a traditional topic, cognitive development. The oldest and perhaps most respected theory of cognitive development is that of Jean Piaget. In this article, Piaget's first proposed stage of cognitive development, the sensorimotor stage, is challenged by author Jean Mandler. Mandler argues that the ability to recognize similarities and differences drives concept development in infancy. The infant's perceptual systems are indeed more active and more complex than we had at first imagined.

In "New Views of Human Intelligence," Marie Winn reviews Howard Gardner's theory of multiple intelligences. Gardner's view challenges the traditional concept of intelligence—that there exists one general form of intelligence. He also challenges the value of traditional IQ tests. According to Gardner, a person could excel at some forms of intelligence but not others. The article reveals that the implications of his theory are being tested in elementary schools and in new approaches to child assessment. Criticisms of his theory focus on the distinctions among abilities, talents, and intelligence.

Gina Kolata, in "Brains at Work," describes how researchers are busy studying metacognition, or thinking about thinking. PET research in which the brain can be scanned as a person thinks suggests that thoughts are extremely localized in the brain. Such research, Kolata reminds the reader, may eventually help computer scientists develop artificial thought in machines. A companion article to this is also included. Sandra Blakeslee writes in "Brain Yields New Clues on Its Organization for Language" that there may not be a specialized center in the brain for language as previously thought. Instead, the brain seems capable of dealing with language in a diversified way.

Scientists are also examining cognitive biases, traps to which we fall prey when we are making decisions and solving problems. Such biases include typicality, availability, and other incorrect heuristics or simple rules of thumb. These biases are difficult to overcome, but they can be overcome to improve our cognitive processes. Cognitive biases are the focus of "Probability Blindness: Neither Rational nor Capricious."

A final article, "Mental Gymnastics" discusses the relationship of cognition to development, especially in the elderly. The author, Gina Kolata, suggests that those who challenge themselves mentally may indeed excel cognitively compared to those elderly who do not.

Looking Ahead: Challenge Questions

What are Jean Piaget's views on cognitive development in infants? Has research upheld him? What do newer data suggest happens in early infancy to promote cognitive development? Which view do you subscribe to, Piaget's or Jean Mandler's?

What are the various types of intelligences described by Howard Gardner? How does his view contrast with that of

traditional psychologists who research intelligence? If Gardner is correct, how must IQ tests change? Can you think of people whom you would call bright by Gardner's definition but not by traditional definitions of intelligence?

Do you ever think about thinking? When you do, why do you do it? What does it mean that thoughts might be highly localized in the brain? What does this suggest about possible damage to various areas of the brain?

What are some of the cognitive traps or biases to which we fall prey? When are we most likely to use each? Do you ever use these biases? Now that you are aware of them, do you think you can change your ways? How?

Should the elderly be mental gymnasts, so to speak? What does the expression "use it or lose it" mean when it comes to cognition? Do you think the "use it" philosophy holds for other age groups besides the elderly?

A New Perspective on Cognitive Development in Infancy

Jean M. Mandler

Jean Mandler received her Ph.D. from Harvard in 1956. She is currently professor of psychology and cognitive science at the University of California, San Diego. Her interests are cognition and cognitive development, with emphasis on the representation of knowledge. She has done research on how our knowledge of stories, events, and scenes is organized and the way in which such organization affects remembering. In recent years her research has concentrated on conceptual development in infancy and early childhood. Preparation of this article was supported by an NSF grant. Address: Department of Cognitive Science D-015, University of California, San Diego, La Jolla, CA 92093.

Over the past decade something of a revolution has been taking place in our understanding of cognitive development during infancy. For many years one theory dominated the field—that of the Swiss psychologist Jean Piaget. Piaget's views on infancy were so widely known and respected that to many psychologists at least one aspect of development seemed certain: human infants go through a protracted period during which they cannot yet think. They can learn to recognize things and to smile at them, to crawl and to manipulate objects, but they do not yet have concepts or ideas. This period, which Piaget called the sensorimotor stage of development, was said to last until one-and-a-half to two years of age. Only near the end of this stage do infants learn how to represent the world in a symbolic, conceptual manner, and thus advance from infancy into early childhood.

Piaget formulated this view of infancy primarily by observing the development of his own three children—few laboratory techniques were available at the time. More recently, experimental methods have been devised to study infants, and a large body of research has been accumulating. Much of the new work suggests that the theory of a sensori-motor stage of development will have to be substantially modified or perhaps even abandoned (Fig. 1). The present article provides a brief overview of Piaget's theory of sensorimotor development, a summary of recent data that are difficult to reconcile with that theory, and an outline of an alternative view of early mental development.

In Piaget's (1951, 1952, 1954) theory, the first stage of development is said to consist of sensorimotor (perceptual and motor) functioning in an

Recent research suggests that infants have the ability to conceptualize much earlier than we thought

organism that has not yet acquired a representational (conceptual) capacity. The only knowledge infants have is what things look and sound like and how to move themselves around and manipulate objects. This kind of sensorimotor knowledge is often termed procedural or implicit knowledge, and is contrasted with explicit, factual (conceptual) knowledge (e.g., Cohen and Squire 1980; Schacter 1987; Mandler 1988). Factual knowledge is the kind of knowledge one can think about or recall; it is usually considered to be symbolic and propositional. Some factual information may be stored in the form of images, but these are also symbolic, in the sense that they are constructed from both propositional and spatial knowledge. Sensorimotor knowledge, on the other hand, is subsymbolic knowledge; it is knowing *how* to recognize something or use a motor skill, but it does not require explicitly knowing *that* something is the case. It is the kind of knowledge we build into robots in order to make them recognize and manipulate objects in their environment, and it is also the kind of knowledge we ascribe to lower organisms, which function quite well without the ability to conceptualize facts. It is the kind of knowledge that tends to remain undisturbed in amnesic patients, even when their memory for facts and their personal past is severely impaired.

In the case of babies, the restriction of functioning to sensorimotor processing implies that they can neither think about absent objects nor recall the past. According to Piaget, they lack the capacity even to form an image of things they have seen before; a fortiori, they have no capacity to imagine what will happen tomorrow. Thus, the absence of a symbolic capacity does not mean just that infants cannot understand language or reason; it means that they cannot remember what they did this morning or imagine their mother if she is not present. It is, in short, a most un-Proustian life, not thought about, only lived (Mandler 1983).

According to Piaget, to be able to think about the world requires first that perceptual-motor schemas of objects and relations among them be formed. Then, symbols must be created to stand for these schemas. Several aspects of Piaget's formulation account for the slow course of both these developments. First, on the basis of his observations Piaget assumed that the sensory modalities are unconnected at birth, each delivering separate types of information. Thus, he thought that one of the major tasks of the first half of the sensorimotor stage is to construct schemas integrating the information from initially disconnected sights, sounds, and touches. Until this integration is

From *American Scientist*, Vol. 78, No. 3, May/June 1990, pp. 236-243. Reprinted by permission of *American Scientist*, journal of Sigma Xi, The Scientific Research Society.

accomplished, stable sensorimotor schemas of three-dimensional, solid, sound-producing, textured objects cannot be formed and hence cannot be thought about.

In addition, babies must learn about the causal interrelatedness of objects and the fact that objects continue to exist when not being perceived. Piaget thought that these notions were among the major accomplishments of the second half of the sensorimotor stage. He suggested that they derive from manual activity—for example, repeated covering and uncovering, poking, pushing, and dropping objects while observ-

represent bottles in their absence.

All the anticipatory behavior that Piaget observed throughout the first 18 months was accounted for in similar terms. Signs of anticipation of future events became more wide-ranging and complex but did not seem to require the use of images or other symbols to represent what was about to happen. Rather, Piaget assumed that an established sensorimotor schema set up a kind of imageless expectation of the next event, followed by recognition when the event took place. He used strict criteria for the presence of imagery—for example, verbal recall of the past

William James described the perceptual world of the infant as a "blooming, buzzing confusion"

ing the results. Handling objects leads to understanding them; it allows the integration of perceptual and motor information that gives objects substantiality, permanence, and unique identities separate from the self. Since motor control over the hands is slow to develop, to the extent that conceptual understanding requires physical interaction with objects, it is necessarily a late development. Much of the first year of life, then, is spent accomplishing the coordination of the various sources of perceptual and motor information required to form the sensorimotor object schemas that will then be available to be conceptualized.

According to Piaget, the development of the symbolic function is itself a protracted process. In addition to constructing sensorimotor schemas of objects and relations, which form the basic content or meaning of what is to be thought about, symbols to refer to these meanings must be formed. Piaget assumed that the latter development has its precursors in the expectancies involved in conditioning. For example, the sight of a bottle can serve as a signal that milk will follow, and babies soon learn to make anticipatory sucking movements. This process, essentially the same as that involved in Pavlovian conditioning, does not imply a symbolic function; there is no indication that the baby can use such signals to

(which implies the ability to represent absent events to oneself) or rapid problem-solving without trial and error. Neither of these can be ascribed merely to running off a practiced sensorimotor schema, but they require instead some representation of information not perceptually present.

Piaget did not observe recall or covert problem-solving until the end of the sensorimotor period. One might think that the fact that infants begin to acquire language during the latter part of the first year would be difficult to reconcile with a lack of symbolic capacity. However, Piaget characterized early words as imitative schemas, no different in kind from other motor schemas displayed in the presence of familiar situations.

Imitation, in fact, plays an important role in this account, because it provides the source of the development of imagery. Piaget assumed that images are not formed merely from looking at or hearing something, but arise only when what is being perceived is also analyzed. The attempt to imitate the actions of others provides the stimulus for such analysis to take place. Although infants begin to imitate early, it was not until near the end of the first year or beyond that Piaget found his children able to imitate novel actions or actions involving parts of their bodies they could not see themselves, such as blinking or sticking out their

Figure 1. According to the Swiss psychologist Jean Piaget, babies like the author's 8-month-old grandson shown here have learned to recognize people, and their smile is a sign of that recognition. However, Piaget believed that babies have not yet learned to think at such an early age and thus cannot recall even the most familiar people in their lives when those people are not present. Recent research suggests that this view may be mistaken and that babies such as this one are already forming concepts about people and things in their environment.

tongues. He took this difficulty as evidence that they could not form an image of something complex or unobserved until detailed analysis of it had taken place; it is presumably during this analysis that imagery is constructed. Piaget's study of imitation suggested that such analysis, and therefore the formation of imagery, was a late development in infancy. To complete the process of symbol formation, then, the anticipatory mechanisms of sensorimotor schemas become speeded up and appear as images of what will occur, thus allowing genuine representation. Finally, by some mechanism left unspecified, these newly created images can be used to represent the world independent of ongoing sensorimotor activity.

All these developments—constructing sensorimotor schemas, establishing a coherent world of objects and events suitable to form the content of ideas, learning to imitate and to form images that can be used to stand for things—are completed in the second half of the second year, and result in the child's at last being able to develop a conceptual system of ideas. Images can now be used to recall the past and to imagine the future, and even perceptually present objects can begin to be interpreted conceptually as well as by means of motor interactions with them. With the onset of thought, an infant is well on the way to becoming fully human.

This theory of the sensorimotor foundations of thought has come under attack from two sources. One is experimental work suggesting that a stable and differentiated perceptual world is established much earlier in infancy than Piaget realized. The other is recent work suggesting that recall and other forms of symbolic activity (presumably mediated by imagery) occur by at least the second half of the first year. I will discuss each of these findings in turn.

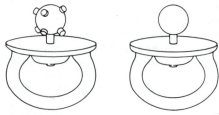

Figure 2. The old idea that the senses are unconnected at birth and are gradually integrated through experience is contradicted by an experiment using bumpy and smooth pacifiers to study the visual recognition of an object that has been experienced only tactilely. A one-month-old infant is habituated to one of the two kinds of pacifiers in its mouth without being allowed to see it. The pacifier is then removed, and the infant is shown both kinds of pacifiers. Infants look longer at the nipple they felt in their mouth. (After Meltzoff and Borton 1979.)

Perceptual development

The notion that the senses are unconnected at birth and that they become integrated only through experience is an old idea that was popularized by William James's (1890) description of the perceptual world of the infant as a "blooming, buzzing confusion." Recent work, however, suggests that either the senses are interrelated at birth or the learning involved in their integration is extremely rapid. There is evidence for integration of auditory and visual information as well as of vision and touch in the first months of life. What follows is a small sample of the research findings.

From birth, infants turn their heads to look at the source of a sound (Wertheimer 1961; Mendelson and Haith 1976). This does not mean that they have any particular expectations of what they will see when they hear a given sound, but it does indicate a mechanism that would enable rapid learning. By four months, if one presents two films of complex events not seen before and accompanied by a single sound track, infants prefer to look at the film that matches the sound (Spelke 1979). Perhaps even more surprising, when infants are presented with two films, each showing only a speaker's face, they will choose the correct film, even when the synchrony between both films and the soundtrack is identical (Kuhl and Meltzoff 1988). In addition, one-month-olds can recognize visually presented objects that they have only felt in their mouths (Fig. 2; Meltzoff and Borton 1979; Walker-Andrews and Gibson 1986). Such data suggest either that the output of each sensory transducer consists in part of the same amodal pattern of information or that some central processing of two similar patterns of information is accomplished. In either case, the data strongly support the view that there is more order and coherence in early perceptual experience than Piaget or James realized.

In addition to sensory coordination, a good deal of information about the nature of objects is provided by the visual system alone, information to which young infants have been shown to be sensitive. For example, it used to be thought that infants have difficulty separating objects from a background, but it ap-

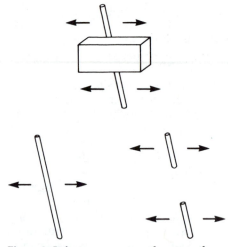

Figure 3. Infants as young as three months can use the perception of relative movement to determine object boundaries. They are habituated to the display shown at the top, which represents a rod moving back and forth behind a block of wood. Then they are tested with the two displays on the bottom: the rod moving as it did before, but with no block in front, or the two pieces of the rod that were visible behind the block, also moving as they did before. Infants tend to continue to habituate to the whole moving rod—that is, they cease to look at it, indicating that it is familiar to them. They prefer to look at the broken rod, indicating that they consider it something new. If the same experiment is done with a stationary rod behind a block, infants exhibit no preference when presented with a whole stationary rod or a broken stationary rod. (After Kellman and Spelke 1983.)

pears that such confusion is a rare event, not the norm. Infants may not "see" that a cup is separable from a saucer without picking it up, but in general they do not have difficulty determining the boundaries of objects. They use information from motion to parse objects from the perceptual surround long before they are able to manipulate them manually. At an age as young as three months, they can use the relative motion of objects against both stationary and moving backgrounds to determine the objects' boundaries (Fig. 3; Kellman and Spelke 1983; Spelke 1988). Even stationary objects are seen as separate if they are spatially separated, whether in a plane or in depth. Infants also use motion to determine object identity, treating an object that moves behind a screen and then reappears as one object rather than two (Spelke and Kestenbaum 1986).

Other work by Spelke and by

Baillargeon (Baillargeon et al. 1985; Baillargeon 1987a; Spelke 1988) shows that infants as young as four months expect objects to be substantial, in the sense that the objects cannot move through other objects nor other objects through them (Fig. 4), and permanent, in the sense that the objects are assumed to continue to exist when hidden. Finally, there is evidence that by six months infants perceive causal relations among moving objects (Leslie 1988) in a fashion that seems to be qualitatively the same as that of adults (Michotte 1963).

From this extensive research program, we can conclude that objects are seen as bounded, unitary, solid, and separate from the background, perhaps from birth but certainly by three to four months of age. Such young infants obviously still have a great deal to learn about objects, but the world must appear both stable and orderly to them, and thus capable of being conceptualized.

Conceptual development

It is easier to study what infants see than what they are thinking about. Nevertheless, there are a few ways to assess whether or not infants are thinking. One way is to look for symbolic activity, such as using a gesture to refer to something else. Piaget (1952) himself called attention to a phenomenon he called motor recognition. For example, he observed his six-month-old daughter make a gesture on catching sight of a familiar toy in a new location. She was accustomed to kicking at the toy in her crib, and when she saw it across the room she made a brief, abbreviated kicking motion. Piaget did not consider this true symbolic activity, because it was a motor movement, not a purely mental act; nevertheless, he suggested that his daughter was referring to, or classifying, the toy by means of her action. In a similar vein, infants whose parents use sign language have been observed to begin to use conventional signs at around six to seven months (Prinz and Prinz 1979; Bonvillian et al. 1983; see Mandler 1988 for discussion).

Another type of evidence of conceptual functioning is recall of absent objects or events. Indeed, Piaget accepted recall as irrefutable evidence

of conceptual representation, since there is no way to account for recreating information that is not perceptually present by means of sensorimotor schemas alone; imagery or other symbolic means of representation must be involved. Typically we associate recall with verbal recreation of the past, and this, as Piaget observed, is not usually found until 18 months or older. But recall need not be verbal—and indeed is usually not when we think about past events—so that in principle it is possible in preverbal infants.

One needs to see a baby do something like find a hidden object after a delay or imitate a previously observed event. Until recently, only diary studies provided evidence of recall in the second half of the first year—for example, finding an object hidden in an unfamiliar location after

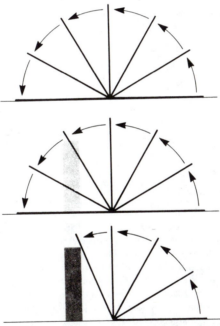

Figure 4. Shown here is a procedure used to demonstrate four- and five-month-olds' memory for the location of a hidden object. At the top is a screen moving through a 180° rotation, to which infants viewing from the right are habituated by repetition. Following habituation, a box is placed behind the screen, and the infants see two test events: an impossible *(middle)* and a possible event *(bottom)*. In the impossible event, the screen continues to rotate 180°, moving "magically" through the hidden box (which the experimenter has surreptitiously removed). In the possible event, the screen rotates only to the point where it would hit the box. The infants' surprise at the impossible event demonstrates that they remember an object they cannot see. (After Baillargeon 1987a.)

a 24-hour delay (Ashmead and Perlmutter 1980). Now, however, similar phenomena are beginning to be demonstrated in the laboratory. Meltzoff (1988) showed that nine-month-olds could imitate actions that they had seen performed 24 hours earlier. Each action consisted of an unusual gesture with a novel object—for example, pushing a recessed button in a box (which produced a beeping sound)—and the infants were limited to watching the experimenter carry it out; thus, when they later imitated the action, they could not be merely running off a practiced motor schema in response to seeing the object again. Control subjects, who had been shown the objects but not the actions performed on them, made the correct responses much less frequently. We have replicated this phenomenon with 11-month-olds (McDonough and Mandler 1989).

Because of the difficulties that young infants have manipulating objects, it is not obvious that this technique can be used with infants younger than about eight months. One suspects, however, that if ninemonth-olds can recall several novel events after a 24-hour delay, somewhat younger infants can probably recall similar events after shorter delays.

There is a small amount of data from a procedure that does not require a motor response and that, although using quite short delays, suggests recall-like processes. Baillargeon's experiments on object permanence, mentioned earlier, use a technique that requires infants to remember that an object is hidden behind a screen. For example, she has shown that infants are surprised when a screen appears to move backward through an object they have just seen hidden behind it (see Fig. 4). In her experiments with four- and five-month-olds, the infants had to remember for only about 8 to 12 seconds that there was an object behind the screen (Baillargeon et al. 1985; Baillargeon 1987a). However, in more recent work with eight-month-olds, Baillargeon and her colleagues have been successful with a delay of 70 seconds (Fig. 5; Baillargeon et al. 1989). This kind of performance seems to require a representational capacity not attributable to sensorimotor schemas. Not only is an absent

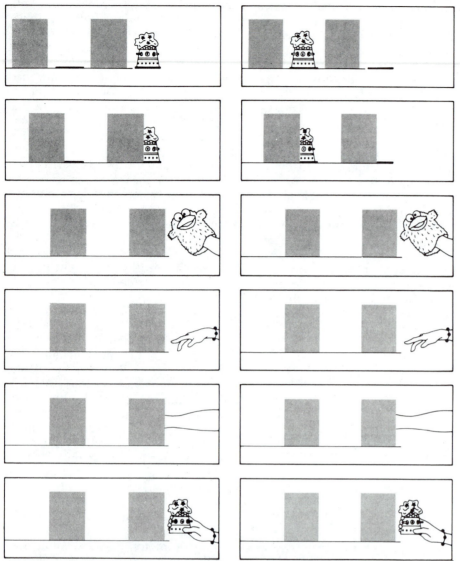

Figure 5. Another procedure involving possible *(left)* and impossible events *(right)* elicits meaningful responses from eight-month-old infants after a delay of 70 seconds. Moving from top to bottom, an object is hidden respectively behind the right or left of two screens; puppets and hand tiptoes are used to keep infants attentive during the delay period; the experimenter reaches behind the right screen and brings the hidden object into view from behind it. (The object was placed there surreptitiously as part of the impossible event.) Surprise at the impossible event indicates memory of the place where the object was hidden. The apparent recall suggests a kind of conceptual functioning that goes beyond the sensorimotor functioning described by Piaget. (After Baillargeon et al. 1989.)

object being represented, but the information is rather precise—for example, Baillargeon (1987b) found that infants remembered not only that an object was hidden but where it was located and how tall it was.

Where do concepts come from?

The data described above indicate that the theory of an exclusively sensorimotor stage of development, in which babies cannot yet represent the world conceptually, is in need of considerable revision. There does not

appear to be a protracted period during which infants have no conception of objects or events and cannot represent them in their absence. A great deal of information is available to and used by infants from an early age, even before they have developed the motor coordination enabling manual exploration that Piaget thought was crucial to conceptual development.

Indeed, a good deal of evidence suggests that we have tended to confuse infants' motor incompetence with conceptual incompetence. Piaget was particularly influenced in his theorizing by the difficulties that

children as old as a year have finding a hidden object, especially when it is hidden in more than one location a number of times in succession. The phenomena he demonstrated have been replicated many times, but it now appears that much of the difficulty infants have in such situations is due not to a lack of understanding of object permanence but to other factors. For example, repeatedly hiding an object in different locations can be confusing and leads to perseverative responding to the same place (see Diamond 1985; Mandler 1988, in press).

If a conceptual system of knowledge has begun to be formed by at least six months and perhaps earlier, where does it come from? Piaget's theory of a transformation of well-developed action schemas into conceptual thought cannot account for conceptual knowledge occurring before the action schemas themselves have developed. On the other hand, perceptual schemas about objects and events develop early. What is needed, then, is some mechanism for transforming these schemas into concepts, or ideas, about what is being perceived, preferably a mechanism that can operate as soon as perceptual schemas are formed.

Little has been written about this problem. One approach is to assume that even young infants are capable of redescribing perceptual information in a conceptual format. I have suggested a mechanism that might accomplish this (Mandler 1988): perceptual analysis, a process by which one perception is actively compared to another and similarities or differences between them are noted. (Such analysis, like other sorts of concept formation, requires some kind of vocabulary; this aspect, still little understood, is discussed below.) The simplest case of perceptual analysis occurs when two simultaneously presented objects are compared, or a single object is compared to an already established representation (i.e., one notes similarities or differences between what one is looking at and what one recalls about it). It is the process by which we discover that sugar bowls have two handles and teacups only one, or that a friend wears glasses. Unless we have engaged in this kind of analysis (or someone has told us), the information will not be accessible for us to think about. Much of the time, of course, we do not make such comparisons, which is why we often can recall few details of even recent experiences.

Although it is analytic, perceptual analysis consists primarily of simplification. Our perceptual system regularly processes vast amounts of information that never become accessible to thought. For example, we make use of a great deal of complex information every time we recognize a face: proportions, contours, subtle shading, relationships among various facial features, and so on. Yet little of this information is available to our thought processes. Few people are aware of the proportions of the human face—it is not something they have ever conceptualized. Even fewer know how they determine whether a face is male or female (this categorization depends on subtle differences in proportions). For the most part we do not even have words to describe the nuances that our perceptual apparatus uses instantly and effortlessly to make such a perceptual categorization.

For us to be able to think about such matters, the information must be reduced and simplified into a conceptual format. One way this redescription is done is via language; someone (perhaps an artist who has already carried out the relevant analytic process) conceptualizes aspects of a face for us. The other way is to look at a face and analyze it ourselves, such as noting that the ears are at the same level as the eyes. The analysis is often couched in linguistic form, but it need not be. Images can be used, but these, in spite of having spatial properties, have a major conceptual component (e.g., Kosslyn 1983).

An infant, of course, does not have the benefit of language, the means by which older people acquire much of their factual knowledge. So if infants are to transform perceptual schemas into thoughts, they must be able to analyze the perceptual information they receive. The perceptual system itself cannot decide that only animate creatures move by themselves or that containers must have bottoms if they are to hold things, and so forth. These are facts visually observed, but they are highly simpli-

fied versions of the information available to be conceptualized.

The notion of perceptual analysis is similar to the process that Piaget theorized as being responsible for the creation of images. He thought that this kind of analysis does not even begin until around eight or nine months and does not result in imagery until later still. However, he had no evidence that image formation is such a late-developing process, and his own description of his children's imitative performance as early as three or four months strongly suggests that the process of perceptual analysis had begun. For example, he observed imitation of clapping hands at that time, a performance that would seem to require a good deal of analysis, considering the difference between what infants see and what they must do. In many places in his account of early imitation, Piaget

noted that the infants watched him carefully, studying both their own and his actions. Other developmental psychologists have commented on the same phenomenon. For example, Werner and Kaplan (1963) noted that infants begin ''contemplating'' objects at between three and five months. Ruff (1986) has documented intense examination of objects at six months (the earliest age she studied).

To investigate contemplation or analysis of objects experimentally is not easy. A possible measure is the number of times an infant looks back and forth between two objects that are presented simultaneously. Janowsky (1985), for example, showed that this measure increased significantly between four and eight months. At four months infants tend to look first at one object and then the other; at eight months they switch back and forth between the two a

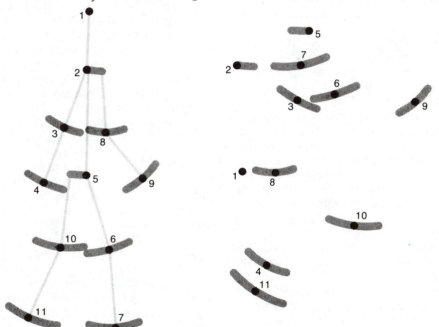

Figure 6. An equally subtle ability is involved in this demonstration of three-month-olds' responses to biological as opposed to nonbiological motion. The infants watch videotapes of computer-generated displays. On the left is a display of 11 point-lights moving as if attached to the head and major joints of a person walking. The motion vectors drawn through each point represent the perceived motions of the display; the lines connecting points, like the numbers and vectors, are not visible to the infants. The display on the right is identical to the normal walker except that the relative locations of the point-lights are scrambled. Correspondingly numbered points in the two displays undergo identical motions. Infants show greater interest in the scrambled display, indicating that they consider it novel. (After Bertenthal et al. 1987.)

good many times. Fox and his colleagues (1979) have reported a similar phenomenon. Interestingly, Janowsky found that the differences in looking back and forth are not associated with differences in total looking time, the rate at which infants habituate to objects (cease to look at them), or accuracy of recognition. So the looking back and forth must serve some other function. I would suggest that it is a comparison process, by which one object is being contrasted with the other.

A vocabulary for concepts

Assuming that perceptual analysis can lead to concept formation, it is still necessary to formulate the vocabulary in which the resulting concepts are couched. But here we face one of the major stumbling blocks in psychological theory: the problem of specifying conceptual primitives (see Smith and Medin 1981). Perhaps because of its difficulty, it has been largely ignored by developmental psychologists, in spite of the fact that any theory of conceptual development must resolve the issue of what the earliest concepts are like, no matter when they may first be formed. Leslie (1988) has offered an analysis of the primitives involved in early causal concepts, and people working on language acquisition have speculated about semantic primitives. For example, Slobin (1985) points out that children must already have concepts of objects and events, as well as relational notions about them, in order for language to be acquired. Since language comprehension begins at around nine to ten months (and perhaps earlier for sign language), some kind of conceptual system must be well established by that time. But we have almost no information as to its character.

Help may come from recent studies by cognitive linguists (e.g., Fauconnier 1985; Johnson 1987; Lakoff 1987). Although the primary goal of these theorists is to understand how language works, their analyses of the root concepts expressed in language may be of use in our search for babies' earliest concepts. For example, Lakoff and Johnson have proposed that image schemas—notions derived from spatial structure, such

as trajectory, up-down, container, part-whole, end-of-path, and link— form the foundation of the conceptualizing capacity. These authors suggest that image schemas are derived from preconceptual perceptual structures, forming the core of many of our concepts of objects and events and of their metaphorical extensions to abstract realms. They demonstrate in great detail how many of our most complex concepts are grounded in such primitive notions. I would characterize image schemas as simplified redescriptions of sensorimotor schemas, noting that they seem to be reasonably within the capacity of infant conceptualization.

The potential usefulness of image schemas as conceptual primitives can be illustrated by the example of the container schema. According to Johnson and Lakoff, the structural elements of this image schema are "interior," "boundary," and "exterior." It has a bodily basis likely to be appreciated by quite young infants, and a perceptual basis that seems to require minimal redescription of the object schemas described earlier. It also has a simple binary logic—either in or not-in; if A is in B and B is in C, then A is in C—that may or may not be the sensorimotor basis of the Boolean logic of classes, as Lakoff suggests, but is certainly a characteristic of concepts as opposed to percepts. (The conceptual system tends to reduce the continuous information delivered by the perceptual system to a small number of discrete values.)

The use of such an image schema might be responsible for the better performance nine-month-old infants show on hiding tasks when a container is used rather than cloths or screens (Freeman et al. 1980). Current work by Baillargeon (pers. com.) suggests that at approximately the same age infants are surprised when containers without bottoms appear to hold things. Of course, these are only fragments of the kind of information needed to document the development of the idea of a container, but

they indicate how we might go about tracking the early establishment of simple concepts.

A more complex concept that may also be acquired relatively early in infancy is that of animacy. Consider some possible sources for such a concept. We know that infants differentiate biological from nonbiological motion as early as three months (Fig. 6; Bertenthal et al. 1987). This perceptual differentiation, although an excellent source of information, does not constitute a concept by itself; it is an accomplishment similar to categorizing male and female faces, which infants have learned to do by six months (Fagan and Singer 1979). As discussed earlier, such perceptual categorization is not accessible for purposes of conceptual thought unless it has been redescribed in conceptual terms. An infant needs to conceptualize some differences between categories of moving objects, such as noting that one type starts up on its own and (sometimes) responds to the infant's signals, whereas the other type does not. An image schema of a notion such as beginning-of-path could be used to redescribe the perceptual information involved in initiation of motion. A link schema (whose elements are two entities and some kind of path between them) could be used to describe the observation of responsivity to self. From such simple foundations might arise a primitive concept of animal, a concept that we have reason to believe is present in some form by at least the end of the first year of life (Golinkoff and Halperin 1983; Mandler and Bauer 1988).

These are some examples of how a conceptual system might emerge from a combination of perceptual input and some relatively simple redescriptions of that input. I have suggested that a mechanism of perceptual analysis could enable such redescription, with the terms of the redescription being derived from spatial structure. The mechanism would not require an extended period of

A good deal of evidence suggests that we have tended to confuse infants' motor incompetence with conceptual incompetence

exclusively sensorimotor functioning but would allow conceptualization of the world to begin early in infancy. The data I have summarized indicate that babies do indeed begin to think earlier than we thought. Therefore, it seems safe to assume that they either are born with or acquire early in life the capacity to form concepts, rather than to assume that conceptual functioning can occur only as an outcome of a lengthy sensorimotor stage.

References

Ashmead, D. H., and M. Perlmutter. 1980. Infant memory in everyday life. In *New Directions for Child Development: Children's Memory*, vol. 10, ed. M. Perlmutter, pp. 1–16. Jossey-Bass.

Baillargeon, R. 1987a. Object permanence in 3.5- and 4.5-month-old infants. *Devel. Psychol.* 23:655–64.

———. 1987b. Young infants' reasoning about the physical and spatial properties of a hidden object. *Cognitive Devel.* 2:179–200.

Baillargeon, R., J. De Vos, and M. Graber. 1989. Location memory in 8-month-old infants in a nonsearch AB task: Further evidence. *Cognitive Devel.* 4:345–67.

Baillargeon, R., E. S. Spelke, and S. Wasserman. 1985. Object permanence in five-month-old infants. *Cognition* 20:191–208.

Bertenthal, B. I., D. R. Proffitt, S. J. Kramer, and N. B. Spetner. 1987. Infants' encoding of kinetic displays varying in relative coherence. *Devel. Psychol.* 23:171–78.

Bonvillian, J. D., M. D. Orlansky, and L. L. Novack. 1983. Developmental milestones: Sign language and motor development. *Child Devel.* 54:1435–45.

Cohen, N. J., and L. R. Squire. 1980. Preserved learning and retention of pattern-analyzing skills in amnesia: Dissociation of knowing how and knowing that. *Science* 210:207–10.

Diamond, A. 1985. The development of the ability to use recall to guide action, as indicated by infants' performance on AB. *Child Devel.* 56:868–83.

Fagan, J. F., III, and L. T. Singer. 1979. The role of simple feature differences in infant recognition of faces. *Infant Behav. Devel.* 2:39–46.

Fauconnier, G. 1985. *Mental Spaces.* MIT Press.

Fox, N., J. Kagan, and S. Weiskopf. 1979. The growth of memory during infancy. *Genetic Psychol. Mono.* 99:91–130.

Freeman, N. H., S. Lloyd, and C. G. Sinha. 1980. Infant search tasks reveal early concepts of containment and canonical usage of objects. *Cognition* 8:243–62.

Golinkoff, R. M., and M. S. Halperin. 1983. The concept of animal: One infant's view. *Infant Behav. Devel.* 6:229–33.

James, W. 1890. *The Principles of Psychology.* Holt.

Janowsky, J. S. 1985. Cognitive development and reorganization after early brain injury. Ph.D. diss., Cornell Univ.

Johnson, M. 1987. *The Body in the Mind: The Bodily Basis of Meaning, Imagination, and Reason.* Univ. of Chicago Press.

Kellman, P. J., and E. S. Spelke. 1983. Perception of partly occluded objects in infancy. *Cognitive Psychol.* 15:483–524.

Kosslyn, S. M. 1983. *Ghosts in the Mind's Machine: Creating and Using Images in the Brain.* Norton.

Kuhl, P. K., and A. N. Meltzoff. 1988. Speech as an intermodal object of perception. In *Perceptual Development in Infancy: The Minnesota Symposia on Child Psychology*, vol. 20, ed. A. Yonas, pp. 235–66. Erlbaum.

Lakoff, G. 1987. *Women, Fire, and Dangerous Things: What Categories Reveal about the Mind.* Univ. of Chicago Press.

Leslie, A. 1988. The necessity of illusion: Perception and thought in infancy. In *Thought without Language*, ed. L. Weiskrantz, pp. 185–210. Clarendon Press.

Mandler, J. M. 1983. Representation. In *Cognitive Development*, ed. J. H. Flavell and E. M. Markman, pp. 420–94. Vol. 3 of *Manual of Child Psychology*, ed. P. Mussen. Wiley.

———. 1988. How to build a baby: On the development of an accessible representational system. *Cognitive Devel.* 3:113–36.

———. In press. Recall of events by preverbal children. In *The Development and Neural Bases of Higher Cognitive Functions*, ed. A. Diamond. New York Academy of Sciences Press.

Mandler, J. M., and P. J. Bauer. 1988. The cradle of categorization: Is the basic level basic? *Cognitive Devel.* 3:247–64.

McDonough, L., and J. M. Mandler. 1989. Immediate and deferred imitation with 11-month-olds: A comparison between familiar and novel actions. Poster presented at meeting of the Society for Research in Child Development, Kansas City.

Meltzoff, A. N. 1988. Infant imitation and memory: Nine-month-olds in immediate and deferred tests. *Child Devel.* 59:217–25.

Meltzoff, A. N., and R. W. Borton. 1979. Intermodal matching by human neonates. *Nature* 282:403–04.

Mendelson, M. J., and M. M. Haith. 1976. The relation between audition and vision in the newborn. *Monographs of the Society for Research in Child Development*, no. 41, serial no. 167.

Michotte, A. 1963. *The Perception of Causality.* Methuen.

Piaget, J. 1951. *Play, Dreams and Imitation in Childhood*, trans. C. Gattegno and F. M. Hodgson. Norton.

———. 1952. *The Origins of Intelligence in Children*, trans. M. Cook. International Universities Press.

———. 1954. *The Construction of Reality in the Child*, trans. M. Cook. Basic Books.

Prinz, P. M., and E. A. Prinz. 1979. Simultaneous acquisition of ASL and spoken English (in a hearing child of a deaf mother and hearing father). Phase I: Early lexical development. *Sign Lang. Stud.* 25:283–96.

Ruff, H. A. 1986. Components of attention during infants' manipulative exploration. *Child Devel.* 57:105–14.

Schacter, D. L. 1987. Implicit memory: History and current status. *J. Exper. Psychol.: Learning, Memory, Cognition* 13:501–18.

Slobin, D. I. 1985. Crosslinguistic evidence for the language-making capacity. In *The Crosslinguistic Study of Language Acquisition*, vol. 2, ed. D. I. Slobin, pp. 1157–1256. Erlbaum.

Smith, E. E., and D. L. Medin. 1981. *Categories and Concepts.* Harvard Univ. Press.

Spelke, E. S. 1979. Perceiving bimodally specified events in infancy. *Devel. Psychol.* 15:626–36.

———. 1988. The origins of physical knowledge. In *Thought without Language*, ed. L. Weiskrantz, pp. 168–84. Clarendon Press.

Spelke, E. S., and R. Kestenbaum. 1986. Les origines du concept d'objet. *Psychologie française* 31:67–72.

Walker-Andrews, A. S., and E. J. Gibson. 1986. What develops in bimodal perception? In *Advances in Infancy Research*, vol. 4, ed. L. P. Lipsitt and C. Rovee-Collier, pp. 171–81. Ablex.

Werner, H., and B. Kaplan. 1963. *Symbol Formation.* Wiley.

Wertheimer, M. 1961. Psychomotor coordination of auditory and visual space at birth. *Science* 134:1692.

New Views of Human Intelligence

A far broader range of important skills and abilities emerges.

Marie Winn

Marie Winn, author of "The Plug-In Drug," writes regularly about child development.

Intelligence—the dark secret of American social science and education—is coming out of the closet. Once intelligence was perceived as a narrow group of mental abilities, those measurable by an I.Q. test. But according to that view great groups of the population turned out to be not very smart or educable. Since these groups were generally composed of poor minorities, nobody liked to talk about intelligence very much—it seemed somehow un-American. In recent years a new definition of intelligence has been gaining acceptance, one which includes a far greater range of mental abilities among the components of human cognition. This conceptual change foreshadows the most far-reaching social and educational consequences.

The idea that intelligence is a single *thing,* a kind of brain power that can be measured by a test the way electric power may be measured by a galvanometer, has informed thinking in the academic and research world for much of this century. Although French psychologist Alfred Binet, creator of the first extensively used intelligence test in 1905, saw intelligence as the exercise of a variety of mental facilities, his disciple Charles Spearman, an English psychologist, added a principle that soon became widely accepted: there is a single factor

common to all these diverse functions. He called this factor "general intelligence" and symbolized it with a lowercase g. All cognitive activity, Spearman proposed, required access to that g factor.

While there was always dispute, sometimes violent disagreement, about whether this factor is basically innate or more or less susceptible to environmental influence, psychologists after Spearman continued to believe in the g factor and worked to create new and better tests to measure it. In 1912 William Stern, a German psychologist, invented the concept of the intelligence quotient, which divided the "mental age" of a person (as discovered through a test) by the chronological age, thereby coming up with a fraction. Four years later, when Stanford University psychologist Lewis Madison Terman came up with an American version of Binet's test that came to be known as the Stanford-Binet—he multiplied the final result by 100, to avoid the fraction—the stage was set for large-scale intelligence testing throughout America.

Yet a curious and strangely neglected fact about I.Q. tests serves to cast doubt on their reliability as a measure of intelligence: while these scores do predict success in school fairly well, there is little correlation between how people score on I.Q. tests and their later success in life. The numbers of people with undistinguished childhood I.Q. scores

who excel in later life, as well as the numbers of certified "geniuses" who come to naught, are legion. Clearly, what the standard I.Q. test measures is but a small part of the complex conglomeration of elements that make up human intelligence, a part that may not have much to do with those cognitive abilities that allow people to function successfully in various walks of life.

Today the g factor concept of intelligence no longer dominates scientific discussion. In its place is a far more pluralistic view. According to John L. Horn, a psychologist at the University of Southern California, "What we see as intelligence, and tend to regard as a whole, is in fact a mosaic of many distinct units." Robert J. Sternberg, a psychologist at Yale, has constructed a "triarchic" theory of human intelligence, which focuses on such areas as common sense and insight. J. P. Guilford, a California psychologist, classified intellectual acts into 120 categories, while one researcher at a recent meeting of psychologists suggested that humans might have 800,000 intellectual abilities.

By far the most intuitively satisfying of the current approaches is Howard Gardner's theory of multiple intelligences, or M.I. theory. Gardner, a psychologist and recipient of a MacArthur Foundation "genius" award, runs a research institution at Har-

Each of Gardner's seven intelligences exists as a discrete entity.

at the University of South Carolina was attended by scholars from across the country. Educational journals regularly feature articles on Gardner's ideas. But the most unexpected testing ground for his theoretical work materialized in the fall of 1985, when eight Indiana school teachers approached Gardner with an audacious plan: to start a public school based on the theory of multiple intelligences.

vard's Graduate School of Education named Project Zero, which is also a fertile testing ground for many of his ideas. Using data from such diverse sources as neurology, anthropology, psychology and pathology, Gardner has come up with seven areas of intellectual competence — intelligences, he calls them — that are relatively independent of one another. A summary of the seven areas, the "end-states" or careers they might lead to and a prominent person proposed by Gardner to exemplify each type of intelligence, follows:

1. Linguistic: sensitivity to the meaning and order of words; poet, translator (T. S. Eliot).

2. Logical-mathematical: the ability to handle chains of reasoning and to recognize patterns and order; mathematician, scientist (Einstein).

3. Musical: sensitivity to pitch, melody, rhythm and tone; composer, singer (Stravinsky).

4. Bodily-kinesthetic: the ability to use the body skillfully and handle objects adroitly; athlete, dancer, surgeon (Martha Graham).

5. Spatial: the ability to perceive the world accurately and to re-create or transform aspects of that world; sculptor, architect, surveyor (Picasso).

6. Interpersonal: the ability to understand people and relationships; politician, salesman, religious leader (Gandhi).

7. Intrapersonal: access to one's emotional life as a means to understand oneself and others; therapist, social worker (Freud).

In his highly regarded book "Frames of Mind" Gardner goes beyond the theoretical by providing physiological evidence that each of the seven intelligences exists as a discrete entity. It is this body of material, based on his own research in neuropsychology at the Boston Veterans Administration Medical Center, that lends the theory its strongest credence.

Gardner provides numerous examples of patients who have lost all language abilities as a result of damage to the speech centers in the left hemisphere of the brain, who nevertheless retain the ability to be musicians, visual artists, even engineers. Most musical abilities appear to be located in the right hemisphere, and thus injuries to the right frontal and temporal lobes cause difficulties in distinguishing tones. He points out that lesions in certain areas of the left hemisphere dramatically affect logical and mathematical abilities.

To buttress his claim for a separate bodily-kinesthetic intelligence, Gardner describes patients whose linguistic and logical capacities have been devastated, but who show little or no difficulty in carrying out complicated motor activities. He cites numerous case histories of patients with right hemisphere injuries who have difficulties with spatial representation and other visual tasks; meanwhile, their linguistic abilities remain intact.

Even for the elusive personal intelligences, there is supporting neurological data. While a lobotomy causes little damage to those intellectual abilities measured on an I.Q. test, the ruinous impact of this surgical procedure on various aspects of the personality is well known.

"I started out thinking that intelligence would break down according to the senses — visual, auditory and so on," Gardner said in a recent interview, "but my study convinced me it didn't work that way. My methodological principle is to look at the mind through a lot of lenses — development, breakdown, cross-cultural material, evolutionary data. And these different lenses all support the existence of multiple intelligences."

Since the publication of "Frames of Mind" in 1983, Gardner's theory has attracted extraordinary attention from both the academic world and the education establishment. A symposium on M.I. theory held last year

ON SEPTEMBER 8, 1987, 150 students arrived at a nondescript building in downtown Indianapolis to take part in a unique educational experiment: a school devised to develop the wide gamut of intelligences identified in Gardner's M.I. theory. What made this theory so attractive to the eight founding teachers was Gardner's belief that while everyone is born with certain strengths and weaknesses in each of the cognitive areas, all people are capable of developing greater proficiency in *all* of them.

The Key School, as it was named, covers a rigorous curriculum devoted to the three R's. This is required by Indiana law, which also mandates periodic standardized testing of all students in these subjects. In a traditional school, that would pretty much sum it up. But at the Key School the daily schedule of every child also includes music, art and physical education — four times the exposure children usually get to these subjects. And every day there is instruction in Spanish and computers. (Federal "magnet" funds have allowed the school to hire eight additional teachers.) A detailed report card evaluates each child in the seven intelligences and provides a far more precise profile of his or her abilities than a conventional report card.

In Room 25 one day last winter, 22 highly concentrated little violinists are eagerly honing their musical intelligence to the tune (or somewhere vaguely near it) of "Frosty the Snowman." In Room 15 teacher Beverly Hoeltke is on the floor, surrounded by a noisy but disciplined group of first, second and third graders exercising their logical-mathematical intelligence. By moving small blocks into circles of varying sizes they are discovering the deeper connections between addition and multiplication: four plus four ends up with the same result as four times two.

A narrow idea of intelligence misleads some children into thinking they are stupid.

In Room 17 Carol Forbes is demonstrating the difference between a small triangle and a large circle — in Spanish — a lesson that combines exercise in both the linguistic and spatial intelligences. In the gym a noisy bunch of kids are playing backboard dodgeball, little realizing, as they gleefully try to bean one another with a large ball, that they are developing their bodily-kinesthetic intelligence.

Intelligences run amok in Room 10, where a two-month-long schoolwide effort has produced a spectacular re-creation of a tropical rain forest. Wildly colorful papier-mâché birds of paradise, parrots and butterflies stare down from the forest canopy at pumas and various primates, which in turn gaze down upon the exotic denizens of the forest floor.

In addition to this splendid manifestation of spatial intelligence, there are charts, graphs and carefully researched reports pinned to the wall giving information on creatures as diverse as tuataras, golden eagles and toucans, demonstrating that the linguistic and logical-mathematical intelligences have not been neglected. The cooperative nature of the project attests to the involvement of the two personal intelligences. Meanwhile, a high level of musical intelligence is revealed in the taped background music, a composition called "Train in the Tropical Forest" written and performed by three upper-graders. It is a remarkable work, filled with unconventional sound effects reminiscent of the composer George Crumb.

It is hard to remember that this is not a special school for gifted children, but one whose racially and ethnically diverse population is chosen entirely by lottery, with more than a third of the students qualifying for free or reduced-price school lunch.

In its third year of operation, the Key School shows every sign of being a runaway success. Scores on standardized tests show that the two intelligences most valued in our educational system are thriving. Only five children in the entire school failed to reach the acceptable level mandated by the school district. Principal Patricia Bolaños also reports: "The test scores reveal that we are diminishing the gap between the achievement levels of our black students and our white students, and it certainly is not because the achievement levels of the white students are diminishing."

Parental enthusiasm, always a litmus test of a school's well-being, is high. "I can't say enough good things about the Key School," says Marilyn Altom, mother of Crystal, who graduated last year, and Alexandra, a second grader. Art teacher Kathy Ann Calwell says: "Crystal Altom was a child who definitely could have been lost in the cracks. She wasn't good in spelling or math or any of the academic areas. But she just flowered, right before our eyes. And in the process of growing confident about her art and music and theater, the other areas got stronger."

IN RECENT YEARS HOWARD Gardner's attention has moved from establishing the multiple intelligences to the more practical area of testing. With David Henry Feldman, a psychologist at Tufts University, he is involved in Project Spectrum, an assessment program that measures a far greater range of abilities than I.Q. tests do. Indeed, it has been designed to touch on all of the seven intelligences. Spectrum evaluates a child's skills over a period of time in the familiar environment of the classroom, and gives a written report on his or her strengths and weaknesses. It is already in use at the Healey School in Somerville, Mass.

The Educational Testing Service, the very institution that administers some of the nation's most widely used standardized tests, has begun to acknowledge the need for change. Drew H. Gitomer, a research scientist at E.T.S., says: "There's a growing recognition that the traditional assessments don't accomplish all that can be done and in certain ways work against educational objectives." E.T.S. is collaborating with Gardner on another alternative assessment program, Arts Propel, which is developing new ways to evaluate children's work in the arts in a number of Pittsburgh public schools.

As the education establishment faces the need for reform, Gardner's ideas are frequently cited. The Education Commission of the States, which serves as a policy resource for the nation's governors, finds his work a promising model. Rexford Brown, the commission's director of communications, says: "Gardner's work has been important in attacking the monolithic notion of intelligence that has undergirded much of our thinking. We are beginning to see that education is not meant merely to sort out a few children and make them leaders, but to develop the latent talents of the entire population in diverse ways."

Gardner's ideas are not without their critics. Sandra Scarr, a professor of psychology at the University of Virginia, looks on M.I. theory as an example of "faulty optimism that leads to dead ends in both theory and practice." She calls it a "lumper theory in which everything good in human behavior is called intelligence."

Robert Sternberg of Yale observes that a person deficient in some of Gardner's cognitive areas, musical intelligence, for example, is not thereby mentally impaired in the way a person lacking in verbal or reasoning skills would be. Sternberg describes Gardner's theory as "a theory of talents, not one of intelligences." He explains: "An ability is a component of intelligence when we cannot get along without it, and a talent when we are not noticeably handicapped by its absence."

Nor is everyone in the education establishment sanguine about Gardner's influence. Chester E. Finn, chairman of the board of governors of the National Assessment of Educational Progress, a Federal testing program, sees this influence as both "good and bad." "The good part," he says, "is the perception that people who aren't very good at one thing can be very good at another and that there are multiple ways of evaluating performance of any given task.

"But his ideas can be turned to ill effect," he continues. "You hear people saying it's all right if kids don't get the right answer as long as they're creative in their approach. But is that good? I firmly believe that every young American ought to have some idea of who Thomas Jefferson and Abraham Lincoln are, and I don't care whether their greatest strength is playing the ukelele or skating backward on the ice."

In his latest book, "To Open Minds," Howard Gardner defends himself against such critics, and expresses a respect for tradition and basic skill development together with the encouragement of creativity in the classroom. As he concluded an interview in his office at Project Zero, he emphasized the value of a more humanistic view of intelligence. "I believe that as long as we have a narrow definition of intelligence — a very scholastic definition — most kids are going to think they're stupid, and they're going to miss the fact that they may have a lot of abilities that could be important vocationally and avocationally. Enlarging the concept of intelligence, and realizing that people may not have the school intelligence but may have other equally important ones — I think that would be an enormously valuable thing to happen."

Gardner pauses and then adds with a smile, "M.I. theory is not the last word. I'm trying to shake things up and pluralize things a bit. To think that there *is* a last word is what's wrong with most intelligence theorists."

Brains at Work

Scientists ponder biochemistry of thought in action

Gina Kolata

The question itself seems audacious: Can the human brain understand what goes on inside itself? Can people, by thinking about thinking, discover what happens when they think? Although all—or even most—of the answers are not in, some researchers believe they are on their way to understanding thought.

The theory of thinking "is a very big area now," said Dr. J. Allan Hobson, a Harvard University psychiatrist who studies brain changes when people dream. "We have to regard it as mainly promising, but the methods are there." Others agree. Dr. Mark Raichle, a neurologist at Washington University in St. Louis, said that recent work with brain imaging "has been more revealing than I ever would have imagined."

Neurologists are exploiting techniques for watching the brain in action to see what parts of it are used when people ponder different sorts of questions. And computer scientists are asking if they can apply hypotheses about human thought to make a machine that thinks.

The neurology research uses relatively new techniques like positron emission tomography, or PET, scans that let scientists see the brain at work. Before that, they could only look at dead brain tissue obtained at autopsy, or at brain structures, seen through computerized tomography, or CT scans, which produce X-ray pictures of living brains.

The PET scan work started several years ago, but because it is slow and difficult, involving thinking tests and scans of multitudes of people, the most intriguing results are only now being published. PET scans use small doses of radioactive glucose, injected intravenously, to indicate on a monitor where blood flows in the brain. When a small area of the brain is unusually active, that area becomes engorged with blood, and that engorgement registers on the monitor. PET scans, Dr. Raichle said, "tell us about the chemistry and pharmacology of the brain in ways we'd never thought of."

Dr. Michael Posner, a researcher at the University of Oregon, said he was struck by the way PET scans showed that very distinct small areas of the brain are turned on when people think. That means rather than being a diffuse process, involving scattered cells throughout the brain, thinking is more concentrated. That means it may be amenable to biochemical analysis. "It's turned out, at least so far, that there is a dramatic localization," Dr. Posner said. "A lot of people hoped that that would happen, but I don't think anyone really expected it."

Dr. Raichle and his colleagues began studying thinking by using the PET-scan technique to see what happens in the brain when people are given words or nonsense strings of letters to read, like tweal or cade, that look like English words but are not. They went on to more complex PET-scan experiments, studying, for example, what happens in the brain when people are asked to quickly find a verb that goes with a noun. They may be given the noun "hammer," for example. Many people will respond with the verb "pound." As people are given more nouns, they become faster at finding verbs to associate with them.

This association task uses parts of the brain that the investigators found, in their initial work, also come into play when people tried to recognize words—a portion on the top along the left side and an area along the mid-line of the brain, where the two lobes come together. But, to their surprise, it also involved a part of the right side of the cerebellum, a part of the brain that was thought to be used only to control movements.

Dr. Raichle and his colleagues recently found a lawyer in his 50's who had a stroke involving that exact part of the cerebellum. Though the lawyer has returned to work and appears to be functioning normally, he cannot learn the noun-verb association task, the researchers found; he never gets faster at finding verbs, no matter how much he practices. "In the context of his daily life, he's fine," Dr. Raichle said. "But if he tried to learn something entirely new, he might have a problem."

Asked whether different people might think in different ways or whether a person who is taught new and better thinking methods might have new areas of their brains start to light up in PET scans, Dr. Raichle said that he and others were still at the very beginning of the PET scan studies, and were not yet able to answer the questions. "These are the sorts of things that you talk about when you put your feet up Friday afternoon when the week is over," he said. "Sure, we think about them, but at the moment, we are only thinking about them."

While scientists like Dr. Raichle

probe the human brain in action, computer scientists are trying to understand thought by looking at hypotheses about how people might think and then testing those hypotheses by building computers that, they hope, will mimic human reasoning.

Dr. Herbert Simon of Carnegie-Mellon University in Pittsburgh, for example, said that the focus of his work for the past few decades had been to make a computer think like a person. "I am directly concerned with finding out how humans think," he said. He explained that he had purposely limited what he let his machines do, holding the computer back from the sorts of procedures that would be impossible for the human mind. For example, he said, "I don't allow computers to look at a million things because people can't look at a million things."

Dr. Simon, who, with his colleagues, has been studying how people make discoveries, said he viewed the human mind as "a big, indexed encyclopedia." An expert, like a scientist who discovers a new law of nature, "responds to cues that a novice wouldn't notice," Dr. Simon said.

He and his colleagues have put into a computer data of the sort Johann Kepler would have known in the 16th century when he developed his laws of planetary motion. The computer looks for regularities in the data and comes up with Kepler's law, Dr. Simon said. Using the same computer program, Dr. Simon can also have the machine "discover" Ohm's law of electricity or any of 30 or 40 other such scientific principles.

"To those who would say there is something special about creativity, I would say, 'Look at the evidence,' " Dr. Simon said. Thinking and making new discoveries "is a matter of having good reasoning processes, having the right encyclopedic knowledge, having the right motivations and living at the right time."

Dr. Marvin Minsky, an artificial-intelligence expert at the Massachusetts Institute of Technology, sees the human mind not so much as an encyclopedia as a "kludge," a computer term for a machine that is clumsy or patched together. Different functions are performed by different parts of the brain linked in an illogical network of connections, he said. Scientists who use the encyclopedia model have not been able to endow computers with some of the very simplest human thinking skills, he added.

Researchers who tried to build thinking machines "are not doing very well at making common-sense machines that do the sorts of things ordinary people do," Dr. Minsky said. He noted, for example, that computers still cannot "understand ordinary language or look around a room and identify the objects visually." And, he said, "there's no machine that can look around and see where the chairs are and where the people are."

But even Dr. Minsky thinks it is possible for people to understand how the mind thinks. He adds, however, that it probably is a good thing we don't know yet because society isn't ready for it. Dr. Minsky predicted, however, that over the next century or two, human societies will learn to live with thinking machines as, at the same time, scientists learn how people think and build machines to do the most routine thinking for them.

Brain Yields New Clues On Its Organization For Language

Better ways of mapping the brain have prompted new ideas about the nature of thought.

Sandra Blakeslee

Christopher, 29 years old, cannot draw simple figures, add 2 and 2 or tie his shoes. Yet he speaks 16 languages, half of them fluently.

Adam, 28, is a stroke patient. He can name man-made objects like saws, screwdrivers and shovels, but the stroke has left him unable to name most animate objects. The curious result is that ducks, foxes, camels and zebras are indistinguishable to him.

Carla, 22, grew up speaking both her native Italian and English. When she began training to become a simultaneous translator, her language ability was localized on the left side of her brain. but after the training, English shifted to her right brain while Italian remained on the left.

Study of special individuals like these, together with sophisticated new instruments like PET scanners, have afforded a startling new insight into how the brain is organized to handle language. Neurophysiologists are beginning to suspect that there is not a single center for language, but rather that the brain distributes language processing over some or many areas. The finding has prompted new ideas about how the brain thinks, including a provocative theory that proposes the brain has "language convergence zones" in which it brings together the separately located attributes of a word or concept.

"The time is ripe for an attack on the neural basis of consciousness" and language, says Dr. Francis Crick, the famous molecular biologist turned neuroscientist. Attempts to infer the nature of language through psychological experiments will never suffice, says Dr. Crick, who works at the Salk Institute in La Jolla. The problem can only be solved by explanations at the neural level.

Among the most interesting new findings about the brain and language are the following:

- Language is not located where people previously thought it was. Rather, each individual has a unique brain pattern underlying his or her language ability.
- Like the Cray computer, a person's first language is tightly organized in terms of nerve cell circuits. Second languages are more loosely organized in the brain, which is why it often takes longer to find words in them. But a stroke in one part of the brain can knock out a native language and leave later learned languages intact—or vice versa.
- Different aspects of language, such as proper nouns, common nouns and irregular or regular verbs, are processed in different areas of the brain. But these areas do not send their signals to a common destination for integration, as if language appeared on a cinemascope screen in the brain. Rather, language and perhaps all cognition are governed by some as-yet undiscovered mechanisms that binds different brain areas together in time, not place.

The most direct insights into the brain's organization for language come from neurosurgeons who take the opportunity to record nervous activity in patients' brains during operations. By mapping the location of nerve cells that produce language, the neurosurgeons are revolutionizing established notions of how language is organized in the brain.

The traditional view holds that spoken and written language are processed in two structures, Broca's and Wernicke's areas, found on the left side of the brain. The right side of the brain was believed to handle spatial tasks and not to be involved in language.

But the brain's language areas are not so neatly compartmentalized, said Dr. George Ojemann, a neurosurgeon at the University of Washington in Seattle who is a leading brain mapper. While it is true that most people have essential language areas on the left side of their brains, he said, some people have them on the right side and others on both sides.

Even more surprising, Dr. Ojemann said, is that each person appears to have a unique pattern of organization for language ability—as unique as facial features or fingerprints. Broca's and Wernicke's areas are indeed important language processing regions in most people, he said, but many additional language areas are found elsewhere in the brain. Two left-brain regions called the temporal and parietal lobes of the left brain are particularly rich in multiple-language areas, he said.

Each essential language area is composed of a sharply defined patch of nerve cells, each about the size of a grape, Dr. Ojemann noted. The cells in each patch appear to be connected to many others located in distant parts of the brain. Different patches govern language functions such as reading, identifying the meaning of words, recalling verbs and processing the words and grammars of foreign languages, he said.

Dr. Ojemann maps language areas in the brains of conscious individuals whose skulls have been opened prior to surgery. In one technique he maps the language-associated area by sticking electrodes into nerve cells on the exposed surface of the brain. In another, he inserts electrodes at random into cells deep within the brain so as to identify the distant nerve cells, or neurons, involved in naming objects.

After probing hundreds of brains, Dr.

Ojemann has found that essential areas for naming things in one's native language are more compactly organized than those for later learned languages. Second languages tend to be diffusely organized, he said, as if neurons devoted to the new language were competing for space in existing essential areas. But when people are gifted bilinguals, Dr. Ojemann said, the brain develops separate, tightly organized essential areas for naming in each language. The same must be true for all language-essential areas, he said.

Brain mapping also shows sex differences in language ability, Dr. Ojemann said. Men tend to have larger essential areas in the parietal lobes, as do women with lower verbal I.Q.'s, he said. Men and women with high verbal I.Q.s tend to have naming sites in an area called the middle temporal gyrus. Dr. Ojemann's research is described in the August issue of the Journal of Neuroscience.

How We Learn
The First 2 Years Are Explosive

The process of learning a language undoubtedly shapes the formation of the essential areas, said Dr. Elizabeth Bates, a professor of psycholinguistics and an expert in child language acquisition at the University of California in San Diego. From birth to age two, she said, the child's brain undergoes an explosive growth of synaptic connections and is primed to learn the sounds and grammar of any language. After the age of 2, she said, language synapses that do not receive inputs from early vocalizations begin to be eliminated or suppressed—a process that continues until about age 15.

Thus Japanese newborns can distinguish the sounds "ra" and "la" but by 2 have begun to lose that ability, Dr. Bates said. Most young children can learn two or more languages without an accent, she said, but most people lose that ability by young adulthood.

Nevertheless, the adult brain can undergo dramatic changes associated with languages, according to Dr. Franco Fabro, a researcher at the University of Trieste in Trieste, Italy. Several years ago Dr. Fabro conducted a study of simultaneous translators, including a young woman named Carla. At the beginning of Carla's training, he said, English and Italian were strongly lateralized in her left brain, as judged by advanced electrical imaging techniques. But after training, the English appears to have shifted to the right side of her brain, he said, perhaps to avoid competing for essential language areas on the left, and Carla was able to shift instantly from language to language.

Dr. Ursula Bellugi of the Salk Institute and Dr. Edward Klima of the University of California at San Diego have studied the rich but silent languages of deaf people. Since these are based on hand movements in three-dimensional space and since the right brain is specialized for tasks involving spatial relationships, Dr. Bellugi wondered if sign language would prove to be localized in the right hemisphere. From deaf people who had suffered strokes, she found that it was lesions to the left brain that impaired the ability to sign. The left brain is strongly predisposed for language, Dr. Bellugi concluded.

Given these biological properties of language, is there a newly evolved organ that gives humans the power to generate language, as M.I.T. linguist Noam Chomsky and his followers say, or, does language ability stem from the general properties of the brain, and hence is widely distributed? An intense debate is under way.

One of the most fascinating pieces of evidence that bear on the debate is the case of Christopher, an idiot savant whose remarkable linguistic abilities support the idea of language as a separate organ. Christopher is socially inept, avoids eye contact and has a nonverbal I.Q. of 65, said Dr. Neil Smith, a linguist at University College London in England. Christopher cannot draw simple figures, carry on a very long conversation nor care for himself in the everyday world. Yet he has learned 16 languages and is a gifted translator.

Dr. Smith recently tested Christopher's grammatical knowledge of foreign languages and found him on a par with gifted polyglots. When Christopher met a speaker of Berber, a new language for him, he asked if the script could be written in Tifanagh, said Dr. Smith. It is a medieval script used by Berber women for writing love poetry.

But further tests reveal that Christopher's language abilities are independent of his cognitive abilities, Dr. Smith said. He never mulls over the meaning of passages and is not able to think about what he translates, he said.

Christopher's case suggests that language is processed in a separate brain organ that can remain intact in a damaged brain, said Dr. Vicky Fromkin, a Chomskyite linguist at U.C.L.A. Conversely, when the language organ is damaged by stroke or other injury, she said, certain aspects of language are permanently lost—as when English speakers with Broca's aphasia lose the ability to use articles of speech: connectives and so-called function words as opposed to nouns and verbs.

Dissenting from the Chomskyite view are scientists who have found that computer networks with randomly assembled connections can learn to categorize words grammatically and produce correct English sentences. The computers even make "speaking" errors just as people do, said Dr. Bates. The finding suggests that a specialized computer or organ is not necessary for learning a language, she said, because a computer with no special structure can be taught.

Also, cross-cultural studies of the loss of language ability suggest that language and grammar are distributed widely across the brain, said Dr. Bates. The same Broca's area lesion that leads English speakers to leave out articles 70 percent of the time, she said, will cause Italian speakers to omit articles 25 percent of the time and German speakers to omit articles 5 percent of the time; in each language articles have different functions.

"This is because articles in English do not carry much meaning," Dr. Bates said, "whereas in Italian they carry information about number and gender and in German the article carries the case, telling you who did what to whom." A German speaker with the identical lesion will struggle to find the article because it is so important, she said, suggesting that knowledge of the language is not gone.

An Explanation
Think About a Styrofoam Cup

Actually, both sides are correct, said Dr. Antonio Damasio, a neurologist at the University of Iowa. With his wife, Dr. Hannah Damasio, he has developed a theory of cognition and language that is receiving rave reviews from linguists and neuroscientists, including Dr. Bates and Dr. Fromkin, who say they rarely agree on anything.

The brain has special areas for processing language very much along the lines of Dr. Ojemann's essential areas, Dr. Damasio said, but these areas do not constitute an independent language organ with little boxes where nouns, verbs and other language features are processed.

Rather, the essential areas can be thought of as "convergence zones" where the key to the combination of components of words and objects is stored. Thus knowledge of words and concepts is distributed widely throughout the brain but needs a third-party mediator—the convergence zone—to bring the knowledge together, during reactivation.

An example helps explain this difficult concept, Dr. Damasio said. "When I ask you to think about a styrofoam cup," he said, "you do not go into a filing cabinet in your brain and come up with a ready-made picture of a cup. Instead, you compose an internal image of a cup drawn from its features. The cup is part of a cone, white, crushable, three inches high and can be manipulated.

"In reactivating the concept of this cup," Dr. Damasio said, "you draw on distant clusters of neurons that separately store knowledge of cones, the color white, crushable objects and manipulated objects. Those clusters are activated simultaneously by feedback firing from a convergence zone. You can attend to the revival of those components in your mind's eye and from an internal image of the whole object."

The same process is true of words, Dr. Damasio said. "When I ask you to tell me what the object is, you do not go into a filing cabinet where the word 'cup' is stored," he said. "Rather, you use a convergence zone for the word 'cup' by activating distant clusters of neurons that store the phonemes 'c' and 'u' and 'p.' You can perceive their momentary revival in your mind's ear or allow them to activate the motor system and vocalize the word 'cup.' "

To read, speak or make other lexical operations about a styrofoam cup, the brain requires a third-party convergence zone that mediates between word and concept convergence zones, the scientist said. "Only then can we operate linguistically and evoke the word from the concept or vice versa," Dr. Damasio said.

Convergence zones are probably established in early childhood during language learning and as memories are formed, Dr. Damasio said. New ones are formed and old ones can be rearranged throughout life.

The convergence zone concept explains the odd language disabilities of his stroke patient Adam, Dr. Damasio noted. When shown a picture of a dog, Adam can say it is man's best friend, has four legs and barks—but he cannot summon the name for dog, Dr. Damasio said. Nor can he distinguish one animal from another by its name. But Adam can name different man-made tools with ease. The explanation: language convergence zones for natural objects are significantly damaged but zones for man-made objects are largely intact.

Recent studies using a powerful brain imaging technique called PET, positron emission tomography, support the idea of convergence zones, said Dr. Steven Petersen of Washington University in St. Louis. Some brain lesions, locatable with PET images, prevent people from reading while other language abilities remain intact, he said. Thus a person can speak the word cup, read the letters 'c' and 'u' and 'p,' trace the word cup and if the word is dictated, he or she can write it, Dr. Petersen said. But a little while later, they cannot read it, he said, even in their own handwriting. The area damaged is a zone for higher order processing of visual word-like forms, he said, possibly a convergence zone for reading.

One critical question about convergence zones remains unanswered. What makes populations of widely distributed neurons activate simultaneously? Dr. Damasio says he believes that the system mechanism is the feedback firing from a convergence zone, but the microscopic nature of the mechanism is a mystery. Many leading scientists, including Dr. Crick, think that the brain creates unified circuits by oscillating distant components at a shared frequency.

Probability Blindness

Neither Rational nor Capricious

Massimo Piattelli-Palmarini

Massimo Piattelli-Palmarini is a principal research scientist at the Center for Cognitive Science at MIT, as well as chairman and organizer of the annual conference of the Cognitive Science Society. He is a contributor to the Times Literary Supplement *and a science columnist for the Italian daily* Il Corriere della Sera.

The city of St. Louis, Missouri enjoys the uncontested privilege of possessing the single largest man-made optical illusion ever built. In fact, strange as it may seem, the celebrated arch is exactly as wide as it is tall. After measuring its picture carefully, we can possibly bring ourselves to believe it, but we still cannot force our *eye* to do the same. We persist in seeing the St. Louis arch distinctly taller than it is wide. Optical illusions are like that: the eye sees what it sees even when the mind knows what it knows. That's just the way we are built.

It should come as no great surprise that phenomena strictly analogous to optical illusions may also happen in the higher chambers of our mind. In fact, several such phenomena have been recently discovered, and they have been rightly labeled "cognitive illusions." Unbeknownst to us, but in ways that have been firmly charted by psychologists over the last fifteen years or so, we fall into all sorts of cognitive traps at almost every moment of our lives. Just as our eye often rebels at corrections from the superior mental tutors, so certain special corners of our thought are relatively impenetrable to the lessons of logic, or arithmetic, or (most of all) to the objective laws of probability. This happens even when these laws and principles are present in another corner of our mind. Two giants in the study of cognitive illusions, Amos Tversky at Stanford and Daniel Kahneman at Berkeley, have beautifully summarized this state of affairs by stating that these intriguing (and, as we will see, rather scary) mental processes are "neither rational, nor capricious."

It is surely not "rational" to continue to perceive the arch as higher than it is wide, once we *know* for sure that it is not. On the other hand, nobody, absolutely nobody, sees the arch as wider than it is tall. The optical illusion always goes in one direction only. It is, indeed, neither rational nor capricious. Just like human nature, of which these illusions, both optical and cognitive, are the inevitable legacy.

Mental Models

Cognitive illusions and cognitive "biases" have been carefully described in a vast and fast-growing body of literature, regularly spanning some 500 professional journals, ranging from psychology to economics, from philosophy to business administration (not counting some early classified reports circulated within the top echelons of the intelligence agencies). A particularly rich field of inquiry is constitut-ed by illusions and biases in the domain of probabilities and by faulty inferences based on statistical data, as the side bars illustrate (see Sidebar A). In modern societies this is the area where they do the most harm. Yet our cognitive biases are vastly more pervasive than that.

Let us start from a well-studied classic domain called syllogistic reasoning, because it will lead us straight into the very heart of the science of all sciences, of the method of all methods. I mean, of course, the lofty realm of pure logic.

Nobody, not even young children, will fail to conclude, and conclude correctly, that from

> *All Ruritanians are rich,*
> and
> *John is a Ruritanian,*
> it follows that
> *John is rich.*

Slightly less intuitive, but still on the easy side, is the following little piece of reasoning (the conclusion is drawn below the solid line, below the two "premises," as logicians have taught us):

> *No sailor is a hunter.*
> *All Ruritanians are sailors.*
> _____
> *No Ruritanian is a hunter.*

But now ask your best and brightest friends what conclusion is to be drawn from the following two premises:

> *All bankers are athletes.*
> *No stationer is a banker.*
> _____
> *? (What follows from the above?)*

Well, since I suggested that you ask your best and *brightest* friends, I am not expecting any of them to come out with the silly answers *No stationer is an athlete* or *No athlete is a stationer.* Even if they do, they will spontaneously bite their lips and recant a few moments later. The interesting result here is that the best and the brightest, *after careful reflection,* are likely to answer that there is *no* relevant conclusion at all to be drawn. The case was studied in the late seventies by the distinguished British psychologist Philip Johnson-Laird (presently a professor at Princeton University) and by his collaborators at the University of Sussex. In order not to spoil your fun (and the fun of your brightest friends), the correct answer (Answer 1) is on page 123. In fact, logic tells us that there *is* a firm

The Framing of Choices

The psychological mechanism called "framing" is well exemplified by the following test.

A certain country in Southeast Asia is faced with a deadly epidemic that threatens the lives of 600 people.

Two kinds of health programs are possible. Let us call them A and B, respectively:

• *If we adopt program A, 200 lives will be saved for sure.*

• *If we adopt program B, there is a ⅓ probability of saving 600 people and a ⅔ probability of saving no one.*

Which program would you recommend?

The reader is invited to pick his or her own preference. The average preference actually expressed by a large sample of subjects is indicated on page 123 (Answer 2).

Now the test is rephrased and a new version is presented to a separate population of experimental subjects which is very similar to the initial one in all relevant respects (age, sex, educational background, etc.). This is the rephrased version:

A certain country in Southeast Asia is faced with a deadly epidemic that threatens the lives of 600 people.

Two kinds of health programs are possible. Let us call them C and D, respectively:

• *If we adopt program C, 400 people are going to die for sure.*

• *If we adopt program D, there is a ⅓ probability that no one dies and a ⅔ probability that 600 people die.*

Which program would you recommend?

Although presenting both versions of the test one after the other is *not* the correct way of proceeding, the reader is again invited to express a preference. The framing effect is sometimes so strong that it shows up even in this kind of blunt sequential presentation.

The median of the choices in *this* version of the test, again expressed by a large sample of experimental subjects, is indicated on page 123 (Answer 3).

(The test of the epidemic is adapted from Amos Tversky and Daniel Kahneman, 1986.)

When choosing between different health programs, as well as when choosing between investments, or between lotteries, economists tell us that there always is a crucial figure to be considered. It is called expected utility, and is simply calculated by multiplying a prize by the probability of obtaining that prize. A sound universal norm of rationality is to always try to maximize expected utility in all our choices. Therefore, a fully rational subject ought to remain totally indifferent between the options indicated above as A,B,C,D.

In 1982, McNeil, Pauker, Sox, and Tversky published similar data in the *New England Journal of Medicine* clearly showing that even physicians are prone to the framing effect in their choice between alternative therapies. They feel uneasy recommending a surgical intervention described as involving an average mortality rate of 7 percent within five years after surgery, but feel significantly more comfortable recommending it when it is described as involving a 93 percent rate of survival within five years after surgery.

We are told that the framing process is governed by two rules of mental economy, respectively called "acceptance" and "segregation." The acceptance rule states that, given a reasonable formulation of a problem involving choice, decision-makers are prone to accept the problem as presented to them, and do not spontaneously generate alternative reformulations. In other words we all have a tendency to accept problem formulations *as they are given*. We remain, so to speak, mental prisoners of the frame provided to us by the experimentalist, or by the "expert," or by a certain situation.

The second rule of mental economy is the "segregation" of the decision problem at hand from its broader context. In accord with this rule, people frame decision problems by focusing on those acts, outcomes, and contingencies that appear most directly relevant to their immediate choice. In other words, we tend to concentrate all our attention on the choice itself, disregarding the global

context, and the overall balance of advantages and disadvantages existing before as well as after the choice we make.

In fact, Tversky and Kahneman have shown that there is a *nearly universal practice* of thinking about problems involving choice in terms of gains and losses, rather than in terms of wealth or final asset positions. In this representation, the part of the outcome that depends on the choice is *isolated* from pre-existing wealth, and segregated from accompanying gifts or penalties.

This practice is best shown by tests of the following kind:

Being first offered a bonus of $300, one then faces the following choice:

a) *win $100 for sure*

b) *50 percent chance to win $200, and 50 percent chance to win nothing*

Most subjects choose a over b. This is typical of a widespread tendency called risk-aversion in situations of possible gain.

But the pattern of choices is reversed in the following situation:

Being first offered a bonus of $500, one then faces the following choice:

a) *a sure loss of $100*

b) *50 percent chance to lose $200, and 50 percent chance to lose nothing*

Now most subjects choose b over a. This is typical of an equally widespread and opposite attitude, called risk-seeking in situations of possible losses. (A typical real-life example is a preference for risky strategems in the domain of taxation, which may avoid taxation altogether, but which may also backfire badly, over simply paying what, for sure, is owed the IRS.)

It is worth stressing that in the above test the two situations are perfectly equivalent in terms of final assets. In fact, the overall final net gain is $400 in both cases and for both choices.

(The psychological mechanisms responsible for these effects have been exhaustively reviewed by Tversky and Kahneman.)

---

conclusion to be drawn, but psychology also tells us that we just do not "see" it. Practically nobody sees it.

The reason we do not "see" the conclusion has been called a "figural effect." Something that is, once more, neither rational nor capricious.

In a nutshell, our problem here (a problem that would presumably not affect either a Martian, or a computer) is that this piece of reasoning starts with grandiose "universal" assertions ("all," "no"),

but then leads quite modestly to a conclusion concerning only "some." Moreover, bankers appear to the left of the first statement, to the right of the second statement and nowhere in the conclusion. Puzzling, isn't it? I mean puzzling *for us*, because the Martian would probably find all of this perfectly obvious. Cognitive psychologists try to explain *why* we fail to see the conclusion. The explanation, again in a nutshell, is that we have to construct one mental picture, or "mental model" in the first syllogism (the one about rich Rurita-

SIDEBAR B

Two Irresistible Temptations: Overconfidence and Hindsight

In 1929, the American educational psychologist T.M. Newcomb did something that went almost unnoticed at the time, but which in retrospect appears truly groundbreaking. In a summer camp for "difficult" adolescents he asked the supervisors of 51 selected campers to keep a detailed daily record of their behavior. At the end of the summer he collected the diaries, read them carefully, and then interviewed the supervisors two months afterwards. The striking result was that the recollection of the supervisors correlated very poorly with what they had written down in their diaries day by day (the statistical correlation was, on average, a scant 27 percent). On the contrary, their recollection of the behavior of a given child correlated quite highly (85 percent) with the "global psychological profile" of that camper, as it had been given to them from the institution at the beginning of the summer. If a child had been labeled as "aggressive," they tended to remember only instances of aggressive behavior. If a child had been labeled "uncooperative" they tended to remember only instances of refusals to participate in the camp's activities, and so forth. Yet, their *own* daily recordings did not support those judgments. Those instructors were totally sincere, acting in good faith, and were quite surprised to discover how poorly their recollections matched their written records.

Ever since Newcomb's pioneering studies, his concept of "illusory correlations" has gained wider currency. From the mid-fifties onward the detailed psychological study of all sorts of pervasive and obdurate "biases," "preconceptions", and "fallacies of hindsight" was to become an important part of psychology. In the late sixties and seventies L.J. Chapman and J.P. Chapman, R.A. Schweder, L. Ross and M.R. Lepper and others, in a series of classic experiments, discovered that we can all be easily and sincerely persuaded to possess outstanding diagnostic insights by simply being *told* that we do, irrespective of the objective frequency of our truly correct guesses. Those experiments were conducted as follows: each subject received a set of psychological profiles of certain individuals,

each profile being paired with samples of personal letters written by that individual. The profiles characterized each individual as normal, or as affected by a certain mental pathology. The individual profiles and the letters had been, as a matter of fact, *randomly* paired. The subjects were then asked to *justify* the profile on the basis of the letters, but were not told that those pairings had been made purely at random. A further interesting situation was created by subdividing the subjects into three groups: subjects in one group received constant and warm encouragement by the experimenter no matter which justification they offered ("You are doing very well," "Remarkable," "Excellent," and so on); another group received constant negative feedback, no matter which justification they offered ("No, this is not correct. Please try harder," or "Are you really sure of what you say? Think twice," and so on); finally the third group received endorsement in 50 percent of the cases and criticism in another 50 percent of the cases. The subjects were assigned to each group at random. Predictably, the subjects in the first group quickly became "overassertive" and "overconfident" in their diagnostic capacities, the subjects in the second group became "underassertive" and "underconfident," and the subjects in the third group became insecure of their diagnostic judgment. But the truly stunning result was that they all *remained* convinced of their diagnostic abilities *even after they were told* how the experiment had been planned and conducted. Those in the first group, for example, stated that their diagnoses were at least right "in principle."

More recent experiments on "overconfidence" have debunked this cognitive propensity in a variety of tasks, including those that elicit a willingness to bet for real money (money which, unbeknownst to the subject, is to be reimbursed at the end of the session). It has been amply confirmed that there is an almost universal tendency to be "overconfident" in one's judgment in certain situations of uncertainty. Particularly scary is the universal tendency aptly labeled "predictability in hindsight." Sketchy but realistic

"profiles" of the overall economic and political situation of a certain country (say, Mexico at the end of the thirties, or Italy in the mid-fifties, or South Korea in the late seventies) are randomly paired with certain subsequent outcomes: inflation, deflation, unrest, stable growth, etc. The subject is told what the outcome was (say, rampant inflation) and asked to justify "in hindsight" that outcome, merely on the basis of the sketchy profile. Subjects, not yet knowing that the pairing has been made at random, *always* find plausible justifications. Once the trick is subsequently revealed by the experimenter, and they are told what the real historical outcome was, they *again* quickly find other justifications for the new pairing. The typical statements are: "Sure, I should have paid more attention to the external debt," or "Indeed, I had neglected the increasing unemployment." It never dawns on them that such forecasts from incomplete and sketchy data are *fundamentally* unreliable. The situation changes dramatically when the *same* sketches are offered to other subjects of comparable age and cultural background, but now as a basis for *actual* forecasts, of outcomes that they must make themselves (not any more as an exercise in hindsight). Here confidence drops significantly.

The lesson here is that we all appear to draw a very sharp line between predictability in the future and "predictability in hindsight." Once the outcome *is* known, we find it irresistible to assume that "we *could* have predicted what was going to happen." Under the spell of this unshakable assumption, we then proceed to show *how* we should have reasoned. These experiments explain, among other things, why the search for the culprit becomes irresistible when things go wrong. And why it is often so easy to persuade someone that he or she *truly* could, and should, have anticipated the disaster. We are ourselves persuaded, but so is the scapegoat-victim, who is also the prey of the same cognitive bias. History has witnessed the somber consequences of combining these purely cognitive biases with equally unshakable emotional and ideological prejudices.

---

nians), two in the second (about hunters and sailors), and no fewer than three, including a rather difficult final one, in the third example. Of course we are not aware that we do construct these mental models. We just do it. And we "just" fail to do it properly in the third case.

If these mishaps befall us even when we are allowed to think carefully and calmly about a problem that has all the elements

explicitly laid out before us, we shudder to think what will happen when we must think and react rapidly, on the basis of incomplete information. In ordinary life this is called decision-making. In the universities it is called "judgment under uncertainty." Let us first examine an instance of rapid intuitive judgment in a perfectly well-defined situation. We will later introduce the additional element of uncertainty. From the domain of logic, we now transfer to domain of simple arithmetic.

A Numerical Illusion

We are asked to compute quickly, say in about ten seconds, the result of the following multiplication:

$$2 \times 3 \times 4 \times 5 \times 6 \times 7 \times 8$$

Please try it yourself, before reading any further. Remember, ten seconds, no more. As shown by Tversky and Kahneman in a study published in 1982, the average response obtained in a vast sample of subjects is 512. (How close did you get in your response? How close did your friends get?)

Now we ask another group of subjects, identical to the first in age distribution and in average cultural background, to multiply rapidly (again in about ten seconds):

$$8 \times 7 \times 6 \times 5 \times 4 \times 3 \times 2$$

This time, the average response is much higher: 2,250. Of course, according to the laws of arithmetic the final result should not change. And this, believe me, all the subjects knew very well. When asked, they showed that they knew the principle in the abstract. Yet, they were driven to compute drastically different results in the two cases. The strategy of our rapid mental calculus is simple: we start multiplying the first three or four figures *left-to-right*, then we extrapolate and round up the final figure. No wonder the result *depends* on the order of the factors.

The mathematically correct answer is far greater than either of these estimates: 40,320. No one goes that high, but there are other really intriguing facts. By telling the subject that he or she has underestimated the result, we easily induce quick self-corrections, but these are *systematically* lower than the true result, and they always remain "anchored" to the initial guess. The lower the initial figure, the lower the final result *after* correction. It is extremely rare that a subject decides to invert the order of calculation and do it right-to-left. It does not help to know that the product does not depend on the order of factors. We know this, but our intuitive estimates cannot use this piece of knowledge. This is what often happens to us: one corner of our mind is unable to use what another corner of our mind knows full well.

This is a simple and easily reproducible instance of the pervasive cognitive illusion called "anchoring." In fact, come to think of it, in a variety of domains once we have made an intuitive estimate, even if we are told that we are wrong, we *still* keep the initial rough estimate as an implicit baseline. We are anchored to it. We are unwilling to neglect it completely and start afresh. I have already used the expression "condemned to" and the word "scary." What follows will further justify such wording.

Ease and Probability

When we add to all this the element of uncertainty, when we are asked to judge on the basis of *incomplete* information, we come closer to real-life situations, and by the same token closer to the vast domain of statistical illusions. One of the most widespread and one of the most resilient, is called "typicality" or "availability" or "ease of representation." To see what is involved, let's try to guess approximately, as an average, the percentage of English words found in a book, or a newspaper, or a magazine . . . that have the following form (the dashes stand for any letters whatsoever):

- - - - i - -

The question is: how many English words, out of a hundred, have seven letters *and* have the letter "i" in the third-to-the-last position?

Try and guess. Difficult? Yes, it is rather difficult, but make a guess all the same. The answer is usually rather low (rarely more than 10 percent, sometimes even less than 1 percent). Tversky collected precise data on these estimates. Then he asked a different group of subjects to make the same guess for English words of seven letters having the following form:

- - - - ing

The result is that the average estimate is now much higher. For reasons that I am going to make explicit in one moment, I hope that some readers' will wonder at this different result. This would be a perfect private self-verification of the tenacity of a cognitive illusion. The estimate *should* be lower here, because the second set of words is a *subset* of the former. For instance, "stylist," "elation," "bonfire," and "verdict" are all words of the former, but not of the latter kind. Even more striking, and contrary to expectation, was Tversky's discovery that the very same initial subjects, when tested on the second estimate a few days after they had been tested on the first, still indicated a greater estimated frequency for words of the second kind. He found it irresistible, at that point, to try to test the same subject for *both* estimates at once, putting one scheme below the other (as I have done here.) It turned out, to his utmost surprise, that a non-negligible percentage of subjects *still* offered greater estimates for the second scheme and *failed to see* that the second case is a particular case of the former.

Another interesting test of intuitive estimates is the following: What percentage of English words begin with the letter "k"? A rather generous estimate usually follows. What percentage of English words have the letter "k" in the third position? A much lower estimate is given. As a matter of fact, the words of the second kind are twice as numerous as the words beginning with "k." But we do not see it.

The key to these illusions is a mental process rightly called "ease of representation." It is *easy* for us to mentally generate instances of words ending with "ing," and instances of words beginning with "k." It is much, much harder to mentally generate instances of words having "i" in the third-to-the-last position, or having "k" in third position. So far so good. This is the way we are mentally built. But here comes the rub, the full-blown and dangerous cognitive illusion: we find it *irresistible* to assign a greater *probability* of occurrence to events that we find easy to imagine. We cannot avoid thinking that, as a matter of fact, in the world, in reality, those sets whose typical members are easy for us to represent mentally are *larger* than those sets whose typical members are hard to represent mentally.

Emotionality Beats Numerosity

We are now ready to understand why this universal and insidious cognitive bias, called "typicality," "availability," and "ease of representation," breeds a typical kind of overconfidence. It explains, among many interesting and frightening phenomena, why we all intuitively judge, contrary to the objective statistics regularly published in the authoritative yearbooks, that more people die every year because of homicide than because of suicide, because of incidents related to fireworks than because of measles; that more women die from the combined effects of pregnancy, abortion and childbirth than from appendicitis. The stark statistical reality would tell us the opposite, but we are the prisoners of our ease of representation. As B. Fishhoff, P. Slovic and S. Lichtenstein demonstrated in 1977, in a pioneering study carried out at the Decision Research Institute in Eugene, Oregon, people are so confident of these intuitive judgments of death-frequencies that they rate the mere possibility of their being wrong as one in a thousand, or even

The Three Boxes

On December 2, 1990 in *Parade Magazine*, Marilyn Vos Savant published several letters (literally containing the exclamation "Shame!") that she had received from distinguished mathematicians who are "probability-blind." She had in fact correctly presented a case that is well-known in the cognitive milieu, and she had offered the right solution. The result was this undeserved volley of insults from top professionals who ought to know better.

I also failed this test when it was first presented to me by my friend and colleague Daniel N. Osherson at MIT about two years ago. I have since then offered it to a number of others, and I have found myself arguing at length about the solution even with distinguished physicists, and I have myself received letters filled with outrage from qualified scientists after I presented it in an Italian magazine and in an interview with a journalist at *L'Unità*. It may be worth offering it again here.

These are the material components of our game (there are different versions of it, but this one will do for our present purposes): three identical boxes, each with a lid, and a certain number of dollar bills. Let's say they are $5 bills. The game is to be repeated a great number of times (say 150 or 300 or 500 times—the actual number is immaterial—the experimenter is just assumed to be rich enough to afford repeating this game many times).

These are the rules for each session of the game, and all sessions are repeated identically: you go out of the room and while you are out, and cannot see what I do, I place a $5 bill in one of the boxes, then I close the lids of all boxes. I know exactly where the banknote is, but you don't. You then come back into the room and you have to guess. For each session, if you guess correctly, you get the $5. There are two stages in each session of the game: first you indicate one of the three boxes at your choice. As soon as you do that, I open the lid of *another* box (not the one you have chosen), and I will *always* open an *empty* box. I can do it in each session, because I always know where I have put the bill.

This means that if by chance, and unbeknownst to you, you have chosen an empty box, I will open the lid of the *other* empty box. If by chance, and unbeknownst to you, you have chosen the right box, I will open at random the lid of one of the other two empty boxes. At this point in each session you are always left with two closed boxes one of which *certainly* contains the $5 bill. Now, after I have opened the empty box,

you are free to stick with your initial choice, or to switch and choose the other closed box. You are free to do this again and again at each new session. If, in your second and final choice, you have guessed correctly, you win the $5. Then you go out of the room again, and we repeat the game over and over.

The question now is: as a rule, should you maintain the initial choice, or should you switch? What is the best strategy?

Think about it. Ask your brightest friends. Do not tell them, though (or at least not yet), that even Nobel physicists systematically give the wrong answer, and that they *insist* on it, and are ready to berate in print those who propose the right answer.

In my experience, the weirdest things happen when this problem is posed. Some state with force that they would always switch. Some state with equal force that they would always maintain the initial choice. Many state that it makes no difference. Or that you can switch 50 percent of the time and maintain the initial choice in the other 50 percent. Believe it or not, many state that it makes no difference *and* that "therefore" they would always switch. Others

*S*uch is human nature. Powerful emotions get mixed in and the cognitive scientist, at that point, exits tiptoeing. It is not his or her business to cope with emotions.

maintain that it makes no difference, and that "therefore" they would always maintain the initial choice. When asked why, many say "For no reason," or "I am a conservative," or "I am always for change." If you offer the problem simultaneously to a whole group of friends real bedlam may ensue.

To put some order into such great mental confusion, it is best to establish that *if it really* makes no difference, if the probability of finding the $5 bill *really* is 50/50, *then* there is no point at all either in switching, or in sticking to your original choice, or in tossing a coin to decide whether to switch or not. That much ought to be agreed on by everyone. And it usually is, *once you make this point clearly*. But is the probability really 50/50?

The intuition here is overwhelming. You have two closed boxes. The banknote is surely

in one of them, but you don't know in which of the two. *Therefore* it *must* be 50/50.

Overwhelming, but *wrong!* In fact, the correct strategy is to *always switch*. The box you have initially chosen had, and will forever have, a ⅓ probability of containing the banknote. The other two *taken together* have a ⅔ probability. But once I open the one that is empty, the other *now* has a ⅔ probability all by itself. Therefore you must always switch. By switching you raise the odds from ⅓ to ⅔. It is horribly counterintuitive, but also rationally impeccable.

Given that even Nobel laureates draw their guns and resist this conclusion, it will be useful to add another way of seeing why you must always switch. If you happen to have chosen the right box, then after my opening the empty box you are *certainly* (not probably) penalized by switching. On the contrary, if you happen to have chosen an empty box, then you are *certainly* (not probably) rewarded by switching. We have now introduced a little element of certainty in all this. Well, let's use it. How often will you happen to choose the right box (and be *necessarily* penalized by switching)? One time out of three. How often will you happen to choose an empty box (and be *necessarily* rewarded by switching)? Two times out of three. Therefore, switching is the right strategy. It pays two times out of three. Sticking with the initial choice is a bad strategy. It pays only one time out of three.

This should be fully convincing. Yet curiously, in my experience, it sometimes is not. Not even these perfectly cogent mini-demonstrations manage to cancel the initial intuition. I have argued forcibly with highly intelligent persons who, after all this is said and done, remain silent for a few moments, then insist that we start all over again. They *insist* that they want "to go back" to the moment when there are two closed boxes and when they do not know in which of the two boxes the banknote is. They *want* to neglect what has happened immediately before that moment. Now, they relish plunging again forcefully, irresistibly, into the intuition that the probability *must* be 50/50. They do not want to move away from that intuition.

I have encountered people who flatly *refuse* to follow the mini-demonstration that one should always switch. They refuse to accept the fact that *after my opening* the two remaining closed boxes have *unequal* probabilities of containing the banknote.

Such is human nature. Powerful emotions get mixed in and the cognitive scientist, at that point, exits tiptoeing. It is not his or her business to cope with emotions. The picture is already complicated enough (and scary enough) even without the further distorting effects engendered by the emotions.

one in a million. They are even ready to bet real money, and lots of it. The illusion of typicality breeds "overconfidence" (see Sidebar B) and this should alarm us vastly more than it does.

The great English mathematician and philosopher Bertrand Russell correctly stated back in 1927 that people tend to draw general conclusions from just a few actual instances they happen to witness, and that these overconfident over-generalizations are based, in Russell's own words "upon the emotional interest of the instances, not upon their number." Homicides, and deaths caused by accidents related to fireworks, impress our imagination, are easily remembered, and are amply reported in the press. On the other hand, suicides, and deaths caused by measles, do not impress us and are understandably neglected by journalists. We find it irresistible to jump to the conclusion that the former are objectively, statistically more frequent than the latter. What is so worrisome is that we are vastly overconfident in these intuitive judgments. We do not know, but we *think we know*. We are ready to bet, not just money, but in certain cases our life, or the lives of others.

Why on earth should objective frequencies of events in nature parallel what is easy for us to represent and remember? In fact, they often don't. Only the most naïve of the Darwinians may assume that the two *must* coincide, but the evolution of our mental aptitudes proves to have been vastly more complicated. What is worse, we are intimately persuaded that we are able to cope with uncertainty, at least in the main. In hindsight, given the pervasiveness and insidiousness of these cognitive illusions, it is hardly surprising that it took so long to discover them, and that even today these stunning discoveries do not attract the public attention they deserve.

For Whom the Bell Tolls

It is worth stressing that these experiments, and those reported in the sidebars, have nothing to do with *individual* degrees of intelligence and with the testing of IQ. The truly interesting cognitive bias, the perfect cognitive illusion, is the one invariably shown by all, or at least most of the members of our species, irrespective of sex, culture, social status, and degree of education. And irrespective as well of emotional biases produced by pride, stubbornness, fear, timidity, and so on. These will increase the intensity of the illusions, and will further protect them from correction. The job of the cognitive scientist is rather to study them in their purest form, once all emotions, all socio-cultural prejudices and all vested interests have been safely removed. After this purification has taken place, certain cognitive biases are still unmistakably detectable in all of us, including Nobel laureates for physics and first-rate mathematicians (see Sidebar C).

In the problem of the three boxes we witness how forceful, elusive and incorrigible a cognitive illusion can be. Luckily enough, there are other cognitive illusions and biases such that, once we become aware of them *in detail*, we become immune. Few seem to be quite so resilient, and so emotion rousing, as the game of the three boxes. With one possible exception: the case of the AIDS test (see Sidebar D), and the perfectly analogous case of the juror's fallacy. Here I have again encountered fierce resistance, and emotions are ready to storm in. I have heard the following comments: "If you are right, then there is no point in making clinical tests!" Even a physician friend of mine told me that. Evidently, for many of us a probability of 6 percent and a probability of 1 percent are *the same*. We are in fact, as literally stated in the technical literature on this subject: "probability-blind near the extremes." Intuitively, we seem to understand only four degrees of probability for an event: very likely, somewhat likely (more likely to happen than not), somewhat

unlikely (more likely not to happen), and very unlikely. Inside those four compartments all is gray. No difference makes any difference. A 6 percent probability appears to us already sufficiently "very unlikely" that the significantly inferior probability of 1 percent is just "the same."

Enter the Miscalculation of Risk

We encounter, alas, in professional publications and in real life many further proofs of our blindness to different degrees of risk. The important lesson to be derived from many scrupulous studies on the subjective perception of risk can be understood even from some homely examples. Subjects have been asked how much they would pay to reduce a risk of one in a million to zero. Let's name this amount to be $100. Now, how much would they pay to reduce that very same risk from two in a million to one in a million? Reason would dictate that they still be ready to pay those fat $100. But that is not the case. Far from that. Now they are ready to pay at most one miserable dollar. Two orders of magnitude less than what they were ready to pay in the previous case, for an identical reduction of risk. Similarly, few would buy an insurance policy that provides protection against earthquakes only on Tuesdays, Thursdays, and Saturdays, or only during the first half of each month. It sounds crazy to buy such a policy. But, suppose a policy is cheap, say ¼ or ⅕ of what a "full" policy would cost? Why not buy it? Is it rational to refuse even to take it into consideration? We are so blind to differences in small probabilities that we judge the "annihilation" of a risk (that is, bringing it to zero) very different from the "mere" reduction of that risk. Is this rational? Or is it rather the compulsory effect of a human trait, known in the profession as "probability blindness near the extremes"? Once more, it is neither rational nor capricious. At the other "extreme," we are ready to pay good money for a lottery ticket that gives us a 99 percent

T he great English mathematician and philosopher Bertrand Russell correctly stated back in 1927 that people tend to draw general conclusions from just a few actual instances they happen to witness.

chance to win a coveted prize, but are *not* ready to pay a penny more to increase that probability to 99.9 percent. We do not *see* the difference. Only this time we are not judging the arch in St. Louis. This time it is not our eye but our mind that refuses to see.

Any Cure for the Common Illusion?

Let's listen to ourselves. We ask in anguish: "Is there *a* risk?" Once we are told that there is a risk, *but* that it is very, very small, we still insist "So there *is* a risk!" We often perceive risks as all-or-nothing. No degrees, no shades of gray. Either there is a risk or there is not. This is all we want to hear. If there is, we want it annihilated, completely removed, obliterated. Cost is immaterial, especially if *others* will pay it. It is not "enough" to merely reduce it even drastically. It is not enough to be told that it is vastly inferior to all sorts of risks we gladly face every day, for instance the risk we face when crossing a city street at rush hours.

In Italy, my native country, a whole network of advanced nuclear power stations was recently dismantled for fear of possible contaminations. The Chernobyl disaster scared everyone stiff and a

The AIDS Test

A patient has a positive AIDS test. You are told that:
- The accuracy of the test is 87 percent.
- The incidence of the disease in the population, independent of any test, is one percent.

How probable is it that the patient really has AIDS, given that the test is positive?

Many subjects answer, candidly and confidently: 87 percent. The piece of reasoning is the following: we know that the test is positive, and we also know that in 87 cases out of one hundred a positive test means that the patient truly has AIDS, therefore the probability is 87 percent. It does not seem to dawn on us that the accuracy of the test is one thing, and that effective risk is another. The accuracy of the test must be *combined* with the average risk that the subject, coming from a given population, may have AIDS independent of the test.

Not everyone jumps to this overconfident conclusion, but still a vast majority of subjects, including many physicians, judge that it is more likely that the patient really has AIDS than not. The estimate is almost invariably higher than 50 percent.

The correct solution, given by a standard **formula known as Bayes's Theorem (see this page), actually is 6.33 percent.**

I expect many readers to find this result simply incredible, even preposterous. How is it possible, we may wonder, that *after* having made a highly reliable test, the probability that the patient truly has AIDS *remain so low?* This shows how far apart our wild statistical intuitions and the rigorous doctrine of probability are.

The correct application of Bayes's Theorem to this case is the following: it is adapted from a paper by D.M. Eddy (1982), in turn based on a paper by R.E. Snyder (1966).

A very similar case is the following:

The Juror's Fallacy

A cab was involved in a deadly hit-and-run accident at night. Two cab companies, the Green and the Blue, operate in the city. You are told that:

- 85 percent of the cabs in the city are Green and 15 percent are Blue.
- a witness identified the cab as Blue.

The court tested the reliability of the witness under the same circumstances that existed on the night of the accident, and concluded that the witness was correct in indentifying the color of the cab 80 percent of the time.

What is the probability that the cab involved in the accident was Blue rather than Green?

The answers here are very similar to the ones for the AIDS test. Many answer: 80 percent. A majority of subjects judge that, at any rate, it is more probable that the cab was Blue rather than Green. Their intuition is based on the *true* fact that the visual acuity of the subject does not depend on the number of cabs circulating in the city. The visual acuity of the witness, in fact, does not, but the *probability* that the cab, indeed, was Blue is a totally different matter. It *does* depend on how many Blue and how many Green cabs circulate. The reliability of the witness and the *a priori* probability of the event have to be *combined*. The correct answer, again based on Bayes's law, is: 41 percent.

In spite of the reliability of the witness, it is slightly *more* probable that the cab was, in fact, Green, not Blue. In technical terms this fallacy is labeled "neglect of base rates." We tend to disregard how probable a certain event is in itself, regardless of any evidence we may have gathered. This constitutes the "old," or "baseline" probability, from which we must now calculate mathematically the *new* probability, the one we now have, *given* the evidence. In cases such as this (and the one about AIDS), we tend to disregard the "base rate" of probabilities, that is, disregard how likely the event is in itself, *irrespective* of the witness (or the test).

The great philosopher David Hume had perfectly summarized the spirit of this principle by stating that no testimony is sufficent to establish a miracle, unless the falsehood of the witness would constitute an even greater miracle than the one he is attempting to establish.

This example, adapted from a well-known test originally introduced by Kahneman and Tversky in 1972, makes it self-explanatory why our blindness to Hume's principle, and to Bayes's Theorem, is also sometimes called "the juror's fallacy."

Bayes's Theorem

The problem of how to calculate "posterior odds," that is, the probability that something really is the case, given evidence in favor of it — for instance a positive clinical test, or a report from a reliable witness, or a sound scientific experiment—was brilliantly and definitively solved in the mid-eighteenth century by Thomas Bayes, a British mathematician and priest.

Bayes's Theorem, applied to our case of the clinical test, combines the following crucial ingredients:

- The "prior probability," that is, the probability that the patient has AIDS prior to, and independent of, the test (in our case 1 percent, that is 0.01).

- The probability that the test is positive, *if* the patient really has AIDS (this is the accuracy of the test, in our case 87 percent, that is 0.87).

- The probability that, if the patient does not have AIDS, the test will still be positive (this is called the "false-positive rate," in our simplified case, it is the complement of 87 percent, or 13 percent, that is 0.13).

- The prior probability that the patient does *not* have AIDS (in our case, it is 99 percent, that is 0.99).

Bayes's Theorem tells us that the "posterior probability," that is, the probability that the patient really has AIDS, *given* that the clinical test is positive, is

$$\text{Prob (AIDS/given the test)} = \frac{(0.87) \times (0.01)}{(0.87) \times (0.01) + (0.13) \times (0.99)} = 0.063$$

or 6.3 percent.

ANSWER 1:
Some athletes are not stationers
ANSWER 2:
[The median of the choices expressed by a large sample of experimental subjects is: 72 percent for A, 28 percent for B.]
ANSWER 3:
[The median of choices in this case shows a reversed pattern: 22 percent for C, 78 percent for D.]

The best therapy is to literally "feel" how our biases constrain us, discretely, insensibly, against our better judgment and against our advantage.

referendum turned into a landslide against nuclear power. But how big, or how small, was the risk of another Chernobyl *in Italy?* It did not seem to matter. Nor did it matter that Italy owns no oil wells, and that standard hydroelectric plants have also proven risky (because of avalanches). Nothing seemed to matter. The nuclear stations had to go. "The" risk had to be removed completely, at all costs.

5. COGNITIVE PROCESSES

Cases of this sort abound. In Florence the Teatro Comunale has now been closed completely and definitively. It may never reopen. In this highly cultural city of noble musical traditions it is presently impossible to stage an opera. Why? Certain asbestos insulators were decreed to increase the risk of cancer. How high was the risk? Nobody has cared to quantify it. There was *a* risk. As Russell had acutely diagnosed, these decisions are made emotionally, not rationally.

Around MIT, where I work, I constantly see, outside of the office buildings, in all weather conditions, small, pathetic platoons of unfortunates who furtively smoke a cigarette, feeling abject and idiotic. There is "*a*" risk that their smoke may harm other people. How high is that risk? It does not matter, for there *is* a risk, and any risk is too much. Innumerable other unfortunates everywhere abstain from a variety of otherwise succulent and tasty foods, gladly eaten for centuries in many cultures, because they contain this or that substance that may constitute a risk to their health. The list may be expanded almost indefinitely.

It is not surprising that these mishaps affect a species that is uniformly probability-blind, from the humble janitor to the Surgeon General, from the modest insurance agent to the Nobel laureate in physics. The only remedy is to become gradually more aware of how we think and how we decide, of who we are, of what we can know, and why we act the way we do. Not in general, in the abstract, but specifically, by learning at least the rudiments of the theory of probability, and by confronting symptomatic instances of illusions and biases like the ones I have offered here, drawn from a vast technical literature. In this domain the best therapy is to literally "feel" how our biases constrain us, discretely, insensibly, against our better judgment and against our advantage.

Whatever one thinks of Freud and his epigones, few doubt that the discovery of an emotional subconscious has been a valuable and fruitful one. Now cognitive scientists such as Amos Tversky and Daniel Kahneman have discovered another realm of the unconscious, and it would be good for us to know about this discovery, too. It may eventually liberate our thinking from all sorts of inconsistencies and dangerous tangles. We should not wait until they receive a Nobel prize for economics. Our self-liberation from cognitive illusions ought to start even sooner.

MENTAL GYMNASTICS

Some scientists are so convinced of the benefits of challenging the brain that they are applying the concept of use-it-or-lose-it to their own minds.

Gina Kolata

Gina Kolata is a science reporter for The New York Times.

At age 55, Ronald L. Graham, a leading mathematician and an administrator at A.T.&T. Bell Laboratories in Murray Hill, N.J., is taking up Japanese and golf. He juggles, does handstands and works out on a trampoline in his backyard. He has learned to speak Chinese, throw a boomerang, play the piano and beat most comers at table tennis.

When you ask Graham what possesses him to master one skill after another, he says he wants to keep his brain active and capable of finding solutions to thorny mathematical problems. His belief is that the more he uses his brain, the better it will perform, and the more he develops diverse mental skills, the more likely it is that he will have a flash of intuition that links seemingly disparate findings. Learning Chinese, he says, "stretches your brain in dramatically different directions." Even his latest juggling challenge—simultaneously juggling four or five balls at three different heights—"is really amazingly tough mentally," he says. It makes him concentrate at every second, which is the sort of mental stimulation he is after.

It's the use-it-or-lose-it idea carried into the sphere of the mind—a principle whose proponents include an increasing number of neuroscientists and psychiatrists. Not that these researchers recommend that everyone become a Ron Graham. But evidence is growing that a mind challenged by reading or an engrossing hobby or paid or volunteer work is a mind likely to remain vigorous and able to learn and create. Not all researchers are convinced by the data, yet even the skeptics admit that people of all ages who continue to use their brains tend to be happier.

Although the brain does change with age, scientists are not sure what bearing this has on the ability to think and reason. Dr. Gene Cohen, acting director of the National Institute on Aging, a Federal research organization in Bethesda, Md., says it is no longer a foregone conclusion that old people will suffer mental deterioration. "Many of the changes that were said to be related to aging," says the 47-year-old psychiatrist, "are now thought to be due to illness." A decrease in mental acuity, for example, has often been considered an inevitable part of the aging process, partly because average test scores of older people are pulled down by the low scores of those who have diseases like Alzheimer's or whose alertness has been affected by medications.

As many as 20 percent of the elderly lose none of their mental faculties as they age. Until recently, however, researchers did not ask whether that was because the 20 percent were healthy or because they continually challenged themselves. That is why a study published last year by Dr. John Stirling Meyer, a 67-year-old neurologist at Baylor College of Medicine in Houston, and his colleagues was unusual in the annals of aging research. It followed a group of *healthy* older people for four years and tried to determine if the members of the group who allowed themselves to stagnate experienced any decline in their mental abilities.

The 94 people in the study were about 65 years old and employed when Dr. Meyer and his colleagues began following them. A third of them continued to hold a job. Another third retired but remained mentally and physically active. They walked or bicycled regularly, for example, or were avid gardeners. Some of them did volunteer work. The rest of the participants were inactive after they retired. Basically, they sat around their houses and did nothing.

At the beginning of the study the researchers gave the participants standard neurological and psychological tests and measured the blood flow to their brains. At this point, all the subjects were at normal levels for their age. Four years later, however, the inactive people had less blood flowing to their brains and did significantly worse on I.Q. tests than the subjects in the other two groups.

"I would definitely say this is cause and effect," Dr. Meyer says. "The study was unlike any other. We had controlled for them being healthy and well at the beginning and they remained in good health," he says of the participants. The only thing that varied was their level of activity.

Other studies that differentiate between active and inactive healthy old people are now in progress, but the results may take years to confirm. In the meantime, the idea that people can maintain their mental skills by continually using them remains controversial, grounded for the most part in animal experiments. Most of the research done so far on humans does not indicate whether people lose some of their mental ability because they do not challenge their minds or whether they do not challenge their minds because their minds have become dull as a result of aging.

But those who believe in the use-it-or-lose-it idea say they are acting on the hunch that what has proved true for animals will prove true for humans. Carl W. Cotman, a 51-year-old neurobiologist at the University of California at Irvine, cites a number of studies that have convinced him that the brain continues to function well only if it is used. In one study, rats that were stimulated by treadmills and other gadgets in their cages as well as the company of other rats had 26 percent more connections between their brain cells than rats raised alone in bare cages. The rats in the enriched environment had an average of 4,546 connections in a cubic thousandth of a millimeter of brain tissue, while those raised in the boring environment had an average of 3,596 connections. The study also showed that the rats raised in the dull environment gained brain cell connections when they were given greater stimulation, while the rats raised in the enriched environment suffered a loss of connections when the stimulation was taken away. This evidence of the value of stimulating the brain, says Cotman, "is very, very solid."

Cotman adds that scientists have learned from laboratory studies that nerve cells stay healthier if they are kept active and firing electrical impulses. The refinement and direction of connections between cells depends on stimulation, he says, and "activity influences how and where connections are made." When investigators blocked nerve receptors from responding to incoming impulses by treating them with toxins, the nerves never made appropriate connections to other nerves.

Scientists have also shown that if an injury destroys brain cells or lops off some of their branches, new branches grow to fill in the gaps. This same process may contribute to a stroke patient's recovery and help compensate for brain cell loss during normal aging. Even people with Alzheimer's disease, in which there is a constant death of brain cells, sprout new cell connections before the disease is too far advanced, Cotman says.

The brain uses a remodeling strategy, explains Zaven Khachaturian, associate director of the neuroscience and neuropsychology of aging at the National Institute on Aging: "It keeps the nerve cells intact but changes their components." As for the use-it-or-lose-it-concept, the 54-year-old scientist says there is no "specific and direct human evidence," but he tries to keep different parts of his own mind stimulated by practicing a variety of skills.

While studying activity in the cat brain, Khachaturian discovered that when he gave the animal something to look at, not only its visual, but also its auditory cortex was stimulated. The brain is not strictly compartmentalized, he says, which is one reason that there are no firm data indicating it is better for people to do several different activities than to work on just one task, like reading something challenging every day. Nonetheless, it is his best guess that by using different parts of the brain, people can coax nerve cells to make connections they might not have made otherwise. This, he says, can only be beneficial.

But Dr. Thomas Chase, a 59-year-old neurologist at the National Institute of Neurological Disorders and Strokes, says he is skeptical of claims that using the brain makes it perform better. "It is not clear that this really occurs in human beings," he says. "I don't know of any evidence that humans sprout new connections except under conditions of injury, and I don't know of any evidence that physiological use confers any advantage." Dr. Chase cautions that "you can't always extrapolate from a rat to a man."

Herbert Weingartner, chief of the section on cognition at the National Institute on Aging, says it may not even be necessary to postulate on the basis of animal studies that the human brain makes more connections in response to stimulation. Researchers already know that when people are mentally engaged, there are biochemical changes in the brain that allow it to function more efficiently in cognitive areas such as attention and memory. This is true in the elderly and middle aged as well as in the young, says the 56-year-old Weingartner. People will be alert and receptive if they "are confronted with information that gets them to think about things because they're interested in them."

"An elderly alert individual," he says, "will do a heck of a lot better than someone who is sleepy. And someone with a history of doing more rather than less will go into old age looking more cognitively intact than someone who has not had an activated mind."

Many experts are so convinced of the benefits of challenging the brain that they are putting the theory to work in their own lives. The idea, says James Fozard, the associate scientific director of the National Institute on Aging, is *not* to learn to memorize long lists. "There are lots of books on how to improve your memory, but most of us don't need those kinds of skills, because we don't have to run between two Greek cities and get the message right," he says. "That kind of specific training is of less interest than being able to maintain a mental alertness."

Fozard and others say they try to use different mental skills as they challenge their brains, both because they enjoy the activities they have chosen and because they are betting that the range of activities will enhance the way their brains work. Fozard, who is 61, plays the trombone in his spare time and leads a jazz band. Khachaturian tries to keep different parts of his mind stimulated by studying languages, playing mental games, woodworking, welding and repairing machines. Cotman does landscape paintings as well as aerobics and calisthenics. He also builds rock walls. "When I do that," he says, "I definitely feel sharper."

Dr. Cohen of the National Institute on Aging suggests that people devise a plan for using their minds in their old age that includes mental and physical activities done alone, like reading, walking or swimming, and those done in groups, like dancing or playing bridge or tennis. He says that people are always being advised to keep physically active as they age, but that studies have shown that older people who keep mentally active are most likely to maintain their intellectual abilities and to be generally happier and better adjusted. "The point is you need to do both," he says. "Intellectual activity is a very important stimulus to the brain. It actually influences brain cell health and size."

Even Dr. Chase, who questions the use-it-or-lose-it concept, says that "if this idea makes people work harder and use their brains more, that's all to the good." He encourages people to stay mentally active. "Most human beings function far below their capacity," he says. "Reasoning and judgment are well preserved into old age."

No one has to tell that to Ronald Graham, the mathematician. "The essence of learning is that you learn how to learn and continue learning," he says. "Once you stop learning, you start to die."

Emotion and Motivation

Janet was a stay-at-home mom, a situation that did not please her since her sister was a working mother and always reminded Janet about her exciting life on the road as a sales representative for a large manufacturing company. Janet loved her children, two-year-old Jennifer, four-year-old Tommy, and newborn Sara. On the particular day of the following incident, Janet was having a difficult time with the children. The baby, Sara, had been crying all day from her colic. Jennifer and Tommy had been bickering over their toys. Janet, realizing that it was already 5:15 and her husband would be home any minute, frantically started preparing dinner. She wanted to fix a nice dinner so that she and her husband could eat after the children went to bed and relax and enjoy each other. This was not to be. Janet sat waiting for her no-show husband. When he finally walked in the door at 9:45, Janet was furious. His excuse that his boss had invited the whole office for cocktails and dinner did not reduce Janet's ire. Janet was angry that her husband did not even call to say that he would not be home for dinner; he could have taken five minutes to do that. Janet yelled and ranted at her husband for almost an hour. Her face was taut and red with rage. Her voice wavered as she escalated her decibel level. Suddenly, bursting into tears, she ran into the living room. Her husband retreated to the safety of their bedroom and the respite that a deep sleep would bring.

Exhausted and disappointed, Janet sat alone and pondered why she was so angry with her husband. Was she just plain tired? Was she frustrated by talking to children all day and simply wanted an adult around once in a while? Was she secretly worried and jealous that her husband was seeing another woman and lied about his whereabouts? Was she combative because her husband's and her sister's lives seemed so much more fulfilling than her own? Janet was unsure just how she felt and why she exploded in such rage at her husband, someone she dearly loved.

This story, while sad, is not unrealistic. There are times we all are moved to deep emotion. On other occasions when we expect waterfalls of tears, we find that our eyes are dry or simply a little misty. What are these strange things we call emotions? What motivates us to rage at someone we love? Why do we autopsy our every mood?

These questions and others have inspired psychologists to study emotions and motivation. The above episode about Janet, besides introducing these topics to you, also illustrates why these two topics are usually interrelated in psychology. Some emotions are pleasant, so pleasant that we are motivated to keep them going. Pleasant emotions are exemplified by love, pride, and joy. Other emotions are terribly draining and oppressive, so negative that we hope they will be over as soon as possible, and are exemplified by the emotions of anger, grief, and jealousy. Emotions and motivation and their relationship to each other are the focus of this unit.

In "Where Emotions Come From," we are reminded that the range of human emotions is vast. Despite this, some individuals fake emotions, thereby adding more emotions to their personal repertoires. Certain genuine emotions are readily identifiable by all of us, including individuals outside of our culture. Some researchers suggest that this is because the brain is intimately involved in the perception of and reproduction of facial movements that express emotion.

Moods are emotional states that are generally more persistent than fleeting emotional states. Are moods catching? If someone is in a good mood, will you feel better if you come in contact with this individual? The answer appears to be "yes," according to Daniel Goleman in "Happy or Sad, A Mood Can Prove Contagious."

Some individuals seem to have persistent emotional levels and patterns that for them portend poor physical health. Such might be true of the cancer-prone and Type A personalities. While not all studies indicate a link between mood or some of the more stable personality traits and physical health, some studies support the link. In "Stress: The 'Type A' Hypothesis," this issue is examined.

Edward Hoffman, author of "The Last Interview of Abraham Maslow," offers us insights into the man and theory that changed how psychologists view human motivation. Maslow took our thinking about motivation beyond the basic motives of hunger, thirst, and survival. In fact, Maslow suggested there are various need states arranged in a hierarchy, with self-actualization at the top. In this interview, Maslow shares his philosophy of motivation as well as his hopes for world peace.

In the final article, a strange human quirk of motivation is revealed. Some of us, while seemingly well-motivated, sabotage our best efforts so that we fail. Bruce Baldwin, the author of "Barriers to Success," discusses self-defeating behaviors and how to overcome them.

Looking Ahead: Challenge Questions

Do you think emotions are triggered by the brain? Or do you believe that something in our environment elicits emotions in us? Do you think that some people are more

emotional than others? From where do you think these individual differences originate? Do some people feel an emotion but do not express it?

Do you think there are disease-resistant and disease-prone personalities? Can people change their typical level of emotionality and therefore change their level of health?

What is the Type A personality? Are all aspects of this personality unhealthy? What can we do to change our own Type A behaviors?

Do you think that what motivates one person serves as a motivator for others as well? What motivates you in particular? Are the stimuli that motivate you different for various situations?

What are Abraham Maslow's notions about human motivation? What makes his views so controversial or unique?

What are self-defeating behaviors or self-sabotage? Can you think of any situations in your own life when you have done this to yourself? How can we terminate or change this strange behavior?

Where emotions come from

Joy and disgust. Sorrow and shame. Science is plumbing the passions that make us human

"We humans are full of unpredictable emotions that logic cannot solve."
—Capt. James Kirk, "Star Trek"

Pop singer Morris Albert crooned about them. Wives complained that their husbands wouldn't discuss them. And by the 1970s, an entire generation of Americans had learned to "get in touch" with their feelings. Scientists, however, were preoccupied with thinking, not emotion. Rational thought, after all, was the faculty deemed by the English philosopher Francis Bacon "the last creature of God." Leagues of researchers devoted their attention to how people solved problems, made decisions, formed opinions and learned skills. Fear and joy, anger and disgust were seen as peripheral, of interest mostly when they interfered with thought or became deviant or extreme, as in mental illness.

It was, in the words of psychologist Silvan Tomkins, an "overly imperialistic cognitive theory." Tomkins, who died last week at age 80, published two thick volumes in the early 1960s arguing that emotions were a crucial component of evolutionary design, even more important than basic drives such as hunger and sex. Anxiety, he pointed out, could drive a man from the bedroom. Fear could pre-empt appetite. Despair could lead to a fatal flirtation with a razor blade.

Tomkins was a lone voice, and he was almost entirely ignored by mainstream psychology. Yet there was a very small core of scientists who took his work seriously, and, building upon it, began to pioneer a new field of emotion research. Today, in disciplines ranging from psychology to neuroscience, from semiotics to genetics and anthropology, emotions have moved center stage. What was once a trickle of journal articles has become a publishing torrent. Researchers have developed methods for mapping the face and measuring emotional responses. They are studying the development of emotions in infants. Their work meshes with the efforts of biologists and neuroscientists who, using increasingly sophisticated technologies, were beginning to trace the "pathways" of emotion in the brain. Cognitive scientists, too, are talking about "hot" cognition, realizing that emotions and moods influence memory, judgment and learning.

It is not that there are, as yet, any solid answers. Even the most elemental question posed by turn-of-the-century psychologist William James — "What is an emotion?" — remains controversial. But researchers are beginning to untangle the first threads of an enormously complex tapestry, finding clues not only to normal emotions but also to how feelings go awry, fear turning to phobia, sadness to debilitating depression.

In the process, they are rejecting the notion of man as simply a "thinking machine," seeing human beings instead as biological organisms whose survival depends upon constant interaction with the environment. In this interplay, evolved over countless centuries and through dozens of steps on the evolutionary ladder, emotions have a critical role. Far from being "trivial," they contain, as one expert put it, "the wisdom of the ages" — warning us of danger, guiding us toward what is good and satisfying, signaling our intentions and our reactions to others. Emotions are the most familiar — and the most intimate — aspect of human experience, and they are gradually yielding their secrets.

Brain researchers, like other scientists, have spent much of the 20th century engrossed in the study of thinking and memory. But earlier investigators took some first steps toward tracing the biological underpinnings of emotion. In the late 1900s, for example, physiologists discovered that surgically removing a dog's cerebral cortex—the brain's thin outer layer of gray matter—did not prevent it from displaying primitive rage responses. By the late 1950s, researchers were identifying specific brain regions that seemed to play a central role in emotion. But only in the last few years have high-tech brain scanners, new methods of staining cells, powerful computers and other developments allowed scientists to begin systematically mapping the highways and traffic patterns of the emotional brain.

Neural pathways. While earlier in-

Anatomy of a smile

Faces of emotion

Not all smiles are the same. Psychologist Paul Ekman describes 18 different types, including the miserable smile, the false "cocktail party" smile and the smile of relief, each marked by different movements of the facial muscles. Most striking is the disparity between the "social" smile and the smile of true enjoyment, called the "Duchenne smile" after French anatomist Duchenne de Boulogne, who first described it in 1862. Smiles of real joy draw in the *Orbicularis oculi* muscle around the eyes, as well as the *Zygomaticus major* cheek muscle (see below). But when people put on a phony expression of pleasure, they smile only with their cheeks, not their eyes. Ten-month-old infants, experts find, are more apt to display a Duchenne smile when their mother approaches, while the approach of strangers often elicits "false" smiles.

ORBICULARIS OCULI MUSCLE. This muscle "does not obey the will," wrote Duchenne de Boulogne, but "is put in play only by the sweet emotions of the soul . . ."

ZYGOMATICUS MAJOR MUSCLE. Faked smiles exercise voluntary cheek muscles; eye muscles remain unsmiling.

ANXIETY. When people are anxious, cerebral blood flow—a measure of brain cell activity—increases in an area at the tips of the brain's temporal lobes just behind the eyes, according to brain scanning studies by University of Arizona psychiatrist Eric Reiman.

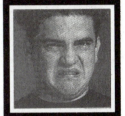

DISGUST. Would you stir your coffee with a new comb? Eat a sterilized cockroach? Most Americans wouldn't, though both are perfectly safe. Psychologist Paul Rozin argues that the things we find disgusting often evoke primitive beliefs about contamination.

HAPPINESS. Moments of intense happiness are not necessarily the key to an overall sense of well-being, says psychologist Ed Diener. Long-term happiness, his studies suggest, depends more on the frequency than the vividness of happy experiences.

EMBARRASSMENT. Darwin believed blushing was like the appendix, a fluke with no purpose. But Wake Forest University psychologist Mark Leary finds that turning red may serve to repair people's social image after they have appeared stupid or incompetent.

---

vestigators probed the emotional roles played by specific brain regions, scientists now put more emphasis upon the complex circuitry that interconnects them. Until recently, the limbic system, a loose network of brain structures beneath the cortex, was thought to do the majority of the work in coding "emotional" information and orchestrating the body's responses. But studies are now linking more and more areas of the brain—both the cortex and in subcortical regions—to the complex mix of perceptions, sensations and judgments we call emotion.

At the same time, brain centers once viewed as intimately involved in emotions are now known to be more marginal. The sea horse-shaped hippocampus,

for example, one of several limbic regions, appears more involved in memory and other cognitive tasks than in emotion, as previously believed. Much more critical, scientists are finding, is a tiny almond called the amygdala, buried deep in the temporal lobe (see diagram).

Indeed, the fingernail-size amygdala, which communicates with many other brain areas, is increasingly being viewed as a kind of "Emotion Central." As far back as 1937, studies showed that damage to the amygdala region produced changes in emotional behavior in monkeys: They became tame and oblivious to normally frightening situations, copulated with other monkeys of the same sex and ate nearly anything they were

offered. Recent work has refined this understanding—showing, for example, that amygdala nerve cells fire selectively in response to emotionally laden stimuli, and that some of these neurons are more sensitive to unfamiliar stimuli.

Quick and dirty. According to New York University neuroscientist Joseph LeDoux, the amygdala may make the first, crude judgment of an event's emotional significance. Consider a man walking through a forest who hears what sounds like a rifle shot at close range. Scientists previously believed that sensory information traveled first to the cerebral cortex, where the sound was consciously perceived. The cortex then sent signals to subcortical areas of the brain like the amygdala, which eval-

An emotional "shortcut"

The brain appears "programmed" to size up the emotional importance of certain stimuli, such as a flash of light, much more quickly than scientists once thought. Researchers previously knew that information taken in by the senses (1) travels to the thalamus (2), an early sensory processing station, then to the cortex (3), where it is consciously taken in and relayed to subcortical areas of the brain such as the amygdala (4). These interior regions then send messages back to the cortex, and also set in motion physiological responses (5). But neuroscientist Joseph LeDoux has found an additional and more direct pathway btween thalamus and amygdala that bypasses the cortex completely. In primitive emotions like fear, nerve impulses transmitted along this route reach the amygdala two to three times faster, allowing a "quick and dirty" judgment of whether the stimulus is something to be afraid of—probably even before it is consciously perceived. This assessment is then elaborated by thinking and memory.

MATT ZANG—USN&WR

CORTEX The thin outer layer of nerve tissue involved in "higher order" processes like planning and logical thought.

Enlarged area

Limbic system

Thalamus

Hippocampus

Amygdala

Shortcut
Original pathway

uated the sound's emotional importance. These "lower" regions then sent return messages back up to the cortex and fired up the autonomic nervous system, producing the pounding heart, rapid breathing and rising blood pressure that are the familiar accompaniments of fear.

But LeDoux's research indicates that, at least for primitive emotions like fear, the brain is constructed to respond even more quickly to potentially threatening events. He and his colleagues have identified in animals an additional nerve pathway carrying impulses directly between the thalamus—an early processing station for sensory input—and the amygdala. Information sent along this "shortcut" reaches the amygdala two to three times faster than that sent

up to the cortex first. Studies also demonstrate that even when the "longer" route through the cortex is destroyed, animals still are able to learn fear of sudden noises, or, in very recent work, flashing lights.

Such high-speed transmission, LeDoux contends, may allow the amygdala to make an almost instantaneous analysis of whether the sound is something to be afraid of, probably even before it is consciously heard or identified. This "quick and dirty" assessment, he speculates, is then elaborated and refined by the neocortex and other brain regions, allowing the hunter to conclude, for example, that the sound was the crack of a tree branch, not a rifle.

LeDoux's findings support the view that at least some emotional processes

take place unconsciously, and that cognition and emotion—though they interact—are separate systems in the brain—both points that have been vigorously debated for decades. In addition, the studies imply that the brain is designed, quite sensibly from an evolutionary standpoint, to react more to some things—loudness, for instance, or abrupt movement—than to others.

No fear of mushrooms. The idea that human beings are "programmed" to be wary of particular events may help explain why some people develop irrational fears of spiders, snakes, heights or close spaces, but never of electrical outlets or daffodils. Northwestern University psychologist Susan Mineka and her coworkers have found that monkeys quickly acquire an exaggerated fear of

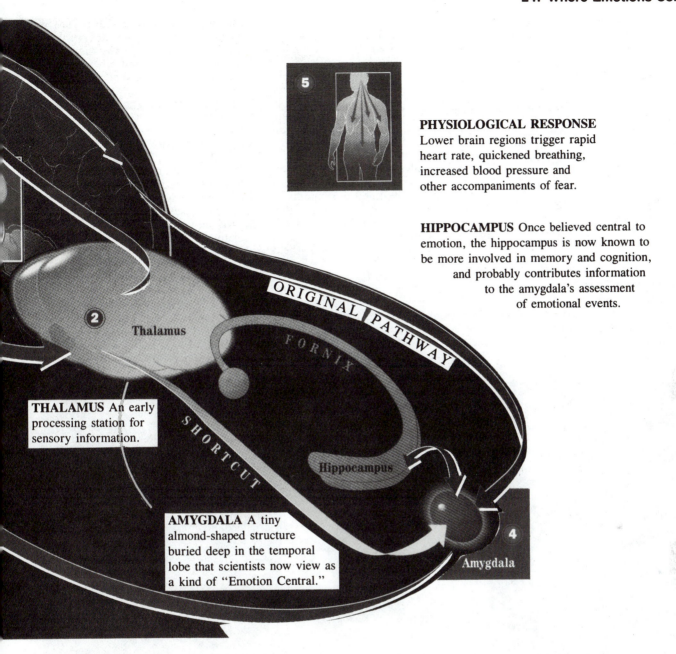

PHYSIOLOGICAL RESPONSE
Lower brain regions trigger rapid
heart rate, quickened breathing,
increased blood pressure and
other accompaniments of fear.

HIPPOCAMPUS Once believed central to
emotion, the hippocampus is now known to
be more involved in memory and cognition,
and probably contributes information
to the amygdala's assessment
of emotional events.

THALAMUS An early
processing station for
sensory information.

AMYGDALA A tiny
almond-shaped structure
buried deep in the temporal
lobe that scientists now view as
a kind of "Emotion Central."

snakes—even toy reptiles that don't move—when they watch videotapes of other monkeys reacting fearfully. But if the same monkeys watch concocted videos of monkey role models jumping in fright at mushrooms or flowers, they remain unswayed.

Twenty years ago, much was made of reports that the brain's left and right hemispheres seemed to "specialize" in different types of thinking, though media accounts of this "right brain/left brain" division were often greatly oversimplified. Now a growing body of work suggests that the two sides of the brain may play distinct emotional roles, perhaps because such a division of labor is more efficient. Neurologists have known for many years that stroke patients whose

right hemispheres have been damaged have trouble both expressing emotion and perceiving the emotional signals of others. They will understand the statement, "I am angry," for example, but fail to detect the speaker's injured tone or the angry expression on his face.

University of Florida neurologist Kenneth Heilman suggests that the right hemisphere may contain a kind of "lexicon" of emotion-laden images, which is impaired when the hemisphere is injured. In a series of studies, Heilman and his colleagues found that patients with right hemisphere damage had great difficulty imagining and describing a smiling face, though they could easily describe imagined objects such as pennies or horses. Yet such patients do retain some

ability to grasp emotional concepts, the scientists have found, perhaps relying upon a combination of logical reasoning and past experience. Told that a man "drank the water and then saw the sign," for example, they can usually figure out that the man is anxious about what he just drank.

The brain's right and left hemispheres may divide negative and positive emotions as well. When subjects report feeling emotions such as fear and disgust, their right frontal lobes show increased electrical activity, according to studies by psychologists Richard Davidson at the University of Wisconsin and Donald Tucker at the University of Oregon. Sadness seems to diminish activity in the left frontal lobe as measured by an electroencephalogram (EEG), while certain positive emotions like happiness and amusement increase it.

Right and left brain asymmetries may even prove to be a marker of differences in overall temperament. In a series of studies, Davidson and his colleagues have found that infants more prone to distress when separated from their mothers show increased activity in the right frontal lobe, as do people with a more pessimistic outlook. People who have at some point in their lives been clinically depressed show decreased left frontal lobe activity compared with subjects who have never been depressed.

Such emotional lopsidedness, Davidson suggests, may be adaptive in a broader, evolutionary sense. Positive emotions draw people toward things that are pleasant or satisfying, engaging them with the world; negative emotions encourage withdrawal from what may be threatening or dangerous. In the hostile environment in which early man evolved, it may have been useful to have approach and avoidance unmistakably delineated in the brain.

"Your face, my thane, is a book where men may read strange matters," Lady Macbeth warns her husband in Shakespeare's great tragedy, knowing that a furrowed brow or curled lip can be a revealing barometer of emotional life. But it remained for psychologists, inspired by Silvan Tomkins, to develop systematic ways to measure and compare the precisely tuned movements of more than 30 facial muscles, and to link the language of sneers, smiles and grimaces to other aspects of emotion.

Their work has challenged long-held assumptions about facial expression. It was widely believed, for example, that the way emotions are expressed by the face was learned after birth and differed from culture to culture. But in cross-cultural studies over the past two decades, psychologists Paul Ekman at the University of California at San Francisco and Carroll Izard of the University of Delaware have demonstrated that facial representations of sadness, fear, anger, disgust and other emotions are remarkably constant and recognizable around the globe.

Darwin's delight. The social roles for displaying emotion *do* vary culturally. The Japanese, for example, are more likely to hold back negative expressions in public. Individuals, of course, also differ in the intensity of their emotional expressions, and to some extent in the events that trigger different emotions. But the researchers found familiar scowls and grins even in members of isolated cultures in New Guinea and Indonesia and in blind children, who cannot learn them by visual imitation.

Such findings would have pleased biologist Charles Darwin, who explored the universality of emotion in his 1872 book, "The Expression of Emotions in Man and Animals" (see box). The findings are equally sweet to modern investigators who believe that humans possess innate,

---

ANCIENT TRADITION

The philosophy of feeling, the biology of barks

The nature of emotion has bedeviled great thinkers ever since Cain slew Abel in a jealous rage. Plato and Aristotle argued over how sharply the "rational" and "irrational" parts of the "soul" were divided—a question that modern scientists, with a modern vocabulary, still quarrel about. Philosophers proposed master lists of "basic" emotions, only to have the next pundit in line revise them or object that there were no such things—an avocation still popular among emotion researchers.

Enlightenment theories of emotion tended to credit mysterious fluids for emotional life, regarding emotions as "provided by God to protect us," says Colby College philosopher Cheshire Calhoun, co-author of "What is an Emotion?" Descartes, for example, explained that the approach of a "strange and frightful figure" triggers the action of "animal spirits" that "proceed thence to take their places partly in the nerves ... and dispose the legs for flight."

In the 19th century, the notion of emotional "instincts" grew stronger. But William James, writing in 1890, contended that the experience of "feeling" followed the physiological sensa-

Darwin's dogs. *Patterns for hostility (bottom) and humble affection (top)*

tions of emotion, rather than the other way around. "We feel sorry because we cry, angry because we strike, afraid because we tremble," James asserted.

But the scientist who first tried to study emotional expression systemati-cally was not a psychologist but a biologist. Charles Darwin, who delved into emotion to gather support for his broader theory of evolution, contended that emotions were universal and not unique to human beings. He described characteristic displays of fear, rage or joy in a variety of animals, including dogs, monkeys, swans and cats. A dog, Darwin pointed out, stiffens, its tail erect, the hairs on its neck bristling when it approaches a stranger. But upon recognizing its master, its demeanor instantly changes to one of affectionate submission.

Human beings required different tactics of study. Darwin sent out questionnaires to missionaries and ambassadors around the globe, asking if emotional expressions were the same in different cultures. Among his questions: "Is astonishment expressed by the eyes and mouth being opened wide, and by the eyebrows being raised?"

Thirty-six questionnaires were returned to the biologist, allowing him to argue his case in his now classic 1872 book, "The Expression of Emotions in Man and Animals." Today, emotion theorists remain split between those who emphasize the contribution of thinking to emotional experience, and those who stress biology. But Darwin's belief that emotions are innate, adaptive mechanisms for dealing with the environment is slowly gaining ground in a field that once scorned such notions.

genetically wired templates of emotional expression and recognition, refined versions of those seen in primates and other "lower order" species.

But how does the face, with its Esperanto of feeling, fit into the larger emotional system—the rising pulse and rapid breathing of a man who has just been called a "sniveling scum bucket," for example, or the intangible experiences we label grief and joy? In an intriguing series of studies, their results still being debated, Ekman and his colleagues Robert Levenson and Wallace Friesen have shown that instructing people to produce the muscular movements of a particular emotional expression—a grimace of disgust, for example—produces changes in autonomic nervous system response, such as heart rate and skin temperature, even though the subjects are not told which emotion they are displaying. The scientists also found that these physiological patterns are, to some extent, specific for different emotional expressions, particularly negative ones such as anger, fear and disgust. The research team recently reported that distinctive heart rate and skin temperature patterns are also produced when subjects are asked to relive the memory of a particular emotional experience.

The person who communicates his feelings is, of course, only half the equation. In a complex social world, we are readers of emotion, too. Using ever more sophisticated tools, researchers are beginning to find out how the brain detects and analyzes emotional signals. Working with monkeys, for example, neuroscientist Edmund Rolls and his colleagues at Oxford University have isolated a group of nerve cells, located in part of the brain's temporal lobe that processes visual information, that respond exclusively to faces and appear capable of recognizing individual faces as well. A second set of neurons, about 2 millimeters away, apparently helps determine which emotion a face displays. Together, Rolls says, the two sets of cells allow monkeys—and probably humans as well—to determine who and what they are dealing with in the environment.

Unfamiliar faces. Just how crucial these mechanisms are is evident in the extraordinary case of a 41-year-old brain-injured patient studied over several years by Massachusetts Institute of Technology neuroscientist Nancy Etcoff. Mr. H., who suffered damage to the temporal lobes of his brain in a car accident many years ago, has no trouble conversing. He holds a responsible job and can quickly distinguish a Mercedes from a Mazda. But he has entirely lost the ability to recognize faces—even those of the people closest to him. He asks his wife to wear a ribbon

in her hair at parties, so he can tell her from the other guests. Arriving at his own house, Mr. H. will stare blankly at the two children in the driveway. "Are those your children?" Etcoff will ask him. "I guess they must be," her patient replies. "They're in my yard."

Yet Mr. H., whose condition is called prosopagnosia, still retains some ability to discern emotions, lending support to the notion that facial recognition and emotional interpretation are separate in the brain. Shown a picture of a sad face, he cannot at first name the feeling he sees. But he *is* able to mimic the downcast expression and in some way, Etcoff believes, this re-creation of sadness on his own face "teaches" his brain, which then correctly labels the emotion in the picture. Still, such maneuvering makes any sojourn into the social world difficult. Says Etcoff: "People who can't recognize facial emotions feel like they

can't read between the lines, and there's a tremendous awkwardness in relating to other people."

The snubbing of emotion in scientific theory was not confined to the study of adults. Child psychologists, too, were riveted by logical reasoning, as if infants and toddlers were, as one expert put it, "little computerized robots dealing with their environment." Even Swiss psychologist Jean Piaget—whose meticulous observations of his own children's intellectual growth serve as a primer for every student of child psychology—barely nodded at emotion, stressing instead the child's developing powers of thought and analysis. Feelings seemed irrelevant to infants, who could not even form goals or distinguish cause and effect.

In the last decade, the scientific work that has reshaped the understanding of emotion has transformed the field of

---

HORMONE OF LOVE

The chemistry of romance and nurturance

The romantic notion that love is a matter of the right chemistry may not be far off the mark. Scientists are now finding links between behavior and the brain's many chemicals; and recent animal studies of one particular hormone, oxytocin, suggest the chemical promotes the social bondings involved in choosing a mate and reproducing. Scientists speculate that the hormone may do the same for humans, fostering friendship, love and nurturance.

Oxytocin is well known for its ability to hasten childbirth and promote lactation, but it is also present in areas of the brain linked to emotions and seems to influence how animals relate to one another. For example, when the hormone is given to two prairie voles, according to zoologist Sue Carter, they immediately form a monogamous bond. In the wild, the small mammals pair up only after sex, when oxytocin floods their systems. In sociable mice, adding oxytocin boosts the instinct for cuddling to a frenzied pitch.

The hormone not only seems to ensure that animals are attracted in the first place, it also appears to promote good parenting later on. Studies by Cort Pedersen and Jack Caldwell at the University of North Carolina and Gustav Jirikowski at Scripps Research Institute show that virgin female rats,

normally nasty to babies, will respond to oxytocin by acting in a more motherly way. Parent rats will even mistreat their children if oxytocin is blocked.

In humans, oxytocin levels rise dramatically during sex, and scientists believe the chemical's presence may promote accompanying feelings of love or infatuation. Some researchers even suspect that oxytocin may play a part in most social behavior. "Human relations are influenced by the model of the parent-child relationship in that they include the notions of nurturing, care, help," says Pedersen. "The deficiency of a hormone tied to that parenting instinct may account for some of the anti-social behavior we think of as psychopathic."

Scientists emphasize that no hormone acts alone. Several dozen chemicals combine in intricate ways to influence emotions. "You will never find one specific hormone for one emotion," neurologist Marsel Mesulam notes. "Rather, it's the overall pattern that's important, just as in music it is the song that makes you feel happy or sad, not a particular instrument." Even so, scientists hope that understanding how oxytocin works may illuminate the most powerful of human emotions.

BY JOANNIE M. SCHROF

child psychology as well. A rapidly expanding body of work now makes it clear not only that infants have emotions, but that they are crucial from the very first moments of life. Nonverbal expressions of enjoyment, anger and other sentiments have been detected in children younger than 8 months old, and even a 10-week-old baby can distinguish his mother's smile of joy from her scowl of anger. "By nine months, the infant is an emotional being," writes Alan Sroufe, at the University of Minnesota.

It is not just that the infant is joyful upon seeing his mother's face or fearful at a loud noise. University of California at Berkeley developmental psychologist Joseph Campos and others argue that emotions are powerful tools for becoming a human being. Through them, children signal their needs and wants and are spurred to satisfy them. Feelings help forge—or sever—bonds with other people. By closely observing the emotional reactions of others—a mother's welcoming look when a stranger approaches, for example—a child also learns to size up uncertain situations, a process Campos and his colleagues call "social referencing."

Language adds sophistication and subtlety both to the expression of emotion and to children's ability to influence the feelings of others. By the age of 20 months, most children possess an emotional vocabulary, voicing in words their distress, pleasure or fatigue: In one study, each of six children said, "I love you" to a parent before his or her second birthday. By 28 months, discussions of feelings take place in a wide variety of contexts, from squabbles with siblings to pretend tea parties given for imaginary guests. And during their third year, children begin to refer to past and future states of emotion, and probe the reasons behind feelings, asking, for example, why an older brother is crying.

Jokes and affection. Experts in child development once devoted their attention mostly to how children learned to "damp down" emotional extremes, controlling tantrums, for example. But in groundbreaking studies, Pennsylvania State University child development expert Judith Dunn has shown that children also actively use emotional expression to obtain comfort, give affection, learn social rules, make jokes, irritate siblings, form friendships and deepen intimacy in relationships.

According to new research by Dunn's group, how much time parents devote to discussing emotions with their children may influence sensitivity to the feelings of others later in life. Studies indicate, for example, an association between the frequency of mothers' exchanges about emotions with firstborn children and the friendly behavior of those children toward their infant brothers and sisters. Dunn and her colleagues have recently suggested that the frequency and content of family conversations about feelings may affect children's ability to recognize emotions in adults six years later.

Even at birth, investigators are finding, children vary in their emotional reactions to people and events, suggesting a hereditary contribution to temperament. Studies of children over a period of time by Harvard University psychologist Jerome Kagan show marked differences between those who are "inhibited"—by which Kagan means shy, quiet and socially withdrawn—and their more talkative, outgoing and sociable peers. Kagan has found that inhibited children have higher and more stable heart rates, react more to stress and may be more prone to depression and anxiety disorders later in life.

Primatologists are now finding that similar temperamental differences are present in monkeys studied in the wild, and may play a role in evolutionary adaptation. Male rhesus monkeys who are highly reactive emotionally, for example, display differences in heart rate similar to those of Kagan's socially inhibited children, according to research by Stephen Suomi and Kathlyn Rasmussen of the National Institute of Child Health and Human Development. These heart rate patterns appear to predict how male monkeys will react at puberty, when they typically emigrate from their own troop and join another. Unusually "shy" monkeys, the scientists found, tend to hang back, working their way into the new group slowly over months or years, while more aggressive monkeys tend to fight their way into the group instead. Both strategies, says Suomi, have pros and cons: "Outgoing individuals have the opportunity to get into the gene pool earlier, but they run a greater risk of getting killed. Shy ones, slower to integrate, are at greater risk for starving to death, but their chances of being killed in a fight are lower."

Sadly, cancer stole the seven more books that Silvan Tomkins hoped to write. But before his death, he completed the final two volumes of "Affect/Imagery/Consciousness," the treatise he began 30 years ago. The books, one just published and the other soon to follow, make their appearance in a vastly changed climate. Emotion research is now everywhere, its importance no longer argued before indifferent auditors. Scientists, finally, are joining the poets in granting the "passions" their rightful place as "the elements of life."

BY ERICA E. GOODE WITH
JOANNIE M. SCHROF AND SARAH BURKE

Happy or Sad, a Mood Can Prove Contagious

Emotions pass from person to person swiftly and subtly.

Daniel Goleman

"Emotions are contagious," wrote the Swiss psycho-analyst Carl Jung. His observation is now being borne out and given precision by scientific studies of the subtle interplay of moods as they are passed from person to person.

The new data depict moods as akin to social viruses, with some people having a natural ability to transmit them while others are more susceptible to contagion. And moods seem to perpetuate themselves by leading a person to do things that reinforce the feeling, no matter how unpleasant it may be.

The transmission of moods seems to occur instantaneously and unconsciously as one person mimics, for example, the physical movement of another's facial expressions. It also appears that a feeling of harmonious interaction between two people is achieved when they synchronize their moods, and this can be done by a series of precisely timed nods and other nonverbal cues.

"Emotional contagion happens within milliseconds, so quick you can't control it, and so subtly that you're not really aware it's going on," said Dr. Elaine Hatfield, a psychologist at the University of Hawaii who presented her findings at a meeting of the American Psychological Society in Washington last June.

The new understanding of who is more likely to pass along emotional contagion and who is more susceptible to picking up someone else's mood comes from psychophysiological studies of how people express their emotions. The data distinguished people by the degree to which their moods were freely expressed in their faces and gestures or in responses of the autonomic nervous system, which controls involuntary activities of the organs, like sweating or a jump in heart rate.

The moods studied are relatively mild, like cheerfulness, melancholy or irritability, because the vast majority of emotional life, researchers have found, is in this range. For example, in a study of more than 5,000 days of people's moods, subjects reported being intensely happy on fewer than 3 days in 100.

Women report being in negative moods about twice as often as men, according to Dr. Ed Diener, a psychologist at the University of Illinois, even though women also say they are, over all, as happy as men. "One reason seems to be that women's moods tend to be more intense than men's," Dr. Diener said. "While they may have unhappy moods more often, they also report more intense joy than men, so it averages out about the same."

The more emotionally expressive people are, the more apt they are to transmit their moods to someone they talk with, said Dr. John Cacciopo, a psychologist at Ohio State University. People who are easily affected by the moods of others, on the other hand, have especially forceful autonomic reactions when they unconsciously mimic someone who is highly expressive, he said.

Such people are far more likely to feel sad after a chat with someone who is depressed, or to feel buoyed by seeing an upbeat commercial, Dr. Cacciopo said. While the spread of strong emotions between people is obvious, the transmission of moods can be almost insidious in its subtlety. For example, in one study, two volunteers simply sat quietly facing each other, waiting for an experimenter to return to the room. The volunteers had been paired because one was highly expressive of emotions, the other more deadpan.

Two minutes later, when the experimenter came back and had them fill out a mood checklist, the mood of the more expressive of the pair had taken over the other person, presumably through body language. The study, reported in the April issue of The Personality and Social Psychology Bulletin, was done by Dr. Ellen Sullins, a psychologist at Northern Arizona University.

The transmission seems to be instantaneous as well as unconscious. "Just seeing someone express an emotion can evoke that mood in you," Dr. Cacciopo said. "This dance of moods goes on between people all the time."

One mechanism at work in this transmission is the tendency for people to imitate the expressions of faces they look at. For example, Swedish researchers reported in 1986 that when people viewed pictures of smiling or angry faces, their facial muscles changed slightly to mimic those faces.

While the changes were fleeting and not visible to [the] eye, they were detected using electrodes that measured electrical activity in the muscles. Dr. Cacciopo repeated the study and found that seeing the faces evoked the moods.

Dr. Cacciopo and Dr. Hatfield theorize in an article to appear later this year in The Review of Personality and Social Psychology that it is through such unconscious mimicry of another person's facial expression, gestures and movements, tone of voice and the like that people create in themselves the mood of the person they are imitating.

SYNCHRONIZATION IS CRUCIAL

This approach has long been used by actors who evoke emotions by recalling times when they felt a particular way and purposely repeat expressions and gestures from that moment.

An ability to synchronize moods with another person appears to be crucial to smooth interaction. "It determines if your interactions are effective or not," said Dr. Cacciopo. "If you're poor at both sending and receiving moods, you'll be likely to have problems in your relationships."

Just how awkward or comfortable people feel together depends to a large extent on how tightly orchestrated their physical movements are as they talk, according to studies by Dr. Frank Bernieri, a psychologist at Oregon State University. His work focuses on the nonverbal markers that punctuate an interaction, like whether one person nods on cue at the precise moment the other makes a conversational point, or whether people shift in their chairs simultaneously or rock at the same rhythm.

"The degree to which people's movements seem orchestrated determines how much emotional rapport they will feel," Dr. Bernieri said. "When people are in sync, it's like watching a long series of volleys in tennis, with one person's movements precisely linked in timing to the other's."

In one study, pairs of volunteers spent 10 minutes trying to teach the other a set of made-up words and their definitions. Analysis of videotapes of their interaction found that those pairs whose movements were in greatest synchrony also felt the most emotional rapport with each other.

"Even if the final mood was something negative, like being bored, if both partners felt the same way, there was greater synchrony in their movements," said Dr. Bernieri.

Such physical synchrony seems to pave the way for the transmission of moods. In another study, Dr. Bernieri had women who scored high on a test of depression come to the lab with their romantic partners and discuss a problem in their relationship.

"The most highly synchronous couples felt lousy after the talk," said Dr. Bernieri. "The men in those couples left feeling as frustrated and depressed as their partners."

People who are feeling an intense emotion like depression seem to choose activities that perpetuate their moods, other researchers have found. While it is no surprise that people in a joyous mood stoke the feeling by, for instance, rehashing a victory, psychologists find that people do the same with unpleasant moods.

SEEKING A CONFIRMING VIEW

The effect is most striking for sadness. For example, William Swann, a psychologist at the University of Texas, had volunteers who scored either very high or very low on a test of depression read what were supposed to be sketches of their personality. Each student saw three sketches, one portraying him or her in a positive light, one neutral and one highly critical.

The volunteers were then told they could meet one of the psychology interns who had purportedly done the sketch. Those volunteers who were least depressed tended to choose the intern who wrote the flattering profile. But those who were most depressed tended to choose the person who had done the critical profile.

"People seek to confirm whatever view they hold of themselves, even if, for the moment, it is a negative one," said Dr. Gordon Bower, a psychologist at Stanford University who is a leader in the research on moods. "In general, you seek out people who are in the same mood you are in."

Much of the research showing how moods perpetuate themselves comes from experiments in which good or bad moods are induced in volunteers, and their actions once in that mood are carefully studied. For example, in research by Dr. Bower's graduate students, volunteers first immersed themselves in recalling an event in their past that made them very happy or very sad. Then they were asked to view an array of slides, half depicting happy moments, half upsetting ones.

"On average, the sad people looked about a second longer at the unpleasant slides, while happy people looked longer at the happy ones," said Dr. Bower.

In a similar study by Dr. Mark Snyder at the University of Minnesota, volunteers who were put into a good or bad mood through hypnosis were then asked to judge snippets of music. Those who were happy preferred light-hearted tunes; those who were sad preferred dirges.

It is perhaps no surprise that people's moods affect how they see their future. But psychologists point out that people are largely unaware that a good or bad mood is creating an optimistic or pessimistic outlook: it simply seems that the facts support one or another view.

Research by Dr. Bower and others shows that moods influence people's judgments by making either positive or negative memories more readily available. Thus a rational weighing of the evidence is swayed in one direction or the other by the bias that moods introduce in what can be brought to mind.

For example, an Australian study found that people who had just seen the comedy "Back to the Future" made positive judgments of such things as how their marriages and careers were working out, while those who had just seen "The Killing Fields" tended to make more negative evaluations.

Stress: The "Type A" Hypothesis

On January 16, 1991, the Gulf War began. Allied planes attacked Iraq, and two days later the Iraqis began to fire SCUD missiles toward Israel. Although world attention centered on the soldiers and civilians who died or were wounded in combat, a different kind of medical crisis was occurring at the Sapir Medical Center near Tel Aviv, within earshot of the missile explosions. More than double the usual number of people were admitted to the hospital with heart attacks in the first eight days of the war. Other hospitals reported a similar surge in cardiac events and sudden deaths, which peaked in the periods immediately after the siren alarms were sounded.

Did the psychological stress of war precipitate the heart attacks among the Israeli civilians? For decades the idea that cardiovascular disease might be caused or made worse by such stress has been a matter of speculation. In 1910 the legendary physician Sir William Osler noted that among a group of doctors who had angina, all were relentless workers. Regardless of their other personal characteristics, "every one of these [physician-patients] had an additional factor — worry; in not a single case under fifty years of age was this feature absent."

Although many pressures of modern life may be unique to our times, Osler's words show that psychological stress is not new, nor is the association between stress and cardiovascular disease. Today, more than 80 years later, the link between head and heart remains controversial. Some investigators contend that the emotions play an important role in the development of cardiovascular disease, and many patients are concerned that their physicians do not seem interested in this aspect of their lives. Recent research has again focused attention on stress as a contributor to hypertension, heart-rhythm disorders, and coronary artery disease. These studies have suggested that psychological stress can also cause *silent ischemia* — that is, brief periods of inadequate blood flow to the heart that do not cause chest discomfort but are detectable on an electrocardiogram.

The conclusion that psychological stress is hazardous to one's health would itself be just one more source of worry if the problem had no solution. But some investigators believe that stress-reducing measures can be useful in both treating and preventing cardiovascular disease, and that recent insights into the impact of stress on the heart can help determine those drug therapies most likely to be effective. Studies focusing on psychological stress have entered the mainstream of medical research and may begin to provide answers to two fundamental questions: what is stress, and what can we do about it?

True to type?

Although events such as loss of a job or a loved one are devastating for everyone, some people are by nature more susceptible to stress. Several studies have suggested that a certain personality or pattern of behavior puts these individuals, said to be *Type A's*, at greater risk for heart disease. In their drive to reach goals that are often poorly defined, Type A's constantly struggle against time and other obstacles. They tend to be aggressive and competitive, to speak quickly and impatiently, to raise their voices, and to finish other people's sentences. In some cases feelings of hostility are barely contained.

Up to 50% of the male population may be considered to exhibit Type A behavior, and some experts believe that this personality pattern is becoming more common. Type B individuals are the opposite of Type A's — relaxed and less aggressive. Despite their low-key demeanor, Type B's may also be interested in success; however, in trying to achieve their goals, their attitude is less hostile.

Hostility: the real culprit?

The first major investigation to suggest a link between Type A behavior and heart disease was the Western Collaborative Study, an epidemiological project completed in 1964. The men who participated were classified as Type A or B based on their behavior and were then followed for several years. For those in the Type A group, heart-disease risk was more than twice that for the Type B men. According to later reports, the more intense the Type A pattern, the greater the likelihood of heart attack. Such behavior appears to increase coronary risk for women as well and in middle-aged persons more than in those over 65. Based on these "positive" results, some researchers believe that not only is a Type A personality a risk factor for heart disease, but it may be on a par with other factors such as smoking, hypertension, and high cholesterol.

Still, two other large trials failed to find a connection between Type A behavior and cardiac problems. In a study of aspirin's effects on heart-attack survivors, Type A behavior was not associated with an increased risk for a second heart attack or death. In addition, in the Multiple Risk Factor Intervention Trial (MRFIT), the personality type of the men enrolled was not related to mortality after seven years of followup. Although neither study was designed to test the Type A hypothesis, such evidence has raised questions about whether that type of behavior is an important coronary risk factor.

Why do some studies suggest this link while others do not? For one thing, the Type A classification may be a poor marker for the behavior pattern associated with coronary artery disease. According to detailed psychological analysis, the real culprits may be pent-up anger and hostility. Competitiveness and job overinvolvement may add to a Type A's risk because these characteristics tend to be associated with such emotions.

Stress tests for the mind

An obstacle to resolving whether Type A behavior actually causes cardiovascular complications has been the problem of defining stress and measuring its effects. Various techniques have been used to evaluate responses to induced stress, including "mental stress tests" designed to challenge a person's intellectual or problem-solving abilities — activities that may seem more like games than medical research.

One common approach involves giving the subject arithmetic tasks, such as continually subtracting 17 from an initial four-digit number — for example, 3245, 3228, 3211, and so on. Another test consists of "mirror drawing," in which the subject is asked to sketch complex figures while viewing only a reflected image of the work-in-progress. In some cases, researchers press the subject even further by pointing out errors or making comments like, "This isn't hard. Why is it taking you so long?" (Whether these subjects volunteer for subsequent studies is not known.)

These mental stress tests cause only temporary anguish, whereas the psychological stresses of real life, such as serious work-related problems, tend to last much longer and cause a more profound kind of pain. Because researchers can subject volunteers to stressful situations for short periods only, some have used harrowing interviews or disturbing movies to study the cardiovascular responses to mental pressure. Another approach is to force the subject to deliver a five-minute speech on his or her personal faults or embarrassing habits in front of two observers.

Using these methods, investigators have shown that Type A's react to stress in ways that may increase their risk for cardiovascular disease. In response to arithmetic tasks and tests of reaction time, Type A's secrete more adrenaline than Type B's do, especially when financial incentives are added. Nevertheless, emotional tension appears to produce biological responses in all of us, regardless of our personality type. In one study the act of speaking in public tripled the amount of adrenaline in the bloodstream within three minutes. Although this surge quickly resolved, the responses to other types of stress may be prolonged. For example, five years after the nuclear-reactor meltdown at Three Mile Island, people living close to the site were found to have abnormally high adrenaline levels.

"White-coat hypertension"

One well-known stress-induced syndrome may be seen in the doctor's office during blood-pressure measurement. In a study conducted in Italy, blood pressure was measured continuously for 24-hour periods in 88 hospitalized patients. Whenever a physician entered the room, systolic pressure rose by an average of 20 mm Hg and diastolic pressure by 10 mm Hg. In some cases the pressure increased as much as 40–50 mm Hg. (When a nurse came in, pressure elevations were less pronounced.) Since the blood-pressure rise seen in white-coat hypertension tends to decrease by more than 50% after about ten minutes, the doctor may postpone this measurement or repeat it if the value was high early in the visit.

Coronary consequences

If Type A behavior truly makes one more susceptible to coronary artery disease, one reason may be its association with hypertension, smoking, and high cholesterol. A recent study noted that only 22% of people with newly detected hypertension had Type B personalities; among those with normal blood pressure, about 40% were Type B's. Psychologists who interviewed the hypertensive subjects felt that their potential for hostility was greater than that of the normotensive group.

Once a person has coronary artery disease, psychological stress can provoke myocardial ischemia. One study at St. Luke's–Roosevelt Medical Center in New York City suggested that patients with coronary disease can be divided into three groups: those without inducible ischemia, those who develop it only with exercise, and those in whom ischemia occurs during exercise *and* mental activities. Using nuclear medicine technology, these researchers visualized heart-wall motion and found that many of the ischemic episodes induced by mental stress did not cause chest discomfort. This phenomenon (*silent ischemia*) may occur in as many as two-thirds of patients after a heart attack.

Brief periods of mental stress also increase the "stickiness" of platelets. These small cells gather at the site of an atherosclerotic plaque and further narrow the coronary arteries, raising the question of whether emotional stress contributes to the development of coronary artery disease even in the absence of other cardiac risk factors. Furthermore, this finding suggests that stress can promote clotting within a coronary artery, thus cutting off blood flow to the heart muscle and causing a heart attack.

Managing stress

Can anything be done to alleviate stress? For many, their job is the major source of psychological duress; on the other hand, being unemployed might be even more distressing. Fortunately, methods for dealing with the stress of work (and other problems) are available; in fact, according, to some studies, these strategies may offer cardiovascular benefits as well.

On examining the relationship between mental stress and the cardiovascular system, research-
ers have noted that efforts at stress management may be particularly useful for controlling mild hypertension. Such training teaches relaxation techniques that may enable individuals to modify their psychological and hormonal responses to mental pressure. Based on pooled data from randomized trials, this type of intervention lowers systolic pressure by an average of 9 mm Hg and diastolic pressure by 6 mm Hg. (In the control subjects in these studies, both systolic and diastolic pressures fell an average of 3 mm Hg.) Although small, these changes sometimes allow people with hypertension to reduce the dose or number of medications they are taking or, less commonly, to forgo such treatment entirely.

Stress-management training may help prevent episodes of ischemia in people already known to have coronary artery disease. In one study of patients who had suffered a myocardial infarction, those given advice about how to control their Type A behavior suffered half as many recurrent heart attacks as did patients who were offered more conventional counseling by their cardiologists.

One response to psychological stress is sympathetic-nervous-system activation, which makes the heart beat faster and more forcefully and prepares the body for physical action. When our cave-dwelling ancestors were threatened by predators, these physiological responses were lifesaving; when one is confronting a belligerent boss, they are less likely to help. Fortunately, certain medications can be used to blunt sympathetic-nervous-system activity. Beta blockers (such as propranolol, atenolol, and nadolol) decrease the electrical activity of the brain associated with aggressive behavior, slow the heart rate, and lower blood pressure; in this way they may prevent myocardial ischemia due to psychological stress. Other drugs, such as dipyridamole, can help keep platelets from clumping in response to stress.

Future research should clarify the impact of stress on the heart and identify those individuals most likely to suffer ill effects. In the meantime, in the words of William Harvey, the seventeenth-century anatomist who was the first to realize that blood traveled from the arteries to the veins and back to the heart, "Every affection of the mind that is attended with either pain or pleasure, hope or fear, is the cause of an agitation whose influence extends to the heart."

The Last Interview of
ABRAHAM MASLOW

Edward Hoffman, Ph.D.

About the author: Edward Hoffman received his doctorate from the University of Michigan. A clinical psychologist on New York's Long Island, he is the author of several books, including The Right to be Human: A Biography of Abraham Maslow *(Tarcher).*

When Abraham Maslow first shared his pioneering vision of a "comprehensive human psychology" in this magazine in early 1968, he stood at the pinnacle of his international acclaim and influence.

HIS ELECTION AS PRESIDENT OF THE AMERican Psychological Association some months before capped an illustrious academic career spanning more than 35 productive years, during which Maslow had steadily gained the high regard—even adulation—of countless numbers of colleagues and former students. His best-known books, *Motivation and Personality* and *Toward a Psychology of Being*, were not only being discussed avidly by psychologists, but also by professionals in fields ranging from management and marketing to education and counseling. Perhaps even more significantly, Maslow's iconoclastic concepts like peak experience, self-actualization, and synergy had even begun penetrating popular language.

Nevertheless, it was a very unsettling time for him: Recovering from a major heart attack, the temperamentally restless and ceaselessly active Maslow was finding forced convalescence at home to be almost painfully unbearable. Suddenly, his extensive plans for future research, travel, and lecturing had to be postponed. Although Maslow hoped for a speedy recovery, frequent chest pains induced a keen sense of his own mortality. As perhaps never before, he began to ponder his career's accomplishments and his unrealized goals.

In 1968 PSYCHOLOGY TODAY was a precocious one-year-old upstart, but such was its prestige that it was able to attract perhaps the country's most famous psychologist for an interview.

Maslow likely regarded the PT interview as a major opportunity to outline his "comprehensive human psychology" and the best way to actualize it. At 60, he knew that time permitted him only to plant seeds (in his own metaphor) of research and theory—and hope that later generations would live to see the flowering of human betterment. Perhaps most prescient at a time of global unrest is Maslow's stirring vision of "building a psychology for the peace table." It was his hope that through psychological research, we might learn how to unify peoples of differing racial and ethnic origins, and thereby create a world of peace.

Although the complete audiotapes of the sessions, conducted over three days, disappeared long ago under mysterious circumstances, the written condensation that remains provides a fascinating and still-relevant portrait of a key thinker at the height of his prowess. Intellectually, Maslow was decades ahead of his time; today the wide-ranging ideas he offers here are far from outdated. Indeed, after some twenty-odd years, they're still on the cutting edge of American psychology and social science. Emotionally, this interview is significant for the rare—essentially unprecedented—glimpse it affords into Maslow's personal history and concerns: his ancestry and upbringing; his mentors and ambitions; his courtship, marriage, and fatherhood; and even a few of his peak experiences.

Maslow continued to be puzzled and intrigued by the more positive human phenomenon of self-actualization. He was well aware that his theory about the "best of humanity" suffered from methodological flaws. Yet he had become ever more convinced of its intuitive validity, that self-actualizers provide us with clues to our highest innate traits: love and compassion, creativity and aesthetics, ethics and spirituality. Maslow longed to empirically verify this lifelong hunch.

In the two years of his life that remained, this gifted psychologist never wrote an autobiography, nor did he ever again bare his soul in such a public and wide-ranging way. It may have been that Maslow regarded this unusually personal interview as a true legacy. More than 20 years later, it remains a fresh and important document for the field of psychology.

Mary Harrington Hall, for PSYCHOLOGY TODAY: A couple of William B. Yeats's lines keep running through my head: "And in my heart, the daemons and the gods wage an eternal battle and I feel the pain of wounds, the labor of the spear." How thin is the veneer of civilization, and how can we understand and deal with evil?

Abraham H. Maslow: It's a psychological puzzle I've been trying to solve for years. Why are people cruel and why are they nice? Evil people are rare, but you find evil behavior in the majority of people. The next thing I want to do with my life is to study evil and understand it.

PT: By evil here, I think we both mean destructive action without remorse. Racial prejudice is an evil in our society which we must deal with. And soon. Or we will go down as a racist society.

Maslow: You know, when I became A.P.A. president, the first thing I wanted to do was work for greater recognition for the Negro psychologists. Then I found that there were no Negroes in psychology, at least not many. They don't major in psychology.

PT: Why should they? Why would I think that psychology would solve social problems if I were a Negro living in the ghetto, surrounded by despair?

Maslow: Negroes have really had to take it. We've given them every possible blow. If I were a Negro, I'd be fighting, as Martin Luther King fought, for human recognition and justice. I'd rather go down with my flag flying. If you're weak or crippled, or you can't speak out or fight back in some way, then people don't hesitate to treat you badly.

PT: Could you look at evil behavior in two ways: evil from below and evil from above? Evil as a sickness and evil as understood compassionately?

Maslow: If you look at evil from above, you can be realistic. Evil exists. You don't give it quarter, and you're a better fighter if you can understand it. You're in the position of a psychotherapist. In the the same way, you can look at neurosis. You can see neurosis from below—as a sickness—as most psychiatrists see it. Or you

can understand it as a compassionate man might: respecting the neurosis as a fumbling and inefficient effort toward good ends.

PT: You can understand race riots in the same way, can't you?

Maslow: If you can only be detached enough, you can feel that it's better to riot than to be hopeless, degraded, and defeated. Rioting is a childish way of trying to be a man, but it takes time to rise out of the hell of hatred and frustration and accept that to be a man you don't have to riot.

PT: In our society, we see all behavior as a demon we can vanquish and banish, don't we? And yet good people do evil things.

Maslow: Most people are nice people. Evil is caused by ignorance, thoughtlessness, fear, or even the desire for popularity with one's gang. We can cure many such causes of evil. Science is progressing, and I feel hope that psychology can solve many of these problems. I think that a good part of evil behavior bears on the behavior of the normal.

PT: How will you approach the study of evil?

Maslow: If you think only of evil, then you become pessimistic and hopeless like Freud. But if you think there is no evil, then you're just one more deluded Pollyanna. The thing is to try to understand and realize how it's possible for people who are capable of being angels, heroes, or saints to be bastards and killers. Sometimes, poor and miserable people are hopeless. Many revenge themselves upon life for what society has done to them. They enjoy hurting.

PT: Your study of evil will have to be subjective, won't it? How can we measure evil in the laboratory?

Maslow: All the goals of objectivity, repeatability, and preplanned experimentation are things we have to move toward. The more reliable you make knowledge, the better it is. If the salvation of man comes out of the advancement of knowledge—taken in the best sense—then these goals are part of the strategy of knowledge.

PT: What did you tell your own daughters, Ann and Ellen, when they were growing up?

Maslow: Learn to hate meanness. Watch out for anybody who is mean or cruel. Watch out for people who delight in destruction.

PT: How would you describe yourself? Not in personality, because you're one of

the warmest and sweetest men I've ever met. But who are you?

Maslow: I'm someone who likes plowing new ground, then walking away from it. I get bored easily. For me, the big thrill comes with the discovering.

PT: Psychologists all love Abe Maslow. How did you escape the crossfire?

Maslow: I just avoid most academic warfare. Besides, I had my first heart attack many years ago, and perhaps I've been unconsciously favoring my body. So I may have avoided real struggle. Besides, I only like fights I know I can win, and I'm not personally mean.

PT: Maybe you're just one of the lucky few who grew up through a happy childhood without malice.

Maslow: With my childhood, it's a wonder I'm not psychotic. I was the little Jewish boy in the non-Jewish neighborhood. It was a little like being the first Negro enrolled in the all-white school. I grew up in libraries and among books, without friends.

Both my mother and father were uneducated. My father wanted me to be a lawyer. He thumbed his way across the whole continent of Europe from Russia and got here at the age of 15. He wanted success for me. I tried law school for two weeks. Then I came home to my poor father one night after a class discussing "spite fences" and told him I couldn't be a lawyer. "Well, son," he said, "what do you want to study?" I answered: "Everything." He was uneducated and couldn't understand my passion for learning, but he was a nice man. He didn't understand either that at 16, I was in love.

PT: All 16-year-olds are in love.

Maslow: Mine was different. We're talking about my wife. I loved Bertha. You know her. Wasn't I right? I was extremely shy, and I tagged around after her. We were too young to get married. I tried to run away with her.

PT: Where did you run?

Maslow: I ran to Cornell for my sophomore year in college, then to Wisconsin. We were married there when I was 20 and Bertha was 19. Life didn't really start for me until I got married.

I went to Wisconsin because I had just discovered John B. Watson's work, and I was sold on behaviorism. It was an explosion of excitement for me. Bertha came to pick me up at New York's 42nd Street library, and I was dancing down Fifth Avenue with exuberance. I embarrassed her, but I was so excited about

6. EMOTION AND MOTIVATION

Watson's behaviorist program. It was beautiful. I was confident that here was a real road to travel: solving one problem after another and changing the world.

PT: A clear lifetime with built-in progress guaranteed.

Maslow: That was it. I was off to Wisconsin to change the world. I went there to study with psychologist Kurt Koffka, biologist Hans Dreisch, and philosopher Alexander Meiklejohn. But when I showed up on the campus, they weren't there. They had just been visiting professors, but the lying catalog had included them anyway.

Oh, but I was so lucky, though. I was young Harry Harlow's first doctoral graduate. And they were angels, my professors. I've always had angels around. They helped me when I needed it, even fed me. Bill Sheldon taught me how to buy a suit. I didn't know anything of amenities. Clark Hull was an angel to me, and later, Edward L. Thorndike.

PT: You're an angelic man. I've heard too many stories to let you deny it. What kind of research were you doing at Wisconsin?

Maslow: I was a monkey man. By studying monkeys for my doctoral dissertation, I found that dominance was related to sex, and to maleness. It was a great discovery, but somebody had discovered it two months before me.

PT: Great ideas always go in different places and minds at the same time.

Maslow: Yes, I worked on it until the start of World War II. I thought that working on sex was the easiest way to help mankind. I felt if I could discover a way to improve the sexual life by even one percent, then I could improve the whole species.

One day, it suddenly dawned on me that I knew as much about sex as any man living—in the intellectual sense. I knew everything that had been written; I had made discoveries with which I was pleased; I had done therapeutic work. This was about 10 years before the Kinsey report came out. Then I suddenly burst into laughter. Here was I, the great sexologist, and I had never seen an erect penis except one, and that was from my own bird's-eye view. That humbled me considerably.

PT: I suppose you interviewed people the way Kinsey did?

Maslow: No, something was wrong with Kinsey. I really don't think he liked women, or men. In my research, I interviewed 120 women with a new form of

interview. No notes. We just talked until I got some feeling for the individual's personality, then put sex against that background. Sex has to be considered in regard to love, otherwise it's useless. This is because behavior can be a defense—a way of hiding what you feel—particularly regarding sex.

I was fascinated with my research. But I gave up interviewing men. They were useless because they boasted and lied about sex. I also planned a big research project involving prostitutes. I thought we could learn a lot about men from them, but the research never came off.

PT: You gave up all your experimental research in these fields.

Maslow: Yes, around 1941 I felt I must try to save the world, and to prevent the horrible wars and the awful hatred and prejudice. It happened very suddenly. One day just after Pearl Harbor, I was driving home and my car was stopped by a poor, pathetic parade. Boy Scouts and old uniforms and a flag and someone playing a flute off-key.

As I watched, the tears began to run down my face. I felt we didn't understand—not Hitler, nor the Germans, nor Stalin, nor the Communists. We didn't understand any of them. I felt that if we could understand, then we could make progress. I had a vision of a peace table, with people sitting around it, talking about human nature and hatred, war and peace, and brotherhood.

I was too old to go into the army. It was at that moment I realized that the rest of my life must be devoted to discovering a psychology for the peace table. That moment changed my whole life. Since then, I've devoted myself to developing a theory of human nature that could be tested by experiment and research. I wanted to prove that humans are capable of something grander than war, prejudice, and hatred. I wanted to make science consider all the people: the best specimen of mankind I could find. I found that many of them reported having something like mystical experiences.

PT: Your work with "self-actualizing" people is famous. You have described some of these mystical experiences.

Maslow: Peak experiences come from love and sex, from aesthetic moments, from bursts of creativity, from moments of insight and discovery, or from fusion with nature.

I had one such experience in a faculty procession here at Brandeis University. I saw the line stretching off into a dim fu-

ture. At its head was Socrates. And in the line were the ones I love most. Thomas Jefferson was there. And Spinoza. And Alfred North Whitehead. I was in the same line. Behind me, that infinite line melted into the dimness. And there were all the people not yet born who were going to be in the same line.

I believe these experiences can be studied scientifically, and they will be.

PT: This is all part of your theory of metamotivation, isn't it?

Maslow: But not all people who are metamotivated report peak experiences. The "nonpeakers" are healthy, but they lack poetry and soaring flights of the imagination. Both peakers and nonpeakers can be self-actualized in that they're not motivated by basic needs, but by something higher.

PT: Real self-actualization must be rare. What percentage of us achieve it?

Maslow: I'd say only a fraction of one percent.

PT: People whose basic needs have been met, then, will pursue life's ultimate values?

Maslow: Yes, the ultimate happiness for man is the realization of pure beauty and truth, which are the ultimate values. What we need is a system of thought—you might even call it a religion—that can bind humans together. A system that would fit the Republic of Chad as well as the United States: a system that would supply our idealistic young people with something to believe in. They're searching for something they can pour all that emotion into, and the churches are not much help.

PT: This system must come.

Maslow: I'm not alone in trying to make it. There are plenty of others working toward the same end. Perhaps their efforts, aided by the hundreds of youngsters who are devoting their lives to this, will develop a new image of man that rejects the chemical and technological views. We've technologized everything.

PT: The technologist is the person who has fallen in love with a machine. I suppose that has also happened to those in psychology?

Maslow: They become fascinated with the machine. It's almost a neurotic love. They're like the man who spends Sundays polishing his car instead of stroking his wife.

PT: In several of your papers, you've said that you stopped being a behaviorist when your first child was born.

Maslow: My whole training at Wisconsin was behaviorist. I didn't question it until I began reading some other sources. Later, I began studying the Rorschach test.

At the same time, I stumbled into embryology and read Ludwig von Bertalanffy's *Modern Theories of Development*. I had already become disillusioned with Bertrand Russell and with English philosophy generally. Then, I fell in love with Alfred North Whitehead and Henri Bergson. Their writings destroyed behaviorism for me without my recognizing it.

When my first baby was born, that was the thunderclap that settled things. I looked at this tiny, mysterious thing and felt so stupid. I felt small, weak, and feeble. I'd say that anyone who's had a baby couldn't be a behaviorist.

PT: As you propose new ideas, and blaze new ground, you're bound to be criticized, aren't you?

Maslow: I have worked out a lot of good tricks for fending off professional attacks. We all have to do that. A good, controlled experiment is possible only when you already know a hell of a lot. If I'm a pioneer by choice and I go into the wilderness, how am I going to make careful experiments? If I tried to, I'd be a fool. I'm not against careful experiments. But rather, I've been working with what I call "growing tip" statistics.

With a tree, all the growth takes place at the growing tips. Humanity is exactly the same. All the growth takes place in the growing tip: among that one percent of the population. It's made up of pioneers, the beginners. That's where the action is.

PT: You were the one who helped publish Ruth Benedict's work on synergy. What's it about?

Maslow: That it's possible to set up social institutions that merge selfishness and unselfishness, so that you can't benefit yourself without benefiting others. And the reverse.

PT: How can psychology become a stronger force in our society?

Maslow: We all should look at the similarities within the various disciplines and think of enlarging psychology. To throw anything away is crazy. Good psychology should include all the methodological techniques, without having loyalty to one method, one idea, or one person.

PT: I see you as a catalyst and as a bridge between many disciplines, theories, and philosophies.

Maslow: My job is to put them all together. We shouldn't have "humanistic psychology." The adjective should be unnecessary. I'm not antibehaviorist. I'm antidoctrinaire.

PT: Abe, when you look back on your own education, what kind would you recommend for others?

Maslow: The great educational experiences of my life were those that taught me most. They taught me what kind of a person I was. These were experiences that drew me out and strengthened me. Psychoanalysis was a big thing for me. And getting married. Marriage is a school itself. Also, having children. Becoming a father changed my whole life. It taught me as if by revelation. And reading particular books. William Graham Sumner's *Folkways* was a Mount Everest in my life: It changed me.

My teachers were the best in the world. I sought them out: Erich Fromm, Karen Horney, Ruth Benedict, Max Wertheimer, Alfred Adler, David Levy, and Harry Harlow. I was there in New York City during the 1930s when the wave of distinguished émigrés arrived from Europe.

PT: Not everyone can have such an illustrious faculty.

Maslow: It's the teacher who's important. And if this is so, then what we are doing with our whole educational structure—with credits and the idea that one teacher is as good as another? You look at the college catalog and it says English

342. It doesn't even bother to tell you the instructor's name, and that's insane. The purpose of education—and of all social institutions—is the development of full humaneness. If you keep that in mind, all else follows. We've got to concentrate on goals.

PT: It's like the story about the test pilot who radioed back home: "I'm lost, but I'm making record time."

Maslow: If you forget the goal of education, then the whole thing is lost.

PT: If a rare, self-actualizing young psychologist came to you today and said, "What's the most important thing I can do in this time of crisis?", what advice would you give?

Maslow: I'd say: Get to work on aggression and hostility. We need the definitive book on aggression. And we need it now. Only the pieces exist: the animal stuff, the psychoanalytic stuff, the endocrine stuff. Time is running out. A key to understanding the evil which can destroy our society lies in this understanding.

There's another study that could be done. I'd like to test the whole, incoming freshman class at Brandeis University in various ways: psychiatric interviews, personality tests, everything. I want to follow them for four years of college. For a beginning, I want to test my theory that emotionally healthy people perceive better.

PT: You could make the college study only a preliminary, and follow them through their whole life span, the way Lewis Terman did with his gifted kids.

Maslow: Oh yes! I'd like to know: How good a father or mother does this student become? And what happens to his/her children? This kind of long-term study would take more time than I have left. But that ultimately doesn't make any difference. I like to be the first runner in the relay race. I like to pass on the baton to the next person.

Barriers To Success

How to examine your self-defeating tactics and overcome the hurdles between you and your goals.

B R U C E A. B A L D W I N

Bruce A. Baldwin is a practicing psychologist and author who heads Direction Dynamics in Wilmington, North Carolina, a consulting service that specializes in promoting quality of life. For busy achievers, Dr. Baldwin has written It's All in Your Head: Lifestyle Management Strategies for Busy People.

When you create goals for yourself, you define what you want out of life. You set about achieving what is important to you. To do this, though, requires a base of successful experiences that have created confidence and a sense of personal control—feelings not always easy to acquire.

Setting and achieving personal goals, however, contributes to emotional well-being, and defining realistic personal goals provides a core of personal meaning from which motivational energy is generated. Frequently, men and women without realistic personal goals develop low self-esteem, and over time they often become lethargic and depressed.

Some men and women have realistic personal goals, but just don't seem to be able to reach them. Although these individuals have the skills and opportunities needed to succeed, they are very frustrated. They do not understand why they can't quite reach their goals, and the personal consequences are negative. The problem here is subtle and often difficult to resolve unless the dynamics involved are understood.

The problem lies within the individual. Rationalizing failure or blaming others for lack of success is human nature. Resistance to success, however, is a personal problem and must be addressed within the individual. To accomplish this, the person must accept full responsibility for his or her behavior.

A pattern to the problem is obvious. Almost always, resistance to success involves a pattern of behavior that is repeated. Sometimes self-sabotage is seen only in specific kinds of situations. In other people the problem is more generalized and emerges more or less across the board.

The reason for self-sabotage is often not in conscious awareness. It would be easy to assume that resistance to success always involves self-defeating acts that are calculated and conscious. While this is occasionally true, more often such patterns operate just below conscious awareness.

The result is failure and lowered self-esteem. No one feels good about repeatedly failing to reach personal goals. Self-sabotage results in erosion of self-esteem and feelings about one's own competence. Over time, motivation to try again often diminishes.

Resistance to success, often beginning in childhood or adolescence, does not necessarily end once adulthood is reached. When resistance does continue in adulthood, the individual's potential is never reached because of self-sabotage. Negative gossip, condescending remarks, put-downs, or even name-calling by family members may develop and make matters worse.

Resistance to success is a most frustrating experience for everyone involved. The problem of self-sabotage and resistance to success *can* be resolved, but first, other dimensions of what is actually taking place must be examined.

The Mechanisms of Resistance

When we recognize self-sabotage, the next level of understanding is to define how personal defeat is carried out. Self-sabotage is manifested through a few well-defined patterns of behavior. While these patterns tend to be quite consistent within individuals, they are often clouded by rationalizations, denials, blaming, and other forms of minimizing.

Each mechanism of resistance serves several psychological purposes. First, the individual never makes an active personal decision to attain a goal or not to do so. Second, each mechanism of resistance gives the individual a built-in excuse, so the decision to proceed (or not) is made by others. The individual escapes responsibility for making that decision or reaching a goal. Here's how it's done.

Choosing an inappropriate peer group. Most of us are influenced by our peer groups. When an individual consistently gravitates toward a peer group that has low academic/work motivation, that legitimizes illegal behavior, or that consistently manifests socially inappropriate values, then a problem develops.

Becoming physically sick. The common personal sabotage technique of becoming physically incapacitated can be observed as early as kindergarten, and it can easily persist into adulthood. Some men and women fake an illness to avoid specific situations that may be stressful or psychologically threatening. More often, an actual illness results from the intense emotional

From *USAir Magazine*, June 1992, pp. 18, 21-25. This article is adapted from B. A. Baldwin's "It's All In Your Head: Lifestyle Management Strategies for Busy People," *Direction Dynamics*, 1985. The book is available from *Direction Dynamics*, 309 Honeycutt Dr., Wilmington, NC 28412 for $11.50 postpaid (NC residents should add 6% sales tax).

turmoil being experienced. Common symptoms include palpitations, severe headaches, diarrhea, nausea, faintness or fainting, dizziness, hyperventilation, and generalized gastrointestinal upset. These symptoms justify avoiding key situations.

Procrastinating until it's too late. Procrastination involves habitually putting off obtaining necessary information, filling out applications, or informing key people of a personal desire or decision. Eventually, this creates a situation where a decision is made for the individual, as for example, when a deadline passes. Such procrastination reflects an individual's inability to make an important decision.

Behaving inappropriately in key situations. Everyone goofs up now and then. But when a consistent pattern of making serious mistakes in critical situations is clear, then an underlying problem involving resistance to success may be present. Inappropriate behaviors include drinking too much at dinner with a potential employer, arriving late for an interview, or making inappropriate remarks that are overheard. The person behaves in ways that prevent a successful outcome. Self-recrimination or rationalizations result, but the real problem remains unaddressed.

Starting strong, giving up at the end. Someone who manifests this pattern typically makes a wonderful start toward reaching a goal. While progress early on is steady, as goal attainment nears, persistence wanes and energy output steadily declines. Why? Because the closer one is to reaching a goal, the more one's underlying ambivalence about achieving it rises to the surface. Toward the end, underlying resistance becomes so strong and performance so impaired that goal attainment is either significantly compromised or sabotaged completely.

The Road to Success

Within each self-sabotaging individual is a personal dilemma that produces resistance to success in life. Usually, the problem is not technical competency or a lack of intellectual ability. This is what is so frustrating. It is also what makes it so difficult for friends, family, and colleagues who know the potential of such individuals and see it not being used. The effect on everyone is disappointment. The long-term effect on the individual is serious self-doubt, damaged self-esteem, and feelings of failure.

While many negative feelings result from lack of progress toward success, deep down in each one of these men and women also lies a secret sense of relief. Why? Because each one has not faced a fear within. Self-sabotage has neatly allowed them to avoid facing important personal issues. While these emotional issues frequently have their origins in the family during the developmental years, part of the problem is that they are not consciously aware of these fears.

Perhaps you recognize yourself in this description. Until critical issues within are resolved, you will continue to be frustrated by internal blocks that impede development of personal maturity and professional success. Here are a number of steps to help confront and resolve these often subtle personal issues.

Define your pattern of avoidance. Uncover the mechanisms of sabotage that are present and determine under what conditions they emerge to impede progress toward personal goals. If possible, pinpoint the very first time that the problem occurred.

Select and dissect one representative incident. If one stands out above all others, use it. If not, then choose a recent example that is still fresh in your memory. Take a few moments to write down exactly what happened before, during, and after the self-sabotage.

Clearly articulate the underlying fear. Ask yourself these questions: "What fear do I associate with success or reaching my personal goals?" "What consequences of success did I avoid through self-sabotage?" Say your answers out loud. The fears usually involve threats to self-image or key relationships.

Look for the origins of your fear. It is helpful to understand where your fear began. Because family dynamics are often involved, try to trace your avoidance pattern back as far as you can. Try to understand the fear, but be careful not to blame others for your problem.

Make an active decision about your directions. This is absolutely critical in breaking this pattern. Decide actively to go forward. If, once considered, the payoffs do not seem to be worth it, then actively decide to stay right where you are. The key is to articulate your decision to yourself.

Obtain support and encouragement. Talk over your decision with one good friend who you know will be objective and have your best interests in mind. Avoid those people who may be part of the problem, who are habitually negative, or who may allow their own interests to influence any support they give you.

Inform others of your decision. After carefully considering all options, let others know what you have decided. This may be the most frightening part of all. Don't vacillate or ask others for permission. Instead, inform them of your decision and your future intentions.

Follow through with direct action. With the positives of your decision firmly in mind, do what you've said you'll do. Recognize that every decision involves something gained and something lost. Don't dwell on the loss. Make yourself do whatever is necessary to implement what you've decided.

When you have completed these steps, you've broken your pattern of self-sabotage. You have overcome unresolved issues from the past and have freed yourself to determine your future. As a result, you've not only reestablished direction for your life, but you've also re-created a sense of internal control, and your self-esteem has increased because you are no longer failing. Winston Churchill once commented, "It's a mistake to look too far ahead. Only one link in the chain of destiny can be handled at a time." You've now broken a negative link to the past and are free to forge your destiny—one link at a time.

Development

The Winstons and the Andrews are parents of newborns. Both sets of parents wander down to the hospital's neonatal nursery where both babies, Joey Winston and Kimberly Andrews, are cared for by pediatric nurses when the babies are not in their mothers' rooms. Kimberly is alert, active, and often crying and squirming when her parents watch her. On the other hand, Joey is quiet, often asleep, and less attentive to external stimuli when his parents monitor him in the nursery.

Why are these babies so different? Are the differences gender-related? Will these differences disappear as the children develop or will the differences become exaggerated? What does the future hold for each child? Will Kimberly excel at sports and Joey excel at English? Can Joey overcome his parents' poverty and succeed in a professional career? Will Kimberly become a doctor like her father or a pharmacist like her mother? Will both of these children escape childhood disease, abuse, and the other misfortunes visited upon some American children?

Developmental psychologists are concerned with all of the Kimberlys and Joeys of our world. Developmental psychologists study age-related changes in such behaviors as language, motor skills, cognition, physical health, and social adeptness. Developmental psychologists are interested in the common skills shared by all children as well as the differences between children and the events that creates these differences.

In general, developmental psychologists are interested in the forces that guide and direct development. Some developmental theorists argue that the forces which shape a child are found in the environment in such factors as social class, quality of stimulation available, parenting style and so on. Other theorists insist that genetics and other physiological factors such as hormones underlie the development of humans. A third set of psychologists, in fact, many psychologists, believe that some combination or interaction of both factors, physiology and environment or nature and nurture, are responsible for development.

In this unit, we are going to look at issues of development in a chronological fashion. That is, we will look at issues at the various life stages from prenatal life to old age. The first article, Putting Children First," discusses social trends, particularly those related to the American family, which often place children at risk. The author of the

article, William Galston, also addresses how to confront the changes to assist families so that children's development is enhanced.

Child abuse is a topic that always captures much attention. In "Sad Legacy of Abuse: The Search for Remedies," Daniel Goleman, a chief behavioral science writer for *The New York Times*, discusses the frequency of abuse and which children are most likely to be victimized. As he reminds us, the effects of abuse need not always be detrimental to the child, especially when a nurturing, supportive adult is available to counteract the abusive parent.

"Children in Gangs," the third article in this unit on development, grapples with the tough issue of youth gangs. The average age of gang members is decreasing, but the number of youths joining gangs is increasing. The article suggests that the best way to intervene is to work with young children so as to prevent them from becoming interested in gang membership.

We next turn our attention to adulthood. Ken Dychtwald and Joe Flower describe changes in the American population in "Meeting the Challenges of an Aging Nation." One notable change is that we have an aging population. That is, the average age of our citizens is increasing. The authors look at the three stages of adulthood as well as the issue of aging in other cultures.

Linda Creighton's contribution, "Silent Saviors," discusses grandparenting. While many grandparents care for their grandchildren once in a while, today some grandparents are called upon to become surrogate parents for their grandchildren because the grandparent's own adult children are addicted to drugs or are victims of violence. The article explores the issues these silent saviors confront.

The ultimate life stage is death. In "Bright Lights, Big Mystery," the mystery of near-death experiences (NDE) is investigated. Individuals who undergo these experiences report common impressions. What these individuals who have come close to death divulge will startle you.

Looking Ahead: Challenge Questions

How has the American family changed over the last decade? Do these changes have enhancing or deleterious effects on the children? What can families do to

protect their children from the damaging effects of some of these trends?

How common is child abuse? What causes child abuse? What are the consequences of abuse to the child who is the victim? What characterizes abusive parents? How can the cycle of abuse be stopped?

Why do children join gangs? Why are there more youth gangs and younger gang members than there were just a few years ago? How can we intervene in gang recruitment to stop the growth of youth gangs?

Our nation is aging. What exactly does this mean? How do we treat our elderly? How are the elderly treated in other cultures? Is our society ready to meet the needs of our ever-growing elderly population? What changes do we need to make to accommodate our elderly?

What is the near-death experience? Do people who encounter death report the same experiences? What kinds of experiences do they report? Does research on this topic change your opinion of or emotional reaction to death or life after death?

Putting Children First

William A. Galston

William A. Galston, the author most recently of Liberal
Purposes: Goods, Virtues, and Diversity in the Liberal
State *(Cambridge University Press), teaches at the University of Maryland, College Park. He is an advisor to
the Washington, D.C.–based Progressive Policy Institute
and a co-editor of* The Responsive Community, *a new
journal that seeks a better balance between rights and
responsibilities. This article is an expanded version of
an essay that appeared in the December 2, 1991, issue
of* The New Republic, *with material drawn from* Putting
Children First: A Progressive Family Policy for the 1990s
by Elaine Ciulla Kamarck and William A. Galston, published by the Progressive Policy Institute.

THE AMERICAN family has changed dramatically in
the past generation, and it is children who have paid
the price. From Ozzie and Harriet to the Simpsons, from
one breadwinner to two, from child-centered nuclear
families that stayed together for the sake of the children
to the struggling one-parent families of today; the revolution in the American family has affected us all. Divorce
rates have surged, and child poverty has risen alarmingly. The signs are everywhere around us that America's
children are suffering—economically, educationally, and
emotionally. Although this fact is obvious, indeed
increasingly obtrusive, it has hardly been discussed by
intellectuals and policy elites until quite recently. Several broad forces—racial conflict, feminism, the culture of
individual rights—help explain this odd silence.

The story begins in 1965, with the publication of
Daniel Patrick Moynihan's *The Negro Family: The Case
for National Action,* which identified the breakdown of
the black family as a growing obstacle to racial progress.
Although intended as the analytical backdrop to major
federal initiatives, it was received as a call for quietism,
even as a subtle relegitimation of racism. Black civil rights
leaders and white liberal scholars argued that the emphasis on family structure would inevitably divert attention

from economic inequalities and would justify "blaming
the victims" for the consequences of discrimination. As
William Julius Wilson has argued, this enraged response
had the consequence of suppressing public debate over,
and serious scholarly inquiry into, the relation between
black family structure and the problems of the ghetto
poor—suppressing it for an entire generation.

Feminism also contributed to the silence. The postwar
American women's movement began as a criticism of the
1950s family. "Liberation" meant leaving the domestic
sphere for the world of work outside the home. It also
meant denying traditional theories of gender difference
that seemed to legitimate inequalities of resources,
power, and self-respect. To be equal was to be the same:
to compete on the same terms as men, with the same
focus on individual separateness and independence. As
Sylvia Ann Hewlett argues, the unquestionable moral
force of the feminist movement muted the voices of
those who, though dubious about its denial of gender differences and deeply concerned about its consequences
for the well-being of children, did not wish to be accused
of a disguised effort to ratify the patriarchal or chauvinist status quo.

Then there was the cultural upheaval of the 1960s,
which yielded an ethic of self-realization through incessant personal experimentation, the triumph of what has
been termed "expressive individualism." An increasingly
influential therapeutic vocabulary emphasized the constraints that relations could impose on personal growth
and encouraged adults to turn inward toward the self's
struggles for sovereignty, to view commitments as temporary or endlessly renegotiable—to behave, in effect,
like adolescents. This vocabulary was anything but hospitable to the discourse of parental continuity, commitment, and self-sacrifice.

A related legacy of the generation just past has been
an impoverishment of moral vocabulary. What some
regard as a descent into relativism is more accurately

Reprinted with permission from the Summer 1992 issue of the *American Educator,* pp. 8-13, 44-46, the quarterly journal of the
American Federation of Teachers.

characterized as the relentless expansion of morality understood as the articulation of the rights of individuals. This development is not alien to the American experience, and it is not wholly to be deplored. Rights, after all, do support self-respect and offer protection against evils. Still, we now know that there is a difficulty: Although systems of rights can guide some spheres of life tolerably well, they can obscure and distort others. In particular, the effort to understand family relations as the mutual exercise of rights led to a legal and emotional cul-de-sac.

IN RECENT years, however, the climate has changed. Debates within the black community, and among social democrats as well as conservatives, have helped to relegitimate the discussion of the links between family structure and a range of social ills. To acknowledge such links, it is not necessary to sever the causal connections between structural inequalities at the political and economic level and disintegration at the family level, or to focus exclusively on the "culture of poverty." The point is, rather, that the cultural effects of past discrimination can take on a life of their own, that they can persist even in the face of changing opportunity structures.

The women's movement is changing, too. In place of equality understood as sameness, feminists such as Sara Ruddick, Carol Gilligan, and Jean Bethke Elshtain have embraced categories of difference, nurturance, and care. Martha Albertson Fineman insists that public policy "recognize and accommodate the positive and lasting nature of mothers' ties to their children." Surely this style of feminist argument will prove far more compatible with traditional understandings of the family than anyone could have predicted a decade ago.

And even broader cultural changes are under way, provoked by demographic shifts. Baby boomers who delayed marriage until their thirties have discovered that the moral universe of their young adulthood is not a suitable place for parents with young children. Others have discovered that the casting off of binding relationships is not necessarily the path to liberation and happiness. A generation that once devoted itself to the proliferation of rights and the expression of individuality has begun haltingly to explore counterbalancing notions of responsibility and community; several polls have documented rapid shifts during the past two years in public attitudes toward a range of family issues.

The most important shift is a welcome expansion of concern beyond narrow bounds of race and class. For too long, worries about children and families focused on such issues as teenage pregnancy, dire deprivation, and collapsing marriage rates. These are serious problems, but they are disproportionately characteristic of the ghetto poor. Such measurements, in other words, enabled the American middle class, scholars as well as citizens, to believe that families and children were someone else's problem. But with increased attention to the clash between work and family, to parental time deficits, and to the impact of divorce, the middle class can no longer sustain such an illusion. The decay of the family is its problem, too. The children of the middle class are also at risk; and its choices can be just as shortsighted, self-

There is growing recognition that we must place the family at the center of our thinking about social issues and children at the center of our thinking about the family.

indulgent, and harmful to the young as any ever contemplated in the culture of poverty.

THESE RECENT trends are at last producing important changes at the level of national politics. For decades, the revolution in the American family evoked a polarized reaction: Liberals talked about structural economic pressures facing families and avoided issues of personal conduct, and conservatives did just the reverse. Liberals habitually reached for bureaucratic responses, even when they were counter-productive, and conservatives reflexively rejected government programs even when they would work.

Both are wrong. Traditional conservatives' support for families is largely rhetorical; their disregard for new economic realities engenders a policy of unresponsive neglect—expressed for example, in President Bush's misguided veto of the Family Leave Act. Conversely, traditional liberals' unwillingness to acknowledge that intact two-parent families are the most effective units for raising children has led them into a series of policy cul-de-sacs.

Recently, however, this clash of conflicting worldviews has begun to give way to a new spirit of accommodation. As E.J. Dionne Jr. has observed, recent proposals for pro-family tax reform reflect the realization that both values and dollars count. Many younger conservatives are addressing social problems long neglected by their movement. Many younger Democrats, meanwhile, are looking for new forms of nonbureaucratic, choice-based public activism as a supplement to the frequently cumbersome and intrusive institutions of the welfare state. There is growing recognition that we must place the family at the center of our thinking about social issues and children at the center of our thinking about the family. We need policies that support and compensate families as they carry out their critical social role—providing for the economic and moral well-being of children. As we will see, a large body of evidence supports the conclusion that in the aggregate, the intact two-parent family is best suited to this task. Making this premise our point of departure takes us toward policies that *reinforce* families and away from bureaucratic approaches that seek to *replace* family functions.

To avoid misunderstanding, I want to make it clear that a general preference for the intact two-parent family does not mean that this is the best option in every case. Nor does it mean that all single-parent families are somehow dysfunctional; that proposition would diminish the achievements of millions of single parents who are struggling successfully against the odds to provide good homes for their children. Rather, the point is that at the level of statistical aggregates and society-wide phenomena, significant differences do emerge between one-parent and two-parent families, differences that can and should shape our understanding of social policy.

I DO NOT mean to suggest that the renewed emphasis on the family is solely the product of cultural and ideological change. Equally important is a broad process of social learning—a growing (and increasingly painful) awareness of the consequences of the choices that we already have made, individually and collectively, over the past generation.

The economic facts are distressing. As Hewlett summarizes the data: Among all children eighteen years and under, one in five is poor, nearly twice the poverty rate for the elderly; among children younger than six, the rate is almost one in four; among children in families headed by adults younger than thirty, one in three; among black children, almost one in two. And noneconomic trends are no less stark. In the past quarter-century, the amount of time that parents spend with their children has dropped by 40 percent, from thirty hours a week to just seventeen; and there is no evidence that these remaining shreds of parental availability represent "quality time." On the contrary: As social historian Barbara Whitehead reports, "Increasingly, family schedules are intricate applications of time-motion principles."

These stress-filled lives reflect changes in the economy that have prompted momentous shifts in the labor force in this country. Since 1973, under the pressure of declining productivity and mounting international competition, family incomes have stagnated while the relative costs of a middle-class existence—in particular, of homeownership, health care, and higher education—have soared. Wage prospects have grown increasingly dismal, especially for young people with no more than a high school education. The surge of women into the work force may have begun three decades ago as a cultural revolt against household roles experienced as stifling, but it has been sustained by increasingly urgent economic necessity. Today two-thirds of all mothers with children younger than eighteen do at least some work outside the home, as do more than one-half of all mothers with children under five.

For tens of millions of American families, the second income means the difference between keeping and losing a tenuously maintained middle-class way of life. To be sure, some adjustments at the margin are possible: Young families can live in smaller houses and stop eating at restaurants. Still, the hope of many moral traditionalists that the 1950s family can somehow be restored flies in the face of contemporary market forces. The tension between remunerative work and family time will not be overcome in the foreseeable future—unless increased income from nonmarket sources allows parents with young children to do less work outside the home. Many thoughtful conservatives are coming to the realization that they must choose between their vision of a well-ordered family and their desire for smaller, less costly government.

THESE TENSIONS and others have clearly taken their toll. Test scores are down, and not just the much-discussed SATs. At BellSouth in Atlanta, for example, only about 10 percent of job applicants can pass exams that test basic learning ability, versus 20 percent a decade ago. Theft, violence, and the use of illicit drugs are far more prevalent among teenagers than they were thirty years ago; and the rate of suicide among teenagers has tripled.

It is tempting to dismiss these data as one sided, or to interpret them as mere cyclical variations within longer-term stability. After all, virtually every generation in every culture has complained of a decline of the family. But this is an alibi. We must face the fact that the conditions we take for granted are the product of a social revolution that has rapidly unfolded over just the past three decades. And at the heart of this revolution lie changes in family structure.

In thirty years, the percentage of children born outside of marriage has quintupled, and now stands at 18 percent for whites and 63 percent for blacks. In this same period, the divorce rate has tripled, as has the percentage of children living with only one parent. Of white children born in the early 1950s, 81 percent lived continuously until the age of seventeen with their two biological parents; the projected rate for children born in the early 1980s is 30 percent. The corresponding rate for black children has fallen from 52 percent in the 1950s to only 6 percent today.

These structural shifts are responsible for a substantial portion of child poverty. As David Ellwood has observed, "[t]he vast majority of children who are raised entirely in a two-parent home will never be poor during childhood. By contrast, the vast majority of children who spend time in a single-parent home will experience poverty." As Ellwood showed in *Poor Support*, in any given year, fully 50 percent of children in one-parent families will experience poverty, versus 15 percent for those in two-parent families; 73 percent of children from one-parent families will experience poverty at some point during their childhood, versus 20 percent for children from two-parent families; 22 percent of children from one-parent families will experience persistent poverty (seven years or more), versus only 2 percent from two-parent families.

These data suggest that the best anti-poverty program for children is a stable, intact family. And this conclusion holds even for families headed by younger parents with very modest levels of educational attainment. For married high school graduates with children, the 1987 poverty rate was 9 percent, versus more than 47 percent for families headed by female high school graduates. Even for married high school dropouts with children, the poverty rate was 25 percent, versus more than 81 percent for families headed by female high school dropouts. Overall, Frank Furstenberg Jr. and Andrew Cherlin conclude, the differences in family structure go "a long way toward accounting for the enormous racial disparity in poverty rates. Within family types, black families are still poorer than white families; but the racial gap in poverty shrinks considerably when the marital status of the household head is taken into account."

> *'The vast majority of children who are raised entirely in a two-parent home will never be poor during childhood. By contrast, the vast majority of children who spend time in a single-parent home will experience poverty.'*

TO BE SURE, the causal arrow could point in the opposite direction: differences in family structure might be thought to reflect differences in economic status. Wilson offered an influential statement of this counterthesis in *The Truly Disadvantaged:* Reduced black marriage rates reflect dramatically higher rates of black male unemployment, which reduces the "male marriageable pool"—under the assumption that "to be marriageable a man needs to be employed." But the most recent research offers only modest support for this hypothesis. Robert Mare and Christopher Winship find that changes in employment rates among young black males account for only 20 percent of the decline in their marriage rates since 1960; they speculate that the various family disruptions of the past three decades may be self-reinforcing.[1] Though Wilson continues to defend the validity of his thesis for the hard-hit central cities of the Northeast and Midwest, he is now willing to say that "the decline in marriage among inner-city blacks is not simply a function of the proportion of jobless men . . . it is reasonable to consider the effects of weaker social structures against out-of-wedlock births."

Along with family non-formation, family breakup is a potent source of poverty, especially among children. According to a recently released Census Bureau study by Susan Bianchi, who identified and tracked twenty thousand households, it turns out that after their parents separate or divorce, children are almost twice as likely to be living in poverty as they were before the split. The gross income of the children and their custodial parent (usually the mother) dropped by 37 percent immediately after the family breakup (26 percent after adjustment for the decline in family size) and recovered only slightly after sixteen months. These findings support the arguments of scholars who have long contended that divorce under current law spells economic hardship for most custodial parents and their minor children.

As Furstenberg and Cherlin show in their admirably balanced survey of current research, there are at least three sets of reasons for this outcome: Many women bargain away support payments in return for sole custody of their children or to eliminate the need to deal with their former spouses; when awarded, child support payments are on average pitifully inadequate; and many fathers cough up only a portion (at best) of their required payments. A Census Bureau report from the mid-1980s showed that of mothers with court-ordered support payments, only half received all of what they were owed, a quarter received partial payments, and the remaining quarter got nothing at all.

IF THE economic effects of family breakdown are clear, the psychological effects are just now coming into focus. As Karl Zinsmeister summarizes an emerging consensus, "There is a mountain of scientific evidence showing that when families disintegrate children often end up with intellectual, physical, and emotional scars that persist for life. . . . We talk about the drug crisis, the education crisis, and the problems of teen pregnancy and juvenile crime. But all these ills trace back predominantly to one source: broken families."

As more and more children are reared in one-parent families, it becomes clear that the economic consequences of a parent's absence (usually the father) may pale beside the psychological consequences—which include higher than average levels of youth suicide, low intellectual and educational performance, and higher than average rates of mental illness, violence, and drug use.

Nowhere is this more evident than in the longstanding and strong relationship between crime and one-parent families. In a recent study, Douglas Smith and G. Roger Jarjoura found that "neighborhoods with larger percentages of youth (those aged 12 to 20) and areas with higher percentages of single-parent households also have higher rates of violent crime."[2] The relationship is so strong that controlling for family configuration erases the relationship between race and crime and between low income and crime. This conclusion shows up time and time again in the literature; poverty is far from the sole determinant of crime.

While the scarcity of intact families in the ghetto is largely a function of the failure of families to form in the first place, in the larger society the central problem is family disintegration, caused primarily by divorce. This pervasive phenomenon has effects that are independent of economics. It is to these studies that we now turn.

In 1981, John Guidubaldi, then president of the National Association of School Psychologists, picked a team of 144 psychologists in thirty-eight states, who gathered long-term data on seven hundred children, half from intact families, the other half children of divorce. Preliminary results published in 1986 showed that the effects of divorce on children persisted over time and that the psychological consequences were significant even after correcting for income differences.[3]

The problems engendered by divorce extend well beyond vanishing role models. Children need authoritative rules and stable schedules, which harried single parents often have a hard time supplying. As Guidubaldi puts it, "One of the things we found is that children who had regular bedtimes, less TV, hobbies and after-school activities—children who are in households that are orderly and predictable—do better than children who [did] not. I don't think we can escape the conclusion that children need structure, and oftentimes the divorce household is a chaotic scene."

The results of the Guidubaldi study have been confirmed and deepened by Judith Wallerstein's ten-year study of sixty middle-class divorced families. Among her key findings:

- Divorce is almost always more devastating for children than for their parents.
- The effects of divorce are often long lasting. Children are especially affected because divorce occurs during their formative years. What they see and experience becomes a part of their inner world, their view of themselves, and their view of society.
- Almost half the children entered adulthood as worried, underachieving, self-deprecating, and sometimes angry young men and women.
- Adolescence is a period of grave risk for children in divorced families; those who entered adolescence in the immediate wake of their parents' divorces had a particularly bad time. The young people told us time and again how much they needed a family structure, how much they wanted to be protected, and how much they yearned for clear guidelines for moral behavior.[4]

Furstenberg and Cherlin offer a nuanced, but ultimately troubling, account of the noneconomic consequences of divorce. For most children, it comes as an "unwelcome shock," even when the parents are openly quarreling. In the short-term, boys seem to have a harder time coping than girls, in part because of an "escalating cycle of misbehavior and harsh response between mothers and sons." Girls more typically respond with internalized disruption rather than external behavior—with heightened levels of anxiety, withdrawal, and depression that may become apparent only years later. These differences reflect the fact that divorce almost always means disrupted relations with the father. It is difficult to overstate the extent of the disruption that typically occurs. Even in the period relatively soon after divorce, only one-sixth of all children will see their fathers as often as once a week, and close to one-half will not see them at all. After ten years, almost two-thirds will have no contact.

These findings are less than self-interpreting, Furstenberg and Cherlin point out, because they must be compared with the effects on children of intact but troubled families. On the one hand, various studies indicate that the children of divorce do no worse than children in families in which parents fight continuously. On the other hand, a relatively small percentage of divorces result from, and terminate, such clearly pathological situations. There are many more cases in which there is little open conflict, but one or both partners feels unfulfilled, bored, or constrained. Indeed, the onset of divorce in these families can intensify conflict, particularly as experienced by children. As Nicholas Zill observes, "Divorces tend to generate their own problems."

Given the profound psychological effects of divorce, it is hardly surprising to discover what teachers and administrators have known for some time: One of the major reasons for America's declining educational achievement is the disintegrating American family. And if we continue to neglect the crisis of the American family, we will have undercut current efforts at educational reform.

Untangling just what it is about family structure that makes for high or low educational achievement is a difficult task. Clearly the economics of the family have a great deal to do with achievement; children from poor families consistently do less well than do children from non-poor or well-to-do families. Nevertheless, income is clearly not the whole story. When studies control for income, significant differences in educational achievement appear between children from single-parent families and children from intact families.

For example, a study conducted under the auspices of the National Association of Elementary School Principals and the Institute for Development of Educational Activities shows that family background has an important effect on educational achievement above and beyond income level—especially for boys. Lower-income girls with two parents, for instance, score higher on achievement tests than do higher-income boys with one parent. At the very bottom of the achievement scale are lower-income boys with one parent.[5]

WHAT SHOULD be our response to these developments? The recent literature suggests three broad possibilities. First, we may applaud, with Judith Stacey, the demise of the traditional (rigid, patriarchal) family and the rise of "postmodern" (flexible, variegated, female-centered) arrangements, which are allegedly far more consistent with egalitarian democracy. Second, we may accept Jan Dizard and Howard Gadlin's suggestion that moral change (in the direction of autonomy) and economic change (in the direction of a two-earner, postindustrial economy) have rendered obsolete the older model of the private family; in its place, they advocate a dramatically expanded public sphere on the Swedish model that assumes many of the private family's functions. And third, there is the response, neither postmodern nor socialist, that might be called neotraditional.

It goes something like this. A primary purpose of the family is to raise children well, and for this purpose stably married parents are best. Sharply rising rates of divorce, unwed mothers, and runaway fathers do not represent "alternative lifestyles." They are, instead, most truly characterized as patterns of adult behavior with profoundly negative consequences for children. Families have primary responsibility for instilling traits such as discipline, ambition, respect for the law, and regard for others; and it is a responsibility that cannot be discharged as effectively by auxiliary social institutions such as public schools. This responsibility entails a sphere of legitimate parental authority that should be bolstered—not undermined—by society. It requires personal sacrifice and the delay of certain forms of gratification on the part of parents. It means that government should devote substantial resources to stabilizing families and to enhancing their child-rearing capacity. But at the same time it must minimize bureaucratic cost, complexity, and intrusiveness, working instead to broaden family choice, opportunity, and responsibility.

The willingness to join the languages of economics and morals, and to consider new approaches to old goals, is increasingly characteristic of public discussion of the family. As Barbara Whitehead notes, this approach suffuses the recent report of the National Commission on Children. The volume edited by David Blankenhorn, Steven Bayme, and Jean Bethke Elshtain is particularly strong along the moral dimension. To be sure, it is easy for this stance to give the appearance of ineffectual exhortation. The editors of *The New York Times* assert that the commission's final report "swims in platitudes." Still, there are eminently practical ways of embedding moral concerns in policies and institutions. Richard Louv argues for moral change focused on the community as much as the individual. He urges us to reweave the tattered "web" of social relationships—parent-school ties, neighborhoods, communal child care arrangements, and the like—that provide a supportive environment for families and help nurture children. Although Louv emphasizes the importance of civil society, he does not imagine that the web can be adequately repaired without major changes in public policy.

Here Louv joins an emerging consensus that differs over details but not over essentials. The point is not to be driven to make a false choice between moral and economic concerns, but rather to combine them in a relation of mutual support. It might well be argued, for example, that the government has a responsibility not to tax away the money that families need to raise children. Four decades ago, the United States had a disguised family allowance: In 1948 the personal exemption was $600 (42 percent of per-capita personal income), while today's personal exemption is only 11 percent of per-capita income. This meant that a married couple at the median income with two minor dependents paid only 0.3 percent of their 1948 income in federal income taxes, compared to today's 9.1 percent. The 1948 couple's total tax bill (federal, state, and Social Security) was 2 percent of personal income. Today that total comes to about 30 percent.

Thus, one proposal now gaining support is to raise the personal exemption from the current $2,050 to at least $4,000, and perhaps eventually to $7,500. To make this more affordable, the bulk of the increase could be targeted to young children, and the increase could be phased out for upper-income taxpayers. Another approach, endorsed by the National Commission on Children, would create a $1,000 tax credit for each child; low-income families that owe no taxes would receive a cash payment for the amount of the credit. (To avoid potentially perverse incentives, this proposal should be coupled with a broader program of welfare reform.)

Reducing the tension between work and family will take changes in the private as well as the public sector. Hewlett, Louv, and many others argue for a "family-oriented workplace" with far more adaptable schedules: more flexible hours, greater opportunities for working at home and communicating by computer, for part-time employment, and for job sharing. Resistance to these changes reflects primarily the ignorance or the obduracy of middle-aged male managers, not negative impact on corporate balance sheets. Much the same is true of unpaid leave for parents following the birth of a child. Studies at the state level indicate that the costs and disruptive effects of such leaves, even when legally mandatory, are minimal. President Bush's opposition to federal family leave legislation is increasingly indefensible.

Adequate reward for labor force participation represents another important link between morals and public policy. If we believe that the presence of a parent who works outside the home furnishes a crucial moral example for his or her children, then surely the community has a responsibility to ensure that full-time work by a parent provides a nonpoverty family income. As Robert Shapiro of the Progressive Policy Institute has argued, the most efficient way to accomplish this goal would be to expand the Earned Income Tax Credit and tie it to family size.

This emphasis on the use of the tax code to promote family opportunity and responsibility is characteristic of a political outlook that has been called "neoprogressive." This is not to suggest that traditional liberal approaches are in every case misguided. Some of them—prenatal care, WIC (the nutrition program for poor women, infants, and children), childhood immunization, and Head Start—efficiently promote the well-being of children and families, and the political consensus supporting their expansion now stretches from KidsPac (a liberal, children-oriented political action committee) and the Children's Defense Fund to the Bush administration and the corporate-based Committee for Economic Development. And yet the neoprogressives are more willing than the traditional liberals to re-examine the programs of the past and to distinguish between what works and what doesn't.

IF THE PRIVATE and public sectors must assume greater responsibility for the well-being of families with children, so must parents. In particular, the moral obligation to help support one's biological children persists regardless of one's legal relationship to them, and the law is fully justified in enforcing this obligation. The 1988 Family Support Act requires states to collect the Social Security numbers of both parents (married or unmarried) at birth, to increase efforts to establish contested paternity, to use (as at least rebuttable presumptions) their guidelines concerning appropriate levels of child support, and to move toward collecting all new support awards through automatic payroll deductions.

These are steps in the right direction, but they don't go far enough. Mary Ann Glendon has argued powerfully that a "children first" principle should govern our spousal support and marital property law:

> The judges' main task would be to piece together, from property and income and in kind personal care, the best possible package to meet the needs of children and their physical guardian. Until the welfare of the children had been adequately secured in this way, there would be no question of, or debate about, "marital property." All assets, no matter when or how acquired, would be subject to the duty to provide for the children.[6]

Moreover, the state-level reforms mentioned above do nothing to address what is in many cases the chief impediment to support collection: fathers moving from state to state to slow or avoid apprehension. Conflicting state laws and a morass of administrative complexity discourage mothers from pursuing their claims across jurisdictions. Ellwood and others have called for the federalization of the system, with payroll deductions remitted to, and support payments drawn from, a centralized national fund. The U.S. Commission on Interstate Child Support, created by Congress to develop a blueprint for reform, is considering this idea.

Even when child support is collected regularly from absent parents who can afford to provide it, payments are typically set too low to avoid tremendous disruption in the lives of custodial mothers and their children. Writing from very different perspectives, Lenore Weitzman, Martha Albertson Fineman, and Furstenberg and Cherlin converge on the conclusion that the laws and the practices of many states leave men in a far more favorable situation after divorce. Furstenberg and Cherlin cite approvingly a proposal to require noncustodial fathers to pay a fixed proportion of their income, 17 percent to 34 percent, depending on the number of minor children; the adoption of this standard nationwide would raise total child support due by roughly two-thirds. Fineman advocates a need-based approach that would (she argues) yield better results for women and children than would ostensibly egalitarian standards.

During the past generation, the presumption in favor of awarding mothers custody of their children has been replaced in many cases by the presumption of equal claims. This development has generated a rising number of joint custody arrangements that do not, on average, work out very well. It has also worsened the post-divorce economic status of custodial mothers and their children: Because women tend to view custody as a paramount issue, they often compromise on economic matters to avoid the custody battle made possible by the new, supposedly more egalitarian, legal framework. And here, too, scholars from various points on the ideological spectrum are converging on the conclusion that the traditional arrangement had much to recommend it. They propose a "primary caretaker" standard: judges should be instructed to award custody of young children to the parent who has (in the words of a leading advocate) "performed a substantial majority of the [direct] caregiving tasks for the child."

THESE AND similar proposals will help custodial mothers and their children pick up the pieces after divorce, but they will do little to reduce the incidence of divorce. For Furstenberg and Cherlin, this is all that can be done: "We are inclined to accept the irreversibility of high levels of divorce as our starting point for thinking about changes in public policy." Hewlett is more disposed to grasp the nettle. While rejecting a return to the fault-based system of the past, she believes that the current system makes divorce too easy and too automatic.

Government should send a clearer moral signal that families with children are worth preserving. In this spirit, she suggests that parents of minor children seeking divorce undergo an eighteen-month waiting period, during which they would be obliged to seek counseling and to reach a binding agreement that truly safeguards their children's future.

The generation that installed the extremes of self-expression and self-indulgence at the heart of American culture must now learn some hard old lessons about commitment, self-sacrifice, the deferral of gratification, and simple endurance. It will not be easy. But other sorts of gratifications may be their reward. Perhaps the old morality was not wrong to suggest that a deeper kind of satisfaction awaits those who accept and fulfill their essential human responsibilities.

REFERENCES

[1]Mare, Robert D. and Winship, Christopher, "Socio-economic Change and the Decline of Marriage for Blacks and Whites." In *The Urban Underclass,* edited by Christopher Jencks and Paul Peterson. Washington, D.C.: The Brookings Institute, 1991.

[2]Smith, Douglas A., Jarjoura, G. Roger, "Social Structure and Criminal Victimization." In *Journal of Research in Crime and Delinquency,* Vol. 25, No. 1, February 1988.

[3]Guidubaldi, J., Cleminshaw, H.K., Perry, J.D., Nastasi, B.K., and Lightel, J., "The Role of Selected Family Environment Factors in Children's Post-Divorce Adjustment." In *Family Relations,* Vol. 35, 1986.

[4]Wallerstein, Judith S., and Blakeslee, Sandra, *Second Chances: Men, Women, and Children a Decade after Divorce.* New York: Ticknor and Fields, 1989.

[5]Sally Banks Zakariya, "Another Look at the Children of Divorce," *Principal Magazine,* September 1982, p. 35. See also, R.B. Zajonc, "Family Configuration and Intelligence," *Science,* Vol. 192, April 16, 1976, pp. 227-236. In a later and more methodologically sophisticated study, the authors try to define more completely what it is about two-parent families that make them better at preparing students for educational success. Income clearly stands out as the most important variable; but the close relationship between one-parent status, lower income, and lack of time for things like homework help and attendance at parent teacher conferences—to name a few of the variables considered—led the authors to say that "the negative effects of living in a one-parent family work primarily through other variables in our model." Ann M. Milne, David E. Myers, Alvin S. Rosenthal, and Alan Ginsburg, "Single Parents, Working Mothers, and the Educational Achievement of School Children," *Sociology of Education,* 1986, Vol. 59 (July), p. 132.

[6]Glendon, Mary Ann, *Abortion and Divorce in Western Law.* Cambridge, MA: Harvard University Press, 1987 (pp. 93-95).

Sad Legacy Of Abuse: The Search For Remedies

Studies aim to learn why some abused children grow up to be abusers, and why most do not.

Daniel Goleman

Children and adults who were victims of child abuse are coming under intensified study by researchers who hope to learn what distinguishes those who go on to become abusers themselves from those who grow up to be good parents.

In the hope of finding ways to break the tragic cycle, the new research is identifying particular experiences in childhood and later in life that allow a great many abused children to overcome their sad legacy.

Studies also now indicate that about one-third of people who are abused in childhood will become abusers themselves. This is a lower percentage than many experts had expected, but obviously poses a major social challenge. The research also confirms that abuse in childhood increases the likelihood in adulthood of problems ranging from depression and alcoholism to sexual maladjustment and multiple personality.

The studies are also uncovering specific factors that help many victims grow into a well-adjusted adulthood, and factors that push others toward perpetuating the pattern of violence. The findings should help therapists improve treatment of abused children or formerly abused adults, helping them recover from their trauma.

"Studies showing that a high proportion of troubled adults were abused in childhood tell only part of the story," said Dr. Richard Krugman, a professor of pediatrics at the University of Colorado Medical School and director of the C. Henry Kempe Center for Prevention and Treatment of Child Abuse and Neglect. "There are substantial numbers of men and women who were abused as children, but who are not themselves child abusers, drug abusers, criminals or mentally disturbed."

Key factors found to worsen the long-term impact of abuse are: abuse that started early, abuse that lasted for a long time, abuse in which the perpetrator had a close relationship to the victim, abuse that the child perceived as particularly harmful, and abuse that occurred within a cold emotional atmosphere in the family. These factors, researchers say, help identify which children need treatment most urgently.

Victims of abuse frequently respond to the trauma by denying that any abuse occurred or by blaming themselves for the abuse, which they often view as justified discipline from adults, the studies show. But many victims can overcome the trauma with the emotional support of a friend or relative or through therapy that makes them aware that they were not to blame for abuse inflicted by their parents. Victims of abuse can almost always benefit from therapy to deal with the psychological effects of being so terribly treated, such as a damaged sense of self-worth and conflicts between wanting to love their parents while recognizing the abuse that happened.

"Child abuse" refers to a range of maltreatment. In addition to physical harm and sexual abuse, researchers also include serious neglect of a child's emotional and physical needs and forms of emotional abuse such as incessant berating of a child. They are finding that the long-lasting effects of all these kinds of abuse share much in common.

In any given year, from 1 percent to 1.5 percent of American children are subject to abuse of some kind, according to Dr. Krugman. By the time they reach adulthood, about one in four men and women have experienced at least one episode of abuse at some point during childhood.

Numerous studies have found those who were victims of child abuse to be more troubled as adults than those who were not. There are disproportionate numbers of victims of abuse among prostitutes, violent criminals, alcoholics and drug abusers, and patients in psychiatric hospitals.

The more severe the abuse, the more extreme the later psychiatric symptoms. For instance, a study by Judith Herman, a psychiatrist in Somerville, Mass., found that among women who had been victims of incest, although half seemed to have recovered well by adulthood, those who suffered forceful, prolonged, intrusive abuse, or who were abused by fathers or step-fathers, had the most serious problems later in life.

Virtually all those who suffer from multiple personality, a rare but severe psychiatric disorder, have a history of being severely abused; the disorder is thought to stem from ways some children try to mentally isolate themselves against the horror of unremitting abuse.

The emotional support of a nurturing adult can help victims overcome the trauma.

A 1985 study of all 15 adolescents in the United States who were condemned murderers found that 13 had been victims of extreme physical or sexual abuse. In nine cases the abuse was so severe—characterized as "murderous" by the researchers—that it led to neurological damage. Similarly, a study of nine women imprisoned for fatal child abuse found that all of them had experienced severe maltreatment themselves.

While all these studies depict an alarming pattern, researchers point out that the statistics do not reflect the large numbers of abused children who do not suffer from these problems.

That abused children need not go on to abuse their own children was shown in a study of more than 1,000 pregnant women, 95 of whom had been abused as children. The report, by William Altemeier, a pediatrician at Vanderbilt University Medical School, and his colleagues, was published in 1986 in the journal *Child Abuse and Neglect*.

Strongest Predictive Factor

The study found that the strongest predictor from childhood of becoming an abusive parent was not having been abused, but rather having felt as a child that one was unloved and unwanted by one's parents—an attitude common, of course, among abused children, but also found in families in which there is no overt abuse.

However, studies in which there have been more careful observations of mothers and their children have found a stronger link between having been abused in childhood and being an abusive parent. In a survey of such studies, Joan Kaufman and Edward Zigler, psychologists at Yale, concluded that 30 percent is the best estimate of the rate at which abuse of one generation is repeated in the next.

Denial that one has been abused is emerging as a source of trouble later in life. Researchers find that many adults who were abused as children do not think of themselves as having been victimized. For instance, three-quarters of men in one study who described punishments that, by objective standards, constitute abuse—such as being burned for an infraction of a minor household rule—denied that they had been abused.

About 30 percent of victims become abusive parents.

That phenomenon is common among those who go on to become child abusers, according to Dr. Krugman, and is part of the cycle by which abused children become abusive parents.

"When you ask them if they were ever abused, they tell you, 'No,' " Dr. Krugman said. "But if you ask them to describe what would happen if they broke a rule, they'll say something like, 'I was locked in a closet for a day, then beaten with a belt until I was black and blue.' Then you ask them, was that abuse? and their answer is, 'No, I was a bad kid and my parents had to beat me to make me turn out okay.' "

While there has been much attention by psychotherapists in recent years on women who were sexually abused in childhood, a more recent focus is on men who suffered sexual abuse. Such men are much more reticent than women about admitting what happened to them and dealing with the trauma, according to Mike Lew, co-director of The Next Step Counseling Centre in Newton, Mass., and author of "Victims No Longer," (Nevraumont) about the problem.

Children fare better after abuse, researchers have found, when they have someone in their life—a relative, teacher, minister, friend—who is emotionally nurturing.

In helping a child recover from abuse, "you need to counteract the child's expectations that adults will be deeply uncaring," explained Martha Erickson, a psychologist at the University of Minnesota.

Among adult victims of childhood abuse who are in therapy, a common refrain from patients is that "it just wasn't that bad," said Terry Hunt, a psychologist in Cambridge, Mass., who specializes in their problem. "The key to their treatment is facing the fact that their parents were so cruel to them; they've bought the parent's word that they were bad and deserved it. The

Many adults refuse to acknowledge that they were abused as children.

damage shows up in their intimate relationships: they're waiting to get hit or used again."

One of the crucial differences between those abused children who go on to become abusers and those who do not, he said, is whether they have the insight that their parents were wrong to abuse them.

Often, Dr. Hunt finds, the most troubled among his patients are those who were told as children, by adults other than their abusing parent, that the abuse was justified.

"If an abused child thinks, 'that was wrong, they shouldn't have done that to me—I'm not that bad,' then he can still love his parents, but decide not to repeat the abuse when he becomes a parent," said Dr. Krugman. "The child somehow gets the message that what happened is not his fault, that he is not to blame."

When parents are not the abusers, how they react to its discovery is crucial. In a study of children who had been involved in sex rings, those who had fewest lasting problems in later years were the children whose parents had been understanding of the child, according to Ann Burgess, a professor of nursing at the University of Pennsylvania medical school.

"These kids recovered with no symptoms, while those whose parents blamed them had the worst outcome," Dr. Burgess said.

The factors that lead some children to become abusers while others become excellent parents is being revealed in research at the University of Minnesota. Psychologists there are currently studying a group of children born to parents with a high probability of becoming abusers. Not all those in the study were abused as children; they were selected instead because they were poor, single, got pregnant at an early age, and had chaotic households—all factors that correlate highly with child abuse.

In addition to physical and sexual abuse—the two varieties most often studied—the researchers are also studying children whose physical care is neglected, those whose parents constantly berate and criticize them and those whose parents are completely unresponsive to their emotional needs.

Followed From Birth

The study, one of the few that has followed children from birth, is finding that there are different emotional effects from each of the different kinds of abuse, and that these effects change from age to age. For instance, children whose mothers were emotionally cold during infancy had emotional and learning problems at the age of six that were as severe as—and sometimes more severe—than those found in children whose mothers had been physically abusive but emotionally responsive during their infancy.

When the same children were studied between the ages of four and six, the most serious problems were found in those whose mothers neglected their physical care.

The study is also finding general effects that come from maltreatment of any kind.

"The earlier the maltreatment occurs, the more severe the consequences," said Martha F. Erickson, a psychologist at the University of Minnesota, who is one of those conducting the study. Dr. Erickson, with Byron Egeland and Robert Pianta, two colleagues, will publish early findings from the study in a chapter to appear in "Child Maltreatment," a book to be published by Cambridge University Press in May.

Many of the lifelong psychological effects of abuse stem from a lack of nurturance, they conclude, a lack that lies behind all the kinds of maltreatment.

The Minnesota researchers report that among those abused children who go on to become abusing parents, there is little repetition of a specific type of abuse.

For instance, of 13 women who had been sexually abused, six were physically abusing their children; of 47 who had been physically abused, 8 were physical abusers by the time their children reached six years, while 8 neglected their children, and 6 had homes where children were being sexually abused, often by a boyfriend of the mother.

Children in gangs

The tragedy of inner-city youth drawn into delinquency and drug trafficking

Carl Rogers

CARL ROGERS,
of the United States, is an
expert on child and family
issues. He serves as the public
policy liaison officer for the
American National Council on
Child Abuse and Family
Violence, a U.S. private sector
initiative for the prevention and
treatment of child abuse,
based in Washington D.C.

THE 1980s witnessed the explosive resurgence of an historic American urban social problem: children and youth in gangs. From New York to Los Angeles, from Chicago to Miami, over forty-five American cities have an identified youth gang problem.

The number of youth gangs in the United States is on the rise and their involvement in the drug trade is resulting in dramatic increases in gang-related violence—including homicide—and arrests for criminal activities in almost every American city. The scope and the nature of the problem vary widely from city to city, but it has been estimated that over 50,000 children and youths are gang members in the city of Los Angeles and that there are over 600 youth gangs in California alone.

Popularized in the 1950s musical *West Side Story,* youth gangs have been a recurring social problem in U.S. cities at least since the second half of the nineteenth century. Their emergence and growth, primarily in poor, urban neighbourhoods, were frequently fuelled by successive waves of immigrants arriving in the United States, and were symptomatic of the problems these groups encountered in trying to adapt to a new and at times radically different culture. Today many youth gangs continue to reflect the difficulties of assimilation of immigrant populations.

Youth gangs are usually defined as groups of young people who frequently engage in illegal activity on a group basis. They are usually territorial in nature, identifying with a particular neighbourhood and protecting their "turf" from encroachment by other gangs. Better organized gangs often control economically motivated crime such as burglary, extortion or drug-trafficking at the neighbourhood level. They may also sell "protection" from criminal activity to legitimate merchants. Youth gangs usually identify themselves by a name ("Crips", and "Bloods" are the names of two Los Angeles-based gangs), and may further distinguish themselves by a particular style or colour of clothing, by use of symbols, or by wearing certain kinds of jewellery.

A MILLION DOLLARS A WEEK FROM CRACK

The recent dynamic growth of youth gangs and related violence is directly attributed by most sources to the increased sale of cocaine, particu-

Courtesy of *The UNESCO Courier,* October 1991, pp. 19-21.

larly in the form known as "rock" or "crack". This lucrative illegal activity is helping to transform gangs into drug trafficking criminal organizations. In 1988 Los Angeles police officials acknowledged that they were aware of at least four gangs in their city grossing over $1,000,000 per week through the sale of cocaine. A recent article in the U.S. magazine *Time* ironically noted that the crack cocaine trade may be one of the biggest job programmes for inner city youth in the United States.

One reason why children become involved in drug trafficking is that the laws governing juvenile crime are more lenient than those governing adult crime. Ironically, as the U.S. "war on drugs" has intensified, with both increasing arrests for drug trafficking and more severe penalties for adults convicted of drug-related crime, the value of youth gang members has increased. While an adult convicted of selling drugs in most states is subject to a mandatory prison sentence of anywhere from two years to life imprisonment, a young person under the age of eighteen will seldom be committed to a correctional facility for a first offence, and even if committed is not subject to mandatory sentence lengths. It has become both increasingly profitable and safer for adult criminals to enroll children and youths in the drug trafficking business.

PEEWEES AND WANNABEES

The average age of youth gang members continues to decline. Most experts place the figure at around thirteen to fifteen years of age, while law enforcement officials in Los Angeles, Chicago and other cities note that children as young as nine or ten years are frequently found in today's gangs. These young recruits, often called "peewees" (slang for little members) or "wannabees" (slang for "want to be" gang members), become casually involved with older gang members who live in their neighbourhood, attend their school, or are members of their own families. Initially, younger children may be asked to perform "favours" for older gang members—to watch for police in the neighbourhood, or to deliver packages which may contain drugs, money or weapons. In exchange, the children often receive expensive gifts or money.

As they demonstrate their trustworthiness and reliability, these children assume more difficult and more dangerous roles. Children as young as ten or eleven years of age are frequently involved in gang-related drug trafficking. Younger children are routinely employed as "spotters" watching and reporting on police activity in their neighbourhood to other gang members, as "weapons carriers" for older gang members, or

in other roles, and earn anywhere from $200 per week to $100 per day. "Runners", usually slightly older children, may earn up to $300 per day keeping street corner dealers supplied with drugs from a hidden cache. Enterprising youths as young as fifteen or sixteen may advance to the level of street corner dealers, routinely earning between $400 and $1,000 per day. In a particularly good market such as New York City, authorities indicate that dealers can make up to $3,000 per day.

Few dealers, however, work full time, and two different studies in Washington, D.C. would suggest that a street corner dealer's average earnings are more likely to be in the range of $4,000 to $7,000 per month. In contrast, most states in the U.S. set a minimum employment age of sixteen years, and most legal entry-level jobs available to young people pay less than $40 per day, or approximately $800 per month.

Once a child is involved with a gang, it may be virtually impossible for him to quit. Gang membership usually leads to truancy and ultimately dropping out of school, closing off escape from a criminal lifestyle through education. The gang member also finds it difficult to give up a more lucrative lifestyle in exchange for unemployment or employment at minimum wage.

The gang member who attempts to quit is also subject to social pressures to continue his or her involvement. At best, attempting to leave the gang may lead to social ostracism; at worst it may lead to direct intimidation.

IMPOVERISHED INNER-CITY NEIGHBOURHOODS

To truly understand the youth gang problem it is important to understand the social context within which the gangs emerge. First, they are almost universally a product of impoverished urban neighbourhoods, where unemployment routinely exceeds 20 per cent of the workforce and in some cases exceeds 50 per cent. Families consist overwhelmingly of single mothers with children and often rely primarily on public assistance for their livelihood. Nationally, 20 per cent of all children in the United States live in families at or below the established federal poverty level. In many inner-city neighbourhoods this figure approaches 100 per cent. These communities are characterized by generally high crime rates, limited legitimate business activity or employment opportunities, and poorly functioning public education systems.

In contrast to the phenomenon of street children in many Third World countries, or to the problem of runaway or "throwaway" children (children, usually teenagers, expelled from their homes by their parents), most youth gang members live at home with their families. Some parents actively support their child's gang involvement or are totally indifferent, but most parents do care. Even the best intentioned parent, however, can find it difficult, if not impossible, to keep his or her child from becoming involved with a local gang. Every neighbourhood has its history of gang revenge against individual children or their families for resisting the gang. The combined factors of intimidation on the one hand and some financial support on the other eventually result in tacit collusion on the part of these parents. An uneasy truce develops where the parent, while not condoning or supporting the child's gang involvement, nonetheless does little to try to stop this involvement and welcomes the child's periodic financial contributions to the family budget.

So far, the overall public policy approach to this social problem has focused on three broad strategies: suppression of drug use and drug trafficking; suppression of youth gangs; and prevention of youth involvement in gangs. To date, while national statistics suggest an overall decline in the use of illegal drugs, this decline appears to have had little effect on the growth of the gangs or on the frequency of gang-related violence. Similarly, attempts at direct suppression of the gangs through law enforcement activities appear to have had limited effects, despite the mobilization of extensive resources. It is argued by many, however, that these efforts have slowed the growth and spread of gangs. Alternatively, some have suggested that efforts at gang suppression through arrest and detention of gang members actually lead to increased levels of gang-related violence as other gangs compete for control of territories once controlled by the suppressed gang.

Most experts agree that the only viable long-term solution to the problem is to prevent children and youths from getting involved in gangs in the first place. Most current programmes seek to provide support for high-risk children and their families. They focus on children between the ages of six and fourteen, since it appears to be generally agreed that prevention efforts must begin before young people develop well-established patterns of delinquent behaviour or become seriously involved with gangs. Key elements in many of these programmes include the provision of social and recreational activities, and educational assistance, as well as efforts to prevent the children from dropping out of school and to enhance their self-confidence and self-esteem. The success of prevention efforts ultimately depends on whether these children and young people have a sense of hope in their own future and a belief that through their own efforts they can lead useful, productive lives.

Meeting the challenges of an aging nation

KEN DYCHTWALD WITH JOE FLOWER/*NEW AGE JOURNAL*

America is aging. The nation that was founded on young backs, on the strength, impetuosity, and hope of youth, is growing more mature, steadier, deeper—even, one may hope, wiser.

The Population Reference Bureau, a non-profit demographics study group in Washington, D.C., has projected that by the year 2025 Americans over age 65 will outnumber teenagers by more than two to one. According to the Census Bureau, by 2030 the median age is expected to have reached 41. By 2050, it's likely that as many as one in four Americans will be over 65. Many demographers consider these projections to be very conservative: By some estimates, the median age will eventually reach 50.

Three separate and unprecedented demographic phenomena are converging to produce the coming "Age Wave":

• *The senior boom.* Americans are living longer than ever before, and older Americans are healthier, more active, more vigorous, and more influential than any other older generation in history.

• *The birth dearth.* A decade ago, the birth rate in the United States plummeted to its lowest point ever. It has been hovering there since, and it's not likely to change. The growing population of elders is not being offset by an explosion of children.

• *The aging of the baby boom.* The leading edge of the boomer generation has now passed 40. As the boomers approach 50 and pass it, their numbers, combined with the first two demographic changes, will produce a historic shift in American life.

Our concept of marriage will change, as "till death do us part" unions generally give way to serial monogamy. In an era of longer life, some people will have marriages that last 75 years, while others will pick different mates for each major stage of life.

The child-centered nuclear family will increasingly be replaced by the "matrix" family, an adult-centered unit that spans generations and is bound together by friendship and circumstance as well as by blood and obligation.

More people will work at careers into their 70s and 80s. Many will "retire" several times during their lives—to raise a second (or third) family, enter a new business, or simply take a couple of years off to travel and enjoy themselves.

Even the physical environment will change. To fit the pace, physiology, and style of a population predominantly in the middle and later years of life, the type in books will get larger and traffic lights will change more slowly. Steps will be less steep, bathtubs less slippery, chairs more comfortable, reading lights brighter. Neighborhoods will become safer. Food might be more nutritious.

But the aging of America will affect more than just our institutions, lifestyles, and surroundings. The demographic changes that rearrange our society will also touch our innermost thoughts, hopes, and dreams. The gift of longevity will make us rethink the tempo of our lives as well as the purposes, goals, and challenges we face in each stage of life.

7. DEVELOPMENT

Indeed, the cumulative effect of all these changes might be an entirely new perspective on the possibilities of old age. A compelling philosophy has recently emerged from the European tradition of adult education that provides a simple yet visionary look at this issue. Referred to as le troisième age—"the third age"—this theory proposes that there are three "ages" of human life, each with its own focus, challenges, and opportunities.

In the first age, from birth to approximately 25 years of age, the primary tasks of life center on biological development, learning, and survival. During the early years of human existence, the average life expectancy of most people wasn't much higher than 25, so the entire thrust of society was satisfying these most basic drives.

In the second age, from about 26 to 60, the concerns of adult life focus on starting and raising a family and on productive work. The second age is filled with social activity; the lessons learned during the first age are applied to the social and professional responsibilities of the second. Until several decades ago, most people couldn't expect to live much beyond 60 and most of society revolved around the concerns of the second age.

Now, however, we are in a new era of human evolution: the third age of humanity. The concerns of the third age are twofold. First, with children grown and many of life's basic adult tasks either well under way or already accomplished, this less pressured, more reflective period allows the further development of the intellect, memory, and imagination, of emotional maturity, and of one's spiritual identity.

The third age is also a period of giving back to society the lessons, resources, and experiences accumulated over a lifetime. From this perspective, the elderly are seen not as social outcasts, but as a living bridge between yesterday, today, and tomorrow—a critical evolutionary role that no other age group can perform. According to Monsignor Charles Fahey, who serves as director of Fordham University's Third Age Center, "People in the third age should be the glue of society, not its ashes."

Of course, this is not a new idea in human history, but it's one that modern society's intense focus on youth has obscured. In other cultures and other times, the elderly have been revered for their wisdom, power, and spiritual force. In ancient China, for example, the highest achievement in Taoism was long life and the wisdom that came with the passing of years. According to writer and social historian Simone de Beauvoir, "Lao-tse's teaching sets the age of 60 as the moment at which a man may free himself from his body and become a holy being. Old age was therefore life in its very highest form."

Among the Aranda people, hunter-gatherers of the Australian forests, extreme old age brings with it a near-supernatural status: "The man whom age has already brought close to the other world is the best mediator between this and the next. It is the old people who direct the Arandas' religious life—a life that underlies the whole of their social existence."

In contemporary Japanese culture, a high value is placed on the unique opportunities for spiritual development offered by old age. According to Thomas Rohlen, an expert on Japanese culture, "What is significant in Japanese spiritualism is the promise itself, for it clearly lends meaning, integrity, and joy to many lives, especially as the nature of adult existence unfolds. It recognizes the inherent value of experience. And for all its emphasis on social responsibility, discipline, and perseverance in the middle years, it encourages these as a means to a final state of spiritual freedom, ease, and universal belonging. . . . Here is a philosophy seemingly made for adulthood—giving it stature, movement, and optimism."

Even in the United States, before modernization shifted our interest from the old to the young, the elderly were the recipients of great reverence. In the early 1840s, the Rev. Cortlandt van Rensselaer said in one of his sermons, "What a blessed influence the old exert in cherishing feelings of reverence, affection, and subordination in families; in detailing the results of experience; in importing judicious counsel in Church and State and private life."

According to Calvinist doctrine, which was profoundly influential during the early 19th century, living to a great age was taken as a sign of God's special favor. The more spiritually evolved elder was considered one of the elect, and therefore worthy of veneration. The elderly were highly honored in all social rituals and on all public occasions. As influential leader Increase Mather commented in the late 17th century, "If a man is favored with long life . . . it is God that has lengthened his days." The soul, the Puritans believed, grew throughout our lives, reaching its highest earthly perfection in old age.

A look at other eras and cultures offers a glimpse of the improvements in American life that can come with an aging population. But whether we can take advantage of this situation depends on whether our society can make the following changes:

• Uprooting ageism and gerontophobia and replacing them with a new, more positive view of aging;
• abandoning the limiting confines that come with viewing life as solely a linear progression and instead emphasizing the cyclical patterns of human existence, which is more appropriate to the shifting needs of an aging population;
• creating a new spectrum of family relationships that takes into account the sexual, companionship, and friendship needs of adults;
• improving the quality and availability of health care;
• providing products and services that will offer older men and women comfort, convenience, and pleasure;
• and achieving cooperation among Americans of all ages in creating a social system that is fair and equitable.

For us as individuals, whether an aged America turns out to be good or bad will depend on whether we can grow beyond the values and expectations of youth to discover a positive and expanded vision of who we might become in our later years.

Silent saviors

Millions of grandparents have stepped into the breach to rescue children from faltering families, drugs, abuse and violent crime

Linda L. Creighton

On a raw, wintry night, Georgie Simmons waited at a hospital in Richmond, Va., for the birth of her first grandson. Nervously pacing the tiled halls, she watched the clock stretch to 4 a.m. Finally a doctor appeared, putting a gentle hand on Georgie's shoulder to guide her to a nursery. There, in an incubator, lay a baby boy, eyes open. Georgie leaned down and whispered, "Welcome to the world, my beautiful grandson." Crying softly, she turned to the doctor and said. "Now I need to say goodbye to my own baby."

Together, they walked down the hall to a darkened room where her 30-year-old daughter, Deborah, shot in the head hours before by a jealous boyfriend, lay comatose, breathing only with the help of a respirator. "You gave him to me," Georgie whispered to her youngest child, "and I'll take care of him." Then the machines that had sustained life long enough for the baby to be born were shut down, and Simmons was left alone with her grief and her grandson.

On that night, DeDongio Simmons became one of the 3.2 million children in the United States who live with their grandparents—an increase of almost 40 percent in the past decade, according to the U.S. Census Bureau. Those, at least, are the known figures; many who are now coming to grips with the trend fear that it could be three to four times worse than that. There is hardly a more frightening leading indicator of the devastation wrought by the nation's manifold social ills, and no class or race is immune. Some 4 percent of all white children in the United States and 12 percent of black children now live with grandparents. Of these, half the families have both grandparents and most of the rest live only with the grandmother. Beyond them are the millions of grandparents who have assumed important part-time child-rearing responsibilities because of the growth of single-parent households and the number of families where both parents work.

The elaborate system of child protection and support agencies throughout the land is more of a hindrance than a help to these beleaguered families. It is very difficult for grandparents to gain unchallenged permanent custody of threatened children. And the financial support they get is less than one third that available to foster families: The national average is $109 per child per month for grandparents who are sole care givers, compared with $371 per child per month for foster parents.

But nothing can really ease the unique burdens these grandparents bear. Many of them are racked by shame and guilt at the fact that their own children have failed as parents—and many blame themselves, wondering where they went wrong as parents. In order to provide safe and loving homes to their grandchildren, some must emotionally abandon their own abusive or drug-addicted children. The stresses are compounded by the fact that some of the children they inherit are among the most needy, most emotionally damaged and most angry in the nation.

There is not a town in America untouched by this version of the extended family. Richmond, capital of the Old Confederacy, is now a very typical home of the nation's new civil wars. It is just like many communities where drugs, crime and financial and emotional distress are splitting families apart and reorganizing them. In the first six months of this year, the city's Juvenile Court handled almost 700 custody cases involving children under 18—many of whom were eventually placed with grandparents.

Richmond's ad hoc way of coping with these problems is fairly typical of other communities. It is the diligence of Wanda Cooper, a resource coordinator at the Richmond Capital Area Agency on Aging, that has begun to convince city officials that special attention must be paid to these new grandparent-led families. In her work visiting homes of senior citizens on fixed incomes, Cooper began to notice more and more small children. She later learned that more than 600 people over 65 were receiving aid to dependent children—the basic welfare program. Now she sees her mission as helping grandparents become parents again and comforting them that they are not alone. It is a message many yearn to hear.

FOGLE FAMILY

Fighting the effects of the drug epidemic is heartbreaking work

Nothing devastated many American families in the 1980s with quite the same malign swiftness as the cocaine epidemic. Katherine Fogle and her two granddaughters are three of its victims. Ask Katherine why she is rearing the girls and she squares off and says, "Drugs." A life rooted in poverty and inner-city hardship has made this 55-year-old strong and unbending. But three of her five children have been stolen from her by drugs, AIDS and hard living, and she is determined her granddaughters will not also be claimed.

That is why, five years ago, Katherine made sure that Melba, then 9, and 2-year-old Katherine, or Kat, were taken

KATHERINE FOGLE, MELBA AND KAT

"I knew I had to take the girls when my daughter looked at me and said, 'Just let me be a junkie.'"

from their cocaine-addicted mother, Penny. For years, Katherine lived across the hall from Penny in a run-down apartment building in New York City and watched her daughter slide into the drug world. Katherine says she had repeatedly tried to intervene, reporting neglect to the child-protection agency, feeding the little girls, washing them and listening for their cries when their mother left them alone. "Melba used to go to school with her clothes turned inside out," says Katherine. "I found out it was because her clothes were so filthy, she was ashamed to wear them right." The animosity between mother and daughter grew until Katherine decided to move home—to Richmond.

But the nightmare only got worse. "I got a phone call from the babies' paternal grandmother, saying Melba was in the hospital. When I asked for what, she broke down and told me Melba, my 9-year-old grandbaby, had gonorrhea. She had been raped." Left by her mother with friends, Melba had been repeatedly assaulted by a young boy. Notified of the rape, the New York Child Welfare Administration placed the girls in protective custody and agreed to let Katherine take them back to Richmond. After nearly five years of extending probationary periods for Penny, authorities finally granted Katherine legal custody of the girls.

In the meantime, Penny had more children, at least two of whom were born drug-influenced. The Sheltering Arms Childrens Service, a private agency that places children throughout the city of New York, contacted Katherine and asked if she would take more of the children to raise. Suffering from diabetes and other health problems, Katherine had to say no. "I'm not physically or mentally capable of taking care of more children," says Katherine. "I held one in my arms and I was tempted. It rode my mind for a long time."

Katherine has refused contact with her daughter for almost five years. And Penny could not be reached for comment for this story. "I'd love to see her get things together, come and take the girls back, but it's just not going to happen," she says. Her eyes soften. "She was my baby, after all." Straightening, she puts her hands together in a firm clasp. "But I just can't think about it that way anymore. I feel like she's just someone I knew." Katherine has come to terms with her own feelings by comforting herself that she did her best as a parent under difficult circumstances: "I never neglected my children, I kept them together. How can I blame myself for what's happened to them?"

In their three-room apartment in a modest, quiet part of Richmond, Katherine holds tight rein on her granddaughters. The girls share a bunk-bedded room. Rising in 6 a.m. darkness, they are on the school bus by 6:45. After-school time and evenings are carefully monitored by Katherine; Melba chafes a bit at not being able to go with friends to places with which Katherine is unfamiliar or to hang out after school talking with friends. "Straight home," says Katherine firmly.

To supplement the $231 a month she receives in ADC benefits, Katherine takes care of a baby during the week. Money for anything extra is tight, and she worries that the girls are being deprived of little extras that give teenagers confidence. On Sundays the three dress in their very best and take a church bus across town to their Baptist church, where they greet everyone by first name and spend the better part of the service waving to friends.

Kat's dark beauty is accentuated by a dazzling grin. At 7, she says she would like to be a teacher when she grows up. She has little memory of her mother, but she listens carefully as Melba speaks of Penny, and it is clear she is curious. "All I know is she's using drugs and she won't take care of us," Kat asserts.

Melba, 14, has inherited her grandmother's grace, but she is a bit uncertain of herself, glancing down as she speaks quietly about her mother: "I love her, but I don't like the things she does. I wish we could be together all in a big house, but I know that probably won't be. I love my grandmother, but I love my mother still, too." Melba talks about the bad things in her life with a steady voice and gaze. "I talked once with a counselor about the rape. But it's just something I need to put behind me." Recently, Melba found letters she had written to her grandmother in Richmond from New York and said: "Mama, I had forgotten what I felt then. It makes me cry now."

Recently, as early evening light began to paint the Richmond streets, Melba walked with her grandmother and sister and giggled self-consciously as a car filled with friends beeped its horn. Safely home, she told her grandmother that night, as she does every night: "Thank you, Mama, for loving me."

MARY AND BRANDY

Some of the worst wounds are the emotional ones that take forever to heal

At 9, Brandy talks a good game. Chin thrust high and eyes narrowed, she does not hold conversations; she challenges. "Yeah, I've got two mothers," she declares. "It's called extra family." Shifting in her seat to face a visitor, she jumps ahead to unasked questions, always ready with a tough reason.

Brandy has had to be strong. She is one of the millions of emotionally scarred and struggling children who must face the fact that their parents couldn't—or wouldn't—care for them. At birth, her mother turned her over to 59-year-old Mary, Brandy's grandmother, and Brandy has lived with her since. Until last year, she thought she had an older sister who lived down the street. Then a neighbor told Brandy the "sister" was her mother. Brandy demanded to know the truth. "I called my daughter and we told her together," says Mary. "I told Brandy, your mother gave birth to you but I raised you. Brandy just sat there and said, 'Now I know.'"

The news had a devastating effect, one Brandy tried desperately to minimize but could not hide. At the William Byrd Community House, where Brandy had been in after-school programs, Elizabeth Moreau says Brandy began to show such hostility toward adults that she felt counseling was in order: "If asked to put away toys, for instance, she would yell, 'You can't make me do anything!' and run out of the room." Her grandmother says Brandy began for the first time to challenge her. "I needed help," says Mary. Finally, this fall, Brandy has begun counseling. "These kids need lots of special care," Mary notes.

This year, for the first time, Brandy gave out two cards on Mother's Day. But her contact with her mother is sporadic and her love and loyalties are defiantly with her grandmother. They asked that their last name not be used here, as Mary has not been able to adopt Brandy.

Bright and a good student, Brandy roller-skates with a hard passion that she hopes will land her in the professionals. But she has more hard roads to travel before she gets to the pros. Mary was diagnosed with emphysema four years ago, and has so far beaten the odds for survival. But she is increasingly tired, and Brandy senses this. "She's talked to me and said she's going to be all right," she says in clipped tones. "She's going to be here to see me get big." Roughly shoving back the bangs that are always in her eyes, she fixes a smile and looks away.

Then the girl with the perfect skin and long black lashes sums up her own soldierly view of life. "There is no such thing as a perfect family," she says. "The only thing I can tell you that's really perfect is heaven." But her time with her grandmother has enabled Brandy to survive and, now, to thrive, and that is a gift that even at 9 she understands. "There are probably some kids who don't feel special living with their grandparents," says Brandy. "I don't have to worry about that because I have a reputation for being very tough. I can beat up anyone in my class who doesn't believe me."

TAYLOR FAMILY

Violent crime turns the world upside down in every way

Until three years ago, Bertha Taylor and her husband, Robert, were living what they felt were their golden years. A respected schoolteacher recently remarried to a successful postal-service truck driver, Bertha was a grandparent for the first time. She and Robert got the usual thrills from visiting her son's 6-month-old baby, Evetta. Then, one night of violence turned their world upside down. Evetta's mother, on her way back from the grocery store, was raped and murdered. Devastated and unable to cope, Bertha's son asked his parents to take Evetta. "Our lives changed completely," says Bertha. "We got her on Saturday, and I thought, 'Lord, what am I going to do? I've got to go to work on Monday.'"

The Taylors became one of the hundreds of thousands of families whose lives were riven by violent crime that year in America. They were financially comfortable and did not have to struggle for the basic needs. "There were a lot of expenses, expenses you never plan for, and I don't know how people making less than our income manage," says Bertha. But there were other things precious to the Taylors—lingering dinners and evenings with friends—that were lost as a baby's schedule took over their lives. "I didn't even have time to go to the bathroom," says Bertha. "Your freedom is gone, your privacy is gone, and you're used to having it." Day care had to be found, and Bertha's work dealing with scores of children all day became exhausting when the end of the day meant a baby waiting for more attention. The marriage underwent stresses neither Bertha nor Robert had expected to con-

☐ **BERTHA TAYLOR AND EVETTA**

"I believe the death of my daughter-in-law happened for a reason. I thank God for putting little Evetta into our lives. If she left us now, there would be a huge void."

front. "Hey, let me tell you, our sex life changed," she says. "You're tired and you've got no time."

With time, the Taylors adjusted and worked out ways of dealing with Evetta's needs. Robert rises early to dress and feed Evetta while Bertha organizes for her day of work at an elementary school. At night, Bertha prepares dinner, Robert does Evetta's bath and together they read stories to her.

Now 3, Evetta could be a star on a family sitcom, her affection and self-confidence bubbling irrepressibly. Though Bertha says she is not spoiling her, Evetta obviously thrives on her grandparents' doting. She is an addition to their relationship, they say, that they could not have foreseen. "If she left us now," says Bertha, "there would be a huge void."

Bertha's son has maintained close contact with the child, and he plans to marry again next year. Bertha says she wants whatever would make him happy, but she and her husband would like to adopt Evetta. As Bertha braids Evetta's hair, she talks of hoping to see "how this little child grows up and turns out." When night falls, a light comes on beside Evetta's bed in her pink satin and toy-filled bedroom. Her tiny voice chimes in with Bertha's schoolteacher singsong of night prayers, and she adds: "God bless all my mommies, and God bless all my daddies."

TOMAN FAMILY

The burden of poverty is worse when it has to be shared with the young

When the Richmond weather turns cold and bitter, 59-year-old May Toman and her two granddaughters pile blankets onto the worn living-room couch and chairs in their rundown row house. There, around an ancient gas burner, they sleep at night. The upstairs is without heat or electricity—and the leaky kitchen ceiling has already fallen in once. But May is afraid to complain for fear the landlord will raise her $110-a-month rent—a development that could leave them homeless.

The girls—Shelly, 8 and Tabatha, 9—make do with thrift-shop clothing, and a steak dinner is a treat remembered for weeks.

Shelly's mother was only 17 when Shelly was born, and soon afterward she and Shelly's father began leaving the baby with friends or near friends, sometimes for long periods without contact. For May, the final straw came when Shelly was 2. May found her alone in the yard one evening. She took Shelly home and called the Richmond Department of Social Services. After an investigation, May got legal custody.

Several years later, May's son, Wayne, ran into marriage problems. When his wife left, he gave his daughter Tabatha, then 7, to his mother and his infant son to his mother-in-law. Tabatha's health had been neglected; her teeth were abscessed. May applied for custody and got it.

The small, frail-looking woman the girls call "Nanny" became their mother, making ends meet by taking in sewing and cutting corners. Up at 7, she walks the girls to school, then cleans house and grocery shops with food stamps. At 3, she meets the girls outside their brick school eight blocks away "so they know there's someone waiting." Together they walk home and do homework until dinner.

One of Shelly's favorite pastimes is studying her baby album, staring intently at the pictures of herself and her mother smiling from behind plastic pages. The album ends abruptly when she is 2, and Shelly turns back to the first page to begin again. She speaks of her Nanny with affection but longs for a reunion with her mother. "I want to live with my mama in a big house," says Shelly, "but I don't really think I'll ever get that." Shelly's mother lives across town and sees Shelly fairly often. But she has another child now, a year old, and says she does not have plans to take Shelly back soon.

Tabatha readily lays her feelings out for inspection: "Well, my daddy lives in the neighborhood, but he can't take me right now. My mama used to call, which made me cry terribly, but she hasn't called now in a long time. She said she was going to send me a birthday card but she never did." Small and polish-chipped fingernails tap determinedly on the table. "I want to stay right here with my Nanny. See, I love my Nanny."

Her father, Wayne, lives next door with two new children and their mother, and though in many ways he and Tabatha are close, he says, "I feel like Tabatha's better off with Nanny."

But Nanny, a high-school dropout with a good deal of worldly wisdom to dispense, is bone weary from trying to make it on $291 a month while solving the typical childhood squabbles and

MAY TOMAN, SHELLY AND TABATHA

"I try to explain about our finances, but it's hard for the girls to understand. At least when they go to bed at night, they know they're going to wake up in the same place."

problems of two kids. Her grandchildren are among the 13.4 million American children who live in poverty—1 out of every 5 children.

May is weary, too, of trying to figure out why she and other grandmothers have ended up raising another generation. "Sometimes I feel like I really failed showing my children what kids mean. I raised mine by myself, and I hung on to them hard. Kids don't have a choice about coming into the world, but adults have choices."

May puts a fragile hand to her forehead. "I put my life on hold for 39 years, raising my own children," she says. "Now it's still on hold, but how much life do I have left? Sometimes I feel like I'm just cracking into sharp little pieces that fall to the ground." Then, running a hand through graying hair, she shrugs a smile and says, "Then I just pick up and go on out to do what I have to do."

FOGG FAMILY

Sometimes, the government child-protection system is no friend of kids

Three winters ago, Brian and Stella Fogg left their warm colonial home in Richmond to drive in a dangerous ice storm to South Carolina. Every half-hour they stopped to scrape the windshield, then slid back onto the interstate. Late in the afternoon they pulled into the parking lot of a K mart store in Beaufort. A 2-year-old boy and a 5-year-old girl climbed hesitantly from a waiting car, each clutching a small trash bag filled with personal possessions. They watched as Brian and Stella came to them with arms outstretched and said, "Now you can come home with Grandpa and Granny."

With that, Brian and Stella saved two of their grandchildren, Justine and Brian, from the system meant to protect them. After their parents' separation and inability to care for them, the children were taken into custody by authorities in South Carolina. Unknown to the grandparents, the children were

then bounced from foster home to foster home for months, finally landing in a shelter for homeless children.

When the Foggs learned of the children's plight from their son, they immediately tracked down South Carolina child-care workers and asked for the grandchildren. Stella still flushes with anger when she remembers the months of futile pleading. Beaufort County officials have refused to comment on the case.

The Foggs were allowed to visit Justine and little Brian once, with a social worker present in a cramped office. Not having seen them in years, the children at first kept their distance from their grandparents. Finally, Justine walked over, put her hand on her grandmother's knee and said quietly, "I think I remember you now. You took me to see Santa once."

Within two weeks of the Foggs' visit, the South Carolina Department of Social Services, Beaufort County, without notifying Brian and Stella, had moved the children to yet another foster home, where Justine and Brian shared a bed with at least three other children. "I understand that the social services are swamped," says Stella. "But with us ready to take them, there was no reason for those kids to suffer any more."

Weeks passed, though, as the Foggs fought to get custody of the children. They thought they had reached a breakthrough four months into the process when they were told they could pick the children up. But they went before a judge who came to their hearing unprepared. He refused to recognize the Foggs' status and made a decision based on faulty information, granting custody to the Commonwealth of Virginia instead of the grandparents. "There is no continuity in the system, no one really looking out for these kids," says Brian. "We were the only ones trying to save them."

The Foggs thought they were prepared to deal with the kids' problems, but they were surprised at their own resentments. After rearing their four sons, they had settled into a new home, made good friends and were savoring each other's company. Now, with two small children, no financial help and no emotional support, they were not happy. They were angry at their son and his wife, and initially argued about whether taking the children was possible. Brian had suffered a bout with cancer, their home had to be remortgaged to support the children and their social life evaporated. "We asked ourselves, is this going to break up our 30-year marriage?" Stella notes. "But we felt we had no choice."

Their income was cut by a third because Brian reduced his business travel schedule as an equipment specialist for

STELLA AND BRIAN FOGG WITH LITTLE BRIAN AND JUSTINE

"Social-service bureaucrats gave us no help at all. I called my congressman, everyone I could think of, and they still balked at giving us the children."

the postal service. They had to pay for extra medical insurance because no local doctor would accept Medicaid patients, and they struggled with the children's emotional scars. Justine's cries for help came when she threatened to burn down the house or rip down the curtains. "There were lots of good days," says Stella. "But never a day when we said we're happy to be doing this."

Three years later, the Foggs say it is never an easy life but they have come to terms with the sacrifices they've had to make and now feel their lives are richer. "Some of our friends say we're crazy, that they would never do this," says Stella. "But if we hadn't done this, in 15 years there might have been a knock on our front door and a young man standing there saying, 'I'm your grandson. Where were you when I needed you, when I lay in bed at night crying for someone to help me?'" The Foggs say that if their son and daughter-in-law's situation does not change soon, they want to adopt Brian and Justine.

On a recent Sunday afternoon, the fireplace in the Foggs' living room snapped with dry logs. Stella brought in a tray filled with tea and hot chocolate, and in her still strong Scottish burr called the kids in from the yard. Racing each other through the leaves, Justine and Brian bounded up the stairs. With small, dirt-dusted hands, they lifted mugs to their lips and stuffed cookies in their mouths. But when Justine talked about what family means and what it is like to live with grandparents, her childishness fell away. "The foster homes were really bad. Mostly the people weren't mean but they didn't like me. And I didn't understand that my parents didn't take care of me. I just thought I got taken away."

Staring at a place on the table, she rested her head in her hand for a moment, then looked up and with an intensity beyond her 8 years said: "At first when I came here to live, I felt kind of sad. I didn't know them. But they act like another kind of parent. They're like they had me out of their own stomachs."

SEXTON FAMILY

After a child has been neglected, the best kind of love is the simple kind

Several weeks ago, 4-year-old James came home from kindergarten crying hysterically. A boy in his class had been given a BB gun, and in a moment of childish bravado told James that he was coming to his house to shoot his parents. Perhaps another 4-year-old boy might have met the challenge with a "Yeah? I'll shoot yours back." But for James, the idea of losing parents is no empty threat. He was taken from his biological parents after he was physically abused. Now James's grandparents, Charlotte and Eddie Sexton, are his parents, and he is afraid of losing them.

From the beginning, say the Sextons, they were worried about the care of James. Neighbors had complained about the baby's treatment. After James's parents showed up at the Sextons' house one afternoon with year-old baby James, asking to leave him, the Sextons readily consented. Desperate to protect the child, Charlotte and Eddie called the Richmond Department of Social Services and, eventually, James was awarded to them on a finding of neglect.

James lived with the Sextons for a year, and then his parents petitioned the court, showing proof of a job and a

CHARLOTTE AND EDDIE SEXTON WITH JAMES

"You have to earn the right to be called Mommy or Daddy. We're trying to. James knows when he's with us, we won't let anyone else hurt him."

new apartment. This time the judge ordered James returned to his parents. "It really looked like they had turned around, so how can you keep James from them?" says Charlotte now. "But we felt like our hearts had been ripped out."

Within a short period, the daughter's husband was jailed for four months in the Richmond City Jail for petit larceny. Almost a year to the day that James was returned to his parents, a social worker called the Sextons to say that he was in a hospital emergency room, with head injuries from a belt buckle. Could they please come to get James?

James has been with the Sextons now for over a year, and they want very much to keep him. "Every child has the birthright to be with his mother and father," says Charlotte. "But sometimes, with some parents, someone has to say 'Enough.' We have reached that point."

"Nobody hands you a pamphlet and says, 'Here, this is what you do when your kid dumps his child,'" says Charlotte. But that didn't stop the Sextons from becoming attached to James. "At first you build a wall," she says. "The longer he's with you, the wall starts to fall." They found free counseling to help deal with James's tantrums and chair throwing, in the process refining their parenting style. "I never felt I had to tell my kids I loved them, I thought they knew," says Charlotte. "With James, we had to start over, like with a baby, nurturing and showing him how much we cared." Now, their parenting combines some pretty tough old-fashioned strictness with newly learned techniques like "time out" to cope with his outbursts.

Charlotte is only 45, and her homespun temperament seems perfect for raising children. Her husband, Eddie, is partial to plaid shirts that do not quite conceal a burly physique kept strong by his work in a tractor-trailer-tire shop, and though his speech is rare, it is sharp and funny. On an annual income of just over $20,000 they feel financially lucky, treating James to burgers or subs occasionally and making Christmas special. "There are times we rob Peter to pay Paul," says Eddie. "But we're OK. Sometimes at the end of the month we actually have 30 or 40 dollars left in the account."

Although James has not yet spoken about his past, he talked for the first time this month about his little brother and sister, a 9-month-old and a 2-year-old still living with his parents. Perhaps he wishes they could be with him.

WHAT GRANDPARENTS WANT

Surer ways to save kids

If grandparents who have become parents again could wave a magic wand, at the top of their wish list would be a liberalization of the laws regulating child custody. Most feel that parental rights are given too much weight in clear-cut cases when custody should be changed. The number of times parents can appeal to get children back should be limited, they say, and it should be possible for grandparents to apply for adoption earlier.

Financially, grandparents suffer an enormous burden, one that might be relieved if resources available to them were more in line with those offered to foster parents. Some states have created "kinship care" programs under which relatives caring for children receive the same amounts as foster parents. Under current rules, though, grandparents are only eligible for such benefits if they give custody of the children to the state. In effect, this makes the grandparents "foster parents" of their own grandchildren, and most grandparents are reluctant to cede their authority to the government. In Los Angeles this month, a child whose aunt was forced to return him to the foster-care system because of financial difficulties was beaten to death in a foster home.

Nationally, there are more than 150 support groups for grandparents. If you want help organizing such a group or finding out what your rights are, here are some organizations that can help:

■ GAP: Grandparents as Parents. Sylvie de Toledo, Psychiatric Clinic for Youth, 2801 Atlantic Avenue, Long Beach, CA 90801, (213) 595-3151.

■ Grandparents Raising Grandchildren. Barbara Kirkland, P.O. Box 104, Colleyville, TX 76034, (817) 577-0435.

■ Second Time Around Parents. Michele Daly, Family and Community Services of Delaware County, 100 W. Front Street, Media, PA 19063, (215) 566-7540.

7. DEVELOPMENT

[ ]

EPILOGUE

It has been nearly a year since the murder of Georgie Simmons's daughter Deborah. For Georgie and her grandson, life has gone on. These days, De-Dongio is a curly-topped smiler who lights up at the sound of his grandmother's voice. He will be walking soon. There is not much chance he will ever get to know his father, who has been convicted and sentenced to life plus 36 years for killing Deborah. Georgie says justice was done, but not for DeDongio.

This season is excruciating because for Georgie it brings back memories of last year's celebrations with her pregnant daughter, especially how Deborah enjoyed eating extra pie at Thanksgiving. And Georgie remembers how excited Deborah was at Christmas when she got a new sweater. This year, Georgie has not yet decorated her house the way she has just after Thanksgivings in times past. But she says she will soon, for DeDongio.

In the meantime, they make regular pilgrimages to Mount Calvary Cemetery in Richmond, where Deborah is buried. Last month, as darkness fell, Georgie wrapped her grandson tightly in a blanket to fight the wind and they made their way across the rows of modest headstones. They stopped at a spot marked by wilted flowers and, as she shifted the blanket, DeDongio's tiny face peeked into the cold. "This is your mama's place," Georgie said softly as the boy gazed up at her. Reaching into her pocket, she took out a small pair of booties and bent to lay them on the grave. "I'm sorry I haven't got you a stone yet, my baby, but I needed the money for DeDongio." For a moment she stood quite still. Then the baby began to cry, and Georgie bundled him up thoroughly again. With one last glance back, she turned into the wind to carry her grandson home.

Bright Lights, Big Mystery

Near-death experiences have become a cottage industry–but how real are they?

JAMES MAURO

"No wonder. No wonder. No wonder."

It's hard, talking to Barbara Harris, not to believe in near-death experiences. Even though she speaks of a Star Wars-like "force" pervading her DNA; even though she describes encountering "a cloud of bubbles, each one representing a different moment of my life"; even though she says her experience led her to a realization about herself that she never had before.

"No wonder I am the way I am," she gasps.

Barbara Harris is like the eight million other Americans who, according to a recent poll by George Gallup, Jr., claim to have had a near-death experience (NDE). They have all had visions of lights, tunnels, and dead relatives greeting them and taking them to a place of beauty, warmth, and peace. And they all say they have been profoundly changed by the experience.

Despite literally thousands of stories such as Harris's, however, science is not yet a true believer: There exists no absolute proof that such experiences are more than the product of fancy, fear, or fever. Indeed, almost all of the research to date relies upon anecdotes reported by "NDErs" rather than empirical corroboration of the events.

Stories of an afterlife have been captivating people ever since the sixth century, when Pope Gregory the Great wrote *Dialogues*, a collection of wonder-tales that included reports of return from death. Although each has the earmarks of a morality tale—with visions of hell instead of heaven—many also contain such elements of modern NDEs as "shining" angels and personality transformations.

But it wasn't until 1975, when psychiatrist Raymond Moody, M.D., wrote a book called *Life After Life*, that fascination with the subject became widespread. Coining the phrase "near-death experience," Moody reported story after story about the same, now-familiar encounter. The book intrigued a cross-section of curious individuals who begged to know more about what to expect when they die.

Fifteen years later, there are no new answers, but there *is* a spate of new books containing, mostly, more anecdotes. There is also a growing acceptance by the scientific community that something may be happening to these eight million people. Regardless of whether they are "meeting God" or simply hallucinating, NDErs routinely report that they have undergone a personality transformation—usually in the form of decreased anxiety about death, less concern with material matters, and a general feeling of peace about their lives.

It is this phenomenon that has finally attracted researchers. Rather than attempting to prove the existence of an afterlife, they have begun to study NDEs in order to learn more about brains, minds, and that elusive quality called well-being. If NDErs have truly benefited from their experience, perhaps they have something to teach us that might advance therapeutic

"There were people I knew who were lit from within. I felt myself pulled toward this bright light. It was so forceful, warm and loving. I never felt anything so peaceful and beautiful."

methods for all kinds of problems—from the dilemmas of suicidal patients to the enduring pain of those who have been abused as children. And possibly, along the way, we just might learn something about what happens when we die.

A Real "Event" or Mass Hysteria?

What exactly constitutes a near-death experience? By examining thousands of reports, researchers such as Seattle pediatrician Melvin Morse, M.D., have identified the common elements that define the experience. In his book, *Transformed by the Light* (Villard; 1992), he lists nine traits that generally characterize a "full-blown" NDE:

1) A sense of being dead: the sudden awareness that one has had a "fatal" accident or not survived an operation.

2) Peace and painlessness: a feeling that the ties that bind one to the world have been cut.

3) An out-of-body experience: the sensation of peering down on one's body and perhaps seeing the doctors and nurses trying to resuscitate.

4) Tunnel experience: the sense of moving up or through a narrow passageway.

5) People of Light: being met at the end of the tunnel by others who are "glowing."

6) A Being of Light: the presence of a God-like figure or a force of some kind.

7) Life review: being shown one's life by the Being of Light.

8) Reluctance to return: the feeling of being comfortable and surrounded by the Light, often described as "pure love."

9) Personality transformation: a psychological change involving loss of the fear of death, greater spiritualism, a sense of "connectedness" with the Earth, and greater zest for life.

Although Morse's compilation of characteristics is drawn from the self-reports of NDErs, that doesn't mean there's noth-

ing to them. In fact, evidence of their validity may be found in the startling consistency of such reports:

"I felt myself floating up, out of my bed. Looking down, I could see myself lying there, motionless."

"I moved through something dark and churning. I guess you could call it a tunnel, or a passageway."

"Suddenly there were people around me, some I knew, who were lit from within. I turned and felt myself pulled toward this bright light. It was so forceful, warm and loving. I never felt anything so peaceful and beautiful."

Yet there are enough variations to lead critics to discount NDEs as mere hallucinations. Morse relates the following story of a 45-year-old Midwestern teacher:

"I entered into a dark tunnel and suddenly I was in a place filled up with love and a beautiful, bright light. The place seemed holy. My father, who had died two years earlier, was there, as were my grandparents. Everyone was happy to see me, but my father told me it was not my time and I would be going back. Just as I turned to go, I caught sight of Elvis! He was standing in this place of intense bright light. He just came over to me, took my hand and said: 'Hi Bev, do you remember me?'."

If such experiences are real and not hallucinations, critics argue, why does Elvis appear in the place commonly inhabited by God? And what about those who see Jesus? Or Buddha? Or children who report seeing pets or parents not yet dead?

Simply stated, there are common elements shared by all NDErs. These seem to be intrinsic to the experience, and usually include the sense of leaving one's body, of traveling through a tunnel, and of seeing a bright light. Along with this so-called core experience come secondary embellishments, which account for the differences in NDE reports. The descriptions of various details and people are more personal aspects of NDEs, which are derived from an individual's life course and cultural background—what they have learned from their religious practices

and what their image is of God and heaven.

To some researchers, the symbols serve to help make sense of the experience. Whereas a bright white light and a feeling of warmth and peace might not fully convey the notion that one has "died," the point is driven home in greetings by dead relatives or pets, as well as a personification of God as Buddha or Jesus—even Elvis Presley. For the Midwestern teacher, Elvis may have inspired the same awe in her life that she felt when she met the Light.

That still leaves open the question whether NDEs are a uniquely Western experience. Does a woman from Boise, say, have the same type of experience as an African farmer? Morse cites the work of Dr. Nsama Mumbwe of the University of Zambia. The African physician wondered whether NDEs were strictly an American phenomenon, and, if not, how the accounts of Third World subjects would differ from those of Westerners.

Studying 15 NDErs in Lusaka, Zambia, Mumbwe found that all had had the same core experience as those in other parts of the world.

That isn't to say there aren't cultural differences:

• Many of the Africans interpreted the event as somewhat evil; half thought the experience signified that they were somehow "bewitched." Another called it a "bad omen."

• Among 400 Japanese NDErs, many reported seeing long, dark rivers and beautiful flowers, two common symbols that frequently appear as images in Japanese art.

• East Indians sometimes see heaven as a giant bureaucracy, and frequently report being sent back because of clerical errors!

• Americans and English say they are sent back for love or to perform a job.

• Natives of Micronesia often see heaven as similar to a large, brightly lit American city with loud, noisy cars and tall buildings.

To Morse and other investigators, these experiences are not as different as they seem. It is merely the individual *interpretations* that differ. Many report that their

NDEs are, like dreams, "difficult to put into words." That forces them to borrow images from personal experience and apply them to their NDE. And the discrepancies found in reports do not signify mass hysteria or hallucinations. On the contrary, the similarities across a wide variety of cultures, ages, and religions support the idea that being near death not only triggers a specific type of experience, but that the experience is "transcendental"—that there is entry into another dimension of being.

A Trip of the Brain or a Journey of the Mind?

There has long been a "medical-school bias"—as Morse puts it—against near-death experiences. Dismissed for years as hallucinations, patients' stories were routinely ignored by their doctors, and grant money for research has been scarce.

Slowly, however, the once-taboo subject is coming under the neuropsychiatric microscope. Decades ago, before the advent of modern neuroscience, the famous Canadian neurosurgeon Wilder Penfield identified an area of the brain that gives rise to near-death experiences. When he electrically stimulated certain sites of the temporal lobe, patients reported retrieving vivid memories as if they were actually "seeing" them. The findings prompted some researchers to search for a neurophysical explanation for NDEs—as some episode of temporal-lobe dysfunction. The implication of this line of investigation is that NDEs take place entirely within the brain, courtesy of some chemical shift or misfiring neuron.

Researchers have pursued endorphins as a cause of the euphoria and visions of heaven; compression of the optic nerve by lack of oxygen as a cause of the tunnel image; and, most recently, the neurotransmitter serotonin, putatively released by the stress of dying, to explain the typical NDE phenomena. But a direct cause-and-effect relationship has yet to be established.

What *is* known is that people who have a large number of paranormal experiences, such as NDEs, also have a higher incidence of anomalous temporal-lobe functioning. "Not abnormal," insists Vernon Neppe, M.D., director of the division of neuropsychiatry at the University of Washington, who developed a set of questions designed to stimulate the temporal lobe of the brain. "Just different. If you stimulate certain areas of the temporal lobe, you'll get certain reactions. And

those subjects with some paranormal experience will react differently."

The finding suggests that some people have a pattern of brain functioning that allows them to experience NDEs. But it does not indicate whether or not these experiences are transcendental—that is, whether the event is a journey into afterlife or a blip in the firing of brain cells. If a spiritual journey occurs entirely in the brain, however, does that make it any less a transformative phenomenon?

Other researchers have attempted to explore whether actually being near death is essential to experience an NDE. Ian Stevenson, M.D., and Justine Owens, Ph.D., of the University of Virginia's Institute for Personality Studies, wondered whether some of those reporting NDEs—and all of their characteristic traits—were not actually near death at the time of their experience, but simply *believed* they were? Surely, they argued, someone who wasn't really dying couldn't transcend into an afterlife, and therefore their experience couldn't be "real."

Stevenson studied the medical records of 40 patients who had reported NDEs, and found that more than half were not close to death at all. He suggested that "the belief of being about to die had been the principal precipitant of their experiences"(*Omega*, Vol. 20, 1989–90). In other words, a psychological reaction to trauma—what the teams calls "fear-death"—had sparked their NDE.

But Stevenson and Owens didn't stop there. They then interviewed 58 NDErs—30 of whom (52 percent) had not actually been near death (*Lancet*; Vol. 336). What they found startled them: A significantly greater number of patients who actually *were* near death reported elements of the core experience—including the bright light—than those who were not. Rather than supporting the psychological explanation, the results actually gave support to the transcendental interpretation. Those who were in a physical state wherein they might transcend into death appeared to do so; the others did not.

Still, whether near-death experiences are neurochemically induced hallucinations, psychological reactions to fear, or transcendental encounters may be moot. As one researcher puts it, in our search for firm answers we may be "overestimating the tether of mind to body."

Encounter-Prone Personalities

For Psychologist Kenneth Ring, Ph.D., author of *The Omega Project* (Morrow, 1992), research into NDEs began with a very down-to-earth approach. He wanted to determine whether there are any dis-

---

NDEs—Real or Imagined?

"I was on the operating table when all of a sudden I felt myself being pulled upward, slowly at first, then faster and faster. Suddenly I was in a black tunnel, and at the end was a light. As I got closer to it, it got brighter and brighter. It wasn't like any light I could describe to you. It was beautiful.

When I was almost at the end, the light was so bright it surrounded me and filled me with a total love and joy. I felt intense-ly pure, calm, and reassured. I just wanted to stay there forever."

"I was floating up near the ceiling and saw myself on my bed. I felt no pain, like an observer between two worlds. In time it seemed as though the ceiling was paved with clouds, and the air seemed sprinkled with gold dust.

It became very bright, and I found myself standing at the entrance to a very long canopy made of blue and silver rays. A powerful light was at the other end, and I felt other presences who were joyous with my coming. Then a doctor started banging on my chest and I opened my eyes."

—*From* Transformed by the Light *(Villard), copyright © 1992 by Melvin Morse, M.D.*

tinguishing features between people who remember and report paranormal encounters and those who do not.

He quickly discovered an extraordinary similarity in the backgrounds of those who had near-death experiences. There was, he says, "a consistent tendency for them to report a greater incidence of childhood abuse and trauma."

One common response to such trauma is dissociation—a psychological phenomenon in which a person separates from a reality that is too painful to process by conscious means, and retreats into a world of their own invention.

In fact, Ring acknowledges that those with histories of child abuse score higher on measures of dissociation, or even develop serious dissociative disorders such as multiple personality. (He cites reports of UFO abductions as possible examples of children dissociating, or "tuning out" from the reality of being abducted by a stranger and forced into an unfamiliar car.)

He sugggests that NDErs are dissociating from the trauma of being near death. But that, for him, does not invalidate the spiritual nature of the experience. Yes, these people are dissociating, he acknowledges, but he sees it as a pathway to another dimension.

"The ability to dissociate makes you more receptive to alternate realities," he explains. "You are dissociating in response to trauma, so you are more likely to register an NDE as a conscious event." By developing a dissociative response style as a psychological defense, you are more able to tune into other realities as well—becoming what Ring calls "an encounter-prone personality."

And that leads back to Barbara Harris, who had her own NDE—actually two experiences within a week—in 1975. A fall in a swimming pool exacerbated her congenital sclerosis and eventually left her in traction, lying immobile in a therapeutic contraption called a circle bed. When a breathing machine failed to allow her to exhale, Harris felt herself "being blown up like a balloon, and then…total blackness.

"Soon, I felt hands and arms around me, and then my grandmother's chest. I experienced myself through my grandmother. It was so much more than words; there was a perfect sharing between the two of us. The darkness was churning and I felt my hands expanding. I could hear a low, droning noise. All of a sudden I was back in my own body."

Afterward, regaining consciousness, she didn't tell anyone about her experience because, she says, "I didn't want to be sedated."

Her second experience was more intense. "I felt myself separating again; saw myself, as if in a bubble. I was one-year-old, in my crib, crying. I kept looking back and forth between my real self lying in bed and as this baby. And the second or third time I turned around, I saw this God-force, if you want to call it that. It moved through me, pervaded my DNA, held me up.

"As soon as I acknowledged it, we moved toward the baby, and it was as though it became part of a cloud of bubbles—each one being a different moment in my life. I relived all the abuse I suffered as a child at the hands of my mother. But I felt detached, the way I did as a kid, and I felt a realization of something I didn't know before. All my adult life I felt like a piece of dirt on somebody else's shoe, and I never knew why. And yet, re-experiencing all of those moments, I realized I had chosen to believe I was bad. I understood why I always felt so worthless.

"And my first thought, watching all this abuse, was, No wonder I am the way I am."

Harris was transformed by her experience: She speaks of acquiring a "general realization about the way everything works." Her experience led her, fittingly, to become a respiratory therapist, and to work with dying patients. She feels she may indeed have something to offer others who are suffering without knowing why.

Yet the question remains: Was Harris, in the face of great pain and trauma, merely dissociating from reality and into a world of her own invention, the way she admits doing as a child in the face of her mother's abuse? Does the coupling effect—her linking of her NDE and the recollection of abuse—reveal a pattern of dissociation, of simply tuning out reality? Or, as she puts it, did her earlier experience with dissociation leave her with a special "pathway" or channel through which she was able to reach such otherworldly levels?

"Yes, I am dissociating," she admits, "but I am also out of my body and I am someplace else. My real separation and tuning out was my misery all my life. When I had my NDE, it was easier for me to slip out of my body because *I already knew how.* The ability was there to

let go. And what I experienced was a sense of who I really am—the person I would have been had I not been abused. I had forgotten her, the part of me that remained intact. The part of me that is the spark of God."

Like Ring and other investigators, Harris believes that childhood dissociation may provide the adult with a kind of "road map" to be followed later, a receptiveness to paranormal experiences. As proof that she did indeed leave her body, she recalls overhearing a nurse's conversation that in fact took place in another room—while she was confined to her circle bed. The conversation was later confirmed by those present.

The Transformative Question

Of all aspects of near-death experiences, personality change is the one most scrutinized for insight into what is actually occurring. It attracts researchers of all persuasions. There are those who feel that the only "real" NDE is one that transforms its subjects. And there are others who are concerned merely with what can be learned from those transformations.

"The public wants to know where they go when they die," contends John Sappington, M.D., professor of psychology at Augusta (Georgia) College. "As scientists, we can't answer that question. Nevertheless, there are ways to study NDErs as a group, things we can learn from them and possibly apply to a therapeutic situation which would benefit a client."

For Sappington and others, the issue is not whether the person is actually meeting God, but why NDErs routinely seem better adjusted, more at peace and content with themselves and the world after their experience. Disregarding, for the time being at least, how they got that way, and focusing on the changes themselves, psychologists would like to borrow this newfound sense of well-being and utilize it in therapy.

Reports are highly consistent and common: "I understand things so much more" and "My senses all seem heightened." Subjects claim "sudden knowledge and comprehension of complex mathematical theorems." Psychologist Ring has identified a consistent set of value and belief changes. They include:
• a greater appreciation for life
• higher self-esteem
• greater compassion for others
• a heightened sense of purpose and self-understanding
• desire to learn

• elevated spirituality

• greater ecological sensitivity and planetary concern

• a feeling of being more intuitive, sometimes psychic.

He also observes "psychophysical changes," including:

• increased physical sensitivity

• diminished tolerance to light, alcohol, and drugs

• a feeling that their brains have been "altered" to encompass more

• a feeling that they are now using their "whole brain" rather than just a small part.

NDErs undergo radical changes in personality, and their significant others—spouses, friends, relatives—confirm these changes, reports Bruce Greyson, M.D., clinical psychiatrist and associate professor at the University of Connecticut. Like Sappington, he is concerned with what can be learned from such new outlooks on life.

Specifically, Greyson wondered whether they could be of help to those of his private clients who were suicidal. "Suicide is generally unthinkable among near-death experiencers," he says. "They exude a peace about death which is very comforting." And yet, ironically, he found, "their experience imparts a sense of purpose to those with thoughts of suicide." Those who are suicidal come away with a "renewed hope in life itself, which actually helps them to go on with their own lives," reports Greyson.

Whether such experiences can be used regularly in therapy is another matter. First, there needs to be some objective

evidence that NDErs are indeed changed by their experience. He would like to see more first-hand accounts of what the subjects felt *before* their NDE. Lacking such information, he says, "we have to rely on the person to tell us that he or she has changed, rather than seeing it for ourselves."

One approach could be standardized psychological testing of patients who for medical reasons may find themselves in near-death situations. For example,

> **"The light was so bright it surrounded me and filled me with a total love and joy. I felt intensely calm; I just wanted to stay there forever."**

Greyson thinks patients suffering from cardiac arrhythmia would be ideal. They often undergo a process known as cardioversion, in which their hearts are stopped for a brief period by a massive electrical charge intended to correct the irregular beating. Many of those who undergo cardioversion report NDEs.

"What I'd like to do is interview each patient before and after this procedure," Greyson explains. And, in order to con-

firm reports of an out-of-body experience—patients often say they floated above the operating table—he would "even plant targets near the ceiling to determine whether or not the subject actually saw them when they rose from their bodies." (Such research of arrhythmia patients is, in fact, about to get underway at the University of Wisconsin.)

Those who report out-of-body experiences often tell of listening in on conversations which took place in another room, or being aware of an event (such as the tipping-over of a tray of operating instruments) that they could not have been witness to inside their bodies. If an unconscious patient later describes the ceiling targets, however, Greyson and others would take it as hard evidence that out-of-body experiences are real.

The Big Question

What, in the end, are near-death experiences? And exactly how far can research go in trying to answer that question?

"People with NDEs routinely report that they had an omniscient feeling—a brief conclusion that they were everywhere at once and that time had no meaning," says John Sappington. "I can't help but wonder what is happening to these people—do they tend toward histrionics in general, or have they had access to information that transcends the beyond?

"Of course we're never going to provide hard proof of an afterlife," he laments. "As a scientist, I find it frustrating that I can't empirically test all these theories. The big question—is there life after death—is still going to remain a mystery."

Personality Processes

Anna and Sadie are identical twins. When the girls were young children, their parents tried very hard to treat them equally. Whenever Anna received a present, Sadie received one, too. Both girls attended dance school and completed early classes in ballet and tap dance. In elementary school, the twins were both placed in the same class with the same teacher. The teacher also tried to treat them the same.

In junior high school, Sadie became a tomboy. She loved to play rough-and-tumble sports with the neighborhood boys. On the other hand, Anna remained indoors and practiced her piano and read poetry. Anna was keenly interested in domestic arts such as sewing, needlepoint, and crochet. Sadie was more interested in reading novels, especially science fiction, and in watching adventure programs on television.

As the twins matured, they decided it would be best for them to attend different colleges. Anna went to a small, quiet college in a rural setting while Sadie matriculated at a large public university. Anna majored in English, with a specialty in poetry; Sadie switched majors several times and finally decided on a communications major.

Why, when these twins were exposed to the same early childhood environment, did their interests and paths diverge in later adolescence? What makes people so unique, so different from one another, even identical twins?

The study of individual differences and commonalties is the domain of the study of personality. The psychological study of personality has included two major thrusts. The first thrust has focused on the search for the commonalties of human life and development. Its major question would be: How are all humans affected by specific events or activities? Personality theories are based on the assumption that a given event, if it is important, will affect almost all people in a similar way, or that the processes by which events affect people are common across events and people. Most psychological research into personality variables has also made this assumption. Failures to replicate a research project are often the first clues that differences in individual responses require further investigation.

While some psychologists have focused on personality-related effects that are presumed to be universal among humans, others have devoted their efforts to discovering the bases on which individuals differ in their responses to environmental events. In the beginning, this specialty was called genetic psychology, since most people assumed that individual differences resulted from differences in genetic inheritance. By the 1950s, the term genetic psychology had given way to the more current term: the psychology of individual differences.

Does this mean that genetic variables are no longer the key to understanding individual differences? Not at all. For a time, psychologists took up the philosophical debate over whether genetic or environmental factors were more important in determining behaviors. Even today, behavior geneticists compute the heritability coefficients for a number of personality and behavioral traits, including intelligence. This is an expression of the degree to which differences in a given trait can be attributed to differences in inherited capacity or ability. Most psychologists, however, accept the principle that both genetic and environmental determinants are important in any area of behavior. These researchers are devoting more of their efforts to discovering how the two sources of influence interact to produce the unique individual.

Given the above, the focus of this unit is on personality characteristics and the differences and similarities among individuals. What is personality? Most researchers in the area define it as "patterns of characteristic thoughts, feelings, and behaviors that persist over time and situations and usually distinguish one person from another" (Phares, 1991).

The foundation for a healthy personality is considered by many psychologists to be good self-esteem. Self-esteem is the general value you place on who you are. If you do not like yourself very much or do not consider yourself a worthwhile person, you have low esteem. If you are a confident person, sure of your self-worth, then you have high self-esteem. Psychologists worry about esteem levels in the average American because those with low esteem are sometimes suicidal.

Self-esteem is the topic of the first article, "Hey, I'm Terrific!" The article focuses on self-esteem as a faddish topic in pop psychology. The authors report that many psychologists feel that the term "self-esteem" is so overworked in our media that it is almost useless.

Gender role is an issue near and dear to personality psychologists. Gender is a concept that speaks to all of the main issues in the field of personality. There exist both similarities and differences between men and women. There also exist similarities and differences within groups of men and within groups of women. From where do these differences come? Nature or nurture, or some combination of both? We look next at two gender issues: one important to girls and women and the other important to boys and men.

In "Girls' Self-Esteem Is Lost on Way to Adolescence, New Study Finds," Suzanne Daley shares with us the work of psychologist Carol Gilligan. Gilligan contends that girls enter their teen years with a healthy self-esteem and emerge with a poor self-image. The article reviews why this is the case.

The next article, "In Search of the Sacred Masculine," pertains to the topic of masculinity. The article discusses how groups of men are forming around the country to assist them in exploring their masculinity, both its benefits and drawbacks. The groups emphasize men's collective heritage and their relationships to other men and women.

Do positive thinkers live healthier, happier lives? Nick Gallo tackles this question in "Tapping the Healing Power of Positive Thinking." Gallo looks at the scientific debate about whether positive attitudes influence our health and weighs the pros and cons of each side of the debate.

Our final article is a companion to Nick Gallo's article. Carolyn Jabs reviews research in "Are You Raising an Optimist?" which discovered that optimistic children do better in school and have more friends than pessimists.

Given these conclusions, the article would be incomplete without some guidelines for parents on how to raise an optimistic child.

Looking Ahead: Challenge Questions

What is self-esteem? What are some of the differences between individuals with low esteem and high esteem? Why do we value high esteem? How can we raise children to have high self-esteem? Why does the self-esteem of girls seem to plummet in adolescence, especially compared to boys'?

What are some of the differences between optimists and pessimists? Are optimists healthier than pessimists? Do optimists really live longer? What differences exist between optimistic and pessimistic children?

What is masculinity? What is femininity? Have men been isolated and alone? Why is this true? How can men change their roles and their attitudes toward each other? Are there differences between the sexes in their expression of affection for members of the same sex? Do other differences exist? Where do you think these differences come from? Are the sexes more similar than they are different?

Hey, I'm Terrific!

The latest national elixir—self-esteem—is supposed to cure everything from poor grades to bad management. Instead, it gives feeling good a bad name.

If you're like most Americans, chances are you never thought you were at risk for low self-esteem. Sure, you felt bad at your kids' school's Career Day when you were the only parent who didn't own his own company. But unless your family psychometrician has administered a Coopersmith Self-Esteem Inventory or the Kaplan Self-Derogation Scale you probably never imagined that a negative self-image might be holding you back in life. You just thought you were no good.

But now you know that there are no bad people, only people who think badly of themselves. You know that "if you really joyfully accept yourself . . . nothing can make you unhappy," in the words of Father John Powell, a specialist in "psychotheology" at Loyola University of Chicago. You know that even famous, successful people like writer Gloria Steinem ("Revolution From Within: A Book of Self-Esteem") have to battle "inner feelings of incompleteness, emptiness, self-doubt and self-hatred." Negative thoughts afflict even paragons of achievement like athlete Michael Jordan, author of this poignant confession in the "self-esteem corner" of the Children's Museum of Denver: "I wish I came in first more often." Ordinary people obviously wish the same thing for themselves. Although only one in 10 Americans believes he personally suffers from low self-esteem, according to a NEWSWEEK Gallup Poll, more than 50 percent diagnose the condition in someone else in their families. And, of course, deviant behavior is prima facie evidence of self-image problems, as in the case of a man being sought in Montgomery County, Md., for a series of rapes. Citizens have been warned by police to be on the lookout for a man in his 30s with a medium build and "low self-esteem."

As a concept, self-esteem can be traced to Freud, who used the term ego ideal. Shame, the emotional expression of low self-esteem, has been a hot topic among therapists in recent years, and is the subject of a new book ("Shame: The Exposed Self") by a prominent developmental psychologist, Michael Lewis. But as a paradigm for analyzing almost every problem in American society, self-esteem is clearly a product of today's relentless search for ever more fundamental and unifying laws of nature. Self-esteem is the quark of social science, a way to make sense of the wildly proliferating addictions, dependencies and 12-step programs jostling for air time on "Donahue." Low self-esteem is a meta-addiction, a state that seems to underlie afflictions as diverse as bulimia and performance anxiety. "People saw that self-esteem was a component of so many other things—teenage pregnancies, dropouts, drugs, school success—and they were hoping we'd found one solution to many problems," says psychoanalyst Nancy E. Curry of the University of Pittsburgh. People always hope that; it's what keeps publishers going, not to speak of religions.

As the distinction between therapy and the rest of American life has eroded, the concept of self-esteem has established itself in almost every area of society. The bulletin of The National Council for Self-Esteem, Self-Esteem Today, lists 10 national and regional conferences this year aimed at extirpating negative self-images from society. Most people, thanks to "Doonesbury," know that California appointed a state commission to promote self-esteem. But the idea is also very big in places like Minnesota (home of the "Very Important Kid" program for "encouraging self-esteem in 3–6 year olds") and in Maryland, where a state task force counted more than 1,000 ways in which citizens were already working to improve the self-esteem of their fellow students, government workers, business executives and cellmates. An outfit called High Self-Esteem Toys Corp. has brought out a fashion doll named Happy To Be Me, whose scale measurements of 36-27-38 are intended to represent a more realistic ambition for a human being than Barbie's exotic mannequin's figure, with its 18-inch waist and 33-inch hips.

Churches have discovered that "low self-esteem" is a less off-putting phrase to congregants than "sin." When Peewee Herman was arrested last year, Jesuit scholar William O'Malley partially exonerated him with the observation that "masturbation isn't the problem, it's lack of self-esteem." (Going further, a Presbyterian Church committee on "human sexuality" last year actually recommended masturbation in cases of severe self-image deficiency. Its example was a man confined to a wheelchair who gains "self-esteem" from the use of an electric vibrator. The committee's report was rejected.)

Businesses have begun to realize that improving employees' self-esteem, usually known in this context as "empowerment," can be a more effective motivator than expensive, old-fashioned "raises." "Self-esteem is a basic building block on which personal effectiveness is based," says management-training consultant Dave Ehlen, head of Wilson Learning Corp. America's corporate managers—the same group whose excessive salaries are elsewhere regarded as a national scandal—have to be made to "believe in themselves . . . to feel good about what they are and where they are going." How does this work in practice? Nancy Stephan, a Minneapolis consultant, was called in to help a medium-size company suffering from a communication problem: the president was yelling at his subordinates. She diagnosed this as a lack of executive self-esteem. By teaching him to "talk to people in a caring way," the company's problem was solved! "Relationships have improved tremendously," Stephan says. They're not actually making any more money, "but they're communicating on a whole different level."

Nowhere has the concept taken root as firmly as in education. Toddlers are encouraged to "reach their full potential" in self-esteem day-care centers. High-school drug and alcohol programs now emphasize self-esteem, on the theory, according to New Hampshire school administrator James Weiss, that "if youngsters feel good about themselves, those temptations won't be so strong." Of course, there are still some kinks to work out. Pamela Smart, the New Hampshire schoolteacher convicted of having her husband murdered, met her teenage lover at a "Project Self-Esteem" workshop in Winnacunnet High School.

The San Diego city school system voted last year to abolish failing grades, a move that was widely misconstrued as an effort to legislate failure itself out of existence. That was not precisely the intention; under the proposal, a student who didn't complete the work would have to repeat the course, but only the subsequent passing grade would show on his record. Nevertheless an outraged public rescued the "F" before the plan could take effect. In any case, it's not clear why anyone believes that too many failing grades are the problem in American schools. Psychologist Harold Stevenson of the University of Michigan found that American schoolchildren rank far ahead of students in Japan, Taiwan and China in self-confidence about their abilities in math. Unfortunately, this achievement was marred by the fact that Americans were far behind in *actual performance* in math. Japanese parents "don't lavish praise on their children—they're concerned they will end up thinking too much about themselves, and not enough about the group," says Lewis. The difference between the cultures "is that the Japanese are trying to be proud, and we're trying to be happy." A new comparison of math and science achievement by schoolchildren in 20 countries, released last week, also showed Americans ranking near the bottom.

As a theory of behavior, self-esteem has intuition on its side, if not necessarily a monopoly on convincing research. It seems to make sense that people who have a low opinion of themselves are more likely to seek momentary pleasures in drugs or sex. Many criminologists believe that delinquency results from youth with low self-esteem trying to show off—a "performance for an audience," in the words of Martin Gold of the University of Michigan's Institute for Social Research. Inevitably, the evidence for this tends to be somewhat anecdotal. The best anecdote is Lewis's account of adolescent boys in a reform school who would punch the offender in the face when one of them passed gas. But does it necessarily follow that "people with low self-esteem confuse being in the presence of someone who farts with the different situation of actually being farted upon"? And what should the nation do about it, anyway?

As a general prescription for child-rearing, self-esteem is unassailable. To develop it, says child psychiatrist Dr. Stanley Greenspan, children need "a constant and loving caregiver . . . a fundamental sense of safety and security." Who could be against that? "A sense of self, grounded in a sense of personal competence and supported by people who think I am a valuable and worthy person, is a requisite for productive learning to occur," says Linda Darling-Hammond, a professor of education at Columbia Teachers College. That also seems intuitively obvious to most Americans today—although 70 years ago it was equally

obvious to many educators that schools had to break down children's "sense of self," the better to fill their heads with facts.

But what is it? Like most things that are intuitively obvious, though, self-esteem can be hard to demonstrate empirically. A recent survey of the literature estimated that more than 10,000 scientific studies of self-esteem have been conducted. Researchers have measured it with more than 200 different tests. (Typically, respondents are asked to agree or disagree with statements such as, "On the whole, I am satisfied with myself.") There isn't even agreement on what it is. Greenspan defines it, tautologically enough, as "the innermost sense of self-worth and value." "I think of it as related to three things: confidence, competence and relationships," says Rutgers University psychologist Maurice Elias, clarifying matters only somewhat. Even the National Council has been unable to agree on a single definition, according to executive director LeRoy Foster, after polling 100 teachers and coming up with "27 distinctly different answers."

The programs aimed at cultivating self-esteem also have a fairly homegrown air about them. "There's a huge self-esteem industry out there, and a lot of it is nonsense," says Lillian Katz, president-elect of the National Association for the Education of Young Children. Everyone gives lip service to the notion that self-esteem must arise from within, from a genuine sense of achievement and worth. But the actual impact of the self-esteem movement has been an explosion of awards, gold stars and happy-face stickers for the most routine accomplishments of childhood. Most children's sports teams now automatically give trophies just for showing up, with the result that the average 12-year-old's bedroom is as cluttered with honors as Bob Hope's den. In Woodland Hills, Calif., the Halsey Schools (nursery through grade 3) holds an awards ceremony *every six weeks*. Each child who enters the Denver Children's Museum is directed to the "self-esteem corner," handed a paper flag and a supply of positive adjectives to trace and stamp on it. The adjectives are supposed to spell out the child's name, so if she happens to be, say, Phyllis, she can anoint herself Patient or Perky, but not Awesome.

A nation of flatterers: And what if Phyllis happens to be Pompous, or just a Pill? There is no self-criticism corner; the museum's goal according to promotion director Leslie McKay is for children to leave "feeling good about themselves." If children are actually fooled by this stuff, the country is in worse shape than anyone imagined. Katz, who is also a professor of education at the University of Illinois, holds to the old-fashioned notion that self-esteem must follow, not precede, real accomplishment. "I'm getting so sick of these empty slogans," she says, citing an example of an Illinois school decked out

with a giant banner reading: WE APPLAUD OURSELVES. "Schools have established award structures—the happy helper of the week, the reader of the week. Teachers think that if they don't do this stuff, the kids won't do the work, but that's ridiculous. We don't need all this flattery. No other country does this."

This is not a prescription for never saying anything nice to children. Children do need encouragement; the problem is that like so much else in life, it is distributed inequitably. "Praise has to be connected with values, with the development of character," says Curry. "Kids need authentic feedback, not praise for walking across the room without falling over." "Too many teachers forget to give children credit for the things they did right, rather than focusing on X-ing what they did wrong," says Darling-Hammond. "We should be remedying that—rather than encouraging Yuppies to be more obnoxious with their kids."

But who wants to be bothered waiting for a child to do something right, when it's so much simpler just to praise him all the time? The Self-Esteem movement hunts down negative thoughts with a holy zeal, a single-minded dedication to knocking some self-esteem into these kids' heads. "101 Ways to Make Your Child Feel Special," by well-known parenting authority Vicki Lansky, recommends that you "tell your child how nice he or she looks . . . even if plaid pants are being worn with a striped shirt!" Do parents really have to suspend judgment to that degree? She also recommends blowing up your child's photo to poster size and hanging it in his room, just the thing if you want to raise a kid with the ego of a rock star. In a pamphlet called "Celebrate Yourself," the Corporation for Public Broadcasting points out that even "handsome 6-foot 1-inch actor Kevin Costner" sometimes criticizes himself: "I wish I were smart . . . more disciplined . . . and better read." If Harold Bloom said this, he would have a self-esteem problem. But a movie star? Isn't Costner just expressing an honest criticism and setting a laudable goal for improvement? Evidently not; this is dismaying evidence that "all of us—even very successful people—put ourselves down."

Self-esteem is a common prescription for African-American youth, who bear the particular burden of a heritage of racial prejudice. "The decks are really stacked against some minorities," says Dr. Alan Stoudemire, a psychiatrist at the Emory Clinic in Atlanta. "They receive powerful messages from family or teachers or society that they are not as good as everyone else." In the absence of real solutions to this problem, slogans and exhortations are being tried instead. Jesse Jackson's famous chant distills the philosophy of self-esteem to its minimalist essence: "I am . . . Somebody!" Others are a trifle more specific. When Jacqueline Ponder, the principal of Atlanta's East Lake Elementary School, noticed that the boys in her classrooms were neglecting to carry books and hold doors for their teachers, she diagnosed the problem as low self-esteem and prescribed a motto: "I Am a Noble African-American Boy!" "Once they have their self-esteem," Ponder asserts, "they don't need anything else. They *are.* And all they have to do is develop that which they are."

As far as the case for self-esteem goes, that says it all. It is a matter less of scientific pedagogy than of faith—faith that positive thoughts can make manifest the inherent goodness in anyone, even 10-year-old boys. Americans are notoriously partial to this brand of naive optimism. As long ago as the 1920s, the French therapist Emile Coué wowed this nation with his formula for self-improvement, based on daily repetitions of the mantra "Every day in every way I am getting better and better." Norman Vincent Peale gave self-esteem (or "positive thinking") a religious dimension. His accounts of industrialists, golf pros and similar role models triumphing over adversity through faith sold millions of books in the 1950s. In the 1980s, the concept got its fullest expression from California television preacher Robert H. Schuller. From the pulpit of the Crystal Cathedral, Schuller preaches

an explicit gospel of self-esteem, which he defines as "the human hunger for the divine dignity that God intended to be our emotional birthright. People who do not love themselves," Schuller asserts, "can't believe in God."

"Like a lot of other words, self-esteem is sort of 'religiously correct' today," agrees Father John E. Forliti, vice president of the University of Saint Thomas in Minnesota. The notion may put off anyone old enough to remember when "Christian" as an adjective was often followed by "humility." But American churches, which once did not shrink from calling their congregants wretches, have moved toward a more congenial view of human nature. The Roman Catholic parish of St. Joan of Arc in Minneapolis is packed every Sunday in part because it won't turn anyone away, including homosexuals and divorced Catholics remarried outside the church. "There's no sense that you broke some law or rule and that you're not good enough," says parish administrator Peter Eichten. In Warren, Mich., the nondenominational Church of Today preaches a doctrine of "empowerment," based on the belief that "the great sin is not the things that people typically see as sins, it's not living up to their own potential." At first glance this seems like a terrific deal for people who *like* doing "the things that people typically see as sins." But self-esteem has a catch to it: like

"grace," if you're living an immoral life, by definition you don't have it. The point is not to abolish ethical distinctions. Wrong actions hurt oneself or others, and no one with real self-esteem would do anything like that. That's why chastising sinners is considered counterproductive: it makes them feel worse about themselves.

The man most responsible for putting self-esteem on the national agenda is not a clergyman or philosopher, but a California state assemblyman named John Vasconcellos, Democrat from San Jose. In his own life Vasconcellos, 59, is a walking advertisement for the importance of self-esteem. He was raised by strict, attentive parents who set high standards for him. This is one of the biggest risk factors for self-esteem problems, next to lax, indifferent parents who don't demand enough. He was college valedictorian, a successful lawyer and politician. Overachievement is a very common sign of low self-esteem, next to underachievement. Yet he was also a troubled legislator, going for three years without cutting his hair and engaging in hostile outbursts against colleagues. Self-esteem problems often contribute to aggression, except when they result in passivity.

The big picture: Psychotherapy helped Vasconcellos correct his own self-esteem shortfall. Then one day in 1983 he stumbled on a theory linking teen pregnancy with low self-esteem. "All of a sudden, the

America Seems to Feel Good About Self-Esteem

How important are the following in motivating a person to work hard and succeed? (percent saying "very important")

89%	Self-esteem/the way people feel about themselves
77%	Family duty or honor
49%	Responsibility to community
44%	Fear of failure
35%	Status in the eyes of others

Is too much time and effort spent on self-esteem?

63%	Time and effort spent is worthwhile
34%	Time and effort could be better spent on work

Who would you say has low self-esteem?

	TOTAL	18 to 29 years old	30 to 49 years old	50 or more years old
Me, personally	10%	7%	8%	15%
Spouse	8%	8%	7%	9%
Child	13%	3%	17%	15%
Other relative	33%	30%	46%	21%

Do you think never giving F's in school to maintain self-esteem and eagerness to learn is a . . .

68% Bad idea	26% Good idea

Which situations would make you feel very bad about yourself?

	18 to 29 years old	30 to 49 years old	50 or more years old
Not being able to pay your bills	51%	57%	80%
Being tempted into doing something immoral	48%	57%	77%
Having an abortion (if male, your wife or girlfriend having an abortion*)	60%	56%	69%
Getting a divorce	57%	52%	73%
Losing your job	50%	53%	65%
Feeling you had disobeyed God	47%	49%	71%
Being noticeably overweight	39%	29%	42%
Doing something embarrassing in public	26%	25%	50%
Being criticized by someone you admire	19%	19%	39%

*Total saying "yes" includes 67% of women, 55% of men. In a differently worded question 10 years ago, 66% of women but only 36% of men said having an abortion would make them feel very bad.

For this NEWSWEEK Poll, The Gallup Organization interviewed 612 adults by telephone Jan. 15-16. The margin of error is plus or minus 5 percentage points. Some "Don't know" and other responses not shown. The NEWSWEEK Poll © 1992 by NEWSWEEK, Inc.

pattern just loomed large," Vasconcellos said. "Maybe violence, drug addiction, crime and other problems were also a product of the same thing."

Eager to share this insight, Vasconcellos helped create a state task force on "self-esteem and personal and social responsibility." Its conclusion—that "lack of self-esteem is central to most personal and social ills plaguing our state and nation"—has inspired five states and nearly all 58 California counties to set up self-esteem task forces. Several groups are urging national legislation. This is a remarkable instance of adopting as a goal of public policy something that is quintessentially private and introspective. It is one thing for the state to discourage welfare dependency, for instance, by requiring recipients to get jobs. It is a big—and thus far unexamined—step for the state to try to do the same thing by tinkering directly with citizens' psyches.

And if it does, it ought at least to be sure it knows what it's doing. Most of what people believe about the public-policy implications of self-esteem come from the task-force report, "Toward a State of Esteem." The report's "key finding" was that "self-esteem is the likeliest candidate for a *social vaccine* [emphasis in original], something that empowers us to live responsibly and that inoculates us against the lures of crime, violence, substance abuse, teen pregnancy, child abuse, chronic welfare dependency and educational failure."

A lot less attention has been paid to the scientific papers prepared for the task force, which were published separately as "The Social Importance of Self-Esteem." Can self-esteem cut drug abuse? The scientists concluded that "there is a paucity of good research, especially studies that could link the abuse of alcohol and drugs with self-esteem." Is it implicated in child abuse? "There is insufficient evidence to support the belief in a direct relation between low self-esteem and child abuse." Crime and violence? "Self-esteem may be positively *or* negatively correlated with aggression." Teen pregnancy? Somewhat embarrassingly, two studies linked *high* self-esteem with increased sexual activity by teens. But there was evidence that girls with high self-esteem were more likely to use contraceptives. Admitting the findings were inconclusive, the authors went on to write that "our approach is to make the strongest case possible, given the research, for the existence of a causal link between self-esteem and teenage pregnancy. We conclude, therefore, that low self-esteem does contribute to the risk of an adolescent pregnancy."

That does seem a remarkable admission in an academic paper, and at least one of the task-force members refused to sign the final report in part because of the gap between the research results and the report's sweeping conclusions. Vasconcellos regards this as pettifoggery. Such criticism comes from "those who only live in their heads, in the intellectual." The research, he says, did what it was supposed to do; it "confirms our intuitive knowledge."

So why be a pedant? How much better it is to think positive thoughts. If you don't have any, the Public Broadcasting pamphlet can supply some, including a list of eight body parts (arms, nose, teeth . . .) and 22 attributes (funny, mature, awesome . . .) it's possible to feel good about. Think of the Halsey Schools, where the word "bad" is never spoken, where everyone gets an award every year, where kindergarten children learn to count by being handed pictures of objects and *told how many there are instead of figuring it out themselves.* Ask yourself: wouldn't it be nice if life were really like this?

And what's going to happen to those kids when they find out it's not?

JERRY ADLER *with* PAT WINGERT *in Washington,*
LYNDA WRIGHT *in Los Angeles,*
PATRICK HOUSTON *in Minneapolis,*
HOWARD MANLY *in Atlanta,* ALDEN D. COHEN
in New York and bureau reports

Girls' Self-Esteem Is Lost on Way To Adolescence, New Study Finds

Suzanne Daley

Girls emerge from adolescence with a poor self-image, relatively low expectations from life and much less confidence in themselves and their abilities than boys, a study to be made public today has concluded.

Confirming earlier studies that were smaller and more anecdotal, this survey of 3,000 children found that at the age of 9 a majority of girls were confident, assertive and felt positive about themselves. But by the time they reached high school, less than a third felt that way.

The survey, commissioned by the American Association of University Women, found that boys, too, lost some sense of self-worth, but they ended up far ahead of the girls.

For example, when elementary school boys were asked how often they felt "happy the way I am," 67 percent answered "always." By high school, 46 percent still felt that way. But with girls, the figures dropped from 60 percent to 29 percent.

Race as a Factor

"It's really quite staggering to see that this is still going on," said Myra Sadker, a professor at American University in Washington, who has spent most of the last decade studying the way teachers treat girls in the classroom. "No one has taken such a large-scale look at self-esteem before, but we have known of this issue for years. And here you see that it is not going away."

Among the girls, race is apparently a factor in the retention of self-esteem, the survey found. Far more black girls surveyed were still self-confident in high school, compared with white and Hispanic girls, and white girls lost their self-assurance earlier than Hispanic girls.

The subject of girls' self-esteem has emerged relatively recently as a field of study, generating considerable controversy. Some academics say the psychological development process of women differs profoundly from that of men; others disagree.

Dr. Carol Gilligan, a professor of education at Harvard and a pioneer in studying the development of girls, said the survey's findings would force a series of more complex questions about what happens to girls' self-esteem during adolescence.

"This survey makes it impossible to say what happens to girls is simply a matter of hormones," said Dr. Gilligan, an adviser on the development of questions asked in the survey. "If that was it, then the loss of self-esteem would happen to all girls and at roughly the same time.

"This work raises all kinds of issues about cultural contributions," she added, "and it raises questions about the role of the schools, both in the drop of self-esteem and in the potential for intervention."

Sharon Schuster, president of the American Association of University Women, a research and advocacy group, said the association had commissioned the study to draw attention to the plight of girls at a time when education changes is a topic of widespread interest.

Are girls still shortchanged in the classroom?

"Generally, most people feel that girls are getting a good education," Ms. Schuster said. "I think this survey shows that the system has some shortfalls. We wanted to put some factual data behind our belief that girls are getting shortchanged in the classroom."

Based on an index of personal self-esteem created by the responses to such statements as "I like the way I look," "I like most things about myself" and "I wish I were somebody else," the study found that overall, boys had a higher sense of self-esteem than girls in elementary school and retained it better over the years.

The study, conducted by Greenberg-Lake Analysis Group Inc., surveyed 2,400 girls and 600 boys at 36 public schools in 12 communities throughout the country last fall. The children, in grades 4 through 10, were asked to answer written questions in the classroom.

The researchers said the margin of sampling error was plus or minus three percentage points for the girls and plus or minus five percentage points for the boys.

Enough girls were questioned for the researches to draw conclusions about race distinctions, but no such conclusions could be drawn about the boys because there were too few boys included in the survey.

The findings among the girls, combined with the answers that black girls gave regarding their relationships with teachers, prompted the researchers to conclude that black girls drew their apparent self-confidence from their families and communities rather than the school system.

Janie Victoria Ward, a Rockefeller fellow at the University of Pennsylvania who is studying the socialization of black families and was an adviser to the study, said one factor that might help black girls is that they are often surrounded by strong women they admire. Black women are more likely than others to have a full-time job and run a household.

Another factor, she said, may be that black parents often teach their children that there is nothing wrong with them, only with the way the world treats them.

"In order to maintain that high self-esteem they are disassociating from school," said Dr. Ward.

Linda Kerber, a professor of history at the University of Iowa, said she, too, found the results about black girls to be particularly interesting.

"This should encourage white people to look with admiration at the black community," Dr. Kerber said. "So often we look at the black family as a locus of problems, but here we can see that they are doing something right."

Dr. Gilligan of Harvard said that what appeared to be happening to black girls had both good and bad consequences. "The danger is that the black girls will miss the opportunity of school," she said. "You can't just romanticize this."

To some degree, the new study supports the work Dr. Gilligan has been doing in recent years. One of her studies looked intensively at about 100 girls enrolled at a private school outside of Cleveland, and fol-

lowed their development closely for more than five years.

Dr. Gilligan also found that adolescence is the moment when girls begin to doubt themselves: while 11-year-olds tend to be full of self-confidence, she said, by 15 and 16 they start to say, " 'I don't know. I don't know. I don't know.' "

But Dr. Gilligan said her study was too small to draw broad-based conclusions about race. "We did see some of these things," she said. "But we could not make the kind of generalizations that this survey allows."

The American Association of University Women's survey also examined children's attitudes toward science and mathematics, finding that girls who did poorly in math tended to see their problems as "personal failures," while boys more often attributed their lack of success or interest in math to a sense that the subject "was not useful."

Indeed, young women who like math are more confident about their appearances than are young men, whether they like math or not, the study found.

In Search of the Sacred Masculine

Benedict Carey

YOU KNOW YOU ARE in the right place because there's a cardboard sign that says MEN in block letters and points toward about two hundred of them, lined up outside an auditorium. If it weren't ten in the morning, these guys might be waiting for a Buffalo Springfield reunion: There are many greying beards, wire-framed glasses, worn Reeboks, domestic midsections.

Suddenly the line tightens and talking ceases. A man in front has opened a side stage door, and he's letting in four or five people at a time, nightclub style. This fellow appears relaxed, but each time he swings the door open an ominous rumbling spills out; a sound that gets louder as you approach, and louder, and then someone whispers in your ear, "Remember your ancestors," and you're inside and *here they are*—not your ancestors but the men!—in a pandemonium of yelping and clapping and bare-chested hooting, and some are pounding conga drums and it is rhythmic, visceral.

And you dance.

"This is a sacred space," an elfin man in his forties tells the audience, once everyone has settled into a seat. "And when you enter a sacred space you might as well dance." The man is Michael Meade, a mythologist and storyteller who, along with Robert Moore, a Chicago psychologist, is leading a two-day seminar at the University of San Francisco to explore the "sacred masculine." Together with Minnesota poet Robert Bly, Meade and Moore

form a sort of trinity in an emerging men's movement that holds that deep in the bosom of every man lies a primal, spiritual maleness, forgotten in the modern world of automatic teller machines, power lunches, and feminism—a world nearly devoid of sacred rituals and meaningful symbols. Across the country, in places as diverse as rural Texas and Midwest college towns and midtown Manhattan, men are attending similar gatherings to rediscover themselves through myth, poetry, ancient ritual, and group therapy.

The emerging movement holds that deep in the bosom of every man lies a primal, spiritual maleness.

It's estimated that these events have attracted nearly 50,000 men since the early 1980s. The 63-year-old Bly, widely acknowledged as the father of the movement, is reaching thousands more: His recent book, *Iron John: A Book About Men*, hit the *New York Times* best-seller list and stayed for months.

"They're talking about the grief men feel from their lack of closeness with

other men, and society's lack of honor for older men," says Harry Brod, an associate professor of Women's and Gender Studies at Kenyon College in Gambier, Ohio, who has edited several collections of essays on men. "These are things our culture hasn't done a good job addressing."

On this Saturday morning the quest for the sacred starts with a fairy tale. To the hypnotic beat of his drum, Michael Meade begins telling Grimm's fairy tale "The Golden Bird," in which three brothers attempt to capture for their father, the king, a great bird that has been stealing golden apples from a tree in the castle's courtyard. The eldest brother sets out first, and by day's end he reaches a village, in which he must choose whether to spend the night at a bright inn or a dark inn—an inn alive with merriment and laughter, or an inn that is abandoned, somber.

Meade stops. "Which would you enter?" he asks.

"The light inn," comes one voice. "I've been in the dark inn for the last twenty years." Another says, "I'd go into the dark inn, because the darkness represents grief, and without dealing with your own grief you cannot move forward." Soon, as the story progresses, and Meade and Moore encourage discussion, men are standing up and offering interpretations of the inns, the bird, the golden apples, relating each symbol to their own lives, their own hopes, fears, and anger. Salesmen and teachers, managers and lawyers, artists and counselors, they have stories of divorce, of alienation from fathers and mothers and children, of family deaths, of losing friends to AIDS, of success and failure.

At one point a man of about 50 with copper-tinged white hair stands up. "I'm a veteran," he says, "and I'll tell you what I'm angry about. I'm angry about what I had to do in Vietnam, and I'm sick and tired of carrying around that anger." Nobody, he says, nobody should have to pull headless bodies of 18- and 19-year-old boys from the insides of tanks.

He pauses. The silence is arctic.

Minutes later a studious-looking man in his mid-forties rises, several seats away. "I'm also a veteran," he says, "only here, at home, in the peace movement. And I want to say that I am angry too about what you had to go through."

For a few seconds they stare at each other, the warrior and the antiwarrior, like ghosts of Khe San and Kent State. Then the combat veteran lurches toward the other man—to hold him in a full-on embrace.

Relief rushes through the audience like a summer wind.

Still, the thought of men going off together and conducting tribal rituals to express pain and anger makes plenty of people uneasy. "The new male macho," Barrie Thorne, a University of Southern California sociologist who studies gender issues, calls it. Kenyon College's Brod, like many outside observers, suspects these men, in trying to preserve some men-only space, are motivated in part by a fear of women. "It's a way of mythologizing the past," he says, "of saying, 'Let's go back to a time when men were men.' Well, there never was a time like that." Bob Connell, an Australian sociologist who has written extensively on the subject of masculinity, says, "At best, it drains energy from any real progressive political needs. At worst it has overtones of a masculine cult."

Yet the men who follow the work of Bly, Meade, Moore, and others have varied and deeply personal reasons for doing so, reasons that defy easy categorization. A 40-year-old San Francisco filmmaker says the mythical images help fortify his resolve when competing for free-lance projects. A professor of military history in New York, a man of about 50, says the sessions have, among other things, strengthened his marriage and helped him understand his disaffection with Catholicism. A 35-year-old high school teacher at the San Francisco conference says he's drawn to the wisdom in the myths and stories, and enjoys telling them to his children.

On the second day of this seminar Meade and Moore directly address men's relationship to women, introducing the topic by reading a few witticisms from celebrities. There's one from Zsa Zsa Gabor: "I'm a marvelous housekeeper. Every time I have a man I keep his house." Then Mae West: "He's the kind of man you'd have to marry to get rid of." And Richard Pryor: "Marriage is about feelings and lawyers."

At this a dark-bearded man of about 30 stands in defiant indignation. "I don't like what you're doing here. Yeah, they're jokes and everybody laughs, but there's so much hurt between men and women, and I think this contributes to it. We should be trying to increase the love between men and women." Some men nod vigorously in agreement; others scoff audibly, at which one man stands and scolds the crowd. "Even if we don't agree with someone, we ought to respect their opinion," he says. This provokes a burst of accusations, followed by debate about whether this sort of humor increases tensions between the sexes, relieves them, or just makes people laugh.

After a while a large, disheveled man with a full grey beard stands and says in a weary voice, "I'm in the middle of my second divorce—the papers aren't final yet. And if I couldn't laugh about it a little, it would be tearing me apart." This seems to settle the issue for now.

Throughout the weekend, during the lunch and coffee breaks, it's clear that Meade's stories and Moore's psychological commentary have stirred genuine fascination. In the foyer outside the auditorium there's a brisk trade in tapes and books, including Bly's *Iron John* and even drums, which start at $200. But by the second day there's also an active exchange of phone numbers and conversation—about work, politics, religion, the Persian Gulf, philosophy—the sort of free-floating, almost giddy back-and-forth that occurs between very old friends and very new ones. Whether these men have connected with the primal, spiritual part of their souls is hard to know; that they are connecting with other kindred male souls, people with real human concerns who want to talk about them, is unmistakable.

On Sunday afternoon this warming companionship spontaneously turns physical. As the crowd pushes into the auditorium after a break there's an excited jostling; then grunts, shouts, and shrieks as several men burst into the open—a grandfather, a college type, and a middle-aged man in a Sikh turban among them—all throwing around a Nerf football. From the looks on their faces, you could swear they'd just rediscovered the joy of sacred ritual.

Tapping the Healing Power of Positive Thinking

How emotions help—or hurt

Nick Gallo

Consider these three brief stories:
• A young mother crawls through a burning house to save her child, not realizing until both have escaped that she has severe burns over most of her back.
• A teenage boy worries so much about his parent's impending divorce that he develops severe stomach pains and must be hospitalized.
• A middle-aged cancer patient lies hopelessly ill in a hospital bed laughing at a stream of humorous books, articles, and movies—which he will later credit for his recovery.

Scientists have long accepted the validity of the first two scenarios. During periods of crisis, the mind is fully capable of turning off pain. And severe emotional turmoil commonly leads to physical symptoms of illness.

What is still open to debate is the third situation. Yet dozens of studies have led researchers tantalizingly close to agreeing that laughter can heal and that hostility can kill. Here's a report on the latest thinking about how your attitudes and emotions can be a force for health—good or bad.

MIND OVER MATTER?

More than a decade ago, Norman Cousins wrote *Anatomy of an Illness*, a personal story of his recovery from a supposedly irreversible disease. In it,

he championed the healing value of life-affirming emotions, such as hope, love, faith, a strong will to live, a sense of purpose, and a capacity for fun.

In recent years, his anecdotal account has been supported by scientific studies. Researchers point to a cluster of emotions and attitudes that seem to be linked to improved health.

Sheldon Cohen, Ph.D., a psychologist at Carnegie Mellon University in Pittsburgh, collected data from a five-year study of 400 people exposed to the common cold. Early results indicate that psychological factors influence your odds of infection.

Fighting spirit. A British study of women with breast cancer reports that women with a "fighting spirit" are more than twice as likely to be alive and well 10 years later than women who hold a helpless, hopeless attitude.

Solid marriage, friendships. Social support seems to contribute to health and lifespan, according to a nine-year survey of 7,000 people. The group with strong social ties—marriage, friendship, group membership—had lower death rates than those who were isolated.

Love, compassion. In a Harvard study, students who were shown a film designed to inspire feelings of love and caring experienced an increase in an antibody that protects against upper respiratory infection.

MIND UNDERMINES MATTER, TOO

Just as positive emotions help health, negative attitudes and emotions seem to undermine one's health. For example, a review of 99 Harvard University graduates who completed personality questionnaires in 1946 found that students who had been most pessimistic at age 25 experienced more severe illnesses at middle-age.

Researchers point to other unhealthy emotions:

Depression. At the University of Chicago, psychologist Richard Shekelle followed the health histories of 2,020 middle-aged Western Electric plant employees and found that those who had been depressed were twice as likely to later die from cancer.

Cynicism and hostility. Researchers at Duke University contend that people with a cynical or hostile attitude are five times more likely to die before age 50 than their calmer, more trusting counterparts.

Loneliness. Rates of illness and death tend to be higher among single and divorced individuals, suggesting that loneliness takes its toll on the immune system.

Stress. Increased illness rates among the recently bereaved suggest that chronic stress affects health. In a study at Ohio State University, medical students nearing exam time suffered a drop in the fighter cells that help the body combat infections.

THE MEANING OF IT ALL

Not everyone is convinced that these statistical associations prove much. How exactly does a positive or negative attitude influence whether you get sick? How can a thought protect you against germs?

Two general theories exist, says David Spiegel, M.D., professor of psychiatry and behavioral sciences at Stanford University. First, people who have a positive mental outlook or strong social support tend to take better care of themselves. They're more likely to go to the doctor regularly, adopt a healthful diet, and avoid smoking, drug use, and other self-destructive behavior.

The second, more radical, idea is that a person's thoughts and emotions act directly on the immune system, the body's disease-fighting brigade. Studies seem to show that emotions may directly stimulate the production of brain chemicals that enhance—or undermine—the immune system.

Beyond the test tube. Various researchers wonder if these effects mean much outside a laboratory. Dr. George Solomon, a UCLA psychiatrist involved in mind-body research, notes that people can lose quite a bit of immune function—in terms of white blood cell counts—and still stay healthy.

Other medical experts claim that any psychological effect would pale in comparison to the biology of a disease such as cancer. Such factors as the type of tumor, its stage, the patient's age, and the treatment are more important than state of mind, believes University of Pennsylvania psychologist Barrie Cassileth, Ph.D., whose studies of cancer patients have not found a link between attitude and length of survival.

Even supporters of mind over health admit that the ultimate value of a positive attitude is unproven. "No matter how probable it seems that the mind influences the immune system, we still don't have enough actual evidence," says Steven Locke, M.D., assistant professor of psychiatry at Harvard Medical School and coauthor of *The Health Within* (New American Library, 1986).

MAKING IT WORK FOR YOU

Although we don't understand the exact connection between health and attitude, research does offer clues on using your mind to stay healthy.

Think positively. University of Pennsylvania psychologist Martin Seligman, Ph.D., author of *Learned Optimism* (Knopf, 1991), believes that your outlook may affect your health.

More than two decades ago he proposed a concept called "learned helplessness." His studies showed that rats who received mild but inescapable shocks wouldn't even try to escape punishment when they were later placed in a box in which they could avoid the shocks. They'd surrendered willpower after deciding that whatever they did didn't matter.

Some humans, too, may lose hope quickly and become passive and depressed when crises strike.

How do you explain a setback to yourself? For some the response is: "It's me; it's going to last forever; it's going to undermine everything I do," says Dr. Seligman. Others are able to say and believe: "It was just circumstances; it's going away quickly, and besides, there is much more in life."

By reviewing and challenging your automatic first thoughts, it's possible to change the habit of saying destructive things to yourself when you suffer disappointments, he says.

"One of the most significant findings in psychology in the last 20 years is that individuals can choose the way they *think*," says Dr. Seligman.

Redford Williams, M.D., a behavioral medicine expert at Duke University and author of *The Trusting Heart* (Times Book, 1989), believes that how you think and feel *about others* affects your health. His studies of Type A people—overcompetitive, hard-driving, hurried—show that hostility ups your odds of heart disease.

In his 12-step program toward a trusting heart, he advises people to reduce their anger and cynical mistrust of others, learn to treat others with kindness and consideration, and to be assertive, not aggressive, in threatening situations.

Other researchers believe there is a health benefit to having some personal control over your surroundings. In a study by psychologists Ellen Langer and Judith Rodin, a group of nursing-home residents who were given a set of responsibilities and greater decision-making showed improvements in health and activities within three weeks. After 18 months, the death rate of this "self-responsibility" group was half that of the other group.

Reach out. One long-range study showed that people with social contact—volunteer work, community activities, support groups—lived longer and were healthier than isolated people.

Use mind-body techniques. Meditation, biofeedback, and numerous other unconventional therapies may help turn on the inner healer. In one study at New England Deaconess Hospital's Mind/Body Clinic, relaxation techniques helped nearly 80 percent of patients with hypertension to either lower their blood pressure or reduce drug dosage. Other studies have used hypnosis to improve the quality of life for cancer patients.

Few experts call these techniques potential cures for illness. "They are meant to complement medicine, not replace it," says Dr. Locke. Yet most doctors agree that a positive attitude—whether optimism or a fighting spirit—plays a role in recovery from illness. And although the evidence is still coming in, there's good reason to believe that a positive outlook on life helps protect you from illness.

Are You Raising An
Optimist?

Carolyn Jabs

Carolyn Jabs believes her optimism comes from her mom, who can find a silver lining in even the blackest cloud. Jabs is passing along that attitude to her children.

Michael and Martin take a surprise quiz on fractions, and both get low scores. That evening, each boy offers his parents an explanation.

Michael: "It was a tough quiz. I hadn't really studied the fraction chapter yet. I'll ace the next one."

Martin: "I'm not very good at quizzes. Math has always been hard for me. I really messed up."

Neither explanation is right or wrong, but Michael's interpretation of the facts shows him to be an optimist whose attitude will help him master not only fractions but whatever obstacles life throws in his path. Martin's version suggests that he is at risk of becoming a pessimist, someone who takes his problems as proof that life is bad and getting worse.

How a child copes with a math quiz might not seem to matter much. Yet evidence is slowly accumulating that people who have an optimistic slant on life enjoy all kinds of benefits. For one thing, they are more likely to succeed in their life's work, perhaps because they aren't discouraged by setbacks. For another, they enjoy more satisfying relationships, probably because it feels good to be around someone who is hopeful. They are at less risk for depression, one of the most debilitating mental conditions, and they are even healthier physically since pessimism triggers the release of hormones that slow the work of the immune system.

For all these reasons, optimism is one of the best gifts a parent can give a child. Giving it, however, does not entail great effort, or mean a working mother must put aside blocks of time in her already crowded schedule. In fact, the way an overworked parent handles the conflicts inherent in juggling her two jobs—the one at home and the one at work—can be a valuable lesson for her child. It is attitude—not preaching—that counts.

Yet many parents actively discourage optimism. In their effort to prepare chil-

Kids who look on the bright side do better in school, have more friends and seem to stay healthier. There's a lot parents can do to encourage a positive point of view

dren for the harsh "realities" of the world, they inadvertently damp down the hopefulness that makes it possible to cope. One woman, for instance, told her daughter regularly that it was extremely difficult to find the "right" man to marry. The girl became so uncertain about relationships that she would stop seeing boys after the first or second date because she "knew" they weren't "right."

Such parents often want more than anything for their children to avoid the pain of making a mistake. Yet there is little joy or fulfillment in a life spent choosing only safe options. Sooner or later, our children will experience failures, and our goal should be to help them learn from the experience rather than be crushed by it. Cultivating healthy optimism doesn't mean letting children grow up oblivious to the world's suffering and sorrow. It does mean giving them a way of explaining life's problems that allows them to persevere despite setbacks.

The Optimistic Difference

Martin E.P. Seligman, PhD, a psychologist from the University of Pennsylvania, has studied optimism exhaustively. In his book *Learned Optimism* (Knopf), he points out that optimists and pessimists start with the same reality but interpret it differently. Specifically, their explanations for bad events differ in three ways.

1. Duration of the problem: Optimists believe difficult circumstances are temporary—"I'm having a bad day." Pessimists tend to project their difficulties into the future—"Things never work out for me." According to Seligman, "This is the most important factor. Optimists believe in the possibility of change over time."

2. Extent of the problem: Optimists tend to isolate their failures. An optimist who doesn't make the cheerleading team will say "I'm not that great at cartwheels." Pessimists use failure as evidence of more pervasive problems—"I'm not popular." Says Seligman, "An optimistic kid doesn't make sweeping statements about a bad event. Instead, he focuses in on the cause of the failure, and sees that this thing has no enormous implications for him as a person."

3. Blame for the problem: Pessimists tend to take responsibility even for things that aren't their fault. If a pessimist asks a friend over and the friend refuses, the pessimist will come up with an explanation that revolves around himself—"He doesn't like me." The optimist is more likely to find an external explanation—"He's probably busy after school."

"We want people to own up to things that are their fault," says Seligman, "but if

From *Working Mother*, September 1991, pp. 42, 44-46. Copyright © 1991 by Carolyn Jabs. Reprinted by permission.

they take blame for things that aren't in their control, they develop feelings of worthlessness."

The Stages of Optimism

Nobody gives optimistic—or pessimistic, for that matter—explanations all the time. However, the tendency toward one or the other is established early in life. On the surface, it seems all children start out as optimists. Anyone who has watched a young child learning to walk recognizes the indomitable spirit that keeps her pulling herself upright despite innumerable spills and bumps.

That spirit persists through preschool. When Susan Nolen-Hoeksema, PhD, a psychologist at Stanford University in Palo Alto, California, asked 94 children, ages four to eight, to give reasons for hypothetical problems, such as a friend not wanting to play, the four-year-olds seldom had pessimistic explanations. Other researchers have found that four-year-olds invariably predict that they will do really well on a test even if they failed the last attempt, and that five-year-olds nearly always believe they are among the best students in their class. "When pre-schoolers fail at a task, they don't experience negative feelings for long, and they don't project the current failure into the future," says Nolen-Hoeksema.

As children get older, they also become more logical. Five-year-olds ask "why" a lot, in part to understand what causes things to happen. The answers parents give to children's questions shape their sense of optimism. If a child asks, for instance, why his favorite toy broke, you can give a general explanation—"Everything around here gets broken"—or one that's more specific—"You threw it on the floor when you were mad." If a child wants to know why he can't go fishing with his older brother, you can supply a reason that's personal—"You always get your feet wet"—or one that has nothing to do with him—"Your brother wants to be by himself." When a child wonders about the war coverage he sees on the TV news, you can give the impression that bad things are permanent—"People are always fighting somewhere" or temporary—"Our leaders are working hard to end the problem as soon as possible." Obviously, no single response fixes a child's sense of how the world works, but the cumulative effect of a parent's explanations shapes the child's assumptions.

Another important influence comes at school age. Around third grade, kids begin to compare themselves to others and come to the conclusion that success is not just a matter of effort but of ability. When Nolen-Hoeksema gave eight-year-olds the same test she gave four-year-olds, the older kids were less confident about their predictions. "Eight-year-olds were coming to grips with what they had been told about their limitations," she says.

At this age, it's not particularly helpful for parents to deny the child's limits. The child with two left feet knows he won't be the star of the soccer team no matter what you say. What you can stress is the value of the attempt, the fun of participating. "Everyone has limitations," says Nolen-Hoeksema. "We want children to maintain the sense that with effort or learning, they can improve in most areas." Researchers have found that when children have similar abilities, the ones who try hardest are those who believe success depends on effort, not talent.

It's also valuable to explain that things which seem impossible now may become easier as the child grows. "It's really empowering to tell a child that with age things will get better," says Nolen-Hoeksema. "Four-year-olds regularly explain their failures by saying 'I'm not old enough.' They know that as they get bigger, they'll gain competence, and this belief is comforting to them." By eight, children are less likely to assume that they will grow into a skill, even though it's every bit as true. Parents may be able to help by pointing out that even they can do things better once they begin trying—"Two years ago, I wasn't a very good runner," a mother might say, "but I've been practicing a lot and now I think I'm ready for a race."

A child's optimism can first be measured around age eight, and psychologists have begun to try to determine which children may be at risk for depression. During the elementary years, a child's style of thinking becomes more and more entrenched until, in adolescence, it becomes what Christopher Peterson, PhD, of the University of Michigan, calls a "cognitive habit" that's likely to persist throughout life. In one remarkable study, Seligman asked women in their 70s and 80s to write essays about their lives; the records were then compared to their teenage diaries. "There was a strong correlation for pessimism," says Seligman. "The women who concluded they were unlovable at seventeen when boys didn't come courting drew the same conclusion at seventy-five when their grandchildren failed to visit."

What Parents Can Do

In other words, the capacity for optimism flourishes or is stunted during early childhood, and can be redirected during the middle years. But by adolescence, the habit is pretty well established. What factors help children to be hopeful? Obviously, there's no single answer, but researchers point to three variables—early life experiences, adult criticism and mother's attitudes—that are associated with optimism. Parents can use all three to give their children what Seligman calls "a psychological immunization."

● **Give your child opportunities to succeed.** "One of the most important predictors of optimism is a long history of success," says Seligman. The role of parents here is subtle. Making the A+ science project for your kid won't help. Only his own efforts will convince him that he can do what he wants to do. "Children need to know they can have an effect," says Peterson. "Video games are so popular in part because they are incredibly responsive to what a kid is doing. All those beeps, buzzers and whistles give him instant feedback."

Parents need not be as flashy as video games, but they should be aware of their child's efforts so they can respond with at least an encouraging smile. They also need to shape new situations, so the child is challenged but not overwhelmed. For the youngest child, this may mean providing a sturdy box the height of a step so he can practice climbing by stepping up and down on it without the risk of a full-size staircase. For a first-grader, it may mean limiting the birthday guest list, so the child can have the success of being gracious rather than overwhelmed. For a pre-adolescent, it may mean helping him write a weekly schedule of what needs to be done so a term paper will be in on time.

Providing arenas for success is particularly important for young adolescent girls. "Girls start out more optimistic than boys," says Nolen-Hoeksema. "Then in early adolescence girls start to believe their choices are limited by their sex. This leads to a sense of helplessness and lack of self-esteem." By late adolescence, girls are statistically more prone to depression, a tendency that persists into adulthood. "Families need to encourage their girls to succeed as much as their boys," says Nolen-Hoeksema. "Support your daughter in her choices and do everything you can to give her a sense of control over her life and her options."

Valuable as it is to help shape events in which children have control, parents also need to realize the damaging effect of situations in which children don't have control. Research shows that a crisis such as divorce, the death of a parent or even going to a new school can put a child at risk for pessimism and even depression. In many cases, parents themselves cannot control what happens, but they can focus special attention on their children during these stressful periods.

Serious events often start a spiral—the child withdraws, so he loses friends and does poorly in school, which persuades him that he isn't a very good person, so he withdraws further. If parents recognize this pattern, they can intervene by refuting the pessimistic belief at the root of the child's sadness. For example, a child whose pet dies may be convinced that he caused the death because he didn't play with the animal enough. A parent can gently question the child's assumption by explaining that he was conscientious about feeding his pet and that it died because it was old or sick. With a parent's help, children can come to limited, temporary, external explanations for most misfortunes. However, drastic problems like divorce or the death of a parent may require professional intervention.

• **Criticize carefully.** All parents need to correct their children, but research shows that the style of criticism has a huge effect on a child's hopefulness. First, try to be as consistent as possible. Optimism and pessimism are attitudes about the future. When a child's world is capricious or chaotic, pessimism becomes a more reasonable theory than optimism. If the youngster doesn't know what kind of behavior will provoke his parent's displeasure, he'll develop a "what's the use?" attitude. On the other hand, a child who knows there'll be a consequence every time he bites a playmate, says a swear word or interrupts while his mom is on the phone gradually learns that his life is under his control: "If I don't bite, swear or interrupt, I'll get to play outside after dinner." That feeling of control is the foundation of optimism.

Second, emphasize the temporary, limited nature of your child's mistakes. If a child spills his milk at lunch, you may want to blurt out "You're so messy," a statement that tells him the fault is both personal and permanent. If you can say instead, "You had an accident," both of

you will see the problem as an aberration in the life of an otherwise competent child. The object is for you—and eventually your child—to perceive failures as opportunities to learn. Whenever possible, give your child a chance to correct his mistake—"Here's a sponge so you can wipe up the milk."

Third, help your child rebut the criticism he hears from other adults. Many children spend most of their time with adults other than their parents, so parents must learn to tune into the messages their children get from other sources. For instance, in choosing a child care provider, notice whether she tends to make broad statements—"You're a bad boy" or specific criticisms—"I don't like it when you take toys away from your friend."

When your child goes to school, the criticism of teachers can be particularly powerful, especially for girls. A study by Carol Dweck, PhD, a psychologist at Columbia University, found that third-grade teachers usually gave boys external rea-

sons for their poor grades—"You were fooling around. You weren't paying attention." Girls, who on the whole behaved better in class, were given personal explanations—"You aren't very good at math. You don't check your work." Nolen-Hoeksema recommends that parents gently challenge a child who brings such assumptions home. "When a child says he's no good at such-and-such, parents should question that reasoning," she says. "Take the child seriously because he believes what he's saying, but help him think about why he believes it."

• **Monitor your own explanatory style.** Research shows that optimistic mothers generally have optimistic children. Surprisingly, the optimism of fathers does not seem to be very significant, though one study did find that optimistic college students tended to remember their fathers as being "happy." Most researchers make the obvious assumption that the tight connection between mothers' attitudes and those of

---

An Optimism Quiz

Many parents don't have a clear sense of whether their children are optimistic or pessimistic. The following quiz will measure your child's sense of the permanence of bad events, one of the key indicators of pessimism.

• **You fail a test.**
A. My teacher makes hard tests. 1
B. The past few weeks, my teacher has made hard tests. 0
• **You fall off your bicycle.**
A. I am not a very cautious person. 1
B. Some days I'm not cautious. 0
• **You try to sell candy, but no one will buy any.**
A. Lots of children have been selling things lately, so people don't want to buy anything else. 0
B. People don't like to buy things from children. 1
• **You don't catch the ball and your team loses the game.**
A. I didn't try hard while playing ball that day. 0
B. I usually don't try hard when I am playing ball. 1

• **You take a bus which arrives so late that you miss a movie.**
A. The past few days there have been problems with buses being on time. 0
B. The buses are always late. 1
• **Your debating club loses.**
A. The club members usually don't speak well. 1
B. That day the club members who were debating didn't speak well. 0
• **Your teacher asks you a question in class and you give her the wrong answer.**
A. I get nervous when I have to answer questions. 1
B. That day I got nervous when I had to answer a question. 0
• **You take the wrong bus and end up getting lost.**
A. That day I wasn't paying attention to what was going on. 0
B. I usually don't pay any attention to what's going on. 1
To figure out your child's score, add up the numbers he or she circled. A score of 4 or more means your youngster is feeling especially pessimistic and may be at risk for depression.

Adapted from *Learned Optimism.* Copyright © 1990 by Martin E. P. Seligman. Published by Alfred A. Knopf Inc.

their children occurs because mothers still are primarily responsible for child care, so children inevitably soak up more of Mom's opinions and philosophies.

Mothers can make use of this information by becoming aware of the messages they give their children, particularly when explaining difficult events. Or, as Seligman puts it, "The first route to improving a child's explanatory style is improving your own." Let's say, for instance, that you have an argument with your husband in the morning and are still fuming when you drive your son to school. At that moment, it's crucial to understand that you have choices about how you'll explain the event to yourself and your child. You might say, "Your father never takes my feelings into account," making it sound as though the problem is permanent and you are powerless. Or you can say, "I think your dad got up in a bad mood. We don't usually quarrel over such little things." The second explanation gives your child the idea that problems can be solved.

In hundreds of day-to-day situations, each of us has the opportunity to give our children explanations that are optimistic or not. Here are just a few examples:

- You break a dish.

Pessimistic: "I'm so clumsy."

Optimistic: "My hands were slippery with soap suds."

- You lose your car keys.

Pessimistic: "I can't get organized."

Optimistic: "I need a special place to keep my keys."

- You lose your temper with your child.

Pessimistic: "I'm a terrible mother."

Optimistic: "It really upsets me when my daughter is disobedient."

Obviously, for your explanations to be convincing, you have to cultivate optimism in yourself, if you don't have the habit already. This may seem daunting given that your own way of explaining what happens has been pretty much the same since you were an adolescent. Can mental habits be changed? "I'm optimistic," says Peterson. "I believe change is possible, but only if people are aware of what they're doing. It's like changing any bad habit. It can't be done overnight."

Parents have a double incentive: Not only will a more optimistic outlook lead to optimism in your child, but it will make it more likely that you will enjoy the rewards of optimism—greater success, better relationships, improved health—in your own life. "Parents need to be hopeful about their own abilities," says Peterson. "They can change—and they can pass optimism along to their children."

Social Processes

Everywhere we look there are groups of people. Your general psychology class is a group, what social psychologists would call a secondary group, a group that comes together for a particular, somewhat contractual reason and then disbands after its goals have been met. Other secondary groups include athletic teams, church associations, juries, committees, and so forth.

There are other types of groups, too. One other type is a primary group. A primary group has much face-to-face contact, and there is often a sense of we-ness in the group (cohesiveness, as social psychologists would call it). Examples of primary groups include sets of roommates, families, sororities, fraternities, etc.

Very large groups or collectives are usually loosely knit, large groups of people. A bleacher full of football fans would be a collective. A line of people waiting to get into a rock concert would also be a collective.

American society and any other large group sharing common rules and norms is also a group—a very, very large group. While we might not always think about our society and how it shapes our behavior and our thinking, society and culture nonetheless have a vast influence on us. Psychologists, anthropologists, and sociologists alike would all be interested in studying the effects of a culture on its members.

Any process found in interpersonal relations is eligible for study by social psychologists. Interpersonal or social distance is one aspect of behavior that fascinates many a layperson as well as social psychologists. We have discovered that various postures and gestures as well as spatial behaviors are used to communicate with other individuals; this nonverbal communication may be more important or influential than communication via language. The discussion of this language without words is the topic of the first article, "Where Do We Stand?" This article by Lisa Davis will convince you that individuals from different cultures often misunderstand one another because the nature of their nonverbal cues is so different.

We next look just at our own society and an issue that does not seem to want to go away—sexism. In "Blame It on Feminism," the women's movement is discussed. Despite the strength and age of this movement, data show that women still do not have the same opportunities as men. Susan Faludi, the author, discusses why.

Many decisions are made and problems are solved by groups. Social psychologists are interested in understanding just how groups make decisions and whether solutions developed in groups are better than those developed by individuals. Psychologists have discovered a peculiar but evidently common group decision-making phenomenon, groupthink, which leads to particularly bad and risky decisions from groups. Groupthink is the topic of Alison Bass's article in this unit. As groupthink unfolds, its symptoms are often apparent, but perhaps not to the group itself. Groupthink feeds upon itself as group members censor themselves from speaking up in disagreement. The group then moves toward a detrimental and risky decision from which there is no fallback position and no mechanisms for corrective action when things do go wrong. Groupthink can be avoided. Bass shows us that some U.S. presidents have been victimized by it, and some have subsequently learned how to avoid it.

Finally, we look at one other group process, conflict—another issue that does not seem to go away. Conflict with others is often created by assumptions we make but which are not true. Conflict, however, can be managed and sometimes even resolved. Sandra Arbetter shares five easy steps to assist us in handling our conflicts with others in "Resolving Conflicts: Step By Step."

Looking Ahead: Challenge Questions

What is spatial behavior? Do spatial behavior and nonverbal communication differ from culture to culture? What are the consequences of misunderstanding or misusing spatial behaviors?

Has the women's movement made gains in equality between men and women? Where have women made gains; where do they fall behind men? What tactics should women use next in their efforts to assure equal opportunity?

What kinds of groups do we use in our society to make decisions? How can groups arrive at high-quality decisions? What is groupthink? How does it develop, and how can it be avoided?

Why is there so much conflict in this world? Why is conflict so bad? Is conflict ever good; that is, does anything positive ever come from conflict? How can conflicts be better managed?

Unit 9

Where Do We Stand?

Lisa Davis

CALL IT THE DANCE of the jet set, the diplomat's tango: A man from the Middle East, say, falls into conversation with an American, becomes animated, takes a step forward. The American makes a slight postural adjustment, shifts his feet, edges backward. A little more talk and the Arab advances; a little more talk and the American retreats. "By the end of the cocktail party," says Middle East expert Peter Bechtold, of the State Department's Foreign Service Institute, "you have an American in each corner of the room, because that's as far as they can back up."

What do you do when an amiable chat leaves one person feeling vaguely bullied, the other unaccountably chilled? Things would be simpler if these jet-setters were speaking different languages—they'd just get themselves a translator. But the problem's a little tougher, because they're using different languages of space.

Everyone who's ever felt cramped in a crowd knows that the skin is not the body's only boundary. We each wear a zone of privacy like a hoop skirt, inviting others in or keeping them out with body language—by how closely we approach, the angle at which we face them, the speed with which we break a gaze. It's a subtle code, but one we use and interpret easily, indeed automatically, having absorbed the vocabulary from infancy.

At least, we *assume* we're reading it right. But from culture to culture, from group to group within a single country, even between the sexes, the language of space has distinctive accents, confusing umlauts. That leaves a lot of room for misinterpretation, and the stakes have gotten higher as business has become increasingly international and populations multi-cultural. So a new breed of consultants has appeared in the last few years, interpreting for globe-trotters of all nationalities the meaning and use of personal space.

For instance, says international business consultant Sondra Snowdon, Saudi Arabians like to conduct business discussions from within spitting distance—literally. They bathe in each other's breath as part of building the relationship. "Americans back up," says Snowdon, "but they're harming their chances of winning the contracts." In seminars, Snowdon discusses the close quarters common in Middle Eastern conversations, and has her students practice talking with each other at very chummy distances.

Still, her clients had better be careful where they take their shrunken "space bubble," because cultures are idiosyncratic in their spatial needs. Japanese subways bring people about as close together as humanly possible, for instance, yet even a handshake can be offensively physical in a Japanese office. And, says researcher and writer Mildred Reed Hall, Americans can even make their business counterparts in Japan uncomfortable with the kind of direct eye contact that's normal here. "Not only do most Japanese businessmen not look at you, they keep their eyes down," Hall says. "We look at people for hours, and they feel like they're under a searchlight."

The study of personal space got under way in the early 1950s, when anthropologist Edward Hall described a sort of cultural continuum of personal space. (Hall has frequently collaborated with his wife, Mildred.) According to Hall, on the "high-contact" side of the continuum —in Mediterranean and South American societies, for instance—social conversations include much eye contact, touching, and smiling, typically while standing at a distance of about a foot. On the other end of the scale, say in Northern European cultures, a lingering gaze may feel invasive, manipulative, or disrespectful; a social chat takes place at a remove of about two and a half feet.

In the middle-of-the-road United States, people usually stand about 18 inches apart for this sort of conversation —unless we want to win foreign friends and influence people, in which case, research shows, we'd better adjust our posture. In one study, when British graduate students were trained to adopt Arab patterns of behavior (facing their partners straight on, with lots of eye contact and smiling), Middle Eastern exchange students found them more likable and trustworthy than typical British students. In contrast, the *mis*use of space can call whole personalities into suspicion: When researchers seated pairs of women for conversation, those forced to talk at an uncomfortably large distance were more likely to describe their partners as cold and rejecting.

Don't snuggle up too fast, though. Men in that study were more irritated by their partners when they were forced to talk at close range. Spatially speaking, it seems men and women are subtly foreign to each other. No matter whether a society operates at arm's length or cheek-to-jowl, the women look at each other more and stand a bit closer than do the men.

It just goes to show that you can't take things for granted even within the borders of a single country. Take that unwilling amalgamation of ethnic minorities, the Soviet Union. According to psychologist Robert Sommer, who along with Hall sparked the study of personal space, spatial needs collide in the republics. "The Estonians are a non-contact people," says Sommer, of the University of California at Davis. "I went to a 'Hands Around the Baltic' event, and nobody touched hands. The Russians, on the other hand, are high-contact. The Estonians say the Russians are pushy, and the Russians say the Estonians are cold."

Nor are things easier within the United States. Researchers have found, for instance, that middle-class, Caucasian schoolteachers often jump to mistaken conclusions when dealing with a child from a different background: If a girl from an Asian family averts her eyes out of respect for her teacher's authority, the teacher may well go on alert, convinced that the child is trying to hide some misbehavior. Ethnically diverse workplaces can be similarly booby-trapped.

> Some cultures do business within spitting distance, while others prefer a couple of feet of personal space.

Such glitches are all the more likely because spatial behavior is automatic— it snaps into focus only when someone doesn't play by the rules. Say an American businessman is alone in a roomy elevator when another man enters. The newcomer fails to perform the national ritual of taking a corner and staring into space; instead, he stands a few inches away, smiling, which is simple politeness in some cultures. "You start to search for a reasonable explanation," says psychologist Eric Knowles, at the University of Arkansas. "In many cases you come up with one without even being aware of it. You say, 'Is this guy a pickpocket? Is he psychotic?' If no explanation seems to fit, you just think, 'This guy's weird, I better get out of here.'"

In fact, such caution is not always unwarranted, because an abnormal use of space *can* indicate that something odd is going on. Research has shown that when people with schizophrenia approach another person, they often either get closer than normal or stay unusually distant. And a small study of prisoners seemed to show that those with a history of violence needed up to three times the space

taken by nonviolent inmates. These are reminders that the human need for space is based in an animal reality: The closer you allow a stranger, the more vulnerable you become.

But the spatial differences among cultures point to something beyond self-protection. Anthropologist Edward Hall suggests that a culture's use of space is also evidence of a reliance on one sense over another: Middle Easterners get much of their information through their senses of smell and touch, he says, which require a close approach; Americans rely primarily on visual information, backing up in order to see an intelligible picture.

Conversational distances also tend to reflect the standard greeting distance in each culture, says State Department expert Bechtold. Americans shake hands, and then talk at arm's length. Arabs do a Hollywood-style, cheek-to-cheek social kiss, and their conversation is similarly up close and personal. And, at a distance great enough to keep heads from knocking together—about two feet—the Japanese bow and talk to each other. On the other hand, the need for more or less space may reflect something of a cultural temperament. "There's no word for privacy in Arab cultures," says Bechtold. "They think it means loneliness."

Whatever their origin, spatial styles are very real. In fact, even those who set out to transgress find it uncomfortable to intrude on the space of strangers, says psychologist John R. Aiello, at Rutgers University. "I've had students say, 'Boy, that was the hardest thing I ever had to do—to stand six inches away when I was asking those questions.'"

Luckily, given coaching and time, it seems to get easier to acculturate to foreign habits of contact. Says Bechtold, "You often see men holding hands in the Middle East and walking down the street together. It's just that they're concerned and don't want you to cross the street unescorted, but I've had American pilots come in here and say, 'I don't want some s.o.b. holding my hand.' Then I see them there, holding the hand of a Saudi.

"Personal space isn't so hard for people to learn," Bechtold adds. "What is really much harder is the business of dinner being served at midnight."

Blame it on Feminism

What's wrong with women today?
Too much equality.

Susan Faludi

To Be A Woman In America at the Close of the twentieth century—what good fortune. That's what we keep hearing, anyway. The barricades have fallen, politicians assure us. Women have "made it," Madison Avenue cheers. Women's fight for equality has "largely been won," *Time* magazine announces. Enroll at any university, join any law firm, apply for credit at any bank. Women have so many opportunities now, corporate leaders say, that they don't really need opportunity policies. Women are so equal now, lawmakers say, that they no longer need an Equal Rights Amendment. Women have "so much," former president Ronald Reagan says, that the White House no longer needs to appoint them to high office. Even American Express ads are saluting a woman's right to charge it. At last, women have received their full citizenship papers.

And yet . . .

Behind this celebration of the American woman's victory, behind the news, cheerfully and endlessly repeated, that the struggle for women's rights is won, another message flashes: You may be free and equal now, but you have never been more miserable.

This bulletin of despair is posted everywhere—at the newsstand, on the TV set, at the movies, in advertisements and doctors' offices and academic journals. Professional women are suffering "burnout" and succumbing to an "infertility epidemic." Single women are grieving from a "man shortage." The *New York Times* reports: Childless women are "depressed and confused" and their ranks are swelling. *Newsweek* says: Unwed women are "hysterical" and crumbling under a "profound crisis of confidence." The health-advice manuals inform: High-powered career women are stricken with unprecedented outbreaks of "stress-induced disorders," hair loss, bad nerves, alcoholism, and even heart attacks. The psychology books advise: Independent women's loneliness represents "a major mental-health problem today." Even founding feminist Betty Friedan has been spreading the word: She warns that women now suffer from "new problems that have no name."

How can American women be in so much trouble at the same time that they are supposed to be so blessed? If women got what they asked for, what could possibly be the matter now?

The prevailing wisdom of the past decade has supported one, and only one, answer to this riddle: It must be all that equality that's causing all that pain. Women are unhappy precisely because they are free. Women are enslaved by their own liberation. They have grabbed at the gold ring of independence, only to miss the one ring that really matters. They have gained

From *Mother Jones*, September/October 1991, pp. 24-29. Excerpt from *Backlash, The Undeclared War on American Women*, published by Crown Publishers.

control of their fertility, only to destroy it. They have pursued their own professional dreams—and lost out on romance, the greatest female adventure. "Our generation was the human sacrifice" to the women's movement, writer Elizabeth Mehren contends in a *Time* cover story. Baby-boom women, like her, she says, have been duped by feminism: "We believed the rhetoric." In *Newsweek*, writer Kay Ebeling dubs feminism the "Great Experiment That Failed" and asserts, "Women in my generation, its perpetrators, are the casualties."

In the eighties, publications from the *New York Times* to *Vanity Fair* to *The Nation* have issued a steady stream of indictments against the women's movement, with such headlines as "WHEN FEMINISM FAILED" or "THE AWFUL TRUTH ABOUT WOMEN'S LIB." They hold the campaign for women's equality responsible for nearly every woe besetting women, from depression to meager savings accounts, from teenage suicides to eating disorders to bad complexions. The *Today* show says women's liberation is to blame for bag ladies. A guest columnist in the *Baltimore Sun* even proposes that feminists produced the rise in slasher movies. By making the "violence" of abortion more acceptable, the author reasons, women's-rights activities made it all right to show graphic murders on screen.

At the same time, other outlets of popular culture have been forging the same connection: In Hollywood films, of which *Fatal Attraction* is only the most famous, emancipated women with condominiums of their own slink wild-eyed between bare walls, paying for their liberty with an empty bed, a barren womb. "My biological clock is ticking so loud it keeps me awake at night," Sally Field cries in the film *Surrender*, as, in an all-too-common transformation in the cinema of the eighties, an actress who once played scrappy working heroines is now showcased groveling for a groom. In prime-time television shows, from *thirtysomething* to *Family Man*, single, professional, and feminist women are humiliated, turned into harpies, or hit by nervous breakdowns; the wise ones recant their independent ways by the closing sequence. In popular novels, from Gail Parent's *A Sign of the Eighties* to Stephen King's *Misery*, unwed women shrink to sniveling spinsters or inflate to firebreathing she-devils; renouncing all aspirations but marriage, they beg for wedding bands from strangers or swing axes at reluctant bachelors. Even Erica Jong's high-flying independent heroine literally crashes by the end of the decade, as the author supplants *Fear of Flying*'s saucy Isadora Wing, an exuberant symbol of female sexual emancipation in the seventies, with an embittered careerist-turned-recovering-"codependent" in *Any Woman's Blues*—a book that is intended, as the narrator bluntly states, "to demonstrate what a dead end the so-called sexual revolution had become and how desperate so-called free women were in the last few years of our decadent epoch."

Popular psychology manuals peddle the same diagnosis for contemporary female distress. "Feminism, having promised her a stronger sense of her own identity, has given her little more than an identity *crisis*, the best-selling advice manual *Being a Woman* asserts. The authors of the era's self-help classic, *Smart Women/Foolish Choices*, proclaim that women's distress was "an unfortunate consequence of feminism" because "it created a myth among women that the apex of self-realization could be achieved only through autonomy, independence, and career."

In the Reagan and Bush years, government officials have needed no prompting to endorse this thesis. Reagan spokeswoman Faith Ryan Whittlesey declared feminism a "straitjacket" for women, in one of the White House's only policy speeches on the status of the American female population—entitled "Radical Feminism in Retreat." The U.S. attorney general's Commission on Pornography even proposed that women's professional advancement might be responsible for rising rape rates: With more women in college and at work now, the commission members reasoned in their report, women just have more opportunities to be raped.

Legal scholars have railed against the "equality trap." Sociologists have claimed that "feminist-inspired" legislative reforms have stripped women of special "protections." Economists have argued that well-paid working women have created a "less stable American family." And demographers, with greatest fanfare, have legitimated the prevailing wisdom with so-called neutral data on sex ratios and fertility trends; they say they actually have the numbers to prove that equality doesn't mix with marriage and motherhood.

Finally, some "liberated" women themselves have joined the lamentations. In *The Cost of Loving: Women and the New Fear of Intimacy*, Megan Marshall, a Harvard-pedigreed writer, asserts that the feminist "Myth of Independence" has turned her generation into unloved and unhappy fast-trackers, "dehumanized" by careers and "uncertain of their gender identity." Other diaries of mad Superwomen charge that "the hardcore feminist viewpoint," as one of them puts it, has relegated educated executive achievers to solitary nights of frozen dinners and closet drinking. The triumph of equality, they report, has merely given women hives, stomach cramps, eye "twitching" disorders, even comas.

But what "equality" are all these authorities talking about?

If American women are so equal, why do they represent two-thirds of all poor adults? Why are more than 70 percent of full-time working women making less than twenty-five thousand dollars a year, nearly double the number of men at that level? Why are they still far more likely than men to live in poor housing, and twice as likely to draw no pension? If women "have it all," then why don't they have the most basic requirements to achieve equality in the work force: unlike that of virtually all other industrialized nations, the U.S. government still has no family-leave and child-care programs.

If women are so "free," why are their reproductive freedoms in greater jeopardy today than a decade earlier? Why, in their own homes, do they still shoulder 70 percent of the household duties—while the only major change in the last fifteen years is that now men *think* they do more around the house? In thirty states, it is still generally legal for husbands to rape their wives; and only ten states have laws mandating arrest for domestic violence—even though battering is the leading cause of injury to women (greater than rapes, muggings, and auto accidents combined).

The word may be that women have been "liberated," but women themselves seem to feel otherwise. Repeatedly in national surveys, majorities of women say they are still far from equality. In poll after poll in the decade, overwhelming majorities of women said they need equal pay and equal job opportunities, they need an Equal Rights Amendment, they need the right to an abortion without government interference, they need a federal law guaranteeing maternity leave, they need decent child-care services. They have none of these. So how exactly have women "won" the war for women's rights?

Seen against this background, the much bally-hooed claim that feminism is responsible for making women miserable becomes absurd—and irrelevant. The afflictions ascribed to feminism, from "the man shortage" to "the infertility epidemic" to "female burnout" to "toxic day care," have had their origins not in the actual conditions of women's lives but rather in a closed system that starts and ends in the media, popular culture, and advertising—an endless feedback loop that perpetuates and exaggerates its own false images of womanhood. And women don't see feminism as their enemy, either. In fact, in national surveys, 75 to 95 percent of women credit the feminist campaign with *improving* their lives, and a similar proportion say that the women's movement should keep pushing for change.

If the many ponderers of the Woman Question really wanted to know what is troubling the American female population, they might have asked their subjects. In public-opinion surveys, women consistently rank their own *inequality*, at work and at home, among their most urgent concerns. Over and over, women complain to pollsters of a lack of economic, not marital, opportunities; they protest that working men, not working women, fail to spend time in the nursery and the kitchen. It is justice for their gender, not wedding rings and bassinets, that women believe to be in desperately short supply.

As the last decade ran its course, the monitors that serve to track slippage in women's status have been working overtime. Government and private surveys are showing that women's already vast representation in the lowliest occupations is rising, their tiny presence in higher-paying trade and craft jobs stalled or backsliding, their minuscule representation in upper management posts stagnant or falling, and their pay dropping in the very occupations where they have made the most "progress."

In national politics, the already small numbers of women in both elective posts and political appointments fell during the eighties. In private life, the average amount that a divorced man paid in child support fell by about 25 percent from the late seventies to the mid-eighties (to a mere $140 a month). And government records chronicled a spectacular rise in sexual violence against women. Reported rapes more than doubled from the early seventies—at nearly twice the rate of all other violent crimes and four times the overall crime rate in the United States.

The truth is that the last decade has seen a powerful counterassault on women's rights, a backlash, an attempt to retract the handful of small and hard-won victories that the feminist movement did manage to win for women. This counterassault is largely insidious: in a kind of pop-culture version of the big lie, it stands the truth boldly on its head and proclaims that the very steps that have elevated women's position have actually led to their downfall.

The backlash is at once sophisticated and banal, deceptively "progressive" and proudly backward. It deploys both the "new" findings of "scientific research" and the dime-store moralism of yesteryear; it turns into media sound bites both the glib pronouncements of pop-psych trend-watchers and the frenzied rhetoric of New Right preachers. The backlash has succeeded in framing virtually the whole issue of women's rights in its own language. Just as Reaganism shifted political discourse far to the right and demonized liberalism, so the backlash convinced the public that women's "liberation" was the true contemporary American scourge—the source of an endless laundry list of personal, social, and economic problems.

But what has made women unhappy in the last decade is not their "equality"—which they don't yet have—but the rising pressure to halt, and even reverse, women's quest for that equality. The "man shortage" and the "infertility epidemic" are not the price of liberation; in fact, they do not even exist. But these chimeras are part of a relentless whittling-down process—much of it amounting to outright propaganda—that has served to stir women's private anxieties and break their political wills. Identifying feminism as women's enemy only furthers the ends of a backlash against women's equality by simultaneously deflecting attention from the backlash's central role and recruiting women to attack their own cause.

Some social observers may well ask whether the current pressures on women actually constitute a backlash—or just a continuation of American society's long-standing resistance to women's equal rights. Certainly hostility to female independence has always been with us. But if fear and loathing of feminism is a sort of perpetual viral condition in our culture, it is not always in an acute stage; its symptoms subside and resurface periodically. And it is these episodes of resurgence, such as the one we face now, that can accurately be termed "backlashes" to women's advancement. If we trace these occurrences in American history, we find such flare-ups are hardly random; they have always been triggered by the perception—accurate or not—that women are making great strides. These outbreaks are backlashes because they have always arisen in reaction to women's "progress," caused not simply by a bedrock of misogyny but by the specific efforts of contemporary women to improve their status, efforts that have been interpreted time and again by men—especially men grappling with real threats to their economic and social well-being on other fronts—as spelling their own masculine doom.

The most recent round of backlash first surfaced in the late seventies on the fringes, among the evangelical Right. By the early eighties, the fundamentalist ideology had shouldered its way into the White House. By the mid-eighties, as resistance to women's rights acquired political and social acceptability, it passed into the popular culture. And in every case, the timing coincided with signs that women were believed to be on the verge of a breakthrough.

Just when women's quest for equal rights seemed closest to achieving its objectives, the backlash struck it down. Just when a "gender gap" at the voting booth surfaced in 1980, and women in politics began to talk of capitalizing on it, the Republican party elevated Ronald Reagan and both political parties began to shunt women's rights off their platforms. Just when support for feminism and the Equal Rights Amendment reached a record high in 1981, the amendment was defeated the following year. Just when women were starting to mobilize against battering and sexual assaults, the federal government cut funding for battered-women's programs, defeated bills to fund shelters, and shut down its Office of Domestic Violence—only two years after opening it in 1979. Just when record numbers of younger women were supporting feminist goals in the mid-eighties (more of them, in fact, than older women) and a majority of all women were calling themselves feminists, the media declared the advent of a younger "postfeminist generation" that supposedly reviled the women's movement. Just when women racked up their largest percentage ever supporting the right to abortion, the U.S. Supreme Court moved toward reconsidering it.

In other words, the antifeminist backlash has been set off not by women's achievement of full equality but by the increased possibility that they might win it. It is a preemptive strike that stops women long before they reach the finish line. "A backlash may be an indication that women really have had an effect," feminist psychiatrist Dr. Jean Baker Miller has written, "but backlashes occur when advances have been small, before changes are sufficient to help many people. . . . It is almost as if the leaders of backlashes use the fear of change as a threat before major change has occurred." In the last decade, some women did make substantial advances before the backlash hit, but millions of others were left behind, stranded. Some women now enjoy the right to legal abortion—but not the forty-four million women, from the indigent to the military worker, who depend on the federal government for their medical care. Some women can now walk into high-paying professional careers—but not the millions still in the typing pools or behind the department-store sales counters. (Contrary to popular myth about the "have-it-all" baby-boom women, the largest percentage of women in this generation remain in office support roles.)

As the backlash has gathered force, it has cut off the few from the many—and the few women who have advanced seek to prove, as a social survival tactic, that they aren't so interested in advancement after all. Some of them parade their defection from the women's movement, while their working-class peers founder and cling to the splintered remains of the feminist cause. While a very few affluent and celebrity women who are showcased in news stories boast about going home to "bake bread," the many working-class women appeal for their economic rights—flocking to unions in record numbers, striking on their own for pay equity, and establishing their own fledgling groups for working-women's rights. In 1986, while 41 percent of upper-income women were claiming in the Gallup poll that they were not feminists, only 26 percent of low-income women were making the same claim.

Women's advances and retreats are generally described in military terms: battles won, battles lost, points and territory gained and surrendered. The metaphor of combat is not without its merits in this context, and, clearly, the same sort of martial accounting and vocabulary is already surfacing here. But by imagining the conflict as two battalions neatly arrayed on either side of the line, we miss the entangled nature, the locked embrace, of a "war" between women and the male culture they inhabit. We miss the reactive nature of a backlash, which, by definition, can exist only in response to another force.

In times when feminism is at a low ebb, women assume the reactive role—privately and, most often, covertly struggling to assert themselves against the dominant cultural tide. But when feminism itself becomes the tide, the opposition doesn't simply go along with the reversal: it digs in its heels, brandishes its fists, builds walls and dams. And its resistance creates countercurrents and treacherous undertows.

The force and furor of the backlash churn beneath the surface, largely invisible to the public eye. On occasion in the last decade, they have burst into view. We have seen New Right politicians condemn women's independence, antiabortion protesters firebomb women's clinics, fundamentalist preachers damn feminists as "whores." Other signs of the backlash's wrath, by their sheer brutality, can push their way into public consciousness for a time—the sharp increase in rape, for example, or the rise in pornography that depicts extreme violence against women.

More subtle indicators in popular culture may receive momentary, and often bemused, media notice, then quickly slip from social awareness: A report, for instance, that the image of women on prime-time TV shows has suddenly degenerated. A survey of mystery fiction finding the numbers of tortured and mutilated female characters mysteriously multiplying. The puzzling news that, as one commentator put it, "so many hit songs have the B word [bitch] to refer to women that some rap music seems to be veering toward rape music." The ascendancy of violently misogynist comics like Andrew Dice Clay, who calls women "pigs" and "sluts," or radio hosts like Rush Limbaugh, whose broadsides against "femi-Nazi" feminists helped make his syndicated program the most popular radio talk show in the nation. Or word that, in 1987, the American Women in Radio and Television couldn't award its annual prize to ads that feature women positively: it could find no ad that qualified.

These phenomena are all related, but that doesn't mean they are somehow coordinated. The backlash is not a conspiracy, with a council dispatching agents from some central control room, nor are the people who serve its ends often aware of their role; some even consider themselves feminists. For the most part, its workings are encoded and internalized, diffuse and chameleonic. Not all of the manifestations of the backlash are of equal weight or significance, either; some are mere ephemera thrown up by a culture machine that is always scrounging for a "fresh" angle. Taken as a whole, however, these codes and cajolings, these whispers and threats and myths, move overwhelmingly in one direction: they try to push women back into their "acceptable" roles—whether as Daddy's girl or fluttery romantic, active nester or passive love object.

Although the backlash is not an organized movement, that doesn't make it any less destructive. In fact, the lack of orchestration, the absence of a single string-puller, only makes it harder to see—and perhaps more effective. A backlash against women's rights succeeds to the degree that it appears *not* to be political, that it appears not to be a struggle at all. It is most powerful when it goes private, when it lodges inside a woman's mind and turns her vision inward, until she imagines the pressure is all in her head, until she begins to enforce the backlash, too—on herself.

In the last decade, the backlash has moved through the culture's secret chambers, traveling through passageways of flattery and fear. Along the way, it has adopted disguises: a mask of mild derision or the painted face of deep "concern." Its lips profess pity for any woman who won't fit the mold, while it tries to clamp the mold around her ears. It pursues a divide-and-conquer strategy: single versus married women, working women versus homemakers, middle versus working class. It manipulates a system of rewards and punishments, elevating women who follow its rules, isolating those who don't. The backlash remarkets old myths about women as new facts and ignores all appeals to reason. Cornered, it denies its own existence, points an accusatory finger at feminism, and burrows deeper underground.

Backlash happens to be the title of a 1947 Hollywood movie in which a man frames his wife for a murder he's committed. The backlash against women's rights works in much the same way: its rhetoric charges feminists with all the crimes it perpetrates. The backlash line blames the women's movement for the "feminization of poverty"—while the backlash's own instigators in Washington have pushed through the budget cuts that have helped impoverish millions of women, have fought pay-equity proposals, and undermined equal-opportunity laws. The backlash line claims the women's movement cares nothing for children's rights—while its own representatives in the capital and state legislatures have blocked one bill after another to improve child care, slashed billions of dollars in aid for children, and relaxed state licensing standards for day-care centers. The backlash line accuses the women's movement of creating a generation of unhappy single and childless women—but its purveyors in the media are the ones guilty of making single and childless women feel like circus freaks.

To blame feminism for women's "lesser life" is to miss its point entirely, which is to win women a wider range of experience. Feminism remains a pretty simple concept, despite repeated—and enormously effective—efforts to dress it up in greasepaint and turn its proponents into gargoyles. As Rebecca West wrote sardonically in 1913, "I myself have never been able to find out precisely what feminism is: I only know that people call me a feminist whenever I express sentiments that differentiate me from a doormat."

The meaning of the word feminism has not really changed since it first appeared in a book review in *The Athenaeum* on April 27, 1895, describing a woman who "has in her the capacity of fighting her way back to independence." It is the basic proposition that, as Nora put it in Ibsen's *A Doll's House* a century ago, "Before everything else I'm a human being." It is the simply worded sign hoisted by a little girl in the 1970 Women's Strike for Equality: "I AM NOT A BARBIE DOLL." Feminism asks the world to recognize at long last that women aren't decorative ornaments, worthy vessels, members of a "special-interest group." They are half (in fact, now more than half) of the national population, and just as deserving of rights and opportunities, just as capable of participating in the world's events, as the other half. Feminism's agenda is basic: It asks that women not be forced to "choose" between public justice and private happiness. It asks that women be free to define themselves—instead of having their identity defined for them, time and again, by their culture and their men.

The fact that these are still such incendiary notions should tell us that American women have a way to go before they enter the promised land of equality.

GROUPTHINK: Taking easy way out of a tough decision

Alison Bass

GLOBE STAFF

At a time when the United States and other nations are desperately seeking a way out of the Iraqi crisis, America's leaders are at enormous risk of making a bad decision, psychologists who study group decision-making say.

In fact, if history is any guide, now is the time when President Bush and his advisers are most vulnerable to the kind of noncritical decision-making that has led to disastrous policy decisions in some previous administrations.

This kind of decision-making gave us the Bay of Pigs invasion and the escalation of the Vietnam War, these psychologists say, and they add that the conditions that set up the Kennedy and Johnson administrations for failure in those crises exist now.

"It's at times like these that you feel the power of needing a consensus," said Clark McCauley, a professor of psychology at Bryn Mawr College in Pennsylvania who studies group dynamics. "The situation in the Middle East right now is like sitting on a burning stove with no relief in sight. There is no easy answer."

McCauley and other specialists interviewed last week say they have no idea how the Bush administration is making decisions about the Iraqi crisis, and thus cannot speculate about how the president and his advisers are proceeding.

But they can say something about forces of human nature that drive group decision-making, and how those forces have sometimes conspired to produce ruinous decisions.

Researchers who study social behavior have long known, for example, that members of a group are often under strong pressures to conform to the majority view. When they don't conform, they risk being isolated or cast aside.

More recently, they have discovered that human beings, whenever they meet in groups, also feel a compelling need to reach consensus. They do so both to preserve the friendly atmosphere and cohesiveness of the group and to continue to be accepted by the group and its leader.

"In all these groups, members tend to evolve informal objectives to preserve friendly intragroup relations, and this becomes part of the hidden agenda at their meetings," wrote Irving Janus, an emeritus professor of psychology at Yale University in his landmark book, "Victims of Groupthink."

Janus studied many different groups in assembling his theory about this unconscious need to reach consensus, which he labeled "groupthink." He and other scholars have expanded their understanding of groupthink through a growing body of experimental studies.

The researchers found, for example, that groupthink almost always interferes with critical thinking. And they discovered that the phenomenon is especially intense in elite, high-prestige groups, which represent the pinnacle of success for their members.

Groupthink is quite different from the more blatant pressures for conformity. Groups that fall prey to the phenomenon are not consciously worried about losing their jobs if they dissent. Rather, they are more concerned about resolving the particular problem or uncertainty at hand without losing the group's clubby atmosphere.

Mutual assurance

"Groupthink is a group-coping mechanism, in the sense that people need to reassure each other and themselves that they are doing the right thing,"

explained Alexander George, a professor of political science at Stanford University and an expert on decision-making. "In the process, they drown out their own and others' inhibitions and uncertainties, and you get a much stronger consensus as a result. It's almost a mutual admiration society."

Groupthink is a more subtle psychological phenomenon than conformity pressures, and researchers believe it may be particularly prevalent in high-level government and corporate decision-making.

In his book, first published in 1972 and revised in 1982, Janus described five cases of major US policy decisions that were dictated (either entirely or in part) by "groupthink" and became unmitigated disasters. Among them were the Bay of Pigs invasion, the escalation of the Vietnam War and Watergate.

He also described two equally important cases where groupthink was avoided and the results were highly successful: the 1962 Cuban missile crisis and the development of the Marshall plan for restoring Europe after World War II.

In both cases, Janus said, the pivotal difference was a leader who had learned to encourage differences of opinion and alternative solutions, without insisting on his own.

"The successful examples come when the president doesn't provide a solution and urges alternative solutions and even appoints a devil's advocate to knock down each solution," agreed McCauley, who expanded on Janus' seminal work in a recently published article. "That seems to increase support and rewards for those in the group who want to think and express thoughts different from the others."

In addition to leadership style, Janus

Reprinted courtesy of *The Boston Globe*, September 10, 1990, pp. 29, 30.

discovered two other conditions that are especially conducive to groupthink: a decision-making group that is homogeneous in social background and ideology and a crisis that appears to have no easy way out.

Those were the conditions in what Janus termed the "perfect failure": the CIA-inspired invasion of Cuba in 1961, widely known as the Bay of Pigs invasion. Led by 1,400 Cuban exiles and aided by the US Navy, Air Force and the CIA, that military disaster left 200 dead, 1,200 exiles as Cuba's prisoners of war and the United States looking like an inept tyrant in the eyes of the world.

Both Janus and McCauley call the decision to invade Cuba a "prototype example" of groupthink. To begin with, there is evidence from later accounts by those who were there that President John Kennedy, even before he consulted his advisers, had decided to aid the anti-Castro rebels.

Despite the president's views, historical documents show, at least two of his advisers harbored serious doubts: Secretary of State Dean Rusk and Harvard historian Arthur Schlesinger, who had been called in by Kennedy as a special adviser. Schlesinger later released a memo he had written to the President at the time expressing his doubts.

But during the crucial meetings, neither Rusk nor Schlesinger voiced their concerns, paving the way for a quick consensus. In his [1989] article, McCauley speculated that both groupthink and conformity pressures played a role in silencing Rusk and Schlesinger.

McCauley noted that there is evidence that all the advisers felt some external pressure to support the plan. At one point, Robert Kennedy took Schlesinger aside and told him the President had made up his mind and it was time for his friends to support him.

But there is also evidence from Schlesinger's later accounts that the advisers desperately wanted to reach a consensus and remain a cohesive group, McCauley and Janus wrote.

Changed approach

By contrast, the same advisers under the same President did express their opinions forcefully in resolving another major test for the Kennedy administration: the Cuban missile crisis. In 1962, after discovering that the Soviets were building missile sites on Cuba, the administration decided to set up a naval blockade around Cuba to prevent Soviet ships allegedly carrying nuclear armaments from getting through. Although the crisis brought the United States and Soviet Union to the brink of nuclear war, it ended successfully when the Soviet ships turned back and Soviet Premier Nikita Khrushchev agreed to remove the missiles.

Kennedy's approach made all the difference in how those crises were handled, according to Janus. In the Bay of Pigs decision, Kennedy thrust a decision on his advisers; in the Cuban missile crisis, although he made an initial decision to respond with some kind of coercive action, he left it up to his advisers to decide what that action would be.

Perhaps, the researchers speculate, Kennedy had learned his lesson from the Bay of Pigs fiasco.

"He asked his advisers for consideration of all possible forms of coercion, deliberately absented himself from some of the earlier meetings of his advisers and appointed Robert Kennedy as devil's advocate to question and attack every proposal offered," McCauley wrote in the August 1989 issue of the Journal of Personality and Social Psychology. "The result was strain, lost sleep, impatience, and anger as the group argued on and on, until finally a majority agreed to recommend a naval blockade of Cuba."

McCauley said struggling to this kind of true consensus is much more arduous for the participants than groupthink, which is why it happens much more rarely. Yet Kennedy's advisers themselves later said the strain of the adversarial procedure itself was crucial in producing the detailed recommendations and contingency planning that made the blockade successful.

George Kennan, a State Department official and architect of the Marshall Plan, voiced similar sentiments in recalling the process that led to that highly successful plan. Given three weeks to come up with a broad plan to extend economic aid to European nations suffering from the aftermath of World War II, Kennan encouraged an open "no-holds-barred" group discussion in which his own proposals were heavily criticized.

"Kennan reported that he went home every night feeling like he had been beat up, but he got a good result out of his group," McCauley said. McCauley and Janus say the group's action was another example of a leader's being able to avoid groupthink.

President Johnson, Janus said, was not as farsighted. He said Johnson took dissent from his war policy as "personal disloyalty" and effectively isolated those who criticized his desire to escalate the Vietnam War. A number of key advisers and senior cabinet members, such as Robert McNamara, McGeorge Bundy and George Ball, left the administration during this time, further evidence that the pressures to conform were enormous.

"If people feel they are going to pay a social cost for expressing their feelings, most won't," McCauley explained. "You have to understand what belonging to the most powerful insiders' group in the world means. It means being invited to the best dinners in Washington, to the best country clubs; it's worth chairmanships on major corporations and big money. It's worth a lot of girls, or boys, if that's what you want."

In the revised version of his book, Janus added yet another example of disastrous decision-making to his list: the Watergate coverup. Even as evidence accumulated that too many people knew too much for the effort to succeed, President Nixon and his close advisers remained unanimous in supporting the coverup. Transcripts from the Nixon tapes show that the president time and again let everyone in the group know which policy he favored. He also discouraged any debate. It was not until John Dean began to be worried more about his own future than about the president's that the consensus unraveled, Janus said.

Pressures always there

Reached at his retirement home in Santa Rose, Calif., Janus said he has no idea how the Bush administration is making decisions about the Iraqi crisis.

"The present administration is extremely secretive," he said. "There is no indication of how they arrived at their decision [to commit troops] and whether they're really setting us up for war or just want a strong presence in the Middle East."

Both Janus and McCauley, however, say the potential for groupthink always exists, along with other pressures to conform to the president's will.

"I'm sure you'll find lots of people who have grave doubts about what's going on in the Mideast, but they're not talking up," McCauley said. "And that's not good. Whenever you do something without thinking about all the possible consequences of what could go wrong, that is bad decision-making."

RESOLVING CONFLICTS
STEP BY STEP

Sandra R. Arbetter, M.S.W.

Jenny couldn't believe how right the world felt. She and Danny had made up. Her mother had stopped nagging her. And her teacher had given her an A on her book report. What had happened to make them all change?

It all started with a speaker who had come to talk to the Students for the Environment club. Instead of talking about the ozone layer or acid rain, the speaker talked about the need for opposing groups in the town to come to an agreement on the proposed building of a multi-story parking garage next to a downtown park. "The problem won't be solved until we resolve the conflicts with those who have opinions different from ours," he told the students, who had been attending city council meetings where there was heated debate on the issue.

Then he talked about what kept people from understanding one another. Jenny couldn't help but see herself in some of the things he said, and it got her to thinking about the conflicts she'd been having lately. She was angry at Danny for spending so much time with the guys. She was angry at her mother for expecting her to make dinner every Tuesday. And she was angry at her teacher for giving her a C in English.

The speaker said that there is nothing basically wrong with conflict. Most people have disagreements from time to time. "Conflicts, in fact, are a way to grow," he said. "Every time we face up to a problem and resolve it, we grow as individuals. We learn to get along better with other people and to take responsibility for our own actions."

Then he came to the part that really made Jenny think. He listed some basic assumptions about life that many people hold. Because these assumptions are not reasonable, they can lead people into conflicts.

Don't Assume

1. *I must have everything my way.* That was Jenny. If she didn't have the last word, she felt others would get in control. So what? Maybe it would be OK to let someone else lead the way for a change.

2. *I must be excellent at everything.* That was Jenny, too. She thought that if she weren't perfect she'd be perfectly awful; there was nothing in between. But no one is perfect and no one but Jenny expected her to have all the answers all the time.

3. *People must be fair to me.* Jenny was big on fairness. If her sister got a new shirt, then Jenny thought she should have one, too. If her friend got an A for a six-page report, then Jenny should, too.

4. *I have no control over the way I feel or act.* Jenny had no problem with this one. She knew there was a difference between feelings and actions and that she had the power to control her actions. Long ago she learned not to blame anyone else for her behavior. Back in third grade, she had told her teacher. "Tommy made me laugh." Both she and Tommy had to write 50 sentences.

5. *I must be liked by everyone.* Jenny didn't like everyone; why should they all like her? Did she *want* everyone to like her? Well, maybe. Did she *need* everyone to like her? Of course not.

The Five Steps

After Jenny thought about what the speaker at the club meeting had said, she was motivated to resolve conflicts with those around her. The speaker had outlined some steps that many experts have agreed upon.

Step 1: Identify the Problem

The first step is to identify the problem. Sometimes it's obvious, sometimes it's not. Jenny and her mother had been arguing about making dinner on Tuesdays. Her mom works that night, but Jenny said she's too busy. The problem wasn't just who would make dinner. The problem was that things had changed a lot since Jenny's mom went to work. Jenny missed the way it used to be, when she could count on her mom always being home and having time to take care of everything.

After talking it over with her mom, they agreed Jenny would make dinner on Tuesdays but be able to choose one weeknight when she wouldn't have any cooking or clean-up chores at all.

From *Current Health 2* September 1991, pp. 14-15. *Current Health 2*, is published by Weekly Reader Corporation. Copyright © 1991 by Weekly Reader Corporation. *Current Health* is a federally registered trademark of Weekly Reader Corporation.

Jenny's conflict with Danny went below the surface, too. She realized that she didn't want him to be with the guys because she thought his best friend didn't especially like her. During one silly fight, she admitted this to Danny. He laughed and said his friend thought that Jenny didn't like *him*. After laughing about this, the three of them got together for a movie and had a good time, and soon Jenny was feeling much more comfortable about Danny having more time with his friends.

Sometimes the problem needs to be viewed in a new way. That's called *reframing*. If you put a new frame on a picture, the picture looks different. If you put a new meaning on a problem, the problem looks different, too. If the child you're baby-sitting cheats at a game you could say he's a sore loser. Or you could reframe it with more understanding and say he's afraid to fail.

Step 2: Look for Solutions

The second step in conflict resolution is to look for possible solutions. Think of lots of them, even if they seem nutty. Good solutions often come from this random brainstorming.

In her conflict about her English grade, Jenny considered boycotting the class, asking her parents to talk with the teacher, redoing the report, accepting the C grade, or talking with her teacher about why she felt she deserved a better grade.

There are some possibilities that are just wishful thinking. Many people hope for some magical rescue—somehow, by someone. They think this might come from their parents, their friends, or people in authority.

Another unrealistic possibility is that if we ignore the problem it will go away. It seldom does, and it often gets worse. Another myth is that it will work to be aggressive—to hurt someone physically, say cruel things, or get revenge. Aside from being unkind, these tactics aren't effective in the long run.

Step 3: Choose One

Third step: Choose the best solution. What's a good solution? It's effective and socially acceptable. It solves the problem, does not hurt anyone or interfere with their rights, and satisfies both parties. There should be no winners or losers; both sides should feel as if they have achieved something. That's called a win-win solution.

Steps 4 and 5: Act, Evaluate

The fourth step is to act. Follow through on one of the solutions.

Finally, evaluate how well your approach solved the problem. If it turns out to be ineffective, don't look on that as a failure. It just means you've eliminated one approach and you're ready to try another. We learn by our mistakes.

At every step, communication is important. Communication doesn't mean just telling someone what *you* want. It means listening to what *they* want. It means establishing eye contact and being sensitive to body language. Bob Woolf, author of *Friendly Persuasion*, says it means not making demands (try suggestions instead) or ultimatums.

Jenny used these guidelines to resolve conflicts at home and at school. The environment club used them in presenting its arguments at the city council meeting. Where can we go from here?

Consider the Consequences

Sometimes feelings get so intense you have the impulse to lash out suddenly, without considering the consequences. Roger Fisher, author of *Getting Together*, gives some hints for impulse control:
- Be aware of your feelings. Although some people are ashamed of their angry, sad, or jealous feelings, you are entitled to any feelings you have. If you're angry, admit it to yourself and express your feeling.
- Take a break if feelings get too hot to handle. Divert yourself. Do something else or go somewhere else.
- Count to 10 slowly. It will give you at least 10 seconds to cool off and think about your approach.
- Consult with someone who has a calming effect on you.

Psychological Disorders

Jay and Harry were two brothers who owned a service station. They were the middle children of four. The other two children were sisters, the oldest of whom had married and moved out of the family home. The service station that these young men operated was once owned by their father who had retired and turned the business over to his sons.

Harry and Jay had a good working relationship. Harry was the "up-front" man. Taking customer orders, accepting payments, and working with parts distributors, Harry was the individual who dealt most directly with the customers. Jay worked behind the scenes. While Harry made the mechanical diagnoses, Jay was the one who did the corrective work. Some of his friends thought Jay was a mechanical genius.

Preferring to spend time by himself, Jay had always been a little different. His emotions had been more inappropriate and intense than other people's. Harry was the stalwart in the family. He was the acknowledged leader and decisionmaker when it came to family finances.

One day Jay did not show up for work on time. When he did, he was dressed in the most garish outfit and was laughing hysterically and talking to himself. Harry at first suspected that his brother had taken some illegal drugs. However, Jay's condition persisted. Out of concern, his family took him to the family's physician who immediately sent Jay and his family to a psychiatrist. The diagnosis: schizophrenia. Jay's uncle had been schizophrenic; the family grimly left the psychiatrist's office. Later they would travel to the local pharmacy to fill a prescription for antipsychotics, medications Jay would probably have to take the rest of his life.

What caused Jay's drastic and rather sudden change in mental health? Was Jay destined to be schizophrenic because of the genes of his family and his uncle? Did competitiveness with his brother and the feeling that he was less revered than Harry by his family cause Jay's decline into insanity? How can psychiatrists and clinical psychologists make accurate diagnoses? Once a diagnosis of mental illness is made, can the individual ever completely recover?

These and other questions are the emphasis in this unit. Mental illness has fascinated and, on the other hand, terrified us for centuries. At various times in our history those who suffered from these disorders were persecuted as witches, tortured to drive out possessing spirits, punished as sinners, jailed as dangerous to society, confined to insane asylums, or hospitalized as simply suffering from an ordinary illness.

Today, psychologists propose that the view of mental disorders as "illnesses" has outlived its usefulness. We should think of mental illness as either biochemical disturbances or disorders of learning in which the person develops a maladaptive pattern of behavior that is then maintained by an inappropriate environment. At the same time, we need to recognize that these reactions to stressors in the environment or to the inappropriate learning situations may be genetically preordained; some people may more easily develop the disorders than others.

Serious disorders are serious problems and not just for the individual who is the patient or client. The impact of mental disorders on the family (just as for Jay's family) and friends deserves our full attention, too. Diagnosis and treatment for various disorders, and the implications of the disorders for the family, are suggested in some of the articles in this section. In this unit, we will explore further the concept of treatment of mental disorders.

Mood disorders, especially depression, are pervasive in American society. Mary-Lane Kamberg, in "Mood Disorders: A Sad State of Mind," assists the reader in recognizing and diagnosing mood disorders, including mania and depression. She also elaborates upon some of the causes. Getting help, she alerts the reader, is not very difficult if one knows the right place to look.

Clinical depression, a very intense feeling of despair and hopelessness, is more common than you might think. Clinical depression also causes most of our suicides in this country. As troublesome as this type of depression is, it can be treated. Its causes and treatments are the focus of "Winning the War Against Clinical Depression."

Obsessive-compulsive disorder is called the secret illness in "The Secret Illness: Obsessive-Compulsive Disorder" by Isabel Forgang. Forgang describes the disorder that is manifested by uncontrollable but persistent and unpleasant thoughts and preoccupations with a behavior. There are successful treatments, though, that can help the obsessive-compulsive live a more normal rather than secretive life.

"Who Am I?" explores the fascinating disorder known as multiple personality. This disorder is often confused with schizophrenia, which is really a split with reality, not a split personality. Nelly Edmondson Gupta reveals that there is an interesting sex difference in multiple personality disorder, too.

Looking Ahead: Challenge Questions

Do you believe everyone has the potential for developing a mental disorder? What circumstances lead an individual to mental illness?

Describe the various mood disorders. How common are they? Do you think Americans are predisposed to them more than people of other cultures? Why? What causes mood disorders? How can they be treated?

What is clinical depression? How is it different from the everyday blues that many of us experience? What are the various treatments for clinical depression?

What is obsessive-compulsive disorder? Why is it called the secret illness? How can individuals who suffer from it overcome their persistent but unwelcome obsessions?

Is multiple personality the same as schizophrenia? What is the typical profile of someone who suffers from split personality? Are there effective treatments for this disorder?

Of all of these disorders, which would you predict you would be most likely to develop? Do you think that individuals suffering from any of these disorders would recognize that they are indeed suffering? Would their symptoms prompt them to seek help or avoid it?

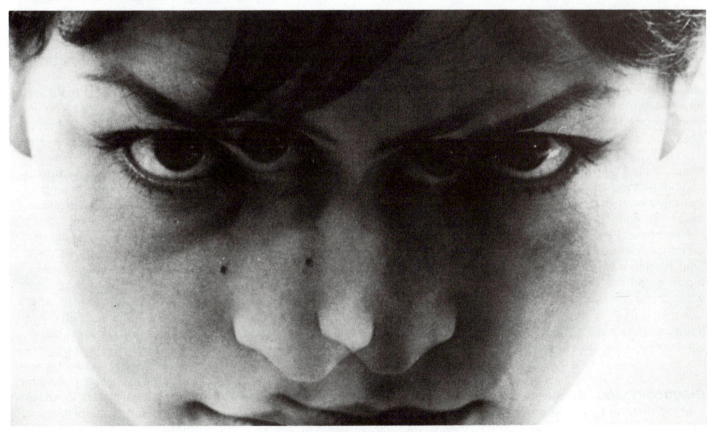

Mood Disorders●●●●●●●●●●●●●

A Sad State of Mind

Mary-Lane Kamberg

When Sally walks down school hallways, she keeps her head down. If she hears people laugh, she assumes they're laughing at her. She feels down in the dumps most of the time, but she alternates between spells when she tires easily and finds concentrating difficult and periods of heightened energy and self-confidence.

Sally describes herself as "an emotional milkshake," unsure how she will react to anything. Doctors have diagnosed her problem as a *mood disorder,* a kind of mental illness that, as the name implies, involves disturbances in a patient's mood. Until recently, these disorders had been called *affective disorders,* but have now been classified as mood disorders.

Nearly everyone feels sad, frustrated, or disappointed some of the time. If someone has a bad day, being in a bad mood is normal. But when those feelings are severe or last a long time, or when a person has a good day and still feels miserable, the cause may be a mood disorder.

Diagnosing Mood Disorders

Mood disorders include *depression, mania,* and a combination of both known as *bipolar disorder.* Symptoms of depression include feelings of hopelessness and worthlessness, sleep and appetite disturbances, suicidal thoughts, and physical symptoms such as headaches and chest pains. Between 30 million and 40 million Americans experience symptoms severe enough to be diagnosed as clinical depression at least once in their life, and between 30 percent and 40 percent of them will have more than one episode. Symptoms can appear at any age—even in infancy—but first onset usually occurs between the ages of 25 and 44. Twice as many women as men get this form of mental illness, and an estimated 6 percent to 7 percent of adolescents are affected.

Symptoms of mania include energy, rapid speech, euphoria, optimism, and overconfidence. The patient may also exhibit hyperactivity and an inability to finish projects begun impulsively. A manic episode typically begins and ends abruptly and can last for a few days or as long as a few months. Mania may appear alone, but, as in bipolar disorder, it is often followed by a period of depression. Bipolar disorder is sometimes called manic-depressive illness. People with bipolar disorder alternate between periods of depression and mania.

Causes: Emotional and Biological

Causes of mood disorders include life events, body chemicals, heredity, other illnesses, and side effects from medication. For example, a reaction to life events, such as sadness from the death of a loved one, is normal, but not if it lingers long after the situation is over.

As research continues, more and more body chemicals are being implicated in mental illness. A substance called *serotonin,* for example, has been linked with depression in a Columbia University study of people who committed or attempted suicide. Serotonin is a neurotransmitter, a brain chemical that helps carry messages throughout the nervous system. Serotonin has been associated with changes in mood, sleep, and appetite, as well as other symptoms of depression. Another body chemical called *melatonin* is manufactured in the pineal gland. Melatonin has been linked with the carbohydrate craving that is characteristic of some kinds of depression.

Heredity plays a part in some mood disorders. A National Institute of Mental Health study of Amish families in Lancaster County, Pennsylvania, discovered a gene that makes a person vulnerable to bipolar disorder. The study, however, did not conclude whether body chemicals or stress from life events triggers onset. Physical illnesses such as diabetes, hepatitis, and thyroid disorders account for onset of some symptoms of mood disorders. Likewise, depression can result from medications such as those for high blood pressure, cancer, and hormone imbalances.

Getting Help

Whatever the cause, people with depression and other mood disorders need help for physical and emotional problems. Fortunately, treatment is available. The three most common treatments are psychotherapy, medication, and electroconvulsive therapy (ECT).

Patients frequently get a combination of drugs and talk therapies. If depression is related to conflicts or emotional difficulties, psychotherapy and other talk therapies may bring relief. Counseling may include cognitive therapy, which teaches patients new ways to look at themselves and their life situations, and behavioral therapy, which seeks to increase the activity of patients who have become socially withdrawn and unmotivated.

If biological factors are involved, or if the person is severely depressed or manic, medication may be necessary. Several kinds of antidepressants are now available, including new medications that correct imbalances of neurotransmitters. New antidepressants have fewer side effects than old drugs and are safer for older patients and those with heart disease or other medical problems. Antidepressants are not addictive, but they often take two to four weeks to exert their full effects. Some patients must try several different prescriptions before finding a drug that helps.

Shedding Light on Seasonal Affective Disorder

About the time daylight savings time ends in the fall, some Americans in northern states start feeling the effects of a newly recognized psychiatric illness called Seasonal Affective Disorder (SAD). Characterized by season-related mood swings, SAD sufferers experience depression, weight gain, sleep disturbance, anxiety, irritability, and a craving for carbohydrates. When the season changes, symptoms diminish, then disappear, only to return the next year.

The best known form of SAD is winter depression followed by disappearance of symptoms in spring. Researchers have also noted a form of SAD triggered by hot summer temperatures. Symptoms of this disorder go away in winter.

Children as young as 9 years old have been diagnosed with SAD, but the illness most commonly begins in the early 20s. Women are four times as likely as men to experience the disorder. No one knows how many people are affected by the winter depression form of SAD—estimates range from 450,000 to 35 million—but researchers know where sufferers live. The disorder is more common at higher latitudes in both the northern and southern hemispheres. The geographic distribution of SAD patients led researchers to suspect that a lack of sunlight is at least partially responsible for the disorder's onset.

Experiments with light treatment found people with winter depression improved with repeated daily exposures to several fluorescent light tubes that gave off the amount of outdoor light available on a sunny spring day. (Indoor lighting provides between 10 percent and 20 percent of this amount of natural light.) Light seems to be connected with the body's production of the two chemicals, melatonin and serotonin, known to be linked to clinical depression and carbohydrate craving. Researchers also learned that the supplemental light must enter the patient's body through the eyes, so tanning salons don't help.

ECT, etc.

Patients who don't respond to medication and those with symptoms too severe to wait for drugs to work can be treated with a modern form of electroconvulsive therapy. ECT is an electric shock that induces a seizure. The seizure is thought to alter transmissions in the brain. ECT is administered under controlled conditions with anesthesia and muscle relaxants. It is the fastest-acting therapy for depression, but disadvantages include memory loss that may be short-term or last a long time. Controversy has sometimes surrounded the use of ECT, but a recent Duke University Medical Center study of its effects found no brain structure changes in

patients who received it. The study used magnetic resonance imaging technology to take pictures of patients' brains before and after ECT.

Nearly everyone with depression and other mood disorders can be helped. Treatment for depression, the most common of the illnesses, works in as many as 90 percent of cases. But experts believe stigma about mental illness prevents some people from getting help. The U.S. Department of Health and Human Services estimates that only about half the people who need help seek treatment. Family doctors or local mental health clinics are good places to get an evaluation and diagnosis of symptoms that may be related to treatable mood disorders.

Winning the War Against
CLINICAL DEPRESSION

"Although we still cannot prevent people from becoming clinically depressed, today's treatments can speed their recovery from an episode of illness and help prevent subsequent ones."

Alan I. Leshner

Dr. Leshner is acting director, National Institute of Mental Health, Rockville, Md.

CLINICAL DEPRESSION is one of the most widespread and debilitating of all mental disorders. Unlike the blue moods and passing periods of sadness and unhappiness everyone experiences, clinical depression is a severe and frequently lifelong mental disorder that recurs and upsets both body and brain functions. It makes life hellish for at least 11,500,000 adult Americans and drains over $27,000,000,000 from our national economy annually, with more than 75% of that sum due to lost social and economic productivity, not the costs of treatment. (Americans miss an estimated 177,000,000 days from work each year due to the ravages of this disorder.) Clinical depression is as debilitating as a chronic heart condition and it, too, can be a killer; it is a factor in up to 70% of all cases of suicide in the U.S.

What is most appalling is that much of the enormous suffering, expense, and loss of life it causes is unnecessary, given the current availability of diagnostic procedures as well as treatment approaches. Although we still can not prevent people from becoming clinically depressed, today's treatments can speed their recovery from an episode of illness and help prevent subsequent ones. We now have a wealth of effective and specific treatments for depression, including many types of medications, several forms of psycho-

therapy, and their combination. Indeed, as many as 80% of patients with this disorder are likely to respond if they are diagnosed and treated properly.

That is a big "if," however. A major national epidemiological survey sponsored by the National Institute of Mental Health (NIMH) has revealed that, in the U.S., only one-third of people with clinical depression receive any professional treatment for their illness. According to a 1986 Roper poll, 78% of respondents said they would live with depression until it passes, and most people who develop the disorder appear to do just that. The NIMH survey also found that some individuals try unwittingly to self-treat their symptoms by abusing drugs and/or alcohol.

Neither approach is prudent, because ignoring clinical depression or subjecting it to inappropriate remedies is an invitation to prolonged suffering and even more severe problems later. Although a single episode eventually will remit, this disorder recurs in 50-60% of cases and is chronic in 15-20%. When clinical depression is untreated, episodes of illness often return, becoming longer and more frequent over time, until most of a person's life is spent being severely mentally ill. For those who become psychotic or suicidal, repeated rounds of expensive inpatient hospitalization—possibly for months on end—may be required.

Given the magnitude of clinical depression—its personal, social, psychological, and economic costs, as well as its potential lethality—why do so many people with this severe mental disorder go untreated?

The reasons include the general public's ignorance about the nature of depression and the likelihood of successful treatment; stigmatization of mental illness, which makes many unwilling to seek help, however much they hurt, and often leads family members and associates to consider depressed individuals lazy or somehow character-flawed, rather than ill; lack of adequate and equitable health insurance coverage for mental disorders, making treatment financially unavailable for some people; the geographic inaccessibility of many health and mental health services, especially in rural areas; and the inability of many health professionals and general medical practitioners to recognize and diagnose depressive illness in their patients—an essential step for appropriate referral or treatment.

Many individuals and organizations, both public and private, are attempting to overcome these problems. Of particular importance is the recent upsurge in organizations focused on advocacy for those with mental illnesses such as depression.

We at the National Institute of Mental Health also have been doing our part. In 1986, we launched a pioneering national campaign to educate the general public as well as health and mental health professionals about the nature of clinical depression and its treatment. The NIMH Depression Awareness, Recognition, and Treatment (D/ART) program, based on the best available scientific information about the disorder, has developed and distributed a wide array of educational materials and has worked closely with local and national groups to stimulate greater public and professional understanding of depression.

The program is conducted cooperatively with D/ART Community Partners—networks coordinated under the leadership of a single nonprofit mental health agency and dedicated to enhancing public awareness of the symptoms and treatment of depression. Partners are active in 24 states and the District of Columbia, organizing a variety of community programs that include speakers bureaus, telephone hotlines, media appearances, public forums, support groups, and professional training.

The latter are addressed to health and mental health practitioners as well as those still in training. Particular attention is given to providing education and mental health consultation for primary care physicians and nurses in rural areas where mental health professionals may be scarce.

In addition to the D/ART Public Education Campaign and its Professional Training Program, a new thrust is focusing on the workplace as a key site for recognizing clinical depression and providing treatment and referral through employee assistance plans. The D/ART Worksite Program also seeks to encourage corporate leadership to adopt health insurance plans and policies that provide appropriate and equitable mental health benefits for treatment outside the workplace.

We have found employers extremely receptive because they recognize that the considerable toll depression takes in absenteeism and reduced productivity can be lowered through appropriate treatment as well as programs and benefits packages that encourage it. One study revealed, for example, that, at the First National Bank of Chicago, inpatient psychiatric charges were reduced by 32% after a comprehensive mental health program was initiated that included prevention and early intervention programs as well as the redesign of mental health benefits.

In addition to efforts to encourage widespread adoption and application of knowledge about the diagnosis and treatment of depression, NIMH is supporting a comprehensive research program that focuses on understanding how psychological and biological factors interact to produce clinical depression, how to treat it more effectively, and how eventually to prevent it. Together, these are helping people with clinical depression spend less time despairing, being impaired and ill, and more time being fulfilled, productive, and healthy. However, removing many of the deeply ingrained barriers to appropriate care will take many more years of consistent, dedicated effort. Making a visible change in the costly pattern of under-recognition and undertreatment we now see will need more than the efforts of a single Federal agency, or a handful of advocacy organizations and their grassroots supporters. It will require all Americans, wherever they live or work, to make an extra effort to learn about clinical depression, encourage people who appear to be ill to seek treatment, and motivate employers to offer benefit plans that provide adequate coverage for mental health as well as health care.

Origins of depression

The causes of depression are many and complex. However, their fundamental mechanisms are becoming increasingly understood, thanks to growing sophistication in the science of mental disorders. Usually, a combination of biological and social/psychological factors is involved, although their specific proportions will vary considerably from one person to another.

Biological factors can be sufficiently powerful—such as inheriting a very strong genetic predisposition toward the disorder, or being exposed to certain drugs or medical procedures—that they alone can precipitate depression. Conversely, disastrous environmental events sometimes can bring on clinical depression virtually by themselves. Most often, however, we believe that a combination of factors is at play.

The role of genetics is a matter of intense research study, but, as yet, the picture remains cloudy. It is known that depression runs in families, and scientists currently are searching for the genetic basis of the disorder. At present, the best that can be said is that some people appear to inherit a predisposition to depression. No specific genetic marker has been found that would allow us to identify who is at particularly high risk of developing this disorder.

Some theorists have argued that depression has its roots in childhood trauma or poor parenting, but there is no well-substantiated long-term research evidence to support this view. Studies have shown, however, that, on average, the offspring of depressed parents are more likely to be depressed than other children. This hardly is surprising. Those of depressed parents face not only the genetic risk of illness, but the environmental possibility of being exposed to an abnormal style of childrearing.

Depression can be a devastating mental disorder, but it also is a very treatable one. We now have a broad array of effective biological and psychological treatments and steadily are improving the ones now available, making it possible for most patients to recover relatively quickly from a depressive episode. These treatments also can help prevent recurrent episodes of depression—an especially important achievement in dealing with a chronic mental disorder. The net effect is that people with clinical depression—many of whom once might have spent most of their lives in a mental hospital—now can be treated on an outpatient basis and lead normal, indeed highly productive, lives.

Studies of depressed people make it clear that depression affects the entire person—thoughts, feelings, and social relationships, as well as the body and brain. In its mental and emotional symptoms, it produces profound despair about the present and a sense of extreme helplessness and hopelessness about the future. Many of the distorted thought patterns of depressed people that help to perpetuate their illness and contribute to suicidal behavior appear to be learned. With therapy, these tendencies can be reversed.

People with clinical depression may develop additional layers of psychological and social problems that can complicate their illness and their recovery. For example, an episode severely may strain or upset a person's relationship with a spouse, child, or lover, and may wreak havoc in the workplace due to absenteeism and severely lowered performance. If hospitalization is required, the person later may suffer the additional burdens of stigmatization as a former mental patient. Often, psychotherapy can help patients—hospitalized or not—cope more effectively with the difficulties of getting their lives back together.

Depressed people have many physical as well as mental symptoms—including disturbances of sleep, appetite, sexual drive, and physical energy—and, when given laboratory tests, reveal additional biological abnormalities. For example, in many depressed patients, the stress hormone cortisol is regulated abnormally, indicating that a key hormone system linking the hypothalamus in the brain, the pituitary just below it, and the adrenal is not functioning properly.

Research also has shown that one or more chemical messenger systems in the brain might be altered during depression. Communication systems that rely upon the neurotransmitters dopamine and serotonin seem to be particularly relevant, as are those involving certain hormone-like brain peptides. Many medications that have been developed can treat depression effectively, normalizing these pathological processes to a certain degree, but through different mechanisms of action. However miraculous the effects of many of these medications may be, it is clear that, at present, the fundamental biological processes underlying depression are just beginning to be understood.

Treatment approaches for clinical depression need to be tailored to meet the specific diagnosis and needs of individual patients. Mild cases of depression may respond well to psychotherapy. Medication often is used, however, during the early stages of an episode, especially if it is severe and there is a strong risk of suicide. (Notwithstanding its unpopularity, electroconvulsive therapy frequently proves to be lifesaving for some severely depressed and suicidal patients who do not respond to medication.) As acute symptoms begin to lessen, psychotherapy may be added to help them understand their illness, strengthen their capacity to cope with its social and psychological consequences, and lessen their vulnerability to situational stressors. Recent evidence from research at the University of Pittsburgh suggests that if, once the episode is over, the patient continues to take standard antidepressant medication on a regular basis, often coupled with periodic psychotherapy services, the likelihood of future episodes is decreased significantly.

For more information on the diagnosis, treatment, and prevention of clinical depression, write: Depression/USA, Rockville, MD 20857.

THE SECRET ILLNESS: OBSESSIVE-COMPULSIVE DISORDER

Fran Sydney, forty-five, had always been compulsively neat. But at age twenty-two, when her first child died at birth, Fran's need for perfection grew all-consuming. Towels had to be folded just so, and the labels on the canned food in her cupboards had to face the same way and be the same distance apart.

As her three children were growing up, her need to "protect" them through neatness and perfection intensified. "We couldn't have visitors, because they would disturb the order of things," she recalls, "and I didn't allow the kids to play with their toys because of the mess. If clothes touched the side of the washing machine when I was taking them out, they had to be washed all over again.

"I was a cleaning machine. Cleaning became a way of controlling something that wasn't controllable," she explains. "It made me feel safe—for about two seconds."

As freakish as Fran's situation sounds, it's all too typical among sufferers of obsessive-compulsive disorder (OCD), an anxiety condition that afflicts millions of Americans. People with OCD experience persistent, unpleasant thoughts, or obsessions, such as preoccupation with dirt and disorder, fear of acting on violent impulses or feeling overly responsible for the safety of others. To offset their anxiety, they feel forced to repeat meaningless actions, or compulsions, such as constant washing, cleaning, checking, counting and arranging. They know their obsessions and compulsions are irrational and excessive, yet they cannot control them.

Although the disorder has been recognized for more than one hundred fifty years, no one knew how prevalent it was until recently. Fearing they would be labeled as crazy, many victims tried to conceal their affliction from others. However, in 1988, a three-year survey by the National Institute of Mental Health found that an estimated 4.5 million adults suffered in secret from this disease.

RECOGNIZING THE SIGNS

"Everyone has occasional fleeting bizarre thoughts," says Michael Liebowitz, M.D., director of the Anxiety Disorder Clinic at the New York State Psychiatric Institute in Manhattan. "You know you won't act on them, so you dismiss them. What is abnormal is if the thought becomes recurrent and intrusive, affecting your ability to function."

A second characteristic of OCD is the sheer amount of time it consumes—often hours a day. "A lot of everyday situations can bring out compulsiveness in many people," says Wayne Goodman, M.D., chief of the OCD clinic at the Yale University School of Medicine. "You may check a couple of times to see that you locked the front door, for example. For someone with OCD, this compulsiveness follows them everywhere. They'll check the lock again and again. At work they're still concerned, so they'll call a neighbor to check."

These pathological doubts separate a person with OCD from someone with an obsessive-compulsive personality, says psychologist Fred Penzel, Ph.D., a member of the science advisory board of the Obsessive Compulsive Foundation, in New Haven, Connecticut. "In OCD, repetitive behaviors are attempts to eliminate anxiety and fear that harm will come to oneself or to others," he explains. "An obsessive-compulsive personality, on the other hand—one that is superclean or superorganized—sees its actions as positive. There is no distress or doubt associated with the behavior."

OCD afflicts both men and women alike. Although researchers don't know why, it often begins in adolescence or the early twenties. However, there are cases of children as young as two years old with the disorder. And while some people may be only compulsive washers or checkers, others are afflicted with multiple symptoms. In short, says Michael A. Jenike,

M.D., director of the Obsessive Compulsive Disorder Clinic and Research Unit at Massachusetts General Hospital, "there's nothing consistent about this disorder."

THE LATEST BREAKTHROUGHS

Definitive knowledge about the cause and treatment of OCD has also been elusive, but experts are making progress. Current research points to a biochemical imbalance in the brain involving the neurotransmitter serotonin, a chemical that affects sleep, appetite, anxiety and repetitive behavior. Exactly how serotonin is implicated, though, remains a mystery. Genetics may also play a part. Studies show that about 25 percent of OCD sufferers have an immediate family member with the disorder.

Researchers have discovered that drugs that act on serotonin seem to be the most effective treatment. Recently, one such prescription drug, clomipramine, which has been available abroad for more than twenty years, was approved by the Food and Drug Administration. Sold under the trade name Anafranil, it's the only drug approved for the treatment of OCD. Two antidepressants, fluvoxamine (or Faverin) and fluoxetine (or Prozac), are being used experimentally to treat OCD. Almost 60 percent of patients are dramatically helped with medication, reports Jenike. But, he and other doctors caution, medication is a treatment, not a cure.

The best answer for most victims, say experts, combines drugs and behavior therapy. With therapy, OCD sufferers are exposed to increasingly large doses of what they fear, while discouraged from performing their anxiety-reducing rituals. Over 90 percent of people with OCD can be helped with this two-pronged treatment, adds Jenike.

For Fran Sydney, medication marked the turning point in her battle with OCD. Today, she says, "I'm able to have a normal life. I can leave things disorganized for a while. I can cope as well as any mother. It's just the normal life cycle that gets to me now!"   —ISABEL FORGANG

For more information about OCD, or for a referral to support groups and treatment centers nationwide, contact the Obsessive Compulsive Foundation, P.O. Box 9573, New Haven, CT 06535; 203-772-0565.

WHO AM I?

She is a wife, a mother—and the victim of one of the most baffling mental illnesses known. Forty-nine personalities—some of them violent—vie for control of her body; many are children, a few are men. And shocking as it is, this woman's condition may be more common than you think.

Nelly Edmondson Gupta

Vickie,* a round-faced brunet of thirty-six, looks like a typical suburban mother in her loose plaid jumper and pink T-shirt. To some extent, that's just what she is; in less than two hours, she will pick up her seven-year-old son, Toby, from school. But suddenly a chilling transformation takes place. She looks down, then shakes her head quickly. And when she starts to speak, she sounds eerily childlike. "I'm Roxette, and I'm seven," she says in a tiny voice. "I enjoy playing house and school. I like to read. I have a book about a unicorn and a book about a magic tree . . . and a bunch of others, too!"

Who is Vickie? She is the thirty-six-year-old mother, the seven-year-old child—and many, many others as well. Vickie suffers from multiple personality disorder (MPD), one of the most complicated psychiatric disorders known. Inside her psyche, forty-nine personalities battle for control of one body. In addition to Vickie and Roxette, there are Rose, the original, or birth, personality, so depressed that she wants only to die; Badla, an often sadistic male personality who

All the personalities' names have been changed to protect the patient's privacy.

usually decides which self will be "out," or in control of the body at any given moment; docile Suzy, who likes to clean house and cook; and Lila, the computer, who keeps track of all the personalities and their memories. There are other personalities, too, some children, some male. And all of them must cope with a painfully fragmented reality. As Vickie—the personality most often in control at this point—puts it, her body is like a lifeless glove; as each personality comes forward, it slips in like a separate, disembodied hand.

Often those changes can be frightening, and even dangerous. "One night when I was driving on the highway," Vickie says, "Badla suddenly put Suzy in control, knowing she can't drive. She hit a lamppost and almost went over a cliff."

Divided minds

Many MPD patients live in the shadows, terrified that others will discover their secret. But Vickie and her therapist, Pamela Hall, Ph.D., a clinical psychologist based in Perth Amboy, New Jersey, and affiliated with Pace University in New York, agreed to talk to the *Journal*

to help others understand the condition. Although many of us already know about MPD through the best-seller *The Three Faces of Eve* (1957) and *Sybil* (1973), the disorder still is widely misinterpreted and misunderstood.

Documented reports of MPD go back for more than four centuries, yet it wasn't until 1980 that the American Psychiatric Association officially recognized it as a bona fide illness. Before that, about two hundred cases were reported; experts now speculate that in the United States alone there may be as many as sixteen thousand people with MPD.

"We now know that MPD is not rare," says Robert Benjamin, M.D., a psychiatrist affiliated with Eugenia Hospital, in Lafayette Hill, Pennsylvania. "Until recently, professionals didn't look for it." As a result, he says, the disorder has been misdiagnosed as everything from schizophrenia to plain old unhappiness.

(Even now, some psychiatrists are cautious about the diagnosis, warning that it may be faddish; severely disturbed people, they say, often exhibit extreme emotional and personality changes during therapy, which overeager practitioners may misinterpret.)

Contrary to the stereotype, only about 6 percent of MPD victims exhibit flagrant personality changes, according to Richard Kluft, M.D., director of the dissociative-disorders unit at the Institute of the Pennsylvania Hospital, in Philadelphia. "Many of the rest have long periods when they're switching off neatly without much strife. In other cases, a single personality may be out for long periods of time."

Experts are also careful to emphasize that MPD differs from schizophrenia, a mental disorder marked by bizarre thought and behavior patterns. For years, schizophrenics were popularly—and wrongly—believed to suffer from a "split personality." And while experts still do not know the cause of schizophrenia—which seems to have chemical or genetic roots—they do know that MPD patients do not usually appear to have the disturbed thought patterns of schizophrenia. For the most part, their internal entities exhibit reasonably clear, purposeful thinking within the context of each separate personality.

A survival strategy

The disorder actually begins as a mental survival strategy that helps children cope with horrendous sexual, physical or emotional abuse. In fact, many experts believe our new sensitivity to the prevalence of child abuse may contribute to the growing awareness of MPD.

"MPD develops when people have been so overcome by early traumas that they have to put up mental partitions in order to function in everyday life," explains Benjamin. MPD patients often have numerous childlike personalities, he says, precisely because much of the abuse occurred early in life and those memories become "frozen" at the ages when the traumas occurred.

Of all those diagnosed with MPD, about 90 percent are women. According to Elizabeth Bowman, M.D., assistant professor of psychiatry at Indiana University School of Medicine in Indianapolis, that may be because females are up to three times as likely as males to be sexually abused.

Some experts believe many undiagnosed male victims of MPD may be out on the streets—or in jail. While female multiples are likely to become depressed and suicidal, males seem more likely to direct their rage outward. "Many criminals—serial killers and others who commit seemingly senseless crimes—could be multiple personalities," says Hall.

Shattered lives

While Vickie has never had the urge to commit a crime, she has been forced into some painful choices because of her disorder. She decided to leave her job as a case supervisor in a child protective services agency after Badla began throwing childish Roxette out at work. "I'd get scared," says Roxette, as Vickie speaks in her little-girl voice. "Vickie had her own office, and I'd close the door. She kept crayons and a coloring book there for me, and I'd play until I could go back inside." Eventually, unable to take the pressure of working under such stressful circumstances, Vickie left. She lives now on medical-disability payments, and most of her former co-workers still do not know the real reason she resigned.

At home, Vickie's conflicting personalities sometimes lead to inconsistent parenting. One self will say, "No candy before dinner," and another, younger self will come out and say, "Let's go eat cupcakes together!" But the changes do not seem to affect Toby, Vickie says: "When Roxette or other child personalities are out with him, he just figures he's got this great mom who can really relate to him and play with him."

Luckily, Vickie has several close friends who are aware of her problem, and on the relatively rare occasions when she feels seriously depressed or self-destructive, she ensures Toby's well-being by having him spend a day or two at their homes. "Vickie would never hurt her child," says Hall. "She has made considerable efforts to be a good parent. He's a really terrific, intelligent kid."

In addition to behaving erratically, Vickie's alternate personalities display annoying physiological differences: For example, Vickie and some of the other adult personalities have asthma, while many of the younger ones don't. In addition, Vicki says doses of barbiturates that calm her make some of her other selves more aggressive. Doctors who work with MPD patients say such differences between personalities are actually quite common.

Roots of an illness

Vickie's childhood, in a rural working-class town on the East Coast, is typical of thousands of MPD sufferers. As far back as she can recall, her mother acted like two completely different people. "In front of others, she was the perfect, storybook mother. She acted very compassionate and loving, made Halloween costumes by hand—the whole nine yards. But when other people left, all hell would break loose. I was beaten unconscious, locked in the basement for entire days; she even put me in the oven with the gas on and nearly asphyxiated me. She was real good at not leaving too much evidence, but when it was there, she always had a good explanation: 'She fell off the stoop; she's uncoordinated; she bumped into my cigarette.' "

Looking back, Vickie says she was probably functioning as a multiple personality even before she learned to talk, although she didn't really understand what was going on. "We knew there were others inside, but we weren't fully aware we were parts of one person," she explains.

Because of the alarming shifts in her mother's behavior, Vickie thinks her mother might have been a multiple personality, too. She could be right. "It's common for MPD to be a familial, multigenerational problem," says Benjamin. Although there is no known genetic component to the disease, he adds, if parents grossly abuse their children, the disorder can be handed down from one generation to the next, especially in those who have a tendency to undergo self-hypnosis—put themselves into trance states—in stressful situations.

"You're a liar"

As a toddler, Vickie tried to tell her legal father about the abuse, but he refused to believe her. "He'd say, 'Your mother would never do that; you have to stop telling such lies,' " she recalls bitterly.

In fact, Vickie's unsuccessful attempts to seek help prompted her mother to abuse her even more. "There's one memory from age four of being tied up and put in a carton. She carried me out to the part of the yard where trash was burned, lit a match and threatened to set the box on fire. Finally, she took me out and said, 'See, I saved you. But if you tell on me again, next time I won't.' "

In school, Vickie found little respite from her troubles. "I was always being accused of lying because one personality would learn a lesson, and the next day another personality who did not know the material would be out," she says.

When she was twelve, Vickie's family moved, and the physical abuse finally stopped. At eighteen, she broke off contact with her relatives and entered college.

There, the personality system made a concerted effort to "pass" as an integrated individual, though her internal divisions were as strong as ever. Rose—the birth personality, who was then most often in control—continued to lose large chunks of time during which she could remember nothing.

"People she didn't know would often say hello to her," says Vickie. "Professors would greet her, but she didn't know she was taking their classes. This caused a lot of stress; in fact, she figured she was crazy."

What was actually happening, says Vickie, was that many of the other selves were often in control. Two personalities—Rose and Rosemary—attended classes. Meanwhile, Vickie worked as a nude model for art classes, and admits now that she was sometimes sexually promiscuous—facts of which Rose was unaware. At the same time, Rose and yet another personality, Marie, held down respectable part-time jobs as a statistics and psychology tutor and as a recreational aide in a group home for troubled teenagers.

After graduation, Vickie met her first husband, Roy, whom she married at age twenty-seven. Although she hid her situation from Roy, a new personality, Cookie, was soon created to cope with married life, and Suzy would often emerge to take care of household chores. But Roy was physically abusive, and in 1983, the couple sought marital therapy. After hearing about Vickie's past—the child abuse she'd suffered, her erratic behavior and the bouts of amnesia—the counselor sent Vickie to a psychologist who suggested that Vickie might be suffering from MPD. Upon receiving the diagnosis, Vickie says, there were many different reactions within the personality system. "Rose didn't believe she had MPD, and it was hard for some of the younger personalities to understand the condition," she says. "I [Vickie] didn't believe the diagnosis at first, though I do now." Badla, she adds, still considers himself a completely separate individual.

A family secret

Difficult as it was for Vickie to face the fact that she had MPD, worse was yet to come. In 1983, right after Toby's birth, she was hospitalized for depression and a psychiatrist gave her sodium amytal—a drug that induces a kind of chemical hypnosis—to help her recall key events from her past. In a trance, Vickie had a searing memory of being raped by her maternal grandfather at age eight. At the same time, says Hall, a younger personality emerged and recalled being told by her paternal grandfather that her mother's husband was not her real father. In fact, he said, Vickie was the product of an incestuous relationship between her other grandfather and her mother. The allegation was unbearable to Rose. "She couldn't deal with it," says Vickie. "So

she left. Since then, the rest of us have pretty much been living her life for her."

Following her hospitalization in 1984, Vickie divorced her husband and tried to find a therapist. About two years ago, she called Kluft at the Pennsylvania Hospital and was referred to Hall, whom she now sees three times a week. "At this point, we're working on *not* splitting into new personalities as a way to deal with stress," says Vickie.

Strange as it sounds, however, she isn't sure at this point that she wants to give up her multiplicity. "My forty-nine personalities are all quite distinct and well developed; it's going to be very hard for them to accept integration," she says. "The real problem is that we're not all playing on the same team. What I want now is mutual cooperation."

Although Hall understands these fears, she hopes Vickie will someday feel differently. If Vickie can learn to accept all the disparate parts of herself, says Hall, "integration would be a natural progression."

A brighter future

These days, Vickie's life is far from easy, but she *is* making progress. About a year and a half ago, she became reacquainted with Tom, an old high-school classmate who returned to her town after seventeen years in Florida, where he worked at a series of jobs and eventually became a computer engineer.

During a phone call shortly after their reunion, Vickie told Tom about her MPD diagnosis. "She blurted it all out," he recalls. "In a way, I think it was sort of a test. I think she felt, 'Let's put this between us now so it won't be between us later.'"

Fortunately, Vickie's difficulties have not come between them; they were married last December. However, Tom does admit having mixed feelings about Vickie's multiplicity. "Sometimes I'm a little spooked; I think, Who is this person next to me?" he says. But he adds: "I really admire her strength; MPD is an indication of incredible resourcefulness and an ability to survive against all odds."

One of the most positive aspects of the relationship, says Hall, is that Tom tries to understand and deal with all of Vickie's selves as they emerge. When Roxette or another child personality is out, he's careful not to make a sexual advance. Tom has also saved Vickie from being hurt by some of the evil personalities.

The most frightening incident took place on May 26, 1988, Vickie's thirty-sixth birthday, when, luckily, she had sent Toby to a friend's house for the night. "She went into the bathroom and stayed there for a long time," Tom remembers. "I called through the door, asking if she was all right. She said, 'Leave me alone; I'm fine,' but her tone of voice made me

suspicious, and I could smell something burning. Finally, I got a hammer and popped the door out of the frame."

What he saw then was terrifying: "Vickie was crouched on the floor burning some black candles and holding a giant kitchen knife. She—it may have been an evil child personality named Samantha—snarled, 'I'm going to hurt her.' I said, 'No. I won't let you do this.'

"I saw a look of indecision pass over her face," Tom continues, "so I grabbed the knife and threw it into the hallway behind me. Then I knelt down and asked if one of her other selves could take control. Eventually, another personality came forward and started weeping. Finally, I led her out of the bathroom. I was terrified for Vickie—and for myself."

Becoming whole

Both Vickie and Tom hope her evil personalities will stop their destructive behavior soon. They want to be able to focus all of their energies on building a better future together. "I want to raise happy kids, and I want to have a solid, nonabusive relationship with my husband," Vickie says. Someday she would also like to return to work at a child protective services agency, and hopes that society will become more alert to the problem of child abuse. "We must realize that people can be pretty horrific, and that parents aren't always what they appear to be on the surface," she says. Nor are patients—and therapists hope they will soon be able to reach out to more MPD sufferers like Vickie, to help them become whole and healthy persons.

Treating MPD

The prognosis for MPD is good—if a person can tolerate what Catherine Fine, Ph.D., program coordinator of the dissociative-disorders unit at the Institute of Pennsylvania Hospital, calls "one of the most difficult therapies a patient can undergo."

The primary treatment is intensive, long-term psychotherapy in which patient and therapist meet for at least an hour one or more times per week. Sometimes antidepressant, antianxiety and other drugs are used to ease symptoms.

Experts often divide therapy into several phases: beginning, middle and termination. During the first phase, the doctor makes the diagnosis, tries to gain the patient's trust and gets to know the personality system: the name, the purpose each serves and when each one split off from the birth personality.

During the second phase, patients must force themselves to go back and recall past traumas in detail. "They must mentally reexperience the abuse that caused their illness," explains Fine. This process, called abreaction, or "remembering with feeling," is so painful that patients sometimes scream, sob and flail about—just as they did during the real event.

As the process continues, the therapist helps the patient break down amnesiac barriers so the personalities can begin to know, understand and help each other. Sometimes, doctors make video- or audiotapes of the personalities, or have patients keep journals so alternate selves can establish a written dialogue. Therapists may also use hypnosis to gain access to buried memories and personalities that don't often emerge, and to encourage interpersonality communication.

Then the therapist must get the personalities to cooperate with each other to accomplish common goals, such as going to the office and making sure childlike personalities do not take control at work. For these constructive changes to occur, the patient must come to terms with all aspects of her self—including uncomfortable feelings such as rage, depression, guilt and shame. As the patient begins to accept herself, barriers between the personalities gradually become less rigid.

"Patients often develop a sense that whereas they used to live only in one room, they are now opening the doors of a large house," says Frank Putnam, M.D., chief of the unit on dissociative disorders at the laboratory of developmental psychology at the National Institute of Mental Health, in Bethesda, Maryland.

Finally, during the third, or postintegration treatment phase, patients learn how to function effectively in the world without creating new selves to cope with life.

Ultimately, say experts, the successfully integrated individual is the sum total of all the feelings, experiences, memories, skills and talents that were previously encapsulated in all of the different personalities. If the patient sincerely wants to integrate—and if she is able to stay in ongoing treatment for at least three to five years—this goal can often be achieved.

Psychological Treatments

Have you ever had the nightmare that you are trapped in a dark, dismal place? No one will let you out. Your pleas for freedom go unanswered and, in fact, are suppressed or ignored by domineering authority figures around you. You keep begging for mercy, but to no avail. What a nightmare! You are fortunate to awake up in your normal bedroom and to the realities of your daily life. For the mentally ill, the nightmare of institutionalization, where individuals can be held against their will in what are sometimes terribly dreary, restrictive surroundings, is the reality. Have you ever wondered what would happen if we took perfectly normal individuals and institutionalized them? In one well-known and remarkable study, that is exactly what happened.

In 1973, eight people, including a pediatrician, a psychiatrist, and some psychologists, presented themselves to psychiatric hospitals. Each claimed that he or she was hearing voices. The voices, they reported, seemed unclear but appeared to be saying "empty" or "thud." Each of these individuals was admitted to a mental hospital, and most were diagnosed as being schizophrenic.

Upon admission, each "pseudopatient" or fake patient gave truthful information and thereafter acted like their usual selves. They no longer said they heard voices. Their hospital stays lasted anywhere from 7 to 52 days. The nurses, doctors, psychologists, and other staff members treated them as if they really were schizophrenic and never really saw through their trickery. Some of the real patients in the hospital did recognize, however, that the pseudopatients were perfectly normal. Upon discharge almost all of the pseudopatients received the diagnosis of "schizophrenia in remission," meaning that they were still clearly construed as schizophrenic; they just were not exhibiting any of the symptoms at the time.

What does this study demonstrate about mental illness? Is true mental illness readily detectable? If we cannot always detect mental disorders, how can we treat them? What treatments are available, and which work better for various diagnoses?

Because depression is so pervasive in our country, we begin by focusing on treatment for depression. While the article "Depression: The Growing Role of Drug Therapies" emphasizes the use of drugs or pharmacologic agents to treat depression, psychotherapy also assists the depressed.

The next article examines self-help groups in which individuals band together to support others with the same problem. The popularity of self-help groups, such as Alcoholics Anonymous, suggests that professional help and medication might not always be necessary. In "Recovery Fever" and "Help Yourself: Self-Care for Emotional Problems," the authors examine the utility of self-care groups and their growth in popularity.

Looking Ahead: Challenge Questions

What is depression? What are the available treatments for it? Why is there a debate over which treatment is best? Which treatment do you think is best and why? What drugs are used to treat depression? What are the side effects of each? Should medication always be the treatment of choice for mental illness? What other treatments are available for mental illness?

How does self-help differ from professional help? Would you prefer a self-help group to professional help? Why? Do you feel that some disorders are more amenable to self-care than others? If so, which ones and why? Why might psychologists and psychiatrists be threatened by the self-help movement?

Unit 11

DEPRESSION
THE GROWING ROLE OF DRUG THERAPIES

As doctors learn more about the biology of mental illness, they are unlocking the mysteries of depression and creating a new science of the mind

PHILIP ELMER-DEWITT

MENTAL ILLNESS CAN WEAR many masks. Most are subtler than the deranged face of schizophrenia, but they can be just as paralyzing. Take the case of Dick Cavett. To many TV viewers, the talk-show host and actor seemed to have it all—wit, charm, fame and fortune. But behind the glib façade, Cavett was falling apart. About 12 years ago, a chronic depression that had haunted him for years rose up and began undermining what he believed was his most valuable asset: his intellect. He became convinced that his brain was "broken" and that life without it was hardly worth living. "Everything seemed to be growing gray," he recalls. "All the things that used to give me pleasure suddenly weren't worth the effort."

Desperate, Cavett checked into a hospital, where for five weeks he was protected from himself while a seemingly mild but potent drug called an MAO inhibitor took effect. Such antidepressants cause subtle changes in the concentrations of certain neurotransmitters, the chemicals that carry electrical messages to and from nerve cells in the brain. The medication, which he still takes on a maintenance dose in conjunction with psychotherapy, worked. His wit, humor and facility for words returned, good as new. And Cavett came away from the experience with a conviction that his disorder was, as he puts it, "absolutely chemical."

That conviction reflects a growing consensus among scientists that dysfunctions like depression and schizophrenia—and indeed most mental disorders—are at their core disruptions of normal brain chemistry and can often be treated as such. The talk-therapy tradition pioneered by Freud and others still has its place. Subconscious issues are believed to affect brain chemistry, and most studies show that drug treatments work best when administered along with some form of talk therapy. But it is the psychopharmacologists, not the psychiatrists, who are making the breakthroughs in mental-health circles.

"There is an explosion of activity," says Richard Wyatt, chief of neuropsychiatry at the National Institute of Mental Health (NIMH) in Bethesda, Md. With computerized scanners, researchers are peering at the chemistry of the working mind. Meanwhile, molecular biologists are beginning to map abnormal behavior to specific strands of DNA. And by tracing the action of drugs like clozapine for schizophrenia and Prozac (fluoxetine) for depression, scientists can link moods and feelings to the action of certain chemicals in the brain. The result is a burst of new ideas about how the mind works—and what is going on when it does not—unequaled since the days of Freud and Jung.

Advances are being made against virtually every affliction to which the human mind is prey. Generalized anxiety can be treated with surprising success with benzodiazepines like Valium, as well as with a new drug called BuSpar (buspirone). Manic depression was effectively treated with lithium long before anyone knew why it worked; now therapy is being fine-tuned with medications like the anticonvulsant Tegretol (carbamazepine) and drugs that ameliorate lithium's side effects. Debilitating panic attacks can be prevented with both antidepressants and benzodiazepines. Hyperactivity, addictive disorders, phobias, sleep disturbances, even dementia—all are succumbing to the new science of the brain.

But it is the treatment of ordinary depression—the crushing despondency that strikes more than 12 million Americans each year and accounts for at least half the nation's suicides—that represents mental health's greatest success story. The condition once called melancholia, and now better known as clinical or major depression, has been the target of an all-fronts research assault over the past decade. The immediate result is a crop of new, highly specific antidepressant drugs that offer fast relief with relatively few side effects. Today depression can be treated—quickly and effectively—in 7 cases out of 10. If a second round of treatment is required, the cure rate jumps to 90%.

Depression comes in many flavors, from seasonal depressions that come and go with the short days of winter to low-level chronic depressions that linger for months. Among the symptoms of clinical depression are weight loss, early waking, diminished sex drive and a general hopelessness. But some people have what are called atypical depressions in which they put on weight and sleep much of the day.

Of course not everyone who has the blues is depressed. Feelings of sadness, frustration and unhappiness are natural reactions to real-life problems—a painful loss, a relationship gone sour, a conflict that won't go away. Psychiatrists refer to such reactions as "adjustment disorders," and the people who suffer from them as the "worried well." A simple rule of thumb prevails: If the symptoms gradually clear up as the problem subsides, you've probably had an ordinary adjustment disorder. If not, you may be suffering from clinical depression.

Increasingly, researchers are seeing depression as a "disregulation" of the brain's reaction to stress. Even a bad case of clinical depression will not go on forever: the disease tends to run its course in nine months to a year. Unfortunately, it often returns. The initial episode has what researchers call a "kindling effect"; it seems to carve a pathway in the brain that leaves 70% of its victims vulnerable to another attack. "While a psychosocial stress can be involved in the onset of the first episode, the triggering mechanism for subsequent depressions can be more autonomous," says Robert Post, the NIMH scientist who developed the kindling theory. "Once someone has a number of depressions, they are likely to happen on their own."

As with Thorazine for schizophrenia, the first breakthrough for treating depression with drugs came accidentally. Doctors using a tuberculosis drug called iproniazid in 1952 discovered that the medicine had a remarkable effect on the mood of their patients: they literally began dancing in the halls.

Five years later, scientists found out why. Iproniazid falls into the category of antidepressant medications known as MAO inhibitors, which work by blocking the breakdown of two potent neurotransmitters—norepinephrine and serotonin—and allowing them to bathe the nerve endings for an extended length of time. A second category of antidepressants, the tricyclics (so named for their triple-carbon-ring structure), raises the level of these neurotransmitters in the brain by slowing the rate at which they are reabsorbed by nerve cells. The third and newest category of medications, represented by the popular Prozac and a number of other drugs, inhibits the uptake of zero serotonin alone. As a result of this specificity, these newest drugs reverse depressive symptoms without the severe side effects of other antidepressants, which can cause low blood pressure, dizziness and blurred vision if not monitored. (Some people allege, however, that Prozac can cause irrational behavior and suicidal tendencies.)

The effectiveness of Prozac, which is the world's top-selling antidepressant, has led some researchers to speculate that serotonin is the key regulator of mood, and that depression is essentially a shortfall of serotonin. But the theory has some serious flaws. If serotonin is so important, why do the tricyclics (which affect both norepinephrine and serotonin) work slightly better than the drugs that act on serotonin alone? And why, since these drugs act quickly to change the serotonin levels in the brain, does it take up to a month for their effects to be felt? Finally, some scientists wonder how a single neurotransmitter could trigger the disruptions of sleep, appetite, memory, learning and sexuality that characterize a typical depressive episode. The nerve endings responsible for these functions, after all, are located in totally different regions of the brain.

Some scientists believe that the neurotransmitters are just links in a chain of reactions and that the real master molecules of mood reside higher up in that chain. One leading candidate: a substance called corticotropin-releasing hormone, or CRH, which is pumped directly into the spinal fluid and thus bathes the entire brain at once. Discovered in 1981 by researchers studying the biochemistry of stress, CRH is known to promote vigilance and decrease interest in food and sex when administered in small doses. In higher doses, it triggers anxiety. When Philip Gold, chief of the clinical neuroendocrinology branch of the NIMH, began looking for the hormone in his depressed patients, he found it was not only elevated, but elevated all the time—even during sleep. What looked like depression was really a state of hyper-arousal, a kind of permanent flight-or-fight response. "In melancholia," explains Gold, "CRH gets stuck."

CRH may be the master molecule of more than just depression. This stress-related substance is also elevated in people suffering from obsessive-compulsive disorders and eating disorders such as anorexia and bulimia. Equally intriguing is the fact that the same drugs used to treat depression are effective against all these conditions and against panic attacks as well. Some researchers have therefore concluded that the diverse disorders may in fact be linked. "Depression may be only the tip of the iceberg of a family of dysfunctions," says James Hudson, a psychiatrist at Harvard.

Much work remains to be done to explain the connection between these disorders and determine why abnormal levels of CRH would lead to one set of symptoms in one person and another in someone else. Genetics may ultimately hold many of the answers. But it is clear that the study of depression and the drugs that relieve it has opened a breathtaking view on the mysterious world of human mood and emotion—and provided new ways to calm some of its most troubling storms. —*Reported by* *Andrew Purvis/New York and Dick Thompson/ Washington*

RECOVERY FEVER

BABY-BOOMERS AND CLUB KIDS ARE TURNING TWELVE STEP PROGRAMS INTO A 90s SCENE

Melinda Blau

"Tonight," Mary announces, "My topic is what we mean by sharing our 'experience, strength, and hope.'"

There are groans. Mary isn't surprised. This Alcoholics Anonymous meeting—in a church basement in East Hampton—is filled with vacationing Manhattanites, tanned, youthful-looking, dressed in weekend chic. Mary, who's leading the discussion, hadn't expected them to like the topic she'd chosen.

"What they really wanted to talk about was relationships," Mary laments after the meeting. "And that's *all* they want to talk about. This isn't what AA used to be!"

She should know: She's a 34-year veteran who joined AA in desperation in 1957, after awakening one pitch-black night in her car, which was wrapped around a fire hydrant. Mary had no idea how she'd got there.

And so—though she was convinced she was joining the "dregs of society"—she ventured into an AA meeting. She was, at 35, by far the youngest person in the room and one of the few women. "Some of the old-timers were skeptical about whether I could really be an alcoholic," she says. "They told me to take the cotton out of my ears and stuff it in my mouth!" Mary thinks some of the newer members she sees these days could do with a little of that old-time advice. She finds it hard to tolerate the way many of them stroll nonchalantly into meetings, acting as if they've just joined the latest social club—as if they're just there to meet people. "Today, we're getting that Me Generation in," she says disdainfully. "A lot of them come in saying they're alcoholics—because the rehabs tell them they are. They just want to belong to something! I wish they would just listen and shut up. It's a chance for them to experience some kind of recovery that isn't so self-centered."

There's no doubt that being "in the rooms" (attending meetings) bears far less stigma than it did in the fifties. Mary is glad that people have lost their sense of shame about getting help and are coming into "the program" younger than they used to. (These days, almost half of the members are 21-to-40-year-olds, and a third of the members are women.)

But there's a downside. The baby-boomers and club kids flooding into the meetings can seem awfully self-involved. Whenever somebody who's been called on to "share" (respond to the speaker's story of his recovery or to the chosen topic) launches into the dread phrase "I've been going through some changes" or "I'm in a lot of pain today," AA veterans get that sinking feeling. They know they're probably in for a fuzzy monologue about the pills the speaker has popped, the cocaine he's snorted, the food she's binged on, arguments he's had with his lover, talk about her rotten childhood, his job anxieties, the Prozac she's been taking for depression, her co-dependency—everything but alcohol.

These maunderings can be plenty off-putting—and, to tentative first-timers, bewildering. "I must have been sober twenty years before I even heard about pain at an AA meeting," Mary snaps. "We used to talk about sober experience, which showed the strength of the program and gave the newcomer hope. Nowadays, 'experience' is whatever happened that day—from which I get neither strength nor hope!" Erin—a fifteen-year AA member—agrees. "These people have this incredible need to draw attention to themselves. They come up to a speaker during the break and say, 'I need to share—please call on me.' That was unheard of years ago! Why can't they just talk to that person then and there? They need the floor!"

WHEN THEY HEAR THE DREAD PHRASE "I'M IN A LOT OF PAIN TODAY," AA VETERANS GET THAT SINKING FEELING.

ONE WONDERS IF EVEN THE VISIONARY BILL WILSON, who co-founded AA in the thirties, could have foreseen the recovery fever that has led so many into the program (membership has more than doubled in New York City since 1978)—and made them so open about it. It's likely he'd find even more amazing the alphabet soup of groups (see box) that have spun off from AA—everything from Anorexic Bulimics Anonymous, Batterers Anonymous, Dual Disorders Anonymous, Families of Sex Offenders Anonymous, and Homosexuals Anonymous to Unwed Parents Anonymous, Workaholics Anonymous, Victims Anonymous, and Youth Emotions Anonymous. Last, and far from least, are the many "co-dependent" and "adult children of" groups set up for people whose lives are entwined with one or another of these sufferers.

Most of the spinoffs base their programs on the Twelve Steps that Wilson and his early colleagues devised to guide AA members into recovery. Step One involves admitting that you are powerless over alcohol. Members are told that their "disease" renders them out of control. Recovery is a matter not of weakness or lack of will but of willingness to "turn it over," which is where Step Two—accepting the notion that a Higher Power exists—comes in. Step Three asks you to rely on that entity—be it a deity, a spiritual force, or the collective power of the group—to guide you. ("Turning it over to a Higher Power" doesn't mean abdicating responsibility: You may have a disease, but you are now responsible for your actions.) Steps Four through Nine encourage you to look at yourself, take an honest "inventory" of your faults, and "make amends" to anyone you've hurt. Finally, Steps Ten through Twelve are about continuing to be honest and open and extending yourself, which includes carrying the message to other alcoholics.

Has AA's popularity—and the development of all those spinoff groups—so watered down the program that it's no longer effective? Many acknowledge that some meetings have lost their focus. But, they say, AA still cleaves to Wilson's original tenets. Alcoholics who have tried years of psychotherapy, antidepressants, or simply trying to "will" themselves away from a drink still find in AA something that finally works. When they walk into a roomful of people like themselves, they find a supportive community that traditional one-on-one psychotherapy can't replicate. "These people are almost intractable by conventional methods," explains Dr. Donald Nathanson, senior attending psychiatrist at Institute of Pennsylvania Hospital in Philadelphia, "but if you group alcoholics together, they know each other's tricks, they begin talking about them, and they begin to heal each other."

Meetings also help people break through their isolation and learn how to trust again. "They talk about feelings," notes Dr. Jonathan Lampert, a psychiatrist at the Ackerman Institute for Family Therapy, who has had extensive clinical experience with alcoholics and addicts and has observed "hundreds" of other kinds of Twelve Step meetings. "It's very compelling to have someone begin speaking what is unspeakable, know what is unknowable. And they have a protocol to follow—the steps—and others with whom they can mitigate the shame. That's very powerful."

Through AA, millions have recovered, and will continue to recover, from the ravages of alcoholism. It boils down to support and identification—the idea of one drunk helping another.

TO FIND MEETINGS THEY LIKE, HOWEVER, TODAY'S NEWcomers may need perseverance as well as the patience to look beyond the confusing digressions and egotistic behavior of some members. Now that rehabs are pouring hundreds of newly sober people into these programs each week and countless others are coming in on their own, the balance between oldtimers (who have stories of long-term recovery that can encourage others) and newcomers (who do not) has become skewed. It's harder than it used to be to find "powers of example"—people who have attained a sense of what serenity is all about and who are willing to extend themselves.

"You don't see people reaching out the way we used to," observes Kelly, a lover of Quaaludes and Jack Daniel's who joined AA ten years ago, when she was 28. "The other night, I heard a woman tell someone that she couldn't pick her up to take her to a meeting [this kind of help for a newcomer was once a common practice]. The driver thought the newcomer lived too far out of her way. What was the woman supposed to do—drink?"

AA's primary purpose, as stated in its preamble, has always been to "stay sober and help other alcoholics to achieve sobriety." ("You learned how to not pick up that first drink—a day at a time," Mary says. "Then you reached out to others.") Though there are greeters at the door at some meetings, gone are the days when most people routinely introduced themselves to whoever sat next to them or made sure they approached a newcomer during a break. Maxi—a nice Jewish girl from the Five Towns whose heroin addiction landed her in jail, in an abandoned building on Ninth Avenue, and finally "in Times Square, turning tricks"—came into AA eleven years ago, when she was 37. "In those days," she says, "someone would announce, 'We're all going for coffee!' That's how I learned to socialize when I came into the rooms. That happens a lot less now."

Today, members are also less willing to "do service"—run a meeting, make coffee, stack chairs, put out program literature, or even be a sponsor (a person who welcomes phone calls and guides newcomers through the steps). Worse, some meetings are run by tightly knit cliques—groups of friends who came into the fellowship around the same time, got sober with one another, and socialize outside meetings as well. As friends embrace in the doorway or shout at one another across the room, a newcomer is likely to feel left out. Many members admit that they don't ask strangers out for coffee as often; they don't use the ten-minute break to talk to someone who seems distressed or lonely; they are more clannish; they just don't take the time.

Georgeanne, in AA for the past ten years, admits she is overwhelmed by the new faces and less willing to give of herself than she was when she first came in. Her attitude sums up a pervasive thirtysomething mentality: "I don't really pay attention to them until they've been coming to meetings for 90 days—to see if they're serious. I've got a husband and a baby and a full-time job, and these newcomers can go on for hours!"

Despite these problems, some veteran AA members are amazed and heartened by the program's growth and the diversity of its membership. "The Woodstock generation has arrived—and I'm glad!" exclaims Steven, 65, who joined AA "when Eisenhower was president." He is unconcerned about the criticism that there's not enough talk of alcohol in AA rooms. "If they listen closely, they'll hear it," he says. "They'll certainly hear about addiction and all the other problems that are common in early sobriety." Moreover, he says, newcomers not only keep the meetings going and growing, they add spice to his life. "I've learned more about rela-

MESSIES ANONYMOUS? DO GROUPS LIKE THIS TRIVIALIZE THE AA CONCEPT?

tionships in these last ten years," he says. "And remember, I came from a closeted era. These young people say things to a roomful of 100 people that I wouldn't say to my parish priest!"

SALVATION OR SELF-INDULGENCE?

THE TERM *recovery*, ONCE APPLIED SOLELY TO ALcoholics and drug addicts, has expanded to include millions more who are afflicted with the maladies of modern living: the people who eat, work, smoke, shop, gamble, exercise, or love too much; the sufferers of certifiable behavioral syndromes; the sex addicts, incest perpetrators, and pedophiles and their victims—the "survivors" of rape, child abuse, molestation.

Messies Anonymous? Emotions Anonymous? Are these fellowships *necessary*? Don't groups with names like these diminish the seriousness of a program like AA, which was founded for people whose disease could cost them their lives?

"We seem to be turning everything into a pathology," complains Daryl, who has been in AA for eleven years. She is puzzled by the proliferation of groups for "co-dependents," the people who coddle the addicted and afflicted. (If you believe the recovery gurus who are trying to sell their books, that's 95 percent of the population.) Daryl points out that women have been *socialized* to put others' feelings and needs above their own—and that's one of the hallmarks of co-dependency as it is defined today. (The term is an outgrowth of "co-alcoholic," someone who is *dependent* on the alcoholic. He has his arms around the bottle; she has her arms around him.) "Caring is a wonderful thing, even in a relationship with an addict, but when we care only about the *other* person, we get into trouble," Daryl believes. "Nor are certain aspects of humanness—like emotions—a 'sickness.'"

"The Twelve Step principles are definitely being commodified," says Frank Riessman, director of the National Self-Help Clearinghouse (25 West 43rd Street, Room 620, 642-2944), which provides information on all kinds of self-help groups. Between 1978 and 1984 alone, the aggressive marketing of recovery treatment resulted in a 350 percent increase in private alcoholic-treatment facilities plus the establishment of rehabs that take in not only alcoholics and drug addicts but gamblers, overeaters, co-dependents, and adult children of any type of dysfunctional family. These inpatient facilities have become the "spas" of recovery.

Riessman reminds us not to forget why all these groups have sprung up. "Recovery therapy arose primarily because other methods were failing to reach large numbers of people," he says. Indeed, Jonathan Lampert maintains, many mental-health practitioners still aren't knowledgeable about addiction, and "they're often overwhelmed by the kinds of extreme behaviors addicts talk about and bring into the office." He believes that for many types of problems, the various Twelve Step offshoots can help people open up. "Many sophisticated people can't stop overeating, but they do it with OA [Overeaters Anonymous]."

Since the newer, less stable programs are works in progress, many of the more recent me-too programs do not have as much to offer as Twelve Step fellowships established prior to 1970—and certainly not as much as AA. They may not be very well defined; members often talk more about problems than about solutions. (When Lindsey, an avid programgoer, recently tried a meeting of Co-Dependents Anonymous—CODA, one of the more popular new additions to the city's menu—she says, "I didn't hear recovery; I heard weekly reports.") Some meetings in these fellowships are not orderly; some are run by the more dominant people in the room and susceptible to personal whims. (In AA,

which is guided by its Twelve Traditions and better organized, "group conscience" guides decision-making.) Some groups, predictably, have already gone by the wayside, like Valium Anonymous. And there's at least one fellowship whose members couldn't be located for interviews—Isolators Anonymous.

That so many people are members of more than one program, even when they are newly sober, makes many veteran AA members suspicious. Maxi maintains, "If alcoholism is your primary disease, you have to get your foundation in AA. When you go to a lot of different fellowships, you may not have to focus on your problems—or on changing your behavior."

Longtime members of Al-Anon—AA's companion program and the oldest and most stable of the "-Anons" (fellowships for families and friends of addicts)—are also distressed. Spouses and other members of alcoholic families used to learn at Al-Anon meetings that they "enabled" the alcoholic by denying, rationalizing, or covering up his drinking, and the program taught them how to change their own behavior. Now just about everybody is a "co-dependent" or worried about being one—and all flock to Al-Anon. "We used to talk about the alcoholics in our lives," says Lilly, an Al-Anon member whose mother is an alcoholic and who also tends to get romantically involved with alcoholics. "Now people in our meetings talk about relationships with their lovers whether they're alcoholic or not."

TWELVE STEPS FOR EVERYBODY?

THERE ARE MANY WHO ARGUE THAT WE DON'T NEED ALL the me-too programs out there. But it's important to resist the tendency to trivialize. The pain one hears in those "other" Twelve Step rooms is no different from the pain of an alcoholic resisting a drink. The woman who goes to an Overeaters Anonymous meeting and admits she hides cookies under her bed to feel safe but that nothing she eats ever makes her feel satisfied, or the man who attends a Gamblers Anonymous meeting because he is afraid he's going to blow a month's pay at Aqueduct, may be talking to someone about these problems and fears for the first time.

Likewise, at a meeting of Sexaholics Anonymous, you're bound to hear the agony of a man (males far outnumber females) who can't stop himself from going to the porn shops on Broadway, from cheating on his wife, or from picking up a prostitute—and that, these days, is as deadly as drug or alcohol addiction.

Dr. Robert DuPont, clinical professor of psychiatry at Georgetown University and a former director of the National Institute on Drug Abuse, applauds the fact that Twelve Step programs have splintered into smaller, very specialized groups whose "cultural specificity" allows people to identify with one another more readily. Some meetings cover particular topics, like incest and being HIV-positive, or serve certain groups—young people, homosexuals, handicapped members.

But does the AA prescription work for behavioral problems—like compulsive gambling or sex addiction? Can someone with a food disorder, for example, be helped by a program originally designed around complete abstinence?

"I've watched people get well," Dr. DuPont insists. By affiliating themselves with these programs, he says, "people are not only saying, 'That's me,' they're finding better ways to live."

Donald Nathanson is more cautious, especially when it comes to programs like Adult Children of Alcoholics and Sex and Love Addicts Anonymous, where the tendency is to point a finger at someone else. "The major focus is not on a person's responsibility for his own behavior but on the inevitability that he behaves a certain way because others made him this way."

Still, Nathanson thinks these programs *can* work—if the person is willing to expend some effort. "If you can think about your inner life once a day, you're doing pretty well," he says. "You reinforce the fact that you're an alcoholic or that you resort to sex as an anodyne or do any of a number of types of behavior that are a detour from facing your own feelings."

Motivation is all—and, according to Nathanson, "some of the people in these other programs haven't suffered as much as alcoholics or addicts. So they don't have as much need and don't go to as many meetings. One has to ask about their problem behavior. 'How long have they been doing it? How much of their world have they lost because of it? And how desperately do they want to change?' "

Psychologist Stan J. Katz, co-author of *The Codependency Conspiracy*—a thoughtful, albeit controversial, critique of the marketing of recovery—has less confidence in using the Twelve Steps for behavior problems. "It's like using penicillin for every disease. AA was developed specifically for alcohol. It is a fairly good program for alcoholics, and the program has a decent crossover for people addicted to drugs. But many people go to meetings for the social life, or because they have other problems that they're trying to cure on a free basis."

Katz maintains that you can't apply a program based on abstinence to food disorders or relationship issues, because you can't completely abstain from eating or being in relationships. Thus, he fears, "the people who need genuine intervention are not getting it—they're going to Twelve Step meetings instead."

Critics of the recovery movement also challenge the widespread use of the "disease model," originally applied only to alcoholism. The theory holds that alcoholics are not morally responsible for their behavior. They have an "allergy" to liquor: The first drink triggers a craving, and then they can't stop themselves any more than a diabetic can control the way his body reacts to sugar.

Labeling all these difficulties "diseases," regardless of their degree of severity, says Katz, is neither scientifically warranted nor helpful to the patient—although it does tend to drum up business for the recovery movement. Katz thinks these labels cause people to perceive themselves as victims, to use the label to excuse their behavior, and to become dependent on the program they're going to: They are eternally "recovering," never "recovered."

Dr. Marc Galanter, professor of psychiatry and director of the Division of Alcoholism and Drug Abuse at New York University Medical Center and director of the alcohol-and-drug-abuse program at Bellevue Hospital Center, has studied cults and religious groups as well as AA. He characterizes Twelve Step programs as part of a "zealous social movement." He maintains that at stress-

THE TWELVE STEP HIT PARADE

ALTHOUGH NOT ALL "ANONYMOUS" OR "-ANON" GROUPS ARE GUIDED BY AA'S TWELVE Steps, nearly 100 self-help groups are. Below is a partial listing of the more popular clone groups for various types of addicts and people affected by their behavior. The information comes from the 1990 edition of *The Self-Help Sourcebook* ($10), available from the American Self-Help Clearinghouse, St. Clares–Riverside Medical Center, Denville, New Jersey 07834 (201-625-7101).

- 1935 **Alcoholics Anonymous**—alcoholics
- 1951 **Al-Anon**—families and friends of alcoholics
- 1953 **Narcotics Anonymous**—addicts
- 1957 **Alateen**—twelve- to eighteen-year-olds who have alcoholics in their lives
- 1957 **Gamblers Anonymous**—compulsive gamblers
- 1960 **Gam-Anon**—families and friends of compulsive gamblers
- 1960 **Overeaters Anonymous**—people with compulsive-eating disorders
- 1967 **Nar-Anon**—families and friends of addicts
- 1970 **Emotional Health Anonymous**—people with mental-health problems
- 1971 **Emotions Anonymous**—people who want to gain better emotional health
- 1971 **Families Anonymous**—relatives and friends of drug or alcohol abusers or of people with behavioral problems
- 1975 **O-Anon**—friends and relatives of people with compulsive-eating disorders
- 1976 **Debtors Anonymous**—credit-card abusers, under-earners, and overspenders

- 1976 **Augustine Fellowship, Sex and Love Addicts Anonymous**—people with obsessive/compulsive sexual behavior or emotional attachment
- 1977 **Sex Addicts Anonymous**—compulsive-sex addicts
- 1978 **Drugs Anonymous** (formerly Pills Anonymous)—chemical addicts
- 1979 **Pill Addicts Anonymous**—those addicted to mood-changing pills and drugs
- 1979 **Sexaholics Anonymous**—people with sexually destructive thinking and behavior
- 1980 **Incest Survivors Anonymous**—incest survivors
- 1982 **Cocaine Anonymous**—cocaine addicts
- 1982 **Survivors of Incest Anonymous**—victims of childhood sexual abuse
- 1984 **Adult Children of Alcoholics**—now interpreted to include adult children of people with other problems
- 1984 **S-Anon**—relatives and friends of sex addicts
- 1985 **Nicotine Anonymous** (formerly Smokers Anonymous)—nicotine addicts
- 1986 **Co-Dependents Anonymous** (CODA)—people who grew up in dysfunctional families and have trouble with relationships

THE TWELVE STEP PHILOSOPHY URGES SUFFERING PEOPLE TO GIVE TO OTHERS—TO GET OUT OF THEMSELVES.

ful times, some people are more susceptible to becoming dependent on the program: "The more you are vulnerable, the more you glom on to something that seems to offer more permanence."

You can usually spot the kind of people who "hide in the rooms." For them, getting sober becomes an end unto itself. But Mary stresses that it's not AA that causes this—it's the individual. "AA is a bridge back to life. It was never meant to *be* your life." Jonathan Lampert notes that the program-shoppers who go from room to room "use therapists the same way!" While he concedes that Twelve Step principles can sometimes be misinterpreted or even abused, he holds that the best starting point for talking about your problems is still a Twelve Step program.

DOES IT WORK IF YOU WORK IT?

A MAJOR STUMBLING BLOCK FOR SOME WHO TRY AA AND its spinoffs is swallowing the idea of a Higher Power. "People think of us as a bunch of religious nuts," admits Nan Robertson, an AA member for the past sixteen years and the author of *Getting Better: Inside Alcoholics Anonymous*. Many people have trouble with the "God part," she says. The word *God* appears in four of the Twelve Steps and is mentioned 132 times in *Alcoholics Anonymous* (better known as *The Big Book*).

Meetings in this city are particularly "New York" in tone—intense, sharp-edged, laced with psychological jargon. But, perhaps because of New York's diverse population, some meetings here don't have the religious overtones one finds in other parts of the country; closing with the Lord's Prayer makes many non-Christian members uncomfortable. Instead, meetings often end with the nonsectarian Serenity Prayer: "God grant me the serenity to accept the things I cannot change, courage to change the things I can, and wisdom to know the difference." Inevitably, that's followed by a rousing "Keep comin' back—it works if you work it!"

But the "God part" keeps some people from "working it." For them, Rational Recovery Systems (RR), a five-year-old organization that's close to 300 groups strong, hopes to provide an alternative.

RR, which is based on psychologist Albert Ellis's rational-emotive therapy, appeals to thinkers, not believers, according to RR's *Small Book*. In RR, the alcoholic's or addict's will and intelligence are called upon to help change his behavior. RR doesn't believe an alcoholic is powerless, nor must he be forever recovering. Alcoholics, RR says, can look within themselves for strength and use "reason to light the way."

Every RR meeting has a professional "adviser," a counselor, therapist, M.D., minister, or nurse who donates time and allegedly has a minor role. An adviser can "spot a problem—like symptoms of suicide," explains Vincent Fox, a member who also sits on the board of directors of RR. For the most part, however, the adviser takes a backseat to the "coordinator," an experienced member who "manages" the meetings. Twelve Step meetings allow no "cross talk" (no advising or answering one another during the meeting); RR is run more like group therapy.

Predictably, there is some AA–bashing at RR meetings, 90 percent of whose members are AA dropouts. And because the organization is so young, it seems to be suffering some of the same growing pains that also beleaguer younger AA offshoots—instability and a lack of long-term sobriety. "We're not at the final stage of our evolution," Fox admits. "Ten years from now, we'll evolve into something more polished, more mature."

A few inpatient institutions now offer RR, in addition to the usual Twelve Step fare, to the newly recovering. To help shore up its claims, RR is submitting to efficacy studies. For now, the jury is out on new groups like RR and Secular Organizations for Sobriety, another non-spiritual alternative.

But then, the flow of bodies into Twelve Step programs has not been inspired by evidence. The truth is, there's very little scientific proof that AA works. The "anonymous" nature of the program, a safeguard incorporated to protect people from the shame of declaring themselves alcoholics (*that's* a bit of an irony, these days), as well as AA's tradition of resisting professional involvement, has made it difficult to monitor.

Dr. Galanter's 1990 study is a noteworthy exception. Galanter and his team surveyed a group of 100 recovering alcoholic or dually addicted doctors who had received inpatient treatment in which AA affiliation was part of the program. They had been clean and sober an average of 33 months at the time of the study.

"After all was said and done," Galanter reports, "they rated their AA experiences as the most influential aspect of their recovery." Though Galanter allows that this was a select and highly committed population, he believes that the findings can be generalized. "There are more than 1 million members nationwide. They wouldn't be going if they didn't think it helped. Certainly, in my experience with the patients I've treated, that's the case."

Robert DuPont adds that many program-bashers, especially his peers in the medical profession, are skeptical about AA and other Twelve Step programs because "it's a language that's alien to professionals. The Establishment sees it as a fringe approach—small, quirky, nonintellectual, cult-oriented, religious—that's the dominant view. They don't understand it."

CLEARLY, TWELVE STEP PROGRAMS DON'T WORK FOR everyone—nor does any one type of treatment. Lampert and others call for an integrated approach, combining self-help with a thoughtful psychological assessment that factors in personality, family history, and the person's context today—his relationships, work situation, socioeconomic status, among other things.

As the AA saying goes, "Some are sicker than others." Some people need only the support of a fellowship and the education and guidance that a Twelve Step program provides. Others may want—or need—what Donald Nathanson calls "a thicker soup: something that allows them to deal with their own personal feelings more on a one-to-one basis."

Many of the criticisms of Twelve Step programs are well taken. People going to these meetings might want to ponder whether they have isolated themselves there, doing only Twelve Step activities with Twelve Step friends. If they feel "stuck" or like victims, or if their conversations repeatedly center on the past or on other people's behavior, it may mean they are dealing with issues that warrant professional treatment. People who are members of more than one fellowship should think about whether they're really getting something different from each one—or whether program-hopping helps them avoid taking responsibility for their lives.

TO PROSPECTIVE AND NEOPHYTE TWELVE STEPPERS, ED Madara, director of the American Self-Help Clearinghouse (see box), which publishes *The Self-Help Sourcebook*, says, "Twelve Step programs constitute the majority of all self-help programs. And people are getting help." But look out, he says. Not all "anonymous" programs are necessarily built on the Twelve Steps. In fact, some groups masquerade as self-help, and some are commercial enterprises. (One doctor, for instance, wrote a book on pathological jealousy and called Madara to network a group called Jealousy Anonymous.)

In the past, it was suggested that you try six meetings of the fellowship you're interested in joining. Most veterans suggest doubling that figure, because nowadays it may take a while to feel comfortable at a meeting and find a group you like. Find a "home group," Mary advises. "If you don't belong to a group, you don't become part of the structure of the program."

A newcomer would be wise to adopt an attitude of cautious optimism. At some meetings—certainly not all—there is considerable whining; some sponsors are controlling; and there are "thirteen-steppers" out there: members who try to get vulnerable newcomers into bed. The point is, one can't assume that all people in

Twelve Step programs are virtuous. As one member put it, "We're sick people getting better, not bad people getting good."

At the same time, the ever-increasing acceptance of the Twelve Step philosophy, which places a premium on "honesty, openness, and willingness," offers suffering people a place to turn. The AA program (and its copies) urges people to be tolerant and to give to others—in essence, to get out of themselves. This is precisely the kind of "moral jogging"—a way to practice selflessness—that psychologist Martin Seligman, author of *Learned Optimism,* prescribes to combat the depression that comes from "overcommitment to the self and undercommitment to the common good." Unfortunately, as Seligman puts it, "giving to others and spending serious time, money, and effort enhancing the common good does not come naturally to the present generation."

Help yourself: self-care for emotional problems

NESHAMA FRANKLIN

I had no choice," Kirsten Nielsen says. "I just had to gut it out." That's how this 42-year-old mother of two sons describes her successful two-year effort to manage her manic-depression without lithium. Nielsen, of Santa Cruz, California, elimi-

Support groups are comforting, non-judgmental, and inexpensive.

What's wrong with therapy?

It is estimated that almost one-third of the population receives professional therapy sometime in their lives. At an average cost of about $65 an hour, psychotherapy is a big business. Although there is no doubt that it is beneficial to many, there is a great deal wrong with it—both the way it is presented to the public and the way it is practiced.

The abuses can be grouped into four categories: misleading promises about its scope and effects; use of one kind of therapy when another is more effective; use of psychotherapy when alternative treatments are superior in results or cost; and too-lengthy terms of treatment.

Promises, promises

Psychotherapy is promoted as useful for all the traditional psychological problems, as well as new problems discovered almost daily: midlife crisis, computer phobia, and conversion to unpopular religious beliefs. Of 500 people who came to one large New York psychiatric clinic for evaluation, therapy was recommended for all but four. Imagine the outcry if surgery were recommended for 99 percent of patients coming to a medical clinic. Whenever a method is universally prescribed, one of two things must be true: The Millennium has arrived or something is seriously wrong.

Another promise of therapy is overwhelming change of personality. Fringe therapies such as primal scream and est are not alone in claiming dramatic change. Psychoanalysis, the oldest and in many people's eyes the most respectable therapy, produces, in the words of Anna Freud, "thoroughgoing personality changes," and some therapists talk about reorganizing or remaking personalities. But as New York psychologist Albert Ellis notes, ther-

apists talk and write about their most spectacular successes; "the poor, partial, or later-relapsing 'successful' cases are much less often published." Only a small percentage of clients are changed to a degree that justifies using terms like "recovery" or "cure."

Which therapy?

The second abuse of therapy is in using a form that is less effective or efficient than another. We now know that certain methods work better for certain problems. Brief sex therapy has demonstrated its superiority for problems like lack of orgasm, premature ejaculation, and erection complaints. Behavioral methods have proven best for phobias, obsessive-compulsive problems, and some social skill deficiencies. Depression can be successfully attacked using specialized short-term therapies. Finally, hypnosis, relaxation training, and cognitive therapy have shown promise in the control of pain.

Since the majority of therapists do not practice behavioral or sex therapy, many problems undoubtedly are being treated with inferior methods. And worse, the patients are not informed of choices.

Alternatives

The third category of abuse is using psychotherapy when alternative treatments are more effective or less costly. Many people who find their way into a therapist's office would benefit from drugs they are not offered. If the therapist is a psychologist, clinical social worker, psychiatric nurse, or marriage counselor, he or she cannot prescribe drugs.

Medication is not the only alternative to psychological therapy. There is considerable evidence that professional therapy is no more beneficial for a number of problems than attending self-help groups (many of which are free or relatively inexpensive), or just talking to

Reprinted from *Utne Reader*, March/April 1987, pp. 33–39. Excerpt from *Medical Self-Care*, Winter 1984. Reprinted by permission of Medical Self-Care Magazine, Point Reyes, CA. One year subscription $15.00.

nated lithium using a unique self-management regimen she developed in partnership with San Francisco psychiatrist Dr. Jeffry Ordover. Ordover warned her that living without lithium would be "the hardest thing she would ever do." Nielsen learned that he was right. Since its introduction in the early 1970s, lithium carbonate has become much more than simply the "drug of choice" to control the debilitating mood swings of manic-depression. Many psychiatrists consider it a "miracle drug."

Nielsen and Ordover are quiet pioneers on the frontiers of the mental health system. They are breaking new ground beyond traditional psychotherapy and drug treatments. The trail is rocky, but they are not alone. Growing numbers of ex-mental patients and people troubled by serious emotional problems are coping successfully with their conditions using alternative therapies based on support groups and other self-care practices.

Numerous self-help and support groups around North America help participants deal with a whole range of personal problems, often as adjuncts to professional therapy and/or medical treatment. Many focus on mental health problems—phobias, compulsions, coping with traumatic events or chronic problems, or just dealing with emotional stress in general. Some ex-mental patients have formed groups that

an interested but untrained person.

Psychologists at Vanderbilt University assigned young men with garden variety neuroses to one of two groups of therapists. The first consisted of the best professional psychotherapists in the area, with an average 23 years of experience; the second group was made up of college professors with reputations of being good people to talk to but with no training in psychotherapy. Therapists and professors saw their clients for no more than 25 hours. The results: "Patients undergoing psychotherapy with college professors showed . . . quantitatively as much improvement as patients treated by experienced professional psychotherapists."

Research indicates that Alcoholics Anonymous is as useful as professional therapy for treating alcoholics. The cure rate isn't high—addictions being resistant to change—but therapy doesn't work any better. Likewise, when it comes to weight problems and drug abuse, no data support the contention that professional therapy is more effective than groups like Weight Watchers. Why induct drinkers, smokers, overweight people, and drug abusers into lengthy, often expensive, and usually fruitless therapy?

How long has this been going on?

The fourth abuse of psychotherapy is carrying it on interminably. Although a good deal of therapy consists of fewer than 20 sessions, much of the brief work is done in clinics and agencies where time limits are enforced. In private practice, where therapists are free to do as they choose, lengthy therapy is often the rule.

What's wrong with therapy taking two, four, or more years? Only one thing: Although for decades the bias among therapists has been that lengthy therapy is best, there is no evidence that longer is better. The few therapies

At an average cost of $65 an hour, psychotherapy is big business. And as is often the case with big business, consumers must be wary.

that have demonstrated effectiveness—behavioral therapy, cognitive therapy, and sex therapy—are all typically brief. Not one of the longer psychotherapies has demonstrated its superiority to briefer treatment for any problem. In the last two decades a small but vocal group of psychoanalysts have called lengthy therapy unnecessary and have offered evidence that changes can be brought about in fewer than 25 sessions.

—Bernie Zilbergeld
Science 86

Excerpted with permission from Science 86 *(June 1986). Time, Inc. has since acquired* Science 86 *and merged it with* Discover *magazine. Subscriptions: $24/yr. (12 issues) from Discover, Time-Life Bldg., 541 N. Franklin Court, Chicago, IL 60611.*

Got a problem? See a friend.

For far too long people have been led to believe that the person suffering from an excess of life's problems needs "expert" medical and psychotherapeutic intervention (thus allowing the "patient" to qualify for "illness") to the ultimate detriment of his mental equilibrium and often at considerable financial cost. Such a view is dangerous nonsense. Clearly there are differences between real psychiatric disease such as schizophrenia and manic-depressive illness and those normal but unpleasant mental states that are an inescapable and often valuable part of everyday living.

I believe we need a redefinition of the proper boundaries of psychological illness. We need a tougher, more rigorous and uncompromising attitude toward what does and what does not constitute disease. Therapists have mistakenly categorized millions of people mentally ill when their chief deficiency is an inadequate approach to problems and unrealistic expectations of what life should give them. A huge therapy industry has created itself to minister to, and profit from, the plight of these "neurotics."

For the therapists to take money for mere talk is, I would argue, in many cases both negligent and, despite the purest of motives, irresponsible. They harm the individual in his pursuit of mental health and encourage dependency and sterile introversion. Above all, they delay interminably that brave confronta-tion of life's problems in which alone salvation lies. The widespread popularity of such an approach comes on the fact that talking about ourselves is strongly pleasurable, that we all like to be the center of attention. In pandering to this mildly unworthy desire, these people do us more than a disservice. For, to the extent that such talk-therapy is pleasant, and its withdrawal difficult and traumatic, I would argue that, like Valium and cocaine, it is psychologically addictive. In the short term it may make us feel better—a quick fix of confidence—but over the years we will pay a considerable price in terms of dependency and lowered self-esteem.

Ostensibly opposed to talk-therapists, but in fact sharing their expert/patient approach, are the medico-biologists. Instead of intellectual insights and exotic theories, their stock-in-trade is chemical panaceas that they dish out like candy to individuals who are not ill. In both cases the end result is the same: a passive "patient" prostrate at the feet of the "healer," suffering the psychological pain of guilt as he learns to like himself less.

Talk therapy and Valium offer no solutions in the absence of real illness. They must be replaced by something of value. I offer Moral Therapy, a philosophy based not on fantasies, pseudo-intellectual gymnastics, or chemistry, but on common sense, on what we know in our hearts. Nobody gets paid for prac-

---

combine mutual support with political advocacy.

At a time when U.S. government agencies have cut back on mental health programs, and when traditional networks such as extended families and neighborhood and religious groups may be unavailable, mutual aid groups can provide crucial support for people who feel stigmatized, ignored, or isolated. They offer welcome relief from the waiting lists and bureaucracies that typify what Ralph Nader's Health Research Group called "the mental health maze." Support

The self-help approach and professional services need not be mutually exclusive nor antagonistic.

groups are comforting, non-judgmental, and inexpensive. Sharing insights and down-to-earth techniques for surmounting serious problems inspire those in the group to "keep on keeping on."

Unfortunately, there has been considerable resistance to—and ignorance about—the self-help/support-group movement from the professional community. Physicians and psychotherapists sometimes have difficulty reconciling them with their own clinical, analytical, illness-oriented model. Some professionals criticize support groups for operating with limited knowledge apart from professional guidance, or for basing their approach on "emotion" rather than "science."

The self-help/support-group approach and professional services need not be mutually exclusive nor antagonistic. In fact, if more mental health workers got involved in support-group work, they might find welcome relief from the burn-out that plagues their profession.

ticing Moral Therapy. Nobody profits from solving the problems of others except in feeling that natural satisfaction we all experience when we have been of service. There are no experts, no training institutes, no degrees or examinations, no gurus. There is nothing but us, our experience of life, our warmth and empathy, the voice of our conscience.

In the absence of psychological illness, we can practice the principles of Moral Therapy on ourselves and on others. Contentedness can exist only if self-respect is high. Only if we like ourselves can we be happy. At all times and in all situations we must obey our own moral codes. Only by doing what we ourselves consider to be right and good can we travel the road to self-respect. Insofar as we disregard our moral imperatives we must suffer the psychological pain of guilt. If we use the guilt mechanism properly and recoil from those actions that cause it to operate, it will serve us well. In the absence of disease, then, guilt is good for us.

With the right help from friends and loved ones, we can all learn to like ourselves more. As concerned and forceful friends, we can become the practitioners of a new Moral Therapy. Into the vacuum created by the disappearance of the paid "expert" will step family, friends, priests, neighbors, husbands, wives, and children. For too long their rightful role has been wrongfully usurped by impostors. The time has come for them to reclaim it.

In particular we should realize and encourage others to realize that self-respect is increased by searching out and achieving more difficult rather than easier objectives. By seeking difficulty and avoiding the easy way in pursuit of what we consider to be worthy ambitions, we will like ourselves more.

—Garth Wood

Excerpted with permission from the book The Myth of Neurosis *(1986, $15.96, $7.95 paperback, Harper & Row, 10 E. 53rd St., New York, NY 10022). ©1983, 1986 by Dr. Garth Wood.*

Many support groups deal with serious mental health problems. Two of the largest are Recovery, Inc., and Emotions Anonymous, which sponsor groups throughout North America. Recovery, Inc., was founded in 1937 by Abraham Low, M.D., a Vienna-trained non-Freudian psychiatrist, to supplement after-care services for ex-mental patients. The organization is now open to anyone. Today Recovery, Inc., sponsors about 1,000 support groups that meet weekly throughout North America and abroad.

The groups are led by members who have attended consistently for at least six months, and who have used the techniques successfully themselves. The organization sees itself as a supplement to—not a replacement for—professional therapy and enjoys broad support among psychiatrists and other therapists. Many participants are referred by a therapist.

The presentations at a typical Recovery meeting follow a strict formula: first a brief description of the traumatic incident, then the symptom(s) it provoked. Recovery calls this "spotting," recognizing problems and the reactions they cause. Next comes "coping," a brief rundown of how the person dealt with the incident using either will power or muscle control. Participants also describe the way they would have reacted before their Recovery training. Finally, they "endorse" themselves, pat themselves on the back for their insights and coping actions. Endorsement is often difficult because most people with emotional problems—for that matter, most people in general—tend to negate their accomplishments.

A young man, who seemed markedly nervous and withdrawn, said he'd been to a party where he felt everyone acted cold toward him. He "spotted" this as "fearful temper." ("Fearful temper" and "angry temper" are two sides of the same coin. The former is self-blame, which leads to depression; the latter is blaming others, which leads to acting out.) He started to shake and in

Most people with emotional problems tend to negate their accomplishments.

pre-Recovery days would have screamed and made a scene, but he was able to control the impulse. The group endorsed him for going to the party in the first place. "It's strengthening to do the things you fear." "It's good that you were 'self-led' and not 'symptom-led'." "It's average to feel uncomfortable when you don't know people." (The concept of "being average" comes up frequently in Recovery groups. It's the recognition that one's symptoms are normal, not pathological.) The phrases in quotes came up frequently. At first they sounded like jargon, but I gradually came to appreciate their value as code words that helped the members recognize their hard-won victories over fears and former habits.

Founded in 1971, Emotions Anonymous (EA) is patterned after the original self-help group, Alcoholics Anonymous (AA). EA adapted the AA program of confession, mutual aid, and 24-hour-a-day telephone support among members.

All the "Anonymous" organizations share a simple, homespun, non-religious spirituality. Weekly meetings open with a prayer: "God grant me the serenity to accept the things I cannot change, the courage to change the things I can, and the wisdom to know the difference." Speakers at EA meetings first admit that by themselves they are powerless over their emotions, then say they could be restored to sanity by a power greater than themselves. This power is open to individual interpretation. For some, it's "The Man Upstairs"; for others it's "Life Itself." The focus is on coping, on learning to live in relative peace despite unsolved problems, and on living life "one day at a time."

Although Recovery, Inc., and Emotions Anonymous deal with a broad range of emo-

tional problems, there are also a host of problem-specific groups and support networks. To find one that meets your individual needs, contact your local community mental health center, or the National Self-Help Clearinghouse (33 W. 42nd St., Room 1227, New York, NY 10036).

Co-Counseling is an approach that trains people to give and accept reciprocal emotional support. Co-Counseling classes themselves serve as support groups, and after the training period, each member gets a list of local members available for counseling sessions.

The National Alliance for the Mentally Ill (NAMI) is a grassroots coalition of friends and relatives of those with serious mental health problems. The organization advocates for the mentally ill by promoting improved services.

The American Schizophrenia Association sponsors support groups for the families of schizophrenics, and explores such issues as residential treatment, relaxation training to reduce the side effects of medications, and orthomolecular therapy with vitamin and mineral supplements.

Studies have shown that success of therapy has less to do with methodology than the mere fact of recognizing a problem and deciding to do something about it. If the process of trying to cope with "the slings and arrows of outrageous fortune" seems beyond your strength, take heart. Whatever your situation, others who face similar challenges are eager to help.

Excerpted with permission from Medical Self-Care *(Winter 1984). Subscriptions: $15/yr. (6 issues) from Medical Self-Care, Box 1000, Point Reyes, CA 94956. Back issues: $2.50 from same address.*

The concept of "being average" comes up frequently in recovery groups.

This glossary of psychology terms is included to provide you with a convenient and ready reference as you encounter general terms in your study of psychology and personal growth and behavior that are unfamiliar or require a review. It is not intended to be comprehensive, but taken together with the many definitions included in the articles themselves, it should prove to be quite useful.

Abnormal Irregular, deviating from the norm or average. Abnormal implies the presence of a mental disorder that leads to behavior that society labels as deviant. There is a continuum between normal and abnormal. These are relative terms in that they imply a social judgment. *See* Normal.

Accommodation Process in cognitive development; involves altering or reorganizing the mental picture to make room for a new experience or idea.

Acetylcholine A neurotransmitter involved in memory.

Achievement Drive The need to attain self-esteem, success, or status. Society's expectations strongly influence the achievement motive.

ACTH (Adrenocorticotropic Hormone) The part of the brain called the hypothalamus activates the release of the hormone ACTH from the pituitary gland when a stressful condition exists. ACTH in turn activates the release of adrenal corticoids from the cortex of the adrenal gland.

Action Therapy A general classification of therapy (as opposed to insight therapy) in which the therapist focuses on symptoms rather than on underlying emotional states. Treatment aims at teaching new behavioral patterns rather than at self-understanding. *See* Insight Therapy.

Actor-Observer Attribution The tendency to attribute the behavior of other people to internal causes and the behavior of yourself to external causes.

Acupuncture The technique for curing certain diseases and anesthetizing by inserting needles at certain points of the body, developed in China and now being studied and applied in the West.

Adaptation The process of responding to changes in the environment by altering one's responses to keep one's behavior appropriate to environmental demands.

Addiction Physical dependence on a drug. When a drug causes biochemical changes that are uncomfortable when the drug is discontinued, when one must take ever larger doses to maintain the intensity of the drug's effects, and when desire to continue the drug is strong, one is said to be addicted.

Adjustment How we react to stress; some change that we make in response to the demands placed upon us.

Adrenal Glands Endocrine glands involved in stress and energy regulation.

Affective Disorder Affect means feeling or emotion. An affective disorder is mental illness marked by a disturbance of mood (e.g., manic depression).

Afferent Neuron (Sensory) A neuron that carries messages from the sense organs toward the central nervous system.

Aggression Any act that causes pain or suffering to another. Some psychologists believe that aggressive behavior is instinctual to all species, including man, while others believe that it is learned through the processes of observation and imitation.

Alienation Indifference to or loss of personal relationships. An individual may feel estranged from family members, or, on a broader scale, from society.

All-or-None Law The principle that states that a neuron only fires when a stimulus is above a certain minimum strength (threshold), and that when it fires, it does so at full strength.

Altered State of Consciousness (ASC) A mental state qualitatively different from a person's normal, alert, waking consciousness.

Altruism Behavior motivated by a desire to benefit another person. Altruistic behavior is aided by empathy and is usually motivated internally, not by observable threats or rewards.

Amphetamine A psychoactive drug that is a stimulant. Although used in treating mild depressions or, in children, hyperactivity, its medical uses are doubtful, and amphetamines are often abused. *See* Psychoactive Drug.

Anal Stage Psychosexual stage, during which, according to Freud, the child experiences the first restrictions on his impulses.

Animism The quality of believing life exists in inanimate objects. According to Piaget, animism is characteristic of children's thinking until about age two.

Antisocial Personality Disorder Personality disorder in which individuals who engaged in antisocial behavior experience no guilt or anxiety about their actions; sometimes called sociopathy or psychopathy.

Anxiety An important term that has different meanings for different theories (psychoanalysis, behavior theory); a feeling state of apprehension, dread, or uneasiness. The state may be aroused by an objectively dangerous situation or by a situation that is not objectively dangerous. It may be mild or severe.

Anxiety Disorder Fairly long-lasting disruptions of the person's ability to deal with stress; often accompanied by feelings of fear and apprehension.

Applied Psychology The area of psychology that is most immediately concerned with helping to solve practical problems; includes clinical and counseling psychology, and industrial, environmental, and legal psychology.

Aptitude Tests Tests which are designed to predict what can be accomplished by a person in the future with the proper training.

Arousal A measure of responsiveness or activity; a state of excitement or wakefulness ranging from deepest coma to intense excitement.

Aspiration Level The level of achievement a person strives for. Studies suggest that people can use internal or external standards of performance.

Assertiveness Training Training which helps individuals stand up for their rights while not denying rights of other people.

Assimilation Process in cognitive development; occurs when something new is taken into the child's mental picture of the world.

Association Has separate meanings for different branches of psychology. Theory in cognitive psychology suggests that we organize information so that we can find our memories systematically, that one idea will bring another to mind. In psychoanalysis, the patient is asked to free associate (speak aloud all consecutive thoughts until random associations tend of themselves to form a meaningful whole). *See* Cognitive Psychology; Psychoanalysis.

Association Neurons Neurons that connect with other neurons.

Associationism A theory of learning suggesting that once two stimuli are presented together, one of them will remind a person of the other. Ideas are learned by association with sensory experiences and are not innate. Among the principles of associationism are contiguity (stimuli that occur close together are more likely to be associated than stimuli far apart), and repetition (the more frequently stimuli occur together, the more strongly they become associated).

Attachment Process in which the individual shows behaviors that promote the proximity or contact with a specific object or person.

Attention The tendency to focus activity in a particular direction and to select certain stimuli for further analysis while ignoring or possibly storing for further analysis all other inputs.

Attitude An overall tendency to respond positively or negatively to particular people or objects in a way that is learned through experience and that is made up of feelings (affects), thoughts (evaluations), and actions (conation).

Attribution The process of determining the causes of behavior in a given individual.

Autism A personality disorder in which a child does not respond socially to people.

Autonomic Nervous System The part of the nervous system (the other part is the central nervous system) that is for emergency functions and release of large amounts of energy (sympathetic division) and regulating functions such as digestion and sleep (parasympathetic division). *See* Biofeedback.

Aversion Therapy A counterconditioning therapy in which unwanted responses are paired with unpleasant consequences.

Avoidance Conditioning Situation in which a subject learns to avoid an aversive stimulus by responding appropriately before it begins.

Barbiturates Sedative-hypnotic, psychoactive drugs widely used to induce sleep and to reduce tension. Overuse can lead to addiction. *See* Addiction.

Behavior Any observable activity of an organism, including mental processes.

Behavior Therapy The use of conditioning processes to treat mental disorders. Various techniques may be used, including positive reinforcement in which rewards (verbal or tangible) are given to the patient for appropriate behavior, modeling in which patients unlearn fears by watching models exhibit fearlessness, and systematic desensitization in which the patient is taught to relax and visualize anxiety-producing items at the same time. *See* Insight Therapy; Systematic Desensitization.

Behaviorism A school of psychology stressing an objective approach to psychological questions, proposing that psychology be limited to observable behavior and that the subjectiveness of consciousness places it beyond the limits of scientific psychology.

Biofeedback The voluntary control of physiological processes by receiving information about those processes as they occur, through instruments that pick up these changes and display them to the subject in the form of a signal. Blood pressure, skin temperature, etc. can be controlled.

Biological (Primary) Motives Motives that have a physiological basis; include hunger, thirst, body temperature regulation, avoidance of pain, and sex.

Biological Response System System of the body that is particularly important in behavioral responding; includes the senses, endocrines, muscles, and the nervous system.

Biological Therapy Treatment of behavior problems through biological techniques; major biological therapies include drug therapy, psychosurgery, and electroconvulsive therapy.

Bipolar Disorder Affective disorder that is characterized by extreme mood swings from sad depression to joyful mania; sometimes called manic-depression.

Body Language Communication through position and movement of the body.

Brain Mapping A procedure for identifying the function of various areas of the brain; the surgeon gives tiny electrical stimulation to a specific area and notes patient's reaction.

Brain Stimulation The introduction of chemical or electrical stimuli directly into the brain.

Brain Waves Electrical responses produced by brain activity that can be recorded directly from any portion of the brain or from the scalp with special electrodes. Brain waves are measured by an electroencephalograph (EEG). Alpha waves occur during relaxed wakefulness and beta waves during active behavior. Theta waves are associated with drowsiness and vivid visual imagery, delta waves with deep sleep.

Bystander Effect Phenomenon in which a single person is more likely to help in an emergency situation than a group of people.

Cannon-Bard Theory of Emotion Theory of emotion that states that the emotional feeling and the physiological arousal occur at the same time.

Catatonic Schizophrenia A type of schizophrenia that is characterized by periods of complete immobility and the apparent absence of will to move or speak.

Causal Attribution Process of determining whether a person's behavior is due to internal or external motives.

Cautious Shift Research suggests that the decisions of a group will be more conservative than that of the average individual member when dealing with areas for which there are widely held values favoring caution (e.g., physical danger or family responsibility). *See* Risky Shift.

Central Nervous System The part of the human nervous system that interprets and stores messages from the sense organs, decides what behavior to exhibit, and sends appropriate messages to the muscles and glands; includes the brain and spinal cord.

Central Tendency In statistics, measures of central tendency give a number that represents the entire group or sample.

Cerebellum The part of the brain responsible for muscle and movement control and coordination of eye-body movement.

Cerebral Cortex The part of the brain consisting of the outer layer of cerebral cells. The cortex can be divided into specific regions: sensory, motor, and associative.

Chaining Behavior theory suggests that behavior patterns are built up of component parts by stringing together a number of simpler responses.

Character Disorder (or Personality Disorder) A classification of psychological disorders (as distinguished from neurosis or psychosis). The disorder has become part of the individual's personality and does not cause him or her discomfort, making that disorder more difficult to treat psychotherapeutically.

Chromosome *See* Gene.

Chunking The tendency to code memories so that there are fewer bits to store.

Classical Conditioning *See* Pavlovian Conditioning.

Client-Centered Therapy A nondirective form of psychotherapy developed by Carl Rogers in which the counselor attempts to create an atmosphere in which the client can freely explore herself or himself and her or his problems. The client-centered therapist reflects what the client says back to him, usually without interpreting what.

Clinical Psychology The branch of psychology concerned with testing, diagnosing, interviewing, conducting research and treating (often by psychotherapy) mental disorders and personality problems.

Cognitive Appraisal Intellectual evaluation of situations or stimuli. Experiments suggest that emotional arousal is produced not simply by a stimulus but by how one evaluates and interprets the arousal. The appropriate physical response follows this cognitive appraisal.

Cognitive Behavior Therapy A form of behavior therapy that identifies self-defeating attitudes and thoughts in a subject, and then helps the subject to replace these with positive, supportive thoughts.

Cognitive Dissonance People are very uncomfortable if they perceive that their beliefs, feelings, or acts are not consistent with one another, and they will try to reduce the discomfort of this dissonance.

Cognitive Psychology The study of how individuals gain knowledge of their environments. Cognitive psychologists believe that the organism actively participates in constructing the meaningful stimuli that it selectively organizes and to which it selectively responds.

Comparative Psychology The study of similarities and differences in the behavior of different species.

Compulsive Personality Personality disorder in which an individual is preoccupied with details and rules.

Concept Learning The acquisition of the ability to identify and use the qualities that objects or situations have in common. A class concept refers to any quality that breaks objects or situations into separate groupings.

Concrete-Operational Stage A stage in intellectual development, according to Piaget. The child at approximately seven years begins to apply logic. His or her thinking is less egocentric, reversible, and the child develops conservation abilities and the ability to classify. *See* Conservation.

Conditioned Reinforcer Reinforcement that is effective because it has been associated with other reinforcers. Conditioned reinforcers are involved in higher order conditioning.

Conditioned Response (CR) The response or behavior that occurs when the conditioned stimulus is presented (after the conditioned stimulus has been associated with the unconditioned stimulus).

Conditioned Stimulus (CS) An originally neutral stimulus that is associated with an unconditioned stimulus and takes on its capability of eliciting a particular reaction.

Conditioned Taste Aversion (CTA) Learning an aversion to particular tastes by associating them with stomach distress; usually considered a unique form of classical conditioning because of the extremely long interstimulus intervals involved.

Conduction The ability of a neuron to carry a message (an electrical stimulus) along its length.

Conflict Situation that occurs when we experience incompatible demands or desires.

Conformity The tendency of an individual to act like others regardless of personal belief.

Conscience A person's sense of the moral rightness or wrongness of behavior.

Consciousness Awareness of experienced sensations, thoughts, and feelings at any given point in time.

Consensus In causal attribution, the extent to which other people react the same way the subject does in a particular situation.

Conservation Refers to the child's ability to understand laws of length, mass, and volume. Before the development of this ability, a child will not understand that a particular property of an object (e.g., the quantity of water in a glass) does not change even though other perceivable features change.

Consistency In causal attribution, the extent to which the subject always behaves in the same way in a particular situation.

Consolidation The biological neural process of making memories permanent; possibly short-term memory is electrically coded and long-term memory is chemically coded.

Continuum of Preparedness Seligman's proposal that animals are biologically prepared to learn certain responses more readily than others.

Control Group A group used for comparison with an experimental group. All conditions must be identical for each group with the exception of the one variable (independent) that is manipulated. *See* Experimental Group.

Convergence Binocular depth cue in which we detect distance by interpreting the kinesthetic sensations produced by the muscles of the eyeballs.

Convergent Thinking The kind of thinking that is used to solve problems having only one correct answer. *See* Divergent Thinking.

Conversion Disorder Somatoform disorder in which a person displays obvious disturbance in the nervous system, however, a medical examination reveals no physical basis for the problem; often includes paralysis, loss of sensation, or blindness.

Corpus Callosum Nerve fibers that connect the two halves of the brain in humans. If cut, the halves continue to function although some functions are affected.

Correlation A measurement in which two or more sets of variables are compared and the extent to which they are related is calculated.

Correlation Coefficient The measure, in number form, of how two variables vary together. They extend from −1 (perfect negative correlation) to a +1 (perfect positive correlation).

Counterconditioning A behavior therapy in which an unwanted response is replaced by conditioning a new response that is incompatible with it.

Creativity The ability to discover or produce new solutions to problems, new inventions, or new works of art. Creativity is an ability independent of IQ and is opened-ended in that solutions are not predefined in their scope or appropriateness. *See* Problem Solving.

Critical Period A specific stage in an organism's development during which the acquisition of a particular type of behavior depends on exposure to a particular type of stimulation.

Cross-Sectional Study A research technique that focuses on a factor in a group of subjects as they are at one time, as in a study of fantasy play in subjects of three different age groups. *See* Longitudinal Study.

Culture-Bound The idea that a test's usefulness is limited to the culture in which it was written and utilized.

Curiosity Motive Motive that causes the individual to seek out a certain amount of novelty.

Cutaneous Sensitivity The skin senses: touch, pain, pressure and temperature. Skin receptors respond in different ways and with varying degrees of sensitivity.

Decay Theory of forgetting in which sensory impressions leave memory traces that fade away with time.

Defense Mechanism A way of reducing anxiety that does not directly cope with the threat. There are many types, denial, repression, etc., all of which are used in normal function. Only when use is habitual or they impede effective solutions are they considered pathological.

Delusion A false belief that persists despite evidence showing it to be irrational. Delusions are often symptoms of mental illness.

Dependent Variable Those conditions that an experimenter observes and measures. Called "dependent" because they depend on the experimental manipulations.

Depersonalization Disorder Dissociative disorder in which individuals escape from their own personalities by believing that they don't exist or that their environment is not real.

Depression A temporary emotional state that normal individuals experience or a persistent state that may be considered a psychological disorder. Characterized by sadness and low self-esteem. *See* Self-Esteem.

Descriptive Statistics Techniques that help summarize large amounts of data information.

Developmental Norms The average time at which developmental changes occur in the normal individual.

Developmental Psychology The study of changes in behavior and thinking as the organism grows from the prenatal stage to death.

Deviation, Standard and Average Average deviation is determined by measuring the deviation of each score in a distribution from the mean and calculating the average of the deviations. The standard deviation is used to determine how representative the mean of a distribution is. *See* Mean.

Diagnostic and Statistical Manual of Mental Disorders (DSM) DSM-III was published in 1980 by the American Psychiatric Association.

Diffusion of Responsibility As the number of witnesses to a help-requiring situation—and thus the degree of anonymity—increases, the amount of helping decreases and the amount of time before help is offered increases. *See* Bystander Effect.

Discrimination The ability to tell whether stimuli are different when presented together or that one situation is different from a past one.

Disorganized Schizophrenia A type of schizophrenia that is characterized by a severe personality disintegration; the individual often displays bizarre behavior.

Displacement The process by which an emotion originally attached to a particular person, object, or situation is transferred to something else.

Dissociative Disorders Disorders in which individuals forget who they are.

Distal Stimuli Physical events in the environment that affect perception. *See* Proximal Stimuli.

Distinctiveness In causal attribution, the extent to which the subject reacts the same way in other situations.

Divergent Thinking The kind of thinking that characterizes creativity (as contrasted with convergent thinking) and involves the development of novel resolutions of a task or the generation of totally new ideas. *See* Convergent Thinking.

DNA *See* Gene.

Double Bind A situation in which a person is subjected to two conflicting, contradictory demands at the same time.

Down's Syndrome Form of mental retardation caused by having three number 21 chromosomes (trisomy 21).

Dreams The thoughts, images, and emotions that occur during sleep. Dreams occur periodically during the sleep cycle and are usually marked by rapid movements of the eyes (REM sleep). The content of dreams tends to reflect emotions (sexual feelings, according to Freud) and experiences of the previous day. Nightmares are qualitatively different from other dreams, often occurring during deep or Stage 4 sleep.

Drive A need or urge that motivates behavior. Some drives may be explained as responses to bodily needs, such as hunger or sex. Others derive from social pressures and complex forms of learning, for example, competition, curiosity, achievement, *See* Motivation.

Drive Reduction Theory Theory of motivation that states that the individual is pushed by inner forces toward reducing the drive and restoring homeostasis.

Drug Dependence A state of mental or physical dependence on a drug, or both. Psychoactive drugs are capable of creating psychological dependence (anxiety when the drug is unavailable), although the relationship of some, such as marijuana and LSD, to physical dependence or addiction is still under study. *See* Psychoactive Drug; Addiction.

Drug Tolerance A state produced by certain psychoactive drugs in which increasing amounts of the substance are required to produce the desired effect. Some drugs produce tolerance but not withdrawal symptoms, and these drugs are not regarded as physically addicting.

Effectance Motive The striving for effectiveness in dealing with the environment. The effectance motive differs from the need for achievement in that effectance depends on internal feelings of satisfaction while the need for achievement is geared more to meeting others' standards.

Efferent Neuron (Motor) A neuron that carries messages from the central nervous system to the muscles and glands.

Ego A construct to account for the organization in a person's life and for making the person's behavior correspond to physical and social realities. According to Freud, the ego is the "reality principle" that is responsible for holding the id or "pleasure principle" in check. *See* Id.

Egocentrism Seeing things from only one's own point of view; also, the quality of a child's thought that prevents her or him from understanding that different people perceive the world differently. Egocentrism is characteristic of a stage that all children go through.

Electra Complex The libidinal feelings of a child toward a parent of the opposite sex. *See also* Oedipus Complex

Electroshock Therapy A form of therapy used to relieve severe depression. The patient receives electric current across the forehead, loses consciousness, and undergoes a short convulsion. When the patient regains consciousness, his or her mood is lifted.

Emotion A complex feeling-state that involves physiological arousal; a subjective feeling which might involve a cognitive appraisal of the situation and overt behavior in response to a stimulus.

Empathy The ability to appreciate how someone else feels by putting yourself in her or his position and experiencing her or his feelings. Empathy is acquired normally by children during intellectual growth.

Empiricism The view that behavior is learned through experience.

Encounter Groups Groups of individuals who meet to change their personal lives by confronting each other, discussing personal problems, and talking more honestly and openly than in everyday life.

Endocrine Glands Ductless glands that secrete chemicals called hormones into the blood stream.

Equilibration According to Piaget, the child constructs an understanding of the world through equilibration. Equilibration consists of the interaction of two complementary processes, assimilation (taking in input within the existing structures of the mind, e.g., putting it into mental categories that already exist) with accommodation (the changing of mental categories to fit new input that cannot be taken into existing categories) and is the process by which knowing occurs. One's developmental stage affects how one equilibrates.

Ethnocentrism The belief that one's own ethnic or racial group is superior to others.

Experiment Procedures executed under a controlled situation in order to test a hypothesis and discover relationships between independent and dependent variables.

Experimental Control The predetermined conditions, procedures, and checks built into the design of an experiment to ensure scientific control; as opposed to "control" in common usage, which implies manipulation.

Experimental Group In a scientific experiment, the group of subjects that is usually treated specially, as opposed to the control group, in order to isolate just the variable under investigation. *See* Control Group.

Experimental Psychology The branch of psychology concerned with the laboratory study of basic psychological laws and principles as demonstrated in the behavior of animals.

Experimenter Bias How the expectations of the person running an experiment can influence what comes out of the experiment. Experimenter bias can affect the way the experimenter sees the subjects' behavior, causing distortions of fact, and can also affect the way the experimenter reads data, also leading to distortions.

Extinction The elimination of behavior by, in classical conditioning, the withholding of the unconditional stimulus, and in operant conditioning, the withholding of the reinforcement.

Extrasensory Perception (ESP) The range of perceptions that are "paranormal," (such as the ability to predict events, reproduce drawings sealed in envelopes, etc.).

Fixed Interval (FI) Schedule Schedule of reinforcement in which the subject receives reinforcement for the first correct response given after a specified time interval.

Fixed Ratio (FR) Schedule Schedule of reinforcement in which the subject is reinforced after a certain number of responses.

Fixed-Action Pattern Movement that is characteristic of a species and does not have to be learned.

Forgetting The process by which material that once was available is no longer available. Theory exists that forgetting occurs because memories interfere with one another, either retroactively (new memories block old) or proactively (old memories block new); that forgetting occurs when the cues necessary to recall the information are not supplied, or when memories are too unpleasant to remain in consciousness. *See* Repression.

Formal Operational Stage According to Piaget, the stage at which the child develops adult powers of reasoning, abstraction, and symbolizing. The child can grasp scientific, religious, and political concepts and deduce their consequences as well as reason hypothetically ("what if . . .").

Frequency Theory of Hearing Theory of hearing that states that the frequency of vibrations at the basilar membrane determines the frequency of firing of neurons that carry impulses to the brain.

Frustration A feeling of discomfort or insecurity aroused by a blocking of gratification or by unresolved problems. Several theories hold that frustration arouses aggression. *See* Aggression.

Functionalism An early school of psychology stressing the ways behavior helps one adapt to the environment and the role that learning plays in this adaptive process.

Gene The unit of heredity that determines particular characteristics; a part of a molecule of DNA. DNA (dioxyribonucleic acid) is found mainly in the nucleus of living cells where it occurs in threadlike structures called chromosomes. Within the chromosomes, each DNA molecule is organized into specific units that carry the genetic information necessary for the development of a particular trait. These units are the genes. A gene can reproduce itself exactly, and this is how traits are carried between generations. The genotype is the entire structure of genes that are inherited by an organism from its parents. The environment interacts with this genotype to determine how the genetic potential will develop.

General Adaptation Syndrome (GAS) The way the body responds to stress, as described by Hans Selye. In the first stage, an alarm reaction, a person responds by efforts at self-control and shows signs of nervous depression (defense mechanisms, fear, anger, etc.) followed by a release of ACTH. In stage 2, the subject shows increased resistance to the specific source of stress and less resistance to other sources. Defense mechanisms may become neurotic. With stage 3 comes exhaustion, stupor, even death.

Generalization The process by which learning in one situation is transferred to another, similar situation. It is a key term in behavioral modification and classical conditioning. *See* Classical Conditioning.

Generalized Anxiety Disorder Disorder in which the individual lives in a state of constant severe tension; continuous fear and apprehension experienced by an individual.

Genetics The study of the transfer of the inheritance of characteristics from one generation to another.

Genotype The underlying genetic structure that an individual has inherited and will send on to descendants. The actual appearance of a trait (phenotype) is due to the interaction of the genotype and the environment.

Gestalt Psychology A movement in psychology begun in the 1920s, stressing the wholeness of a person's experience and proposing that perceiving is an active, dynamic process that takes into account the entire pattern of ("gestalt") of the perpetual field. *See* Behaviorism; Associationism.

Glia Cells in the central nervous system that regulate the chemical environment of the nerve cells. RNA is stored in glial cells.

Grammar The set of rules for combining units of a language.

Group Therapy A form of psychotherapy aimed at treating mental disorders in which interaction among group members is the main therapeutic mode. Group therapy takes many forms but essentially requires a sense of community, support, increased personal responsibility, and a professionally trained leader.

Growth The normal quantitative changes that occur in the physical and psychological aspects of a healthy child with the passage of time.

Gustation The sense of taste. Theory suggests that the transmission of sense information from tongue to brain occurs through patterns of cell activity and not just the firing of single nerve fibers. Also, it is believed that specific spatial patterns or places on the tongue correspond to taste qualities.

Habit Formation The tendency to make a response to a stimulus less variable, especially if it produced successful adaptation.

Hallucination A sensory impression reported by a person when no external stimulus exists to justify the report. Hallucinations are serious symptoms and may be produced by psychoses. *See* Psychosis.

Hallucinogen A substance that produces hallucinations, such as LSD, mescaline, etc.

Hierarchy of Needs Maslow's list of motives in humans, arranged from the biological to the uniquely human.

Higher Order Conditioning Learning to make associations with stimuli that have been previously learned (CSs).

Hippocampus Part of the cortex of the brain governing memory storage, smell, and visceral functions.

Homeostasis A set of processes maintaining the constancy of the body's internal state, a series of dynamic compensations of the nervous system. Many processes such as appetite, body temperature, water balance, and heart rate are controlled by homeostasis.

Hormones Chemical secretions of the endocrine glands that regulate various body processes (e.g., growth, sexual traits, reproductive processes, etc.).

Humanism Branch of psychology dealing with those qualities distinguishing humans from other animals.

Hypnosis A trancelike state marked by heightened suggestibility and a narrowing of attention that can be induced in a number of ways.

Debate exists over whether hypnosis is a true altered state of consciousness and to what extent strong motivating instructions can duplicate so-called hypnosis.

Hypothalamus A part of the brain that acts as a channel that carries information from the cortex and the thalamus to the spinal cord and ultimately to the motor nerves or to the autonomic nervous system, where it is transmitted to specific target organs. These target organs release into the bloodstream specific hormones that alter bodily functions. *See* Autonomic Nervous System.

Hypothesis A hypothesis can be called an educated guess, similar to a hunch. When a hunch is stated in a way that allows for further testing, it becomes a hypothesis.

Iconic Memory A visual memory. Experiments suggest that in order to be remembered and included in long-term memory, information must pass through a brief sensory stage. Theory further suggests that verbal information is subject to forgetting but that memorized sensory images are relatively permanent.

Id According to Freud, a component of the psyche present at birth that is the storehouse of psychosexual energy called *libido*, and also of primitive urges to fight, dominate, destroy.

Identification The taking on of attributes that one sees in another person. Children tend to identify with their parents or other important adults and thereby take on certain traits that are important to their development.

Illusion A mistaken perception of an actual stimulus.

Imitation The copying of another's behavior; learned through the process of observation. *See* Modeling.

Impression Formation The process of developing an evaluation of another person from your perceptions; first, or initial, impressions are often very important.

Imprinting The rapid, permanent acquisition by an organism of a strong attachment to an object (usually the parent). Imprinting occurs shortly after birth.

Independent Variable The condition in an experiment that is controlled and manipulated by the experimenter; it is a stimulus that will cause a response.

Inferential Statistics Techniques that help researchers make generalizations about a finding based on a limited number of subjects.

Inhibition Restraint of an impulse, desire, activity, or drive. People are taught to inhibit full expression of many drives (for example, aggression or sexuality) and to apply checks either consciously or unconsciously. In Freudian terminology, an inhibition is an unconsciously motivated blocking of sexual energy. In Pavlovian conditioning, inhibition is the theoretical process that operates during extinction, acting to block a conditioned response. *See* Pavlovian Conditioning.

Insight A sudden perception of useful or proper relations among objects necessary to solve the problem.

Insight Therapy A general classification of therapy in which the therapist focuses on the patient's underlying feelings and motivations and devotes most effort to increasing the patient's self-awareness or insight into his or her behavior. The other major class of therapy is action therapy. *See* Action Therapy.

Instinct An inborn pattern of behavior, relatively independent of environmental influence. An instinct may need to be triggered by a particular stimulus in the environment, but then it proceeds in a fixed pattern. The combination of taxis (orienting movement in response to a particular stimulus) and fixed-action pattern (inherited coordination) is the basis for instinctual activity. *See* Fixed-Action Pattern.

Instrumental Learning *See* Operant Conditioning.

Intelligence A capacity for knowledge about the world. This is an enormous and controversial field of study, and there is no agreement on a precise definition. However, intelligence has come to refer to higher-level abstract processes and may be said to comprise the ability to deal effectively with abstract concepts, the ability to learn, and the ability to adapt and deal with new situations. Piaget defines intelligence as the construction of an understanding. Both biological inheritance and environmental factors contribute to general intelligence. Children proceed through a sequence of identifiable stages in the development of conceptual thinking (Piaget). The degree to which factors such as race, sex, and social class affect intelligence is not known.

Intelligence Quotient (IQ) A measurement of intelligence originally based on tests devised by Binet and now widely applied. Genetic inheritance and environment affect IQ, although their relative contributions are not known. IQ can be defined in different ways; classically it is defined as a relation between chronological and mental ages.

Interference Theory of forgetting in which information that was learned before (proactive interference) or after (retroactive interference) the material of interest causes the learner to be unable to remember the material.

Interstimulus Interval The time between the start of the conditioned stimulus and the start of the unconditioned stimulus in Pavlovian conditioning. *See* Pavlovian Conditioning.

Intrauterine Environment The environment in the uterus during pregnancy can affect the physical development of the organism and its behavior after birth. Factors such as the mother's nutrition, emotional, and physical state significantly influence offspring. The mother's diseases, medications, hormones, and stress level all affect the pre- and postnatal development of her young.

Intrinsic Motivation Motivation inside of the individual; we do something because we receive satisfaction from it.

Introspection Reporting one's internal, subjective mental contents for the purpose of further study and analysis. *See* Structuralism.

James-Lange Theory of Emotion Theory of emotion that states that the physiological arousal and behavior come before the subjective experience of an emotion.

Labeling-of-Arousal Experiments suggest that an individual experiencing physical arousal that she or he cannot explain will interpret her or his feelings in terms of the situation she or he is in and will use environmental and contextual cues.

Language A set of abstract symbols used to communicate meaning. Language includes vocalized sounds or semantic units (words, usually) and rules for combining the units (grammar). There is some inborn basis for language acquisition, and there are identifiable stages in its development that are universal.

Language Acquisition Linguists debate how children acquire language. Some believe in environmental shaping, a gradual system of reward and punishment. Others emphasize the unfolding of capacities inborn in the brain that are relatively independent of the environment and its rewards.

Latency Period According to Freud, the psychosexual stage of development during which sexual interest has been repressed and thus is low or "latent" (dormant).

Law of Effect Thorndike's proposal that when a response produces satisfaction, it will be repeated; reinforcement.

Leadership The quality of exerting more influence than other group members. Research suggests that certain characteristics are generally considered essential to leadership: consideration, sensitivity, ability to initiate and structure, and emphasis on production. However, environmental factors may thrust authority on a person without regard to personal characteristics.

Learned Helplessness Theory suggests that living in an environment of uncontrolled stress reduces the ability to cope with future stress that *is* controllable.

Learned Social Motives Motives in the human that are learned, including achievement, affiliation, and autonomy.

Learning The establishment of connections between stimulus and response, resulting from observation, special training, or previous activity. Learning is relatively permanent.

Life Span Span of time from conception to death; in developmental psychology, a life span approach looks at development throughout an individual's life.

Linguistic Relativity Hypothesis Proposal by Whorf that the perception of reality differs according to the language of the observer.

Linguistics The study of language, its nature, structure, and components.

Locus of Control The perceived place from which come determining forces in one's life. A person who feels that he or she has some control over his or her fate and tends to feel more likely to succeed has an internal locus of control. A person with an external locus of control feels that it is outside himself or herself and therefore that his or her attempts to control his or her fate are less assured.

Longitudinal Study A research method that involves following subjects over a considerable period of time (as compared with a cross-sectional approach); as in a study of fantasy play in children observed several times at intervals of two years. *See* Cross-Sectional Study.

Love Affectionate behavior between people, often in combination with interpersonal attraction. The mother-infant love relationship strongly influences the later capacity for developing satisfying love relationships.

Manic-Depressive Reaction A form of mental illness marked by alternations of extreme phases of elation (manic phase) and depression.

Maternalism Refers to the mother's reaction to her young. It is believed that the female is biologically determined to exhibit behavior more favorable to the care and feeding of the young than the male, although in humans maternalism is probably determined as much by cultural factors as by biological predisposition.

Maturation The genetically-controlled process of physical and physiological growth.

Mean The measure of central tendency, or mathematical average, computed by adding all scores in a set and dividing by the number of scores.

Meaning The concept or idea conveyed to the mind, by any method. In reference to memory, meaningful terms are easier to learn than less meaningful, unconnected, or nonsense terms. Meaningfulness is not the same as the word's meaning.

Median In a set of scores, the median is that middle score that divides the set into equal halves.

Memory Involves the encoding, storing of information in the brain, and its retrieval. Several theories exist to explain memory. One proposes that we have both a short-term memory (STM) and a long-term memory (LTM) and that information must pass briefly through the STM to be stored in the LTM. Also suggested is that verbal information is subject to forgetting,

while memorized sensory images are relatively permanent. Others see memory as a function of association—information processed systematically and the meaningfulness of the items. Debate exists over whether memory retrieval is actually a process of reappearance or reconstruction.

Mental Disorder A mental condition that deviates from what society considers to be normal.

Minnesota Multiphasic Personality Inventory (MMPI) An objective personality test that was originally devised to identify personality disorders.

Mode In a set of scores, the measurement at which the largest number of subjects fall.

Modeling The imitation or copying of another's behavior. As an important process in personality development, modeling may be based on parents. In therapy, the therapist may serve as a model for the patient.

Morality The standards of right and wrong of a society and their adoption by members of that society. Some researchers believe that morality develops in successive stages, with each stage representing a specific level of moral thinking (Kohlberg). Others see morality as the result of experiences in which the child learns through punishment and reward from models such as parents and teachers.

Motivation All factors that cause and regulate behavior that is directed toward achieving goals and satisfying needs. Motivation is what moves an organism to action.

Motor Unit One spinal motoneuron (motor nerve cell) and the muscle fibers it activates. The contraction of a muscle involves the activity of many motoneurons and muscle fibers. Normally we are aware only of our muscles contracting and not of the process producing the contraction, although biofeedback can train people to control individual motor units. *See* Biofeedback.

Narcotic A drug that relieves pain. Heroin, morphine, and opium are narcotics. Narcotics are often addicting.

Naturalistic Observation Research method in which behavior of people or animals in the normal environment is accurately recorded.

Negative Reinforcement Any event that upon termination, strengthens the preceding behavior; taking from subject something bad will increase the probability that the preceding behavior will be repeated. Involves aversive stimulus.

Neuron A nerve cell. There are billions of neurons in the brain and spinal cord. Neurons interact at synapses or points of contact. Information passage between neurons is electrical and biochemical. It takes the activity of many neurons to produce a behavior.

Neurosis Any one of a wide range of psychological difficulties, accompanied by excessive anxiety (as contrasted with psychosis). Psychoanalytic theory states that neurosis is an expression of unresolved conflicts in the form of tension and impaired functioning. Most neurotics are in much closer contact with reality than most psychotics. Term has been largely eliminated from DSM-III.

Nonverbal Behaviors Gestures, facial expressions, and other body movements. They are important because they tend to convey emotion. Debate exists over whether they are inborn or learned.

Norm An empirically set pattern of belief or behavior. Social norm refers to widely accepted social or cultural behavior to which a person tends to or is expected to conform.

Normal Sane, or free from mental disorder. Normal behavior is the behavior typical of most people in a given group, and "normality" implies a social judgment.

Normal Curve When scores of a large number of random cases are plotted on a graph, they

often fall into a bell-shaped curve; there are as many cases above the mean as below on the curve.

Object Permanence According to Piaget, the stage in cognitive development when a child begins to conceive of objects as having an existence even when out of sight or touch and to conceive of space as extending beyond his or her own perception.

Oedipus Complex The conflicts of a child in triangular relationship with his mother and father. According to Freud, a boy must resolve his unconscious sexual desire for his mother and the accompanying wish to kill his father and fear of his father's revenge in order that he proceed in his moral development. The analogous problem for girls is called the Electra complex.

Olfaction The sense of smell. No general agreement exists on how olfaction works, though theories exist to explain it. One suggests that the size and shape of molecules of what is smelled is a crucial cue. The brain processes involved in smell are located in a different and evolutionarily older part of the brain than the other senses.

Operant Conditioning The process of changing, maintaining, or eliminating voluntary behavior through the consequences of that behavior. Operant conditioning uses many of the techniques of Pavlovian conditioning but differs in that it deals with voluntary rather than reflex behaviors. The frequency with which a behavior is emitted can be increased if it is rewarded (reinforced) and decreased if it is not reinforced, or punished. Some psychologists believe that all behavior is learned through conditioning while others believe that intellectual and motivational processes play a crucial role. *See* Pavlovian Conditioning.

Operational Definitions If an event is not directly observable, then the variables must be defined by the operations by which they will be measured. These definitions are called operational definitions.

Organism Any living animal, human or subhuman.

Orienting Response A relatively automatic, "what's that?" response that puts the organism in a better position to attend to and deal with a new stimulus. When a stimulus attracts our attention, our body responds with movements of head and body toward the stimulus, changes in muscle tone, heart rate, blood flow, breathing, and changes in the brain's electrical activity.

Pavlovian Conditioning Also called classical conditioning, Pavlovian conditioning can be demonstrated as follows: In the first step, an *unconditioned stimulus* (UCS) such as food, loud sounds, or pain is paired with a neutral *conditioned stimulus* (CS) that causes no direct effect, such as a click, tone, or a dim light. The response elicited by the UCS is called the *unconditioned response* (UCR) and is a biological reflex of the nervous system (for example, eyeblinks or salivation). The combination of the neutral CS, the response-causing UCS, and the unlearned UCR is usually presented to the subject several times during conditioning. Eventually, the UCS is dropped from the sequence in the second step of the process, and the previously neutral CS comes to elicit a response. When conditioning is complete, presentation of the CS alone will result in a *conditioned response* (CR) similar but not always the same as the UCR.

Perception The field of psychology studying ways in which the experience of objects in the world is based upon stimulation of the sense organs. In psychology, the field of perception studies what determines sensory impressions, such as size, shape, distance, direction, etc.

Physical events in the environment are called distal stimuli while the activity at the sense organ itself is called a proximal stimulus. The study of perceiving tries to determine how an organism knows what distal stimuli are like since proximal stimuli are its only source of information. Perception of objects remains more or less constant despite changes in distal stimuli and is therefore believed to depend on relationships within stimuli (size *and* distance, for example). Perceptual processes are able to adjust and adapt to changes in the perceptual field.

Performance The actual behavior of an individual that is observed. We often infer learning from observing performance.

Peripheral Nervous System The part of the human nervous system that receives messages from the sense organs and carries messages to the muscles and glands; everything outside of the brain and spinal cord.

Persuasion The process of changing a person's attitudes, beliefs, or actions. A person's susceptibility to persuasion depends on the persuader's credibility, subtlety, and whether both sides of an argument are presented.

Phenotype The physical features or behavior patterns by which we recognize an organism. Phenotype is the result of interaction between genotype (total of inherited genes) and environment. *See* Genotype.

Phobia A neurosis consisting of an irrationally intense fear of specific persons, objects, or situations and a wish to avoid them. A phobic person feels intense and incapacitating anxiety. The person may be aware that the fear is irrational, but this knowledge does not help.

Pituitary Gland Is located in of the brain and controls secretion of several hormones: the antidiuretic hormone that maintains water balance, oxytocin that controls blood pressure and milk production, and ACTH that is produced in response to stress, etc. *See* ACTH.

Placebo A substance that in and of itself has no real effect but which may produce an effect in a subject because the subject expects or believes that it will.

Positive Reinforcement Any event that, upon presentation, strengthens the preceding behavior; giving a subject something good will increase the probability that the preceding behavior will be repeated.

Prejudice An attitude in which one holds a negative belief about members of a group to which he or she does not belong. Prejudice is often directed at minority ethnic or racial groups and may be reduced by contact with these perceived "others."

Premack Principle Principle that states that of any two responses, the one that is more likely to occur can be used to reinforce the response that is less likely to occur.

Prenatal Development Development from conception to birth. It includes the physical development of the fetus as well as certain of its intellectual and emotional processes.

Preoperational Stage The development stage at which, according to Piaget, come the start of language, the ability to imitate actions, to symbolize, and to play make-believe games. Thinking is egocentric in that a child cannot understand that others perceive things differently.

Primary Reinforcement Reinforcement that is effective without having been associated with other reinforcers; sometimes called unconditioned reinforcement.

Probability (p) In inferential statistics, the likelihood that the difference between the experimental and control groups is due to the independent variable.

Problem Solving A self-directed activity in which an individual uses information to develop answers to problems, to generate new problems, and sometimes to transform the process by creating a unique, new system. Problem solving involves learning, insight and creativity.

Projective Test A type of test in which people respond to ambiguous, loosely structured stimuli. It is assumed that people will reveal themselves by putting themselves into the stimuli they see. The validity of these tests for diagnosis and personality assessment is still at issue.

Propaganda Information deliberately spread to aid a cause. Propaganda's main function is persuasion.

Prosocial Behavior Behavior that is directed toward helping others.

Proximal Stimulus Activity at the sense organ.

Psychoactive Drug A substance that affects mental activities, perceptions, consciousness, or mood. This type of drug has its effects through strictly physical effects and through expectations.

Psychoanalysis There are two meanings to this word: it is a theory of personality development based on Freud and a method of treatment also based on Freud. Psychoanalytic therapy uses techniques of free association, dream analysis, and analysis of the patient's relationship (the "transference") to the analyst. Psychoanalytic theory maintains that the personality develops through a series of psychosexual stages and that the personality consists of specific components energized by the life and death instincts.

Psychogenic Pain Disorder Somatoform disorder in which the person complains of severe, long-lasting pain for which there is no organic cause.

Psycholinguistics The study of the process of language acquisition as part of psychological development and of language as an aspect of behavior. Thinking may obviously depend on language, but their precise relationship still puzzles psycholinguists, and several different views exist.

Psychological Dependence Situation when a person craves a drug even though it is not biologically necessary for his or her body.

Psychophysiological Disorders Real medical problems (such as ulcers, migraine headaches, and high blood pressure) that are caused or aggravated by psychological stress.

Psychosexual Stages According to Freud, an individual's personality develops through several stages. Each stage is associated with a particular bodily source of gratification (pleasure). First comes the oral stage when most pleasures come from the mouth. Then comes the anal stage when the infant derives pleasure from holding and releasing while learning bowel control. The phallic stage brings pleasure from the genitals, and a crisis (Oedipal) occurs in which the child gradually suppresses sexual desire for the opposite-sex parent, identifies with the same-sex parent and begins to be interested in the outside world. This latency period lasts until puberty, after which the genital stage begins and mature sexual relationships develop. There is no strict timetable, but, according to Freudians, the stages do come in a definite order. Conflicts experienced and not adequately dealt with remain with the individual.

Psychosis The most severe of mental disorders, distinguished by a person being seriously out of touch with objective reality. Psychoses may result from physical factors (organic) or may have no known physical cause (functional). Psychoses take many forms, of which the most common are schizophrenia and psychotic depressive reactions, but all are marked by personality disorganization and a severely reduced ability to perceive reality. Both biological and environmental factors are believed to influence the development of psychosis, al-

though the precise effect of each is not presently known. *See* Neurosis.

Psychosomatic Disorders A variety of body reactions that are closely related to psychological events. Stress, for example, brings on many physical changes and can result in illness or even death if prolonged and severe. Psychosomatic disorders can affect any part of the body.

Psychotherapy Treatment involving interpersonal contacts between a trained therapist and a patient in which the therapist tries to produce beneficial changes in the patient's emotional state, attitudes, and behavior.

Punishment Any event that decreases the probability of the preceding behavior being repeated. You can give something bad (positive punishment) to decrease the preceding behavior.

Rational-Emotive Therapy A cognitive behavior modification technique in which a person is taught to identify irrational, self-defeating beliefs and then to overcome them.

Rationalization Defense mechanism in which individuals make up logical excuses to justify their behavior rather than exposing their true motives.

Reaction Formation Defense mechanism in which a person masks an unconsciously distressing or unacceptable trait by assuming an opposite attitude or behavior pattern.

Reactive Schizophrenia A type of schizophrenia in which the disorder appears as a reaction to some major trauma or terribly stressful encounter; sometimes called acute schizophrenia.

Reality Therapy A form of treatment of mental disorders pioneered by William Glasser in which the origins of the patient's problems are considered irrelevant and emphasis is on a close, judgmental bond between patient and therapist aimed to improve the patient's present and future life.

Reflex An automatic movement that occurs in direct response to a stimulus.

Rehearsal The repeating of an item to oneself and the means by which information is stored in the short-term memory (STM). Theory suggests that rehearsal is necessary for remembering and storage in the long-term memory (LTM).

Reinforcement The process of affecting the frequency with which a behavior is emitted. A reinforcer can reward and thus increase the behavior or punish and thus decrease its frequency. Reinforcers can also be primary, satisfying basic needs such as hunger or thirst, or secondary, satisfying learned and indirect values, such as money.

Reliability Consistency of measurement. A test is reliable if it repeatedly gives the same results. A person should get nearly the same score if the test is taken on two different occasions.

REM (Rapid-Eye Movement) Type of sleep in which the eyes are rapidly moving around; dreaming occurs in REM sleep.

Repression A defense mechanism in which a person forgets or pushes into the unconscious something that arouses anxiety. *See* Defense Mechanism; Anxiety.

Reticular Formation A system of nerve fibers leading from the spinal column to the cerebral cortex that functions to arouse, alert, and make an organism sensitive to changes in the environment. *See* Cerebral Cortex.

Retina The inside coating of the eye, containing two kinds of cells that react to light: the rods that are sensitive only to dim light and the cones that are sensitive to color and form in brighter light. There are three kinds of cones, each responsive to particular colors in the visible spectrum (range of colors).

Risky Shift Research suggests that decisions made by groups will involve considerably more risk than individuals in the group would be willing to take. This shift in group decision depends heavily on cultural values. *See* Cautious Shift.

Rod Part of the retina involved in seeing in dim light. *See* Retina.

RNA (Ribonucleic Acid) A chemical substance that occurs in chromosomes and that functions in genetic coding. During task-learning, RNA changes occur in the brain.

Role Playing Adopting the role of another person and experiencing the world in a way one is not accustomed to.

Role Taking The ability to imagine oneself in another's place or to understand the consequences of one's actions for another person.

Schachter-Singer Theory of Emotion Theory of emotion that states that we interpret our arousal according to our environment and label our emotions accordingly.

Schizoid Personality Personality disorder characterized by having great trouble developing social relationships.

Schizophrenia The most common and serious form of psychosis in which there exists an imbalance between emotional reactions and the thoughts associated with these feelings. It may be a disorder of the process of thinking. *See* Psychosis.

Scientific Method The process used by psychologists to determine principles of behavior that exist independently of individual experience and that are untouched by unconscious bias. It is based on a prearranged agreement that criteria, external to the individual and communicable to others, must be established for each set of observations referred to as fact.

Secondary Reinforcement Reinforcement that is only effective after it has been associated with a primary reinforcer.

Self-Actualization A term used by humanistic psychologists to describe what they see as a basic human motivation: the development of all aspects of an individual into productive harmony.

Self-Esteem A person's evaluation of oneself. If someone has confidence and satisfaction in oneself, self-esteem is considered high.

Self-Fulfilling Prophecy A preconceived expectation or belief about a situation that evokes behavior resulting in a situation consistent with the preconception.

Senses An organism's physical means of receiving and detecting physical changes in the environment. Sensing is analyzed in terms of reception of the physical stimulus by specialized nerve cells in the sense organs, transduction or converting the stimulus' energy into nerve impulses that the brain can interpret, and transmission of those nerve impulses from the sense organ to the part of the brain that can interpret the information they convey.

Sensitivity Training Aims at helping people to function more effectively in their jobs by increasing their awareness of their own and others' feelings and exchanging "feedback" about styles of interacting. Sensitivity groups are unlike therapy groups in that they are meant to enrich the participants' lives. Participants are not considered patients or ill. Also called T-groups.

Sensorimotor Stage According to Piaget, the stage of development beginning at birth during which perceptions are tied to objects that the child manipulates. Gradually the child learns that objects have permanence even if they are out of sight or touch.

Sensory Adaptation Tendency of the sense organs to adjust to continuous, unchanging stimulation by reducing their functioning; a stimulus that once caused sensation no longer does.

Sensory Deprivation The blocking out of all outside stimulation for a period of time. As studied experimentally, it can produce hallucinations, psychological disturbances, and temporary disorders of the nervous system of the subject.

Sex Role The attitudes, activities, and expectations considered specific to being male or female, determined by both biological and cultural factors.

Shaping A technique of behavior shaping in which behavior is acquired through the reinforcement of successive approximations of the desired behavior.

Sleep A periodic state of consciousness marked by four brain-wave patterns. Dreams occur during REM sleep. Sleep is a basic need without which one may suffer physical or psychological distress. *See* Brain Waves; Dreams.

Sleeper Effect The delayed impact of persuasive information. People tend to forget the context in which they first heard the information, but they eventually remember the content of the message sufficiently to feel its impact.

Social Comparison Theory proposed by Festinger that states that we have a tendency to compare our behavior to others to ensure that we are conforming.

Social Facilitation Phenomenon in which the presence of others increases dominant behavior patterns in an individual; Zajonc's theory of social facilitation states that the presence of others enhances the emission of the dominant response of the individual.

Social Influence The process by which people form and change the attitudes, opinions, and behavior of others.

Social Learning Learning acquired through observation and imitation of others.

Social Psychology The study of individuals as affected by others and of the interaction of individuals in groups.

Socialization A process by which a child learns the various patterns of behavior expected and accepted by society. Parents are the chief agents of a child's socialization. Many factors have a bearing on the socialization process, such as the child's sex, religion, social class, and parental attitudes.

Sociobiology The study of the genetic basis of social behavior.

Sociophobias Excessive irrational fears and embarrassment when interacting with other people.

Somatic Nervous System The part of the peripheral nervous system that carries messages from the sense organs and relays information that directs the voluntary movements of the skeletal muscles.

Somatoform Disorders Disorders characterized by physical symptoms for which there are no obvious physical causes.

Somesthetic Senses Skin senses; includes pressure, pain, cold, and warmth.

Species-Typical Behavior Behavior patterns common to members of a species. Ethologists state that each species inherits some patterns of behavior (e.g., birdsongs).

Stanford-Binet Intelligence Scale Tests that measure intelligence from two years of age through adult level. The tests determine one's intelligence quotient by establishing one's chronological and mental ages. *See* Intelligence Quotient.

State-Dependent Learning Situation in which what is learned in one state can only be remembered when the person is in that state.

Statistically Significant In inferential statistics, a finding that the independent variable did influence greatly the outcome of the experimental and control group.

Stereotype The assignment of characteristics to a person mainly on the basis of the group, class, or category to which he or she belongs. The tendency to categorize and generalize is a basic human way of organizing information.

Stereotyping, however, can reinforce misinformation and prejudice. *See* Prejudice.

Stimulus A unit of the environment that causes a response in an individual; more specifically, a physical or chemical agent acting on an appropriate sense receptor.

Stimulus Discrimination Limiting responses to relevant stimuli.

Stimulus Generalization Responses to stimuli similar to the stimulus that had caused the response.

Stress Pressure that puts unusual demands on an organism. Stress may be caused by physical conditions but eventually will involve both. Stimuli that cause stress are called stressors, and an organism's response is the stress reaction. A three-stage general adaptation syndrome is hypothesized involving both emotional and physical changes. *See* General Adaptation Syndrome.

Structuralism An early school of psychology that stressed the importance of conscious experience as the subject matter of psychology and maintained that experience should be analyzed into its component parts by use of introspection. *See* Introspection.

Sublimation Defense mechanism in which a person redirects his socially undesirable urges into socially acceptable behavior.

Subliminal Stimuli Stimuli that do not receive conscious attention because they are below sensory thresholds. They may influence behavior, but research is not conclusive on this matter.

Substance-Induced Organic Mental Disorders Organic mental disorders caused by exposure to harmful environmental substances.

Suggestibility The extent to which a person responds to persuasion. Hypnotic susceptibility refers to the degree of suggestibility observed after an attempt to induce hypnosis has been made. *See* Persuasion; Hypnosis.

Superego According to Freud, the superego corresponds roughly to conscience. The superego places restrictions on both ego and id and represents the internalized restrictions and ideals that the child learns from parents and culture. *See* Conscience; Ego; Id.

Sympathetic Nervous System The branch of the autonomic nervous system that is more active in emergencies; it causes a general arousal, increasing breathing, heart rate, and blood pressure.

Synapse A "gap" where individual nerve cells (neurons) come together and across which chemical information is passed.

Syndrome A group of symptoms that occur together and mark a particular abnormal pattern.

Systematic Desensitization A technique used in behavior therapy to eliminate a phobia. The symptoms of the phobia are seen as conditioned responses of fear, and the procedure attempts to decondition the fearful response until the patient gradually is able to face the feared situation. *See* Phobia.

TAT (Thematic Apperception Test) Personality and motivation test that requires the subject to devise stories about pictures.

Taxis An orienting movement in response to particular stimuli in the environment. A frog, for example, always turns so its snout points directly at its prey before it flicks its tongue. *See* Orienting Response.

Theory A very general statement that is more useful in generating hypotheses than in generating research. *See* Hypothesis.

Therapeutic Community The organization of a hospital setting so that patients have to take responsibility for helping one another in an attempt to prevent patients from getting worse by being in the hospital.

Token Economy A system for organizing a treatment setting according to behavioristic principles. Patients are encouraged to take greater responsibility for their adjustment by receiving tokens for acceptable behavior and fines for unacceptable behavior. The theory of token economy grew out of operant conditioning techniques. *See* Operant Conditioning.

Traits Distinctive and stable attributes that can be found in all people.

Tranquilizers Psychoactive drugs that reduce anxiety. *See* Psychoactive Drug.

Trial and Error Learning Trying various behaviors in a situation until the solution is hit upon; past experiences lead us to try different responses until we are successful.

Unconditioned Response (UR) An automatic reaction elicited by a stimulus.

Unconditioned Stimulus (US) Any stimulus that elicits an automatic or reflexive reaction in an individual; it does not have to be learned in the present situation.

Unconscious In Freudian terminology, a concept (not a place) of the mind. The unconscious encompasses certain inborn impulses that never rise into consciousness (awareness) as well as memories and wishes that have been repressed. The chief aim of psychoanalytic therapy is to free repressed material from the unconscious in order to make it susceptible to conscious thought and direction. Behaviorists describe the unconscious as an inability to verbalize. *See* Repression.

Undifferentiated Schizophrenia Type of schizophrenia that does not fit into any particular category, or fits into more than one category.

Validity The extent to which a test actually measures what it is designed to measure.

Variability In statistics, measures of variability communicate how spread out the scores are; the tendency to vary the response to a stimulus, particularly if the response fails to help in adaptation.

Variable Any property of a person, object, or event that can change or take on more than one mathematical value.

Weber's Law States that the difference threshold depends on the ratio of the intensity of one stimulus to another rather than an absolute difference.

Wechsler Adult Intelligence Scale (WAIS) An individually administered test designed to measure adults' intelligence, devised by David Wechsler. The WAIS consists of eleven subtests, of which six measure verbal and five measure performance aspects of intelligence. *See* Wechsler Intelligence Scale for Children.

Wechsler Intelligence Scale for Children (WISC) Similar to the Wechsler Adult Intelligence Scale, except that it is designed for people under fifteen. Wechsler tests can determine strong and weak areas of overall intelligence. *See* Wechsler Adult Intelligence Scale (WAIS).

Whorfian Hypothesis The linguistic relativity hypothesis of Benjamin Whorf; states that language influences thought.

Withdrawal Social or emotional detachment; the removal of oneself from a painful or frustrating situation.

Yerkes-Dodson Law Prediction that the optimum motivation level decreases as the difficulty level of a task increases.

Source for the Glossary:

The majority of terms in this glossary are reprinted from *The Study of Psychology,* Joseph Rubinstein. © by The Dushkin Publishing Group, Inc., Guilford, CT 06437.

The remaining terms were developed by the Annual Editions staff.

Credits/ Acknowledgments

Cover design by Charles Vitelli

1. Science of Psychology

Facing overview—Medical World News.

2. Biological Bases of Behavior

Facing overview—WHO photo. 27—Illustration by Lewis E. Calver. 28—(top right) Hank Morgan—Rainbow; (middle left and bottom right) Buchsbaum; (middle right) Dan McCoy—Rainbow; (bottom left) Howard Sochurek. 29—(top & middle) Courtesy Haier & Buchsbaum; (bottom) courtesy Buchsbaum. 33—Carol Donner. 34—Tomo Narashima. 35—Patricia J. Wynne; courtesy of Clement Fox, Wayne State University, © Williams & Wilkins Co.

3. Perceptual Processes

Facing overview—United Nations photo by Shelley Rotner. 60-63—Johnny Johnson.

4. Learning and Remembering

Facing overview—United Nations photo by Marta Pinter. 82—United Nations photo by John Isaac.

5. Cognitive Processes

Facing overview—United Nations photo by John Isaac.

6. Emotion and Motivation

Facing overview—United Nations photo by Margot Granitsas.

7. Development

Facing overview—United Nations photo by John Isaac.

8. Personality Processes

Facing overview—United Nations photo by Margot Granitsas.

9. Social Processes

Facing overview—Courtesy of Daniel Hand High School, Madison, CT.

10. Psychological Disorders

Facing overview—WHO photo by Jean Mohr.

11. Psychological Treatments

Facing overview—United Nations photo by G. Palmer.

ANNUAL EDITIONS ARTICLE REVIEW FORM

■ NAME: _____ DATE: _____

■ TITLE AND NUMBER OF ARTICLE: _____

■ BRIEFLY STATE THE MAIN IDEA OF THIS ARTICLE: _____

_____

_____

_____

_____

■ LIST THREE IMPORTANT FACTS THAT THE AUTHOR USES TO SUPPORT THE MAIN IDEA:

_____

_____

_____

_____

_____

_____

■ WHAT INFORMATION OR IDEAS DISCUSSED IN THIS ARTICLE ARE ALSO DISCUSSED IN YOUR
TEXTBOOK OR OTHER READING YOU HAVE DONE? LIST THE TEXTBOOK CHAPTERS AND PAGE
NUMBERS:

_____

_____

_____

_____

_____

_____

■ LIST ANY EXAMPLES OF BIAS OR FAULTY REASONING THAT YOU FOUND IN THE ARTICLE:

_____

_____

_____

_____

■ LIST ANY NEW TERMS/CONCEPTS THAT WERE DISCUSSED IN THE ARTICLE AND WRITE A
SHORT DEFINITION:

_____

_____

_____

_____

ANNUAL EDITIONS: PSYCHOLOGY 93/94
Article Rating Form

Here is an opportunity for you to have direct input into the next revision of this volume. We would like you to rate each of the 50 articles listed below, using the following scale:

1. Excellent: should definitely be retained
2. Above average: should probably be retained
3. Below average: should probably be deleted
4. Poor: should definitely be deleted

Your ratings will play a vital part in the next revision. So please mail this prepaid form to us just as soon as you complete it.
Thanks for your help!

Annual Editions revisions depend on two major opinion sources: one is our Advisory Board, listed in the front of this volume, which works with us in scanning the thousands of articles published in the public press each year; the other is you—the person actually using the book. Please help us and the users of the next edition by completing the prepaid article rating form on this page and returning it to us. Thank you.

Rating	Article	Rating	Article
	1. Psychology: The Core Discipline		27. The Last Interview of Abraham Maslow
	2. Liberal Educaiton, Study in Depth, and the Arts and Science Major—Psychology		28. Barriers to Success
	3. Ratting on Psychologists		29. Putting Children First
	4. Mapping the Brain		30. Sad Legacy of Abuse: The Search for Remedies
	5. Mind and Brain		31. Children in Gangs
	6. What a Child Is Given		32. Meeting the Challenges of an Aging Nation
	7. Study Links Genes to Sexual Orientation		33. Silent Saviors
	8. A Pleasurable Chemistry		34. Bright Lights, Big Mystery
	9. Sizing Up the Sexes		35. Hey, I'm Terrific!
	10. The Legacy of Gestalt Psychology		36. Girls' Self-Esteem Is Lost on Way to Adolescence, New Study Finds
	11. Are We Led by the Nose?		37. In Search of the Sacred Masculine
	12. Research Probes What the Mind Senses Unaware		38. Tapping the Healing Power of Positive Thinking
	13. Consciousness Raising		39. Are You Raising an Optimist?
	14. How Kids Learn		40. Where Do We Stand?
	15. The Town B. F. Skinner Boxed		41. Blame It on Feminism
	16. Gone But Not Forgotten		42. Groupthink: Taking Easy Way Out of a Tough Decision
	17. Dreams of a Rat		43. Resolving Conflicts: Step By Step
	18. A New Perspective on Cognitive Development in Infancy		44. Mood Disorders: A Sad State of Mind
	19. New Views of Human Intelligence		45. Winning the War Against Clinical Depression
	20. Brains at Work		46. The Secret Illness: Obsessive-Compulsive Disorder
	21. Brain Yields New Clues on Its Organization for Language		47. Who Am I?
	22. Probability Blindness: Neither Rational nor Capricious		48. Depression: The Growing Role of Drug Therapies
	23. Mental Gymnastics		49. Recovery Fever
	24. Where Emotions Come From		50. Help Yourself
	25. Happy or Sad, a Mood Can Prove Contagious		
	26. Stress: The "Type A" Hypothesis		

(Continued on next page)

ABOUT YOU

Name_____ Date_____

Are you a teacher? ☐   Or student? ☐

Your School Name _____

Department _____

Address _____

City _____ State _____ Zip _____

School Telephone # _____

YOUR COMMENTS ARE IMPORTANT TO US!

Please fill in the following information:

For which course did you use this book? _____

Did you use a text with this Annual Edition?   ☐ yes   ☐ no

The title of the text? _____

What are your general reactions to the Annual Editions concept?

Have you read any particular articles recently that you think should be included in the next edition?

Are there any articles you feel should be replaced in the next edition? Why?

Are there other areas that you feel would utilize an Annual Edition?

May we contact you for editorial input?

May we quote you from above?